THE ROYAL HORTICULTURAL SOCIETY
GARDENERS' CALENDAR

THE ROYAL HORTICULTURAL SOCIETY
GARDENERS' CALENDAR

A guide to gardening through the year

Consultant Editor John Main, Curator at the RHS Garden, Wisley

Guild Publishing London

A *Macdonald Orbis* BOOK

© Macdonald Orbis 1987

This edition published 1987 by
Book Club Associates
by arrangement with Macdonald & Co (Publishers) Ltd
London & Sydney

Filmset by Wyvern Typesetting Limited

Printed and bound in Italy by New Interlitho

Senior Editor: Judith More
Editor: Julie Dufour
Text editors: Lizzie Boyd, Denys de Saulles
Art Editor: Simon Webb
Designer: David Cook
Indexer: Freda Wilkinson

CONTENTS

PREFACE

Written by the Wisley team who have become familiar faces on TV's *Gardener's Calendar*, this book is based on a unique fund of gardening experience. Enormously practical, it distils the knowledge of men and women who work in a setting that has become every gardener's Mecca. There could be no better teachers, for each is an expert in certain aspects of gardening, a fact reflected by their appearances on television and their contributions to this book.

In a sense, we ordinary gardeners, too, must learn to become specialists. This is because every garden presents problems of its own, such as sticky soil, excessive shade, exposure to wind, or the gardener's own shortage of time. It follows that there is no simple set of rules to suit us all. Yet it is this very diversity that helps to make each garden an individual achievement and a source of endless pleasure.

And pleasure, surely, is what it is all about. Gardens are for relaxing in, for drawing a little closer to nature in a harsh and troubled world. We obscure the purpose if we become over-ambitious, or fret too much about failures. This philosophic approach is certainly in evidence among the Wisley team. They, too, have their problems – and bear in mind their critical audience – but they have learned that there is always another season, another opportunity.

CHAPTER ONE

GROUNDWORK

Gardening, like any other hobby, begins with a thorough understanding of the raw materials, the most important of which is the soil. The following pages analyse the basic types, from light sandy soil to heavy clays, the scope and limitations imposed on them, and the cultural remedies that can alter their structure, fertility and water-holding capacities. Understanding your particular soil makes maintenance with well-chosen tools that much easier. Regular applications of garden compost, fertilizers and manures are needed to keep up nutrient levels, and constant watering and mulching to satisfy moisture requirements.

The vagaries of the British climate present constant challenges to the gardener, and aspect may influence the range of plants that can be grown. Such limitations must be accepted, but much can still be done to reduce the weather damage: winds can be filtered through hedges and shelter belts; frost pockets can be located and avoided; heavy rainfalls can be countered with adequate drainage and droughts with deep mulching.

The joy of gardening lies in the cultivation of plants, but in time they will succumb to old age, accidental injury or disease. Happily they are all capable of producing new generations by one or more methods of propagation.

S oil is a mixture of mineral particles and organic matter (plant and animal remains). Air and water fill the spaces between, the water containing dissolved nutrients.

In the soil live many kinds of algae, bacteria and fungi, insects and worms. Most of these feed on the organic matter, breaking it down and recycling plant foods stored in the dead tissues. In this way they create a rich, fertile soil in which seeds can germinate and plants grow.

Topsoil is the upper, fertile layer. It may vary in depth from several feet in deep river valleys to a scant few inches on chalk downland. Below this is the subsoil, which is usually lighter in colour. Although infertile, it may contain some useful nutrients, and roots may penetrate it for anchorage and in search of moisture.

The entire topsoil may have been removed from a new building site during construction, in which case more may have to be bought in. The depth of the topsoil can be checked by digging a trench or by studying nearby excavations.

TYPES OF SOIL

Soils are classified according to the varying amounts of sand, silt and clay that they contain:

Loam This is an ideal blend of clay, silt and sand particles, together with essential organic matter. It is easily cultivated, retains moisture well, and is suitable for most crops. So-called heavy loam has an above-average clay content; light loam has a higher level of sand particles.

Clay This soil is difficult to cultivate, consisting of fine particles that cling closely together. It is moisture-retentive, and tends to be sticky when wet. When dry, it shrinks and the surface cracks. A soil high in clay will, when wet, smear under thumb pressure, leaving the surface smooth and very shiny.

Clay soils are disliked by commercial growers as they are slow to warm up and only become workable in spring. This makes them unsuitable for early cropping, while in wet autumns it may be difficult to harvest crops. They are commonly termed 'heavy' soils.

Nonetheless, clay soils are usually rich, holding applied fertilizers well and releasing them slowly. They can be improved to some extent by making the drainage better and by adding dressings of sharp sand and grit. Organic matter, such as coarse peat, processed tree bark, leaf litter and strawy manure, is particularly valuable in improving their texture.

Lime, when applied to acid clays, improves the texture by causing the particles to flocculate (cluster together and form crumbs). However, it is of no value on clays that are already chalky or alkaline. Proprietary soil conditioners may bring about a moderate improvement in some clays.

Sandy soils These are made up of large particles, with bigger air spaces through which water drains freely. Rubbed between the fingers, sandy soil feels sharp and gritty, and a squeezed handful crumbles rapidly.

Soils of this type are easy to cultivate at all seasons. They warm up early in the spring and are therefore good for early cropping. Their main drawbacks are that they dry out rapidly and that plant foods are quickly washed out by rain or irrigation. They are often termed 'poor' or 'light' soils, and the key to improvement lies in heavy dressings of organic matter, such as garden compost or well-rotted manure.

Silt soils These consist of particles intermediate in size between clay and sand. They show little response to liming and need regular applications of organic matter to maintain good texture and fertility.

ACIDITY AND ALKALINITY

Soil pH is a term used to describe the degree of acidity of soils, pH 7 being neutral. In the British Isles, test readings lower than 4.5 (very acid) and higher than 8.5 (very alkaline) are rare.

Most plants, including vegetables and fruit crops, grow best on slightly acid soils (pH 6 to 6.5), but some are lime-hating and require soils below pH 6. This applies, among others, to rhododendrons, camellias and most heathers. Plants indigenous to chalk and limestone regions usually grow best at pH 7 or above.

Soil testing kit
Simple testing kits can be used to determine soil activity. Take samples of garden soil and mix with barium sulphate powder and the test solution. Compare the liquid in the test tube with the colour chart indicating soil acidity/alkalinity.

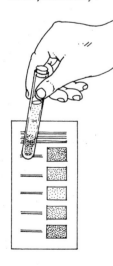

Calcium is continually being removed from the soil, either in the water that drains away after heavy rain or else absorbed by the plants. In this way soil acidity gradually increases, slowing down bacterial activity. Organic matter is broken down at a reduced rate, and fewer nutrients are available to plants. As a result, essential foods may become 'locked' in the soil, so that plant growth suffers and deficiency symptoms become apparent.

Liming will correct this condition, but excessive liming may itself give rise to similar deficiency problems. It is advisable, therefore, to check the soil pH before liming, testing it every two or three years on heavily-cropped land.

Simple soil-testing kits can be bought from most garden centres, allowing several tests to be taken and giving a rough but workable guide. Kits are also available which measure nutrient levels, but assessment can be difficult. Alternatively, samples can be sent to a professional soil analyst from time to time – a worthwhile step to guard against both deficiencies and excesses.

Having established that lime is needed, apply it in winter, after digging. Rain will wash it in, and it will be thoroughly mixed with the soil during the final preparations for sowing and planting. Calcium carbonate (ground chalk) is the quickest-acting material, but calcium hydroxide (garden lime) is usually cheaper and is widely used in horticulture.

DRAINAGE

In poorly drained soils, water may fill the spaces between soil particles to within a few inches of the surface for several months of the year. Roots of most plants will rot under these conditions, or fail to penetrate far. Roots that are restricted to the top few inches provide poor anchorage, and plants will achieve below-average growth.

Low-lying ground is especially liable to waterlogging, but in most gardens the water level – or water-table, as it is called – is usually well below the surface, and many soils drain naturally and freely.

Poor drainage may be due to the soil structure, notably when closely-packed,

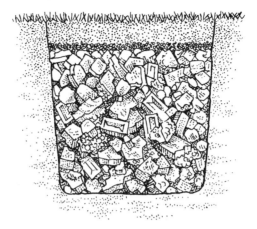

fine particles of clays and silts impede the passage of water. In soils rich in iron, a hard layer, or 'iron-pan', may develop at as little as 30–60 cm (1–2 ft) down, impeding drainage and root development. This needs to be broken up by double digging, or by driving an iron bar through it at intervals.

On new housing developments, the soil may have been compressed by heavy vehicles, impeding drainage. Ditches or existing land drains may have been filled in or destroyed.

To improve a small area of poorly-drained land, a single line of short clay pipes (or longer ones made of plastic) can be laid, or a herringbone system placed to cover a larger area. Lay the pipes 60–90 cm (2–3 ft) deep, on a bed of gravel, with an overall fall or slope of about 1 in 40. The main pipe channels the water into a nearby ditch or watercourse, or a soak-away excavated in a suitably out-of-the-way corner of the garden.

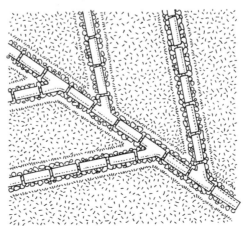

Soak-away
An artificial drainage system must discharge the collected water into a soak-away. Dig a hole about 1.2 m (4 ft) square into which the pipes can run. Fill it with coarse brick rubble or clinkers, top with a layer of gravel and level off with the surrounding surface.

Drainage system
Pipes are laid in a herringbone-pattern to improve drainage over a large area. Lateral pipes channel water into the main pipe which discharges into the soak-away. Cover the pipes with a deep layer of pebbles or coarse gravel (*below*) to prevent them becoming dislodged.

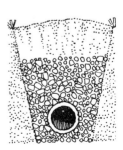

Gardeners moving from one part of the country to another may find themselves faced with totally different conditions from the ones with which they are familiar. Even neighbouring gardens may have micro-climates different from their own – north-facing, cold and open, as opposed to south-facing, warm and sheltered.

These differing conditions determine the kinds of plants and crops that can be grown successfully.

PLANT HARDINESS

In tropical and sub-tropical regions, plants showing drought tolerance may be termed 'hardy', but in northern Europe the most important survival factor is frost-hardiness. Plants from warmer climates which do not usually survive an average winter outdoors are termed 'tender'; those which tolerate frost are termed 'hardy'.

MAJOR CLIMATIC FACTORS

Coastal The seas surrounding the British Isles have a moderating effect on our climate. In winter, coastal areas are warmer than those inland, particularly those in the south-west and along the western seaboard, where the influence of the Gulf Stream is felt.

In winter, overall sea temperatures remain slightly higher than land temperatures. Conversely, coastal areas may be cooler in summer; as land temperatures rise, cooler air moves in from the sea.

Altitude and latitude Mountainous and hilly areas are colder than lowland areas. Spring is a little slower to arrive and winter starts earlier, giving a shorter growing season. Similarly, the growing season at higher latitudes – Scotland and the north of England, for instance – is shorter than in the south of England.

Wind and rainfall Winds blow from all quarters, but the strongest and most damaging are usually westerlies from the Atlantic. Milder south-west air streams bring rain, most of which is precipitated over more mountainous western regions, with drier conditions prevailing to leeward.

Easterly winds blowing from northern Europe bring cold, dry conditions to the eastern seaboard and lowlands, the regions of lowest rainfall.

Urban areas In larger towns and cities, average winter temperatures may remain higher than in the surrounding open countryside. This favours earlier growth and flowers in spring, and allows the cultivation of less-hardy plants.

Overall climatic pattern The overall pattern is of cool, dull summers, with mild, wet winters in the south and lower temperatures in the north. These are conditions in which a very wide range of temperate-climate plants can be grown.

However, the pattern is occasionally broken by hot, dry summers, during which even well-established plants may succumb to drought, and by occasional very cold winters, during which plants with low frost tolerance may be killed.

FACTORS WITHIN THE GARDEN

Aspect Plants vary in their growing needs, some preferring coolness and shade, others sun and warmth. For most gardeners, the ideal is a garden open to the south and sheltered to the north and east.

A south-facing slope receives the maximum amount of sun, warmth and light. The soil warms up rapidly in early spring, giving a long growing season. A north-facing slope is slow to become warm and receives only low-angle sunlight for much of the year. This gives a shorter growing season and, with most plants, poorer growth and cropping.

Sun and shade There are few gardens without some areas of shade. Large, deciduous trees may bring shade to much of a garden during the summer, or a garden may be overshadowed by nearby buildings. Tall conifer screens or windbreaks, hedges and fences will all cast shadows.

Some areas of the garden may be in permanent shade. Others will be in shade for varying periods each day as the sun moves across the sky. The pattern changes from season to season, the extremes being December 21st, when the sun is at its lowest, and June 21st when the sun is at its highest in the sky. When house-buying in dull weather, it is well worth taking a compass along with you.

The first step in garden planning should be to mark in the areas of shade on a site plan, so that, as far as possible, warm, sunny areas can be allocated to fruit and vegetables, to flower borders and rose beds, and, most important, to the siting of a greenhouse. Areas of permanent shade are more suited to the needs of plants adapted to cool, poorly lit woodland or to a shaded hedgerow habitat.

Wind Gardens on high ground, and on open flat-lands, such as parts of East Anglia, may frequently be exposed to strong winds. Constant air movement causes moisture to be lost more rapidly from both foliage and the soil. Gale-force winds, particularly from the west and south-west, may cause damage to trees and shrubs and endanger greenhouses, frames and conservatories.

In spring, cold, dry, northerly and easterly winds may desiccate and scorch the foliage of evergreen shrubs and damage tender young growths. In flat, open country, topsoil may be displaced and carried by the wind.

Wind is best countered by planting a hedge or erecting a screen that will filter the wind. In contrast, the barrier presented by

Providing shelter
Shelter belts that filter the wind and reduce its velocity are preferable to solid barriers. Tall hedges, durable wooden fences and tough wattle hurdles make excellent windbreaks.

a solid wall or fence gives rise to down-draughts and strong turbulence a short distance to leeward.

A moderately dense hedge or a lath fence is suitable, or a screen can be erected from the heavy-duty plastic sheeting sold especially for this purpose. A screen that filters out about 60 per cent of the wind is ideal. A barrier of this sort will reduce wind speed considerably, with little turbulence, for distances up to twenty times its height. Where space is available, two or three staggered rows of screening trees will form an effective, taller shelter belt.

In coastal areas, however, gales often damage plants for considerable distances inland, due to the salt they carry. A hedge or screen makes little difference, so it is important to choose salt-tolerant species for coastal planting and screening.

Frost Like water, cooling air flows downhill and accumulates in low-lying areas and hollows. As it chills during winter nights or cold, sunless days, it forms 'lakes' or 'frost-pockets' of below-freezing air.

Frost pockets may be created unwittingly by erecting a solid fence or planting a dense hedge across sloping ground. Instead, use slatted timber fencing, or something similar, that will allow cold air to permeate through.

It is important to recognize and take account of frost pockets in order to avoid having tender plants damaged and the blossoms of fruit trees and bushes destroyed. A frost pocket may be restricted to only part of a garden, but in low-lying areas may encompass many gardens.

Snow The quantity, frequency and duration of snowfalls may vary considerably from region to region and year to year.

When snow falls during a cold spell it sifts through the branches of trees and shrubs, blanketing the ground and protecting plants from subsequent severe frost. However, plants may be in danger when the snow follows a period of milder weather, and large, moist flakes accumulate on branches and stems.

Conifers and other evergreens are especially at risk, for they may snap under the weight of wet snow. Prompt action is necessary to dislodge the snow.

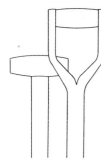

Spade handles

Spade blade

Much the same set of tools is needed whatever one plans to grow. Additions can be made later if interest develops in a more specialized aspect of gardening. Whatever you buy, the basic rule is to go for quality. Good tools, well cared for, will give a lifetime of service. Cheap tools are usually less robust, less effective and less comfortable to use.

DIGGING TOOLS

The spade takes pride of place in any garden shed, being the main tool required for soil preparation. This is one of the heavier gardening tasks, but a good spade helps to make it easier.

Most spades are made from forged steel, and preference should be given to one with an ash handle. This wood retains a certain amount of resilience, so is less likely to break. A spade with a tread is easier to use and avoids damage to footwear.

Stainless steel spades cost substantially more but the blade's smooth surface cuts through the soil more easily, especially on clay. After use, soil can be removed by washing and the blade need not even be dried. These advantages apply also to other stainless steel tools, and the extra expense is well repaid.

Spade handles are either T-shaped or D-shaped, most gardeners finding the latter more comfortable. The question of comfort is one of the main points to consider when buying tools. Good balance and a snug grip ensure easier working.

A large four-tined fork has many uses in the garden and may even be used instead of

a spade on stony soil. Points already made about choosing a spade apply equally to forks, except that they do not require added treads. This is because they are made from thicker metal.

In addition to a full-size digging fork, a scaled-down version is useful for turning the soil in herbaceous borders and in other places where space is limited or deep digging unnecessary. These are correctly called border forks, although the term ladies' fork is often used. There are also small hand forks, with handles of various lengths, which are useful for weeding and for pricking the soil around bulbs.

Although not essential, a shovel can be a good investment. It is the best tool for mixing compost and for handling sand or gravel. Often, it is possible to use a spade instead, but never with the same degree of comfort and efficiency. A glance at the blade will show that it is shaped quite differently from that of a spade, with curved edges to enable materials to be lifted without spilling. Also, the handle of a shovel is set at an angle that enables it to be used with less strain on one's back.

SEED BED TOOLS

A hand cultivator, usually with three or five hooked tines mounted on a 1.5 m (5 ft) handle, provides the easiest means of breaking down soil before sowing or planting. When drawn through the ground with a little downwards pressure, the tines open up the surface and help to produce a crumb-like structure.

There are also smaller versions, with handles from 45–90 cm (1½–3 ft) long. These are useful for aerating the soil in confined spaces and around plants.

An iron rake, with either flat or round teeth, is needed for levelling seed beds. Both shapes work well, but choose one where the teeth are not too close together or every little stone will be removed, which is neither necessary nor desirable.

The other point to check is that the head is fixed securely to the handle. The action of drawing the rake towards you puts some strain on the fastening, and it is frustrating if the head falls off every few minutes due to an insecure fitting.

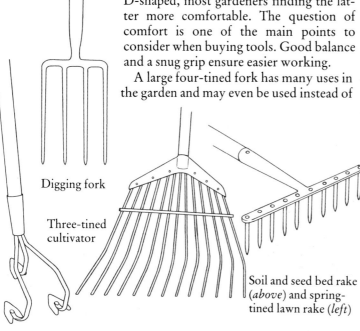

Digging fork

Three-tined cultivator

Soil and seed bed rake (*above*) and spring-tined lawn rake (*left*)

Two other types of rakes, with long wire or rubber tines, are used for scarifying lawns and collecting leaves.

HOES

There are two basically different designs – draw hoes and push hoes. Their names describe the action with which they are used. Although draw hoes (also called swan-neck hoes) can be used for weed control, their main purpose is for forming seed drills and for earthing up such crops as potatoes. When used to sever weeds, a proportion of the smaller ones will inevitably be partially buried and perhaps grow again.

Some draw hoes have square blades, others are of half-moon shape. There are also short-handled types, called onion hoes, which are useful in confined spaces and for weed control around small plants.

The Dutch hoe is perhaps the best-known push type, but the so-called push-pull design offers definite advantages. As the name implies, it works in two directions, both the front and back of the blade having a sharpened edge. Once the knack of using it has been acquired, it is faster and more accurate than a Dutch hoe, largely because its design makes it easier to see exactly where you are hoeing. It can even be used alongside small seedlings.

PLANTING AIDS

A garden line, preferably made from nylon, is essential if you plan to grow vegetables. A line is also needed for marking out paths, borders and other features when making a garden. A reel attached to one end, and a pin for the other, will make it easy to use and store.

A trowel is indispensable for planting. There are two designs: those pressed out from a single piece of metal, and others with a strong forged joint between the blade and the handle. The former are much weaker, and liable to bend and eventually break. A thin-bladed stainless steel trowel is ideal.

Some gardeners like to use a dibber, especially for planting vegetables. One with a D-shaped handle, and not more than 30 cm (1 ft) long, is best, while a metal-tipped point makes it easier to obtain a clean hole.

SECATEURS

There is a wide range of types and prices, but the cheapest often prove the most costly in the long run. After a while they cease to cut cleanly, leaving torn and snagged ends which lay the plants open to infection. Good quality secateurs will last a lifetime, with some makers offering free service for an indefinite period.

There are two basic types: those with a single blade that cuts against a flat surface, and others with a scissor action. Both are satisfactory, but it is especially important to keep the former type sharp by regular honing on a whetstone.

Long-handled loppers give greater leverage for cutting through thicker wood. There is no call for them in many small gardens, but they are invaluable for tackling overgrown shrubs and fruit trees.

LAWN EDGERS

A half-moon edging iron is invaluable for giving a lawn neat edges, and for keeping them that way. Avoid cheap designs made from pressed steel clamped round the handle like a child's seaside spade. They soon break. Those spiked into the bottom of the handle are stronger, and the downward pressure exerted during use helps to keep the fastening secure.

SPRAYERS

A small pressurized sprayer is an almost essential aid for controlling pests and diseases. One with a capacity of 2¼ litres (½ gal) is sufficient for most needs. It should give long service if lubricated occasionally and washed out thoroughly after use. If you apply weedkiller with a sprayer, it is advisable to keep one especially for this purpose, and to label it.

CARING FOR TOOLS

More tools get ruined by neglect than get worn out by normal use. Get into the habit of cleaning them before putting them away, and always store them in a dry place. If tools are unlikely to be used for a while, wipe the metal parts with an oily rag.

Draw hoe

Push-pull hoe

Two blade secateurs

Hand sprayer

Reel-mounted garden line

MAKING GARDEN COMPOST

The compost heap remains a neglected area in many gardens. This is unfortunate, for it can provide a regular source of nourishing humus, so essential for the fertility of the soil. The need is particularly great in towns, where manure is often not easily obtainable.

With a little care, the heap need not look unsightly. If it cannot be tucked away out of view, it should be easy enough to provide camouflage in the form of a small hedge or by erecting a frame to support a climbing plant. Keep the heap well clear of wooden boundary fences as the damp organic material may result in rotting.

Although a single heap is valuable, it is a great advantage to have two. This will allow one heap to be left to mature while a start is made on the second.

COMPOST CONTAINERS

A choice has to be made between buying proprietary bins or constructing your own. The drawback of ready-made bins is that they are mostly rather small and also relatively expensive. By making your own bin, you can save money and produce a more substantial container where the materials will decompose better.

The simplest form of home-made bin consists of chicken wire supported by corner posts. Stronger side cladding, such as welded wire mesh, would be an improvement, while wooden slats will make a really sturdy construction. If you do use timber, make the front slats removable so that the bin can be filled and emptied more easily. An earth floor is best.

The size of the bin, or bins, should relate to the likely amount of material, but anything less than 1.2 m (4 ft) sq and 1.2 m (4 ft) high slows down decomposition.

COMPOST MATERIALS

As a rule, all types of soft, disease-free garden waste can be added to the bin to make compost. This includes annual weeds, soft prunings, vegetable waste, leaves, lawn mowings, kitchen waste, spent compost from plant pots, and so on. But some discretion is needed with two of these materials – lawn mowings and leaves.

The problem with mowings is that they are almost too abundant throughout the summer. If placed on the heap in thick layers, they tend to become a soggy mass that will not rot properly and may even be difficult to remove from the bin. The best solution is to mix them with straw, which will prevent compaction and add bulk.

Although straw may not be available in towns, or be very expensive, it should be easy enough to buy a couple of bales during a weekend outing to the country. It makes no difference if they are weather-damaged, but they will be easier to bring home if you have some dustbin sacks and a roof rack.

Leaves, too, are a problem where large quantities are concerned, the difficulty being that they are often too dry or leathery to decompose satisfactorily. By all means add fairly small amounts to the general heap, but for large amounts it is better to make a separate heap and allow them to rot down at their own rather slow pace. The resultant compost, known as leaf mould, is ideal for mulching.

Hard, woody waste, such as rose prunings, cabbage stalks and perennial weeds, is best burned and the ashes added to the compost heap.

MAKING COMPOST

Place the materials in the bin to a depth of about 23 cm (9 in) and firm this by treading. Now sprinkle sulphate of ammonia over the surface at the rate of 15 g per sq m (½ oz per sq yd) and water this in with 9 litres of water per sq m (2 gal per sq yd). As more waste becomes available, add this until the next layer is 23 cm (9 in) deep and

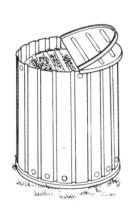

Ready-made bin
Purpose-made compost bins are made from PVC panels which slide up to give access to the compost at the bottom.

Home-made bin
Wooden compost bins are best constructed as three-sided boxes, with front boards to slip into position as the heap builds up.

MAKING GARDEN COMPOST

firm it well. This time add lime at 125 g per sq m (4 oz per sq yd), followed by another watering as before.

Continue building up the heap in similar layers, spreading sulphate of ammonia and lime alternately. These are the least expensive 'activators', but there are a number of proprietary types which may be used instead. They give satisfactory results if the makers' instructions are followed.

Another method is to mix small amounts of farmyard manure with the garden and kitchen waste. This will set up the necessary bacterial action, and no other activator is then necessary.

It is best to keep the heap covered so that it does not become saturated by heavy rain. The easiest way is to lay black polythene over the top, anchoring the sheet with stones or bricks at the corners to prevent it from being blown away. It takes only a moment to remove the plastic when adding to the heap.

Once it has been built up to its full height of about 1.2 m (4 ft), the heap should be left for between four and six weeks, or a week or two longer in winter. Then turn over all the material with a fork, moving the partly rotted material at the outside of the heap to the inside. After another six weeks the compost should be ready for use – a moist, crumbly material that is evenly rotted throughout. Well-made compost is never cold and soggy.

Owners of small gardens may find that things do not work out in quite this fashion. With only small amounts of material to add at any one time, the heap is less likely to heat up satisfactorily. In this case, make the most of your own or neighbours' lawn mowings, mixed with straw, and also add household waste of vegetable origin. Cover shallow layers of material to prevent them drying out and be ready to turn the heap more than once if the top and outside are slow to decompose.

Although garden compost is excellent for adding to the soil as a conditioner, it is not very suitable for mulching. This is because it generally contains many weed seeds, thereby defeating one of the main purposes of mulching – weed suppression.

Building a compost heap
Compost is made from soft, disease-free garden rubbish and kitchen waste, with straw for added bulk and chemical activators to speed decomposition. Build up the heap from 23 cm (9 in) layers of vegetable rubbish mixed with straw, thoroughly moistened. Sprinkle the layers alternately with sulphate of ammonia and lime, or use a proprietary compost activator.

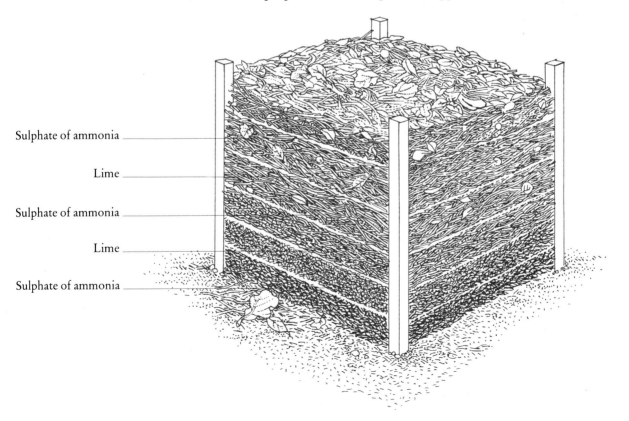

Sulphate of ammonia

Lime

Sulphate of ammonia

Lime

Sulphate of ammonia

Most soils contain all the elements needed for plant growth. As evidence, almost any newly-disturbed piece of land will soon be covered by a healthy crop of weeds.

However, plants growing in the wild are adapted to particular soil conditions. For example, slow-growing, lime-hating heathers are found on acid, sandy, moorland soils. Yet the average garden contains plants from many different habitats, and it is inevitable that some will find the conditions less to their liking than others.

Also, many plants, particularly food plants, have been bred for rapid growth and high yields. Often they have only a short growing season. To obtain these qualities, particularly in vegetable crops, the plants have to be provided with extra food in the form of fertilizers or manure.

The difference between manure and fertilizer is essentially one of bulk. Fertilizers contain plant foods in concentrated form and are applied in small quantities. They usually supply one or more of the three major elements – nitrogen (N), phosphate (P) and potassium (potash) (K).

Manure contains only small amounts of N, P and K, but it also supplies trace elements and organic matter. The latter decays to become humus, an essential material for binding soil particles together and improving soil texture.

FERTILIZERS

There are two basic types of fertilizer, organic and inorganic.

Organic fertilizers These are of plant or animal origin, such as hoof and horn meal (13% nitrogen); bone meal (4% nitrogen: 16–20% phosphate); wood ash (variable, 5–10% potassium preferably ash from young, sappy shoots as ash from older wood contains very little potash).

The nutrients that these organic fertilizers contain are not available to plants until the materials are broken down by soil bacteria. For this reason they are often described as slow-acting, bacterial activity being particularly slow in cold conditions. When applied in spring they provide little immediate stimulus and are more useful for crops and plants that make most of their growth during summer and autumn.

Inorganic fertilizers These are manufactured materials, by-products of industrial processes, or mined natural deposits. They are sometimes called chemical, or artificial, fertilizers and are sold in powder or granular form.

The nutrients they contain are usually available to plants soon after application and so they are often quick-acting. Even so, Nitroform persists for about six months; sulphate of potash, and triple superphosphate for a full growing season or more.

Examples of fertilizers supplying nitrogen include sulphate of ammonia (21%); ammonium nitrate (35%); Nitro-chalk (ammonium nitrate plus calcium carbonate) (21%); nitrate of soda (15.5%); Nitroform (38%). Those supplying phosphate include superphosphate (18%); triple superphosphate (47%).

Fertilizers supplying potassium (potash) include sulphate of potash (48–50%); potassium nitrate (45%, plus 13% nitrogen). The latter dissolves easily in water and, with urea, is used in the preparation of liquid feeds.

Liquid fertilizers These products are manufactured from fully soluble substances, sometimes with seaweed as their base. They usually contain the three main nutrients – nitrogen, phosphorous and potash – in various ratios, and may also contain trace elements such as magnesium.

Liquid fertilizers are sold in concentrated form or as soluble powders. They are used mainly for feeding greenhouse plants and house plants, but are also suitable as supplementary feeds for any garden plants in need of a boost during the growing season. They should be applied to moist soil or compost.

Slow-release fertilizers Their purpose is to provide a regular supply of nutrients, for up to a full growing season, as the pellets or spikes containing them slowly disintegrate in the soil. They are also available in cartridge form for tree feeding.

Fritted trace elements These contain various trace elements, such as iron, boron, molybdenum, etc. They are prepared by

Clever design can make suburban gardens appear larger than they are. Curving lines and meandering paths lead the eye on detours round a shrub border to the rock garden, while the complementary colours create a beguiling vista.

Small is beautiful, and a town garden can become an oasis of green tranquility. Foliage plants, like mahonias, hostas and ferns are especially suitable for town gardens, though many roses and hydrangeas will flower well in shade.

A climbing rose trained over a door and beds packed with a multicoloured array of shrubs, herbaceous perennials and bulbs are the hallmarks of the nostalgic cottage garden style.

A typical country garden is stocked to the brim with old-fashioned favourites including gladiolus and zinnias, phlox and cornflowers, roses and dahlias. The dense rows of flowers hide the vegetable garden from view.

being coated with a soft, glass-like covering which decomposes slowly in the soil. Release is gradual, over a long period.

Fritted trace elements are used in loam-less composts. They are needed, too, when plants, such as rhododendrons, are suffering from chlorosis through trace elements being locked up in soil that has become too alkaline.

Foliar feeds Plant nutrients may be applied to the foliage as a fine spray. Foliar feeding, as it is called, is useful for providing a growth stimulus to plants that have suffered root damage, perhaps because of drought or transplanting; it should not be used as a substitute for feeding through the soil where healthy roots are present.

USING MANURE AND FERTILIZERS

Manure is usually dug into the soil during the routine winter digging of any land not carrying overwintering crops, or it may be applied in spring as a surface mulch around roses, fruit bushes and other plants. When dug in, it provides a steady supply of nutrients during the growing season for the first and second years following application, but not subsequently. The chief value of manure is in providing fibre and humus to maintain a good soil texture.

Spring is a critical period for renewed plant growth, but the soil is still cold, with little bacterial action, and little nitrogen being released from manure in the soil. To ensure that adequate nitrogen is available early in the year it is necessary to apply quickly-available, inorganic fertilizers in granular or powder form.

Surface dressings These are applied in early spring to the soil surface around established plants. Do this when the soil is moist, then allow rain to wash them in. If planting was done during the previous autumn or winter, the fertilizer may be hoed in lightly to carry it nearer to the roots. Do not hoe deeply around established plants, however, or their roots may be damaged.

Base dressing Vegetable crops, in particular, need an adequate supply of plant foods from the time they start to grow. This is best achieved by applying fertilizer to the roughly prepared plot, then working it well into the soil with a hoe or fork – if possible, two or three weeks before sowing or planting so that the nutrients are available in the root area as soon as the plants or seedlings need them. If left on or near the surface, some nutrients move down through the soil to the roots too slowly to be of immediate use.

For the same reason, to give a boost to growth during the growing season – for example, to leafy vegetable crops – it is advisable to use a readily soluble inorganic fertilizer, such as sulphate of ammonia, or a liquid feed. An organic fertilizer, such as bone meal, or a granular fertilizer would be too slow-acting.

Base dressings also provide the nutrients in all types of proprietary composts and growing mixtures.

SOME TERMS EXPLAINED

Nutrient levels or content of the three major nutrients These are legally required to be given in percentages on all fertilizer packs – for example, 10% N (nitrogen), 10% P_2O_5 (phosphorous), 5% K_2O (potassium).

The total *pure* nutrient level is, therefore, 25%, the remaining percentage being made up of associated elements, such as sulphur, impurities and inert 'filler' materials.

Balanced fertilizer One that contains equal amounts of nitrogen, phosphorous and potash – Growmore, for instance, contains 7% of each.

General or compound fertilizer One that contains two or more nutrients. It may or may not be 'balanced', and may be specially formulated for a particular crop, such as chrysanthemums or tomatoes.

Straight fertilizers These contain only one nutrient – for instance, sulphate of potash (potassium) – and are used where there is a deficiency of a single nutrient. For example, sulphate of ammonia (nitrogen), applied in early spring, encourages vigorous leaf growth.

Complete fertilizer This is a term sometimes, incorrectly, used for a compound fertilizer. A fertilizer could be 'complete' only if it contained every element needed for plant growth.

Everyone knows that plants need watering during hot, dry weather, but gardeners often set about it in the wrong way. Frequently, the hose is turned on during the evening and the whole garden watered in as little as half an hour. Afterwards, the soil looks damp, so it is assumed that all is well.

The trouble is that the small amount of water splashed over the ground has almost certainly not reached the roots. Frequent wetting of the surface in this manner encourages plants to develop new, shallow roots, often at the expense of the deeper ones. Once this has happened, failure to water every day or two can prove fatal to the plants – which can be a serious problem at holiday times.

It follows that it is much better to give one good watering every ten days or so during dry periods, wetting the soil thoroughly, than to apply it in dribs and drabs. Obviously, this method calls for some discretion, for few plants will grow in water-logged soil. Although there are inexpensive meters that show how moist the soil is, the surest method of checking is to dig a hole 15–20 cm (6–8 in) deep. At that depth the soil should be noticeably damp.

Another point to check is that you have the legal right to use water in your garden. In some areas the use of a hose and sprinkler is covered by the water rate, which is based on the rateable value of the property. In others, a separate hose-pipe licence is needed, possibly with a further charge for a sprinkler. If in doubt, ask your supplier or contact the Water Board Authority. Restrictions may be imposed under drought conditions, though seldom a total ban.

Whatever appliance you use for watering, bear in mind that a fairly fine spray is preferable to large droplets. As well as damaging the plants, the latter will certainly cake the surface of the soil, slowing down penetration and causing puddling.

Water plants before they begin to flag, for damage may have started even before this happens. Remember, too, that plants can absorb nutrients only in liquid form. So starvation as well as dehydration will result from failure to water in time.

Without going into detailed figures and statistics, it is interesting to note that about 2.5 cm (1 in) of moisture is lost from the soil every ten days by evaporation during a dry spell in summer. Leafy plants, including many vegetables, may extract as much as 4.5 litres per sq m (1 gal per sq yd) every summer's day from the soil.

Although established plants, including shrubs and perennials, may be watered at any convenient time of day, the evening is usually the best time. Because evaporation is slower then, this allows more time for the water to penetrate the soil.

There is a widespread belief that daytime watering may result in scorching, due to the sun shining through the water droplets. This is unlikely to happen, as is obvious from the lack of damage during bright but showery weather. Indeed, most plants benefit from having their foliage sprayed, for this washes away dusty deposits from their leaves. As a result, the plants are able to 'breathe' and transpire more easily.

Fine spraying with a hose can be extremely beneficial to young plants that have to be transplanted during sunny, windy weather in spring. Transpiration is rapid under such conditions and losses may be heavy – particularly where young conifers are concerned.

Overhead watering of older plants is best avoided, however, while they are in flower, for this often damages the blooms. It may also encourage fungus infection, especially in strawberries. Low-level watering, perhaps with a trickle hose, is preferable.

During a drought, when there are restrictions on the use of water, it helps to conserve precious supplies if plants are watered individually. A good deal is wasted if it is splashed around over dry, bare soil.

Climbing plants grown close to a wall or fence need special attention. In both cases they may be shielded from much of the rain that does fall, while a wall can absorb a great deal of moisture from the soil. For this reason, the roots should always be set 30–38 cm (12–15 in) away from the base, and watering needs to be particularly generous to compensate.

SEED SOWING

There are a few special points to observe when sowing seeds outdoors. Either water the soil thoroughly a day or two before sowing, or else draw the seed drills, water them well and allow the excess moisture to drain away before sowing the seeds. Either way, there should then be sufficient moisture until the seeds have germinated. For pelleted seeds, the drills must remain moist until the clay covering has disintegrated.

Subsequent watering, after germination, should be with a can fitted with a fine rose, the latter directed upwards so that the water falls gently over the seedlings. Let the water fall first on bare ground alongside the row, otherwise the initial dribble may wash some of the seedlings out of the soil.

VEGETABLES

There are a few special rules relating to vegetables. Bearing in mind that, to a large extent, water produces leaf, it is obvious that cabbages, lettuces and spinach are crops that respond particularly well to irrigation. If left dry for long periods, they become tough and unpalatable.

Again, marrows, courgettes and cucumbers contain a large percentage of water, so liberal irrigation – rather more than for most other vegetables – is bound to help. Note, however, that although watering generally increases fruit size and yield it does not necessarily improve flavour.

Watering young peas and beans makes for leafy plant but does not necessarily increase yields. They respond better if watered when flowering starts, giving an improved 'set' of the flowers, and again as the pods begin to swell.

If tomatoes or carrots have been allowed to become very dry, sudden, heavy watering will result in splitting.

Water seedboxes and pots before transplanting vegetables or other plants. This will keep the rootball intact and help the plants to become established more quickly.

EQUIPMENT

Watering will be easier and quicker if you have suitable equipment. A 1.5 cm (½ in) braided hose, for instance, may cost a little more than the cheapest types, but it is kink-resistant. Sound tap fittings are essential, especially if you have to make use of a kitchen tap.

Either buy a hose reel, or at least get into the habit of rolling the hose. Avoid dragging the hose about the garden as friction will result in holes.

Modern hose-end fittings and connectors are easy to fix in place. Should the hose be rather stiff, simply dip the end in hot water and it will then become more pliable.

Watering equipment This ranges from ordinary plastic hoses to electronically controlled irrigation systems. In between are sprinklers, with a fixed head or with rotating or oscillating heads. Hose pipes last for years if properly used and attached to a reel, mounted on a trolley or fixed to a wall.

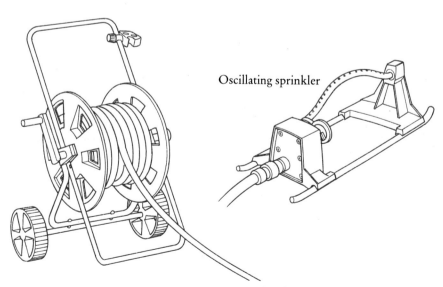

Oscillating sprinkler

Hose reel and trolley   Rotating sprinkler

WATERING AND MULCHING

Perforated hoses provide a simple method of dispersing the water. There are two basic types – lay-flat tubing with perforations to eject a mist of water on each side, and polythene tubing with small holes that allow little jets of water to squirt out for just a few inches.

There are fixed or rotating types of garden sprinklers that cover a fairly small circular area, oscillating types that cover a square or rectangular area (usually adjustable), and pulse-jet sprinklers that cover a whole or part circle with a long throw.

There are also travelling sprinklers that move slowly back along the hose, laid out over an area where water is needed, sprinkling water on each side. At the end of the hose, they switch off the supply.

An even greater degree of automation is possible with a battery-powered water line, programmed to turn the water on or off at pre-set intervals. Linking this system with a moisture gauge prevents overwatering during damp weather. The hose can be connected to a sprinkler or used with a drip-feed system.

MULCHING

Eliminating or reducing competition from other plants helps a crop to make the most of available soil moisture. Weed eradication is one method; allowing extra spacing between plants is another. Also, well-chosen ground cover plants help to reduce evaporation due to wind or sun.

Mulching is another method of conserving soil moisture. This involves covering the soil with a 5–8 cm (2–3 in) layer of leaf mould, peat, spent mushroom compost, pulverized bark or well-rotted manure. As well as reducing evaporation, mulching suppresses weeds. Manure also leaches small amounts of nutrients into the soil. Care is needed, however, to keep it away from the stems of plants, which it might damage.

Mulching is particularly valuable in the vegetable garden, for it provides the cool, moist root conditions that such crops as peas and beans enjoy. Straw placed under strawberries is another form of mulching, for it shades the soil as well as helping to keep the fruits clean.

Paper and plastic mulches of various kinds have become popular in recent years. In particular, covering the soil around newly-planted trees with black polythene has proved very effective.

Pine needles are one of the few organic materials not recommended as a mulch. They contain large amounts of resin and can be harmful to most plants, so they are best burned. However, if mixed with well-rotted leaves they appear not to harm such plants as rhododendrons and azaleas.

Conversely, acid-loving plants react badly to a mulch of spent mushroom compost, which contains lime.

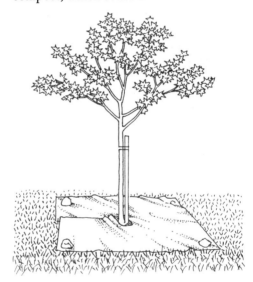

Mulch for trees and shrubs
Mulches are used to keep the soil round growing plants cool and moist, and to suppress weeds. Organic mulches are popular, but purpose-made strips or sheets of black polythene are less messy and ideal over the root area of newly planted trees and shrubs. Water the ground thoroughly before covering it with a polythene mulch suitably weighted down.

Mulch for strawberries
A straw mulch round strawberry plants serves several purposes. It keeps the fruits off the ground and eliminates competition from annual weeds. Apply the straw when the berries begin to swell, or use black polythene strips or proprietary strawberry mats.

PLANT PROPAGATION

Reproduction from seed is a natural characteristic shared by most plants. However, when plants fail to produce seeds, or if they are of hybrid origin, it is necessary to use vegetative methods. It is this art of multiplying plants by 'artificial' means that forms such a fascinating and rewarding part of gardening.

Thanks to the various aids that have been introduced over the years, what were formerly professional skills are now within the grasp of any keen gardener wishing to try his or her hand at plant raising.

SEEDS

Most seeds ripen in the autumn. If collecting them yourself, simply put the dry seeds in paper envelopes or bags, not plastic, close and store loosely in a cool, dry place.

With berried plants, which normally rely on birds to eat their fruit and so disperse the seeds, a different storage technique is needed. Instead of allowing the seeds to become dry, damp sand is placed in a flower pot and the seeds either mixed with it or spread in layers. The pot is put outside for the winter, suitably protected from birds and rodents. The name of this technique, stratification, derives from the layering process. Stratification serves to break the dormancy of the seeds.

With small amounts of seed, the same result can be achieved by placing the seeds in a polythene bag, first mixing them with damp peat or sand, and then placing the bag in a refrigerator for the storing period.

Certain plants, including primulas and meconopsis, produce seeds that have a short life and thus need to be sown as soon as they ripen. So, in order to grow plants from home-saved seeds, it is as well to check first the correct time for sowing the particular plants you are trying to raise.

Successful germination is governed by a number of factors, and the needs of particular plants vary. Temperature is an obvious case in point. For instance, a plant from the tropics will need a high temperature – possibly 25 °C (77 °F). Conversely, some seeds – notably varieties of the Butterhead lettuce – refuse to germinate at temperatures over 20 °C (68 °F).

Light is another requirement for some seeds but not for others. Those needing light to germinate are in the minority, but it would be worth experimenting with various degrees of light, and perhaps with cooler conditions, if you experience difficulty in germinating some of the less familiar types of seeds.

Timing is important for seedling growth. For instance, low levels of light during the winter may result in drawn, weak seedlings which are prone to disease and unlikely to grow into sturdy plants. So unless artificial lighting can be given, it is generally best to avoid sowing seeds during the harsh winter months.

There are exceptions, however. Some seeds, including those of hellebores, peonies, gentians and many alpines, are best sown outdoors in late autumn or early winter in order to undergo a period of freezing before germination.

When raising plants that need a long germination period, including many trees and shrubs, the best plan is to sow in the autumn – no later than September – when there is sufficient natural light to produce strong seedlings. These can be kept growing slowly under glass through the winter. Pricking out these seedlings in February or March will result in almost two years' growth in one.

This technique is particularly useful for primulas and meconopsis, already mentioned as having short-lived seeds, and also for rhododendrons and allied species which are very slow growing.

Biennial plants, and those grown as biennials (wallflowers and sweet williams, for instance) need somewhat similar timings, although they are sown earlier, usually in June or July. The plants are put in their flowering positions before the winter and are then ready to flower the following spring.

Spring is the main sowing time, although if you have a heated greenhouse or heated propagator it can begin as early as the second half of January – especially for such plants as begonias. The important thing is to have plants just ready for setting out when the danger of frost is over and the soil is warming up.

Stratification
Exposure to frost helps to soften the hard or fleshy coats on seeds from trees and shrubs, and thus to hasten germination. The seeds are layered, in boxes or pots of damp sand, and placed outdoors for the winter, with a top covering of fine-mesh wire-netting to prevent entry by rodents.

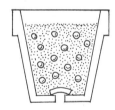

CUTTINGS

Plants grown from cuttings, unlike those raised from seeds, need to be encouraged by various means. Principally, this involves keeping them in good condition for as long as it takes to produce the roots with which they will support themselves. This done, they will grow into replicas of the plant from which the original material was taken.

This is the essential difference between propagating from cuttings and growing from seed. A seedling is unique in itself and may differ from the parent, whereas cuttings are replicas of the mother plant.

From the collecting of the material and throughout its processing the main aim must be to prevent loss of moisture. A polythene bag is invaluable for keeping material moist. Kept cool and out of bright light, it will remain fresh for a few days. Nevertheless, the sooner the cuttings are in a propagating frame the better.

Cuttings may be of soft or semi-ripe growth, of ripened wood or hard wood. Softwood cuttings are taken from the immature tips of shoots. Semi-ripe cuttings are current season's shoots that have become woody near the base but still have soft tips. Ripe cuttings are firm, mature growths. Hardwood cuttings are taken from hard, woody shoots at the end of their first growing season.

Soft cuttings The speed with which these cuttings, taken in June or July, can be removed from the parent plant and placed in their new environment has a direct bearing on the chances of success. Use a container of a size to suit the number of cuttings, placing in it a compost mixed from equal parts of moss peat and gritty sand. It is better to keep each batch of cuttings separate, for this simplifies subsequent hardening off and growing on.

The condition of the softwood cuttings needs to be just past the soft, floppy stage, usually indicated by a general darkening of the stem. Do not make the cutting any longer than necessary – about 5–10 cm (2–4 in) of stem is suitable. If the cutting has a pithy or hollow stem, cut through a joint, but otherwise just cut to length. Reduce the leaves to three or four per cutting.

Do not use hormone rooting powder. Any advantages are likely to be cancelled out by the burning which often occurs with cuttings of this type.

As the cuttings are soft, a dibber is needed to make holes in the compost before inserting them. Afterwards, water them in with a fine-rose watering can and place them in a close, humid atmosphere. A propagator with a plastic lid is suitable, or you can place the containers on peat in a deep box, with a sheet of glass over the top, or in a pot covered with a plastic bag.

Mist propagation provides the conditions most likely to result in successful rooting, and quite small units are available for the greenhouse. These devices spray the cuttings at intervals with a fine mist of water, the frequency depending on the humidity at any given time. The control is automatic and very sensitive.

Semi-ripe and ripened cuttings Use a polythene bag to collect the material as for soft cuttings. However, speed is not quite so important. In fact, if there is likely to be some delay between collecting and inserting the cuttings, semi-ripe and ripened

SOFT CUTTINGS

1 Take soft tip cuttings in early summer, from young non-flowering shoots.

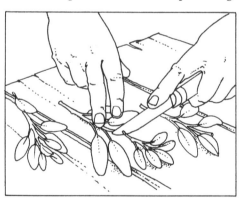

2 Trim cuttings to no more than 10 cm (4 in).

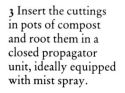

3 Insert the cuttings in pots of compost and root them in a closed propagator unit, ideally equipped with mist spray.

cuttings, taken from mid-July until the end of August, are the most suitable.

The cuttings can be a good deal longer— some 15 cm (6 in)—than a soft cutting, although they are prepared in the same way. If hollow or pithy, cut through a joint or at a heel; otherwise just cut to length. Remove sufficient leaves, or cut the leaves in half, to give a good balance between stem and leaf.

This type of cutting differs from a softwood cutting in that it is an advantage to wound the lower part of the stem. Wound by removing a slither of rind about 2.5 cm (1 in) long. It is not fully understood why wounding stimulates rooting but it is probably due to improved absorption of water and to the larger area that can be treated with a root-stimulating hormone.

Having prepared the cuttings, immerse them in a solution of benomyl fungicide at the rate that is recommended by the manufacturer.

After allowing the surplus solution to drain, dip the wounded area into a proprietary hormone rooting powder, first tipping a small amount into a suitable container. Do not return any surplus to the main supply. Maintain the effective life of the powder for as long as possible by storing it in a cool, dark place.

Insert the prepared cuttings in a compost consisting of equal parts of peat moss and gritty sand and place the container in a greenhouse where heat is available to keep the compost at about 16 °C (60 °F). Water them in and cover with thin, transparent polythene – the type used by dry cleaners is ideal. Place the plastic so that it is in actual contact with the cuttings and seal the edges by tucking them under the container.

Every ten days or so take the polythene off, remove any dead or diseased material, check whether more water is needed and then give a light watering with benomyl solution. Reverse the polythene and replace it for the next ten days, when the process should be repeated. The thin plastic film soon mists over and this will help to protect the cuttings from scorching. Even so, additional shade may be needed during a very hot and sunny summer, both on the greenhouse glass and over the plastic.

SEMI-RIPE AND RIPENED CUTTINGS

1 Trim semi-ripe cuttings to a length of 15 cm (6 in).

2 Remove a slither of rind and dip in benomyl solution.

3 Coat cuttings with rooting compound and insert in compost.

4 Cover with clear plastic and place in a warm greenhouse.

When the plants start to grow away, perhaps with roots protruding from the base, harden them off gradually by slitting the polythene in stages until they are able to stand uncovered without flagging.

Hardwood cuttings These are the easiest to strike, October being the best month. Taken as a rule from deciduous species and fully ripened shoots, a minimum of moisture is lost through transpiration. Because of this, good plants can be produced by inserting them outdoors in a sheltered border during the autumn. Each cutting should be 23–30 cm (9–12 in) long and inserted for two thirds of its length.

The usual practice is to plant them 10–13 cm (4–5 in) apart in a slit made with a spade. It is helpful, but not essential, to place some gritty sand in the bottom of the slit. Lift the cuttings a year later and plant them out to grow on.

Fully ripened cuttings taken from evergreens, such as cotoneaster and berberis, are best rooted in a cold frame in October or November. Remove 10–15 cm (4–6 in) of soil from the frame and replace with a

Hardwood cuttings
Take cuttings up to 30 cm (1 ft) long, in autumn, and root them in the open. Set them 10 cm (4 in) apart and up to two-thirds their length, in a trench lined with coarse sand. They take about a year to root.

Root cuttings
Root cuttings are taken during dormancy. Slice off a strong root near the crown of a lifted plant (1). Remove side roots and slice the cutting into 4 cm (1½ in) pieces (2), making a straight cut at the top and a slanting cut at the base of each (3). Insert in pots of gritty compost, straight-cut level with the top (4) and cover with sand (5).

compost mixed from two parts sand to one of peat moss. Prepare as described for semi-ripe cuttings, then plant them in rows with a dibber. Little attention is needed, except that some shading will be required the following spring.

It is an odd fact that when hardwood cuttings are planted in a bundle, instead of being lined out individually, more of them root and overall root growth is stronger. If you care to experiment, plant your cuttings in bundles, then lift them the following spring and plant them out individually.

Root cuttings Most plants with thick, fleshy roots, such as *Primula denticulata*,

can be propagated from root cuttings. Winter is the best time, preferably December.

The mother plant needs to be vigorous and healthy, and, if possible it should be lifted completely. This is no problem with such herbaceous plants as *Papaver orientale* (oriental poppy) and the cultivars of *Anchusa azurea*, but if a plant is too large to be lifted easily, the root nearest the main stem will give satisfactory results.

When removing a root from the plant to be propagated, make a right-angle cut nearest to the plant and a diagonal cut at the opposite end, otherwise you may forget which end is which. Shoots will grow from the end that was nearest to the plant and roots from the other end.

After washing soil from the roots, cut them into 4 cm (1½ in) lengths, using the same technique to identify the ends, then dust with fungicide. Fill some 9 cm (3½ in) pots to within 2 cm (¾ in) of the rim with well-drained gritty seed compost. Using a dibber, insert the cuttings upright, the straight-cut ends level with the top of the compost. If the root cuttings are less than 1.5 cm (½ in) in diameter, put two in each pot. Finally, cover the cuttings with 1.5 cm (½ in) of sand.

Roots that spread just below the surface, and have buds spaced evenly along their length, can also be propagated by this means. *Romneya* (tree poppy) and *Tropaeolum speciosum* (flame flower) are examples. In this case, cut the roots into 4 cm (1½ in) lengths and place them horizontally on the surface of the compost. Regulate the number of cuttings in each pot by their thickness – that is, the larger they are, the fewer to the pot – then cover with sand as for cuttings with fleshy roots.

Some warmth is helpful for stimulating these root cuttings into growth.

LAYERING

Layering is a natural method of propagation for many plants, and in many cases they need no more than a little encouragement. Heather shoots, for instance, will form independent roots when pegged down under a covering of compost. Carnations simply need pegging down onto the

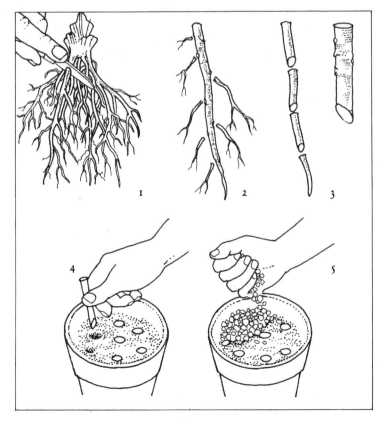

LAYERING

1 Layer young and pliable outer shoots of woody-stemmed plants in autumn. Begin by making a shallow oblique cut, thus forming a tongue.

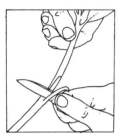

2 Peg the shoot into position (see detail), keeping the tip upright and securing it to a bamboo cane.

surrounding soil. Blackberries and related plants form thickets when their growing tips root into the ground.

To layer a tree or a shrub there must be a convenient branch near the ground. Given this, most can be propagated in this way.

Select a pliable shoot on the branch and peg it down securely. This is important, for no roots will form if there is any movement. Bend the end of the shoot upright and secure it to a bamboo cane. Wound the part of the stem in contact with the soil by scraping it or cutting a tongue in it, then cover the wounded area with compost. The plant must not be severed until it has made sufficient roots to stand on its own, which takes a minimum of a year.

Air layering may be tried when conventional layering is not possible. This long-established technique, made easier with the aid of polythene film, can be used on shrubs growing outside and also on indoor plants. A rubber plant (*Ficus elastica*) that has lost its lower leaves can have the top layered and the lower part discarded.

Spring is the best time to air layer, though this is not so important for plants growing indoors. The same method is used for all species.

Select a healthy shoot with a strong tip – preferably about the thickness of a pencil. If only weaker shoots are available, some additional support will be needed. With a sharp knife cut a tongue into the stem 15–20 cm (6–8 in) from the tip of the shoot, taking care not to cut any deeper than a quarter of the way through. Insert a little moist sphagnum moss into the tongue, sufficient to keep it open. Now place a tube formed from polythene film, 10 cm (4 in) wide, over the end of the shoot and use adhesive tape to secure it 5–8 cm (2–3 in) below the tongue.

Next, fill the sleeve with moist, clean sphagnum moss and secure the upper end the same distance above the tongue. If you form the tube yourself from sheet polythene, place the overlap on the underside to prevent water entering. If the layer is on a weak shoot, either tie it to a nearby branch or support it with a bamboo cane.

Inspect the layer every week or so to check that water has not got in. If it has, remove the tape and squeeze out surplus moisture. As soon as sufficient roots have grown, cut the layer from the plant, take off the polythene and the piece of stem below the roots and pot the new plant into John Innes potting compost no 1, or a soil-less equivalent. It will need protection in a frame or greenhouse, and must be shaded from sun until established.

Layering is not used to any great extent commercially these days, except for the production of fruit rootstocks. An interesting variant, called French mound layering, is sometimes used to propagate *Cotinus coggygria* (smoke bush).

Air layering
Woody plants without pliable shoots can be propagated by air layering. Select a young shoot, strip it of most of its leaves and make a cut about 15 cm (6 in) from the tip. Keep the tongue open with sphagnum moss and cover it with a polythene sleeve, packed with moist moss, above and below the cut.

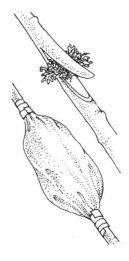

PLANT PROPAGATION

This method starts with a plant pruned hard back to produce strong, whippy growths from ground level. In the following spring, a strong shoot is pegged down parallel to and just above the soil. The laterals will then grow upright and at right-angles to the pegged-down shoot.

When the laterals are 10 cm (4 in) or so long, soil is mounded around them progressively and the roots will grow into this. By the following autumn, each lateral will have formed a separate, rooted plant and can then be severed.

GRAFTING AND BUDDING

Grafting consists of putting together two pieces of plant material in such a way that they will grow together and form a single plant. The part providing the root is called the stock; the part that will produce the stem, flowers and fruit is called the scion.

This means of propagation is used principally for fruit trees and for certain shrubs. Rootstocks are selected according to their vigour, so determining the size of the tree or bush. The scion is cut from a parent plant of the chosen species or cultivar, a form of vegetative propagation that ensures an exact replica of flowers, fruits and other characteristics, excluding vigour.

The key to joining the scion and the stock is the matching up of the cambium layers – the layer of cells situated between the bark and the inner wood of a plant. A successful graft brings the cambium layers into contact, and stock and scion will unite if given suitable growing conditions.

Grafting is principally a technique for nurserymen, most gardeners having no need to undertake it themselves. It can take a number of different forms, some concerned with rejuvenating old or damaged trees, but the aim is essentially the same in each case – that of joining parts of two or more living plants so that they can grow on a single rootstock.

Budding is essentially the same procedure. However, instead of a scion being inserted (which consists of a portion of the stem and, sometimes, leaves as well) a bud is inserted into the stock.

Some skill is needed, together with a strong, sharp knife, for successful grafting.

Gardeners interested in this rather specialized subject should study one of the several books that explain the techniques in detail.

Few ornamentals are now propagated by budding, but budding and grafting are still the standard propagation methods for fruit trees. At one time roses were produced exclusively by budding but they are now propagated in large numbers by Meristem culture in the laboratory, a method not available to amateur gardeners.

This technique involves removing tiny growth tips with the aid of a microscope. These growth buds, which may be a mere half millimetre across, are placed aseptically into a nutrient solution and sealed in glass flasks, which are moved continuously. When the tiny pieces have grown to perhaps five or six millimetres, they are cut into four and grown on in flasks until they, in turn, are divided. Within a year – theoretically, anyway – many hundreds of plants can be raised, each one an exact reproduction of the original.

DIVISION

As the name implies, this involves dividing the plants into pieces, each having a root system and so forming a new plant. Herbaceous perennials lend themselves to this method; in fact, the majority benefit from being divided every three to four years and the old centre of the plant being discarded. Exceptions include peonies, veratrums, lythrums and kniphofias, which are better left for a longer period unless extra plants are needed. Plants with fleshy roots can be cut into portions, provided each piece has at least one bud or crown of leaves.

Many different plants can be increased by division, but it needs doing with care. Often, a large clump that looks just right for division is actually on a single stem.

Generally, division should take place in the autumn or spring and the pieces potted or planted immediately. Spring is the better season, and plants should be divided in the autumn only if the soil is light and sandy.

Tubers and corms can be divided, too, by cutting them into portions in the same way as plants with fleshy roots. Each piece must have a bud from which to produce top growth.

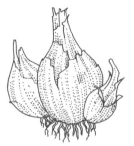

1 Gladiolus corm

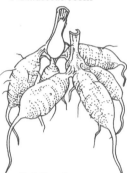

2 Dahlia tuber

Propagating corms and tubers
Separate cormlets (1) from the parent corm in autumn and grow them on in a nursery bed. Divide tubers (2) by cutting upwards through them so that each section contains part of the main stem.

Bulb offsets
Many bulbs form offsets next to the mother bulb. These can be removed and grown on in a nursery bed until they reach flowering size.

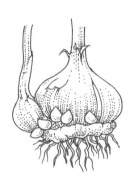

PLANT PROPAGATION

Potatoes can be cut into pieces before planting; the tuberous begonia may be cut in half, and dahlia tubers divided. As a precaution against infection, allow the cut surfaces to dry naturally before planting, or dust them with a fungicide.

BULBS AND CORMS

Both bulbs and corms can be grown from seed, but in many cases it will take a long time for them to attain flowering size. From five to seven years is not unusual, and for this reason vegetative propagation methods are generally preferred.

Bulbs and corms are composed of swollen underground leaves or stems which act as food stores to sustain the plant during the dormant period. When in active growth, the leaves manufacture food, which is passed down to this store, so promoting a continuing growth cycle from year to year.

Corms differ from bulbs in that most die after a year's growth, a new corm replacing the old one. Exceptions to this include gloxinias, begonias and cyclamen, where the corm does not die annually but goes on increasing in size.

In addition to producing a new corm each year, gladiolus forms cormels or spawn. When lifting gladioli in the autumn, the spawn can be removed and then stored dry through the winter. The following spring they can be planted in a nursery bed and grown on for two or three seasons until they reach flowering size.

Some bulbs similarly produce small bulbs, or offsets, which can be removed and grown on to increase the stock. Sometimes the bulb will itself divide, making two or three smaller bulbs, and these can be used as a method of increase.

Lilies can be propagated from scales – a task for the dormant season. Remove sound, healthy scales from the outside of a newly-lifted bulb, dust them with sulphur and then mix them with damp peat moss. Place this mixture of scales and peat in a polythene bag, seal the opening and place it in a warm, dark place.

Inspect the scales from time to time. When they show signs of fresh growth, remove them from the bag and plant them

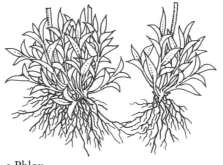

1 Phlox

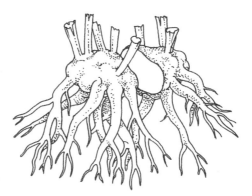

2 Delphinium

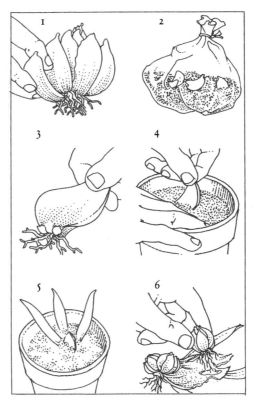

Dividing perennials

Division of perennials is best done in spring. Split overgrown clumps of fibrous plants (1), if need be with two garden forks back to back to prise them apart. Replant only outer sections and discard the centre. Plants with tough woody crowns (2) can be difficult to divide. Split the lifted plants, using a sharp knife, into sections, each with roots and growth buds.

Propagating lilies from scales

Lilies may be increased from scales. Detach a number of plump scales from the base of a healthy bulb (1). Place the scales in a polythene bag of moist peat moss (2); after about 6 weeks bulbils should appear (3). Pot the scales (4), and when shoots appear (5), separate the small bulbs (6), pot them up singly and grow on for several years.

Lily bulbils
Some lilies produce bulbils in leaf axils. Pot in seed compost to reach flowering size in 3 years.

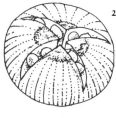

Hyacinth offsets
Make 2–3 wedge-shaped cuts across a dormant bulb base (1); place it on moist sand, in the dark, and wait for small bulbs to appear (2).

in a container of potting compost, where tiny bulbs will form at the base of each scale. The small bulbs will need to be grown on for a season before being hardened off and planted out.

Some lilies – including *Lilium lancifolium* (syn. *L. tigrinum*) and *L. speciosum* – produce tiny bulbs in the axils of their leaves, a habit that can be encouraged by removing the flower buds before they open. Grow on the bulbils as you would bulbs propagated from scales.

Hyacinths produce offsets very slowly, so some encouragement is needed. The right time is during the dormant season. With a knife, take out two wedges at right-angles to each other across the base of the bulb. Place on sand, with the cuts upwards, in a warm, dark place. After eight to ten weeks, remove and grow on the small bulbs that will have grown from the cut surfaces.

PROPAGATION – THE LATER STAGES

Whichever method was used, the after-care of newly-propagated plants is much the same. A basic rule, for instance, is to make changes of environment as gradual as possible. So, when moving plants outdoors from a greenhouse, frame or propagator, increase the degree of exposure over a period of several days. Similarly, for newly-rooted cuttings that are growing in a warm, humid atmosphere, increase the ventilation slowly, over a period of six or seven days.

Shade seedlings from strong sun for a few days after they have been pricked out. They will do better if set fairly close together in boxes rather than pricked out individually into pots. Cuttings, too, make better growth if placed near each other in small pots, and then potted on into larger containers as they develop. Outdoors, set them in nursery rows at first, not in their final positions.

Never pot in ordinary garden soil, which will become compacted and may also harbour disease organisms. Either mix your own potting compost or else buy one of the proprietary types. Take care over the preparation of outdoor nursery beds.

Unless rooted early in the year, cuttings from deciduous plants struck under glass should not be disturbed. Leave them until growth appears in the following spring, then transplant them when the dormant buds start into growth.

COMPOST

A good seed compost can be made with equal parts of peat moss, sterilized loam and gritty sand. To this add a compound slow-release fertilizer at the rate of 1½ tablespoons per 4.5 litres (1 gal). Unless you are germinating the seeds of plants that require acid conditions, add ground chalk or limestone at half the rate of the fertilizer.

Whether boxes, pots or pans are used for seed sowing, good drainage is essential. Even the best-textured compost will become too wet if surplus water is unable to drain away.

A general guide to sowing depth under glass is that it should be roughly twice that of the thickness of the seed. Outdoors, where the surface soil is liable to dry out and there are birds and mice to contend with, somewhat deeper sowing is usual.

For fine seeds sown under glass, it is better not to give a covering of compost. After germination you may need to dust the surface lightly with fine sand if the first tiny roots spread along the surface instead of penetrating the compost. This often happens with the germinating seedlings of rhododendrons and primulas.

If it is expected that germination will be slow – and this applies to many of the alpine plants – it is a good idea to cover the sown seeds with a thin dusting of grit. This acts as a mulch, keeping the surface of the compost moist and free from mosses. Alternatively, some very small seeds are best sown by sprinkling them on the grit and then watering them into the gaps between the particles.

Growing any plant from seed, whether an easy bedding plant or a rare gem, is possibly one of the most exciting and rewarding aspects of gardening. At Wisley we are still experimenting with certain seeds to find the varying combinations of warmth and cold, over precise periods, to unlock their protective mechanisms.

CHAPTER TWO

GARDEN PLANNING & SPECIAL INTERESTS

Garden making is a continuous process, changing over the years as plants mature or outgrow their allotted space, and as the family needs alter or energy diminishes. Few people acquire the garden of their dreams; sometimes it starts out as a virgin building site, on other occasions it can be a neglected wilderness, and often it is a well-tended but unimaginative plot. In all cases, the sensible thing is to plan the garden's development, assessing its possibilities and deciding on the features it should contain. Finances may not allow the installation of a greenhouse immediately, but in a well-designed garden a suitable site would be allotted to it from the outset. The same applies to such permanent features as rock gardens and pools, terraces and patios and raised beds, the construction of which is described and illustrated in this chapter.

Small gardens – even miniature ones like balconies, roof gardens and tiny basement areas – need just as careful planning. Many plants, trees and shrubs included, are ideally suited to container growing, and alpines especially show to advantage in sinks and troughs.

Peat beds permit the cultivation of those acid-loving plants that would otherwise die in a limy soil, and a properly-equipped greenhouse extends the gardening season to a full twelve months in a year.

In many ways it is easier and more satisfying to plan a garden when the plot is brand new and undeveloped – as left by the builders, in fact. When taking over an existing, well-kept garden there is less incentive to put one's own stamp on it, while a neglected or derelict plot has to be reclaimed before worthwhile reconstruction can start.

Even so, the basic stages are the same in each case. First, an assessment of the site must be made to see what conditions and features it has to offer. Next, you have to think carefully about what sort of garden you want and what it should contain. Finally, armed with this knowledge, a detailed design can be mapped out.

ASSESSING THE SITE

Soil and aspect are fundamentals, affecting everything you will grow and do. Elevation and the degree of exposure come close behind. See also *Getting to Know Your Soil* and *Coming to Terms with Climate*.

You will also have to take stock of buildings – including the shade that they cast. Apart from the house, there may be a garage and one or more sheds to consider. Paths, a driveway, large trees and existing local bye-laws are other features that will influence the eventual design.

Garden site plan
A site plan is essential for good garden design. For awkward plots, divide the sketch into units of squares or triangles (*right*), or mark in a base line from which measurements can be taken to the right and left (*below*).

On a more mundane level, such items as the refuse bin, clothes line, compost bin and incinerator will all have to be found a home. It is easier to take them into account right from the start rather than have to fit them into a finished design. Remember that an open, sunny position is needed for clothes drying, the same conditions that suit so many flowering plants.

Site plan At this stage it is as well to start getting things down on paper. It is much easier to alter a drawing than to rectify mistakes made in the garden. It should be emphasized, though, that the drawing is only a means to an end. Its purpose is to provide a fairly accurate site plan on which to work out ideas gathered while actually 'on the ground'.

The important thing is that it should be in proportion. With this in mind, the first step is to prepare a rough sketch on which to record measurements taken on site. From this, a finished outline plan can then be drawn.

Nothing elaborate is needed, but to get the measurements you will require a long tape measure and a helper. If the garden is not symmetrical it may be easier to make a plan by dividing it into squares, rectangles and triangles. In the case of a really oddly-shaped site, a 'base line' may be drawn and the measurements taken from this at right-angles.

Obviously, you will have to work to a definite scale. If you prefer metric measurements, the scale can give a reduction of 50 or 100 times (that is, 1 cm on the drawing can represent either 50 or 100 cm). In imperial measurements, reductions of 48 times or 96 times are convenient, so that 1 in can represent 4 ft or 8 ft.

Choice of scale depends on the size of the garden and what drawing paper you have on hand. A sheet of A3 paper will allow lines of 40 cm (16 in) and 28 cm (11 in). Based on a metric scale of 1:100, this would be suitable for a site measuring 40 m × 28 m (about 131 ft × 92 ft).

DECIDING WHAT YOU WANT

This is not the time to choose individual species but to decide what broad types of plants you wish to grow and to consider such features as a lawn, a rock garden, a greenhouse and so on. Choosing the right position for each can be quite critical, especially if part of the garden is often in shade. For instance:

Lawn This needs placing fairly centrally and requires a reasonably open and sunny position. Central placing allows a lawn to be used as a link between other garden features and to serve as a foil to colourful plants around it. When deciding its position, remember also that it will act as a leisure area for relaxing and playing.

Roses, annuals, greenhouse and rock garden All of these also need a reasonably sunny and open site, away from overhanging trees. A rock garden does best if it has a southerly aspect and it often provides a good use for sloping ground.

If you plan to add a greenhouse in a few years' time, lay the electricity cable now so that you do not have to dig up the lawn or a path later on.

Herbaceous border Although a sunny position is fine, many perennials will grow in semi-shade. This may prove a considerable help when planning a garden overshadowed by trees or buildings.

Shrubs Just as with herbaceous perennials, there are types to suit nearly every soil and situation. Remember, too, that they can be invaluable for screening.

Fruit and vegetables The ideal spot would have well-drained soil in an open, sunny position, with protection from cold winds. Frost pockets are not really suitable. If a fruit cage is planned, allow for access into it and around it.

Pool A fairly sunny position is needed, not too close to trees. Often, a pool forms part of a rock garden layout, perhaps with a cascade or waterfall. The latter, or a fountain, will need a supply of electricity, so it should not be too far from the nearest mains circuit.

Though filling and emptying are only occasional tasks, position the pool within reach of a hose and in a spot where the contents can be siphoned off as needed.

Peat beds The retaining walls are made with peat blocks, which need to be kept moist in order to prevent shrinking. A shady position makes this easier and is also essential for many of the plants that thrive in such a bed. A peat bed or a retaining wall is also a good way to make use of a north-facing slope.

Trees Their choice and placing needs careful thought, for trees are often the dominant feature in a small garden and will usually outlast the gardener. In particular, consider the shade a tree will cast and its effect on your garden or a neighbour's.

MAKING THE DESIGN

Having decided roughly where things should be, the next step is to create a pleasing design around them. This is a very different matter from drawing attractive curves and patterns on a sheet of paper and then trying to fit in the features you would like to include. Although every design will be different, there are a few basic rules.

1) The centre of the garden should be kept open and uncluttered.
2) Curves should be gentle.
3) Although straight paths provide the shortest route, they are not necessarily the most attractive. On the other hand, too devious a route will tempt people to take short cuts. It is a good idea to walk a proposed route a few times before committing yourself.
4) Aim for a surprise or two, rather than having the whole garden visible at a glance.
5) Plan for some 'views' and focal points to draw the eye.
6) Remember, a garden is primarily for plants.

Style A garden can be its owner's original creation or else be based on a definite style – formal, informal, Elizabethan, cottage, Japanese and so on. Where a style would clash with such alien items as a garage or oil tank, the answer is to restrict it to just one part of the garden. In this way, different styles can co-exist, but in separate areas.

AN EXERCISE IN GARDEN PLANNING

To suggest how these theoretical considerations work in practice, the following is an account of how one medium-size garden, attached to a semi-detached house, was planned and developed.

The site is long and narrow, bordered on the south by a private road and on the east by a public road. In addition to its awkward shape, the plot slopes slightly to the north, while the eastern boundary is open to bitter winds in winter. Mature oaks and chestnuts in the field on the east side cast shade, and there were already four mature trees within the garden to be taken into account.

The soil is a sandy loam over clay, the topsoil being well-worked and fertile. The new occupier chose to develop the plot in the style of a cottage garden.

ROUGH-SKETCH STAGE

This drawing, which is not to scale, includes the basic elements as they existed before the garden was developed. The main measurements are noted, together with the positions of buildings and the trees below.

- (A) *Metasequoia glyptostroboides*
- (B) *Chamaecyparis lawsoniana*
- (C) *Robinia pseudoacacia* 'Frisia'
- (D) *Chamaecyparis obtusa* 'Crippsii'

SITE PLAN

As often happens, the scaled drawing looks very different from the rough sketch, stressing its value for accurate planning. North has been indicated on the rough sketch, together with a line showing the extent of the shade cast by buildings in winter. It will be seen that the sunniest part of the garden is at the end furthest from the house.

A scale of 1:100 was chosen for the site plan. This reduces the longest measurement (40 m) to 40 cm.

The finished plan The two mature trees, although about 9 m (30 ft) tall, at the far end of the garden present no shade problem. Being fine specimen trees they were retained at either end of the kitchen garden which also includes those service areas which, though essential, have no ornamental value.

In this way, the potting shed, compost bins and incinerator are hidden from view. The frame, on the northern boundary, is partly shaded while the two greenhouses are exposed to the sun, even in winter. Both will need shading in sunny, hot periods.

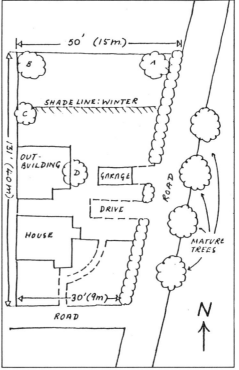

Rough sketch
Before redesigning a garden, make a rough sketch, incorporating all existing features, compass points, prevailing winds and shady areas. Include any mature trees it may be worthwhile to retain:
A *Metasequoia glyptostroboides*
B *Chamaecyparis lawsoniana*
C *Robinia pseudoacacia* 'Frisia'
D *Chamaecyparis obtusa* 'Crippsii'

Measuring 3.6 m × 5.5 m (12 ft × 18 ft), the fruit cage fits in snugly and allows access all round. Vegetables, based on the 'bed' system, completed the planning of this 'utility' area.

The weakness of this part of the garden is its general unattractiveness. It was decided to plant a shrub border to serve as a screen between the kitchen and the ornamental garden, with both deciduous and evergreen species providing year-round interest. Medium-size species were chosen, to avoid casting too much shade on the vegetables.

This shrub border also helps to enclose the 'heart' of the garden, which extends from here to the buildings. The centre is occupied by a lawn, with a rock garden set into it, and the other edges are bounded by a herbaceous border, a peat bank and bed and another shrub border.

The specimen *Robinia pseudoacacia* 'Frisia' (golden false acacia) was semi-mature and a lovely tree. Being on the western boundary, the shade it cast did not cause many problems, so it was retained.

Nearer the house, the narrow strip between the garage and outbuilding makes the garden 'wasp-waisted'. This was accentuated with further shrub plantings so that it becomes necessary to peep into the secret garden beyond. Instead of a path, which would tend to cut the open centre in half, a series of stepping stones leads across the lawn to the utility area.

There were two main viewpoints – from the drive and from the house. With these in mind, two focal points were planned – a *Cornus kousa* var. *chinensis* in the shrub border, which would be seen from the house, and a stone sundial in the herbaceous border, to be seen from the driveway.

The remaining *Chamaecyparis* provides a canopy over the wasp-waisted area and serves to increase the effect of this narrow opening. It also casts shade over an area where it is needed. For all these reasons it was decided to retain it.

Moving closer to the house, a small area was earmarked for a patio. Although in shade, it provides a cool sitting-out area in summer. Nearby, a bed alongside the garage is in full sun and ideal for sun-loving shrubs, helping to screen the building.

Outside the kitchen is a small enclosed area which contains refuse bins and a removable rotary clothes drier. There is also room for a garden seat, plant containers and a bird table. Climbing plants, chosen always for aspect, will be sited at various positions around the garden.

The south-facing side of the house constitutes the front garden. It is sheltered by hedges and provides the perfect site for choice, less-hardy plants on one side, and a heather and dwarf conifer bed on the other side of the front path.

Hedges A fast-growing hedge was considered a priority for planting along the eastern side in order to give protection from bitter winds. X *Cupressocyparis leylandii* (Leyland cypress) was chosen. It will eventually be topped at 2.4 m (8 ft), at which size it will make for much better growing conditions within the garden.

The hedge at the southern end, bordering the private road, is *Elaeagnus* x *ebbingei*. Although vigorous, it will be kept to about 1.8 m (6 ft). The dark green leaves of this evergreen shrub have a silvery reverse, looking most attractive when they flutter in the wind.

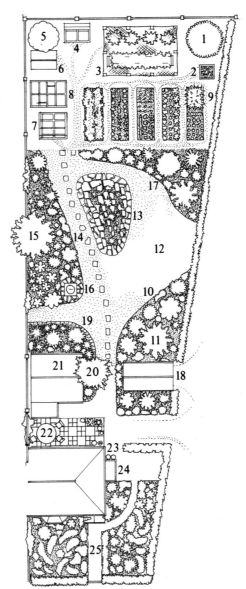

Finished garden plan
The finished plan cleverly separates the kitchen garden and utility area from the ornamental garden in the centre. Mature trees have been retained and incorporated in a design of curving lines that obscure the irregular shape.

1 *Metasequoia glyptostroboides*
2 Compost heap, incinerator
3 Fruit cage
4 Frame
5 *Chamaecyparis lawsoniana*
6 Potting shed
7 Greenhouse (food crops)
8 Greenhouse (ornamentals)
9 Vegetable beds
10 Shrub border
11 *Cornus kousa*
12 Lawn
13 Rock garden
14 Herbaceous border
15 *Robinia pseudoacacia*
16 Sundial
17 Shrub border
18 Garage
19 Peat bank
20 *Chamaecyparis obtusa*
21 Outbuilding
22 Patio
23 Refuse bins
24 Clothes drier
25 Front garden

An overgrown garden
Neglected plots are usually a tangle of weeds and brambles. These are best cleared by cutting them down, then disposed of by burning or by throwing in a hired skip.

Plunging in haphazardly with herbicides or a cultivator is the worst way to set about remaking a neglected garden. The former may destroy worthwhile plants that have survived beneath the weeds. A cultivator will multiply perennial weeds by chopping up their roots and may itself come to grief on any bricks, wire or old iron concealed in the undergrowth.

The first step, therefore, should be a careful examination of the site. If you find any interesting plants, either dig them up (if the season is right) or mark them with prominent sticks so that they can be avoided during subsequent clearance.

At the same time, remove any large obstacles, perhaps hiring a skip if there is a considerable amount of rubbish to dispose of. Remember, though, that bricks, pieces of stone and other rubble may be needed as a sub-base for a patio or paths, and in this case are better removed to an out-of-the-way corner.

Undulations in the ground may indicate old flowerbeds and paths, or even an overgrown rock garden or pool. You may well deduce where the lawn was, though whether any of these features are worth restoring will depend on their condition and, in due course, on the plans that you have for the garden.

While exploring in this fashion, note any wet spots that you find. If they persist, you will have to attend to soil drainage.

Clearing weeds and scrub Weeds and other unwanted growth will have to be cleared away before cultivations can start. Between spring and late summer you may, if you prefer, kill this growth with a herbicide before cutting it down. Weedkillers are less effective during the autumn and winter, when growth is slow or plants are dormant. They work much more rapidly when plants are growing actively.

Alternatively – and especially if the garden is only small – you may prefer to cut the weeds down by hand or with a machine while they are still active. The best hand tools are a sickle or a short-bladed scythe. Suitable powered aids for larger gardens include a motor scythe, a heavy-duty rotary grass-cutter and a petrol-powered brushcutter. All of these can be hired.

If you decide on the latter course you will still have to contend with subsequent growth of any perennial weeds. The answer is either to apply a herbicide to the secondary growth that will soon appear, or to fork out the roots by hand.

Which course you take will be governed by the size of the area and the number of perennial weeds present. If the plot has been neglected for only a short time, so that few perennial weeds have become established, annual weeds may in due course be turned in with a motor cultivator or dug in with a spade.

The best way to dispose of cut weeds, brambles and so on – whether or not treated with a herbicide – is by burning, but only if there is sufficient space to do this in safety and without annoying neighbours. Heap the cut material well away from fences or buildings, then wait for a still day on which to burn it so that smoke is not blown across nearby gardens. Where space is lacking, or there is a risk of sparks spreading the blaze, dispose of the material in a hired skip or at the local council tip.

Planning and assessment It is at this stage, before cultivations are started, that a plan of the garden's main features should be decided. What you need to know is where the soil should *not* be disturbed.

Paths, patios and foundations of all sorts are best laid on ground that is thoroughly consolidated, so these areas should be left as they are.

This is a good moment, also, to assess the depth and nature of your soil – which may well vary in different parts of the garden. For this purpose, take out a number of spade-depth holes to see how far the topsoil extends before the lighter-coloured subsoil. In subsequent cultivations it is essential not to mix the two.

If water appears rapidly in any of the holes, plunge a digging fork into the bottom in an attempt to penetrate and break up the subsoil. If this results in the water draining away after a time, you will know that there is a hard layer, or 'pan', which will need breaking up by deep digging. If the water remains, there is a drainage problem.

Cultivation Forking out perennial weeds by hand is a tedious business, but it is essential unless you use a type of herbicide that will kill both top growth and roots. This is how to set about it:

1) Mark out a rectangle as long as needed and about 1.8–3 m (6–10 ft) wide.

2) Mark a strip across one end of the rectangle about 60 cm (2 ft) wide, fork out the weeds carefully and cart them away.

3) Remove the soil from this clean strip to just beyond the far end of the rectangle, leaving a trench about 30 cm (1 ft) deep.

4) Work backwards from the trench with a fork, teasing out all perennial roots and throwing the cleaned soil forwards to maintain a trench. This hollow will form a natural separation between the worked and unworked soil.

5) Fill in the final trench with the original soil, then move to a second rectangle and start again.

6) Repeat the job in a few weeks' time if the soil was very heavily infested and there is renewed growth. Fortunately, the second clearance can be done in a fraction of the time.

Once the ground has been cleaned in this way, normal digging and manuring can go ahead (a motor cultivator may be used to speed up the work).

Reclaiming a lawn Whether reclamation is possible depends on the degree and period of neglect. It is worth attempting it if the finer lawn grasses still predominate, even if there are patches of coarser types and a large amount of weed growth.

However, if the grass has not been cut for more than a year or two, the coarse grasses will probably have taken over. In this case the only answer is to make a new lawn by seeding or turfing.

Spring or early summer are the best times to make a start with renovation. Reduce the height of the overgrown grass progressively over several weeks until the blades are set at about 2 cm (¾ in). A rotary grass cutter is ideal for this. Do not mow lower than this until the finer grasses are growing strongly.

Apply a turf fertilizer, watering it in should the weather be dry. When the effect is visible, and assuming that there are

Removing perennial weeds
Mark out a 1.8–3 m (6–10 ft) wide rectangle, with a 60 cm (2 ft) wide strip across one end. Remove the weeds and the first ft of soil, leaving a 30 cm (1 ft) deep trench. Work backwards, 60 cm (2 ft) at a time, teasing out roots and throwing cleaned soil forwards. Fill in the final trench with the original soil, mark out a second rectangle and begin again.

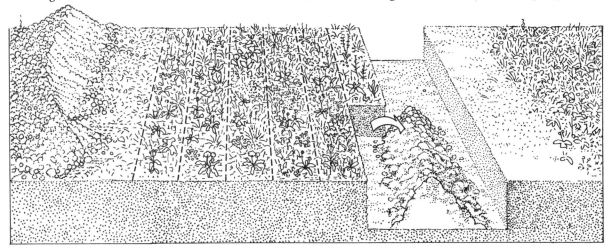

weeds present, apply a lawn weedkiller based on 2,4–D, repeating as necessary.

If there are bare patches – perhaps where weeds have been killed – loosen the surface, work in a dusting of fertilizer and sprinkle some grass seed. It is a good plan to mix this with fine soil before sowing. Cover with cotton or netting to keep the birds off and be prepared to water frquently, using a fine rose on the can, if the weather is dry.

It is surprising what a transformation can be made in a few months. It is essential, however, not to let the recovering lawn become too dry. A second feed may be given between six and eight weeks later, during July or August, if the first was applied in spring. In September, scarify and aerate the lawn and apply an autumn-grade lawn fertilizer.

Shrubs Shrubs that are overgrown and unpruned are fairly easily restored to more orderly growth.

If they are not in too bad a state you will need to know in each case whether they flower on the current year's growth or on that of the previous season. This will tell you which wood to cut out and which to leave, and you can then follow the normal pruning method for the species.

However, if a shrub has been neglected for some time, and is really straggly, it may be better to cut the branches right back and start again, even if this means losing a season's flowers.

This hard pruning must be done while the plants are dormant, between December and February, and it is the species flowering on year-old wood that will miss a season's blooms. Those flowering on shoots produced the following spring will not be affected.

After such drastic pruning, be sure to keep the plants watered during dry spells. Mulch well and feed generously until they are fully re-established.

Roses Treat shrub roses just like other shrubs, if necessary cutting hard back to encourage a fresh framework of branches. This can also be attempted with large-flowered bush roses (hybrid teas) and cluster-flowered bush roses (floribundas), but the chances of a full restoration after a long period of neglect are not so good.

Make sure that the pruning cuts are above the old grafting point, visible as a knob or a bulge at the base of the stem. Cutting too low will encourage suckers from the rootstock – one or two of which may well appear in any case.

Do not be tempted to add new roses to an old bed. The soil must be replaced or sterilized, or a new site chosen.

Herbaceous plants The remnants of a border will include the strong-growing, common and somewhat coarser species. They are likely to be entangled with weeds. Renovation is best carried out between autumn and spring and is usually done by hand, as described here, but a weedkiller may be used instead.

First, dig out the plants and place them temporarily in spare ground. Next, fork out the perennial weeds as described. Dig the border over to a spade depth, adding plenty of good manure or compost, and leave it to settle for a few weeks.

Divide any plants that are worth saving, at the same time teasing out weed roots

Pruning shrubs
Overgrown shrubs, including roses, can often be reclaimed by drastic pruning in the dormant season. Remove all dead wood and cut main branches hard back, if necessary to just above the ground. With mulching and feeding, new strong shoots should grow from low down; no flowers can be expected in the first season.

with great care. Replant fist-size pieces from the outsides of the clumps, or even single-stem divisions. Space these in groups, well apart, and purchase new, choice plants to fill the gaps.

Pools Spring is the best time to empty a pool and take stock of its condition and contents. Make a temporary container in which to place the fish, if any, and pieces of plants that you wish to retain.

Small cracks in concrete pools can be repaired with a special plastic paint sold for the purpose. If the cracks are extensive, however, it would be better to install a PVC or butyl liner, first covering the concrete with a fibreglass blanket.

Repair kits are also available for liners and fibreglass pools that are leaking due to a puncture.

Rock gardens If annual weeds are the only problem, careful hand-weeding is all that is needed. However, the chances are that creeping perennial weeds will be growing under and between the rocks. In this case, the conventional solution is to remove the rocks, clean the site meticulously and then rebuild. Alternatively, a herbicide may be used.

If you decide to rebuild, look out for desirable, healthy plants, planting these temporarily in weed-free ground until you are ready to re-stock the rock garden.

CLEARANCE WITH WEEDKILLERS

A garden deteriorates into a wilderness in fairly well-defined stages. In particular, the type of weed growth alters, and this helps to determine the choice of weedkiller.

During the first year of neglect, many annual weeds will appear in areas that are regularly cultivated, including the vegetable garden and borders that are usually planted with summer bedding. The second year will see the appearance of perennials, and by the end of the third year annuals will mostly have been replaced by grasses and broad-leaved perennials.

Well-planted shrub borders may resist the establishment of annual weeds, except along their edges, but some of the stronger-growing perennials may soon appear. This applies particularly to scramblers, such as blackberry and bryony, and to the shrubby

elderberry, all originating from seeds dropped by birds.

When comparing weedkillers, note that some are a good deal more costly than others for treating a given area. As already mentioned, the type of weed is another factor to take into account, and so, too, is the site to be treated. Can it be left vacant for some months or do you plan to re-plant the garden almost immediately? Is there a risk of harming the roots of any trees or shrubs you want to retain?

Unplanted areas (vegetable plots, etc.) Where perennial weeds are not yet well-established, a simple method during the growing season is to spray with paraquat/diquat. The top growth will soon become brown and dead. It can then be cleared and the site dug, removing by hand the roots of any perennials. Planting or sowing may follow immediately.

Where perennials are well established, and there are no underlying tree or shrub roots, weed growth may be sprayed with sodium chlorate or ammonium sulphamate at the start of or during the growing season. Ammonium sulphamate may persist in the soil for up to twelve weeks. Sodium chlorate on the other hand can persist for up to twelve months.

Vegetation sprayed with sodium chlorate becomes highly inflammable, so be sure to use a brand containing a fire suppressant. Both chemicals are corrosive to most metals, so it is advisable to use plastic sprayers or cans.

Alternatively, spray the weeds with glyphosate. The best times are when the weeds are growing very strongly and approaching flowering, or after they have flowered but before growth begins to die in the autumn. Spraying early in the year is seldom very effective.

Glyphosate will kill many perennial weeds, checking even deep-rooting, persistent types, such as horsetail and convolvulus. It is also very effective against couch grass.

Glyphosate is inactivated on contact with the soil, so there is no risk of damage to underlying tree and shrub roots. Sowing or planting can begin as soon as the treated weeds are dead.

Couch grass
A persistent perennial weed, couch grass spreads by underground rhizomes. In uncultivated ground, treat couch grass with glyphosate. Treated plots can be dug as soon as the weed foliage has died down.

Grass weeds Where the weed growth is largely or entirely composed of grasses, including couch grass, either alloxydim-sodium, dalapon or glyphosate may be applied at a time when the grasses are growing strongly.

Alloxydim-sodium and glyphosate may be used in areas where there are underlying tree and shrub roots, and planting can take place three or four weeks later. Dalapon should not be used where there are underlying roots, except at low-dosage, maintenance rates. It is residual for some six to eight weeks.

A single treatment of either alloxydim-sodium or dalapon may not give complete control of couch grass. If the site is dug after a single treatment, bury the surviving roots (rhizomes) as deeply as possible.

Grasses and broad-leaved weeds Apply dalapon or alloxydim-sodium to the grasses while they are growing strongly. Follow this with spot-treatment of clumps or patches of broad-leaved perennials, such as nettle or dock, when they are approaching flowering or after flowering. For this spot treatment use ammonium sulphamate, mixtures of 2,4–D with dicamba, or glyphosate, choosing glyphosate where there are underlying tree or shrub roots. Alternatively, glyphosate can be used as an overall treatment.

Planted areas Couch and other perennial grasses can be controlled in neglected ornamental plantings – such as shrub borders, rose beds, herbaceous borders and rock gardens – by repeat overall spraying with alloxydim-sodium at a time when growth is vigorous.

If such areas are heavily infested with broad-leaved weeds, but the garden plants are healthy, reclamation may be possible by careful spot treatment. If most of the plants are in poor condition, remove any particularly desirable specimens, or take propagation material, then treat as for an unplanted area.

Tree and bush fruits An overgrowth of perennial weeds such as ground elder is best treated by repeat spraying with paraquat/diquat, carefully directed.

Paved areas Apply dichlobenil granules to weeds established in crevices between paving stones, in the gaps between bricks laid as patios or paths or in other inaccessible corners.

Woody weeds After several years' neglect, shrubs and hedges may largely disappear under a tangle of brambles and elderberry. Sycamore saplings may fill corners where there is sufficient light for germination, unhampered by overhead cover.

Woody-stemmed weeds such as these are most effectively controlled by treatment with mixtures of 2,4–D with dicamba, or with ammonium sulphamate.

Brambles A tangled mass of brambles is difficult to spray, so first cut the stems down to about 30 cm (1 ft) and remove them elsewhere to be burnt. Spray the freshly-cut stumps with 2,4–D/dicamba, or ammonium sulphamate, wetting them thoroughly.

Much the same treatment can be carried out where brambles are growing through a shrub or hedge. Begin by cutting through the bramble stems a few centimetres above the soil, then, wearing rubber gloves and using a soft brush, carefully apply the weedkiller solution to wet the stumps. Take great care to keep the weedkiller off the shrub or hedge and do not allow it to run off into the surrounding soil.

Ivy Sever the stems close to ground level, then treat the stump as advised for brambles. If the stems are rooted into soil or old brickwork, spray with 2,4–D/dicamba during the winter.

Tree saplings Small saplings, or large seedlings too well-rooted to be tugged out, should be cut back to 30 cm (1 ft). Apply a proprietary mixture of 2,4–D with dicamba, or a solution of ammonium sulphamate, to the freshy-cut stump surface, and also to the stem down to soil level.

Sever larger saplings about 90 cm (3 ft) above ground level and treat similarly. This longer stem will provide useful leverage when digging up the dead stump.

If not chemically treated, the stumps of sycamore and other saplings may produce strong regrowth or troublesome root suckers. Other unwanted trees or shrubs originating from bird-dropped seeds, such as elderberry, dog rose and hawthorn, may be treated in similar fashion.

Treating bindweed Spot treatment with glyphosate will kill the invasive bindweed (convolvulus) after repeat applications during the growing season. The weedkiller is inactivated on contact with the soil.

GROWING PLANTS IN CONTAINERS

I t is remarkable what can be grown in tiny town gardens and backyards where there is no space for conventional beds. The secret lies in containers, imaginatively planted and tended with loving care. They also have a part to play in larger gardens, brightening walls and window areas and bringing life and colour to otherwise drab paving.

The 'loving care' behind successful displays is, indeed, the key to growing plants that cannot extend their roots into ordinary soil. Being entirely dependent on the gardener for food and water, the quality of the display is in direct proportion to the time and care expended on them.

Hanging baskets, for instance, which have all their surfaces exposed to sun and drying winds, may need watering two or three times a day to make them flourish. So unless you are prepared to go to some trouble, it might be better to avoid containers altogether.

The choice in containers is enormous, but some are designed more for their own appearance than for the well-being of the plants. This applies especially to some stone and terra-cotta containers, where the planting surface is so often too small (Ali Baba pots, for example) or where a large surface area lacks an adequate depth for soil. The latter is a key point when choosing or making containers for plants. A depth of about 30 cm (1 ft) is the minimum for pots and tubs, although a little less will do for window boxes.

Good drainage is essential. If a container has no drainage holes, some should be made or else the vessel rejected. Rather than place it on a flat surface, which will effectively block the drainage outlets, stand it on bricks or similar supports so that the holes are clear.

The compost must be of a sort that allows water to drain freely. Ordinary garden soil is unlikely to do this. Instead, use John Innes potting compost No. 3, which is loam-based, or else a proprietary peat-based compost. The fertilizer contained in either should be of a slow-release type. Always leave a 2.5–5 cm (1–2 in) space at the top of the container to allow for thorough watering.

Plants in containers should not be fed too generously, otherwise flowers will be sacrificed for leafy growth.

HANGING BASKETS

Traditional wire baskets are still popular, but others, made of plastic, or plastic-covered wire, are now commonplace. There are also plastic and fibre types with solid or perforated sides, looking more like shallow bowls than baskets. However, the original idea of creating a lush 'hanging garden' remains unchanged, and both the style of a 'basket' and the material from which it is made become irrelevant once trailing plants have grown sufficiently to conceal it.

Moss is the traditional lining for hanging baskets, but there are now synthetic substitutes even for this. Purpose-made liners can be bought for fitting inside, fulfilling the same object of containing the soil while allowing it to drain.

The plants used traditionally for hanging baskets are not completely hardy and so must not be exposed to frosts or cold winds. This means rather late planting and development – say, from late May onwards, even in the south of Britain – unless you have a greenhouse or conservatory in which to hang the planted basket for a few weeks before moving it outside.

To fill and plant a basket – two jobs which should be done together – first rest it on a suitable stand, such as an old paint tin. Assuming that you are using moss, place this and the compost in layers, easing

Window boxes
Choose boxes that are sturdy and at least 23 cm (9 in) deep, to allow for drainage material, compost and plant roots. Perennials, like trailing ivies and pelargoniums, have deeper roots than surface-rooting annuals and bedding plants.

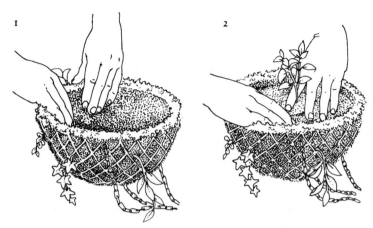

Filling a hanging basket
Traditional open-mesh hanging baskets are lined with moss (1), to conserve moisture and retain the compost. Insert trailing plants through the bottom and sides and cover the roots with compost before positioning the next layer. Set upright plants in the centre at the top (2), to give height to the composition.

plants through the wire walls at intervals and covering their horizontal roots with the next layer of compost.

Once planted, water the compost thoroughly and leave it to drain. If you have not already done so, fix a sturdy bracket or hook well able to carry the considerable weight. Bracket screws must be securely plugged into the wall. A suitable height for the basket is best judged by standing back and considering how it will look in the surroundings, also bearing in mind that it must be accessible for watering.

The range of suitable plants is not very extensive, for they have to flower over a long period, remain of a suitable size for the container and not require too-frequent dead-heading.

Trailing lobelias, planted through the moss, are ideal for the sides, and they may also be set around the top edges. Four good ones are 'Blue Cascade', 'Cambridge Blue', 'Red Cascade' (rosy red with a white eye) and 'Sapphire' (deep blue with a white eye).

Impatiens (busy lizzie) is a good choice and especially useful for a shady position. Indeed, the basket could be planted exclusively with *Impatiens*, which may be planted through the sides as well as on top. There are hybrids in a number of colours.

Pendulous begonias, as well as the fibrous-rooted bedding types, are worth considering, together with some of the larger-flowered cultivars. *Begonia* 'Pink Avalanche', an F_1 hybrid raised especially for containers, has a graceful, arching habit with cascading pink flowers.

The centre planting might be composed of zonal pelargoniums, so often called geraniums, and there is a range of colours from which to choose. Ivy-leaved pelargoniums make attractive trailing plants for the sides.

Fuchsias figure strongly in the list of candidates, and baskets made up entirely of these plants can be very striking. 'Cascade' is a popular cultivar, the white flowers having shades of carmine. There are numerous others and it would be as well to consult a nurseryman, explaining that the plants are needed for baskets.

Some of the 'silver leaf' plants are rather strong-growing for hanging baskets, but *Helichrysum petiolatum*, which throws out long stems, may be kept in check by judicious pruning.

WINDOW BOXES

A box may either rest on the sill – if necessary, supported by angled chocks to counteract the slope – or else be placed on sturdy brackets beneath the sill. The latter will permit a reasonably deep box to be used, allowing a greater depth of soil, without intruding on window space. This will also permit a box to be used that would be a little too wide to fit on the sill.

Whatever its position, the box must be secured to the wall or window frame so that it cannot become dislodged. This is doubly important above a public or frequently-used pathway.

The minimum satisfactory depth for a box is 23 cm (9 in), bearing in mind that 5–8 cm (2–3 in) of this will be occupied by drainage material, with a further 2.5 cm (1 in) watering space at the top. An inch or two extra would be an advantage.

Traditionally, window boxes are constructed from timber. The longest-lasting, and most expensive, are made of oak, teak or cedar. Softwoods are widely used, too, and give quite long service if treated with a suitable preservative, such as Cuprinol – not creosote. A lining of plastic sheeting will also delay rot, as will charring the inside with a blowlamp.

The joints are the most vulnerable part of a wooden box, which is being wetted continually. In addition to structural failure, they may allow water to leak out without wetting the soil, engendering false confidence that the plants are receiving all the moisture they need.

Plastic boxes provide an alternative to wood and there are also plastic inserts for placing in a wooden surround. Provided their appearance is satisfactory – especially colour, which can be odd – these are well worth considering.

Plants suitable for window boxes are the same as those listed for free-standing containers.

FREE-STANDING CONTAINERS

The range of potential containers is limitless, from expensive, purpose-made stoneware to boxes, half barrels, discarded wheelbarrows, troughs and even hollowed-out logs. There are, too, many quite inexpensive proprietary containers, including plastic and earthenware pots. The importance of planting area and adequate depth has already been stressed.

When planting small containers, give some thought to colour combinations and plant associations. It is better to use related or soft shades rather than lurid colours. But for really large containers, amounting almost to small beds, brighter-coloured plants are more acceptable.

For summer displays, including window-box plantings, there is almost no limit to the range of half-hardy annuals and perennials, but remember the need for a continuous display. A few plants that have the right qualities are *Ageratum*; *Begonia semperflorens*; *Dianthus*; *Heliotropium*; *Impatiens*; *Kochia trichophylla*; *Lobelia*; *Lobularia (Alyssum maritimum)*; *Tagetes* (French and dwarf African marigolds) and also cultivars of *T. signata* var. *pumila*; *Matricaria*; *Nicotiana*; *Petunia* (especially the 'Resisto' group); cultivars of *Salvia splendens*; *Verbena* – both the annual named sorts and *V. venosa*.

Foliage plants that can be raised from seed include *Centaurea candidissima*, with large silvery leaves; *C. gymnocarpa*, with silver leaves that are fern-like; *Cineraria* (syn. *Senecio*) *maritima*, with silvery cut foliage; *Chrysanthemum (Pyrethrum) ptarmiciflorum*, another silvery plant with foliage that is very finely cut; *C. parthenium* 'Aureum' has golden-yellow leaves.

While most of the plants listed are discarded at the end of the season, half-hardy perennials may be over-wintered either as plants or as cuttings. Zonal pelargoniums are an obvious example, although they may also be raised annually from an early sowing. Fuchsias, *Helichrysum petiolatum* and ivy-leaved pelargoniums may also be over-wintered.

A limited but reliable combination of bulbs and biennials will take care of the spring display. The shorter-growing narcissi and tulips, such as *Tulipa greigii* hybrids, are ideal for window boxes in combination with *Myosotis*. In more substantial containers, the larger spring bulbs can be grown with wallflowers.

If there is a problem, it is to maintain any sort of display during the winter and to overcome the pause between the planting and flowering of summer bedding. For the former, dwarf evergreen shrubs and conifers do provide out-of-season interest. Early-sown, well developed half-hardy plants can reduce the late-spring gap.

An effective alternative, if you have a greenhouse, is to use liners made from plastic or wire mesh, planting these up some time before a display is required. They can be swapped to give an instant effect, if necessary being grown on under glass in the meantime.

Containers
Free-standing containers are available in a range of materials, including wooden half-barrels, plastic bowls and fibre-glass tubs, earthenware pots, and real or reconstituted stone troughs. Choose plants and containers that harmonize in shape and size.

CREATING A COTTAGE GARDEN

The term 'cottage garden' evokes an image of thatch and lavender, of beds bright with pinks and pansies against a taller backdrop of hollyhocks, lupins, phlox and bellflowers. Somewhere in the scene will be an arch or a pergola in the close embrace of a honeysuckle.

This familiar picture – revered by romantics and town-dwellers – has been perpetuated on countless chocolate boxes and jigsaws. Yet it is a fairly recent creation and is certainly not true of cottages in bygone days.

Until fairly recent times, cottages were houses that were 'tied' to the job. Indeed, a large proportion of a cottager's wages were represented by his home, and produce from his garden was also considered as part of his earnings. It was essential, therefore, to use every inch of available space.

Usually, livestock were confined to the back-garden, with the area in front of the cottage planted with fruit and vegetables. It is not uncommon to see front gardens still used in this fashion. Only when offspring left home, and the need for garden produce diminished, would ageing cottagers allow themselves the luxury of flowering plants.

During this century, circumstances and occupational changes have altered the role of cottage gardens. Over the years the drift from the land left many cottages empty, and these were gradually taken over by more affluent home-owners. In the transition, vegetables, fruit and livestock, if any, were relegated to the end of the garden, while the remainder of the ground was given over to plants grown for love, not from necessity. Prettiness took pride of place over functional, and so the cottage garden evolved and became stylized.

It took the second World War, with the national call for home-grown food, to check the trend. Now, with the need for self-sufficiency much reduced, nostalgia is again the order of the day and there are many who seek to re-create simple, 'cottage-style' beauty around their homes.

In order to understand, and possibly adopt, the style, it is helpful to break it down into its main elements – setting, plants, continuity and method.

Suitable herbaceous perennials

Althaea rosea (hollyhock).
Anemone x hybrida (Japanese anemone).
Aquilegia vulgaris (columbine).
Aster species and hybrids (michaelmas daisy).
Campanula pyramidalis (chimney bellflower).
Delphinium species and hybrids (perennial larkspur).
Dianthus species and hybrids (pinks).
Helenium species and hybrids (sneezewort).
Kniphofia species and hybrids (red-hot-poker).
Korean chrysanthemums.
Lupinus species and hybrids (lupin).
Lychnis species (campion).
Lythrum salicaria (purple and loosestrife).
Monarda didyma (bergamot).
Nepeta x *faassenii* (catmint).
Phlox paniculata.
Rudbeckia species and hybrids (coneflower).

Rudbeckia

Sedum spectabile (iceplant).
Valeriana officinalis (valerian).

Suitable biennials include:

Cheiranthus x *allionii* (Siberian wallflower).
Cheiranthus cheiri (wallflower).

Cheiranthus cheiri

Dianthus barbatus (sweet william).
Digitalis species (foxglove).
Hesperis matronalis (sweet rocket).
Lunaria annua (honesty).
Myosotis species (forget-me-not).
Oenothera biennis (evening primrose).
Pansy.
Polyanthus.
Primula.
Viola tricolor (heartsease).

Larger shrubs include:

Buddleia davidii (butterfly bush).
Buddleia davidi var. *nanhoensis.*
Shrub roses, such as *Rosa glauca,* syn. *R. rubrifolia.*
Ribes sanguineum (flowering currant).

Smaller shrubs include:

Hypericum perforatum (St. John's wort).
Lavandula species (lavender).
Perovskia species.

Salvia Officinals

Rosmarinus species (rosemary).
Ruta graveolens (rue).
Salvia officinalis (sage).

Suitable annuals include:

Amaranthus caudatus (love-lies-bleeding).

Centaurea cyanus

Calendula officinalis (pot marigold).
Centaurea cyanus (cornflower).
Centaurea imperialis (sweet sultan).
Eschscholzia californica (Californian poppy).
Helianthus annuus (sunflower).
Lobularia maritimal (sweet alyssum).
Matthiola bicornis (night-scented stock).
Reseda odorata (mignonette).
Setaria italica (millet).

Suitable bulbs, corms, etc. include:

Convallaria majalis (lily-of-the-valley).
Crocosmia species and hybrids.
Crocus species.
Endymion non-scriptus (bluebell).
Fritillaria imperialis (crown imperial).
Iris species.
Lilium candidum (madonna lily).
Lilium regale (royal lily).
Narcissus pseudonarcissus (daffodil).
Paeonia species and hybrids (peony).
Tulipa (tulip).

CREATING A COTTAGE GARDEN

THE SETTING

A half-timbered thatched cottage is not easily purchased these days. There are, of course, many other dwellings that provide a cottage garden setting, but if you think that your home is too alien to the style, you may content yourself with a border or a bed. This should be situated away from the building, where a fence, hedge or backcloth of shrubs will help to provide a sympathetic setting.

The soil should be well-worked and weed-free but should not be over-rich. A garden around a house will provide a variety of conditions, but a bed or border, given a choice, needs to be sunny in order to suit the majority of 'cottagey' flowers.

PLANTS

Many plants fit into this concept, but there is an indispensable nucleus which epitomizes the image. These old and trusted varieties are robust, and generally lack the lurid colours of modern hybrids.

For the most part they have widely-used common names. Nevertheless, botanical names are included to avoid confusion. The lists are not exhaustive, and many gardeners will have other favourites of their own.

Biennials and a few early perennials form the bulk of the garden's spring display. The hardy annuals are sown where they are to grow and flower. Half-hardy annuals are not included, as they are often more exotic in appearance and thought to be unsuitable for this sort of planting scheme.

An apple tree seemed a prerequisite in any cottage garden, and some very old trees survive to this day. These may support a few climbers, as will pergolas, rustic fencing and sheds. Suitable climbers include *Lonicera* (honeysuckle) *Clematis vitalba* (old-man's beard) and the *montana* and larger-flowered types of clematis. Rambler roses are especially suitable, and climbers too. If you fancy a vine, choose one with culinary value that looks good.

Dry-stone walls should not be without *Sedum acre* (stonecrop) and *Sempervivum* species (houseleek). *Fumaria officinalis* (fumitory), *Valeriana officinalis* (valerian), *Cheiranthus cheiri* (wallflower) and even *Antirrhinum majus* (snapdragon) will seed and establish themselves without assistance. You may also wish to add *Aubrieta* and *Alyssum saxatilis* (golden alyssum).

Plants that will find their way into crevices include *Armeria maritima* (thrift), *Dianthus deltoides* (maiden pink) and *Viola tricolor* (heartsease).

CONTINUITY

A cottage garden will survive, flourish and diversify by self-seeding, and all biennials depend on this process for continuity. Indeed, it may be necessary to reduce the very large numbers of seedlings that do germinate, although care must be taken not to lose the random effect when thinning and transplanting.

Deadheading also controls seeding, but it is as well to leave occasional plants or stems untouched for the same reason.

Hardy annuals and some perennials will also set seed, and it is worth noting, too, that some plants help to decorate the garden with their seedheads – *Nigella damascena* (love-in-a-mist) and *Lunaria annua* (honesty) are outstanding examples.

METHOD

'If you get simple beauty, and naught else,
You get about the best thing God invents.'
 – Browning

Part of the charm of a cottage garden stems from the fact that there is no real method; no hard and fast rule; no blue-print for construction. Such a garden is individual, random and personal.

How do you copy the handful of daffodil bulbs strewn across a lawn for a natural and random effect? Only by plotting each bulb with baseline and tangents, as in surveying. But what a bore and how contrived! Certainly, a cottage garden could be plotted in this way, but on whose creations and style would it be based?

Choose plants from the lists; take note of their height but do not be too pedantic with their placings. Avoid contrived colour schemes and forms (leave that to the herbaceous border planners). Play around with plant spacings. Aim for associations and combinations employing, mostly, the single plant or occasionally a bold group.

ROCK GARDENS, RAISED BEDS AND SCREES

So-called 'rockeries' tend to be formed from heaps of stones and broken concrete, laid on a pile of earth and, as often as not, placed under a tree. As sites for growing alpines, everything about them is wrong!

The stones and concrete are supported by the soil, instead of the other way round. The light under the tree is poor, while in the autumn the leaves will put paid to any plants that do survive.

CONSTRUCTING A ROCK GARDEN

The chief requirements for a rock garden are good drainage, plenty of light and a site away from trees and shrubs. There is a real risk that falling leaves may encourage botrytis if they are left to cover the plants in autumn. Trees and shrubs in the immediate area can be tolerated only if leaves are picked up as soon as they fall – a tedious and repetitive chore.

A somewhat limited range of plants can be grown if the light is less than perfect, but there can be no compromise over drainage. Neither should there be any water running on to the site from above. Another requirement is freedom from perennial weeds, such as docks, dandelions, oxalis, creeping buttercup, ground elder and bindweed, all of which may extend their roots under the rocks and prove difficult to eradicate.

Ideally, the rock garden should be built on a slope of 20 degrees or more, facing between south-east and south-west. Failing an adequate slope, a scree bed would be preferable, or else a raised bed. It is difficult to construct a convincing rock garden on a flat site.

If there is insufficient space for any of these features, alpines may be grown in a sink or trough.

The rocks The easiest rocks to lay are those with an angular shape. These can be fitted against one another, making it simpler to retain the soil of the terrace which they edge. Failing this, you will have to do the best with what you can get, though avoid those with a pronounced rounded shape, if possible.

Planning a rock garden
On a large scale, a rock garden will consist of several terraces, rising gently (*below*). They should curve slightly into the slope (*left*) so as to suggest a natural rock outcrop. As construction proceeds, set the plants in place, in niches between the rocks, with trailing plants to spill over the rock faces, choice alpines on the terraces, and dwarf conifers and miniature shrubs and trees on upper levels.

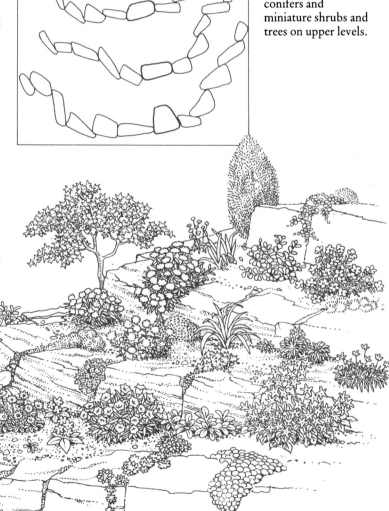

Local stone, if that exists, is usually the cheapest because it will have cost less to transport. Also, it is more likely to fit in with the local landscape and buildings.

Overall, it is better to construct just a few terraces with large rocks than to make a greater number with smaller ones, or the rocks may appear to outnumber the plants.

The principal types are sandstone and limestone. Plants of any kind will grow alongside sandstone, but lime-loving plants should have pride of place in a limestone rock garden.

Rocks are sold by weight, but your own calculations will be concerned with the number and sizes of stones needed. The best plan is to visit the supplier's premises so that you can see what he has to offer and make your requirements clear. First, though, you must do some initial planning.

To estimate the quantity and sizes of rocks to order, lay rope or thick string in jagged curves at different levels on the site, representing the tiers to be built. Measure their length, adding ten per cent extra for overlaps. When you visit the supplier it will then be fairly easy to calculate how many rocks are needed to form these tiers.

When considering the size of the rocks needed, allow for the bottom layer being set about 5 cm (2 in) into the soil. Subsequent layers should be buried about the same length below the tops of the rocks in the tier beneath them.

The height of each tier can be about the same throughout its length. The front-to-back measurement of the rocks is not critical, but each piece should be substantial enough to give support during subsequent maintenance work. It is an advantage if widths vary, with some quite broad pieces over which plants can trail, interspersed with smaller rocks that will provide plenty of crevices.

On most sites it is easier to place the largest rocks, giving the highest rise, at the base. The smaller ones can be lifted over them to form the higher terraces.

Having completed this preliminary planning it should be possible to give a rough specification of the sizes and numbers of rocks wanted. What you actually get is bound to be rather different, but any

particularly large rocks can, if necessary, be buried more deeply. Should there be any obvious strata lines, these will need to be kept parallel and not too far from the horizontal.

Construction Starting at the lowest point on the site, lay the largest rock as a keystone. This can go on the existing soil. Lean it gently into the slope, followed by other rocks to left and right of it. The line of rope laid earlier should be taken as a rough guide only, for the shapes of the stones may suggest a rather different pattern to follow.

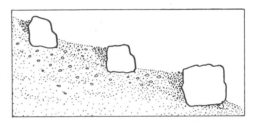

The rocks on one side of the keystone can be placed with their sides touching or else just behind the stone next in line. On the other, the overlap must be reversed. In this way, all the rocks will be wedged together, with only the keystone having its front face fully exposed.

If it is impossible to achieve a reasonably snug fit between rocks, cut them to shape and size with either a 2.5 cm (1 in) cold chisel or a bolster – the latter having a 10 cm (4 in) blade. Small gaps can be filled with off-cuts fitted in from behind and held in place with the soil that must be packed in after each rock is laid.

Avoid straight lines of rocks. The ends of each tier should 'bend' into the slope, disappearing into the soil (or into steps, where these are laid).

Lay the second and subsequent layers of rocks in the same way as the first, with their bases up to 5 cm (2 in) below the tops of the previous tier. This, together with close-fitting joints, will prevent soil erosion.

Planting in the niches between rocks must be carried out during construction. The best place is where two rocks form a narrow angle, providing space for the roots, and where the head of the plant will lie flush with the rock face. After planting,

Placing the rocks (left)
In each tier, lay the largest rock first, as a keystone, with the smaller rocks on either side. Tilt them into the slope at a slight angle so that water can percolate through to the roots; pack the soil behind each rock.

fill any gaps with wedges of stone placed from behind.

When all the rocks have been laid, remove 23–45 cm (9–18 in) of soil from behind each tier and replace it with John Innes potting compost No 2, with 25 per cent extra grit – approximately 2 mm (⅛ in) grains – and 25 per cent extra sedge peat, which has already been wetted.

To allow for settlement, fill with this compost to above the height of the rocks. The lighter the soil, the less of this soil mix is needed. About 23 cm (9 in) is sufficient for sandy soils, but a full 45 cm (1½ ft) is desirable on clay.

Constructing steps Build these while you are making the rock garden, forming them as a continuation of the tiers. Individually, the steps will not be so high, however, and two or three steps can 'run into' a single line of rocks.

Choose angular rocks, with at least one reasonably flat face, for the treads. Rounded or irregularly-shaped rocks are more difficult to walk on.

RAISED BEDS

Site and planning A flat site, or one with a gentle slope of less than 20 degrees, is more suitable for a raised bed than for a rock garden. Sited in an open position, this can provide everything needed to grow alpines successfully, although its appearance will inevitably be more formal.

Construction is straightforward, the sides being built with the fairly small stones sold for walling. No mortar is used to fill the joints, and there is no need to lay a concrete base. There are suitable plants for all aspects.

Any formal shape is suitable – including a curved rectangle, a half moon or an L-shape – and the bed can be as long as you wish. However, its width – the front-to-back measurement – must depend on its height.

For a bed up to 45 cm (1½ ft) high, the width should not exceed 1.2 m (4 ft), although this need not apply if stepping stones are laid on its surface.

For a bed 45–60 cm (1½–2 ft) high, the width can be increased to 1.5 m (5 ft), while a bed 60 cm (2 ft) or more high can be up to

1.8 m (6 ft) wide. This is because a taller wall can be leant against with your knees or thighs while weeding or planting.

Constructing a raised bed The site should not have been loosened for some time before construction. If it has, firm it thoroughly overall so that the wall does not settle unevenly.

After marking out the shape – and, on sloping ground, starting at the lowest point – choose some of the larger stones and lay them as the base for one of the walls. The bottom of each stone should be just below soil level. Continue right round the bed in this fashion.

From this stage, build up the corners a little ahead of the walls, choosing fairly substantial stones with two good faces, and then infill between them with courses of stones bonded one above the other as in a brick wall. The face of each wall should lean inwards by about 5 cm (2 in) for each 30 cm (1 ft) of rise.

Fill in with soil behind the walls as each course is built, ramming it firmly to give maximum support. Use the same soil

Raised bed
A raised bed can often replace a conventional rock garden; it is easier to construct and maintain, and the scale is more sympathetic to a small garden. Most rock garden plants thrive in a raised bed, though size will limit the choice of dwarf shrubs and the more sprawling alpines.

mixture as for rock gardens, except that the lower part of taller walls can be made up of any spare garden soil available.

With walls 30 cm (1 ft) or more high, it is well worth setting plants between some of the stones, and this must be done while the wall is being built, placing them from the front between narrow stones.

Any sample of walling stones is likely to contain some that are bigger than most of the others. Use these as 'jumpers' – pieces that occupy two or three courses. They should be fairly well separated, however, as they interfere with the bonding pattern.

The final course of stones should appear level to the eye, though not necessarily to a spirit level. To allow for settlement, the final layer of soil should be a little higher than the walls.

SCREES

A number of rock plants are adapted to growing in the litter of stones often to be found on a hillside. Scree conditions, as they are called, can be simulated in the garden, first-class drainage being the main need. Less space is required than for a substantial rock garden, while construction is both cheaper and easier.

Choosing the site In addition to good drainage, most scree plants need abundant light. For this reason the site should be clear of shadows cast by buildings, fences or trees. The site may face in any direction, provided that the slope does not exceed 20 degrees, although a north slope is the least favourable.

Avoid places close to trees or shrubs, where fallen leaves may accumulate. Remove or kill all perennial weeds, as they will be difficult to control once the rocks have been placed.

A scree bed can be of virtually any size, a gentle slope being the main need. In addition to a covering of small stones, typical of a natural scree on a hillside, a number of larger rocks should be included. As well as helping to vary the contour, these serve as stepping stones and so help to avoid compacting the soil.

Preparation Mark out the site with rope or thick string, then remove the topsoil and any turf. Dispose of the turf, unless it is

quite free from weeds and weed-type grasses. Put the topsoil on one side.

Now remove the subsoil, and dispose of it, to give an excavation with an overall depth of about 30 cm (1 ft). If any turves were saved, place these upside down in the bottom of the trench.

The next step depends on what type of soil you have. If this is anything but clay, return the topsoil to the hole. Should it be clay, however, it would be better not to use it, filling the hole instead with the gritty compost described under Construction of a Rock Garden.

A clay base is acceptable, provided that the whole scree does not form a sump into which water drains from the area around. If just the bottom is wet, this would be a good place for bog plants.

Rocks The type and size of the rocks will depend on the scale of the scree. Those with interesting shapes can be used in isolation, or groups of two or more can be placed together as outcrops. Local stone is usually the least expensive.

Although it is better to avoid pieces with regular angles, some fairly flat rocks are needed as stepping stones, enabling you to reach all parts of the scree. These apart, the chief purpose of the rocks is to provide free-draining high-spots suitable for cushion-forming plants, particularly those with hairy and blue-grey foliage.

Construction Mix some gritty but moisture-holding compost to spread over the replaced topsoil – or directly on the base in the case of clay. The mix already recommended for rock garden construction is

Scree bed
A scree bed is another variation on the rock garden theme, and suited to a gentle slope. A couple of large rocks and dwarf conifers among the surface cover of small stones add height and realism to the composition. Flat stepping stones may be incorporated into the design. The best choice of plants are those alpines which remain attractive in leaf when the flowers are over.

suitable. Spread this in layers, each well trodden in, to within 5–8 cm (2–3 in) of the surrounding ground level.

Lay the rocks on top of the soil, or just slightly buried, aiming for a balanced but informal effect. Tilt each rock slightly so that any strata lines disappear back into the slope. Ideally, the strata lines of all the rocks should be parallel and just a little off horizontal – certainly never vertical.

Over the remaining area spread a 5–8 cm (2–3 in) layer of small, broken stones to bring the surface level with the surrounding ground. These should be of the same material as the rocks, and between about 2.5–5 cm (1–2 in) thick.

Planting Plants may be placed directly in the scree material or in the surface of the soil. Those planted in the stones will soon send roots down into the soil, their necks remaining on top of the free-draining scree material.

First plant conifers and small shrubs, choosing positions where they will show to best advantage. Next place the hairy and blue-grey foliage plants immediately behind the rocks, then plant all the other chosen alpines.

Throughout, tread only on the flat rocks placed as stepping stones. It will be impossible to loosen the soil by forking if it becomes compacted, for the scree surface will be over the soil.

TUFA

This irregularly-shaped porous rock has no strata lines, and can be used in a sloping scree, or even on a flat site, in conjunction with limestone scree material. Tufa rocks may also be placed in an area of paving if one or more slabs are first removed.

Because the rock is soft, it is a simple matter to cut planting holes in it, using a club hammer and a 2.5 cm (1 in) cold chisel or a drill. Keep turning the chisel as you hammer, until holes about 5–8 cm (2–3 in) deep are formed. These are best used for lime-loving plants, which will send their roots into the rock itself.

Choosing fibrous-rooted seedlings or cuttings, preferably at the pricking-out stage, place some scree-type compost in the bottom of a hole and ease the plant into the

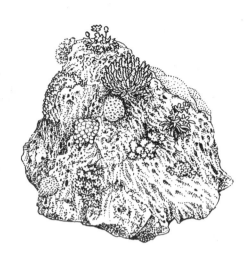

Tufa block garden
Tiny rock gardens can be made from tufa blocks. Planting holes are easily drilled in the soft limestone rocks, and once planted they need little care apart from watering. Tufa may be free-standing, but being porous the rocks are better set in a scree bed or embedded in soil. Limestone loving plants like ramondas, saxifrages and dianthus species are suitable alpines.

cavity. Use a pencil or the blunt end of an old ball-point pen as a tamper and a potato peeler as a trowel.

Trickle more compost around the roots, tamping it gently but firmly around them until the hole is filled. The neck of the plant should be flush with the mouth of the hole. For holes that are not vertical, cover up the lower two-thirds of the opening with a mortar mix of three parts builder's sand to one part cement. This will prevent the compost from falling out.

The whole rock will soak up moisture, so water it liberally. Frequent watering is needed in warm weather, especially during the first season.

Raised beds introduce different planting levels, and plants are easier to cultivate and to view. Even a small, north-facing site will accommodate prostrate and miniature conifers for year-round interest.

When selecting plants for a rock garden, bear in mind that alpines thrive on a rocky site. However, as most are low-growing, it is a good idea to include some dwarf conifers in your planting, as here, to add height.

Splashes of vivid colour – like the profusely flowering begonias and fuchsias in the hanging baskets and containers on this west-facing patio – will brighten a grey expanse of paving.

This roof garden illustrates the stunning effects that can be achieved in a small area. Pots and troughs contain a variety of plants – including roses and fuchsias – to create a delightful mixture of colours and shapes.

Containers for roof gardens

For roof gardens – and balconies – the best containers are lightweight fibreglass tubs and boxes. Filled with plants and compost, they withstand wind buffeting. Also, they strain the bearing capacity of the structure less than heavy stone and pottery containers.

Growing plants on a roof-top or a balcony has something in common with patio gardening, but certain aspects make it a good deal more difficult than growing plants at ground level.

First, one has to be absolutely sure that the structure is sufficiently strong to bear the extra weight of beds and containers. When building a new house this can be taken into account from the start, but expert advice should be sought before using an existing structure in this way.

Access can be a problem, for usually it will be necessary to carry containers, soil and plants through the house. Fortunately, much of this work has to be done only once, or quite infrequently, but there is the continuing chore of supplying the plants with water – perhaps as many as two or three times daily during high summer.

An external water tap is a boon, although it can be difficult to provide one at roof level. A hose may sometimes be the answer, while a rainwater butt can be used to store water if there is an adjacent roof at a higher level. During very dry weather, small pot plants can be placed in a shallow container of water, though a careful watch should be kept for signs of waterlogging.

Finally, there is the matter of exposure. Both balconies and roofs are often subjected to strong and drying winds. Balconies facing south or west may become heat traps, both from the sun itself and from hot, dry air currents rising from below and reflected off the walls of the house.

So much for the problems. They are seldom insoluble, but it is as well to be aware of them before beginning. Also, some of these factors will have a bearing on the choice and care of plants.

Having decided to go ahead, you may consider that some form of protection is desirable. An 'open' structure, such as strong trellis or a purpose-made wire mesh support, is better than solid panels. Clad with climbing plants, it will filter the wind, whereas a solid barrier will create turbulence. The screen needs to be strong, though, and securely anchored.

The tough climber *Lonicera periclymenum* (common honeysuckle) and the wall plant *Chaenomeles speciosa* are both deciduous and so offer little resistance to powerful winter winds.

Fairly substantial containers are needed for strong-growing shrubs and climbers such as *Camellia*, *Rhododendron* and *Wisteria*, not only to provide root space but also for anchorage. A half-barrel would not be too large. On the other hand, the restrictions of a container may help to keep vigorous plants in check and some trees can also be controlled by this means.

Although peat-based composts are lighter than loam-based mixtures, they may not be sufficiently dense to support top-heavy plants. Unless weight is a crucial factor, it would be better to settle for a loam-based compost.

The overall effect, together with the choice of plants, will be determined by whether you are content with an annual display or whether you are seeking something more permanent. Only the hardiest plants should be used for the latter, especially on a roof-top that is completely exposed.

Given space and adequate support, beds can be established for growing smaller plants to complement the larger ones grown in pots. In shade, camellias, *Fatsia*, x *Fatshedera*, oriental strains of *Helleborus*, *Hosta* and rhododendrons would be suitable choices for pots or other containers. For early colour, the floor-level planting might be made up of *Anemone blanda* and *A. nemorosa*; dwarf narcissi and *Tulipa* species; *Erythronium dens-canis* (dog's tooth violet); *Galanthus* (snowdrop); *Primula vulgaris* (primrose); pulmonarias and *Scilla sibirica*. If you propose growing annuals, with their more flamboyant colouring, choose a sunny spot a little distance away.

Unless you have achieved a good degree of shelter, avoid plants of a fragile nature. Petunias, lovely as they are, could take a battering from the wind, although the 'Resisto' varieties, which recover well after rain, might be tried. Container-grown shrubs generally need supporting, at any rate during their first season or two. Other categories of plants worth considering include herbs and dwarf conifers.

A sheltered patio
A sunken patio becomes a sheltered suntrap.

Paving materials
Paving slabs, concrete blocks and bricks are available in several colours. They can be laid as irregular slabs (1), brick and concrete blocks (2) or 'patchwork' bricks (3).

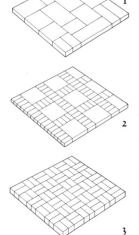

Providing a sort of half-way house between home and garden, a patio is a place for relaxing, for taking summer meals and for entertaining. The best position is usually at the rear or side of the house – whichever provides the best combination of privacy, access and a pleasant aspect.

Full sunshine is by no means essential, although it does extend the season of use. An awning or umbrellas may be needed for a south-facing patio, and a northerly or easterly aspect can be a positive advantage during a really hot summer.

There is no need to despair if the area immediately alongside the house is unsuitable. A sunny, secluded area of paving can often be laid elsewhere in the garden, linked to the house by a hard path. This is especially practical if a summerhouse can be erected alongside for storing furniture.

THE PAVING

When considering how large to make the patio, allow for gatherings of family or friends at barbecues and on other occasions. Remember that furniture will occupy some of the space and that you will probably also want plant containers.

The floor of a patio needs to be firm and free-draining. When positioned alongside the house, it should slope towards the garden and have its higher edge at least 15 cm (6 in) below the damp-proof course of the house. This is especially important if you propose including beds for plants along the house wall.

As for the surface itself, plain concrete – laid on a hardcore base – is one possibility, although the result will not be particularly attractive even if a pigment is added. Crazy paving is another, but this must be laid on a concrete base and requires a lot of work.

Bricks can either be laid on concrete or vibrated into a 5 cm (2 in) bed of sharp sand. This method may also be used for small, interlocking concrete blocks, and the result in both cases is a durable, free-draining and handsome surface. The vibrator can be hired from a plant-hire firm, but it is important to get advice on the correct technique – and also to get rid of all perennial weeds before you start work.

More widely used than any of these materials are the many types of concrete or reconstituted stone paving slabs now available. These are made in a number of colours and sizes, and some have a 'riven' finish or resemble cobbles. You may also be able to obtain second-hand York paving. All except the smallest slabs can be laid directly on thoroughly consolidated soil, with a blob of mortar placed under each corner and another in the centre.

Whether you lay blocks, bricks or larger slabs, consider leaving occasional, well-placed spaces for subsequent planting. If the space is small, set a pot into the ground and lay the slabs around it, withdrawing the pot later and making good with gritty compost. In the case of a larger space, a slab can be removed and the soil replaced with compost when slab-laying is finished.

THE SURROUNDS

Some form of overhead structure may be considered, perhaps as a support for climbing plants that will give shade during the summer. This is of dubious value, however, bearing in mind the drips, plant debris and insects liable to fall from it.

There is every advantage in growing plants on one or more sides, however, especially if these will give a greater sense of privacy. It may be possible to increase the height of an existing fence or wall by a trellis extension at the top – a perfect support for climbing plants.

Depending on the site, the illusion of an 'outdoor room' may also be fostered by erecting a pergola, lattice fence or even a low retaining wall across the width of the patio. A hollow wall, suitably planted, looks charming.

If the patio is likely to be used by anyone who is disabled – perhaps confined to a wheelchair – consider the possibility of a raised bed along one or more sides. For preference, choose walling blocks to match the paving material. To put them within reach of a person in a wheelchair, such beds should not be more than 1.2 m (4 ft) wide and 53 cm (21 in) high.

Other features worth considering are a small aviary or a pool. Both need a fair amount of space – especially the latter, as very small pools suffer from temperature fluctuations which affect both the plants and the fish.

FURNITURE

Two sorts of furniture will be needed if you are to use your patio to the full – a table and set of upright chairs for dining, together with reclining chairs or loungers for relaxing. You may consider investing in a swing hammock. Furniture is available in the following range of materials: wood, cast metal, tubular steel and moulded plastic.

Hardwood, including teak and iroko, is durable and weatherproof. An occasional treatment with preservative (follow the maker's advice) is all the care needed. Fitted cushions, which can be stored indoors, are available for some types.

Cast metal furniture, usually painted white and nowadays generally of aluminium, is strong and it dries quickly after rain. It is ideal for outdoor dining suites.

Tubular metal is the material used for many types of loungers and easy chairs. These are light and relatively inexpensive, but their robustness varies a great deal. When buying, consider the strength of hinges and rivets, which are generally the first parts to break.

All-plastic furniture is weatherproof, light and often attractive to look at. The better sorts are strong and well designed, but these qualities may be lost at the lower end of the price range. Both dining suites and loungers are made of plastic – often based on polypropylene – and cushions are generally available at extra cost.

Barbecues are extremely popular nowadays. The choice lies between a portable unit, which can be placed strategically to suit the wind direction, or a fixed structure built from bricks or concrete blocks. If you like the idea of the latter, there are firms who specialize in supplying the grill pans, and other fittings are readily available from hardware stores.

As an alternative to charcoal, you may prefer either a gas or electric unit. There is much less delay while these reach cooking heat, the power source in both cases heating volcanic rocks over which the food is grilled.

PLANTS FOR PAVING

These should be low-growing, with a spreading habit and the ability to survive being trodden on occasionally. If they are scented, so much the better.

The list right includes both spreading and hummock plants, and one or two that are scented – the latter marked with a +. The figures refer to heights.

PLANTS FOR PATIO WALLS

Walls, fencing or trellis alongside a patio provide an opportunity to grow some of the more tender climbers and wall plants. These can be planted in a bed at the foot of the vertical surface or grown in containers. *Sollya heterophylla* (bluebell creeper), growing to about 1.8 m (6 ft), is an excellent candidate for such a position. It has sky-blue, bell-shaped flowers during summer and autumn. *Eccremocarpus scaber* (Chilean glory flower) grows to about 3 m (10 ft) and is covered with orange flowers throughout the summer. *Calceolaria integrifolia*, with yellow flowers during the second half of summer, is unlikely to exceed about 1.2 m (4 ft). *Aloysia triphylla*, syn *Lippia citriodora*, (lemon-scented verbena) has leaves that smell of lemon when crushed. It grows to about 1.5 m (5 ft) and needs protection with straw or bracken in winter.

Plants for paving

Erinus alpinus

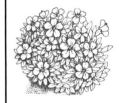

Silene acaulis

Acaena buchananii, 2.5–5 cm (1–2 in).
Acaena microphylla, 2.5–5 cm (1–2 in).
Achillea argentea, 15 cm (6 in).
Antennaria dioica, 5 cm (2 in) upwards.
Armeria caespitosa, 5–8 cm (2–3 in).
Campanula arvatica, 5 cm (2 in).
Dianthus alpinus, 10 cm (4 in).
Erinus alpinus, 8 cm (3 in).
Erodium chamaedryoides 'Roseum', 2.5–5 cm (1–2 in).
Hutchinsia alpina, 5–8 cm (2–3 in).
+*Mentha requienii*, 2.5 cm (1 in).
Saxifraga – both the mossy (Dactyloides) and Kabschia types; heights from about 2.5 cm (1 in).
Sedum spathulifolium, 5–8 cm (2–3 in).
Sempervivum species, 1.3–2.5 cm (½–1 in).
Silene acaulis, 5 cm (2 in).
+*Thymus serpyllum*, 5 cm (2 in).
Veronica prostrata, 8–15 cm (3–6 in).

Peat gardens are a fairly recent development, the first reference to 'Peat Walls' being in the 1927 Journal of the Royal Horticultural Society in an article about Logan Garden, near Stranraer. They can be likened to rock gardens, but blocks of peat are used instead of rocks to create the terraces.

A peat garden need not be large. Just a few square metres will enable the interested gardener to choose from a wealth of plants. The conditions provided by the peat are cool and moist.

Unlike rock, which lasts for ever in the garden, peat blocks slowly deteriorate and therefore will probably require replacing after about fifteen years. Their life can be extended by setting some of the plants directly into the blocks, and this will also help to prevent birds from tearing the fibre from the blocks when they are looking for nesting material.

The site is important. It should face to the north, north-west or north-east, providing partially shaded conditions and so assisting the blocks to remain moist. This is one of the few garden features that can be sited on the north side of a building, at the base of a north-facing wall or on the shady side of shrubs or small trees. Even so, it should not be beneath them, as most plants dislike being dripped upon or being covered by leaves.

The ideal site is one that slopes gently to the north, at about 20 degrees, where the peat blocks can be built up in terraces to support the soil. On well-drained soil an area can be excavated to form a depression, if needed.

This form of gardening is most successful in areas with acid soils. The site should drain freely, yet retain moisture, and it must be cleared of any perennial weeds before construction begins.

Peat blocks can be bought from most large peat firms. When purchasing, it is best to obtain them wet because if they have been allowed to dry out they will have to be soaked before use. This can be a slow and laborious task.

The best blocks are dug and cut from the area just beneath the shrubby surface-vegetation, where the root fibres are still contained within the block. Ideally, each should be a 30 cm (1 ft) cube, as this will give stability to the walls, but it may be necessary to improvise from materials that are available locally.

The most difficult types of block to work with are those that have been cut for fuel, because they are small and bone-dry.

Building a terraced peat garden
Using a sharp edging iron to trim the peat blocks to shape, lay the blocks tightly together and sloping slightly back into the soil for stability. Fill in behind each peat wall with topsoil.

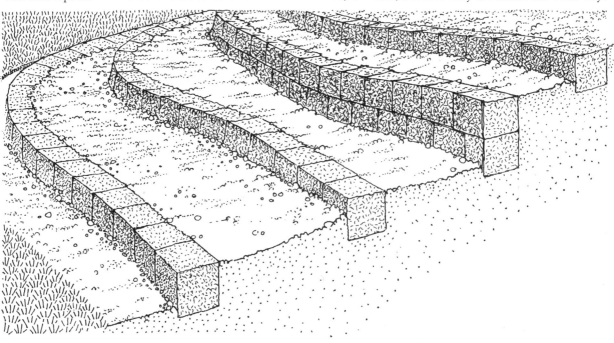

Therefore this type should be used only as a last resort.

The ideal peat garden is one that gives the appearance of a moorland where subsidence and erosion have left behind banks, walls and level terraces. Unlike rocks for a rock garden, peat blocks can be moulded and cut into shape to produce the desired effect. Sculpt the soil roughly to the shapes and contours needed before starting to build with the blocks.

When laying the blocks, ensure that the bottom of each is laid just below the level of the soil, for if left high and dry they will quickly dry out. To obtain height, lay the blocks like bricks, with the wall gently sloping back into the soil for stability. If they are the small type used for fuel, lay them lengthwise into the slope.

It is usually best not to construct walls any higher than two blocks, although it is possible to build three high if they are the best sort. As the walls are constructed, fill in behind with gently-firmed top soil until the desired height is reached.

Place the blocks as tightly together as possible so that no gaps are left. Trim any curves with a sharp edging iron, using the same tool to shape blocks during building. With maintenance in mind, it is essential to place stepping stones on the terraces so that the plants can be tended without standing on the peat walls. This would cause the blocks to crumble away.

On the terraces, between the walls, fork in a good quantity of granulated peat, firm this gently and apply a balanced fertilizer at the rate of 20 g per sq m (¾ oz per sq yd).

General maintenance consists chiefly of weeding and watering. The peat blocks should never be allowed to dry out, or they will shrink and twist, allowing the soil to fall between the terraces. Each spring the plants will benefit from a dressing of balanced fertilizer at the same rate as the initial one, and a top-dressing of peat.

Having constructed the peat garden, now comes the exciting part of choosing the plants. Those listed right are intended to give a start to the planting, but many more can be added. The figures refer to heights. If there is sufficient room, the larger plants will provide a good backdrop.

Background plants
Dactylorhiza elata.
60–75 cm (2–2½ ft).
Deep purple.
May.
Gentiana asclepiadea
(willow gentian).
60–90 cm (2–3 ft).
Bright blue,
heavily spotted.
August–September.
Glaucidium palmatum.
Up to 1.2 m (4 ft).
Pinkish-mauve.
May.
Lilium canadense.
Up to 2.4 m (8 ft).
Orange.
July.
Lilium japonicum.
45–90 cm (1½–3 ft).
Pale pink.
June–July.
Lilium martagon
'Album'.
Up to 2 m (6½ ft).
White.
June.
Meconopsis grandis.
1 m (3½ ft).
Blue.
May.
Primula cockburniana.
30–45 cm (1–1½ ft).
Bright orange.
May.
Ranunculus lyallii
(New Zealand
buttercup).
45 cm (1½ ft).
Semi-double, white.
June.
Thalictrum chelidonii.
Up to 2.1 m (7 ft).
Yellow stamens,
large mauve sepals.
June–July.
Trillium grandiflorum.
45 cm (1½ ft).
White.
April.
Uvularia grandiflora.
30 cm (1 ft).
Yellow.
May.

Shrubs
Amdromeda polifolia
var. *compacta.*
Up to 15 cm (6 in).
Pink.
May–July.

Arctostaphylus uva-ursi.
Up to 15 cm (6 in).
Pinkish.
April–May.
Bruckenthalia
spiculifolia.
15 cm (6 in).
Deep pink.
May–July.

Arctostaphylus
uva-ursi

Cassiope 'Edinburgh'.
23 cm (9 in).
White.
April–May.
Cassiope mertensiana
var. *gracilis.*
15 cm (6 in).
White.
April–May.
Cassiope 'Muirhead'.
10 cm (4 in).
White.
April–May.
Cyathodes colensoi.
15–23 cm (6–9 in).
White.
April–May.
Gaultheria
nummularioides.
Hugs the ground.

Flowers pinkish,
fruit black.
July–August.
Gaultheria procumbens
(wintergreen or
partridge berry).
8 cm (3 in).
Flowers pink, fruit
bright red.
July–August.
Gaultheria trichophylla.
Hugs the ground.
Flowers white, flushed
pink, fruit greeny-blue.
May.
Kalmiopsis leachiana.
30–40 cm (12–16 in).
Pink.
April.
Leiophyllum
buxifolium.
30 cm (1 ft).
Pink in bud,
opening to white.
May–June.
Pernettya prostrata var.
pentlandii.
Prostrate.
Flowers white, fruit lilac
turning deep purple.
May–June.
Phyllodoce aleutica.
23–30 cm (9–12 in).
Lemon-yellow.
April–May.
Phyllodoce caerulea.
15–23 cm (6–9 in).
Blue-purple.
April–May.
Phyllodoce x *intermedia*
'Fred Stoker'.
30 cm (1 ft).
Pink.
April–May.
x *Phyllothamnus*
erectus.
30 cm (1 ft).
Pink.
April–May.

Trillium grandiflorum

Background shrubs (cont.)

Rhododendron campylogynum.
30 cm (1 ft).
Pink, light purple, and shades of rose.
May.
Rhododendron 'Chikor'.
30 cm (1 ft).
Yellow.
April.
Rhododendron fastigiatum.
23 cm (9 in).
Purple.
April–May.
Rhododendron hanceanum 'Nanum'.
15 cm (6 in).
Yellow.
April–May.
Rhododendron impeditum.
Up to 60 cm (2 ft).
Purple.
April–May.
Rhododendron keleticum.
30 cm (1 ft).
Deep purple, with blood-red sepals.
June.
Rhododendron yakushimanum.
Up to 1.2 m (4 ft).
Pink, fading to white.
May.
Salix apoda (male form).
Up to 15 cm (6 in).
Silvery-white catkins with golden stamens.
April.
Sorbus reducta.
60 cm (2 ft).
Autumn tints and pinkish fruits.
May.

Primula gracilipes

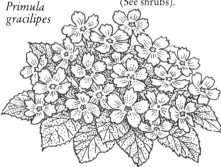

Vaccinium nummularia.
Hugs the ground.
White with pink tips.
April–May.

For growing on top or at the base, of peat walls

Arcterica nana.
4 cm (1½ in).
Creamy-white.
April.
Cassiope mertensiana var. *gracilis.*
(See shrubs).
Cornus canadensis.
15 cm (6 in).
White floral bracts.
June.
Cyananthus lobatus.
8 cm (3 in).
Purple-blue.
August–September.
Gaultheria nummularioides.
(See shrubs).
Gaultheria procumbens.
(See shrubs).
Gaultheria trichophylla.
(See shrubs).
Phyllodoce nipponica.
15 cm (6 in).
White.
April–June.
Primula edgeworthii.
8 cm (3 in).
Lavender, with a white centre.
March–April.
Primula gracilipes.
8 cm (3 in).
Pink.
March–April.
Primula whitei.
8 cm (3 in).
Ice-blue.
March–April.
Rhododendron campylogynum.
(See shrubs).

Cypripedium calceolus

Rhododendron forrestii var. *repens.*
8–15 cm (3–6 in).
Bright scarlet.
May.
Rhododendron pumilum.
8–15 cm (3–6 in).
Pink.
May.
Salix reticulata.
Prostrate.
Male catkins yellow, female catkins purplish.
April.
Shortia soldanelloides.
18 cm (7 in).
Deep to light pink.
April.
Shortia uniflora.
8–15 cm (3–6 in).
Pink.
April.

For growing on terraces

Arisarum proboscideum (mouse-tail plant).
Up to 15 cm (6 in).
Brownish-purple.
March.
Astilbe glaberrima var. *saxatilis.*
10 cm (4 in).
Pink.
June–July.
Calceolaria tenella.
Hugs the ground.
Yellow.
July–August.

Codonopsis vinciflora.
Will climb through dwarf shrubs.
Bright blue.
July–August.
Corydalis cashmieriana.
8 cm (3 in).
Sky-blue.
April.
Cypripedium calceolus (lady's slipper orchid).
30 cm (1 ft).
Pale yellow/ chocolate-maroon.
May.
Dodecatheon jeffreyi (American cowslip or shooting stars).
Up to 60 cm (2 ft).
Purple.
June.
Fritillaria pyrenaica.
Up to 60 cm (2 ft).
Dark purple to dark green.
May.
Galanthus nivalis.
15 cm (6 in).
White.
Jan–March.
Gentiana sino-ornata.
8 cm (3 in).
Blue.
September–October.
Heloniopsis orientalis, syn. *H. japonica.*
Up to 15 cm (6 in).
Pink.
April.
Jeffersonia dubia.
15 cm (6 in).
Lilac-purple.
April–May.
Meconopsis quintuplinervia (harebell poppy).
45 cm (1½ ft).
Lilac.
April–May.
Nomocharis aperta.
60 cm (2 ft).
Rosy purple.
July.
Omphalogramma elegans.
10 cm (4 in).
Bluish-purple with a white, hairy throat.
April–May.
Ourisia caespitosa.
Prostrate.
White.
May.

Primula calderiana.
23 cm (9 in).
Maroon to purple, with a yellow eye.
June.
Primula capitata.
30 cm (1 ft).
Violet.
June–August.
Primula ioessa.
15 cm (6 in).
Lilac.
June.
Primula vialii.
Up to 45 cm (1½ ft).
Pale violet.
June–July.
Ranunculus amplexicaulis.
15–23 cm (6–9 in).
White.
April–May.
Scoliopus bigelovii.
8 cm (3 in).
Striped green and reddish-purple.
March–April.
Synthyris reniformis.
Up to 15 cm (6 in).
Blue.
April.
Tricyrtis formosana.
45 cm (1½ ft).
Purple-spotted lilac.
July.

Nomacharis aperta

There is something intriguing, even exciting, about a garden pool, and there are few more restful sounds than the murmur of gently-moving water. A thundering waterfall has no place in a small garden!

If the surface is sufficiently large, the water will reflect the area around it, so the size of garden pools is important. All too often they are not large enough.

Also, the larger they are, the less the temperature of the water will fluctuate.

An isolated pool set in grass must be big enough to be noticeable. The pool at the base of a rock garden ought to be at least one-third the size of that feature, making the rock garden itself look twice as large. The same principle applies when the pool is at the base of a scree, or where at least a third of it is surrounded by plants.

The depth of the pool is important, too. If less than 60 cm (2 ft) deep, problems may arise during very cold weather, when the water may freeze for most of its depth. Herons can wade into pools with less than this depth of water to take the fish. During hot weather, the 'balance of life' in a shallow pool may be difficult to maintain, with algae multiplying rapidly in the over-heated water.

TYPES OF POOL

The most expensive and least adaptable pools, although the easiest to install, are those pre-formed from fibreglass. They can be bought as waterfall pools, base pools, or used on their own.

Pools made with liners are commonest, and it is easy to build shelves for marginal plants into the sloping sides. Unlike fibreglass pools, which also have sloping sides and shelves, they can be as large – and as deep – as you like. There are four main types of liner.

The cheapest and shortest-lived material is black polythene, of 250 gauge upwards. PVC is stronger and longer-lasting, reinforced PVC having a life of about ten to twelve years, which is slightly longer than ordinary PVC. By far the longest-lasting lining material (but also the most expensive) is butyl, which has a life of fifty years or more.

Although some liners are supplied in a variety of colours, black is the best choice, for it looks the most natural and helps to check the growth of algae. Being virtually invisible, it makes the pool appear deeper than it really is. In any case, algae will soon cover the liner, whatever its colour.

Concrete pools might seem to be the strongest type, but in practice it can be difficult to make them completely water-proof. Their only real advantage is that the sides can be vertical, making it easier to link the water with any feature – such as a rock garden – built beside it. Rocks can be laid right to the edge without damaging the pool. Obviously, the combination of concrete and liner creates extra work and expense, and the rather slight advantage may be insufficient to persuade many gardeners that it is worthwhile.

If the idea is pursued, only the sides need to be lined with concrete. After this has hardened, the concrete is covered with a fibreglass blanket, and soft sand is laid over the earth floor of the pool. The liner is then laid in just the same way as for a non-concreted liner pool.

Fibreglass pools Buy the largest – and deepest – that you can afford. Mark and dig out a rectangular area around where the pool is to be set in the ground. If the hole is limited to the shape of the pool, filling in afterwards will be more difficult.

The depth of the hole will depend on how you propose to finish off around the edge. If the pool is to be set in grass, a border of thin, flat stones placed to project very slightly over the water will conceal the edges of the fibreglass. In this case, the

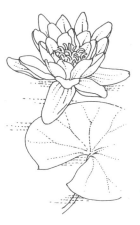

Water lily

Installing a fibreglass pool
Fibreglass pools are easy to install, after initial ground preparation. Make sure that the excavated base is even and free from stones, in an area large enough to accommodate the pool comfortably. Check that the pool is level before and during the infilling of soil.

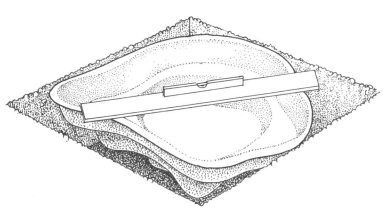

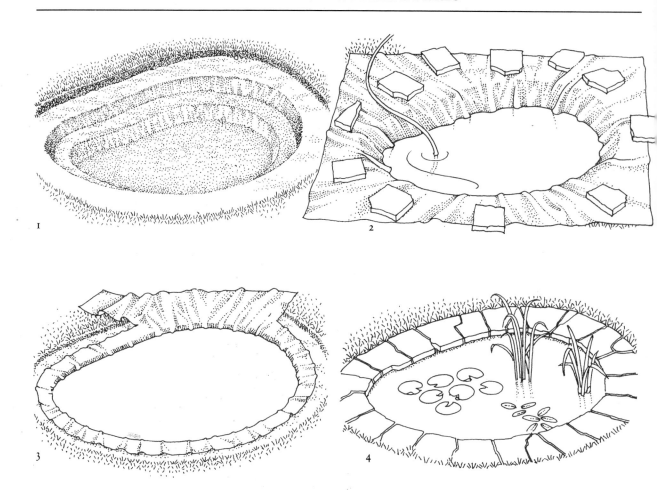

Installing a pool liner

Liner pools made from reinforced PVC are durable and long-lasting. Dig out the pool shape to the required depth and size, ideally with a raised shelf for marginal plants (1). Spread the liner over the hole, allowing plenty of overlap, and keep it in place with stones while water is run in (2). As the liner stretches, adjust the weights; remove them and trim the edges (3) when the pool has been filled. Hide and secure the edges of the liner with a surround of flat stones (4).

pool's rim will need to be sufficiently below ground level for the tops of the stones to lie flush with the turf, allowing a mower to run over them.

However, if you do not propose such an edging, the rim of the pool should be at ground level and the hole can be shallow.

Remove any sharp stones from the hole and cover the base and sides with sand or sifted soil. Set the pool in place, using a spirit level to ensure that the rim is quite level. Fill in any awkward crevices first, then replace the soil around the pool in 15 cm (6 in) layers, tamping these firmly with a wooden stake. Build up all the way round in this fashion until the top lip is reached.

Herbaceous perennials, low shrubs or grasses are the most suitable plants for growing around a fibreglass pool.

Liner pools PVC liners, reinforced or otherwise, can be bought in a number of ready-made sizes. So can butyl, and in both cases it is possible to get virtually any other size made to order. Black polythene, which

is unlikely to last for more than five years, is not recommended for a permanent pool.

To judge how big a pool is needed, choose a level site and mark out the proposed shape with rope, thick string or a hosepipe. Within this boundary place further strings to represent the spread of the plants that are to be grown. At least two-thirds of the surface should remain exposed in order to give a reflecting and enlarging effect of the area around it, and of the pool plants. It is surprising how large an area of water is needed for this.

A site that is not absolutely level will spoil the finished effect. Water will spill over the edge on one side, while some of the liner will be exposed on the other.

To calculate the size of liner needed, first measure the pool's maximum length and width. To each of these figures add twice the maximum depth of the pool, plus another 30 cm (1 ft) to allow a 15 cm (6 in) overlap all round the pool. The minimum recommended depth is 60 cm (2 ft).

Cut out the grass, if any, and topsoil, from the site. Use the grass as compost material, or for patching up worn areas of lawn. Use the topsoil for other areas of the garden, perhaps for a rock garden.

Next, cut out the subsoil, with the sides at an angle of 70 degrees. The subsoil could be used as the base for a raised bed.

Allow for a shelf 23 cm (9 in) deep and wide on which to grow marginal plants, either all the way round or at intervals along the edge of the pool. Dig out the base to the planned depth, making it flat and removing all sharp obstructions.

Cover all surfaces with soft sand, then, with helpers, lay the liner so that it covers the hole with an equal surplus all round. Do not try to press in all the angles. Instead, lay weights, such as heavy stones, all the way round and start running water into it. Held by the stones, the pool liner will stretch into place, though the weights will need adjusting as the pool fills.

The edge of the liner may now be trimmed, but leave 15 cm (6 in) surplus all round. This edging may be covered in a number of ways, depending on the immediate surroundings.

For a pool in a lawn, the turf can be taken right up to the water's edge, or an edging of paving slabs or fairly flat stones can be laid. If there is a bed alongside, bury the edge of the liner under the soil, sloping it down at an angle of 45 degrees.

While keeping soil from dropping into the water, bury as much of the edges as possible. Exposure to ultra-violet light will reduce the life of the liner.

Waterfall pools Moving water, even a modest trickle tumbling through a rock garden, can be exciting. But do bear in mind that water lilies need calm water, so plant them as far away from the splash point as possible.

One or more small pools, each of which should be at least 30 cm (1 ft) deep, can be effective in linking the terraces of a rock garden, although a depth of 60 cm (2 ft) is advisable if you plan to stock them with plants or fish. Concrete provides a simple building material, combined with a continuous length of liner to make both the pools and the linking stream waterproof.

Fibreglass waterfall pools are easily installed, but they are shallow and look artificial. When measuring up for a liner to cover the proposed route, remember to allow for twice the depth of each pool and extra, also, for changes of direction. Lay the liner, with a fibreglass blanket beneath it, from the base upwards, taking at least 30 cm (1 ft) of the liner into the base pool.

Lay the liner before placing rocks over which the water will tumble, so ensuring that any leak from behind and under them eventually reaches the pool below.

This principle applies for each terrace of rock, each waterfall and each small concrete pool, so that the liner and fibreglass blanket act, in effect, as a buffer between rocks and concrete. When making a stream, hide the butyl by strewing stones throughout its length.

The points of connection between pools and waterfall rocks should be disguised with a mortar mix of three parts builders' sand to one part cement, adding a proprietary brand of waterproofing powder. A colourant – preferably black – can also be added.

PIPES, CABLES AND PUMPS

To take water to the top, a 15 cm (½ in) hosepipe is laid from the base while the rock garden is being constructed. Where it goes into the top pool, poke a stiff wire into the hose and then bend it over so that the water is expelled vertically.

An electric cable will have to be laid from the nearest convenient mains source to the foot of the lowest waterfall, where a submersible pump should be installed. Get a qualified electrician to do this, preferably sooner rather than later if it will have to run under any planned garden constructions.

Submersible pumps are relatively cheap to buy, inexpensive to run, and easy to remove for maintenance during the winter. The output is perfectly adequate for garden pools of limited size.

For larger projects, an above-ground pump is necessary. These are more expensive to install and maintain, although their output is spectacular. Take advice from a specialist supplier on the sort most likely to suit your needs.

Waterfalls
Rock and water are natural companions. Space permitting, a waterfall spilling from one rock terrace into a pool at the foot of another makes an attractive feature. If deep enough, the pool can be stocked with fish and aquatic plants; water lilies do not flourish in moving water.

GROWING ALPINES IN SINKS AND TROUGHS

Miniature gardens
Sinks and troughs, in real or simulated stone, make handsome miniature gardens, and have the advantage that compost can be selected to suit the chosen plants. Ensure drainage by raising the troughs off the ground.

Weathering a glazed sink
Glazed sinks can be given a weathered-stone look with hypertufa, a mixture of peat, silver sand and cement. Be sure to leave the drainage hole intact.

Growing alpines in a miniature landscape, such as that provided by a stone sink, is a fascinating form of gardening. It also raises the plants to a more comfortable working level. Furthermore, this method of growing alpines allows excellent control over drainage, the most important single factor in their cultivation.

Should you be lucky enough to own a genuine stone sink or trough, then you have a container that makes a feature in itself. More likely, though, you will have to make do with a white or buff-coloured glazed sink. In this case, easily the most effective disguise is a covering of 'hypertufa' – a really very simple material to make.

Covering a glazed sink The covering consists of a mixture of two parts (by bulk) sifted moss peat, one part silver sand and one part cement. Moisten the dry mix to a consistency where water can just be squeezed out.

Having cleaned the sink, coat it with a PVA adhesive or bonding agent. Apply the mix by hand to give a covering about 2 cm (¾ in) thick. Take the covering just under the sink base and also 8 cm (3 in) down the inside, so that no glaze will be visible. Leave the surface fairly rough and uneven.

Cover the sink with a polythene sheet to prevent it from drying out too rapidly. In winter, it is essential to protect it from frost until the covering has set.

After a couple of days make some 'chisel marks' to further the illusion of hand-hewn stone. A coating of neat liquid fertilizer will encourage moss to grow, and so help the ageing process.

1 Coat the outside of the cleaned sink with a bonding agent.

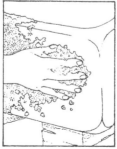

2 Apply hypertufa, 2 cm (3 in) thick, to sides and over edge.

3 Wrap the sink with polythene so hypertufa dries out slowly.

GROWING ALPINES IN SINKS AND TROUGHS

After about three weeks, when the covering is quite hard, place the sink on some stones or bricks so that its top is about 45 cm (1½ ft) from the ground. An open, sunny site is best, and the supports should be as unobtrusive as possible.

Preparing for planting From this stage the preparation is the same for any sort of sink or trough, whether stone or earthenware. Having made sure that the sink is level (not tilted towards the drainage hole), use pieces of broken clay pot to cover the hole and place coarse gravel over these to prevent soil blockage later.

Use John Innes potting compost No. 2 for filling, with an extra 25 % of sharp grit added. Fill the sink in 5 cm (2 in) layers, rather than pouring the compost in all at once and then having it settle later. Firm the compost well, especially at the corners of the sink.

Before planting, arrange a few interesting rocks to suit the size of the container. After planting, top-dress with a 2 cm (¾ in) layer of sharp grit. This will help to conserve moisture, prevent heavy rain splashing soil on to the plants, and also give the miniature garden a 'finished' appearance. The grit should be of similar type to the rocks embedded in the surface.

Water the sink thoroughly, until it actually runs out of the drainhole and, for the first season at least, two or three times every week during dry weather.

The greatest care should be taken when choosing plants for a sink or trough, avoiding the temptation to overplant and so run the risk of overcrowding.

Trailing or edging plants

Alyssum serpyllifolium. Rounded golden flowers in early summer on a carpet of silver-grey leaves.

Artemisia assoana. Fine-cut leaves of intense silver. The insignificant flowers should be removed.

Asperula nitida var. *puberula.* Forms a neat, dense mat of grey-green leaves, with pink, tubular flowers during late spring.

Cyananthus microphyllus. A herbaceous plant, with purple-blue, funnel-shaped flowers at the end of each shoot in late summer.

Dryas octopetala 'Minor'. A semi-evergreen mat of toothed leaves, with pure white, anemone-like flowers in early summer. Fluffy seed heads follow.

Helianthemum alpestre 'Serpyllifolium'. Small mats of tiny grey leaves, with masses of golden blooms in early summer.

Phlox douglasii 'Crackerjack'. Bright crimson blooms in late spring over a neat cushion of soft-green, spiky leaves.

Salix pyrenaica. A red-stemmed bushlet, some 15 cm (6 in) high. Grey-green leaves, and red catkins with yellow stamens.

Sedum cauticolum. Flat crimson flower-heads in late summer. Glaucous fleshy leaves. Attractive to butterflies.

Plants for height and form

Helichrysum selago 'Minor'. A bushlet with whippy stems, each having overlapping, scale-like leaves. The small fuzzy flowers, in summer, smell of honey.

Ilex crenata 'Mariesii'. This rigid-stemmed little holly has tiny, leathery, dark green leaves. Black berries in autumn and winter. Very slow-growing.

Juniperus communis 'Compressa'. A neat, candle-flame column of blue-green, spiky growth. This conifer is ideal for sinks, as the annual growth is only 2.5 cm (1 in).

Salix x *boydii.* This fascinating pygmy willow has grey leaves with 'netted' veining. Very slowly, it forms a gnarled bush to 30 cm (1 ft).

Teucrium subspinosum. Spiky stems some 10 cm (4 in) high. Tiny grey leaves; small crimson flowers in late summer.

Cushion and crevice plants

Aquilegia saximontana. A pygmy columbine, with blue-green leaves and short stems that carry short-spurred blue and white flowers in spring.

Campanula raineri. Mid-summer flowering. Large, open, blue bells over ash-green leaves. Has a wandering habit.

Carex firma 'Variegata'. Stiff green leaves, with cream margins, make this tiny sedge an attractive trough plant.

Dianthus alpinus 'Joan's Blood'. A neat plant with crowded bronze leaves. Blood-red flowers on short stems during early summer.

Draba bryoides. A dense, low mat of emerald green, moss-like foliage. Small yellow flowers in spring.

Erodium reichardii. Dark green mats and an unusually long succession of white, red-veined flowers during the summer.

Gentiana verna 'Angulosa'. Vivid, deep blue 'stars', with a central white eye, form a stunning display during late spring.

Potentilla eriocarpa. Forms a small mat of grey-green leaves, with short-stemmed yellow flowers throughout the summer and autumn.

Primula 'Beatrice Wooster'. A vigorous hybrid that bears short-stemmed, rose-pink flowers during early spring, each having a central white eye.

Ramonda myconi. For the shady side of a rock. Crinkled, dark-green leaves; purple-blue, flat-faced flowers in spring.

Saxifraga carniolica. Tightly-packed leaves of silver-grey with exquisite 'beading' down each margin. Creamy-white flowers in early summer.

S. 'Marie Louise'. Snowy-white blooms often appear during late December and January. Perfectly-shaped, silver-grey rosettes.

S. oppositifolia 'Ruth Draper'. Rose-pink, stemless flowers in very early spring. Best in part shade to avoid leaf-scorch.

Silene keiskei 'Minor'. A late-summer-flowering, campion-like herbaceous plant. The blooms are deep pink.

Teucrium aroanium. An attractive, grey-leaved sub-shrub bearing hooded, lavender-coloured flowers during the summer.

Thalictrum kiusianum. A neat, wiry-stemmed plant with leaves resembling those of a maidenhair fern. Fuzzy, purple flower-heads in spring. Herbaceous habit.

Wahlenbergia pumilio, syn. *Edraianthus pumilio.* Tufts of grey-green leaves. Upturned, funnel-shaped flowers in varying shades of blue during the summer.

Alpine staging
The ideal staging is deep and solid enough to constitute a plunge bed of sand or fine gravel. Clay pots and pans are buried to their rims in the drainage material which is kept moist during the growing season.

Shading alpines
Alpines under glass need a cool atmosphere and good air circulation. Blinds with narrow wooden laths provide essential shade in hot sunny weather.

The alpines covered by this article are true mountain plants, not the assortment of small or slow-growing species that many gardeners tend to think of under this heading. True alpines are found between the climatic limit of tree vegetation and the zone of permanent ice or snow cover, which occurs in the Arctic and Antarctic, as well as in temperate and tropical mountain regions.

So why should the protection of a house be needed for plants adapted to such severe conditions?

In the wild, alpines survive the winter beneath a layer of snow where they remain dry and protected from the desiccating effects of cold winds. Although the temperature is low it does stay constant; in contrast British climate tends to be damp and cloudy, with fluctuating temperatures. Our springs are often prolonged, with periods of drying winds and little rain – conditions that are almost the opposite of those required by alpine plants.

An alpine house will at least ensure that plants remain dry, if not dormant, during the winter. Although they are little affected by cold, the dampness of a British winter may cause them to rot.

Alpine houses have been used in Great Britain for about 100 years. Traditionally, they are constructed from wood, with a low-pitched roof and continuous ventilation in both the roof and sides. This ensures plentiful movement of air through the house, helping to keep the plants dry in winter and cool in summer.

Purpose-made structures of this sort are apt to be expensive, but most ordinary greenhouses can be adapted for growing alpines. Bear in mind that the larger the house, the easier it is to manage, for temperature fluctuations are greater in small greenhouses.

When buying a new greenhouse for this purpose, obtain as many extra roof and side ventilators as possible. When converting an existing greenhouse, it is a fairly simple matter to remove panes of glass in the side walls and replace them with louvre units. Although wooden structures are favoured by most alpine gardeners, aluminium houses are just as good. The space under the staging in glass-to-ground models can be used for plants needing some shade.

Frames are also used for alpines. They may well provide a first stage before embarking on a full-scale alpine house, for many of the plants can spend most of the year in a frame, being brought into the larger structure only when in flower.

Having erected the house in an open, sunny situation in the garden, the next item to consider is the staging. This, like the size and quality of the house, is dependent on the depth of one's pocket.

If plain, slatted staging, which is the cheapest, is used, the plants will dry out quickly in summer. They will suffer if left unattended all day. Trays containing gravel or sand are to be preferred, but best of all is staging that will allow the pots to be plunged up to their rims in sand. This will be heavy, so a sturdy structure is needed.

This system is particularly effective when used with clay pots. If the sand is kept moist during the summer, water will seep through the pots to the plants' roots. The sand is kept much drier during the winter, but for plants needing some moisture the sand around the pot can be watered. This makes it easier not to dampen cushion plants, possibly causing them to rot.

If you have only the open type of staging, it is advisable to double-pot the more difficult plants. This is done by placing the pot in which the plant is growing inside a larger one, filling the space between the two pots with sand. One of the drawbacks is that more space for each pot is required on the staging.

During the summer, shading is important in order to keep the plants cool and prevent them from being scorched. The best method is to use roller blinds made from wooden laths, suspended about 23 cm (9 in) above the glass. They can be lowered during sunny weather and rolled up when it is cloudy or wet. This system provides the correct degree of shading and does not allow the plants to become drawn during cloudy weather.

Other methods are to suspend plastic shading over the roof of the house, and possibly down the sides and ends, depending on the position of the house in the garden. Alternatively, the glass can be painted with special shading paints which, provided they are applied when the glass is dry, will not be washed off by rain. The great disadvantage of the last method is that the material remains on the glass until it is removed in the autumn, and plants may suffer during cloudy weather.

When it comes to buying pots, choose either clay or plastic, but do not mix the two sorts on the same staging. They require different watering techniques, and most alpine growers prefer clay.

There are many soil mixtures that can be used, the most essential factor being free drainage. No plant will grow well in containers if the drainage is poor.

A good mixture for a wide range of plants can be made up from 2 parts loam, 1 part peat or leaf-mould and 1 part sharp sand or grit. (If preferred, the 1 part sand can be made up of 50% sand and 50% grit.) To every 35 litres (1 bushel) add 60 g (2 oz) of a well-balanced fertilizer. While it is true that alpines do not require heavy feeding – which will make them grow lush and lose their natural habit – healthy growth does demand some nutrients.

This basic compost can be adapted for growing very specialized plants.

Alpines should not be given too large a pot. Instead, choose one that will hold the roots comfortably. It will be necessary to repot into larger pots from time to time, and this is best carried out in the spring or immediately after flowering. Repotting should be done only when the pot has become full of roots or, in the case of cushion plants such as androsaces and dionysias, when the cushion has reached the side of the existing pot.

Top-dress all pots with chippings or pieces of rock, ensuring that this material is tucked underneath the plants to help their necks remain dry.

Another growing method worth considering is that of planting out the alpines to suggest a landscape on the staging in the house. The plants will respond well, but the disadvantage is that you will not be able to grow as large a collection because the plants cannot be moved between the house and frames.

Apart from repotting, general maintenance consists principally of watering, particularly during the warmer months of the year. A weak liquid feed can be given three or four times in the growing season.

Watering is a difficult technique to master. While it is true that many plants are killed by over-watering, some, such as *Raoulia eximea*, can be killed by being kept too dry in the later part of the winter. This stresses that a careful eye has to be kept on the plants at all times of the year.

In addition to shading, electric fans can be installed to lower the temperature during the summer. They are also effective in the autumn and winter for giving air movement on still days, helping to keep the atmosphere dry. Make sure, though, that fans are turned off during long spells of frost, because they can desiccate the plants.

De-humidifiers can be used in winter to remove surplus moisture from the air.

Pests and diseases are always liable to give trouble when plants are grown out of their natural environment. A careful watch needs to be kept for aphids during the growing season; also for botrytis, which can cause the plants to rot during the autumn and winter. One other troublesome pest is the larvae of the vine weevil, which chew the roots off primulas in particular.

Overall, alpines can be among the most difficult of plants to cultivate successfully. Any gardener seeking a challenge need look no further.

Growing alpines under glass
Alpines grown on a small scale in the greenhouse are best double-potted. Plant and pot are sunk in a larger pot of sand kept permanently moist so that the correct balance of moisture and drainage is maintained.

A greenhouse adds greatly to the scope and pleasure of gardening. Even a small one enables flowers and vegetables to be raised for planting outdoors, together with a variety of plants for growing in the greenhouse itself. The range will be that much greater if the greenhouse is heated.

Bear in mind, though, that a greenhouse does demand some time and effort. Plants require daily attention, and this is true even if automatic aids are used. Friends and neighbours can be helpful at holiday times but there are no real short cuts in terms of day-to-day management. However, far from being a drawback this detailed care is a source of interest and pleasure to those with a love of plants.

CHOOSING A GREENHOUSE

Before going ahead, there are certain basic needs to consider. For instance, is there a site for the greenhouse that will get plenty of sun and not be overshadowed by trees or buildings for much of the day? Ideally, it should be sheltered from the worst of the wind. It does not matter greatly which direction the greenhouse faces, though an east-west orientation will admit more light during the winter.

The choice of a particular greenhouse will be governed, in part, by the kinds of plants that are to be grown. For instance, if there is to be a tomato crop during the summer, and maybe lettuce in the winter, a structure with glass right down to ground level will provide the abundant light needed.

On the other hand, a greenhouse constructed on low walls is a better choice if plants are to be grown in pots on benches. A compromise, with glass to the ground on one side and a low wall on the other, is possible if you are likely to grow plants in the border as well as needing a bench for pot plants.

Size is important, too. Make sure that there is sufficient head-room for yourself – and not only at ridge level – as well as for tall-growing crops such as chrysanthemums. Fortunately, there is a current trend towards higher eaves. If necessary, the height of a glass-to-ground house can be increased by placing it on two or three rows of bricks or on railway sleepers.

Within reason, it is sensible to go for as large a greenhouse as space and money allow. The greater volume of air in a substantial greenhouse reduces temperature fluctuations. Also, as you gain experience you will almost certainly wish to grown an ever-larger range of plants. A

Greenhouse types
Greenhouses are either free-standing or lean-to. They vary greatly in shape, size, material and cost. Some are made with a cedarwood frame (1), others with aluminium (2); some have glass right to the ground (3), others have part wooden walls (4). The sides may be straight or sloping, the roofs domed, angled or polygonal, and the material can be glass or heavy-gauge polythene.

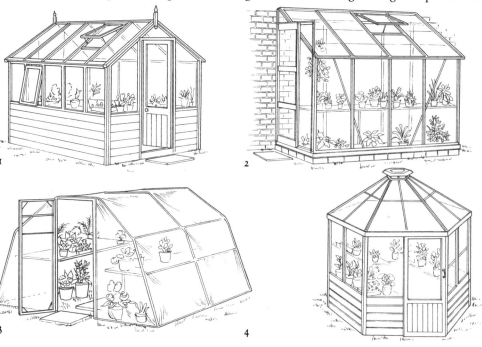

compromise would be to choose a house that could be extended at some future date – always a point to check when buying.

The need for heating will depend, like the design of the structure, on what you propose growing. Some plants, notably alpines, can be grown without any heat, but a 'cold greenhouse', as it is termed, does have severe limitations. In winter, it will not remain frost-free during prolonged cold spells, but should give protection from frost when the outside temperature drops to around -3 °C (26 °F).

A cold greenhouse does, however, protect plants from wind and rain, and it advances growth early in the year. Later, when the risk of frost has passed, less hardy plants can be grown.

A so-called 'cool greenhouse', where a minimum temperature of 4 °C (40 °F) is maintained, provides the right conditions for a wide range of interesting plants. Fuel costs are not excessive, and a great many greenhouse owners settle for this relatively modest degree of warmth.

With a minimum night temperature of about 13 °C (55 °F), a wide range of exotic foliage plants may be grown, many of which make excellent houseplants. A structure of this type is classed as a 'warm greenhouse'. The cost of heating is substantially greater, but it may be possible to partition off a high-temperature section in an otherwise cool greenhouse. Both sections need independent ventilation.

As with most hobbies, and whatever the heating policy, a certain amount of expenditure must be balanced against the pleasure and satisfaction gained. In the case of a greenhouse, this is a more realistic approach than expecting the plants to pay for themselves in cash terms.

TYPES OF GREENHOUSE

Choosing from the many greenhouse designs becomes easier when you know the advantages and disadvantages of each of the main types and makes available.

Free-standing greenhouses with vertical sides and even-span roofs provide the largest possible amount of bench space for the area of ground occupied. Most standard fittings can be easily fixed.

As a slight modification, some have sloping sides. This assists stability and, provided the side walls run east to west, also admits more light during the winter when the sun is low.

A lean-to structure, designed to fit against a wall, can best be described as half a traditional greenhouse. When built against a house wall, easy access to gas and electricity provide big advantages, while heating costs will be much reduced if use can be made of the central heating. A south-facing wall is generally best.

Dome-like structures made from triangular aluminium frames are extremely strong. The shape is eye-catching, but it is not so easy to make use of the growing space inside. Fittings, such as staging, have to be of special design, while the shape and style of such a greenhouse may not fit easily into the average garden.

Interesting shapes are also provided by the polygonal types. These have six, seven or even nine sides and make a most attractive garden feature. However, they can be expensive in relation to the growing area provided and need special fittings.

Plastic-covered greenhouses are, in effect, miniature versions of the plastic tunnels that commercial growers have used successfully for years. Polythene film is supported by a steel or aluminium frame, providing a relatively inexpensive way of protecting a given area of ground.

There are snags, however, Comparatively little protection is given during periods of hard frost. Fairly frequent re-cladding is necessary, though this is a simple operation. Tall plants cannot be grown at the sides, and fittings are difficult to attach. (Further points are discussed under *Glass versus plastic.*)

So-called mini-greenhouses have space only for the plants. With no standing room for the gardener, they have to be tended from outside. Positioned against a wall, they occupy little space, but their small volume can lead to rapid temperature changes. A wall facing south-east or south-west is best; one facing due south may prove too hot at mid-day.

Metal or wood? Nowadays, a great many garden greenhouses are made from aluminium. This metal is strong, needs virtually no maintenance and is less expensive than timber. The glass is secured by clips, a quick and simple method. There is a very wide choice, especially among the less expensive types. Aluminium the colour of dark wood is available for those who dislike the usual bright, metallic appearance. Note, though, that metal is a poor insulator, so condensation occurs when it cools at night. Therefore make sure that the glazing bars have adequate drip channels.

In spite of metal having some practical advantages, there is no denying the attractive appearance of wooden greenhouses. They seem to fit more readily into a garden setting. The favourite timber is western red cedar, which is resistant to rot and distortion. Even so, it benefits from regular treatment with wood preservative. Fittings are easy to attach, while the sections often come ready-glazed for easy erection. Condensation on the timber frame is minimal.

The disadvantages of timber are its relative expense and weakness. Because of the latter, the glazing bars have to be thicker, with a consequent reduction in light. Timber splits fairly easily and moisture trapped in it causes iron fittings to corrode. Unlike metal structures, ready-made bases are seldom available, so foundations have to be built.

Glass *versus* plastic Glass remains the favourite cladding material for greenhouses. Besides being a good transmitter of light, it traps the long-wave radiation that warms the inside of the structure. It is easily cleaned and, because of its rigidity, it makes for a stronger building. Water, in the form of rain or condensation, runs off steadily.

Against this, polythene is inexpensive and very light, so a correspondingly lightweight and inexpensive structure will suffice. However, light transmission is poor and it becomes progressively worse due to deterioration caused by the sun's ultra-violet rays. The sheeting has to be replaced every two or three years. Heat is lost rapidly and ventilation is not so straightforward as with a glazed structure. Also, because water is not shed so readily, drips of condensation can be a problem.

PVC sheeting, a possible alternative, is more expensive than polythene but should last for up to five years before being replaced. It is somewhat less flexible.

Polycarbonate sheeting is rigid, light, virtually unbreakable and transmits about the same amount of light as glass. Unfortunately, it is a good deal more expensive, although it might be considered as an alternative to glass for vulnerable positions. It is not totally scratch-proof.

Ventilation Most greenhouses for amateurs do not have enough ventilators to allow adequate ventilation, especially at the ridge, so it is worth checking whether additional units can be bought (and fitted). The guideline here is that ventilation at the ridge should equal at least one fifth of the floor area. Side ventilation is important, too, and in aluminium greenhouses it usually takes the form of louvres. Hinged ventilators are more usual on wooden types, while additional sliding ventilators set into dwarf walls allow even more air to circulate.

Ventilation controls temperature, humidity and air circulation. The smaller the greenhouse, the more critical it becomes. A combination of side and ridge ventilation produces the so-called 'chimney effect', which cools the house thoroughly at all levels. Ridge ventilation on its own results in the 'wind effect', which functions fairly well but is more difficult to control.

Points to check Following are some of the detailed points to look for when choosing a greenhouse.

If the building has a sliding door, make sure that it moves backwards and forwards quite freely. Doors of all types should be sufficiently high and wide for people and barrows; but avoid a high sill, which will get in the way of both feet and wheels.

If buying an aluminium greenhouse, check that the frame does not have sharp corners – always a potential hazard.

Examine the guttering, if fitted. It should be the same size as house guttering, or a little smaller, otherwise it may be unable to cope with heavy rain. It will be a good deal stronger if it forms an integral part of the side frame.

The base plates on which metal greenhouses rest are invariably sold separately, so take this into account when calculating the cost. They should be made so that they fit accurately at the corners, with no gaps.

GARDEN FRAMES
A frame is an essential adjunct for both cold and heated greenhouses. Its main function is to provide an intermediate stage of protection for greenhouse-raised plants before they are planted outdoors – the vital 'hardening-off' period.

Early crops of radishes, carrots and lettuce can also be grown in frames, followed in summer by tomatoes, cucumbers and melons. However, this presupposes additional space, as bedding plants, cuttings and the like must be given priority for a good part of the year.

As a rule, a south-facing site provides the warm, rapid-growing conditions required for most purposes, but a north-facing frame provides the necessary cool conditions for the initial growth of pot plants such as cinerarias and calceolarias. Frames facing east or west offer an acceptable compromise if not too exposed.

In addition to provision for ventilation, shading is needed during the summer. Matting or some other additional covering is required for protecting plants during frost nights in spring and autumn.

EQUIPMENT AND TECHNIQUES
Heating Basic heating can be provided by an open-flame paraffin burner, but do not expect too much of this during severe weather. Far superior, though suitable only for large greenhouses – perhaps 18 sq m (200 sq ft) – are specially-designed paraffin burners that do not have wicks and that lend themselves to fairly precise thermostatic control.

Natural-gas, open-flame heaters are effective but, together with paraffin heaters, they can produce harmful gases and will increase the level of humidity. With both, a small amount of top ventilation is needed at all times. The same is true if bottled gas is used instead of natural gas.

Electric fan heaters are efficient and they do not increase the level of humidity.

When required, the fan may be used on its own to create air movements. Electric tubular heaters are excellent, too, though they occupy more space.

Heating by hot water pipes remains the best method, whether the boiler is fired by gas, oil or electricity. In lean-to greenhouses, attached to the home, it is often possible to extend the central heating. Make sure, though, that the greenhouse heating can be operated independently even when indoor radiators are shut off.

Ducted hot air, carried in large-diameter polythene tubing, is another possibility for the larger greenhouse. Using either gas or paraffin as a heat source, an electric fan forces the air through perforations in the tubing.

Outputs of the various heating systems are expressed either as kilowatts or as British Thermal Units per hour. (1 Kw = 3412 BTU/H.) The needs for a particular greenhouse can be calculated by using the following formula:

The required BTU/H = surface area of glass (ft²) × 1.4 × temperature lift.

Temperature lift is the number of degrees the temperature needs to be raised above the likely minimum temperature in a given part of the country. As a general guide, a large part of Great Britain and Northern Ireland can expect to go down to at least −10 °C (14 °F), with only the coastal areas of southern England, East Anglia, Wales, Ireland and most of Cornwall and Devon having −5 °C (23 °F).

Therefore, if a minimum temperature of 4 °C (40 °F) is required, and if the recorded minimum for the district is −10 °C (14 °F), the necessary temperature lift is 14 °C (26 °F).

On this basis, a greenhouse measuring 2.4 m × 1.8 m (8 ft × 6 ft) needs a 1.5 Kw heater. One measuring 3.6 m × 2.4 m (12 ft × 8 ft) requires 2 Kw.

It is important that all electrical and gas installations should be fitted by a qualified contractor.

Insulation It has been calculated that 80 per cent of the heat in a greenhouse is lost through the glass, 12 per cent as leakage and 8 per cent through the floor. Clearly, insulation will reduce this heat loss.

Heating a greenhouse
Electric fan heaters distribute the heat evenly throughout the greenhouse in winter, and help to circulate air in summer. Fan and tubular heaters can be controlled thermostatically.

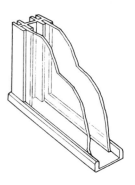

Insulating a greenhouse
Double-glazed greenhouses are available, but they are very costly and tend to cut out the light. Bubble or clear plastic insulation, erected 2 cm (¾ in) from the glass, is cheaper and easily removed.

Plastic sheeting can be laid over the floor, except where plants are being grown directly in the soil. Paving and gravel may be placed on top of the insulation.

It is a considerable help to clad glass side walls, using either plain polythene sheeting or, for preference, bubble plastic. To get the best results, leave at least 2 cm (¾ in) between the glass and the insulation material. This can be pinned to the framework of timber houses or secured with special clips to aluminium glazing bars.

Reduced light and increased humidity are two problems that arise with insulated houses especially during really cold weather. However, superior types of insulation film are now available. One, covered with aluminium foil, is suitable for the north side of the house, where it improves insulation and reflects extra light.

Significant draughts, perhaps from a badly-fitting door, should be excluded, but slight air movement does help to counter condensation. Take care, though, that plants are not placed in a direct draught.

Thermal screens, made of porous material to reduce condensation, may be drawn over plants at night or during particularly cold weather to retain warmth at a lower level. Current thinking is that many plants are able to cope with relatively low night-time temperatures so long as they receive reasonable warmth by day.

Ventilation aids Automatic ventilator openers are particularly useful for greenhouses left untended for any length of time. The kind in widest use is activated by a heat-sensitive compound contained in a small cylinder. A piston in the cylinder causes the ventilator to open or close, and the same system can be used to control louvred vents in the side walls.

Electrically-operated extractor fans give a positive movement of air, though it is still necessary to provide an air inlet. As a rule, such fans are thermostatically-controlled. It is usual to place the fan above the door, choosing one with a cubic capacity (per minute) seven and a half times greater than for a corresponding floor area – 7½ cu ft per minute for each sq ft of floor.

Shading Nearly all greenhouses, but especially small ones, need some form of temporary shading in spring and summer as a further aid to cooling and to prevent bleaching and possible scorching of both flowers and foliage.

The simplest method is to apply a shading liquid to the glass by either painting or spraying. This can be a proprietary type, including the sort that becomes translucent when wet, or else made at home from one part of flour to six parts of water. The drawback of liquid shading is its inflexibility, for it also reduces light and warmth during dull, cool spells.

An ideal form of shading is provided by an external blind that can be lowered or raised to suit the weather. Slatted wooden roller blinds are excellent, but they are both costly and heavy. A form of venetian blind is used by at least one greenhouse manufacturer. Ideally, blinds should be 23–30 cm (9–12 in) above the glass.

Light hessian, close-woven netting and coloured plastic sheeting may also be used as roller blinds, attached to frames hung on the roof or merely hooked directly on the superstructure. It is even possible to have them controlled automatically, according to the weather. Whatever method is chosen, ensure that blinds are well secured during windy weather.

Blinds can be fitted inside the greenhouse, but they are less efficient and may get in the way of tall plants.

Watering The correct watering of plants under glass calls for care and observation. As a broad rule, plants are less likely to be harmed by under-watering than by over-watering, but there is a general tendency to give insufficient during the summer.

The weight of a pot plant provides a good indication of its dryness, or otherwise. Feeling the top 6 mm (¼ in) of compost is a fairly reliable guide, while a clay pot containing dry compost will emit a ringing sound if given a sharp tap. Wilting is another clue, though every effort should be made to water plants before this occurs. Wilting may also be due to persistent over-watering.

If at all possible, lay on a water supply to the greenhouse, burying the pipes below frost level and lagging them carefully. Collect as much rainwater as possible if

Ventilating a greenhouse automatically Greenhouse ventilation is essential for correct temperature and humidity levels. Automatic systems consist of heat-expanding compounds which activate pistons that open and shut the vents.

you grow calcifuges (lime-hating plants), such as ericas or azaleas, and live in a hard-water area. It may be difficult to store sufficient, however, and it is safe to use tap water for damping down – spraying paths, walls, soil surfaces and staging with water to lower the temperature during hot weather and to increase humidity.

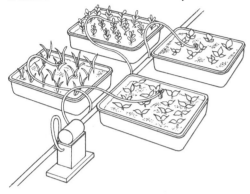

Watering of pot plants can be automated by means of capillary matting or fine sand. Both must be placed on polythene sheeting or in purpose-made plastic trays.

Matting is light, but in time it will become covered by algae and will have to be cleaned or replaced. A simple way to keep it moist is to let the front edge dip into a gutter kept topped up with water.

If fine sand is used, the edges of the polythene must be turned up and supported to provide a depth of 5–8 cm (2–3 in). The wet sand represents a considerable load, so the bench must be strong.

Both matting and sand can be kept moist by hand-watering, but it is quite easy to automate the system by means of an inverted container from which water runs into a shallow reservoir and which, in turn, overflows on to the capillary surface. For full automation, a water main connected to a cistern and ball cock can govern an intermittent outflow on to the bed.

Use plastic pots, as the thin material and many drainage holes will bring the compost into direct contact with the moist base. If fine sand is used, even better contact is assured if the pots are nestled in it to a depth of 1.3 cm (½ in).

Neither form of capillary watering is successful during the winter, when soft and excessive growth makes the plants vulnerable to both cold and disease, so it is better to revert to watering by hand.

There are also methods of automatic watering based on pipes, with perforations or drip nozzles supplying individual pots and plants. The supply may be regulated by a time clock or flow uninterrupted from a small reservoir. Plants needing humid conditions are particularly responsive to such systems.

However, although all these methods can save time and effort, they in no way reduce the need to keep a close eye on individual plants and containers. They are non-selective, and the gardener must ensure that plants receive just the amount of water they need for healthy growth.

Staging and shelving Slatted staging is supplied as an optional extra for most greenhouses. Unless solid benching is erected – usually in alpine houses or for capillary watering – it provides an excellent form of support for pots and seed trays. Slatted staging is particularly suitable in glass-to-ground greenhouses, where other carefully-chosen plants may be grown in the bed beneath. Even if the greenhouse has a wall up to staging level, the area underneath is suitable for forcing such crops as chicory, rhubarb and seakale.

Staging should be about 75 cm (2½ ft) high, with a maximum width of about 75 cm (2½ ft). In a lean-to or conservatory it can be erected in tiers to show off the plants to better advantage.

Solid benches not used for capillary watering can be covered with about 2.5 cm (1 in) of 1 cm (⅜ in) clean shingle or with a proprietary clay aggregate, obtainable in several sizes. If the surface is corrugated – stronger than a flat surface – ensure that the ridges are well covered, otherwise the pots will not stand level.

Although shelving can extend the available growing space, it is something of a mixed blessing. If positioned beneath the ridge, head room is reduced and the plants will be more prone to sun-scorch and drying out. If fixed to the side walls, the shelves will cast shade onto the staging, and the plants below may suffer from drips falling on them.

Supports Many plants need some form

Supporting growbag tomatoes
Attach lengths of string to overhead wires stretched from one end of the greenhouse to the other. Tie the other end of each length of string to the base of a plant and twist the string round it as it grows.

Ring culture
Place open-ended pots or rings on a bed of aggregate kept permanently moist; feeding roots develop inside the ring, drinking roots in the aggregate.

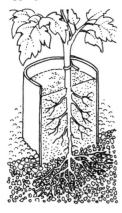

of support, tomatoes and cucumbers being obvious examples. Simple, temporary supports will suffice for short-lived plants but others need to be fixed permanently.

Bamboo canes and wooden stakes provide good, neat supports. Both these and the ties should be as unobtrusive as possible for ornamental plants, with soft garden twine or raffia being the best materials for tying. Use tarred twine for ties that will have to last for a good while.

It can be difficult to support tomatoes in a growing bag placed on a solid floor. Special support frames are sold for the purpose, but a length of strong string (baler twine is ideal) will do instead, provided that the upper end can be secured to a hook screwed into a glazing bar. First secure the bottom end as a loose loop round the base of the stem, then tie the top to the hook. As the plant grows, twist the string gradually round the stem.

Plants growing against the wall of a lean-to greenhouse can be trained on a wooden framework. A purpose-built frame, made on the square, often looks more pleasing than the widely-available diamond trellis. Treat the timber with preservative, but avoid creosote unless the wood can be weathered for six months.

If you prefer to use wire fixed to eyes, space 14 or 16 gauge wires horizontally 23–30 cm (9–12 in) apart. Wire, plastic or cord netting provides a simple but effective form of support for many greenhouse climbing plants.

Greenhouse beds Plants can be grown in the greenhouse soil, provided it is in good physical condition and fertile. For the first couple of years it will be sufficient to dig in well-rotted manure, peat or mushroom compost, together with a dressing of general fertilizer, but thereafter there may be a build-up of pests and diseases, especially if a single crop, such as tomatoes, is grown.

In a small greenhouse it is fairly easy to replace the soil. Otherwise, soil sterilization is a possible course, though the most effective chemicals are not available to amateurs.

Garden disinfectants containing phenols or alkyl quaternay compounds or dichlorophen can be used to help control fungal disorders in the soil. Grow nothing in the soil for at least a month, then sow a test crop of mustard and cress to ensure that there are no residual effects.

Growing bags If the soil cannot be replaced, and sterilization is difficult, a simple answer is to use growing bags. These are long, plastic bolsters filled with a special peat mix. They are simply laid on the greenhouse floor and the plants inserted through holes cut in the top.

The bags may be used for a second crop. For instance, strawberries, winter lettuces or radishes can follow tomatoes or cucumbers. If this is done, loosen the peat with a hand fork and mix in a good handful of Growmore fertilizer or John Innes Base Fertilizer. After the second crop, spread the peat as a mulch in the garden.

Watering needs special attention. A mature crop of tomatoes usually needs twice-daily watering during warm weather. This, in turn, means extra feeding.

Ring culture Although largely superceded by growing bags, this method is still preferred by some gardeners who have an inexpensive supply of potting compost. Bottomless pots ('rings'), filled with compost, are placed on a clean, free-draining layer of ballast, coarse sand or weathered ashes. This inert material must be at least 15 cm (6 in) deep, 45 cm (18 in) wide, and must be contained in a polythene-lined trench.

Once the plants become established, and their roots penetrate the ballast, this should be kept continuously moist. Feed is applied only in the ring and, in theory, only the base material should be watered. In practice, it is often necessary to water the ring as well during warm weather.

Nutrient film This recently-introduced method of growing tomatoes and cucumbers is used by some commercial growers and is available in a simplified form.

Polythene troughs hold strips of capillary matting, through which is passed a nutrient solution. Plants placed on the matting extend their roots over it and take up the food they need. The troughs are laid with a slight fall so that the nutrient can be collected at the lower end and pumped back to the top.

Seed and potting composts The choice

rests between loam-based John Innes composts and those with peat as their main ingredient. Both can give excellent results, but certain points are worth noting.

The term 'John Innes' refers to a formula and is not a brand name. Unfortunately, some suppliers use ingredients of inferior quality, and products bearing this name are not as uniformly reliable as they should be. When buying, look for packs bearing an official seal of approval.

John Innes seed compost is for sowing seeds and striking some cuttings. John Innes potting compost is divided into three grades, depending on fertilizer and chalk content, J I potting compost No 1 having the least fertilizer and J I potting compost No 3 the most. J I potting compost No 1 is for seedlings and slow-growing plants, with the other two grades intended for established and more vigorous plants.

Proprietary peat-based composts are for the most part reliable and are both light and reasonably clean to use. In addition to seed and potting grades, there are universal types that serve both purposes.

Peat-based composts do have some disadvantages. For instance, their light texture and weight may be insufficient to hold tall pot plants upright. There is a greater risk of over-watering, though peat is difficult to moisten thoroughly once it has been allowed to dry out. Plants grown in peat-based composts need supplementary feeding sooner than those grown in loam.

Propagators Some form of propagator, however small, is invaluable for raising seedlings and for rooting cuttings. There are proprietary models of various sizes, heated by electric elements and thermostatically controlled, but it is quite easy to make one's own from a wooden frame, with a polythene sheet to roll over the top. An electric heating cable, with thermostatic control, can be embedded in a sand base, or a small paraffin heater placed underneath the frame.

Mist propagation provides a more sophisticated means of striking cuttings. Intermittent bursts of fine mist ensure that the plant material never dries out. Because the cuttings are not shaded, photosynthesis continues and earlier rooting results.

Proprietary propagator Automatic propagator units are heated by soil- warming cables plugged into the mains electricity supply. The transparent plastic cover provides a sealed, humid and warm environment in which to germinate seeds and root cuttings.

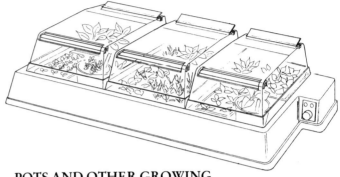

POTS AND OTHER GROWING METHODS

Most plants are still grown in pots, but plastic pots have largely taken over from clay ones. The results they give are just as good, if not better, and they are lighter, stronger and easier to clean. They are non-porous, so less water is lost. No drainage material is needed in the base, except for alpines, which need very sharp drainage.

Flimsy 'pots' made from black polythene, with large holes punched in their bases, are adequate for such plants as tomatoes and chrysanthemums. They are available in many sizes.

Pots made from impregnated paper or thin cardboard are suitable for short-term growing. Some, made from compressed peat, do not need separating from the plant when potting into a larger pot or straight into the ground.

Another sort of compressed peat pot, which swells when soaked in water, is suitable for the initial stages of growth – whether seedlings or cuttings. Similar use can be made of special peat-based compost that is compressed into small blocks, using a hand-operated gadget. The blocks are best placed on a flat tray.

Seed trays, made from plastic or wood, are the best choice where a substantial number of seedlings or cuttings are to be grown. They are made in two depths, and in half sizes as well, the shallower ones being used for seed sowing or for growing on plants that are not too vigorous.

GARDENING ROUND THE YEAR

Plants make the garden come alive. Carefully chosen and positioned, they echo the changing seasons, awakening in the darkest months with winter-flowering heathers, trees and shrubs, the first rhododendrons and early snowdrops, to be followed by a host of colourful spring bulbs and dainty alpines. High summer belongs to the brilliant annuals and perennials, to the glory of roses, scented climbers and majestic lilies that merge into early autumn's dahlias and chrysanthemums before giving way to autumn tints and berries.

The green sward of a well-tended lawn holds the composition together, with hedges to frame the picture, wall plants and climbers to lift it to the third dimension, and specimen trees to provide focal points of interest.

Some gardeners favour a little of everything, others specialize in alpines, water plants or hardy ferns, variegated shrubs or dwarf conifers, vegetables and fruits, greenhouse plants or orchids. The following pages describe them all: their appearance and outstanding qualities, cultural needs, and cropping qualities.

In addition, the accompanying calendars detail month-by-month the necessary jobs that ensure healthy growth, perfect bloom and worthwhile crops: sowing of annuals and vegetables in the open and under glass, pruning of roses, training of maiden fruit trees, feeding of lawns, or division of border plants.

Herbaceous borders have for long been a treasured part of our gardening scene. In particular, very substantial borders used to be found in the gardens of large country houses, with a range of plants that matched the available space. Today, rising costs have reduced the number of such displays, but much of the former grandeur may still be seen in properties taken over and restored by the National Trust. Gardens with particularly splendid mixed borders include Hidcote Gardens, Hampton Court, Edinburgh's Royal Botanic Garden and, of course, Wisley.

However, herbaceous plants are not only for those with unlimited space. Like shrubs, they have much to offer the owners of quite small gardens. Because each plant will remain in place for several years, there is a significant saving in cost and time when compared with annuals, biennials and bulbs grown for bedding.

SOIL PREPARATION AND PLANNING

To a considerable degree, success depends on good soil preparation. It becomes increasingly difficult to add further humus to the soil during the three to five years that plants remain undisturbed. The ideal preparation is to double-dig the ground at the start, mixing in plenty of manure or garden compost with the lower spit. Be sure, though, not to mix the more fertile topsoil with the subsoil.

There are no hard and fast rules as to planting time. In the north of Britain, and also in the south on heavy soil, spring planting will reduce the risk of losses. Autumn planting is safe on free-draining soils in the south, and can continue throughout the winter on light land if conditions are neither too wet nor too cold.

Given these conditions, the chief advantage of early planting (before spring) is that the plants are able to develop their root systems, even though there are few signs of above-ground growth. As a consequence, they grow away rapidly with the warmer weather in spring. In contrast, if planted in light soil in spring, watering will be needed at once should dry weather follow before the roots have had a chance to develop.

These considerations apart, there are one or two slightly tender herbaceous plants that are better planted in spring whatever the soil conditions. Among these are *Agapanthus* and *Kniphofia*, but to be on the safe side you should check others with the nurseryman when ordering.

A plan of the border is needed in order to judge how many plants of each kind to buy. This warrants a little trouble, for there are several considerations to keep in mind when deciding which perennials to grow and where to place them, such as colour, height and flowering period.

Herbaceous borders These are most successful when planted with a mixture of foliage plants, like the handsome hostas, and flowering perennials that come into bloom successively.

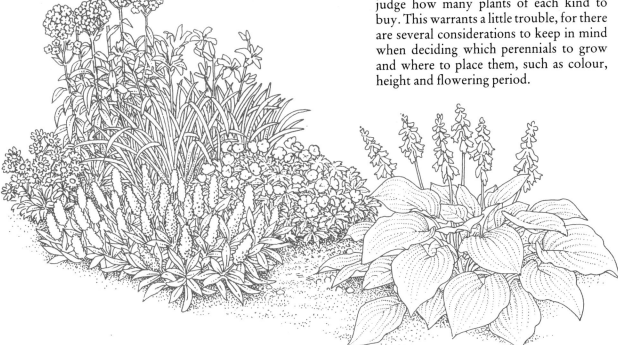

It is more effective to grow herbaceous plants in groups of three or five than to dot them about individually. You may decide to have a layout based on overall colour, perhaps starting with light shades and working through to deeper ones. A border divided into clearly defined colours is another possibility and, indeed, probably the majority of gardeners prefer this greater variation, provided the colours are chosen to harmonize with one another. It is important, too, to take account of flowering times so that colour is maintained in the border for as long as possible.

As a rule, the taller plants should be at the rear of the border, but this advice should not be followed too rigidly. A slightly undulating effect is preferable. Also, early-flowering plants of medium height, such as *Dicentra* or *Doronicum*, set near the rear can easily be hidden, after flowering, by a group of taller, later plants placed in front of them. Spacing between plants varies, of course, with the taller types needing the most room. A solid barrier, such as a wall or fence, enables climbing plants to be grown as a backdrop for the herbaceous flowers.

Most borders are backed by a fence, a wall or a hedge. If space allows, it is a good idea to leave a path up to 60 cm (2 ft) wide between the plants and this boundary. As well as allowing a better circulation of air, this will provide access for staking some of the taller plants.

Herbaceous plants may also be grown in island beds, although it is better to avoid the taller sorts if space is very limited. The most satisfactory layout is a fairly large, irregularly-shaped bed, with some high points created by fairly tall plants and shorter ones forming valleys between them; remember it will be viewed from all sides. Plant in groups, as for a border.

PLANTING

Having drawn a plan and ordered the plants, the next step is to transfer the plan to the border or bed. This can be done by scratching furrows to mark the edges of each small planting area, or, if preferred, by using pegs. If the plants have arrived bare-rooted this preparation will ensure that they can be set in the ground without delay. Make the planting holes sufficiently large for the roots to be spread out and then firm the soil well once the plants are in position. Should the weather turn frosty after planting, check that the plants are still firmly in position when the weather warms up again.

Support the plants with stakes quite early in the season, for it will be too late to do a good job once the wind has loosened them. The right time is when they are about 45 cm (1½ ft) high, and the developing foliage will soon cover the sticks.

Pea sticks, wire frames, or canes and string may all be used. Choose supports that are tall enough to do their job but not so high that they will still be visible when the plants are fully grown.

AFTER-CARE

Dead-heading will prolong the flowering period and conserve the plants' vigour. Cut the stems back gradually as they turn yellow but on no account cut into any green stems. In the autumn, when the plants start to look old and bedraggled, cut most of them down to 5–8 cm (2–3 in) of the ground. The exceptions are some of the more tender species that will benefit from winter protection by having the dying foliage wrapped around their crowns. Remove this as soon as the weather breaks in spring.

With this autumn trimming completed, and after all the leaves have been shed by nearby trees, fork the border over lightly. Three years after the original planting, some of the more vigorous plants may be divided and replanted – a process that can be repeated during the next two years until the whole border has been replanted. This gradual approach not only spreads the work-load but also ensures continuity of display year by year.

Each spring, apply a dressing of either bonemeal or a balanced organic fertilizer at 65–100 g per sq m (2–3 oz per sq yd). A 5 cm (2 in) layer of peat or spent mushroom compost will help to suppress weeds and conserve moisture, and this mulch should be applied to damp soil once it has started to warm up in spring.

Popular herbaceous perennials

Make use of nursery catalogues to help choose from the many plants available. Among those specially recommended are:

Achillea filipendulina 'Coronation Gold' or 'Gold Plate'. Height 90–120 cm (3–4 ft). Large heads of yellow flowers, which can be cut and dried for flower arranging. June to August.

Achillea ptarmica 'The Pearl'. Height 60 cm (2 ft). Quite different from the above, with small white flowers, which can be cut and dried for flower arranging. June to August.

Agapanthus Headbourne Hybrids (African lily). Height 60–75 cm (2–2½ ft). Blue flowers. July to August.

Hemerocallis hybrid

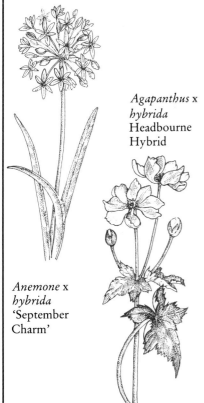

Agapanthus x *hybrida* Headbourne Hybrid

Anemone x *hybrida* 'September Charm'

Bergenia 'Ballawley'. Height 30 cm (1 ft). Has large evergreen leaves and red flowers. Forms good ground cover. April to May.

Dicentra spectabilis (bleeding heart). Height 60 cm (2 ft). Red and pale pink flowers. May to June.

Doronicum plantagineum 'Miss Mason', single-flowered, or 'Spring Beauty', double-flowered, both yellow. Height 30–45 cm (1–1½ ft). Good choice for an early display. April to May.

Geranium pratense 'Johnson's Blue' (crane's-bill). Height 30 cm (1 ft). May to August. *G.* 'Russell Prichard', pink flowers. June to September. Will grow quite well in dry soil and in shade.

Rudbeckia 'Goldsturm'

Anemone 'September Charm'. Height 45 cm (1½ ft). Pink flowers from August to October. Dislikes being disturbed too often.

Aruncus dioicus, syn. *A. sylvester*. Height 1.2–1.5 m (4–5 ft). Produces white plumes and is good for shady and moist positions. June to July. 'Kneiffii' is similar, but only 60–90 cm (2–3 ft) high.

Hemerocallis (day lily). Height 60 cm (2 ft). Many good cultivars, 'Golden Chimes' being more compact than most. June to August.

Hosta (plantain lily). Height up to 90 cm (3 ft). There are numerous species and cultivars from which to choose, the foliage usually being more attractive than the flowers. Best grown in moist soil, with some shade.

Phlox paniculata. Height 60–90 cm (2–3 ft). There are many good cultivars, all needing reasonably heavy soil with good water retention. Many shades, mostly white, pink, red, lavender and purple. July to September.

Schizostylis coccinea

Polygonum bistorta 'Superbum'. Height 60–90 cm (2–3 ft). Pink flowers. May to August.

Rudbeckia 'Goldsturm' (cone flower). Height 60 cm (2 ft). Golden, black-eyed flowers. July to October.

Schizostylis coccinea 'Sunrise' (kaffir lily). Height about 60 cm (2 ft). Star-shaped flowers carried on spikes in October and November. Only for the south of England, and may need protection even there.

Sedum 'Autumn Joy' (ice plant). Height 45–60 cm (1½–2 ft). Fleshy foliage good throughout the summer. Pink or red flowers. Best in a sunny position and attractive to butterflies. August to October.

Solidago (golden rod). Height 30–135 cm (1–4½ ft). The modern cultivars are a vast improvement, all in varying shades of yellow and flowering July to September.

BORDER CARNATIONS AND PINKS

Border carnations, flowering in July and August, are hardy in almost any situation. Because they become straggly after flowering, they are best treated as biennials.

Carnations may be propagated from seed but the plants will produce poor-quality blooms. Layering, a much better method, is done during August. Pinks are best increased by cuttings taken in July. These should be of shoots that have yet to flower and that are neither too woody nor too soft. Plant out in September or October, or as soon as possible in the spring.

Both carnations and pinks will grow in a variety of soils provided these are well-drained and not acid. They do best in an open, sunny position where plenty of organic matter, such as well-rotted manure or compost, has been dug in and the bed left to settle for about a month before planting. Hoe a dressing of lime or ground chalk into the surface and avoid re-planting on a site recently used for the same plants.

There are numerous cultivars of border carnations, including 'Alfred Galbally', 60 cm (2 ft), white, heavily flecked and rimmed with dull crimson; 'Forest Sprite', 60 cm (2 ft), pale lemon-apricot, rimmed and flecked with pink; 'Golden Cross', 50 cm (20 in), self-coloured yellow.

Pinks may be left where planted for a number of years, but their centres will become increasingly bare. In the south of England flowering usually starts in May, with the main flush in June. If dead-headed regularly, many cultivars will flower until the end of September. Flowering starts progressively later further north. It can also be affected if aphids are not checked.

Recommended cultivars of modern pinks include 'Christopher', 45 cm (1½ ft), deep salmon-pink, with a darker flush and flecking; 'Doris Varlow', 30 cm (1 ft), pale pink; 'Valda Wyatt', 20 cm (8 in), pink with a rose-pink eye.

TYPICAL CARNATIONS AND PINKS

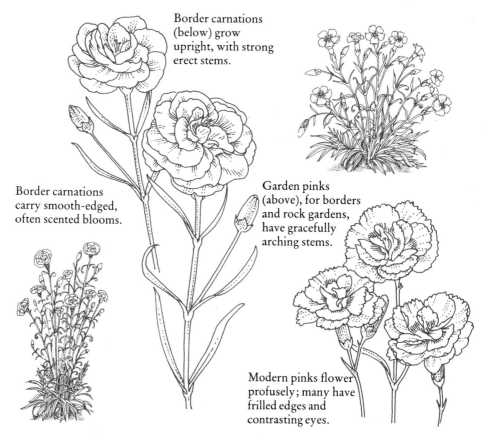

Border carnations (below) grow upright, with strong erect stems.

Border carnations carry smooth-edged, often scented blooms.

Garden pinks (above), for borders and rock gardens, have gracefully arching stems.

Modern pinks flower profusely; many have frilled edges and contrasting eyes.

JANUARY

Planning and preparation If you plan to raise hardy perennials from seed (a simple and inexpensive means of propagation), study seed catalogues and order now.

Other indoor jobs include preparing labels, especially for new plantings, and ensuring that you have sufficient canes and stakes ready for when they are needed. If supports put away hurriedly in the autumn are in poor condition, it may be possible to shorten them back to sound material.

Outside work If the soil is not too wet or frozen, complete any unfinished digging for new borders without delay.

Tidy up existing borders, removing leaves and any remaining dead foliage that may harbour slugs. However, it can be left on tender plants to afford some protection. If severe weather is forecast, and such tender subjects as *Agapanthus* have not already been given protection, wrap bracken or straw lightly round their crowns.

After tidying beds, fork the soil over lightly, preferably with a border fork. Following hard frosts, check to see whether recently-planted perennials have lifted in the soil; if necessary firm them in again.

Preparing for cuttings If delphiniums or michaelmas daisies were boxed up in the autumn, remove them from the cold frame and place them in the greenhouse. A little warmth will help to promote growth to provide material for cuttings.

FEBRUARY

Established beds Complete the forking over of established beds by the end of the month, taking care to remove all perennial weeds. Sprinkle a general fertilizer around the plants at 65–100 g per sq m (2–3 oz per sq yd).

Preparing for planting Weather permitting, make final preparations for planting. The soil must be broken down to a reasonable tilth and a balanced fertilizer worked into the surface at 65–100 g per sq m (2–3 oz per sq yd).

Now mark out the bed in accordance with your plan. If soil and weather allow, you may be able to start planting towards the end of the month.

If plants arrive during a spell of bad weather, place them in a greenhouse or shed. Unless they are in containers, cover the roots with peat, straw or something similar to prevent them from drying out or being damaged by frost.

Carnations and pinks Should bad weather have stopped you from planting out pinks and border carnations in the autumn, do this as soon as possible. Space them 38 cm (15 in) apart in each direction.

Sowing seeds The first of the perennial seeds may be sown this month, for planting out during the autumn. Sow the seeds thinly, in gentle warmth, in a seed tray nearly filled with seed compost and cover them lightly.

MARCH

Planting Although there may be plenty to do, keep off the soil if it is sufficiently wet to stick to your boots. Compaction of wet soil, especially the heavier types, damages its structure. In borderline cases it helps to work from boards, which spread the load over a greater area.

In the south, try to finish planting herbaceous perennials by the end of the month. In the north, they can be left for another two or three weeks. Make sure that the holes are large enough to allow the roots to be fully spread. Fill in carefully and firm well.

A combination of March winds and sunny weather may cause young plants to wilt. Usually, there should be sufficient moisture in the soil to prevent this, but occasional damping of the foliage with a fine spray is a great help.

Tender plants In the south, remove the covering from tender plants if they start to make fresh growth during mild weather. Left on, it may harm the young shoots. It may be as well to wait a little longer in the north.

Sowing seeds Further sowing of perennial seeds may now be made, including *Delphinium; Aquilegia; Papaver orientale* (oriental poppy); *Eryngium; Armeria* (thrift); *Gypsophila; Limonium* (statice). If sown in gentle heat they will germinate in two or three weeks and make good plants by the autumn.

Cuttings Michaelmas daisies, and delphiniums brought into the greenhouse in January should now have made sufficient growth for cuttings to be taken.

Stem cuttings of asters are easily taken in the usual way. Delphiniums are a little more difficult, having hollow stems, and the following method will be found easier:

Delphinium cuttings You will need a jam jar or honey jar that is not too deep, as it is better to keep most of the foliage out of the container. Place a thin layer of sharp sand on the bottom, with about 2.5 cm (1 in) of water.

Take 10–15 cm (4–6 in) long cuttings from low down on the

crown so that the base is solid. Prepare them in the usual manner, trimming off the lower leaves, and stand a number of them in the container.

All that is needed is to keep the water topped up to the 2.5 cm (1 in) mark. Roots should have appeared within about three or four weeks and the cuttings can then be potted up. They need handling with care, however, as roots produced in water tend to be brittle and do not become readily established.

Propagating delphiniums
Overwinter under glass. In spring, sever cuttings cleanly from the crown.

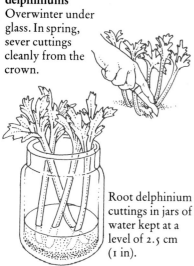

Root delphinium cuttings in jars of water kept at a level of 2.5 cm (1 in).

APRIL

Tender plants Any protective material remaining on tender plants in northern gardens should now be removed. If required, they can be lifted and divided.

Ease your way gently round the plants, lifting them with a strong fork. Care is needed, as many of them have large, strong root systems and there is a real risk of breaking the fork.

Having removed the plant from the soil, look carefully to see where it can be divided without

Dividing perennials
Divide overgrown perennials at the start of the growing season.

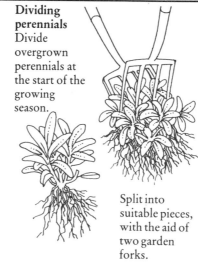

Split into suitable pieces, with the aid of two garden forks.

causing too much damage and insert a fork downwards through the plant at this point. Then insert a second fork, back to back with the first one. Lever the handles apart to divide the plant, repeating as necessary to produce pieces of a size suitable for planting.

Mulching Once the soil has started to warm up, apply a mulch to prevent weeds growing and also to conserve moisture. Do not be in too much of a hurry, however, as it will prevent cold soil from becoming warmer and in this way inhibit growth of the plants.

As well as being warm, the soil should be moist, so spread the mulch after rain has fallen or after watering. If you decide to use wood chippings or bark – just two of the many suitable materials – sprinkle a nitrogenous fertilizer, such as sulphate of ammonia, over them at about 30 g per sq m (1 oz per sq yd).

For new borders, where the plants are small, it would be better to omit a mulch during the first season and to keep weeds under control with a hoe until the plants are fully established.

Routine tasks Any empty spaces in the border can be filled with gladioli, which will give some

colour in August. Plant them 10 cm (4 in) deep.

Cuttings of michaelmas daisies taken last month should now be ready for planting.

Better flowering will be encouraged by a little thinning of new shoots on established border plants such as *Phlox*, which should by now be growing strongly. Use a sharp knife to cut out the weaker, spindly growths, leaving the stronger ones spaced evenly over the clump.

Keep an eye on any irises planted in the border, as rhizome rot can be a problem during wet spells. The tall bearded varieties are particularly at risk. Early yellowing of the foliage is the first sign, and the rhizomes will be found soft and pappy.

Staking must begin once plants reach a suitable height. A few, even quite tall plants do not need support, however, including *Anemone*; *Echinops* (globe thistle); *Eryngium*; *Kniphofia* (red hot poker).

MAY

Staking Plants should be given support before they become too large, when the task will be more difficult. Also, early support allows the developing growth to hide the stakes. A variety of materials may be used.

One common and effective method is to insert three or four canes of suitable height around each plant. As the plants grow, tie string between the canes every 23–30 cm (9–12 in). Other methods are to place a circle of large-mesh wire netting, supported by canes, around each clump, or to support a flat section of large-mesh netting on stakes or canes for stems to grow through.

STAKING METHODS

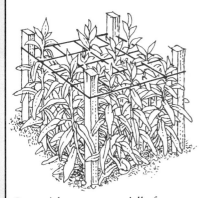

Use pea sticks to support weak-stemmed plants, bending the tops of the sticks to form a canopy.

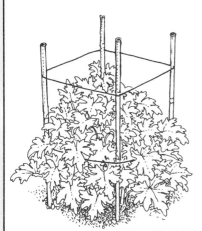

Perennials grown especially for cut flowers can be supported with large-squared wire mesh secured to posts.

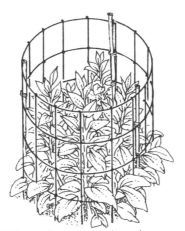

Bamboo canes and twine are ideal for delphiniums. Insert 3 or 4 canes round the clump and tie string between the canes at regular intervals.

Tall-growing perennials are best supported with wire-mesh cylinders kept rigid with strong canes tied to the inside of the cylinders.

Pea sticks are excellent but they need replacing annually. After one season they become brittle and are liable to snap just when their support is needed most.

A good method of using pea sticks is to trim the base to produce supports about 30–45 cm (1–1½ ft) taller than required. Push them firmly into the soil around the plant, then bend the surplus over at right angles towards the centre of the circle. This enables the plants to grow through the twigs, the horizontal sections of the twigs providing additional support.

The flower spikes of tall bearded irises may need supporting; they become especially top-heavy and vulnerable during wet weather. A few thin 90 cm (3 ft) canes placed round each plant will allow the spikes to be tied separately.

Sowing seeds If you do not have a greenhouse, many perennials can now be sown outdoors. Among those that should produce good plants by the autumn are *Achillea; Anchusa; Delphinium; Lupinus* (lupin); *Lychnis chalcedonica* (campion); *Catananche caerulea; Chrysanthemum maximum* (Shasta daisy); *Chelone barbata*. Seeds of *Campanula* should be sown in a greenhouse or frame.

Draw out shallow drills and, if the surface is dry, water the drills before sowing. Sow thinly to avoid too much disturbance should thinning be necessary.

Cuttings Delphinium cuttings taken in March will now be ready for planting. To help them grow into strong plants, remove all their buds so that they do not flower during the first season.

Mulching If mulching was not completed last month, do this now.

JUNE

Pests and diseases From now on, pests are liable to multiply rapidly if not checked at an early stage. See also *Plant Health*. Aphids are the most common but are fairly easy to control if sprayed when first seen. Left untreated they soon get out of control and do extensive damage.

Leaf miners may appear, too, with the tell-tale silvery lines appearing on the surface of the leaves, which eventually turn yellow and die. If left unchecked, the burrowing insects that cause the damage will in time drop to the soil and there may be a second, possibly more severe, infestation later in the season.

Peonies may need attention, especially during wet weather. This is the time when peony wilt is most likely to occur, the stems first becoming soft and then collapsing. Remove the dead growth to prevent the infection spreading, then dust a fungicide over the base of each plant.

Routine tasks Any gaps that have appeared in the borders may be filled with annuals.

Remove flower heads as soon as they start to die. This helps the plant to maintain its strength and, with some species, it may lead to a second flush of flowers later on.

Tying needs regular attention, for wind and rain may cause serious damage if the ends of long shoots are left unsupported.

Do not allow the soil to become too dry before watering. Plants may be under stress well before the signs are apparent.

Hand-weed frequently to keep weeds in check in borders that have not been mulched.

JULY

Delphiniums After they have flowered, cut delphiniums down to about 10–15 cm (4–6 in) from the ground. If kept moist they will soon make fresh growth, producing a second flush of blooms in late September or October. These will not be as large as the earlier ones, but they will provide welcome colour when many other plants have finished flowering.

Irises Prepare the soil now if you plan to re-plant bearded irises next month, giving them time to become established before the winter. They are fairly shallow-rooted, so single-spit digging is sufficient unless the drainage is particularly poor. Add some well-rotted manure as you dig.

If the soil tends to be acid, add lime at about 130 g per sq m (4 oz per sq yd), raking this into the surface after digging; leave the bed to settle, ready for planting.

Michaelmas daisies Perennial asters, widely known as Michaelmas daisies, provide a lovely show late in the season. Sadly, they have lost a good deal of their former popularity, mainly because they are so vulnerable to mildew. However,

provided they are sprayed with fungicide early enough and regularly (before the leaves become silvery white) there should be no great problem.

An occasional change of sprays reduces the risk of the fungus developing immunity to one type.

Seedling care Seedlings of perennials sown outdoors in May should now be growing strongly. Thin them as necessary, keep weeds under control and do not allow the small plants to dry out. At this stage they have only very shallow roots and will soon die if neglected.

Cuttings of pinks The main flush of flowers on pinks will finish this month and material will be available for cuttings. Non-flowering shoots that have appeared from the base of the plant are the ones to use. Those nearest the base are generally small, the ones at the top rather spindly, so take the intermediate ones instead. Avoid weak or stunted growths.

Remove the cuttings by pulling downwards gently. If taken correctly and at the right time, a small piece of bark from the flowering stem will remain attached. If a large piece of bark comes away, the cuttings are hard, having been taken too late. The opposite is true if there is no bark at all.

In either case the cuttings should be discarded. Unfortunately, it is impossible to give a precise guide to timing, but one soon learns with experience. Plants from which cuttings are to be taken should be kept well watered.

With a sharp knife, carefully remove the small piece of bark from the base of each cutting and trim off the lower pairs of leaves, leaving about 2.5 cm (1 in) clear stem. Insert the cuttings in pots of sandy compost, up to the base of

the next pair of leaves; place the pots in a garden frame or cold greenhouse, shaded from the sun. They will have rooted, ready for potting up, in about four weeks.

Dead-heading Continue to remove dead flower-heads as a routine task so that they are unable to set seeds.

AUGUST

Routine tasks Continue with weeding, watering and dead-heading, not forgetting young plants sown in May. While carrying out these tasks, look out for signs of pests and diseases. Take prompt action if any are seen.

Dividing irises Lift and divide bearded irises every three years or so, or when they appear crowded. Pull the new rhizomes away carefully from the old, unproductive

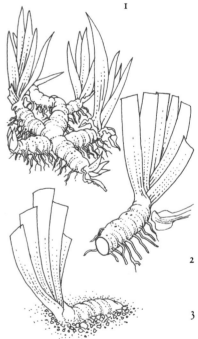

Propagating irises
Divide irises (1) in late summer, severing new rhizomes from old (2). Plant rhizomes shallowly (3).

rhizome in the centre of the plant. Discard this old material and prepare the new pieces for planting.

Trim the end of each new rhizome where it was pulled away from the old plant, using a sharp knife to make a clean cut. Trim the foliage, too, to leave about 23–30 cm (9–12 in). This looks neater if cut at an angle from either side up to the centre.

Plant firmly, leaving half of each rhizome exposed above soil level. Keep them moist for two or three weeks.

Layering carnations Select some strong, non-flowering shoots if you wish to increase your stock of border carnations by layering. Loosen the soil around the plant and pile an 8 cm (3 in) deep mound of sandy compost over this area.

Remove the lower leaves from the stems to be layered, leaving about five or six pairs at the top. Just below the joint next to the lowest pair of leaves, make a cut from one side upwards through the joint to about the same distance above. Take care not to cut into the joint that does have leaves.

INCREASING PINKS AND CARNATIONS

Propagate pinks in July, taking cuttings from non-flowering shoots.

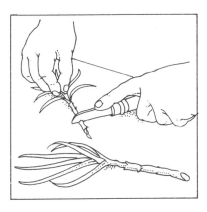

Remove the lower leaves, cut cleanly below the joint and pot the cuttings.

The layer is now attached by only half its stem, the cut having formed a tongue. Remove the small portion of the tongue below the joint. Bend the stems down carefully and insert the tongue in the compost, 12 mm (½ in) deep, and secure with a short length of wire; a hair pin is ideal.

When you have inserted as many layers as required, water them thoroughly and make sure that the compost does not dry out until the layers have rooted. This will take about four weeks.

Once they have rooted, sever the layers from the parent plants. Lift them after a further week, either planting them out or potting them up for later use.

SEPTEMBER

Routine tasks While tidying up, remember to check that the supports for late-flowering perennials are both adequate and secure. Other routine jobs are dead-heading, pest control, and weeding or hoeing.

Double digging Preparations may be made now for planting next month if you are planning a new herbaceous border. However, autumn planting is inadvisable in the north of the country, and even in the south on heavy soil. As the plants will be in position for the next three or four years, give the best possible treatment by double digging to a depth of 45–50 cm (18–20 in), adding plenty of compost or manure.

If the area is large enough, open up a trench 60 cm (2 ft) wide and one spit deep at one end. Place a good layer of manure in the trench and fork it into the lower spit, then mark out another 60 cm (2 ft) strip and use the top spit from this to fill the first trench. Repeat until the

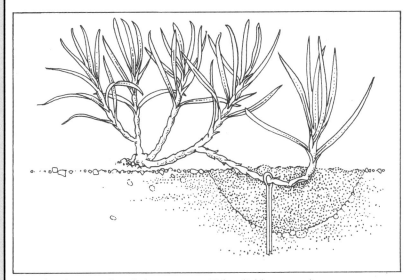

Layer border carnations in late summer. Take pliable young shoots, remove lower leaves and cut through stem and joint. Open tongue and pin into soil.

whole area has been double-dug. Use the soil from the opening trench to fill in the final one.

Finalize your planting plan ready for next month.

Seedlings and cuttings Move young seed-raised plants from the seedbed to their permanent positions as soon as space is available.

Plant out rooted cuttings of pinks, taken in July, and the rooted carnations that were layered in August.

Dividing peonies Peonies that are getting too large may be divided now. However, they should not be disturbed unnecessarily as they frequently fail to flower for a year or two after being lifted.

OCTOBER

Planting A new border dug last month for autumn planting should now be given its final preparation. Cultivate the soil to break down lumps, then rake into the surface bonemeal or a balanced organic fertilizer at about 100 g per sq m (3 oz per sq yd). Mark out the positions for the plants and, if weather permits, proceed with planting. This is also a good time to divide existing plants, taking material for replanting from around the outer edges of the old clumps. (See April.)

Autumn planting gives a distinct advantage, provided you have well-drained soil and live in the southern part of Britain. As the soil is still reasonably warm, the plants will start to make fresh roots before the winter. This helps them to grow rapidly the following spring, promoting a better first season's display – especially of early-flowering varieties.

If you live in the north, or have heavy soil, have the border ready for planting in March.

Cutting back perennials
Remove dead stems of perennials, cutting back to ground level.

Clearing the border With flowering now coming to an end in established borders, most plants may be cut back almost to ground level. Burn the woody stems but place soft and green material on the compost heap.

Remove stakes, canes, peasticks and netting. Stand sound material under cover, where it can be cleaned and stored ready for next year. Pea sticks and any rotten stakes should be burned.

Renovating a border Now is the time to undertake any changes or renovation that may have occurred to you during the summer. If a whole section is to be renewed, lift the plants with a reasonable ball of soil and heel them in on a spare patch until you are ready to divide and replant them.

Prepare the ground by double digging (see September), ready for planting later.

Preparing to take cuttings The best way to maintain a supply of good delphiniums and perennial asters is by propagating new cuttings each spring. In preparation for this, lift a few plants, box them up in compost and keep them in a cold frame until January (to protect them from excessive wet).

NOVEMBER

Planting Complete any remaining planting without delay. After the first week or so of the month it will be too late on all but the lightest soils and will have to be left until the spring.

If you will be planting perennials in the spring, double dig the ground if this has not been done already (see September). To help improve the texture of heavy soil, spread lime so that it can be washed in by rain during the winter. Order plants now.

Routine tasks Keep fallen leaves cleared from beds, to discourage both rotting and slugs.

Keep some dry material handy – such as straw or bracken – for protecting tender plants during severe weather.

DECEMBER

Digging Try to finish digging by the end of the year in readiness for spring planting. Many soils are too wet to work from about the middle of this month onwards.

Clay soils can be improved by spreading some sharp sand, old potting compost or well-rotted leaf-mould over the surface after digging. Spring cultivations will mix this in with the surface layer.

Established borders Continue cleaning up whenever soil conditions allow. After removing dead growth, leaves and perennial weeds, fork the ground over to a depth of 5–8 cm (2–3 in) – enough to bury any small weeds but not to harm the roots of the plants.

It is best to leave the surface knobbly, neither large lumps nor too fine. A fine tilth will be flattened by rain, making it difficult for surface water to drain.

Eye-catching herbaceous borders are carefully planned. Clumps are graded for height, with tall growers at the back; for colour, pastel shades merging into strong tones; and for flowering periods so as to maintain continuity.

A pool can make a very attractive garden feature if filled with plants like waterlilies and reeds, and edged with attractive paving and colourful border plants.

A greenhouse in the traditional style has a ridge-spanned roof, wooden frame and slatted staging. Even an unheated house ensures stable growing conditions for half-hardy crops like tomatoes and cucumbers.

Ornamental grasses are available in a range of attractive colours and foliage patterns. They vary in height from the 3–3.6 m (10–12 ft) tall pampas grass to plants as low as 15 cm (6 in).

Perennial ornamental grasses are often overlooked when planting plans are drawn up. This is a pity, for they are available in a great variety of colours, including glaucous blue, gold, silver, green and variegated. These grasses vary in height, from as low as 15 cm (6 in) to the 3–3.6 m (10–12 ft) attained by some noble specimens.

Often, flowers are of less importance than the foliage effect, although the feathery plumes of pampas grass add grace to any garden. Some are useful, when dried, for flower arrangements.

Given ample space, a pleasing bed of mixed grasses can be planted, but in most gardens they have to take their place in the herbaceous border. Although it is generally advised that plants should be grouped in threes or fives, some grasses are altogether too expansive for such treatment. For instance, although it would be acceptable to have a group of *Festuca glauca* growing towards the front of the border, just a single plant of *Cortaderia selloana* 'Sunningdale Silver' would suffice, and this near the back.

Another important point, particularly in small gardens, is to consider the root systems of the various species and cultivars. Some are very invasive, with roots that encroach like those of couch grass. Gardeners who have encountered this weed will know the problems it can cause.

There are three basically different types of roots: creeping stems (stolons) above the ground that take root almost anywhere; underground roots (rhizomes) that grow through any other plant that may be in their path, and, lastly, the tufted types. It is to the latter that we should look for plants, as they remain reasonably compact and can be treated just like other herbaceous perennials.

Ornamental grasses have one big advantage over most other herbaceous plants. Whatever their size, their stems are strong enough to support the flowers and seed heads, so no staking is required. They need little attention during the season, while pests and diseases present few problems.

Most grasses do best in an open, sunny position, with soil that is well-drained and on the light side but that contains a reasonable amount of humus for moisture retention. Ideally, it should be low in nutrients, for too rich a soil will make the foliage grow vigorously, at the expense of flowers or seed-heads. Some species and cultivars grow well in a marshy area.

Although the soil at Wisley is acid and very sandy, grasses seem to thrive, no doubt appreciating the rapid surface drainage. Plants that stand in cold, wet soil throughout the winter are particularly affected by frost.

Most grasses die back during the winter but it is as well to allow the dead foliage to remain until early spring, for it helps to protect the crown. It may be an advantage to remove any seed-heads that have not been gathered for house decoration in order to avoid unwanted seedlings.

When removing foliage, be careful of the saw-edged leaves of pampas grass, which may cut your hands unless you wear strong gloves. An alternative method for this particular species is to burn the foliage, but there is a risk that if too much heat is generated the crown will be destroyed.

The small tufted species and cultivars that do not die back will benefit from being trimmed in spring, as the new growth that appears seems to be better coloured.

Grasses, like herbaceous plants, need lifting and dividing from time to time. There are no fixed rules, but the plants can be left alone as long as they are growing well and not getting too large for the area they occupy.

At least five years should elapse before lifting and division becomes necessary. Then, it should be carried out in the spring as new growth begins to appear. Autumn division will often fail, the roots having no time to re-establish themselves before the winter.

Anyone thinking of planting grasses should make an effort to see them growing before deciding which to buy. Among the places where collections of such plants can be seen are University Botanic Gardens at Oxford and Cambridge, Royal Botanic Garden, Edinburgh, the Royal Horticultural Society Garden at Wisley and the Royal Botanic Gardens, Kew.

ORNAMENTAL GRASSES

Bamboos also come within the general category of grasses, but although some are attractive they do require plenty of room and the roots are very invasive. Nevertheless, they can form useful windbreaks, and the plants will provide garden canes – although not for three years or more.

Sedges (listed as *Carex*) are suitable for damp ground, although some will survive in drier situations.

Annual grasses Most annual grasses are quite easy to grow. However, they tend to finish rather early and, in an annual border, they then look untidy while other plants are still at their best, particularly during a wet season. Their greatest value is for use in dried flower decorations, and it is quite a good idea to set aside a small area of the garden especially for growing them. Alternatively, mix them in with other types of plants, not just annuals.

Seeds can be sown directly in the ground but the difficulty will be to distinguish the seedlings from those of self-sown annual weed grasses. A better method is to grow a few seeds in individual pots containing John Innes seed compost. Sow the seeds in late March in 8 cm (3 in) pots, or slightly smaller, and then water them in with Cheshunt compound to control damping off. When the seeds have germinated, thin the seedlings out to give them space to grow. Leave them to grow on, eventually hardening them off in a cold frame before planting out in early June.

A few species are very susceptible to frost damage, so take care not to plant these out before the danger of late frosts has passed. These include *Eragrostis elegans*, *Pennisetum villosum*, *Setaria italica*, *S. viridis* and *Sorghum nigricans*.

Prepare the site for annual grasses by cultivating to a fine tilth and raking in a balanced organic fertilizer at 65–100 g per sq m (2–3 oz per sq yd). A planting distance of 30 cm (1 ft) is satisfactory for most annual grasses. Water the young plants generously at first to get them established, after which one good watering a week in dry weather should be sufficient. Stop watering once the flowers and seed-heads appear.

Cut the heads for drying on a warm, dry day before the seed has set, otherwise they will become overripe and begin to scatter. After cutting, they are best wrapped, not too tightly, in newspaper, and hung up to dry in a warm but airy and dark place.

Choosing annual grasses

Briza maxima (quaking grass). Height 45 cm (1½ ft). One of the annual grasses most grown for decoration, this has large, nodding spikes, which dry exceptionally well.
Hordeum jubatum (squirrel tail). Height 45 cm (1½ ft). An ornamental barley with silky, long-haired tassels.
Lagurus ovatus (hare's tail). Height 45 cm (1½ ft). Another favourite, with soft and fluffy, creamy-white plumes.
Setaria italica (foxtail millet). Height 60 cm (2 ft). Large, nodding, green heads that turn golden when dried.

Choosing perennial grasses

Cortaderia selloana 'Pumila' (pampas grass). Height 1.2–1.8 m (4–6 ft). Compact and suitable for small gardens.
C. selloana 'Sunningdale Silver'. Slightly taller at about 1.8–2.1 m (6–7 ft), with very good silvery plumes.
Festuca glauca. Height 23 cm (9 in). Blue-grey. One of the best evergreen edging grasses.

Briza maxima

Lagurus ovatus

Glyceria aquatilis 'Variegata'. Height 60 cm (2 ft). Best for a wet situation. The leaves have white, yellow and green stripes, the white appearing pinkish on young growths.
Miscanthus sinensis 'Silver Feather'. Height 2.1 m (7 ft). This bamboo-like grass provides a good display during September and October, with silky flowerheads.
Miscanthus sacchariflorus. Suitable for a windbreak, strong-growing but not invasive. It will grow 1.8–2.7 m (6–9 ft) in one year. The grass grows from the base each year but the dead stalks remain during the winter.
Pennisetum orientale. Height 45 cm (1½ ft). Forms plenty of brown-green flower spikes from July to September.
Phalaris arundinacea 'Picta'. Height 90 cm (3 ft). This also prefers moist conditions, but can be very invasive. It has white and green-striped leaves.

Drying flowers
Pick just-open
everlastings; tie them
in bundles and hang
up to dry.

HARDY ANNUALS

Providing a carpet of colour from mid-June until the autumn frosts, hardy annuals are among the most brilliant of summer flowers. They are easy to grow, and certainly give maximum value for space during their relatively brief lives.

Annuals may be used to make good any gaps left in borders where spring bulbs have died down or where plants have failed to survive the winter. They can fill spaces in a newly-planted shrub border or be planted in hanging baskets and window boxes. Trailing varieties are especially effective in such containers, while climbing species will soften the appearance of bare walls and fences. Most striking of all is a bed given over entirely to hardy annuals, where they will form a patchwork quilt of contrasting colours, textures and forms. The outlay is low but the results are beautiful and quickly achieved.

Thanks to the work of plant breeders, it is now possible to grow a wider range of hardy annuals even more easily than in the past. In particular, many now come into flower much more rapidly than formerly. The plants that do this are the F_1 hybrids, grown from seeds resulting from a cross between two pure-bred and closely related strains. Although usually costing a little extra, their improved size, uniformity and overall performance can be a revelation.

Position Hardy annuals need all the sunshine they can get if they are to flower well right through the summer. So choose an open position and, if possible, grow them in a bed that can be viewed from all sides. Climbing nasturtiums are a good choice for covering a fence, shed or even a pergola.

Qualities that were considered in compiling the list below and overleaf include length of flowering period, ability to withstand heavy thunderstorms, and minimum need for support.

'Everlasting' hardy annuals, suitable for drying

Grasses. There are a number from which to choose (see Ornamental grasses, opposite). Their main value is for inclusion in arrangements of dried flowers.

Helichrysum bracteatum (straw flower or everlasting flower). Height 30–90 cm (1–3 ft). There are both tall and short varieties in a range of colours. Free-flowering.

Helipterum roseum. Height 30–45 cm (1–1½ ft). Daisy-like everlasting flowers in shades of pink, red, white.

Helipterum manglesii. Height 30 cm (1 ft). Carmine, rose and silvery-white flowers with yellow or dark brown centres.

Scabiosa stellata 'Drumstick'. Height 45 cm (1½ ft). Powder-blue flowers which, when mature, form bronze-coloured, globe-shaped seed-heads.

Xeranthemum annuum. Height 60 cm (2 ft). Wiry-stemmed plants with paper-like flowers in white, rose-pink and lilac. Single and semi-double blooms.

Popular hardy annuals

Adonis aestivalis. Height 30 cm (1 ft). Outstandingly beautiful, with deep crimson, cup-shaped flowers and almost black stamens. Good for the front of a border.

Anchusa capensis 'Blue Angel'. Height 23 cm (9 in). Compact and good for the front of the border. Deep blue flowers.

Atriplex hortensis 'Rubra'. Height 1.8 m (6 ft). A good background plant, with attractive deep red foliage. A sound choice for flower arrangers, as the seed pods can be dried or preserved with glycerine.

Cacalia coccinea. Height 30–45 cm (1–1½ ft). Bright scarlet and orange, tassel-like flowers. Very free-flowering.

Calendula officinalis (pot marigold). Height 30–45 cm (1–1½ ft). A wide range of colours and shades, including cream, yellow, gold and orange. Possibly the easiest annual to grow, it provides continuous colour throughout the summer.

Centaurea cyanus (cornflower). Height 30–75 cm (1–2½ ft). A mixture of colours that includes blue, mauve, pink, red and white. Some are almost black. Very free-flowering, an excellent cut flower and may also be dried for the winter. The taller varieties may need some support.

Centaurea moschata (sweet sultan). Height 60 cm (2 ft). Cornflower-type flowers in a mixture of colours. Dislikes rich soil but will do well in partial shade.

Chrysanthemum coronarium (annual chrysanthemum). Height 75 cm (2½ ft). Striking colours and shades. Free-flowering over a long period and an excellent flower for cutting.

Clarkia elegans. Height 60 cm (2 ft). As a rule, supplied only in mixtures of white, pink, red, lavender and purple. Does well in semi-shade.

Convolvulus minor (syn. *C. tricolor*). Height 30 cm (1 ft). A showy annual, with flowers similar to those of the climbing species. A number of clear, jewel-like colours.

Convolvulus minor

Popular hardy annuals (cont.)

Cynoglossum amabile (hound's tongue). Height 45 cm (1½ ft). The flowers, a lovely deep turquoise, are produced freely all summer.

Delphinium consolida (larkspur). Height 38–90 cm (15–36 in). The erect stems are more than half covered with florets in many different colours. It flowers over a long period and the spikes can be dried for winter decoration. May be sown outdoors in the autumn for earlier blooms.

Dimorphotheca aurantiaca (star of the veldt). Height 20–30 cm (8–12 in). Predominantly orange flowers make a dazzling spectacle on a sunny day. Must be planted in full sun, otherwise the flowers will not open.

Echium plantagineum (bugloss). Height 30 cm (1 ft). Borage-like flowers in striking shades of blue, lavender and pink, with occasionally some white. Blooms for weeks on end.

Eschscholzia californica (Californian poppy). Height 30 cm (1 ft). Bright, poppy-like flowers and will grow in any soil provided the position is sunny. Will seed itself in mild areas.

*Eschscholtzia
californica*

Euphorbia marginata. Height 60 cm (2 ft). Grown mainly for its striking green and white foliage, and a good choice for flower arrangers. The milky-white sap can irritate the skin if not washed off immediately.

Godetia grandiflora. Height 30 cm (1 ft). Azalea-like flowers which are semi-double and coloured pink, salmon, crimson, cerise and white. They have the appearance of crushed silk. Long-lasting as a cut flower.

Helianthus annuus 'Sungold' (sunflower). Height 60 cm (2 ft). These miniature

Papaver
('Shirley')

sunflowers have almost ball-shaped flowers up to 15 cm (6 in) across, carried on rigid stems. A sunny position is needed.

Iberis umbellata (candytuft). Height 15–30 cm (6–12 in). The flowers of this fast-growing annual are mainly red, pink or white. Free-flowering and a good edging plant.

Lavatera trimestris (mallow). Height 75 cm (2½ ft). Lovely trumpet-shaped flowers, mainly pink or white, that are produced continually. Although tall, the stems are strong and need no support.

Linaria maroccana (toadflax). Height 23 cm (9 in). Dainty and variously-coloured antirrhinum-like flowers, some of the most striking being crimson and gold. Good edging plant.

Linum grandiflorum (flax). Height 30–45 cm (1–1½ ft). Saucer-shaped, scarlet and blue flowers that look especially beautiful when swayed by the wind. Suitable for planting near the front of the border.

Lobularia maritima (alyssum). Height 8–10 cm (3–4 in). Many varieties, in shades of white, pink and purple. Suitable for tubs and as an edging plant.

Lupinus 'Lulu' mixed. Height 45–60 cm (1½–2 ft). Long-lasting and in a range of beautiful colours. A further batch of flowers later in the season can be encouraged by removing the seed-heads as soon as they form.

Malcolmia maritima (Virginian stock). Height 20 cm (8 in). Good for edging paths. Flowers in various shades of red, lilac and white.

Nemophila insignis (baby blue eyes). Height 15 cm (6 in). Sky-blue flowers with white centres. Grow in full sun. Useful for edging beds and borders.

Nigella damascena (love-in-a-mist). Height 38–45 cm (15–18 in). Cornflower-type flowers in various shades of blue, rose, red, mauve, purple and white,

surrounded by a mist of green, finely-cut leaves. The odd, balloon-like seedpods are good material for flower arrangements.

Papaver (poppy). Height 30–90 cm (1–3 ft). Among the most striking of annuals, varying from large, peony-type flowers in the 'Shirley' strains, to the small, single, black-spotted, red flowers of 'Ladybird'.

Reseda odorata (mignonette). Height 30 cm (1 ft). An old-fashioned flower, the seeds of which were sent by Napoleon to Josephine on one of his campaigns. The superb perfume makes up for the rather ordinary flowers.

Scabiosa atropurpurea (pincushion flower). Height 38–90 cm (15–36 in). Usually sold in mixed colours, these ranging from dark purple through blue, red and pink to white. Both the flowers and the seed pods provide material for arrangements.

Senecio elegans, syn. *Jacobaea erecta*. Height 45 cm (1½ ft). The flowers are daisy-like, in shades of carmine and red. Very showy if planted in bold patches.

Tropaeolum majus (nasturtium). Height (bedding types) 30 cm (1 ft). Both the bedding and climbing types grow well on poor soil, preferably in a sunny position.

*Tropaeolum
majus*

Germination tends to be unreliable. Bedding types are available in many bright colours and some have variegated leaves.

Climbing nasturtiums, height to 2.4 m (8 ft), are useful for hiding sheds and fences and for covering pergola posts.

Viscaria oculata. Height 25 cm (10 in). Small, five-petalled flowers in various shades of pink, blue, red and white. The massed effect is striking.

Xeranthemum annuum. Height 60 cm (2 ft). The daisy-like flowers dry well for winter use. Cut when just open, remove foliage and hang upside down in a cool, airy place to dry. White, rose, lilac and purple flowers.

SWEET PEAS

These hardy annuals are prized for their beauty and versatility. For planting near the front of the border, and needing little or no support, there are dwarf cultivars such as 'Jet Set', 'Snoopee' and 'Super Snoopee'. Plant them in groups of three or four, with 30 cm (1 ft) between groups.

The taller Spencer and Multiflora types are more suitable for the back of the border. Growing to around 1.8 m (6 ft) in height, they need the support of canes or pea sticks. Plant 15–20 cm (6–8 in) apart.

The seeds may be sown at various times. For the best results, sow in a greenhouse or frame during October, then plunge the potted seedlings in a cold frame for the winter. They need covering only during very cold or wet weather, but take precautions against mice. Plant out during the second half of March.

Alternatively, sow in January in a heated greenhouse, hardening the plants off in a cold frame as growth progresses. They will be ready for planting out in early May. Another way is to sow the seeds in late March or early April directly into the bed. It will aid germination if each seed is nicked with a sharp knife before sowing, avoiding the area round the 'eye' of the seed.

If the plants are to form groups in the border, sow seven or eight seeds in a 15 cm (6 in) pot, reducing these to five or six if all germinate. They can then be planted without disturbing the roots.

If plants are to be grown singly, sow in a seed tray. Pot the seedlings individually into 8 cm (3 in) pots or sweet pea tubes when they are large enough, eventually planting them 15–20 cm (6–8 in) apart, or 30 cm (1 ft) for cordons.

The cordon system is used to obtain high-quality blooms for exhibition. It is very time-consuming, however, and not the most practical method for garden display. The method involves growing the plants on a single stem, which entails frequent removal of side-shoots and tendrils, tying-in as the plants grow.

Mottling and discoloration of the leaves are signs of virus disease. Remove and burn affected plants, washing your hands afterwards. Keep aphids in check by spraying.

Cultivars that are particular favourites include 'Cream Beauty', with large, frilled, cream-coloured flowers; 'Grace of Monaco', which has soft pink, waved and fragrant blooms; 'Lady Diana', another very fragrant cultivar, is pale violet; 'Red Ensign' has scented, bright red flowers.

Sweet peas
These produce a profusion of scented blooms throughout summer.

SUPPORTS FOR SWEET PEAS

Pea sticks
Dwarf sweet peas need little support, but taller-growing types require a framework. Pea sticks provide ready footholds.

Netting
Wire, plastic or string netting, secured to upright posts or fencing panels, make good supports on exposed sites.

Inclined pea sticks
For group displays in the garden, set tall pea sticks at an incline. This allows air circulation round the plants.

Cane wigwam
Alternatively, grow sweet peas against a wigwam support of tall bamboo canes. The leaf tendrils will twine round the smooth canes.

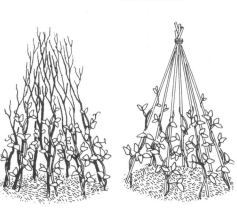

Popular biennials

Campanula medium (Canterbury bell). Height 38 cm–1.2 m (15 in–4 ft). A magnificent spectacle, with subtle shades of pink, lavender and purple. The taller varieties may need supporting but there are also some most attractive short varieties.

Campanula medium

Cheiranthus × allionii (Siberian wallflower). Height 30–45 cm (1–1½ ft). Excellent for spring bedding, being more compact than ordinary wallflowers and sometimes a little earlier. Bright orange is the usual colour, but there are variations.

Cheiranthus x allionii

Cheiranthus cheiri (wallflower). Height 30 cm (1 ft). A superb range of colours, including the usual shades of red, orange and yellow. On light, sandy soil, allow a break of at least three years before replanting wallflowers in the same bed. This will help to combat club root.

Dianthus barbatus (sweet william). Height 30–45 cm (1–1½ ft). Deep burgundy shades and other lovely colours. Good for cutting. If left, and the dead leaves cleared, it may last for another year.

Myosotis alpestris (forget-me-not). Height 15 cm (6 in). The current trend is away from the original deep blue colour, with pink, white and other shades of blue taking its place.

Perennials treated as biennials

Primula polyantha (polyanthus). Height 23 cm (9 in). Few plants can rival the polyanthus for colour and length of flowering. The blooms are carried on trusses well clear of the leaves and come in many shades of yellow, blue, pink, red and white. They will grow in sun or partial shade and need moisture-retentive soil.

Viola 'Blue Tit'. Height 15 cm (6 in). A splendid little plant that will flower for months on end if consistently dead-headed. Best propagated from cuttings, which strike very easily.

Dianthus barbatus

BIENNIALS

These plants develop over two seasons, from the seedling stage to the production of ripe seeds. Growth is made during the first year; they flower, fruit and die in the second.

A problem with sweet williams and Canterbury bells is that they may not flower until June or even early July, so bear this in mind when planning your beds. It is a good idea to have a spare box of annuals handy for filling up the gaps left when they have finished flowering.

HALF-HARDY ANNUALS

The term 'half-hardy' describes plants that will grow outdoors without protection only when the risk of frost has passed. Half-hardy annuals have to be raised under glass – in a greenhouse or frame – before being planted out to flower during the summer.

Often known as 'bedding plants', they are widely available at nurseries, garden centres and local shops. If you buy plants instead of raising them yourself, reject any that are not green, sturdy and healthy-looking. Avoid any that are spindly or have yellow leaves.

The other essential point is to delay buying and planting them until the risk of a late spring frost in your area has passed. This will be late May or early June, depending on whether you live in the south or the north of the country. Even then, the plants should have been gradually hardened off to accustom them to cooler conditions.

Detailed instructions for raising and growing half-hardy annuals are given in the month by month calendar at the end of this section. A few of the bedding plants described opposite are, in fact, perennials, though grown as annuals.

Popular bedding plants

Ageratum species. Height 20–25 cm (8–10 in). With its powder-puff flowers, this is an excellent plant for edging. Mainly blue, but also some white varieties. Grows anywhere except full shade. Sow mid-March.

Amaranthus tricolor 'Splendour'. Height 60 cm (2 ft). A fine foliage plant, the mottled red, orange or yellow colouring deepening as it matures. Avoid overhead watering, which spoils the foliage. Sow late February.

Antirrhinum majus (snapdragon). Height 20–90 cm (8–36 in). A tremendous colour range, with the flower forms varying between single, double, butterfly and azalea types. There are some dwarf, carpet-bedding varieties. Early sowing is advisable – either late January or early February.

Begonia semperflorens. Height 23–30 cm (9–12 in). A wide range of varieties, with various shades of foliage and red, pink or white flowers. Flowering is over a long period, and the plants grow quite well in shade. Sow January or early February.

Cineraria maritima (syn. *Senecio bicolor*) 'Silver Dust'. Height 60 cm (2 ft). Striking grey foliage that provides a gentle background for some of the more dazzling bedding plants. Sow mid-February.

Cleome spinosa (spider flower) Height 1 m (3½ ft). An unusual-looking annual in lovely shades of delicate pink – also white. Take care when handling, for it is armed with sharp thorns. Sow late March.

Cobaea scandens. Height 3 m (10 ft). A rather unusual climber, with bell-shaped flowers in shades of mauve and greenish white. Suitable for fences and pergolas, but it needs full sunshine. Sow late March.

Cosmos bipinnatus (Mexican aster). Height 60–90 cm (2–3 ft). This fairly tall annual has lovely fern-like foliage and single orange, pink or rose-crimson flowers. Sow late March.

Cuphea miniata 'Firefly'. Height 30 cm (1 ft). Reddish, tube-like flowers grow freely from the axils of the leaves. Sow mid-March.

Dahlia hybrids. Height 60–75 cm (2–2½ ft). Bedding dahlias provide colour right into the autumn. Several different types, include Collerette, Coltness hybrids and Double-flowered. If you wish, the tubers that develop may be stored for the following year just like those of the large-flowered varieties. Sow late February/early March.

Dianthus hybrids. Height 20–38 cm (8–15 in). There are many lovely colours and interesting flower forms. Some are

Salvia superba

sweetly scented and all flower over a long period. Sow late February.

Impatiens (busy lizzie). Height 23–38 cm (9–15 in). Popular as a pot plant, it is also a good choice for bedding and for planting in hanging baskets and other containers. Good for shaded sites. A remarkably wide colour range. Sow early February.

Ipomoea tricolor (morning glory). Height 3–3.6 m (10–12 ft). Lovely trumpet-shaped flowers. The blue ones are particularly fine, but there are also red, pink, lavender, chocolate and violet varieties. Good for covering walls, fences and pergolas. Sow in February.

Lobelia erinus. Height 10 cm (4 in). Its dwarf habit makes it a good edging plant for any display of annuals. There is also a trailing kind for hanging baskets and window boxes. The flower colours range through blue, crimson and white. Sow between January and March.

Nicotiana

Matthiola incana (stock). Height 45–60 cm (18–24 in). The highly-scented flowers produce a wonderful show from June onwards. Many tints and shades of pink, purple, cream and white. Sow in February or March.

Nicotiana (tobacco plant). Height 25–45 cm (10–18 in). Since the introduction of the 'Nikki' strain, this has become one of the most popular bedding plants. Plants of this type have a compact habit and are in a range of colours, including red, pink, rose and white. Like most nicotianas, they are fragrant, especially during the evening. Sow between February and April.

Pelargonium (geranium). Height 25–38 cm (10–15 in). The new types are a great advance on the older varieties. A February sowing will provide flowers from June until the autumn frosts. The colour range has also been extended.

Petunia. Height 15–30 cm (6–12 in). In addition to a wide range of single colours, many beautiful bicolours are now available with either single or double flowers. A sunny position is needed but their flowering period can be shortened by wet weather in August. The 'Resisto' varieties are a little more tolerant of rain. Sow between January and March.

Phlox drummondii. Height 15–30 cm (6–12 in). Bright, showy blooms, useful for small arrangements of cut flowers. A wide range of colours. Sow between February and April.

Rudbeckia (gloriosa daisy). Height 45–75 cm (1½–2½ ft). A striking flower with a prominent, conical centre. The petals are in magnificent shades of orange, yellow, brown and mahogany. Sow in February or March.

Salvia. Height 23–60 cm (9–24 in). The flowers are a blaze of colour during the summer, and there are other shades from which to choose in addition to the usual scarlet.

Tagetes erecta (African marigold). Height 30–75 cm (1–2½ft). Gold, orange and yellow flowers over a very extended period. Sow in March.

Tagetes patula (French marigold). Height 15–30 cm (6–12 in). The colour range is even wider than for African types, for it includes red. One of the newest introductions, 'Burpees White', is a beautiful ivory colour. Sow in March.

Zinnia. Height 23–60 cm (9–24 in). Brightly-coloured flowers in a variety of shades and forms. Pot the seedlings individually, handling them with care and never pressing the stems. Avoid watering overhead or when the sun is on the plants. Sow in March or April.

JANUARY

Sweet peas Sow in pots or seed trays (see October) and germinate at gentle heat.

Biennials After spells of cold weather, check over-wintering plants, such as wallflowers, stocks, sweet williams and polyanthus, to see whether they have been lifted by frost. If they have, firm them in.

Half-hardy annuals Antirrhinums and begonias may be sown this month in a heated greenhouse. A temperature of 16–18°C (60–65°F) is needed for germination. Alternatively, sow early next month.

If your greenhouse is heated to only about 7°C (45°F), a small electric propagator will provide suitable conditions for germination. Afterwards, the seedlings can be grown on in the cooler temperature of the greenhouse.

Sowing the seeds Use clean pots or seed pans. To ensure good drainage, cover the base of the container with broken crocks or with rough, fibrous material. Fill to within 12 mm (½ in) of the top of the pot with seed compost and press this down firmly.

Soak the compost thoroughly and leave it to drain for half an hour, then sow the seeds thinly on the damp surface. It is easier to distribute very fine seeds, such as begonias, more evenly if they are first mixed with a little silver sand.

Finally, sift a shallow covering of seed compost over the seeds and firm lightly. Place a sheet of glass over the pot and cover with paper. Turn the glass over every day, making sure that condensation does not drip on to the soil.

When the first seedlings appear, remove the glass and paper. Place the seedlings as near to the greenhouse glass as possible. This will prevent them from becoming drawn and leggy. For the first two or three days protect the seedlings from bright sunlight, covering them with paper when necessary.

FEBRUARY

Hardy annuals Towards the end of the month, finish thinning autumn-sown annuals, if and when soil conditions allow. (On no account walk on sticky soil.) Leave a little more space between autumn-sown seedlings than spring. (See May.)

Sweet peas Move seedlings from a January sowing to a cold frame.

Biennials If the soil shows signs of drying out, take the opportunity to weed among spring bedding plants and to loosen the surface of the soil. If possible, replace any plants that have died.

Polyanthus seeds may be sown now under glass. (See January, half-hardy annuals.)

SOWING SEEDS

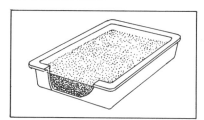

1 Cover tray bases with clay pot shards and top with seed compost.

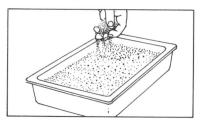

3 Cover seeds lightly with compost. Water well and leave to drain.

Half-hardy annuals Sow seeds of trailing *Lobelia*, which is useful for hanging baskets; also *Impatiens* and *Phlox drummondii*.

Pricking out Seedlings raised last month should now be large enough to prick out. This means transferring them to boxes from the pots in which they were sown, which gives the seedlings more room to develop freely.

The time to start pricking out is when the first pair of true leaves appears. These are the 'rough' leaves that develop soon after the first, smooth pair of leaves, known as seed leaves or cotyledons.

The box should have ample drainage holes, with a layer of rough material, such as coarse peat, placed over the bottom. Fill to within 6 mm (¼ in) of the top with John Innes potting compost No. 2, or a similar, soil-less compost. Smooth the surface level and press it down fairly firmly.

It will be easier to handle and insert the seedlings if you make use of two small sticks. Use a wooden plant label with a V-shaped notch cut in one end and a rounded stick with a blunt point.

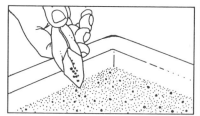

2 Firm the compost before scattering the seeds evenly and thinly.

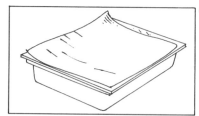

4 Place a sheet of glass and newspaper over the tray to conserve moisture.

PRICKING OUT

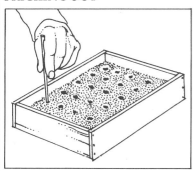

1 For seedlings, space planting holes evenly in boxes of potting compost.

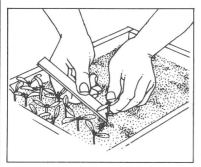

2 Use a V-notched plant label to prise the seedlings from the seed trays.

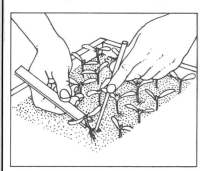

3 Insert the seedlings in the holes, pushing down the roots with a stick.

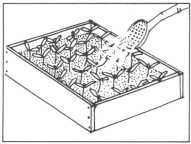

4 Water the seedlings with a fine rose; grow them on in good light and heat.

Use the notched stick to prise up and lift the seedlings, assisting with the other one if necessary. Use the rounded stick to make the planting holes, spacing these 5 cm (2 in) apart in each direction.

Push the roots into the hole gently with the pointed stick, then fill in the space round the seedling by pressing down the sides of the hole. When the box is full, smooth out any remaining depressions.

Use a fine rose to damp over the box of seedlings. Put the box back on to the greenhouse staging, covering it with a sheet of paper if it is sunny. This will be necessary only for the first few days.

Never let the compost dry out, but do not over-water it either. Once the seedlings start to grow they must be watered as needed.

MARCH

Hardy annuals Towards the end of the month, and provided that the soil is not at all sticky, spread a dressing of bonemeal – about 65 g per sq m (2 oz per sq yd) on the bed prepared last November for sowing annuals. Then break up the surface with a pronged cultivator.
Sweet peas Plant out October-sown seedlings, soil and weather permitting.
Biennials If you have been unable to cultivate the soil among your biennials, do so now.

Sow seeds of pansies. (See January, half-hardy annuals.)
Half-hardy annuals Sow seeds of *Ageratum; Dahlia; Tagetes* (French and African marigolds); and *Zinnia*. (See January.)

Seedlings pricked out last month can be moved to a cold frame, weather permitting, at the end of the month. Keep the frame closed unless the weather is very warm. If there is any fear of frost, cover it with sacking or some suitable alternative at night.

Seeds sown last month should now be large enough to prick out. (See February.)

APRIL

Hardy annuals Tread over the prepared bed (see March) to firm it evenly, then rake the surface to a fine tilth.

Annuals look most effective if planted in drifts of varying sizes. Mark out the shapes of the drifts with a pointed stick, referring to the plan made in December.

Seed sowing can start from about mid-April, but only if the soil is sufficiently dry for a tilth to be created. On no account work on sticky soil. Start with the annuals that take a little longer to germinate. These are: *Adonis; Alyssum; Anchusa; Atriplex; Cacalia; Centaurea* (cornflower and sweet sultan); *Chrysanthemum; Clarkia; Convolvulus; Cynoglossum; Echium; Euphorbia; Godetia; Helianthus* (sunflower); *Helichrysum* (straw flower); *Lavatera* (mallow); *Linaria* (toadflax); *Linum* (flax); *Lupinus* (lupin); *Nigella* (love-in-a-mist); *Papaver* (poppy); *Reseda* (mignonette); *Tropaeolum* (nasturtium); *Viscaria; Xeranthemum.*
Sowing hardy annuals It is better to sow the seeds thinly in parallel drills than to scatter them at random. This makes it much easier to distinguish the seedlings from weeds during the early stages, allowing hand weeding or even hoeing with an onion hoe. Sowing in drills also enables you to tread on the bed without damaging the seedlings.

Use a pointed stick to make the

drills, which should be 6–12 mm (¼–½ in) deep. If you are sowing a bed of mixed annuals, draw the drills in adjacent drifts at different angles, helping to disguise the fact that they are in straight lines. This will not be apparent once the plants start to grow.

The correct spaces between drills are as follows: 15 cm (6 in) between annuals that grow to 23–30 cm (9–12 in); 23 cm (9 in) for plants 30–45 cm (1–1½ ft) high; 30 cm (1 ft) for plants 45 cm (1½ ft) high and over.

Cover the newly-sown bed with brushwood to discourage cats and birds.

Sweet peas Weather permitting, make outdoor sowings where the plants are to flower.

Biennials Canterbury bells may need support, particularly if planted in a windy position. The rest of the biennials should be flowering freely and need little attention.

Half-hardy annuals Sow *Matthiola incana* seeds (ten week stock).

Continue placing pricked-out plants in the cold frame as they become ready. In mild weather remove the top of the frame, but be wary of cold east winds.

MAY

Hardy annuals The rest of the hardy annuals may now be sown.

Thinning out Even if annuals are sown thinly it will still be necessary to thin out the seedlings. Those sown last month should now be ready for this.

Thinning is best started as soon as the seedlings can be recognized. It is better to do it in three stages than attempt to complete it in a single operation. If the ground is dry, water the seedlings well the night before, using a fine rose on the watering can. Water again after thinning. Repeat this task twice again at about weekly intervals, with the final thinning leaving the plants at the following distances.

Allow about 10 cm (4 in) between plants that grow 23–30 cm (9–12 in) high, 15 cm (6 in) for plants between 30–45cm (1–1½ ft), and 20 cm (8 in) for plants of 45 cm (1½ ft) upwards.

It may be necessary to water the seedlings once or twice after thinning. However, once the plants are about 10 cm (4 in) high, and growing well, stop watering. They are now quite able to survive without further attention.

Sweet peas Plant out hardened-off seedlings from January sowings.

Biennials Prepare a small area of ground to sow some biennial seeds for flowering next year. Give a top-dressing of bonemeal at the rate of 65 g per sq m (2 oz per sq yd) before sowing.

Rake the surface and sow the seeds in drills 12 mm (½ in) deep. Space the drills 20 cm (8 in) apart to allow a hoe to be used between the rows.

Half-hardy annuals Planting may begin once the plants have been well hardened off and all danger of frost is over. The last week in May is the earliest safe time in most areas.

As a general rule, planting can be a little earlier in the south and west, but it should always be delayed if cold winds are blowing from the north or east.

Planting out Before starting to plant, make sure that the soil in the boxes is well moistened. If it is dry, soak it thoroughly and wait for an hour or two. If the bed is dry, soak it thoroughly the day before you wish to plant.

Bump each side of the box on the ground, then tip the plants out

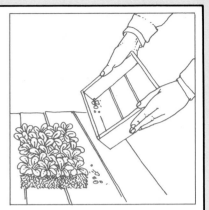

Separating seedlings
Tip out hardened-off seedlings en bloc and pull them gently apart.

en bloc. Pull them gently apart with your fingers, leaving the roots intact. At all stages, the less check they receive the better.

Once the plants start to grow away, stop watering. Hardy annuals do not as a rule need irrigating, except when very dry.

JUNE

Hardy annuals Thin out seedlings as required.

Half-hardy annuals Plant out the remaining half-hardy annuals to complete the bedding scheme and also to fill any empty spaces in a mixed border.

JULY

Hardy annuals Try not to walk between the plants unless absolutely necessary. This might damage them and shorten their lives. Remove faded flowers at once to encourage new buds to form. Remove any large weeds by hand.

Biennials Plant out biennial seedlings into nursery beds, spacing them 15 cm (6 in) apart in the row and 30 cm (1 ft) between the rows. Water the plants if necessary.

Half-hardy annuals As with hardy annuals, try to avoid walking on the bed. Regular dead-heading will help to keep the plants flowering. Remove weeds by hand weeding or hoeing.

AUGUST

Hardy annuals Continue to remove faded flowers and keep the bed free from weeds. Of course, if you wish to save your own seeds you will have to leave one or two flowers to mature. However, there is no point in saving F_1 hybrid seeds, as they will not come true.

Drying 'everlastings' Cut the flowers on a dry, warm day when there is a minimum of moisture on the leaves and flowers. Never pick material to dry when it is raining or dew is forming.

As a general rule, choose flowers just before they come into full bloom. Fully-open blossoms, or flowers that have already begun to set seed, will merely shed petals and seeds during drying.

Air drying Pick the flowers and remove the leaves from the stems. Leaves that are left on will simply wither and become tangled as they dry. If the flowers are fairly small, divide them into small bunches and tie them with string or plastic, leaving a loop to slide onto a line or hook.

If you have chosen material with large flower-heads, hang them singly, otherwise they may be damaged when you try to disentangle the dried florets. As the material dries it tends to shrink, so you may need to tighten the ties to hold the stems securely.

Hang the prepared bunches, well apart, on a line or hooks in a cool, dry, airy place – not in bright sunlight.

Drying time The length of drying time varies enormously. Delicate material, such as grasses, may take only a week. Heavier flowers, containing more moisture, may need three weeks or more.

Check the material to see if it feels quite dry and dehydrated before removing it for storage. Store the dried material in cardboard boxes in a dry, cool place. Do not use polythene bags.

Half-hardy annuals Follow the advice given for hardy annuals.

SEPTEMBER

Hardy annuals In the south of the country, many hardy annuals may now be sown in the open where they are to flower next year. (See April). Annuals suitable for sowing now include: *Calendula* (pot marigold); *Centaurea* (cornflower); *Clarkia; Echium* (bugloss); *Eschscholzia* (Californian poppy); *Godetia; Iberis* (candytuft); *Linaria* (toadflax); *Lobularia* (alyssum); *Nigella* (love-in-a-mist); *Papaver rhoeas* (annual poppy).

Biennials Prepare the soil for planting out biennials next month. Fork the soil over, adding some well-rotted manure or compost. Rake a dressing of bonemeal into the surface – 130 g per sq m (4 oz per sq yd).

OCTOBER

Hardy annuals Once the plants have been killed by frost, remove the dead growth so that the site is ready for digging next month.

Thin annuals sown last month, but not as drastically as you would those sown in spring. The final thinning will be done in February.

Sweet peas This is the best month

for sowing in a cool greenhouse or a cold frame. Sow in pots, or in trays for cordon-trained plants.

Biennials It is now time to plant biennials in their spring flowering positions. This should be completed before the end of the month, if possible, so that they become established before the weather gets too cold and frosty.

If there is a prolonged dry spell, set the plants out and water them for a few days after planting.

Should you consider planting tulips between the biennials, be sure to plant the biennials first, otherwise you could easily damage the bulbs.

Half-hardy annuals Clear up the bed, as for hardy annuals. Send for seed catalogues.

NOVEMBER

Hardy annuals Dig the area that will be sown with annuals next year, leaving it rough for frosts to break it down. Add garden or spent mushroom compost, but avoid cow or pig manure. An over rich soil will result in lush foliage at the expense of flowers.

Sweet peas Move seedlings to a cold frame for the winter. For cordon-trained plants, prick out the seedlings individually, in 8 cm (3 in) pots.

Biennials If it was not possible to finish planting last month, complete the job by the middle of November at the very latest.

DECEMBER

With the new seed catalogues on hand, now is a good time to draw up plans for next year's annual border and bedding schemes. When this has been done, place your seed order.

No wonder roses are so widely grown and admired! They are surely among the most diverse and beautiful of all flowering plants, yet it is well within the power of every gardener to grow them successfully.

Perhaps the most puzzling aspect for beginners is the classification of the various kinds. Only when this is understood can a sensible choice be made from the many species and cultivars. Unfortunately, even the familiar terms 'hybrid tea' and 'floribunda' have now been superseded by a new classification, which is gradually being adopted by growers. Basically, this divides roses into modern and older kinds.

'Modern Roses' are made up of large-flowered (hybrid tea) and cluster-flowered (floribunda) bush roses, miniatures, many shrub roses, and also the majority of climbers and ramblers.

'Old Garden Roses', the second major category, include old-fashioned shrub roses, together with some of the older ramblers and climbers.

There is a third group, classified as Species Roses, which takes in most of the original species of shrub roses, and also a few climbers.

So where does this leave the ordinary gardener? There is still the same wide choice, but the roses may be offered under different names. 'Hybrid tea' and 'large-flowered bush' mean exactly the same thing. So do 'floribunda' and 'cluster-flowered bush'. It remains to be seen how quickly the new terms will gain general acceptance.

Large-flowered (H.T.) bush roses are prized for the beauty of their individual blooms, which generally appear in flushes during the summer. Cluster-flowered (floribunda) types carry their flowers in trusses and, as a rule, keep flowering more or less continually throughout the warmer summer months.

Miniature roses, mostly about 30–38 cm (12–15 in) in height, flower throughout the summer and are useful for edging, for growing in containers and also for planting in rock gardens.

Modern shrub roses, for the most part

hybrids, are a good deal taller and broader than either the large-flowered (H.T.) or cluster-flowered (floribunda) types. They make fine specimen plants for placing in prominent positions, as a rule flowering throughout the summer.

Climbing roses vary a great deal in vigour and flowering characteristics. Thus, some will cover a wall 7.6 m (25 ft) or more high, while others will barely attain 3 m (10 ft). There are varieties that will produce only a single flush of flowers, but a good many others that will bloom the summer long. This cannot be said of ramblers, which blossom just once during the summer, with a brief but memorable glory.

The older shrub roses, which include such groupings as the bourbons, gallicas, rugosas and moss roses, are a diverse bunch and perhaps not an obvious choice for the smaller suburban garden. Yet many are supremely lovely, even if their flowering period is brief, and there is often the bonus of seductive scent or attractive autumn hips.

WHERE TO GROW ROSES

Roses do best in a sunny situation, but avoid parts of the garden that are especially hot. Some cultivars suffer from scorch under such conditions.

Along with plenty of light, a good circulation of air is needed for healthy growth. Avoid beds surrounded by dense hedging or overhung branches.

A rich, free-draining, slightly acid loam is the ideal soil. Roses will tolerate quite a wide range of conditions, provided the soil does not become waterlogged.

Large-flowered, cluster-flowered and miniature roses are best grown on their own. They appear to resent competition from other plants. Modern shrub roses and species roses will mix quite happily with shrubs and herbaceous plants, provided they get plenty of light, but do avoid overcrowding.

PREPARING THE SOIL

Autumn is the best time to prepare beds for planting roses. This includes measures that must be taken if the bed has previously been used for this purpose.

ROSES

Large-flowered bush
rose (hybrid tea)

Cluster-flowered
bush rose
(floribunda)

Shrub rose

Standard rose

Climbing rose

Modern roses
Modern roses include
large-flowered and
cluster-flowered bush
types, and have an
almost continuous
display of blooms,
borne singly in the
former, in clusters in
the latter. Height
averages are 75 cm
(2½ ft) for hybrid
teas, 90 cm (3 ft) for
floribundas, with
miniatures at 25 cm
(10 in).

Modern shrub roses
Hybrids between
Species Roses and
Old Garden Roses,
these differ in being
repeat-flowering, and
carry their blooms
singly or in small
clusters. They grow
to a height and spread
of 1.5 m (5 ft).

Standard roses
Budded on bare briar
stems 90–100 cm (3–
3½ ft) high, the
blooms are either
large-flowered or
cluster-flowered
varieties; weeping
standards are budded
with rambler roses.

Climbing roses
These roses have a
complex parentage.
Some are climbing
sports of large or
cluster-flowered bush
roses, which are
repeat-flowering,
while others derive
from Species Roses,
with one massed
display in June and
July. True climbers
are more vigorous
than ramblers which
have one period of
bloom only.

Large-flowered (hybrid tea) roses

'Ace of Hearts' Height 60 cm (2 ft). A true red rose, with shiny, dark green foliage. Excellent for cutting, lasting up to two weeks in water.

'Adolf Horstman' Height 75 cm (2½ ft). Bronze-apricot blooms on long, straight stems. Good foliage and excellent for cutting.

'Alpine Sunset' Height 75 cm (2½ ft). Large, peach-pink blooms that are quite fragrant. Upright habit with dark, glossy foliage.

'Doris Tysterman' Height 75 cm (2½ ft). Tangerine blooms on long, sturdy stems, with bronzy foliage.

'Dr. Darley' Height 60 cm (2 ft). Large pink blooms on thick, sturdy stems. Rather short habit; dark green, glossy foliage.

'Evening Star' Height 75 cm (2½ ft). An excellent white rose of American origin. It flowers freely, the foliage being dark green.

'Fragrant Hour' Height 90 cm (3 ft). Large, salmon-pink blooms, which are nicely shaped and beautifully scented. Rather a tall rose, with dark green foliage.

'Just Joey' Height 90 cm (3 ft). Coppery-orange, with large, slightly scented blooms. These are borne on strong, upright stems, with bronze-green foliage. It is a free-flowering variety.

'L'Oreal Trophy' Height 1.2 m (4 ft). This has orange blooms and tall, upright growth. It is a very showy variety, being continuous-flowering and with excellent foliage.

'Loving Memory' Height 1.2 m (4 ft). Large, crimson-scarlet blooms of excellent quality. It has little fragrance, a rather vigorous habit and dark green foliage.

'Mala Rubinstein' Height 90 cm (3 ft). Fine, shapely blooms of camellia-rose and well scented. Quite a vigorous variety, with good foliage.

'Pot o' Gold' Height 60 cm (2 ft). Golden-yellow blooms; a first-class variety. It flowers in profusion on short, sturdy stems. The foliage is mid-green.

Prima Ballerina' Height 90 cm (3 ft). Deep rose-pink blooms with good shape and scent. This rose has quite a vigorous, upright habit and is well clothed with dark green foliage.

'Princess Margaret of England' Height 1.2 m (4 ft). Large pink blooms on strong, sturdy stems. An upright habit and good foliage.

'Pristine' Height 1.2 m (4 ft). Blooms of a delicate ivory-pink, very fragrant and often with several buds to a stem.

Vigorous, upright growth, and mid-green foliage.

'Silver Jubilee' Height 75 cm (2½ ft). One of the best large-flowered bush roses, with pink blooms on strong, upright stems. Disease-resistant, free-flowering; glossy foliage.

'Simba' Height 60 cm (2 ft). Clear, bright yellow blooms of good shape. A fairly short rose, with rigid stems and mid-green, healthy foliage.

'Sunblest' Height 75 cm (2½ ft). Golden-yellow flowers that hold their colour well. They are slightly fragrant. Fairly vigorous, upright bush, with mid-green glossy foliage.

'Troika' Height 75 cm (2½ ft). Orange-bronze, well-shaped blooms. A free-flowering variety, with upright growth, bright green foliage and moderate scent.

'Tynwald' Height 1.2 m (4 ft). Creamy-white blooms are carried on upright stems. The foliage is deep green and shiny, and the plant is resistant to disease.

'Whisky Mac' Height 90 cm (3 ft). Golden blooms with bronze buds – a fragrant, free-flowering and compact bush. The young foliage is bronze-green.

'Troika' (Large-flowered)

Cluster-flowered (floribunda) roses

'Amsterdam' Height 60 cm (2 ft). A free-flowering variety, with bright red blooms in large clusters. The stems are short and sturdy, the foliage shiny.

'Anne Harkness' Height 1.2 m (4 ft). Soft apricot blooms are carried in large clusters, with each individual bloom on a long stem. This makes it a good flower-arranging rose, and the flowers are particularly long-lasting. This variety flowers up to a fortnight later than most bush roses.

'Bobby Dazzler' Height 60 cm (2 ft). The orange-pink flower clusters are bright and eye-catching. The short, sturdy habit and plentiful mid-green foliage makes it a sound choice for small gardens.

'Brown Velvet' Height 75 cm (2½ ft). This variety provides a new colour break, being russet-brown in the early stages and taking on reddish tints when mature. The petals are like velvet and it is certainly a flower arranger's rose. Medium-sized growth is combined with a free-flowering habit.

'Burma Star' Height 90 cm (3 ft). This apricot rose is an outstanding variety, with strong, sturdy growth and large trusses of freely-borne blooms. The foliage is dark green and shiny, and the plant is disease-resistant.

'Congratulations' Height 1.5 m (5 ft). A strong-growing variety, with soft pink blooms carried on long, sturdy stems. It is free-flowering, and the foliage is dark green.

'Copper Pot' Height 1.4 m (4½ ft). An excellent rose, with coppery flowers on strong stems. The foliage is dark green, shiny and disease-resistant.

'Eyecatcher' Height 75 cm (2½ ft). Bright pink-apricot blooms make this a striking rose. The growth is short and sturdy, with good foliage.

'Eyepaint' Height 1.5 m (5 ft). The single blooms are scarlet, with a white eye and bright yellow stamens. The flowers are borne in large clusters. Growth is vigorous and the foliage bright green.

'Escapade' Height 90 cm (3 ft). The semi-double blooms are magenta coloured, with a white eye when fully open, and scented. The flowers are borne in large clusters. Growth is sturdy and the foliage disease-resistant.

'Fervid' Height 1.2 m (4 ft). This rose, with its red, single flowers, always gives an excellent display. The flowering season is very long indeed, and the growth habit strong.

'Fragrant Delight' Height 90 cm (3 ft). Coppery-salmon blooms are freely produced and they have a strong fragrance. Growth is vigorous.

'Georgie Anderson' Height 75 cm (2½ ft). The blooms are apricot at the bud stage, turning to peachy-pink when fully open. This variety is free-flowering over a long period. Other features are sturdy, rather short growth, medium scent and good, disease-resistant foliage.

'Grace Abounding' Height 90 cm (3 ft). The creamy-white blooms are carried in large trusses on thick, sturdy stems. The foliage is dark green and disease-resistant.

'Harry Edland' Height 75 cm (2½ ft). The mauve blooms are possibly the best of their type, being beautifully scented, of good shape and borne freely. Sturdy growth holds the flower trusses erect.

'Ice White' Height 90 cm (3 ft). This free-flowering, clear white variety has fully double blooms, borne in large trusses on firm, sturdy stems. A good all-round, disease-resistant variety.

'Intrigue' Height 50 cm (20 in). Possibly the deepest red cluster-flowered variety available. The deep crimson blooms, with a dark, velvety appearance, show bright yellow stamens when fully open. Large trusses of these blooms are borne on short, sturdy stems, making this a neat, low-growing variety.

'John Crossley' Height 90 cm (3 ft). Well-shaped yellow blooms are carried on strong stems. The foliage is attractive and the plant free-flowering.

'Southampton' (Cluster-flowered)

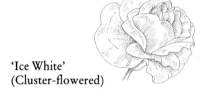

'Ice White'
(Cluster-flowered)

'Judy Garland' Height 90 cm (3 ft). This yellow and red rose is very much like the old 'Masquerade', though possibly stronger growing. It has large trusses of flowers on thick stems, and is both free-flowering and disease-resistant.

'Kerryman' Height 75 cm (2½ ft). The large, hybrid tea-type blooms are a rather unusual shade of pink. Good-sized trusses are borne freely over a long period. The foliage is attractive and disease-resistant.

'Kiskadee' Height 75 cm (2½ ft). The outer petals of this beautiful golden-yellow rose are veined red. The dark green, shiny foliage is disease-resistant.

'Korresia' Height 75 cm (2½ ft). The yellow blooms are hybrid-tea shape, fragrant and borne freely on sturdy stems. The plant has a branching habit, with dark green, disease-resistant foliage.

'Liverpool Echo' Height 1.2 m (4 ft). This quite tall, free-flowering, salmon-pink variety is outstanding. The small blooms are of perfect shape, carried in very large trusses of flowers on thick, sturdy stems. The mid-green foliage is disease-resistant.

'Margaret Merril' Height 90 cm (3 ft). A beautifully scented variety that carries pearly-blushed flowers turning to pure white. It is sometimes sold as large-flowered (H.T.). By any standards it is a superb rose, with a bushy, branching habit, a continuous display of flowers and dark green, glossy foliage.

'Mary Sumner' Height 90 cm (3 ft). A vermilion-shaded variety, carrying large trusses of blooms on strong stems. The glossy green foliage is resistant to disease.

'Matangi' Height 90 cm (3 ft). A free-flowering variety, with double, orange-vermilion blooms that have silver shading at the base and on the reverse of the petals. They are slightly fragrant and carried in large trusses on strong stems.

'Meggido' Height 75 cm (2½ ft). The bright red flowers are truly striking, being an unusual shade. The beautifully-shaped blooms are borne freely on good stems. The habit is rather bushy, with good foliage.

'Memento' Height 75 cm (2½ ft). Salmon-vermilion blooms, opening flat, are unusually weather-resistant. The large trusses of flowers are borne on sturdy stems and backed by dark green foliage.

'Princess Michael of Kent' Height 75 cm (2½ ft). Clear yellow blooms are carried freely in large clusters. The variety has a bushy habit, with disease-resistant, mid-green foliage.

'Ripples' Height 90 cm (3 ft). This is one of the mauve varieties, possibly the best of its type. It is free-flowering, with large trusses of blooms and healthy foliage.

'Rob Roy' Height 90 cm (3 ft). Crimson-scarlet, hybrid-tea type blooms. These are fragrant, form perfect buds and give a continuous display until late autumn.

'Rocky' Height 90 cm (3 ft). A brilliant vermilion-scarlet, with a silvery-cream reverse. The large clusters of semi-double blooms stand out against vigorous, lush foliage.

'Satchmo' Height 75 cm (2½ ft). Well-formed, double, scarlet blooms are borne freely on this rather bushy, vigorous plant. The foliage is attractive and healthy.

'Southampton' Height 1.2 m (4 ft). It has orange flowers with a yellow reverse. They are fragrant, semi-double and borne in large trusses.

'Wembley Stadium' Height 90 cm (3 ft). Red flowers, in large trusses, are carried on strong stems. Attractive foliage.

'Young Venturer' Height 90 cm (3 ft). The flowers, on strong stems, are sweet-scented, apricot-gold and well-shaped. The foliage is a dark, glossy green and disease-resistant.

Miniature roses

'Angela Rippon' Height 30 cm (1 ft). Double, bright salmon flowers.

'Colibre' Height 20–30 cm (8–12 in). Rich apricot, with a slight fragrance.

'Coralin' Height 38 cm (15 in). The flowers are coral-pink to deep coral-red. It is a vigorous plant, with bronze-tinted foliage.

'Dresden Doll' Height 25–30 cm (10–12 in). Shell-pink, small double blooms are preceded by dainty buds covered in light green "moss" – the miniature moss rose.

'Frosty' Height 25–30 cm (10–12 in). Pale pink buds open to pure white double flowers, with a pleasant fragrance.

'Gold Pin' Height 45 cm (1½ ft). Semi-double, buttercup-yellow blooms on bushy, vigorous growth.

'Green Diamond' Height 20–25 cm (8–10 in). The tiny pom-pom flowers have a distinctive green shading from the time the buds open.

'New Penny' Height 20 cm (8 in). Orange-red buds open to coral-pink flowers with a slight fragrance. The foliage is good and the habit compact.

'Royal Salute' (Miniature)

'Pour Toi' Height 20–25 cm (8–10 in). The well-shaped white flowers have a hint of cream at the base of their petals. A compact rose with an upright habit.

'Royal Salute' Height 75 cm (10 in). Fragrant, double, carmine-pink blooms, freely borne on a bushy plant.

'Starina' Height 25–30 cm (10–12 in). Scarlet and orange flowers with glossy foliage. The habit is vigorous and bushy.

'Wee Man' Height 20–25 cm (8–10 in). Semi-double, fragrant blooms, light crimson in colour.

Modern shrub roses

'Anna Zinkersen' Height 1.4 m (4½ ft). Spread 90 cm–1.2 m (3–4 ft). The pale lemon blooms are very fragrant and the variety is repeat-flowering. It has a rather bushy habit, with good, dark green foliage.

Angela Rippon' (Miniature)

'Butterfly Wings' Height 1.2 m (4 ft). Spread 1 m (3½ ft). The blush-white petals have rose-red edges. It forms a spreading bush, with good foliage.

'Charles Austin' Height 90 cm (3 ft). Upright habit. This is one of the newer introductions, with *Rosa centifolia*-type flowers but a hybrid-tea or floribunda habit. The apricot-shaded blooms are strongly scented and the variety is repeat-flowering.

'Charmian' Height and spread 1.2 m (4 ft). Closely identified with 'Charles Austin', the flowers are a beautiful deep pink and very fragrant. It has a rather spreading habit.

'Cécile Brunner' Height 90 cm (3 ft). One of the old-fashioned polyantha roses. Delicately scented, tiny, pale pink flowers are perfectly formed and freely borne in clusters throughout summer. It can also be obtained as a climber.

'Fountain' Height 1.8 m (6 ft). Upright habit. With double, well-shaped blooms of crimson velvet, this is a vigorous plant. The foliage is dark green and shiny.

'La Sevillana' Height 60 cm (2 ft). Spread 1.4 m (4½ ft). Vermilion blooms, in large trusses, are carried on sturdy short stems. It flowers continuously over a very long period and is an outstanding variety.

'Cécile Brunner' (Modern shrub)

'Lavender Lassie' Height 1.8 m (6 ft). Spread 1.5 m (5 ft). A continuous-flowering variety with attractive lavender-pink blooms. Rather strong growth and good foliage.

'Marjorie Fair' Height 75 cm (2½ ft). Spread 50 cm (20 in). Carmine-red flowers, with a white eye, on short, strong stems. It will continue flowering until late autumn, making an attractive, compact bush.

'Mountbatten' Height 1.8 m (6 ft). Spread 1.5 m (5 ft). Although often listed as cluster-flowered (floribunda), this variety develops into a large bush, best thought of as a modern shrub. Scented, clear yellow flowers are carried in profusion over a long period, set off by shiny, dark green foliage.

'Olive' Height 1.8 m (6 ft). Upright habit. The large blooms, on strong, thick stems, make good cut flowers. Dark green, glossy foliage clothes the rather tall, upright stems.

'Pearl Drift' Height 1.2 m (4 ft). Spread 1.5 m (5 ft). Prized for its continuously-produced creamy-white flowers. It has a rather spreading habit, with good foliage.

'Marjorie Fair' (Modern Shrub)

'Radox Bouquet' Height 1.8 m (6 ft). Upright habit. The rose-pink flowers, with a lovely fragrance, often split into quarters when they are fully open. This is a good cut rose, of tall, upright habit, dark green, shiny foliage and considerable resistance to disease.

'Robusta' Height 1.8 m (6 ft). Spread 1.5 m (5 ft). This shrub rose is covered with single, scarlet blooms over a very long period.

'Sally Holmes' Height 1.5 m (5 ft). Spread 1.2 m (4 ft). It carries large trusses of fragrant, creamy-white flowers, having a compact, bushy habit and good foliage.

'Saga' Height 1.5 m (5 ft). Spread 90 cm (3 ft). With the blooms a striking shade of buff on white, it flowers early in summer and again in the autumn. The habit is upright and bushy.

Climbing roses

'**Bantry Bay**' Height 3 m (10 ft). Pink, semi-double blooms and a vigorous habit. Glossy foliage. Repeat-flowering.

'**Climbing Cécile Brunner**' Height to 7.5 m (25 ft). Pale pink, beautifully-shaped small blooms are produced in profusion. A vigorous, summer-flowering rose.

'**Coral Dawn**' Height 3 m (10 ft). A variety with double, soft pink blooms in large clusters. Repeat-flowering.

'**Dreaming Spires**' Height 3.6 m (12 ft) or more. The fragrant, double blooms are golden-yellow, the buds being marked with deep red. It has vigorous, upright growth with dark green foliage. Repeat-flowering.

'**Golden Showers**' Height 2.4 m (8 ft). Well-shaped golden-yellow buds open into semi-double blooms. This is a particularly free-flowering variety, putting on an almost continuous display throughout the summer. It will flower quite freely in a shaded spot.

'**Grand Hotel**' Height 2.4 m (8 ft) or more. With beautiful red blooms, well shaped and freely borne, this is a good pillar rose. Repeat-flowering.

'**Handel**' Height 2.4–3 m (8–10ft). The creamy-white blooms, flushed pink at the edges, are of perfect shape. Growth is vigorous, the foliage dark green. A good pillar rose, and repeat-flowering.

'**Leverkusen**' Height 3–3.6 m (10–12 ft). The blooms are creamy-yellow and rosette-shaped. Though with the habit of a rambler, it usually blooms again in the autumn.

'**Mermaid**' Height up to 9 m (30 ft). With prominent amber stamens, the large, single, primrose-yellow flowers are borne from mid-summer onwards. The foliage is particularly glossy. This variety grows

'Mermaid' (Climber)

well on a north-facing wall, but it is not completely hardy in the coldest winters.

'**Pink Perpetue**' Height 1.8–2.4 m (6–8 ft). Bright rose-pink blooms are freely borne in large clusters throughout summer. This is an excellent rose for a sunny wall.

'**Swan Lake**' Height 2.4–3 m (6–8 ft). A variety with well-shaped, large, white blooms and a vigorous growth habit. The foliage is mid-green and leathery. It makes a good pillar rose and is repeat-flowering.

'**Sympathie**' Height 3–3.6 m (10–12 ft). The full, fragrant blooms are scarlet, with a velvety texture. It is quite vigorous, with good foliage, and is very hardy. Repeat-flowering.

'Dorothy Perkins' (Rambler)

Rambler roses

'**Dorothy Perkins**' Height 5.5 m (18 ft). Rose-pink blooms appear in large clusters in early summer. This is a vigorous grower.

'**Félicité et Perpétue**' Height 3 m (10 ft). Small, pale cream flowers are borne in large clusters, with small hips in the autumn. The light green foliage is almost evergreen. It has very vigorous growth and is suitable for growing through and up trees.

'**Paul's Scarlet**' Height to 4.5 m (15 ft). Semi-double, bright scarlet blooms are borne in rather small clusters. It has light green foliage, and a vigorous growth habit.

'**Purity**' Height 3.6 m (12 ft). With large, pure white, semi-double flowers, this robust plant has light green foliage.

'**Seagull**' Height 6 m (20 ft). Pure white

flowers are borne profusely in large clusters.

'**The Garland**' Height 4.5 m (15 ft). White, semi-double, fragrant blooms are flushed pink and carried in large clusters. A good variety for climbing into small trees.

Roses for ground cover

'**Fairyland**' Height 75 cm (2½ ft). Spread 1.8 m (6 ft). A variety that grows into a mound of dainty foliage. Pretty, light pink flowers cover the whole of the plant.

'**Fairy Prince**' Height 75 cm (2½ ft). Spread 1.8 m (6 ft). This resembles 'Fairyland' in every detail, except for the colour, which is geranium pink.

'**Pink Bells**' Height 60 cm (2 ft). Spread 1.2 m (4 ft). Other varieties are 'Red Bells' and 'White Bells'.

'**Pink Wave**' Height 90 cm (3 ft). Spread up to 1.2 m (4 ft). A variety with a rigorous habit and soft pink double flowers.

Old roses grown for their hips

R. × *highdownensis*. Height 1.8 m (6 ft). Spread 1.5 m (5 ft). Single crimson flowers, orange-red hips.

R. moyesii. Height 2.4 m (8 ft). Spread 1.5 m (5 ft). Deep blood-red single flowers, orange-red hips.

R. rugosa 'Scabrosa'. Height and spread 1.5 m (5 ft). Mauve and pink flowers; large, bright red hips.

R. sweginzowii. Height 2.4 m (8 ft). Spread 1.2 m (4 ft). Pink flowers, bright red hips that are earlier than most.

Rosa moyesii (Species)

Old-fashioned shrub roses

'Buff Beauty' (Hybrid Musk). Height 1.2 m (4 ft). Spread 1.8 m (6 ft). The clusters of double, rosette-shaped flowers are apricot-yellow, shaded buff, and very fragrant. It gives a good second display in late summer. With its spreading habit, this rose can be trained on wires to form a hedge. It is apt to suffer from mildew during August, so must be watched and sprayed when necessary.

'Penelope' (Hybrid Musk). Height 1.2 m (4 ft). Spread 1.8 m (6 ft). Salmon-pink buds pale almost to white as the scented blooms mature. There is a second flush quite late in the summer. This rose can also be grown as a hedge.

'Fantin-Latour' (Centifolia). Height and spread 1.5 m (5 ft). The beautiful, pale pink cupped blooms deepen in colour at the centre of the open flowers. One summer display only.

Rosa centifolia. Height 1.5 m (5 ft). Spread 1.2 m (4 ft). Often called the 'cabbage rose', or the 'Provence rose', this old favourite has clear, deep pink flowers that are delightfully fragrant.

'Nuits de Young' (Moss). Height and spread 1.2 m (4 ft). The colour is deep maroon-purple, outstanding yellow stamens. Summer-flowering. The buds are heavily mossed.

'William Lobb' (Moss). Height and spread 1.8 m (6 ft). The newly-opened blooms are dark crimson, but fade to lavender-mauve with white tints in the centre. Rather a tall habit; attractive dark green foliage on thorny stems.

'Mme Hardy' (Damask). Height 1.5 m (5 ft). Spread 1.2 m (4 ft). A beautiful pure white rose, with excellent dark green foliage. A 'must' for any garden where space allows.

Rosa damascena **'Versicolor'** (Damask). Height and spread 1.5 m (5 ft). This is the York and Lancaster rose, with blooms of varying colours – pale pink, white or a mixture of both. It has vigorous, dark green foliage.

'Charles De Mills' (Gallica). Height and spread 1.5 m (5 ft). This compact, upright bush flowers profusely, in June and July, causing some branches to bow almost to ground level. The blooms are full petalled and whorled, giving them an exotic appearance with their shades of maroon and rich, dark purplish-red.

Rosa Mundi (Gallica). Height 90 cm (3 ft). Spread 1.5 m (5 ft). This is one of the most popular of the old roses, with almost flat, open flowers. These have a mixture of red and white markings, with golden stamens, and are certainly eye-catching.

'Paul Neyron' (Hybrid Perpetual). Height 1.2 m (4 ft). Spread 90 cm (3 ft). The fragrant, deep rose-pink flowers are large and peony-shaped, carried on sturdy stems. These are clothed with pale green foliage.

'Frau Dagmar Hastrup' (Rugosa Hybrid). Height 90 cm (3 ft). Spread 1.2 m (4 ft). Noted for its neat, compact habit, the silvery-pink single blooms are followed by attractive deep red hips. Disease-resistant foliage.

'Pink Grootendorst' (Rugosa Hybrid). Height 1.8 m (6 ft). Spread 1.5 m (5 ft). Small, picotee-edged pink flowers are borne in large clusters, making a magnificent sight over a long period.

Rugosa Hybrid rose 'Frau Dagmar Hastrup'

'William Lobb' (Moss)

'Buff Beauty' (Hybrid Musk)

'Fantin-Latour' (Centifolia)

'Paul Neyron' (Hybrid Perpetual)

'Mme. Hardy' (Damask)

'Rosa Mundi' (Gallica)

JANUARY

Soil preparation Complete remaining preparation of new beds as soon as weather and soil allow. (See October.) If the ground has already been dug – and especially if it is heavy loam or clay – break down the surface with a pronged cultivator, weather permitting.

FEBRUARY

Planting Weather and soil permitting, roses may be planted from the second half of the month onwards. This includes any plants that had to be heeled in until the arrival of more suitable weather.

Final soil preparation consists of applying bonemeal at 65 g per sq m (2 oz per sq yd), working this into the surface, treading the ground firm and then raking.
Preparing bushes for planting Trim some 5–8 cm (2–3 in) off each root, cutting it back to sound,

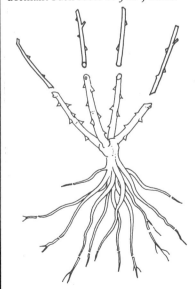

Preparing bush roses for planting
Before planting, prune the stems on dormant bush roses to 3 or 5 buds.

healthy growth and using a sharp knife or secateurs to ensure a clean cut. Prune back each of the stems to between three and five buds, always cutting just above one that faces outwards.

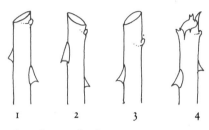

Pruning methods
Pruning cuts, to outward-facing buds, should slope level with the bud (1). Shallow or distant cuts (2 and 3) lead to die-back; ragged cuts (4) invite disease.

Do not trim climbing varieties harder than is necessary to remove any dead wood or weak growth.
Planting distances Allow 45 cm (1½ ft) between large-flowered (hybrid tea) bushes, and 68 cm (27 in) between cluster-flowered (floribunda) types. Leave 23–30 cm (9–12 in) between miniatures, depending on their eventual size.

Shrub roses, too, should be spaced according to size, within the range of 1.2–1.5 m (4–5 ft).
Planting method Dig a hole large enough to take the roots, with a little space to spare all round and deep enough to ensure that the graft (the bulge just above the

Planting method
Plant roses so that the swelling of the graft union is just below the soil level.

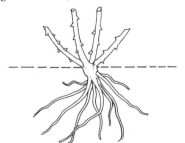

roots, where the rose was budded) is just below soil level. Spread the roots out as evenly as possible and fill in carefully with soil, treading gently but firmly around the bush to ensure that there are no air pockets in the soil.
Pruning climbers True climbing roses may be pruned this month. (Leave ramblers until September.) Thriving plants will have produced a number of strong shoots last summer, and you should aim to keep from five to seven strong, well-placed growths. Remove as many as possible of the older stems that have already flowered.

Sometimes there are insufficient young growths, and in this case retain some of the younger flowered stems. To encourage new growth during the coming season, prune back all side-shoots to within three buds of their base.

Tie all shoots securely to the support, taking care not to cross the stems.
Pruning shrub roses Weather permitting – which excludes frosty spells – shrub roses may be pruned from the second half of February onwards. Although heavy pruning is not required, some restriction of size is usually needed, especially in particularly small gardens.

Those classed as old shrub roses are best treated as individuals, rather than following some general technique. As a rule, flowers are more freely produced on the previous year's growth, so the aim is to encourage new growths from the base of the bush. It is also necessary to remove older, unproductive branches and any that cross in the centre.

A few modern shrub roses throw long, vigorous shoots from near the base. Shorten these by up to a third to reduce wind-rock and to keep the bush within bounds.

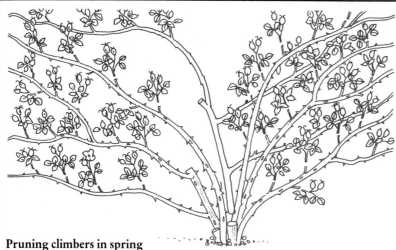

Pruning climbers in spring
Remove old stems which interfere with the shape; tie in young replacement shoots. Shorten side shoots, made the previous summer, to 2–3 buds.

MARCH

Pruning Early March is a good time for pruning if you live in the south of Britain. In colder, northern areas it would be as well to wait for another week or two. In any case, it is better not to prune during frosty weather.

Generally, strong-growing varieties need the least severe pruning. It is the weaker types that need cutting back fairly hard, for hard pruning encourages growth. Always cut back to a dormant, outward-facing bud, and make sure that your secateurs are really sharp before you start. A clean cut is essential.

You may sometimes find that an apparently healthy shoot is brown inside when you make a pruning cut. This is particularly common after a severe winter, especially on the large-flowered (hybrid tea) and cluster-flowered (floribunda) varieties. It is essential to cut back to white, healthy wood, even if this means cutting down to ground level. If possible, burn all rose prunings immediately.

Pruning large-flowered (hybrid tea) roses First, remove damaged or weak growths completely. Cut back strong, healthy growths to within three or five buds of the base – always to an outward-facing bud. Aim for about five stems on each bush.

The aim with these and cluster-flowered varieties is to keep the centre of the bush open, allowing air to circulate freely. Roses grown for show may be cut back to two buds to promote extra vigour.

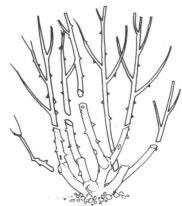

Pruning bush roses
Prune established bush roses hard back, to 3–5 buds on large-flowered, 5–7 buds on cluster-flowered types.

Pruning cluster-flowered (floribunda) roses The process is much the same as for hybrid teas, although not quite so severe. Prune to between five and seven buds from the base of each stem, maintaining five or six stems on each plant.

Pruning standard roses Prune according to their type – that is, hybrid tea or floribunda – along the lines already advised. While pruning, take the opportunity to check the stakes and ties.

Weeping standards may be pruned now if this was not done in late summer last year. (See September.)

Pruning miniature roses Pruning should be relatively severe. After removing old or dying wood, cut back weak-growing varieties to about three buds from the base, stronger types should be cut back to four or five buds.

Occasionally, an old plant will produce one or more exceptionally strong shoots. Remove these entirely to help maintain a symmetrical shape.

Pruning modern shrub roses With heights varying from about 90 cm–2.1 m (3–7 ft), pruning methods are variable and there are no strict rules. The general aim should be to remove sufficient growth to allow the plant to develop well and make plenty of young wood.

For a large crop of flowers, just tip the shoots. For large blooms, prune more severely, to perhaps half the length of shoots.

Spraying against disease After pruning, weed the rose beds and spray the plants with a fungicide as a precaution against mildew and black spot. Make sure that every stem and shoot is well covered with spray.

Underplanting roses Although opinions about underplanting differ, there is no doubt that the fibrous, surface-feeding roots of roses can be damaged if other plants are grown in the same bed. It is therefore better to avoid this, and for the same reason it is as well not to fork over the surface soil between roses.

Rabbit damage Rabbit damage to roses can be quite a problem in rural gardens, the main harm being done after pruning when the buds break.

Wire netting 90 cm (3 ft) high, and with a 2.5 cm (1 in) mesh, is the best safeguard. Turn the bottom 15 cm (6 in) outwards and bury it under the soil or turf. Leave it in place until early June.

APRIL

Feeding and top-dressing Roses planted in well-manured ground (see October) do not require a spring fertilizer dressing. Established roses, however, should be given a dressing of balanced fertilizer – either Growmore, at 65 g per sq m (2 oz per sq yd) or a proprietary rose fertilizer. In the case of a proprietary fertilizer, check the application rate on the packet. Rake or hoe the dressing into the top inch or two of the soil.

Once the plants have started into growth, and the soil has become warmer, a top-dressing or mulch of organic material will help to nourish the plants, conserve moisture and suppress weeds. Wait until the soil is moist after rain before spreading it.

Suitable materials include well-rotted cow manure and spent mushroom compost. The latter has the great advantage that it does not contain living weed seeds. Peat has no food value, but it helps to stifle weeds and to keep the soil

moist. Garden compost is not ideal, unless it is well-rotted and has heated sufficiently to kill weed seeds.

Whatever your choice, a layer 5–8 cm (2–3 in) deep is needed for effective results. Both new and older roses will benefit, the latter deserving priority if you are short of suitable material.

Weed control Failing a top-dressing, you will have to keep your rose beds hand-weeded throughout the summer. This is simple enough in a small garden, but weedkiller may be the answer where a fair amount of space is concerned. (See *Weed Control*.)

Aphid control Because they sometimes break into growth earlier than other roses, shrub roses are vulnerable to aphid attack even as early as April, should the weather be mild. Spray with a suitable insecticide as soon as any appear, but avoid the period between 10 am and 4 pm on sunny days, when there is a risk of the shoots being burned.

MAY

Late planting There is still time to replace any roses that were damaged or killed during the winter. Select container-grown plants, as they can be placed in the planting hole without disturbing the soil ball and root system.

Water the plants thoroughly, allowing time for the moisture to soak into each root ball. Dig a hole that is slightly oversize, then cut through the plastic container with a sharp knife. Keeping the soil ball intact, place the plant in the hole and fill in around it with good soil.

Remove any pruned stems that have died back. Keep the plant watered if a dry spell should follow planting.

Pest and disease control Aphids multiply at an alarming rate unless they are spotted at an early stage and action taken at once. Systemic insecticides give control for a longer period, and there are also combined insecticide and fungicide sprays to control diseases as well as sap-sucking insects.

Do not spray in wet or windy weather, or when rain is likely during the next four hours or so. Spray either in the early morning or during the evening.

Caterpillars and leaf-rolling sawflies are among other pests that may prove troublesome on roses. See also *Plant and Soil Pests*. Measures for dealing with black spot and other rose diseases are explained in *Plant Diseases and Disorders*.

JUNE

Tying-in climbers As new growths on climbing roses develop, tie them in loosely to avoid wind damage. If this is done regularly and gradually, they will be in position to replace the older wood due to be pruned out next spring. Left untied, they may well break or at least be more difficult to secure in place later on.

Note that these young shoots should on no account be cut off if you wish to maintain a healthy, free-flowering plant.

Removing suckers Do not confuse new shoots – whether on climbers or on bush roses – with suckers. The latter come from below the graft joint, which is visible as a swelling near the base of the stem. Often they emerge through the soil, being shoots from the rootstock on to which the named variety of rose was budded. Such shoots must be removed. They usually have either more or fewer thorns than the rest

Removing suckers
Trace suckers back to the point of
origin; cut or pull them away.

of the plant, and the wood is likely
to be a much paler green. Suckers
do not occur on roses grown on
their own roots, such as Old
Garden Roses and Species Roses.

Remove suckers with a knife as
soon as you spot them, severing at
the point where they join the
rootstock. It may be necessary to
scrape some soil away to see where
this is. The job is even easier with a
small tool that is made especially
for this purpose.

Pest and disease control Keep a
watchful eye for signs of pests and
diseases. Spray as necessary, never
letting them gain a firm hold.

JULY

Dead-heading The first flush of
flowers will be over by mid-July,
and the sooner the dead blooms
are removed the better. Cut down
the flower stem by about one
third, which amounts to a form of
summer pruning. An important
exception, however, is any rose,
like the Old Garden Roses, grown
for autumn hips.

Summer feeding Unless the soil
is particularly fertile, established
roses will benefit from another
fertilizer dressing. About 65 g per

sq m (2 oz per sq yd) of a balanced
product will encourage further
blooms, but do not give this later
than the third week of the month.
The risk, if you do, is that it will
promote the growth of young
stems that will not ripen before the
onset of the cold weather.

Pest and disease control The rose
sawfly may be troublesome at this
time of year. The larvae, which are
almost transparent, consume the
inner tissue of leaves, leaving a
pale skeleton. Spray as for the
leaf-rolling sawfly.

Also spray both sides of the
leaves with a fungicide as a precaution against mildew. Spraying is
seldom effective once blisters
are seen and a white, powdery substance appears on the undersides.

Routine jobs Continue looking
for suckers and remove as necessary. (See June).

Tie in new growths on climbing
roses. (See June.)

Remove weeds, including any
that have penetrated the top-
dressing if this was applied during
the spring. Soft thistles, which
serve as a host plant for aphids, are
a particular nuisance.

Making plans This is a good time
to consider any changes that you
may wish to make to your rose
beds, or to plan additions. When
visiting gardens or nurseries, take
particular note of the newer
varieties, checking how well they
flower, whether they take a rest
after the first flush, whether they
show signs of mildew or black
spot, and so on.

Soon it will be time to order
new roses. For popular types it
may be necessary to get your
order in early.

AUGUST

Routine jobs Continue with

dead-heading, tying-in shoots of
climbers, and regular spraying.

Although aphids cease to be a
problem about now, rose rust may
enter the scene. Like black spot, it
will thrive on under-nourished
plants, especially when the soil is
excessively dry. Spray at once and
apply a foliar feed.

Ordering new roses Try to place
your orders for roses by the end of
the month. Ideally, buy from a
nursery in your own district. Failing this, choose a nursery that is in
an area colder than your own.

SEPTEMBER

Routine jobs Remove seedpods,
which appear very rapidly now on
modern roses; the hips on old-
type roses are attractive and useful
for indoor decoration.

Continue spraying against mildew and black spot, making sure
that each plant is covered thoroughly with the liquid.

Continue to tie in the young
growths of climbers, making them
secure for the winter.

Pruning rambler roses The middle of the month is the best time
for pruning, first untying all the
stems from the supports as an aid
to sorting them out.

Ideally, cut out the old wood
completely, leaving about six
lengths of new growth on each
plant. If this would leave the plant
virtually stripped, save some of
the old wood but prune the
growths on them quite severely.

Cut each side-shoot back to
three buds – usually about 2.5 cm
(1 in) from the stem. The harder
you prune, the better the chance of
young stems growing from near
the base.

Tie the stems that are retained
back to the supports, spreading
them evenly. Use tarred twine of

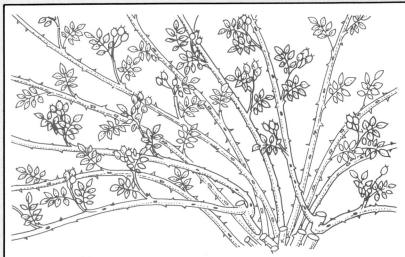

Pruning ramblers
After flowering has finished, cut out all old stems on rambler roses. Then tie in replacement shoots.

medium thickness for this – not thinner material, which cuts into the young wood. Allow a little space for the stems to swell.

A slightly different routine is needed in the case of varieties that seldom produce basal growths. In such a case, remove old wood wherever possible, leaving young shoots that may have developed lower down the stems. If there are none, removing one or two old stems may well encourage young shoots to grow from the base.

Pruning weeping standards
The method is the same as for rambler roses. Remove thin, weak and crossing branches, retaining as many young growths as necessary. Prune severely any older stems that have to be retained.

Propagating roses from cuttings
As many of the older varieties are no longer readily obtainable, propagation from cuttings is an excellent idea if a relative or friend has a variety that you would like to grow. This is the month to take them.

An advantage of roses grown from cuttings – in other words, not budded on to a different rootstock – is that no suckers are produced. Any growth from below ground level comes true to type. This can be useful if shoots are destroyed by rabbits or deer, and also when severe weather cuts bushes back to ground level. Provided the roots are not damaged, the plants will make fresh growth.

The cuttings should be from well-ripened, strong stems. Make a clean cut at each end, just beyond a bud, to leave a cutting about 30 cm (12 in) long. Do not remove any of the buds.

Using a spade, form a narrow, V-shaped trench about 23 cm (9 in) deep, three-quarters filling it

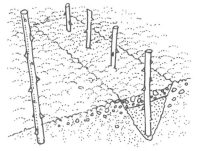

Propagating Old Garden and Species Roses
Take hardwood cuttings; set in a trench to root.

with sharp sand. Place the cuttings 15 cm (6 in) deep in the trench and about the same distance apart. Firm the soil around them by treading. The rooted cuttings should be ready for planting out in a year's time.

OCTOBER

Routine jobs When necessary, keep spraying against pests and diseases until the month's end.

Preparing new rose beds If you are planning to replant an existing rose bed, or to make a new one, this is a good month to prepare the soil. It is worth going to some trouble, for the plants may last for around fifteen years and will perform a great deal better if conditions are to their liking.

There is another point to bear in mind if you plan to replant an existing bed. After a long period of growing roses – say, ten or twelve years – soil is likely to be 'rose-sick'. Due to a build up of soil parasites and a depletion of mineral reserves, newly-planted roses may not do at all well, even if the previous plants have appeared reasonably healthy.

The answer is either to change the top 30–38 cm (12–15 in) of soil or to sterilize it chemically. You may even prefer to plant the new roses elsewhere using the previous bed for other plants.

Roses will not grow in water-logged soil, so attend to drainage if necessary.

Changing the soil Dig out the top 30–38 cm (12–15 in) of soil and exchange it with soil from the vegetable garden or an empty border. Before placing the fresh soil in the rose bed, dig over the bottom and empty in a good layer of rotted manure, compost or peat. Allow the replaced soil to settle naturally during the winter before planting.

Sterilizing the soil To sterilize a bed, dig it to a depth of 30 cm (12 in) while the soil is still fairly warm, adding a good layer of manure or other organic material. Apply a soil sterilant at the maker's recommended rate, then cover with polythene for at least a month to retain the fumes so they have time to act on the soil.

Making a new bed If the chosen area is turfed, remove this for placing in the trench when you are digging.

Deep cultivation is essential, which is best achieved by double-digging. To do this, remove a spit of soil across the width of the plot, leaving a trench the depth of the spade. Dig over the subsoil with a fork, mixing in manure or other organic material, then turn the next spit of topsoil on top of it. Continue across the bed, filling the final trench with the soil removed from the first one. If you have turves to bury, place these upside down on the subsoil before covering with topsoil.

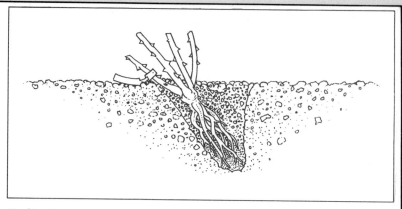

Heeling-in roses
Heeling-in new roses until planting is possible by laying them in a shallow trench. Cover the roots with soil to prevent them drying out.

NOVEMBER

Pruning Large-flowered (hybrid tea), cluster-flowered (floribunda), standard, miniature and modern shrub roses may all be pruned now if you live in a mild, sheltered area. (See March.) However, many rose-growers prefer to wait until spring, when the hardest frosts are over.

If you decide not to prune now, it is still worth cutting back any particularly long growths by half. This will reduce wind buffeting, which can loosen the stem at ground level and allow water and frost to penetrate, sometimes with fatal results. If you notice a 'fun-

nel' formed in this way, firm the soil back with your foot.

Heeling-in and planting As soon as the ordered roses arrive, unpack them at once and heel them in so that the roots cannot dry out. To do this, dig a trench and place the bushes close together in this, with the soil just above the graft union, until you are ready to plant them out.

If plants arrive when the ground is frozen, put the plants temporarily in a frost-free shed, covering them with sacking or straw (not polythene).

Should the ground be unsuitable for planting, the roses can remain heeled-in until February. Otherwise plant them now in a prepared bed (see October), following the method outlined in February. However, do not prune until March.

Cleaning beds Remove weeds and dead leaves from beds. Burn rose leaves if there have been signs of black spot, rust or mildew during the growing season.

DECEMBER

Soil preparation and planting New beds may still be dug, and

old ones renovated, for planting in late February or March. (See October.) The soil needs time to settle, so do not do any planting this month.

However, roses may be planted in beds that were dug in October, provided the soil is neither sticky nor frozen. Give the bed a final dressing and raking, as outlined in February.

Routine jobs Clear fallen leaves from rose beds, burning them if there have been traces of black spot, rust or mildew during the growing season.

Check that the supports for standard roses and climbers are firm and that ties are secure without being too tight.

Checking equipment If sprayers were put away uncleaned, rinse them with warm water containing a little detergent. Undo the nozzle and clean the inside. After drying, lubricate washers and 'O' rings with some petroleum jelly.

If secateurs are not cutting cleanly, sharpen the angled side of the blade – never the flat, inside edge – on an oil stone or fine carborundum. The same abrasive surface will do for knives. Afterwards, put a drop of oil on pivots; smear blades with an oily rag.

So-called ground cover plants – slow-growing, spreading species that need a minimum of maintenance – serve a number of purposes. Chief among these is their ability, once established, to keep soil practically weed-free. Many are attractive plants, suitable for growing on their own or beneath shrubs or trees.

In addition, they are valuable for planting in problem areas where little else will grow. These may include dark, shady patches under trees, and also dry banks where garden plants struggle.

Under natural conditions such sites would soon become colonized by strong-growing weeds, such as ground elder and perennial nettle – effective, if uninvited, ground-covering plants. Fortunately, many ornamental species will serve the same purpose.

Qualities to look for in ground cover plants are a relatively low and spreading habit, combined with growth dense enough to deter weed germination and growth. The best kinds are fast-growing and evergreen, so that a well-spaced planting will, within a year or two, provide up to 100% cover throughout the year.

Other important qualities are minimum maintenance needs and a reasonable degree of permanence. Where ground cover plants are prominent, they should have attractive foliage, a pleasing growth habit and, ideally, an annual show of flowers.

Among the most effective types are carpeting plants that form roots at leaf nodes along spreading stems, and also plants that spread by means of underground suckers, shoots or stolons.

In addition there are hummock-forming plants, such as *Calluna vulgaris*, with low, central stems from which radiate a large number of branches. There are also clump-formers – herbaceous perennials, such as hostas – with foliage that dies down in winter. These do leave the site at some risk from winter-germinating weeds. Hummock and clump-forming types both need closer spacing than colonizing plants.

In selecting plants it is important to choose types that are suited to the particular situation and soil. Some are suited to shade, others to hot, dry conditions, but there are also a number of ground cover plants that will thrive in most situations.

LARGE AREAS

Owners of large gardens often try to reduce costs by altering the lay-out. Labour-saving changes may also be sought by older gardeners who find it increasingly difficult to keep borders weed-free and lawns regularly mown.

One solution is to enlarge existing shrub borders or to plant new ones, but it will be some years before these become established and the ground beneath relatively weed-free. In the meantime they have to be kept weeded, mulched and pruned. Also, tall shrubs may in time impede views and alter the basic concept of a well-designed garden.

It is more satisfactory to extend permanent planting by using suitable ground cover plants. It is important to choose attractive kinds if they are to be planted in prominent areas, and both soil conditions and site must be considered. For substantial areas choice can include such stronger-growing shrubs as listed on page 120.

These may be planted in groups, with the inclusion of occasional taller shrubs, or conifers, to give a contrast in height. On acid soils, heathers may be used in the same way, with conifers or tree heaths providing the height contrast.

SHADED SITES

Shade is not always constant. In some gardens the area affected varies from season to season as the days lengthen or shorten and the sun's height alters. In other gardens there may be an area on the north side of the house that is always in shade. Under large, heavy-branched, deciduous trees shade may be intense in summer, yet a considerable amount of low-angled sunlight may fall there from late autumn until the spring.

Soil conditions in shade are equally variable. Under a heavy canopy of branches, the soil is often poor, dry and impoverished, with many roots near the surface. In the permanent shade of a large building, protected from drying sun and

GROUND COVER PLANTS

wind, the soil may remain cold and damp. In open woodland, the soil and leaf litter is often very moist during the winter and early spring when the trees are leafless. And the soil is dry throughout the summer when trees screen it.

If you are uncertain about the extent of shade in a garden, wait for a sunny day in spring or autumn, when the shade pattern is at neither extreme, and use canes to mark out the extent of shaded areas. Note where there is deep overhead shade and also where there is light shade, open to the sky but screened from direct sun by a building or by trees.

An area receiving only two or three hours of sunlight in early morning or late evening is best regarded as shaded. It should be considered sunny if it receives several hours of direct sunlight in the middle of the day.

Planting under trees is best done in the autumn, first preparing the site thoroughly by forking in plenty of organic matter. If you plant before leaf-fall, do not allow the plants to be smothered by leaves. They will then be able to start growing early the following spring, before conditions become shadier and drier as the leaf canopy develops. Evergreens must be watered in after planting.

Growing conditions in deep shade are particularly testing. The plants included in the list on page 120 are among the best for such areas.

SLOPES AND BANKS
Unless backed by higher ground, slopes and banks are usually well-drained. If in full sun and, perhaps, on light soil, they are likely to be very dry in summer. Often, they are sown with fine lawn grass as an extension of the lawn, but banks are difficult to mow and often deteriorate into coarser, infrequently-mown turf. Replacing with ground cover plants makes for easier maintenance.

On a steep slope there is a real risk of soil erosion on the lower part after planting and before the ground cover becomes well established. This can be countered by setting a temporary, angled line of land drains along the upper part of the slope to reduce the run-off. Where there is a risk of erosion, plant in spring.

On gentle slopes, plant in shallow, lipped hollows, so that plants can be mulched and watered in during the early stages without fear of erosion. On steeper slopes it may be helpful to create small terraces, using short lengths of board held in place with pegs. Remove the boards after a season or two.

On a slope of crumbling rock, plant in soil-filled pockets chipped from the rock face. If you are faced with a hard rock surface, with earth at either the foot or the top of the slope, plant climbers to scramble up the rock or trail down from above.

Where a bank is newly formed and unstable, peg fibrous (non-plastic) matting firmly to the surface – ideally, a sort that will rot down within a few weeks. Make incisions at intervals and plant small, well-rooted carpeting or stem-rooting plants through the matting into large handfuls of leafy soil. The matting will soon accumulate debris, as will the plants themselves, to provide good integrated cover by the time the fabric has rotted away.

PLANTING AND AFTER CARE
Most ground-cover planting is done in difficult situations and on poor soils, so first dig in a good dressing of organic matter. Young plants which have been raised in relatively rich compost will then be encouraged to extend their roots into the surrounding soil.

Better results will be achieved by planting groups of small, well-rooted young plants, sensibly spaced, than by using larger plants widely spaced.

Until the plants are well-established, feed them in early spring with a general or slow-release fertilizer, following this with a mulch while the soil is still moist. Watering may be needed during the first spring and early summer, so check the soil regularly.

Keep weeds under control until they are smothered by the increasingly dense cover. Remove fallen leaves in autumn. Examine the plants annually, ideally in late winter, and prune back any that have become at all straggly.

General-purpose ground cover

The following evergreens grow rapidly and may, in time, become invasive:

Cotoneaster salicifolius 'Autumn Fire'. A low-growing, semi-evergreen shrub with willow-like leaves. White flowers in early summer followed by red berries.

C.s. 'Gnome'. A prostrate shrub. Bright red fruits in autumn.

C.s. 'Skogholm'. A prostrate shrub with bright orange fruits in autumn.

Hedera colchica 'Dentata Aurea' and *H.c.* 'Sulphur Heart', syn. 'Paddy's Pride, are forms of Persian ivy with variegated leaves.

H. helix var. *hibernica* (Irish ivy) is a vigorous form of the common ivy, with glossy, dark green leaves.

Hypericum calycinum (rose of Sharon). A suckering evergreen or semi-evergreen shrub, up to 38 cm (15 in) high. Bright yellow flowers in mid-late summer.

Vinca major (greater periwinkle) is a vigorous, trailing shrub, 15–23 cm (6–9 in) high, with blue flowers in spring.

V. minor (lesser periwinkle) which is 8–10 cm (3–4 in) high, has smaller leaves and a more pronounced trailing habit.

Waldsteinia ternata. A carpeting plant with dark, glossy leaves and small, bright yellow flowers in spring.

The following evergreens have a slow or medium growth rate:

Bergenia 'Ballawley' and *B. cordifolia* 'Purpurea'. Rhizomatous perennials with glossy leaves and, in spring, clusters of white, pink or red-purple flowers.

Cotoneaster microphyllus. A wide-spreading shrub, 30–45 cm (1–1½ ft) high. Small, glossy leaves and, in autumn, bright red berries.

Euonymus fortunei 'Carrieri'. There are a number of variegated-leaved forms of this small, spreading shrub. These include 'Carrieri', 'Coloratus', 'Emerald 'n' Gold', 'Silver Queen' and 'Variegatus'.

Juniperus horizontalis. A prostrate or dwarf, spreading conifer, 8–23 cm (3–9 in) high. Cultivars, with green, grey-green or blue-green foliage, include 'Bar Harbor', 'Emerald Spreader' and 'Glauca'.

J. sabina var. *tamariscifolia.* A low-growing conifer, 38–45 cm (15–18 in) high, with a dense, mounded, bushy habit.

J. x *media* 'Pfitzerana'. This wide-spreading conifer, 60–90 cm (2–3 ft) high, has dense branches with drooping tips.

Lonicera pileata. A small-leaved shrub, 45–60 cm (1½–2 ft) high, with strong, flat and spreading branches.

Mahonia aquifolium. Growing from 30–60 cm (1–2 ft) high, this shrub bears fragrant yellow flowers in late winter.

Pachysandra terminalis. A shrubby, spreading evergreen bearing spikes of white flowers in spring.

Prunus laurocerasus 'Otto Luyken' and *P.l.* 'Zabeliana'. These are small, shrubby forms of the cherry laurel. Both carry attractive spikes of small white flowers in spring.

The following deciduous and herbaceous plants have a medium or rapid growth rate:

Campanula portenschlagiana (syn. *C. muralis.*) A spreading perennial, 8–10 cm (3–4 in) high, with bell-shaped purple flowers throughout the summer.

Geranium. These hardy perennials, 15–60 cm (6–24 in) high, are clump-forming or spreading. The summer flowers are white, pink, red or blue. Among the best for ground cover are 'Johnson's Blue', *G. macrorrhizum*, *G. procurrens*, *G. sanguineum* and *G. endressii* 'Wargrave Pink'.

Hemerocallis species/hybrids (day lily). Clump-forming plants, 45–60 cm (1½–2 ft) high with spikes of lily-like flowers in mid summer.

Hosta. Clump-forming, large-leaved plants up to 45 cm (1½ ft) high. There are many species and cultivars, with a range of leaf shapes and colours and bearing spikes of lily-like flowers in summer.

Nepeta x *faassenii.* Clump-forming, with aromatic foliage and bearing lavender-blue flowers in summer.

Polygonum affine. Mat-forming, with lanceolate leaves that turn bronze in winter. Short spikes of tiny flowers in summer. 'Darjeeling Red', with red flowers, and 'Superbum', pink, are good cultivars.

Symphytum grandiflorum (comfrey). Height 15 cm (6 in). Rough-textured leaves and small heads of creamy, pink or blue flowers.

Hypericum calycinum

Prunus laurocerasus

Bergenia cordifolia

Hosta cultivar

Plants for deep, dry shade, including banks

Galeobdolon argentatum (*Lamium galeobdolon* 'Variegatum'). Long, trailing stems, nettle-like leaves, yellow flowers in early summer. Invasive.

Gaultheria shallon. An evergreen shrub, up to 1.2 m (4 ft) high, with white or pinkish bell-shaped flowers in summer. Lime-free soil only.

Hedera helix var. *hibernica.* (See General-purpose ground cover, Evergreen.)

Iris foetidissima. Grass-like foliage, 45 cm (1½ ft) high. Dull mauve flowers followed by scarlet seeds.

Luzula sylvatica (woodrush). An evergreen rush, 30 cm (1 ft) high. 'Marginata' has cream-edged leaves.

Mahonia aquifolium. (See General-purpose ground cover, Evergreen.)

Pachysandra terminalis. (See General-purpose ground cover, Evergreen.)

Prunus laurocerasus 'Otto Luyken' and *P.l.* 'Zabeliana'. (See General-purpose ground cover, Evergreen.)

Rubus calycinoides. A prostrate evergreen shrub with small, dark green leaves.

Sarcococca humilis. This evergreen shrub, up to 38 cm (15 in) high, has fragrant white flowers in winter.

Vinca major and *V. minor.* (See General-purpose ground cover, Evergreen.)

Waldsteinia ternata. (See General-purpose ground cover, Evergreen.)

Plants for deep, moist shade

Asarum europaeum. A herbaceous carpeting plant, 8–10 cm (3–4 in) high, with dark, glossy leaves.

Brunnera macrophylla. Herbaceous, 30 cm (1 ft) high, with bright blue flowers in spring.

Convallaria majalis (lily of the valley). The white, bell-shaped flowers, delightfully fragrant, appear in spring.

Lamium maculatum (dead nettle). About 8–10 cm (3–4 in) high, with trailing, self-rooting stems and whorls of magenta flowers.

Tiarella cordifolia. An evergreen, up to 15 cm (6 in) high, with spikes of creamy-white flowers in spring.

Vancouveria hexandra. Some 15 cm (6 in) high, this rhizomatous plant has delicate leaves and, in spring, long sprays of white flowers.

Plants for sunny banks

Cotoneaster conspicuus 'Decorus'. An evergreen shrub, up to 1.5 m (5 ft) high, with arching branches and scarlet berries.

C. salicifolius 'Autumn Fire'. (See General-purpose ground cover, Evergreen.)

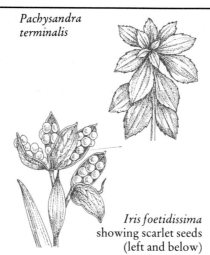

Pachysandra terminalis

Iris foetidissima showing scarlet seeds (left and below)

Asarum europaeum

Euonymus fortunei 'Variegatus'. (See General-purpose ground cover, Evergreen.)

Genista pilosa. Height 30 cm (1 ft). Densely-branched, carrying yellow, broom-type flowers in early summer.

Hedera colchica 'Dentata Aurea' and *H.c.* 'Sulphur Heart', syn. 'Paddy's Pride'. (See General-purpose ground cover, Evergreen.)

Helianthemum (rock rose). Shrubby, evergreen plants, 15–23 cm (6–9 in) high. Several cultivars, with white, yellow, orange or red flowers in summer.

Hypericum calycinum (rose of Sharon). (See General-purpose ground cover, Evergreen.)

Juniperus horizontalis. (See General-purpose ground cover, Evergreen.)

Plants for steep, rocky banks

Clematis montana and cultivars. Vigorous and scrambling. White or pink flowers in May. *C. orientalis* has a similar habit, but the bell-shaped flowers, in late summer, are yellow.

Hedera (ivy). There are several kinds, some with glossy green leaves, others variegated.

Lonicera henryi. An evergreen or semi-evergreen honeysuckle, with small yellow and red flowers. *L. japonica* 'Halliana' has white flowers, changing to yellow, that are very fragrant and long-lasting.

Parthenocissus quinquefolia (Virginia creeper). A vigorous deciduous climber or creeper, the leaves turning brilliant orange and scarlet in autumn.

Stronger-growing shrubs for the larger areas

Berberis verruculosa. This evergreen shrub, about 90 cm (3 ft) high, bears golden-yellow flowers in spring.

Cistus x *corbariensis.* Up to 90 cm (3 ft) high, evergreen and one of the hardiest of the genus. White flowers in June. Needs full sun.

Genista hispanica (Spanish gorse). Height 60 cm (2 ft). A deciduous, spiny shrub with yellow flowers in early summer.

Hebe rakaiensis. An evergreen shrub, up to 60 cm (2 ft) high, with a dense habit. White flowers in summer.

Juniperus x *media* 'Pfitzeriana'. (See General-purpose ground cover, Evergreen.)

Lonicera pileata. (See General-purpose ground cover, Evergreen.)

Mahonia aquifolium. (See General-purpose ground cover, Evergreen.)

Prunus laurocerasus 'Otto Luyken' and *P.l.* 'Zabeliana'. (See General-purpose ground cover, Evergreen.)

Senecio 'Sunshine'. Growing to 60–90 cm (2–3 ft), this evergreen shrub carries clusters of daisy-like flowers in summer.

Stephanandra incisa 'Crispa'. The arching branches of this deciduous 60 cm (2 ft) shrub bear small, greenish flowers in early summer. The leaves are a rich gold in autumn.

Symphoricarpos x *chenaultii* 'Hancock'. A 60 cm (2 ft) deciduous shrub with a suckering habit. The tiny yellow-green flowers are followed by pink or purple berries.

Viburnum davidii. An evergreen shrub, up to 75 cm (2½ ft) high. The white flowers, in summer, are followed (on female plants) by turquoise-blue berries.

DAHLIAS

Although so widely grown today, it is a mere 200 years since dahlias first appeared in Britain. They came in the form of seeds from France and Spain, but it was a few years before the technique of growing these plants was mastered. They are named, incidentally, after Dr. Andreas Dahl, the famous Swedish botanist, although Mexico is their country of origin.

An early development was the introduction of fully double types from France and Belgium in about 1814. But it was not until the 1830s that English hybridists became really involved, resulting in up to 1000 cultivars being listed by the middle of that decade.

Dahlias are produced in a number of flower shapes and sizes, with about six main classifications. Pompons, which are the smallest, carry large numbers of domed flowers, each about 5 cm (2 in) in diameter. These make delightful small flower arrangements and are best left to grow naturally, without disbudding. Next in size are the Ball types, which bear spherical flowers suitable either for garden or indoor decoration.

Decorative varieties are grouped in four categories, Small, Medium, Large and Giant. All have good, compact flowers, but with a flatter base than those already described.

Cactus and Semi-cactus dahlias, particularly the latter, bear flowers of a spidery form, again in Small, Medium and Large sizes. Decoratives are correctly in a class of their own, being the largest-flowered – about 25 cm (10 in) in diameter – and grown mainly for exhibition.

There are also some minor groups, including Anemone-flowered, Collerette and Water Lily types. These produce single flowers, often bicoloured, which are much favoured by flower arrangers. Overall, the colour range of dahlias is wide, from white, yellow, orange, pink and red to shades of mauve and purple.

Dahlias are grown to provide cut flowers, for garden decoration and for exhibition. They are mostly 90 cm–1.2 m (3–4 ft) high, but there are also several dwarf types, some 45–60 cm (1½–2 ft) high, which have been developed progressively during the present century.

Formerly, the great drawback of these more compact plants was their abilitiy to reproduce true from seed. However, this was overcome with the introduction of the Coltness Hybrids, around 1950. This advance greatly increased their popularity, and seed-raised dwarf dahlias are now widely used for bedding.

Growing bedding dahlias If you would like to grow bedding dahlias, sow the seeds in warmth in March, prick the seedlings off into boxes, and then harden them off before planting in late May or early June when the danger of frost is over.

They will start to flower almost at once, but it is as well to remove the first blooms to help the plants become established. Subsequently, dead-heading is most important. Although watering is necessary during very dry weather, watering at other times may result in excessive foliage at the expense of the flowers. With attention to these details, bedding dahlias should provide continuous colour in your garden for at least three months.

Choosing and ordering The best way to start with the larger, perennial dahlias is by buying rooted cuttings from a reputable grower. The first step is to send off for some catalogues so that you can study and compare the various types and cultivars. This done, you should be clearer about your purpose in growing dahlias.

If the intention is to grow flowers for cutting, there is little point in having plants that will produce blooms 25 cm (10 in) in diameter. On the other hand, these and almost any other cultivars will serve for garden decoration and, perhaps, for exhibiting at local horticultural shows.

Having determined which plants to order, you must also decide when you wish them to be delivered – that is, within the period specified by the grower. This, in turn, will depend on whether you have a heated greenhouse, a cold greenhouse or, perhaps, only a cold frame. Obviously, the more warmth you can provide, the earlier you can safely take delivery.

Early delivery offers two advantages. For one thing, the first ten or so cuttings

Single dahlia
The single-flowered dahlia, originally from Mexico, is superseded by named garden varieties.

Supporting dahlias
Dahlias need strong supports. Tie the stems to single stout stakes or contain the plants with triangles, with string tied at intervals to hold the stems in place.

taken from a tuber are likely to produce the best plants, and these are the ones you will get if you are quick off the mark. Secondly, an early start will enable you to grow the plants on into larger, 13 cm (5 in) pots, giving them a flying start at planting time and, as a result, earlier flowers.

Preparation of the border An open, sunny site is best. Frost pockets are unsuitable, as each end of the growing season will be shortened. The soil should be water-retentive, but without any tendency to become waterlogged. If you have light soil, add plenty of organic material in the form of farmyard manure or garden compost.

Spring cultivation consists of breaking the surface down to a fine tilth and mixing with it a balanced organic fertilizer at 60–100 g per sq m (2–3 oz per sq yd). The time to do this is from about the middle of April onwards.

Supporting After preparing the bed, but before setting the plants out, mark where the plants are to go and put supporting stakes in position. These should be 2.5 cm (1 in) square. If this is left until after planting, the tubers may be damaged.

There are two widely-used methods, one being to provide a single stake for each plant, with all growths tied in, and the other to set three stakes in a triangle around each position. In this case you should leave sufficient space for a 13 cm (5 in) root-ball, and splay the tops outwards to form a larger triangle. Ties can be secured round these stakes as the plants grow.

The three-stake method is easier in the long run and time-saving, but the outlay is considerably greater.

Planting and after-care The last week in May or the first week in June is the time for planting, but the young dahlias must be hardened off in a cold frame for the previous fortnight to prepare them for the change of environment. Firm the plants in well and keep them watered if the weather is dry. If allowed to become too dry, growth will cease and the stems will become woody, thus putting them back by several weeks.

As the plants develop, remove their growing points (often a bud) to encourage side growths and a bushier habit. At about

this stage, too, it is helpful to spread a 5–8 cm (2–3 in) layer of spent mushroom compost or well-rotted manure around the plants to help retain moisture and keep the roots cool.

Although not essential for garden decoration, it is a good idea to remove growths from the leaf axils of the top two pairs of leaves. These usually consist of wing buds from the upper pair, and new shoots from the lower pair. This will allow the individual flowers to develop better and thus be slightly larger. It also produces longer stems for cut flowers.

Remove all dead-heads as soon as possible. They are unsightly and may cause disease problems, while, if seed sets, this will retard the growth of any later flowers. To ensure further blooms, take care not to cut the stems below the level at which the side growths have been removed.

Well-grown dahlias give few problems but, should yellowing of the leaves suggest that they need a little extra nourishment, a foliar feed would be a good choice. The two most troublesome pests are black fly and, during a hot summer, red spider mite. (See *Plant and Soil Pests.*)

Dahlias will continue flowering until the first frosts, which may be well into October, or even November in the south of England. Once the foliage has been blackened to about half its length, cut it down to within 15–23 cm (6–9 in) of the ground. Lift the tubers carefully with a fork, attach labels, and place them upside down in a cool, frost-free shed unheated greenhouse or garage to dry.

After about two weeks they will be ready to turn up the right way again for storage. First check that all the tubers are sound, cutting off any parts that show signs of rotting and dusting the wounds with sulphur. Also dust the area around the crown, where moulds may otherwise form.

Next, place the tubers in boxes and fill the space around them with dry peat or sawdust, taking care to leave the crowns exposed. A temperature of about 4 °C (40 °F) is adequate for storage, but it must never be allowed to fall to freezing point. Check the tubers once or twice during the winter to ensure that all is well.

RAISING DAHLIAS

1 Start dahlia tubers into growth at gentle heat.

2 On 8 cm (3 in) basal shoots cut off leaves and stem below joint.

3 Root the cuttings in pots of peat and sharp sand.

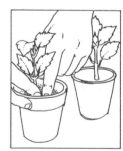

4 Pot the rooted cuttings individually and grow on.

Propagation If you do not have a greenhouse for raising cuttings, re-plant last year's tubers in a prepared bed around mid-April. However, if you are able to take cuttings, they will certainly produce the best plants and will also provide an easy way to increase your stock.

February is the time to start the tubers into growth, the exact timing being governed by the available heating. The necessary temperature is 16 °C (60 °F).

First remove the tubers from their storage boxes, check them over carefully and remove any unhealthy-looking material. Then re-box them in moist peat or John Innes seed compost, again leaving the crown exposed. Do not be tempted to moisten the dry peat in which they were stored, for it will be water-resistant and become far too wet in the process.

Keep the compost moist, but not wet, and take care not to let the crowns become wet. As growth gets under way you will have to moisten the compost more often.

Take the cuttings when the growths are about 8 cm (3 in) long. Sever each shoot just above its first basal joint, which will allow further growth for later cuttings. Remove the lower pair of leaves and make a clean cut through the stem about 3 mm (⅛ in) below the joint. Dip the base of the cutting in water, then in hormone rooting powder, and shake off the surplus.

Use small pots – 5 cm (2 in) – for each individual cutting, or insert four or five cuttings around the edge of an 8 cm (3 in) pot. Equal parts of sharp sand and peat, with no added fertilizer, provides the best rooting mixture.

After making a hole with a pencil, insert the cutting about 2·5–5 cm (1–2 in) deep and firm gently round it. If possible, spray with water two or three times daily to prevent flagging.

After about three weeks, when the cuttings should have rooted, pot them individually into 8 cm (3 in) pots containing John Innes potting compost No. 1. They will suffer from starvation if left much longer than this in the rooting mixture. Later, transfer to 13 cm (5 in) pots containing John Innes potting compost No. 2.

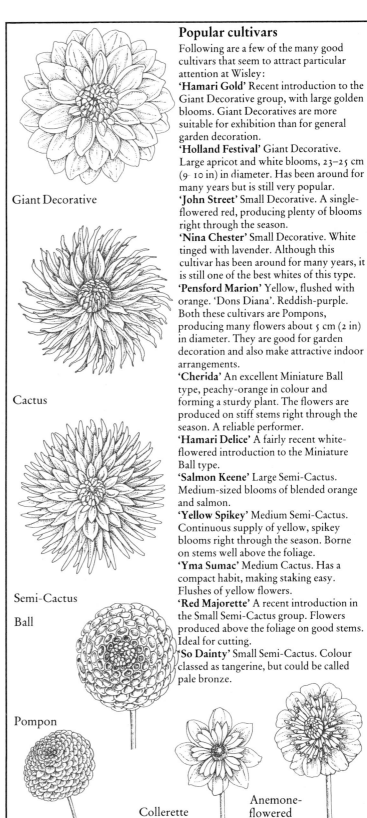

Giant Decorative

Cactus

Semi-Cactus

Ball

Pompon

Collerette

Anemone-flowered

Popular cultivars

Following are a few of the many good cultivars that seem to attract particular attention at Wisley:

'Hamari Gold' Recent introduction to the Giant Decorative group, with large golden blooms. Giant Decoratives are more suitable for exhibition than for general garden decoration.

'Holland Festival' Giant Decorative. Large apricot and white blooms, 23–25 cm (9–10 in) in diameter. Has been around for many years but is still very popular.

'John Street' Small Decorative. A single-flowered red, producing plenty of blooms right through the season.

'Nina Chester' Small Decorative. White tinged with lavender. Although this cultivar has been around for many years, it is still one of the best whites of this type.

'Pensford Marion' Yellow, flushed with orange. 'Dons Diana'. Reddish-purple. Both these cultivars are Pompons, producing many flowers about 5 cm (2 in) in diameter. They are good for garden decoration and also make attractive indoor arrangements.

'Cherida' An excellent Miniature Ball type, peachy-orange in colour and forming a sturdy plant. The flowers are produced on stiff stems right through the season. A reliable performer.

'Hamari Delice' A fairly recent white-flowered introduction to the Miniature Ball type.

'Salmon Keene' Large Semi-Cactus. Medium-sized blooms of blended orange and salmon.

'Yellow Spikey' Medium Semi-Cactus. Continuous supply of yellow, spikey blooms right through the season. Borne on stems well above the foliage.

'Yma Sumac' Medium Cactus. Has a compact habit, making staking easy. Flushes of yellow flowers.

'Red Majorette' A recent introduction in the Small Semi-Cactus group. Flowers produced above the foliage on good stems. Ideal for cutting.

'So Dainty' Small Semi-Cactus. Colour classed as tangerine, but could be called pale bronze.

JANUARY

Advice given for February also applies this month.

FEBRUARY

To propagate from cuttings, which produce the best plants, start the tubers into growth by re-boxing them in moist peat or compost. Do not simply moisten dry peat used for winter storage. A temperature of about 16 °C (60 °F) is needed. Remove the cuttings when the shoots are 5–8 cm (2–3 in) long.

MARCH

Sow seeds of bedding dahlias at a temperature of 18 °C (64 °F). Prick off the seedlings into boxes or into pots.

Take cuttings from tubers started into growth last month. Once the cuttings have rooted, which takes about three weeks, pot them individually into 8–9 cm (3–3½ in) pots.

APRIL

Continue taking cuttings from tubers and potting up the rooted cuttings individually as they become ready (after about 3 weeks).

Outdoors, prepare dahlia beds from about the middle of the month. After adding organic matter and fertilizer, and reducing the surface to a fine tilth, mark planting positions and insert supporting stakes.

Towards the end of the month plant last year's dormant tubers outdoors if you are not taking cuttings from them.

MAY

Harden off bedding dahlias and rooted cuttings, ready for planting out once frost is not a risk.

In the south, plant out from the last week of the month onwards, provided plants have been hardened off in a cold frame for at least a fortnight. In northern counties and Scotland delay planting for another week or two.

Watch for aphids on young shoots, spraying if necessary.

JUNE

Remove the growing points on plants to encourage side growths. Remove growths from the leaf axils of the top two pairs of leaves.

Tie plant stems to the supporting stakes.

Spread an organic mulch around growing plants.

JULY

Remove all dead flowers to ensure continued flowering.

Continue to tie growing plants to their supporting stakes.

Spray against aphids and other pests as necessary.

AUGUST

Continue July's routine tasks.

A liquid fertilizer, applied as a foliar feed, will help to keep plants growing and flowering during the later months of summer.

SEPTEMBER

Dead-head, feed and spray against pests as necessary.

OCTOBER

When frost has blackened the upper half of the foliage (which may not happen until November) cut the stems down to within 15–23 cm (6–9 in) of the ground. Lift and label the tubers, then place them upside down under cover to dry.

NOVEMBER

Lift and dry the tubers if this was not done during October. After a fortnight examine the tubers for signs of rotting. Remove damaged parts, dusting these and around the crowns with sulphur. Place the tubers in boxes of dry peat or sawdust, crowns exposed, and store in a cool but frost-free place for the winter.

DECEMBER

Advice given for November also applies this month.

Overwintering dahlias
As soon as autumn frosts blacken the foliage, cut down dahlia stems to about 23 cm (9 in). Lift the tubers, stand them upside down to drain before storing them in boxes of dry peat, in a frost-free place.

For cutting and for garden display, few plants can rival the shapes and colours of dahlias. Best grown in a bed of their own, they range from low-growing types through medium and large decoratives to the giant cactus dahlias.

Like most chrysanthemums, the attractive colour, incurved petals and long flowering period of this handsome
outdoor chrysanthemum 'Bonigold' variety are hard to rival. Its vase life is also longer than that of other flowers.

The large-flowered bush rose (Hybrid tea) 'Silver Jubilee', with silver-pink blooms of exquisite form, made its first appearance at the Chelsea Flower Show in 1977 to mark the Silver Jubilee of Her Majesty Queen Elizabeth.

A bed of colourful annuals will give a carpet of colour from mid-June to the autumn frosts. These easy-to-grow plants can be used to fill spaces in a border where bulbs have died down or where plants have failed to survive the winter.

The proud title given to this class of chrysanthemum is 'Queen of the autumn'. It is well deserved, for from late summer until early winter it has no equal either as a garden plant or as a cut flower. Its vase life is much longer than that of most other cut flowers.

Left to grow naturally, but with the growing point pinched out at quite an early stage, the plants will develop like miniature bushes, each bearing a mass of small blooms. In this form they are known as spray chrysanthemums, and some cultivars have been developed especially for this form of cultivation.

Alternatively, the plants can be partially disbudded. Although fewer in number, the buds that are left will develop into much larger flowers. They will also be somewhat earlier than those on plants not disbudded, so the risk of frost damage is reduced. Cultivars suited to this treatment are available with several different types of blooms, including incurved and reflexed.

Both methods of growing chrysanthemums are popular, the essential point in each case being to start off with good-quality rooted cuttings from a reliable source. Subsequently, it is a simple matter to take your own cuttings, provided you have a greenhouse where a moderate amount of heat can be provided.

Chrysanthemums grow best in well-drained, fertile soil. With this in mind, dig the soil during the winter, incorporating a heavy dressing of well-rotted farmyard manure or garden compost. Digging well before planting time will give the soil a chance to settle, for chrysanthemums are most likely to thrive in firm soil.

PLANTING

Insert a stake at each planting position before placing the plants. The roots may be damaged if this is left until later. Allow 30 cm (1 ft) between plants if you plan to restrict them by disbudding, 45 cm (1½ ft) for the bushier plants grown as sprays.

Chrysanthemums are not deep-rooting, so set the roots firmly but quite shallow. When the plants are about 23 cm (9 in) high – and regardless of whether or not they are to be disbudded – pinch out their tips. This

Stopping
Removal of the growing tip, known as stopping, encourages the formation of side shoots. Spray and pompon chrysanthemums need stopping once only.

will cause them to produce a number of side-shoots, known as 'breaks'. Spray cultivars need no other stopping.

After-care Having 'stopped' the plants, start to feed them with a well-balanced granular or liquid fertilizer. Continue doing so until the buds start to show colour. Give plenty of water throughout the growing period, but restrict this to the base of the plants once they start to flower. At this stage, keep both the foliage and the flowers as dry as possible, or they may show symptoms of damping-off.

Once the breaks are growing strongly on plants that are to be disbudded, select five of the strongest and remove the remainder. In mid-summer, the selected shoots will themselves produce side-shoots, which must be removed.

A little later still you will see that a 'crown bud' has formed at the tip of each break. Remove the surrounding side buds once you are satisfied the crown bud is strong and healthy and that the others can be pinched out without damaging it.

On spray chrysanthemums, apart from pinching out the main growing tip, all the growths and buds should be left. All you need do is pick off the dead flowers.

Keep a careful watch for potential pests and deal with these immediately.

Korean Spray

Recommended cultivars

Disbudded
'Fundraiser', pale lemon
'Sheila Orr', white
'Cornish', cream
'Ian Rodger', yellow
'Golden Market'
'Paint Box', red
'Pink Julie Ann'
'Yvonne Arnaud', purple
'Red Rose Stevens'
'Bronze Yvonne Arnaud'.

Spray
'Margaret', pink
'Gold Margaret'
'Apricot Margaret'
'Bronze Margaret'
'Yellow Heidi'
'Golden Pamela'
'Emilia', pale pink
'Pennine Rose'
'Pennine Song', deep pink
'Pennine Ace', pink.

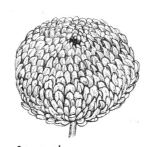

Incurved

Pompon

Reflexed

Spray

PROPAGATION

To take cuttings from your own plants, start in November by cutting down the main stems to about 23 cm (9 in), trimming any basal growth to soil level. Lift these 'stools' and replant them in boxes 10 cm (4 in) deep, covering the roots with a light, porous compost. Water them sparingly and place them in a cold frame.

In early February, bring the boxes into the greenhouse, place them on the staging in full light and start to water them. A minimum temperature of 7 °C (45 °F) will encourage new shoots to develop between late February and mid-March.

Cut these shoots off, trimming them just beneath a leaf joint to a length of 5 cm (2 in) and removing the lowest leaf. Insert the cuttings 5 cm (2 in) apart in trays of John Innes potting compost No. 1, which should be 5 cm (2 in) deep. Place the trays where a bottom heat of 13–16 °C (55–60 °F) can be maintained. Rooting should then take place in about three weeks.

Pot the rooted cuttings into 8 cm (3 in) pots of John Innes potting compost No. 1, gradually getting them accustomed to cooler, more airy conditions. Alternatively, plant them in a frost-proof frame, 10 cm (4 in) apart. Either way, they should be ready for planting about mid-May.

A disbudded chrysanthemum

JANUARY

Advice given for February also applies this month.

FEBRUARY

Early in the month, bring into the greenhouse 'stools' overwintered in a cold frame. Water the plants and place in full light. A temperature of 7 °C (45 °F) is sufficient.

MARCH

As the shoots develop on the stools, remove and trim the cuttings and insert them in trays of equal parts peat and sand, or a proprietary potting compost. Pot rooted cuttings individually into John Innes compost No. 1.

Outdoors, prepare the bed for planting if this was not done during the winter. Aim to give it as long as possible to settle before planting in May.

APRIL

Rake a general fertilizer into the bed where chrysanthemums will be planted next month.

Start to harden-off rooted cuttings in preparation for planting out in May.

MAY

Insert supporting stakes before setting plants out in the middle of the month. If you are a beginner, or need new plants, this is also the time to buy rooted cuttings.

JUNE

Pinch out the tips of all plants when they reach about 23 cm (9 in) high. From this stage on feed regularly with liquid fertilizer until the buds start to show colour. Give plenty of water, too, throughout the growing season.

JULY

If plants are to be disbudded in order to promote larger flowers select the five strongest shoots on each plant and remove the remainder. In due course, remove the side-shoots that will form on the five selected shoots.

Continue with watering, as needed, and feeding. Keep new growth tied to the supports.

AUGUST

Leaving the crown bud at the tip of each break, remove side buds, first satisfying yourself that the crown bud is strong and healthy and that the others can be pinched out without damaging it.

SEPTEMBER

Dead-head, feed and spray against pests as necessary.

OCTOBER

Dead-head as necessary.

NOVEMBER

If you plan to take cuttings next spring, cut down the main stems of plants to 23 cm (9 in) and remove any basal growth. Then lift plants and place the stools in boxes of compost in a cold frame. Water sparingly.

DECEMBER

If possible, dig next year's chrysanthemum bed. Add compost.

STOPPING AND DISBUDDING
Controlled stopping and disbudding result in large and early blooms.

 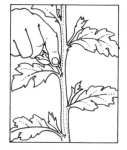 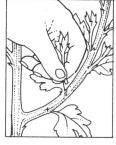 

1 Remove the growing tip of young outdoor plants when they are 23 cm (9 in).

2 After stopping, only allow 5 'breaks' to grow on.

3 Pinch out all side shoots as they appear on the selected shoots.

4 Disbudding for large blooms consists of removing all but the crown bud.

Besides being among the easiest of plants to grow, shrubs provide us with colour and interest right through the year. There are innumerable species and varieties, offering beauty of form and foliage, lovely flowers, autumn tints and other attractions. To make the most of this invaluable group of plants we therefore need to plan with some care – choosing the right ones for our tastes and needs, and then placing them sensibly in relation to one another and to suit the site and the soil.

This is no less true when shrubs are planted as a screen, to provide privacy or to conceal the compost heap. It becomes quite essential when setting out a complete border. Fortunately, the range is so wide that there are types to suit gardens of every size, in sun or shade and on any but waterlogged soils.

Note that there is a world of difference between a well-planned shrub border and a 'shrubbery'. The latter is made up of close-planted specimens which soon merge into one another to give a massed, but confused, effect. Shrubs in a carefully-planned border have sufficient space to mature individually – far more satisfying to view and much easier to manage.

Making the plan Sketch out the shape of the border on a piece of paper. Using a scale suitable for the paper's size, square up the drawing in metres or yards. Mark the aspect, together with any nearby objects likely to give either shade or protection. Each of these features has a bearing on the choice of plants. Note, also, the places where one or more eye-catching shrubs might be positioned to provide focal points when seen from the house or an approach path or drive.

Now you have an informative picture on which to scheme the sort of planting effect you would like to achieve. The squares, in particular, will give you an accurate basis for determining just how many of the chosen shrubs can be planted in the available space.

Although the plan is two-dimensional, you must try to create in your mind an image of the plants themselves – their heights, and how they will associate one with another. It will certainly be easier to develop the planting plan if you stand at the site where you can get the 'feel' of what will look right.

As a broad rule, tall plants are best placed at the back of a border, or at the centre of an island bed, and others of lesser stature graded towards the front. Even this needs doing with discretion, however, in order to avoid too formal an effect. Some taller plants should be brought forward, and smaller ones pushed back, to provide an undulating contour.

Different forms and textures, carefully interposed, can create interesting associations. Apart from avoiding obvious clashes, colour is largely a matter of personal taste. Bear foliage colour in mind, as well as that of the flowers. Note that blues tend to recede into the background, while red shades are more prominent and aggressive.

A shrub border
Plan carefully, allowing for eventual height and spread, contrasting or complementary leaf and flower colours and textures, autumn tints and berries, and winter profiles.

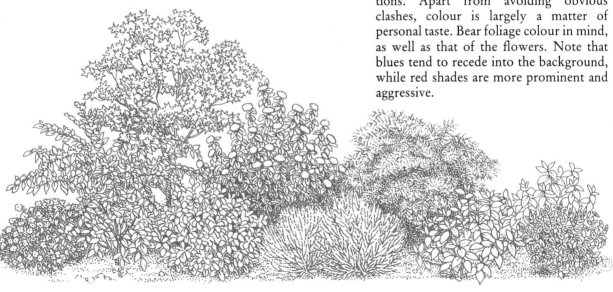

And a final point: although many shrubs are large enough to be planted singly, some of the smaller ones look better in groups. Remember this when completing the planting plan and, eventually, compiling your shopping list.

Weeding and feeding A shrub border will be much easier to manage if the plants go into well-prepared ground that has been cleared of perennial weeds. (See the calendar, October.) The best way to suppress subsequent weed growth is by laying a mulch of peat, spent mushroom compost or pulverized bark, 5–8 cm (2–3 in) deep, immediately after planting. Replenish this each May, first applying a balanced fertilizer around the plants.

Selected shrubs Below and overleaf is a selection of garden-worthy shrubs, many obtainable at local garden centres, and others more likely to be found at specialist nurseries. Most will grow best in a neutral soil, but will tolerate acid or alkaline conditions. Any exceptions are noted in the descriptions. All the shrubs are deciduous unless otherwise stated.

CLIMBERS AND WALL PLANTS

Climbing plants are able to support themselves with little or no help from the gardener. They do so by twining around poles or stems, or by gripping vertical and horizontal surfaces with adhesive pads, aerial roots or even thorns. Some climbers, such as ivies and Virginia creepers, attach themselves to wall surfaces without any aid, but the majority need support in the form of wires, plastic or wooden frameworks or trellis. Following are some examples of climbing plants and their methods of support:

Twining stems *Lonicera* (honeysuckle); *Wisteria*; *Humulus* (hop).

Twining leaf stalks *Clematis.*

Tendrils *Vitis coignetiae* (vine).

Hooks and barbs *Rosa* (rose); *Rubus* (brambles).

Adhesive pads *Parthenocissus quinquefolia* (Virginia creeper).

Aerial roots *Hydrangea petiolaris*; *Hedera* (ivy).

Unlike true climbers, wall plants have to be supported by tying to wires or frameworks. Many can also be grown as free-standing shrubs; they are sited against a wall to show their flowers or foliage to advantage or to obtain shelter.

Wall plants need regulative pruning and tying-in in order to achieve a regular shape and a flat profile. This apart, they are subject to the same general rules of pruning as any other shrub.

Recommended garden shrubs

Abelia 'Edward Goucher'. Height and spread 90 cm (3 ft). A sunny, sheltered position is best for this semi-evergreen, which produces small pink flowers in abundance during mid-late summer.

Berberis. There are numerous species, both deciduous and evergreen, of this widely-grown genus. One of the most popular is *B. darwinii*, height and spread 2.4 m (8 ft), an evergreen with orange-yellow flowers in spring followed by blue berries. The leaves are holly-like. *B.d.* 'Nana' is barely half its size.

 B. thunbergii, of which there are several forms, has a height and spread of 1.2 m (4 ft) or more. It is a compact, deciduous, small-leaved shrub, with yellow spring flowers, scarlet berries and lovely autumn colouring.

Buddleia davidii (butterfly bush). Height and spread 3 m x 2 m (10 ft x 6½ ft). It has lilac-purple flowers in late summer and, like all buddleias, is lime-tolerant.

Varieties include 'Black Knight', deep violet; 'Empire Blue', violet-blue; 'Harlequin', variegated foliage and red-purple flowers. *B.d.* var. *nanhoensis* is a dwarf form growing to only 1.5 m (5 ft), with smaller racemes of lavender flowers.

 B. fallowiana can grow to 3 m (10 ft), with a spread of 1.8 m (6 ft). It has woolly, silver leaves, lavender-coloured flowers in late summer and needs a sheltered site. Along with *B. davidii*, it does best in a sunny position. *B. globosa* (orange ball tree) has a height and spread of about 3 m (10 ft) and bears globes of orange flowers in late spring. It is a semi-evergreen and does best in shade.

Caryopteris x *clandonensis*. Height and spread 90 cm (3 ft). There are several named cultivars, all with small, blue or blue-violet flowers appearing in late summer. It needs a sunny position and a well-drained soil.

Clerodendrum trichotomum var. *fargesii*. Height and spread 4 m × 3 m (13 ft ×

10 ft). White, strongly-scented flowers open in August, followed by blue berries clasped in crimson calyces.

Cornus alternifolia 'Argentea' (dogwood). Height and spread 2.4 m × 1.8 m (8 ft × 6 ft). One of the best silver-variegated plants, it does best in neutral or acid soil and in a sunny position. Several other *Cornus* are grown for their coloured stems, which look attractive in winter and should be cut back hard in March to encourage new growth.

Cotoneaster. These shrubs, both evergreen and deciduous, are prized for their massed display of white flowers and for the berries that follow. One of the best is *C. conspicuus*, height and spread 1.5 m (5 ft), an evergreen with an arching, spreading but graceful habit, white flowers in early summer and large quantities of red berries from early autumn. A sunny position is best.

Shrubs (cont.)

Cytisus battandieri (Morocco broom).
Height and spread 3.6 m (12 ft). This is an
open-growing shrub that produces
terminal spikes of yellow, pea-like
flowers, smelling of pineapples, in late
spring. The silver leaves resemble those of
the laburnum. A sunny position in neutral
or alkaline soil suits it best, but it will also
grow well under acid conditions.

Deutzia scabra. Height and spread 3 m ×
1.5 m (10 ft × 5 ft). Clusters of white
flowers, in June, are the attraction of this
erect shrub. They are borne on the
previous year's wood. *D.s.* 'Plena' is a
double form with rosy suffusions. Grow
in sun or light shade.

Deutzia scabra

Elaeagnus. These tough shrubs can help to
provide shelter for others. Both those
described will grow in sun or partial
shade. *E.* x *ebbingei*, height and spread
3 m (10 ft), is a fast-growing evergreen. Its
deep green leaves flutter in the wind,
revealing silver under-surfaces.
Insignificant, but highly-scented, silver-
white flowers appear in late autumn.
E. pungens 'Maculata', height and spread
3.6 m (12 ft), is moderately vigorous and
another evergreen. The variegated leaves
splashed with gold.

Euonymus alatus. Height and spread
2.4 m (8 ft). Scarlet autumn foliage is the
chief attraction of this slow-growing
shrub. *E. fortunei*, an evergreen, has a
scrambling or climbing habit, with a
spread of about 1.5 m (5 ft).

E.f. 'Emerald 'n' Gold' is rather more
bushy, with green and yellow variegations
that become red as the weather grows
colder. *E.f.* 'Silver Queen' is compact,
with a greater proportion of green in its
colouring. The two cultivars mix well.

E. japonicus 'Aureopictus', height
about 3.6 m (12 ft) and spread 1.5 m (5 ft),
has an erect habit, with bolder, yellow-
splashed variegations. It, too, is an
evergreen. All *Euonymus* grow well in sun
or partial shade.

Forsythia. An exceedingly popular shrub,
grown for its beautiful spring flowers.
Among the best cultivars is *F.* 'Beatrix
Farrand', height and spread 4 m × 3 m
(13 ft × 10 ft). *F.* 'Lynwood' is very
similar. *F. ovata*, height and spread 1 m ×
1.5 m (3½ ft × 5 ft), is an early-flowering
species, but may suffer from damage by
birds. Grow in sun or shade.

Fuchsia. Those mentioned here are the
hardier sorts, which may nevertheless be
cut to the ground in severe winters. They
usually recover with fresh growth in
spring, but height and spread is
determined by winter hardiness. They will
grow in sun or light shade.

F. magellanica. Average height and
spread is about 1.5 m × 90 cm (5 ft × 3 ft).
The flowers, in late summer, are crimson
and purple. *F.m.* 'Versicolor' has a more
spreading habit, the leaves acquiring
creamy variegations. *F.* 'Riccartonii'
makes a much larger plant, especially in a
mild district, with a typical height and
spread of 90 cm–2.4 m (3–8 ft).

These and other hardy fuchsias add a
distinctive form to a border.

Garrya elliptica. Height and spread 2.7 m
(9 ft). The long, grey-green catkins that
hang from the branches in winter and
early spring make this a much-planted
evergreen. Male plants have the boldest
tassels but females carry them, too, and
produce seed if planted near a male. A
sunny position is best.

Hamamelis (witch hazel). The two main
species are *H. japonica* and *H. mollis*,
which with their hybrid *H.* x *intermedia*
have several attractive named forms.
Perhaps the best way to choose is by
visiting a garden such as Wisley or a plant
centre in January, when plants may be
seen in flower. One particularly striking
cultivar is *H. mollis* 'Pallida', with a height
and spread of about 4.5 m (15 ft). Its
scented flowers are sulphur-yellow, and
the autumn leaves are yellow.

Hebe. Beautiful evergreen flowering
shrubs, but very few are reliably hardy in
severe winters. Over-wintered rooted
cuttings will ensure succession if older
plants are killed. Hebes will grow in most
soils, in a sunny or partially shaded
position and preferably with some shelter.

H. speciosa grows to barely 90 cm (3 ft).
It has glossy, dark green foliage and bears
purple flowers from mid-summer

onwards. The flowers of *H.* 'Alicia
Amherst' are violet, those of *H.* 'Simon
Delaux' deep crimson. Both need
protection. *H.* 'Waikiki' is hardier and
somewhat smaller, with narrow, bronzed
foliage and flowers of lavender-blue.

H. x *franciscana* 'Blue Gem', too, is
reasonably hardy, with bright blue
flowers. Height and spread 1.2 m (4 ft).

Hypericum calycinum (rose of Sharon).
This will grow almost anywhere. It
reaches about 38 cm (15 in) and has an
indefinite spread, making it a useful
ground-cover plant. Golden flowers are
borne from June until the end of summer.
H. 'Hidcote', a semi-evergreen, makes a
more upright shrub, with a height and
spread of 2 m (6½ ft). Bright yellow
flowers are carried from July to October.

H. x *inodorum* 'Elstead', with a height
and spread of 90 cm (3 ft), has smaller
flowers than *H.* 'Hidcote', but they are
followed by conspicuous red fruits. Prone
to rust disease.

Kerria japonica. Height and spread
1.2–1.8 m (4–6 ft). This is prized for its
abundant orange flowers, borne in April
and May. It will grow in sun or partial
shade. *K.j.* 'Pleniflora' (bachelor's
buttons) has a height and spread of 1.2 m
× 45 cm (4 ft × 1½ ft), making a slender,
upright shape. Arching stems carry
double, ball-shaped flowers. *K.j.*
'Variegata', height and spread 90 cm (3 ft),
is a low, wiry shrub with variegated
foliage and single yellow flowers.

Leucothoë fontanesiana. Height and
spread 90 cm–1.5 m (3–5 ft). This is an
evergreen with a spreading habit. It carries
pitcher-shaped white flowers in May, and
the leaves take on plum-purple tints in
winter. It needs a lime-free soil and grows
best in semi-shade. The leaves of
L.f. 'Rainbow' are variegated cream,
yellow and pink.

Lonicera (honeysuckle). The following
are all deciduous or occasionally semi-
evergreen shrubs and produce their
fragrant, creamy flowers in winter –
L. fragrantissima, L. x *purpusii* and
L. standishii. Average height and spread is
1.8–2.4 m (6–8 ft), and they will grow on
most soils and in sun or partial shade.

Mahonia japonica. Height and spread
1.8 × 3 m (6 × 10 ft). This is an evergreen grown for the graceful racemes of
fragrant yellow flowers that are carried in
winter and early spring. The leathery,
spiny-edged leaves are attractive, too. Its
hybrid, *M.* 'Charity', is a somewhat taller
plant, with larger inflorescences and
foliage. Neither is suitable for an exposed
site, but they will tolerate light shade.

Philadelphus (mock orange). This has acquired its name from the orange-blossom scent of its white flowers that open in early summer. *P. coronarius*, height and spread 4 m (13 ft) makes a dense bush that will grow in any soil in an open position. *P.* 'Belle Etoile', with a height and spread of 2 × 1.5 m (6½ × 5 ft) is more compact.

Sambucus nigra (common elder). This has a number of forms, with an average height and spread of 4.5 m (15 ft). They are grown for their shiny autumn berries as well as for their attractive foliage and creamy-white June flowers. Almost any soil suits them, and either sun or partial shade. *S.n.* 'Aurea' has golden-yellow leaves; *S.n.* 'Laciniata' (fern-leaved elder) has finely-cut leaves; the young foliage of *S.n.* 'Purpurea' is flushed purple.

S. racemosa 'Plumosa Aurea' has golden, deeply-cut foliage. Varieties grown primarily for their foliage should be pruned hard in spring to produce larger, well-coloured leaves.

Spiraea x *arguta* (bridal wreath or foam of May). This is aptly named. With a height and spread of 1.5 m (5 ft), the slender, arching branches are hidden by tiny white flowers in mid spring. *S.* x *bumalda* is about the same size, but the flowers are pink, in flat clusters, and the leaves are variegated cream and pink. The young leaves of *S.* x *b.* 'Goldflame' are orange-yellow. Choose a sunny position.

Syringa (lilac). Still widely planted for their fragrant spring flowers, lilacs will grown on all soils, including chalk, and in sun or light shade. Many varieties, with large flowers of various shades, will be found in catalogues under *S. vulgaris*. The exceedingly large, rose-pink flower panicles of *S.* x *josiflexa* 'Bellicent', height and spread 3 m (10 ft), make it an excellent specimen plant.

S. velutina, height and spread 90 cm–1.5m (3–5 ft), is a small, dense-growing shrub with lilac or lilac-pink flowers.

Viburnum opulus 'Sterile' (snowball bush). The common name provides a good description of the shrub's appearance in mid-summer, when large, round heads of pure white flowers are carried. It grows to about 3.6–4.5 m (12–15 ft). *V. plicatum* 'Mariesii', height and spread 3 m (10 ft), makes a tiered plant with masses of white flowers. Both are suitable for full sun or partial shade.

Weigela. The funnel-shaped flowers in early summer are the chief attraction of these shrubs. Height and spread average about 1.8 m (6 ft). *W.* 'Bristol Ruby' has ruby-red flowers, *W. florida* pink.

W.f. 'Foliis Purpureis' has purple leaves. *W.f.* 'Variegata' has creamy-white leaf margins.

Weigelas will grow in most soils, and in sun or partial shade.

Climbers

Actinidia kolomikta. A spectacular and vigorous deciduous climber grown principally for its foliage. The base of each leaf is green; the rest, white flushed with pink. A sunny wall is ideal. Leaves do not always colour white and pink on young plants.

Campsis radicans (trumpet vine). This supports itself by aerial roots. Orange and red flowers appear in late summer. It is deciduous and needs a sunny wall.

Celastrus orbiculatus (staff vine). A vigorous, deciduous twiner with autumn fruits that glow orange, with paler, yellow surrounds. Good fruiting depends on planting both male and female forms. The support may be in sun or light shade.

Clematis. Selecting from this extensive family of deciduous climbers is a matter of personal choice. Among recommended favourites are *C. montana* 'Elizabeth', which has faintly fragrant pink flowers in late May, and *C.m.* 'Tetrarose', with deep rose flowers above bronze foliage.

C. orientalis and *C. tangutica* are both yellow-flowered species that have fluffy seed-heads later in the season.

The rule for all clematis is 'roots, cool; head in the sun'.

Hedera (ivy). This comes in many forms, but it would be hard to better

H. canariensis 'Gloire de Marengo', which has silvery-white edged leaves. It needs a sheltered wall. Another fine one is *H. colchica* 'Sulphur Heart', syn. *H.c.* 'Paddy's Pride', with yellow variegations.

All the ivies are evergreen and there is none tougher than *H. helix*, which has a number of named forms.

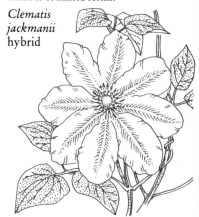

Clematis jackmanii hybrid

Humulus lupulus 'Aureus'. A yellow-leaved hop that makes entirely fresh growth each year. Given a sunny wall, it is very vigorous indeed.

Hydrangea petiolaris. A climbing *Hydrangea*, this attaches itself by aerial roots if given some initial assistance. A deciduous plant, it carries typical lacecap, creamy-white hydrangea flowers in June. Suitable for any wall.

Lonicera periclymenum (common honeysuckle). This is mainly deciduous, vigorous and sweetly-scented, and bears

Weigela florida

Passiflora caerulea

Climbers (cont.)

yellow, red-flushed flowers through the second half of summer. *L.p.* 'Serotina' is somewhat later and has deeper-toned flowers.

Honeysuckles will grow in all positions. *Passiflora caerulea* (passion flower). Requires a warm wall, the further south in the country the better. It is evergreen in the mildest areas, given sheltered conditions.

Schizophragma. Related to, and often mistaken for, *Hydrangea petiolaris*, it has a similar climbing habit. Conspicuous white bracts make *S. hydrangeoides* and *S. integrifolium* very distinctive. Both are deciduous and the plants grow best in light shade.

Wisteria. Some flower sparsely or not at all, though this may also be because they are seedlings or because the soil is poor.

The two species most worth considering are *W. floribunda* (Japanese wisteria) and *W. sinensis* (Chinese wisteria). It is an odd fact that the former twines clockwise, the latter anti-clockwise. Both do best in full sun.

W. floribunda has dark blue flowers. There is a form, *W.f.* 'Macrobotrys', with racemes up to 90 cm (3 ft) long. *W. sinensis* is a free-flowering species with fragrant, deep-lilac flowers. The white form, 'Alba', makes a spectacular show when scrambling along a garden hedge.

Wall plants

Abeliophyllum distichum. Height and spread up to 1.5 m (5 ft). A slow-growing deciduous shrub that needs frequent tying-in to keep it tidy. White flowers,

Abutilon megapotamicum

flushed with pink, appear in February on the previous year's growth and are highly scented. The plant will grow in sun or shade.

Abutilon megapotamicum. Height and spread about 1.8 m (6 ft). A deciduous species that carries pendulous flowers over a long period. Each has a red calyx, buff-yellow petals and purple anthers. A sunny south or west wall is best.

Aloysia triphylla, syn. *Lippia citriodora* (lemon-scented verbena). Height 1.5 m (5 ft), spread 1.2 m (4 ft). Though somewhat tender, this is worth growing for its scented foliage. It is deciduous and needs a warm wall.

Azara microphylla and *A. serrata.* Two fast-growing evergreen shrubs, both reaching a height of at least 3 m (10 ft), with an obliging fan-shaped habit of growth. They will cover a large wall – preferably a sunny one – but pruning (after flowering) will keep them within bounds. The flowers are yellow and appear, on *A. microphylla*, in early spring; those on *A. serrata* are borne in summer and are more conspicuous.

Buddleia crispa. A deciduous shrub with white-felted leaves and scented lilac flowers. Height 1.8–3 m (6–10 ft), spread 1.2–2.4 m (4–8 ft). It looks especially good when set against a wall of dark bricks.

B. colvilei, which is semi-evergreen, and tender when young, is more vigorous (height up to 5.5 m (18 ft)) and needs a substantial wall. It is worth growing for its handsome panicles of deep rose flowers. Both species do best in a warm position.

Ceanothus dentatus, C. impressus, C. thyrsiflorus and *C.* x *veitchianus.* Height and spread 3 m (10 ft). These are the most commonly grown members of this lovely genus. All are evergreen and have deep green leaves. A warm wall suits them best.

Chaenomeles. These should be trained and pruned like espalier apples, for their apple-type flowers, and subsequent quince-like fruits, are produced on short spurs. *C. speciosa* offers a range of named forms, in many shades from white to deep red. The same is true of *C.* x *superba*, with the added advantage of hybrid vigour. Average height and spread for all 1.8 m (6 ft). A wall of any aspect suits them.

Cotoneaster horizontalis. A familiar and much-loved deciduous wall plant. Height and spread to 2.4 m (8 ft), or more. It shows to best advantage in its variegated form, *C.h.* 'Variegatus'. In autumn and winter the branches, in a distinct herring-borne pattern, are clustered with bright red berries.

C. microphyllus, an evergreen, is particularly hardy. It is almost prostrate, but wide-spreading and may be used for ground cover as well as for growing against a wall.

Itea ilicifolia. An evergreen with holly-like leaves of a glistening green. These are joined, in late summer, by racemes of insignificant but scented flowers. A partially shaded wall suits it best. Height and spread about 3 m (10 ft).

Pyracantha coccinea 'Lalandei'. Height and spread 3–4.5 m (10–15 ft). In early summer, a multitude of small white flowers brings this evergreen alive with the hum of bees. Later, the orange-red berries are borne in equal profusion, and, but for the birds, they would last until spring. Any wall suits it, but it is best with a north or east aspect.

Rosa. These must be trained when grown against a wall. All are deciduous and are dealt with more fully elsewhere (see page 104), but one or two are worth special mention.

When trained vertically, *R. ecae*, and especially its hybrid *R.e.* 'Helen Knight' (height 1.5 m (5 ft)), makes a splendid fan of ferny leaves, enhanced by a myriad of small yellow flowers. Of the Bourbon roses, both 'Zéphirine Drouhin', height 2.7 m (9 ft), and 'Kathleen Harrop', height 2.1 m (7 ft), are thornless and have pink flowers. Sadly, both are prone to mildew.

R. 'Mermaid', which needs a warm wall, bears beautiful yellow flowers, though its lethal thorns make training a challenge. Height up to 7.5 m (25 ft).

Solanum crispum (Chilean potato-tree). Height about 4.5 m (15 ft). A semi-evergreen 'scrambling' plant that is tougher than generally supposed. It bears purple flowers throughout the summer.

Solanum crispum

JANUARY

Shrubs If vulnerable shrubs have not already been given protection, as they should have been, take steps now without delay. Prevent heavy snow from damaging evergreens by shaking it off at intervals.

Climbers and wall plants

Pruning This is a good time finally to shorten summer growths of wisterias to two buds. These are the same whippy growths that were reduced to about 30 cm (1 ft) in September. The purpose of this two-stage pruning is to concentrate food in the shoots to assist the formation of flower buds.

If a wisteria fails to bloom satisfactorily, one likely cause is incorrect pruning. Other possible reasons include planting too close to a wall, where the roots dry out, and lack of nourishment.

Remember that a strong, drying east wind may cause evergreens to become dehydrated. A protective screen can make all the difference to their survival.

Securing Prepare for February and March winds by checking that plants remain firmly secured to their supports.

FEBRUARY

Shrubs Protection against cold and snow is still needed this month. Cold, drying east winds are a particular hazard, to some extent to deciduous species but in particular to evergreens. Leaves of the latter may shrivel and fall, or turn brown in early spring. Over-wintering flower buds on the tips of branches are also at risk, and this applies to both deciduous and evergreen shrubs.

A solution is to erect a temporary screen. Brushwood, hurdles or chestnut palings are suitable, or you could buy purpose-made plastic windbreak material.

Planting Except in a sheltered spot, planting is better delayed until the worst of winter is over.

Pruning As *Hamamelis* species finish flowering, prune out any misplaced branches, removing either the section concerned or the entire branch.

Climbers and wall plants Do not allow snow to settle too heavily on bulky evergreen wall plants. The weight may damage not only the plant but also the supports. An occasional shake will dislodge most of it.

At the end of the month, cut back the Jackmanii and Viticella groups of *Clematis* to within 30 cm (1 ft) of the ground. If early flowers are required, prune less severely.

Shrubs Complete the planting of bare-rooted, deciduous shrubs by the end of this month, weather permitting. Evergreens are better left until April or May, although container-grown plants can go in whenever the weather and soil are suitable.

In some instances, Group 2 shrubs (see March) need pruning down to the ground, the annual routine being based on the 'stool' system which is designed to encourage the growth of young stems. Species in this category include *Cornus alba* and *C. stolonifera* (dogwood), and *Salix alba* 'Chermesina'.

There are also some hypericums, and the hardy *Fuchsia*, which can be cut down to ground level this month, if desired, in situations where cold weather has not already done this.

In addition to these two broad groupings there are shrubs that do not need regular pruning, their flowers being carried on the tips of an extending framework. Some examples are hebes, tree peonies and *Buddleia globosa*. These and some evergreens, will need the occasional misplaced stem or branch removed to maintain shape. Either take this right out or cut to a point where there is new growth.

Finally, remove dead, diseased or damaged wood as soon as you spot it, whatever the season or type of shrub. If you are uncertain when to prune a particular shrub, wait until you can determine when it flowers, and on what wood this occurs, then apply the rules outlined here.

Pruning this month In addition to the Group 2 shrubs already mentioned, others that need pruning either at the end of March or early in April, depending on the season, include *Caryopteris*, deciduous *Ceanothus*, such as *C.* 'Gloire de Versailles' and *C.* 'Topaz', and also species and cultivars of the genus *Sambucus* grown for foliage effect.

Treat *Cornus alba* and *C. stolonifera*, grown for their coloured stems, as already described, and such willows as *Salix alba* 'Chermesina', *S.a.* 'Vitellina', *S. daphnoides* and *S. irrorata*. If cut hard back annually, they need a general fertilizer dressing and a rich mulch; otherwise, cut them back every other year.

Climbers and wall plants Whether you buy bare-rooted plants (which must go in before the end of March) or those grown in containers, it is as well to fix the permanent supports in place first.

Pruning The same general pruning principles apply for climbers and wall plants as for shrubs, already explained in this month's entry.

Where *Pyracantha* is grown as a

wall plant, any long growths – other than extensions of the framework – must be shortened to within a couple of buds of the main frame. Although autumn is the best time for doing this, prompt action now is better than leaving the shrub unpruned.

To rejuvenate old, overgrown cultivars of *Clematis patens*, prune them hard this month, even though this will mean losing most of this year's early flowers. Watering and an occasional feed will help the plants to recover.

The Jackmanii and Viticella groups of *Clematis*, which flower on the current season's growth, should be pruned hard back early in March if this was not done in February. Cut back to within about 30 cm (1 ft) of the ground.

Protection Keep the protective material handy, if removed because of a mild spell, in case of a return to more severe weather.

MARCH

Shrubs March sees the start of the annual pruning cycle, in this case concentrating on shrubs that will flower later this year on the growths they make during the next few months. Beginners are often confused about the purpose and timing of pruning, so following is an explanation of why and when it is carried out.

Why prune? Failure to prune will result in a large, untidy plant with flowering shoots that become progressively weaker, often with smaller flowers. The purpose of pruning is to enhance shape and vigour, the latter being closely allied to health. The purpose is *not* to restrict the plant's size to a particular area for, if this is necessary, it suggests that the wrong shrub was chosen in the first place.

When to prune Shrubs needing regular pruning fall into two distinct groups – those (Group 1) that flower on growths (wood) formed the *previous* season and others (Group 2) that flower on the *current* season's growths.

Group 1. Flowering on shoots that developed and ripened the previous year, the majority bloom during the earlier part of the season. Clearly, pruning once the shoots have started to grow would mean loss of potential flowers. For this reason, Group 1 shrubs are pruned as soon as they finish flowering, removing as much flowered wood as possible and cutting close to suitable new growths lower down the stem. The new shoots will then have the rest of the season to grow and ripen. Plants in this category include *Forsythia*, *Philadelphus*, *Weigela* and some *Spiraea*.

Group 2. In this case, flowers are carried on shoots that have formed during the same growing season. If such shrubs were left unpruned, the new shoots would emerge towards the ends of last year's wood, resulting in an open,

lanky plant with poorer flowers.

Pruning consists of removing last year's shoots almost to their point of origin, cutting back to the first good bud, or pair of buds, at the base. This will result in sound, healthy new shoots, the tips of which will flower later in the year.

Late March or early April is the ideal time for doing this, for the emerging shoots will be spared the worst of the frosts. Examples of shrubs in this group are *Buddleia davidii* and *Perovskia*.

APRIL

Shrubs Complete any pruning that was due in March but had to be delayed because of cold weather. Continue to prune early-flowering shrubs as they finish blooming.

After a hard winter there may be a number of shrubs that appear at least partly dead. It may be necessary to wait until well into this month, or even into May, for signs of new growth so that the real damage can be ascertained.

Some *Ceanothus*, for instance,

Pruning Group 2 shrubs
With shrubs like *Buddleia davidii*, cut back to the first good buds, or pair of buds, in March or April.

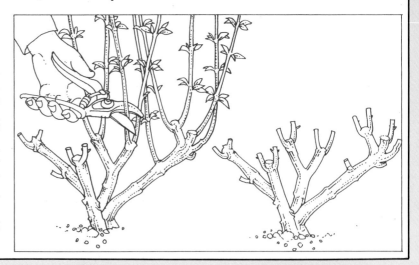

may start sprouting at the base of the laterals even though they had every appearance of being dead. The correct action is to prune back the laterals to live wood.

Similarly, shrubs that have been frosted to ground level will take a while to make fresh growth. As with *Ceanothus*, cut back to live, healthy wood once the extent of the damage can be determined.

Neglected shrubs Old and neglected shrubs may be revitalized at the beginning of April. If there are young, year-old shoots sprouting from the base, remove all other growths. If there are no new shoots, cut the whole lot to the ground anyway.

Shrubs likely to respond to this drastic treatment include *Forsythia × intermedia, Ligustrum ovalifolium, Viburnum × bodnantense, Deutzia, Philadelphus* and *Syringa.*

If in doubt, the best advice is to at least make the attempt. Should the treatment fail, you will have lost only an indifferent shrub. If the plant does revive, normal pruning will then keep it in very good order.

Reversion Keep a watchful eye for reversion – to green in the case of plants with variegated foliage, to upright growth on a weeping tree. Prune out the offending part immediately.

Planting April is a good month to plant evergreens that were not planted out last September or October.

Climbers and wall plants Before the season gets fully under way, check whether ties are still secure. Loosen them or re-tie, as required.

Pruning As advised for shrubs, give winter-damaged plants an opportunity to recover before attempting to prune them. When the extent of the damage is clear, prune back to healthy wood, even

if this means cutting to ground level. If in doubt, check with your thumbnail to see if the bark is still greenish in colour, a sign that the shoot is alive.

When *Abeliophyllum distichum* has finished flowering, cut the old flowered shoots hard back to suitably-placed emerging shoots lower down. Tie these in as soon as they develop.

Prune deciduous types of *Ceanothus* as for *Buddleia davidii* to encourage fresh flowering growth. (See Shrubs, March.)

Planting If the ground against a wall or fence is poor, dig out a planting hole 45 cm (1½ ft) deep and replace it with better soil, working in some rotted manure or compost. If the ground is dry, first fill the hole two or three times with water, allowing each filling to soak away, before filling with soil and planting.

Plant with the stem about 30 cm (1 ft) away from the wall or fence and lean the plant towards it. In the case of a grafted plant, it is better to have the graft on the outside so that it will not come under stress when the stem is bent against the wall.

Provide an initial support until the main support is reached. Canes will do for wall plants, a few twigs or wire mesh for climbers. Bear in mind that some climbers, such as *Clematis*, like to have their heads in the sun but their roots in moist, cool shade. This can be achieved by planting them in the shade of a shrub, around the corner of a wall or fence or by placing a slab over the root area.

MAY

Shrubs Apply a balanced fertilizer around shrubs after ensuring that the ground is weed-free.

Water recently-planted shrubs if the ground is dry. Apply a generous mulch of well-rotted manure, spent mushroom compost, leaf-mould or peat. Home-made compost is suitable provided that it heated sufficiently in the heap to destroy weed seeds.

Damaged shrubs Basal growths may yet appear on winter-damaged shrubs, so be patient. Two frequent late-developers are the broader leaved hebes and *Indigofera potaninii.*

Planting A period of wet weather in May is a good time to plant *Ilex* (holly) and other evergreens. These will be either balled – their roots wrapped in hessian – or container-grown. These plants need a warm soil if they are to avoid a check, and for this reason September planting is best of all. Old plants do not take kindly to moving, and neither do bare-rooted plants at this time.

Pests and diseases Keep a watchful eye for a build-up of pests or signs of disease. Shrubs are troubled less than many other plants, but this is a time when aphids in particular, are starting to become active. If spraying proves necessary, add a foliar feed to stimulate growth.

Climbers and wall plants Check winter-damaged plants again, as advised in April.

Pruning Keep new growths of wall plants tied in. Prune any strong growths that are growing inwards or outwards, thus retaining a flat profile.

If you have any *Chaenomeles* (japonica) note how the blossoms are positioned at the base of last year's wood. This knowledge will guide you when you start pruning next month.

Clematis montana needs pruning only if the plant has grown out of hand. Do this immediately after flowering, cutting hard back to encourage strong new growths that will bear next year's flowers.

JUNE

Shrubs Even if you have applied a mulch, a good soak will be needed during prolonged dry spells.
Pruning During June, a number of shrubs will be flowering on last year's wood and will therefore need pruning as soon as the blooms have faded. The principles will be those outlined for Group 1, in March, except that new wood will now be that much more advanced.

Among the more popular shrubs needing this treatment are *Buddleia alternifolia*, *Deutzia*, *Philadelphus* and *Weigela*.

On some shrubs – *Deutzia*, for example – there may be young, healthy shoots growing from the base as well as from old stems. Retain a proportion of both, but discard those that are too high on the old stems. Precisely which shoots to keep is a matter of gauging the future shape and balance of the bush.

After flowering, prune *Buddleia alternifolia* back to the pair of shoots at the base of the old stem. This will prevent any significant increase in size from year to year and is typical of the pruning method for shrubs that flower on the previous season's wood.
Climbers and wall plants As *Pyracantha* comes into bloom, the new growths may be shortened sufficiently to reveal the flowers. Though only a temporary check to growth, this treatment will encourage fruiting spurs to form. It is a good idea to do the job in the late evening, otherwise you may disturb bees gathering nectar.

Although not essential, regular pruning of the evergreen *Ceanothus* will prevent the shrub protruding too far from the wall. After the tips have flowered, prune back short spurs to within a few buds of the main stem.

After flowering, prune back lateral growths of *Chaenomeles* to about five buds. There will probably be some regrowth, and further pruning (in late summer) will reduce them to two buds – the ones that will flower next year.

JULY

Shrubs Bushes pruned hard back in spring will now be coming into flower. New growths on shrubs that flowered in the spring will be starting to ripen and will benefit from a dressing of high-potash fertilizer. Either give a generous sprinkling of sulphate of potash around the roots, watering this in afterwards, or apply tomato fertilizer as a foliar feed.
Pruning For a second, though less spectacular, crop of flowers on *Buddleia davidii*, remove the terminal flowers as they deteriorate. The new blooms will appear just below the old ones, so be careful not to cut too much off.
Routine care Overall, keep a watchful eye for pests and diseases, spraying as necessary. Water thoroughly during prolonged dry weather.
Climbers and wall plants As *Weigela florida* and its cultivars finish flowering, you will see that fresh new shoots lower down the plant are growing quite strongly. These will bear next year's flowers. Remove the old, flowered wood down to these growths, tying the latter in to the supports. Also remove completely any very old, exhausted wood.

Plants of this type lend themselves to a formal fan shape, covering a wall or fence, if pruned and tied in with this in mind.

AUGUST

Shrubs Last month's advice on feeding, pest and disease control, and watering still applies.

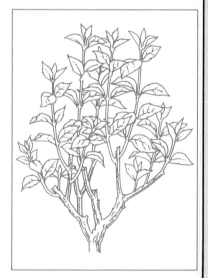

Pruning shrubs
Cut out faded stems on shrubs that flower on the previous year's wood.

Retain shape by pruning old stems back to where new shoots appear.

Climbers and wall plants Check to ensure that ties are not constricting growth, loosening any that are. Water liberally during dry periods, especially plants growing against walls.

Feeding Apply a high-potash fertilizer to plants with wood now maturing that will carry next year's display. The potash will help the wood to ripen and assist bud formation. Tomato fertilizer or sulphate of potash may be used, the latter sprinkled over the planting area and watered in.

SEPTEMBER

Shrubs Cuttings of doubtfully-hardy shrubs taken this month can be given the protection of a greenhouse or cold frame during the winter. These will provide replacements should the older shrubs not survive.

Planting Root-balled evergreens may be planted towards the end of the month. This time and October provide the best conditions, for the soil is still warm enough to encourage root development.

Climbers and wall plants Towards the end of the month start planting climbers and wall plants. The warmth left in the soil will encourage root action without forcing too much top growth, setting plants up for winter.

Pruning Early in the month, shorten the long, whippy shoots of wisteria to about 30 cm (12 in) from their source.

To help show pyracantha berries to full advantage, cut back laterals to about two or three buds from source. Give the same treatment to fresh growths on laterals shortened in early summer. Leave unpruned any leading shoots earmarked to extend the plant, tying these in as necessary.

OCTOBER

Shrubs Evergreens may still be planted – the sooner the better, while the soil is still warm.

Pruning In an exposed garden, remove part of the stems of tall, late-flowering shrubs as the blooms fade. This will help to prevent wind damage during the winter. The remainder of the stems will be removed next spring and it would be as well not to cut back too far at this stage, otherwise a mild winter may induce basal growth vulnerable to cold winds and frost.

Leave other late-flowering shrubs untouched, not only for their own winter protection but also, in some cases, for the beauty of their stems. *Perovskia* is a good example.

Preparing for planting This is a good time to start preparing the soil for a shrub border. It will then be ready for bare-rooted shrubs planted during the dormant season or for container-grown plants purchased in the winter or spring.

Double-digging is well worthwhile, bearing in mind how long the shrubs will occupy the site. Add plenty of well-rotted organic matter to the lower spit, remove the roots of all perennial weeds and allow the soil to settle for some weeks before planting.

Climbers and wall plants On heavy soil, complete any planting as soon as possible, before the ground becomes wet and cold. On such soil, container-grown shrubs are better left unplanted in a sheltered but airy place until spring. Evergreens will need light too. Never let pots dry out completely, especially those with evergreens.

Where planting is planned, erect the supports in readiness.

NOVEMBER

Shrubs Deciduous shrubs of all sorts – ball-rooted, container-grown or bare-rooted – may be planted in well-drained soil prepared last month. With the ground still retaining some summer warmth, there is time for the roots to make a little fresh growth before winter sets in. Do not allow the roots to become dry.

On clay soils it would be as well to wait until the end of winter as the ground will remain cold and wet until spring.

Climbers and wall plants The planting advice given for shrubs applies equally to climbers or wall plants. Whatever the soil, the planting of evergreens is now better left until April.

DECEMBER

Shrubs Some shrubs, both deciduous and evergreen, are of suspect hardiness, especially while still young. A warm wall may give them the protection they need, or it may be provided by other shrubs in a well-planned border. As an alternative, a wattle screen can be erected to filter the wind.

Another way to protect tender shrubs in cold areas is by covering them with bracken or straw, securing this with string or wire netting, if necessary. Cut bracken on a dry day and pack it into sacks.

Climbers and wall plants Protective materials suggested for shrubs will serve also for climbers and wall plants. They can be secured in place with netting. Alternatively, a covering of hessian will keep off the worst of frost and wind. Do not put protection in place until needed and be ready to remove it if prolonged mild spells occur.

Finding the right-sized tree for a small garden is not always easy. What seemed an attractive little specimen at the garden centre may outgrow its space after a few years, casting shade where it is not wanted and looking altogether out of proportion to its surroundings.

However, some quite tall trees are so slow-growing that they will remain a reasonable size within the lifetime of the gardener who planted them. Again, some trees with a column-like (fastigiate) habit may occupy comparatively little ground space even though they grow quite tall. For both reasons, ultimate height is not necessarily the sole guide.

Particular trees may be chosen for many reasons, in addition to providing a focal point or shade. Interesting foliage, flowers, fruit, scent, autumn colour or attractive bark are among desirable qualities, and sometimes one species may have three or more of these.

Five genera are so large that only a limited selection of species can be made here. They are *Acer, Crataegus, Malus, Prunus* and *Sorbus*. A good catalogue will give further suggestions and a visit to a tree nursery will be well repaid.

Height is influenced by situation and soil, and by general care. The heights given in the lists are for average trees near maturity.

WEEPING TREES

Quite a few genera have species or forms with a weeping (pendulous) tendency. Their height may be regulated by encouraging or discouraging this habit. In some cases, a long shoot is needed to serve as a leader and provide height. Removing this will keep a tree low.

Some weeping trees remain narrow and so occupy little ground space. Others, such as the weeping beech, tend to sprawl and may take up a large area.

On page 144 are brief details of some attractive species. All are deciduous, unless otherwise stated.

CONIFERS

Some species sold as 'dwarf' are slow-growing but eventually develop into quite large trees. Speed of growth is, in some cases, tortuously slow, and slow-growing forms may occur in genera that are normally quite large and fast-growing. These are certainly points to bear in mind when choosing conifers for small gardens.

Trees for small gardens

Acer (maple). Trees in this genus range from forest specimens to mere shrubs. The main appeal of the smaller trees is their vivid autumn colouring, attractive bark and winged fruits. Mostly they need moist, well-drained, lime-free soil, plus protection from direct sunlight and cold, drying winds.

There are many attractive forms of *A. japonicum* and *A. palmatum*, both known as Japanese maples. Average height is 6 m (20 ft). *A.j.* 'Aconitifolium' has deep lobed leaves which are crimson in autumn. 'Aureum' is slow-growing, with yellow leaves turning red in autumn; 'Vitifolum' turns a rich ruby-red in autumn.

The leaves of *A. palmatum* turn to orange and red in autumn. The purple summer foliage of *A.p.* 'Atropurpureum' becomes more intense as the season advances. 'Osakazuki' shows several changes of shade. 'Senkaki' (coral bark maple) has young branches of a lovely coral red during the winter.

Acer palmatum

The so-called snake bark maples have distinctively striated or marbled bark in addition to good autumn colouring. Under this general heading come *A. capillipes, A. davidii* 'George Forrest', *A. forrestii, A. grosseri* and its variety *hersii, A. henryi, A. pensylvanicum, A.p.* 'Erythrocladum', *A. rufinerve* and *A.* 'Silver Vein'. Average heights are 4.5–6 m (15–20 ft).

Other small maples of note include *A. ginnala*, 3–4.5 m (10–15 ft), which has beautiful red autumn foliage, and *A. griseum* (paper bark maple) growing to 12 m (40 ft) with age. This name refers to the peeling bark, revealing a reddish-brown trunk. Distinctive trifoliate leaves turn bright orange-red in autumn.

Finally, there is *A. pseudoplatanus* 'Brilliantissimum', which is very slow-growing and has young foliage of a striking shrimp-pink. A worthy specimen tree may attain about 6–9 m (20–30 ft). *Alnus* (alder). Hardiness and a preference for damp, heavy soil make this a useful genus of deciduous trees for situations where many others might not prosper. Alders will, in fact, grow in most soils other than shallow chalk.

A. firma, reaching 3 m (10 ft), is worth considering for its interesting cone-like fruits. *A. glutinosa* 'Imperialis', height 10–20 m (33–66 ft) is a tall, graceful tree but grows only slowly. It has lovely feathery leaves.

Trees for small gardens (cont.)

A. incana (grey alder) eventual height 18 m (60 ft), is a very tough tree with leaves that are grey beneath. *A.i..* 'Aurea' is smaller and slower-growing, reaching about 3–12 m (10–40 ft). The young shoots are red and the early foliage yellow.

Amelanchier (snowy mespilus). This deciduous rival, in both spring and autumn, to the flowering cherries has a multi-stemmed habit and grows well under similar conditions to the alders. *A. lamarckii*, height 6–9 m (20–30 ft), is laden with white blossom in spring, while the autumn foliage is ablaze with red and crimson.

Amelanchier lamarckii

Aralia elata (Japanese angelica tree) is a deciduous species of variable height. Of shrubby habit, a tree-like form is obtained by removing suckers, this giving a small, exotic-looking tree with large, pinnate leaves. The flowers, whitish and foamy, rise above the top cluster of leaves in early autumn. There is a variegated form which is even more attractive but in short supply.

Cercis siliquastrum (Judas tree). Height 6 m (20 ft). This is a slow-growing deciduous tree of great charm, the purplish-pink, pea-like flowers appearing in clusters ahead of the delicate olive-green leaves. In a good season the flowers 'set' to produce masses of brown pods, which persist all winter.

Cornus (dogwood). This variable genus ranges from ground-cover plants to shrubs and small trees. Of particular appeal is *C. kousa* var. *chinensis*, which attains a height of about 6 m (20 ft).

The masses of white flowers, in June, are for the most part bracts. The small central flowers turn to 'strawberries' in a good season. As autumn approaches, the foliage becomes plum-coloured and then crimson. When this has fallen, the patchily-coloured bark remains attractive. Not for alkaline soils.

Cotoneaster frigidus, height 7.6 m (25 ft), makes a welcome addition to the garden when trained to a single stem. It is semi-evergreen and heavy-fruiting, with persistent red berries. *C.f.* 'Fructuluteo' has yellow berries.

Crataegus (ornamental thorn). Few trees are tougher, for they will withstand extremes of climate and are tolerant of most soils. Growing from about 4.5–7 m (15–23 ft), they mostly attain the size of an orchard apple tree.

The flowers are generally white, opening in May, and are followed by red-berried fruits, or 'haws'. All species are deciduous. Some of the many attractive species include:

C. crus-galli (cockspur thorn). Glossy leaves, colouring in autumn. Long-lasting berries. *C. flava* (yellow haw) has orange-yellow berries.

C. monogyna 'Biflora' (the Glastonbury thorn) sometimes flowers in winter as well as in spring. *C.m.* 'Stricta' is a more erect form, suitable for restricted areas.

C. oxyacantha. This species offers a wider range of flower colours. Among the more worthwhile forms are 'Aurea', with yellow berries; 'Paul's Scarlet', with double scarlet flowers; 'Plena', with double white flowers; 'Rosea Flore Pleno', with double pink flowers.

C. x prunifolia is notable for its good autumn colouring and persistent, showy, red berries. It makes an attractive specimen tree. *C. tanacetifolia* is very nearly thornless, with greyish, tansy-like leaves and yellow, apple-like fruits.

Eucalyptus niphophila grows to about 5 m (16 ft) and, like others of the genus, is evergreen. It is, perhaps, the hardiest of the smaller species, but avoid exposed positions and also alkaline soils. The trunk displays a patchwork of greys, greens and browns, and the young foliage is particularly attractive.

Ilex (holly). Separate male and female plants occur in this evergreen genus. Although some of the females bear a reasonable crop of berries when planted alone, better results are produced when there is a male nearby. *I. x altaclarensis* and *I. aquifolium* are by far the most widely grown, and there are a good many named forms of each.

I. x altaclarensis 'Camelliifolia', a female, has splendid glossy leaves which are almost spineless, and large berries. Height is up to 9 m (30 ft).

I. aquifolium 'Golden Queen' is, oddly enough, a male form. The leaf margins are yellow. Height up to 10.5 m (35 ft). *I. a.* 'J. C. van Tol', a female but reasonably

Ilex aquifolium

self-fertile, makes a tall tree of 10 m (33 ft) and over. It is almost spineless and bears masses of red berries.

Laburnum (golden chain). The common species, *L. anagyroides*, which grows to about 4.5–6 m (15–20 ft) has green leaves, but those of *L.a.* 'Aureum' are golden. All laburnums are deciduous. Unfortunately, the seeds are poisonous, a danger which may be lessened by growing *L. x watereri* 'Vossii'. This sets less seed than others.

Malus (crab apple). Grown primarily for their flowers and fruits, the range of species and varieties is quite extensive. In general, these deciduous trees differ little from culinary apples, and the larger forms may be kept within bounds by similar pruning.

M. coronaria. Height to 5.5 m (18 ft). Fragrant pink flowers and good autumn colouring. *M.* 'Dorothea' is a slow-growing tree that remains a dainty 3 m (10 ft) after many years, but may be difficult to obtain. *M. floribunda*. Height 3.6–4.5 m (12–15 ft). Laden with pinky-white flowers that open from crimson buds in May.

The young leaves of *M.* 'Profusion' are copper-coloured, the fragrant flowers a mass of red. It grows 4.5–6 m (15–20 ft). *M.* 'Royalty', growing to a similar height, has crimson flowers and reddish-purple leaves.

Prunus. Within this genus of deciduous trees come the flowering cherries, of which there are very many. Choice should be governed not only by their flowering qualities but also by autumn colouring.

P. x hillieri 'Spire' makes a narrow tree up to 7.6 m (25 ft) high. It has pink flowers, and crimson leaves in autumn. *P.* 'Kursar' grows slowly up to 9 m (30 ft) high. The pink flowers are borne quite early in spring, and the autumn colouring is early, too. *P.* 'Pandora', attaining 4.5–

Trees for small gardens (cont.)

6 m (15–20 ft), has an upright habit and carries pink blossom as early as March. The autumn tints are red.

Two trees of special note among the Japanese cherries are *P.* 'Amanogawa' and *P.* 'Jo-nioi', both up to 7.6 m (25 ft) high. The former makes a narrow column and has double, shell-pink flowers which are scented. The latter has a more spreading habit, with strongly perfumed, single white flowers.

Rhus trichocarpa, growing to 4.5–6 m (15–20 ft), makes a splendid small tree; the downy leaves are green when young but turn deep orange in autumn. A better-known species is the suckering *R. typhina* (stag's horn sumach) which attains 3–4.5 m (10–15 ft), tolerates a wide range of growing conditions and displays superb leaf colouring from late summer onwards. *R.t.* 'Laciniata' has deeply-cut leaves. All species of *Rhus* cultivated outdoors in Britain are deciduous.

Robinia pseudoacacia (false acacia) is a deciduous tree well worth planting for its fragrant flowers in late spring and for its attractive pinnate leaves. It grows to about 9 m (30 ft) high, and the creamy-white blooms are carried in racemes.

R.p. 'Frisia', which has golden yellow leaves, can be pruned to keep it under control if it becomes too large.

Sorbus aria (whitebeam) is noted for the silvery undersides of its oval leaves. It grows to about 6 m (20 ft) and, like other *Sorbus* species, is deciduous. Creamy, hawthorn-like flowers open in May, and the autumn leaves are tinted. The young leaves of *S.a.* 'Lutescens' are creamy-white.

S. aucuparia (rowan or mountain ash) is unrivalled for the colouring of its fruits and autumn leaves. 'Chinese Lace' is worth considering for its delicate foliage. This turns reddish-purple in autumn and the fruits are red. Height 4.5–7.6 m (15–25 ft).

Styrax (snowbell). A moist but well-drained lime-free soil in a sheltered position suits this deciduous tree. If these conditions can be met, consider planting *S. japonica*, which grows to about 3 m (10 ft). In June, bell-shaped white flowers are carried in pendulous bunches.

Syringa (lilac). The following plants are sufficiently tree-like to be included here. Other lilacs will be found in Planning a Shrub Border. All are deciduous and grown for their late spring flowers.

S. vulgaris, (common lilac) grows to 6 m (20 ft). Some of the more attractive forms are 'Charles X', with single purple-red flowers; 'Mme. Lemoine', double white; 'Primrose', single pale yellow.

Weeping trees

Alnus incana 'Pendula'. Height 3–10 m (10–33 ft). A handsome grey alder.
Betula pendula 'Youngii' (Young's weeping birch). Height about 5 m (16 ft).
Cotoneaster 'Hybridus Pendulus'. Evergreen. Grafted, it grows to a height of 3 m (10 ft). Red autumn fruits.
Crataegus monogyna 'Pendula'. Height about 5 m (16 ft). A graceful weeping thorn, with white flowers in spring and crimson leaves in autumn.
Ilex aquifolium 'Pendula'. Height about 5 m (16 ft). Evergreen. A free-fruiting holly.
Laburnum alpinum 'Pendulum' (Scotch laburnum). Height about 3 m (10 ft). A slow-growing tree. *L. anagyroides* 'Pendulum' (common laburnum) Height about 3 m (10 ft).
Malus 'Echtermeyer' (syn. *M.* x *purpurea* 'Pendula'). Height about 4 m (13 ft). A weeping crab apple, rosy-pink flowers and purple fruits. *M.* 'Red Jade'. Height about 5 m (16 ft). Pink and white flowers, persistent red fruits.
Morus alba 'Pendula' (weeping white mulberry). Height about 5 m (16 ft).
Prunus 'Hilling's Weeping'. Height about 4 m (13 ft). Superb white spring flowers and autumn colouring. *P. subhirtella* 'Pendula'. Height about 3 m (10 ft). A lovely canopy of white flowers. *P.* 'Kiku-shidare Sakura'. Height about 7 m (23 ft). Bronze foliage, pink flowers.
Pyrus salicifolia 'Pendula' (weeping silver pear). Height about 5 m (16 ft). Graceful, willow-like leaves.
Salix caprea 'Pendula' (Kilmarnock willow). Height about 3 m (10 ft). Stiffly pendulous branches. *S. purpurea* 'Pendula' (purple osier). Height 3 m (10 ft) at most. Spring catkins before the leaves.
Sophora japonica 'Pendula' (Japanese pagoda tree). Height about 3 m (10 ft). Creamy flowers in late summer.
Sorbus aria 'Pendula'. Height about 3 m (10 ft). A small, weeping whitebeam.
S. aucuparia 'Pendula'. Height about 5 m (16 ft). A wide-spreading mountain ash.
Ulmus glabra 'Camperdownii'. Height 3 m (10 ft). A small but elegant elm.
U. x *hollandica* 'Hillieri'. Height at most 1.5 m (5 ft). A miniature weeping elm.

Conifers

Cedrus atlantica 'Aurea' (golden Atlas cedar) eventually reaches 3–5 m (10–16 ft). Its rate of growth is much less than the species. *C.a.* 'Glauca Pendula' a weeping form of the blue Atlas cedar, makes a fine specimen planting. Its dimensions may be about 1.5–2.4 m (5–8 ft) after 10 years.
C. deodara 'Aurea' (golden deodar) grows to 3–4.5 m (10–15 ft) after perhaps 25 years.

C. libani 'Nana' is a very slow-growing version of the cedar of Lebanon, eventually reaching 3 m (10 ft).
Cephalotaxus harringtonia var. *drupacea* (cow's tail pine). More shrub than tree, it barely reaches 3 m (10 ft). This yew-like species will grow in shade and chalky soil, the female plants bearing olive-like fruits.
Chamaecyparis lawsoniana 'Columnaris' may be tall – 8 m (26 ft) – but its narrow form occupies little ground space. Its growth rate is 5 m (16 ft) after 20 years, and its blue-grey foliage forms a striking focal point. *C.l.* 'Ellwoodii' grows slowly to form a blue column some 6 m (20 ft) high.

C. nootkatensis 'Compacta' makes a globular column, with light green foliage, some 3–4 m (10–13 ft) high. Its rate of growth is moderately slow. *C. obtusa* 'Crippsii' slowly reaches 5 m (16 ft). The foliage is a rich gold.

C. pisifera 'Boulevard' is a soft-foliaged 'bush' reaching some 3–4 m (10–13 ft) high. It has steel-blue foliage tinged with purple in winter. *Cryptomeria japonica* 'Elegans' is an attractive conifer that grows at varying rates, depending on position, to about 6–8 m (20–26 ft). The blue-green foliage becomes bronze-coloured in winter. *C.j.* 'Globosa Nana' is a rounded compact bush which may eventually reach 1 m (3½ ft).
Ginkgo biloba (maidenhair tree). Although growing to 20 m (66 ft), this distinctive tree, which does not look like a conifer, grows extremely slowly and remains acceptably small for decades. The deciduous fan-shaped leaves turn bright gold in autumn.

Ginkgo biloba

As days shorten and nights grow colder, deciduous trees and shrubs prepare to discard their leaves. A barrier forms between leaf and stem, depriving the former of its supply of sap – a simple process, but the manner in which some leaves react provides one of the glories of nature. Individually, the leaves of many species develop subtly beautiful colours. Overall, the massed effect of autumn tints can be overwhelming.

Gardeners wishing to make the most of this phenomenon have a wide range of species from which to choose. Although autumn colours are, to some extent, subject to the vagaries of the weather, those described here may be relied upon for a brilliant display in most years. The list includes large trees that may be seen in the countryside, and also in arboreta and other gardens open to the public.

Large trees As autumn approaches, oaks, beeches, hornbeams, chestnuts, birches and ash trees provide massed displays in the countryside. If you are lucky enough to have elms left, enjoy their yellow autumnal tints while you can. Field maples also colour beautifully, but to see the cultivated varieties you will have to visit large gardens or parks.

Acer platanoides (Norway maple) is a medium-sized tree with a rather capricious performance, yet it never fails to provide some display of yellow and sepia tints. *A. rubrum* (red maple) is a large tree with red and scarlet autumn colours; *A.r.* 'Scanlon' is a more upright cultivar that colours just as well.

After delighting us with silver rustling all summer, the leaves of *A. saccharinum* (silver maple) offer attractive autumn tints. *A. saccharum* (sugar maple), another large tree, takes on tints of crimson, orange and gold. It tends to be a poor grower in the British Isles. 'Temple's Upright' is a narrower form of the sugar maple, slowly making a column of warm orange tints. Its autumn colouring is not as reliable in Britain as in the U.S.

The tupelo and the sweet gum are two of Wisley's most noble trees. Although neither is unduly large, they do need to be given reasonable space. *Nyssa sylvatica* (tupelo) forms a pyramid of fire, the individual leaves glistening with colour. The display, however, is short-lived.

Liquidambar styraciflua (sweet gum) lasts much longer and progresses from a dull plum colour to scarlet, with exciting shades in between. The foliage is aromatic and, given a still, dry period, fallen leaves form saucers of iridescent beauty.

A fair amount of space is also needed for both *Phellodendron amurense* and *Parrotia persica*, which are wide-spreading. The former must be allowed freedom for its canopy of glowing butter-yellow. *Parrotia persica*, although supreme for autumn tints, has an annoying habit of marring a collective display by shedding its leaves before others have started.

Liriodendron tulipifera (tulip tree) offers an unusual leaf shape, with glowing yellow colouring. It can become a large, somewhat rangey tree, but the cultivar 'Fastigiata' takes up less ground space.

Another tree with unusual attributes is *Ginkgo biloba* (maidenhair tree) with fan-shaped leaves that turn bright gold. As with *Liriodendron*, there is a narrower form.

It seems almost too much that a tree that heralds spring so decoratively should also supply us with a splendid autumn display. Yet this is true of many flowering cherries. *Prunus sargentii* may grow to 10 m (33 ft), but if you can accommodate this size you will be rewarded with a brilliant display of orange and crimson. *P. serrulata* var. *hupehensis* (Chinese hill cherry) makes a well-shaped medium tree, clothed in crimson during the autumn. There are also some smaller *Prunus* worth considering.

Medium-size trees The shape of *Prunus* 'Hilling's Weeping' is somewhat bizarre, not unlike tumbling water. Its display of

Parrotia persica
The wide-spreading but slow-growing *Parrotia persica* assumes crimson and gold autumn tints.

Liriodendron tulipifera
Conspicuous for its tulip-shaped flowers in summer and its butter-yellow autumn foliage.

Sorbus 'Joseph Rock'
Displays amber-
yellow fruits among
orange-red, copper
and purple leaves.

spring blossom is equalled in autumn by a cascade of orange, red, yellow and olive leaves. Both *Prunus* x *hillieri* and *P.* x *h.* 'Spire' are superb for their autumn display, but while the former may reach 10 m (33 ft), *P.* x *h.* 'Spire' will be somewhat shorter and certainly more slender.

Pyrus communis (garden pear) may not seem a likely candidate for autumn colour, but see the drift of cultivars at Wisley's fruit field and judge for yourself. *P. ussuriensis* offers a rich autumn display.

Among the crab apples, *Malus tschonoskii* is a splendid choice for both form and colour. An upright tree, it is clothed in a mixture of colours, from yellow to scarlet.

Famed for its colourful berries, *Sorbus aucuparia* (rowan or mountain ash) also sports rich autumn colours. Most rowans colour well, but some of the best are 'Embley', 'Eastern Promise' and 'Joseph Rock', the latter somewhat upright in habit; also *S. pohuashanensis*, which has a spreading habit. These, and others, offer exciting combinations of red, orange, copper and purple. Seen in close-up, the leaves display beautiful mixtures of colours.

Sorbus aria (whitebeam) is a handsome small tree with large leaves that are silver on the underside. In some variants these turn yellow. Of these, 'Chrysophylla' and 'John Mitchell' are good examples.

The genus *Crataegus* (ornamental thorn) provides us with fine autumn displays. Of these, *C. crus-galli* (cockspur thorn) has particularly handsome red and orange tones, while *C. prunifolia* is a most attractive and reliable thorn for autumn colour.

Cornus kousa var. *chinensis*, which makes a small tree or shrub, starts off its autumn display with a rusty olive and ends in a rich plum or crimson. *Picrasma quassioides*, which eventually attains 6 m (20 ft), is a valuable asset in autumn, when it glows buff-orange.

Small trees and shrubs *Amelanchier* (snowy mespilus) rivals flowering cherries in both spring and autumn. *A. lamarckii*, especially, is suitable for group planting, and the massed spectacle of rich crimson is truly exhilarating.

The genus *Cotinus* (smoke tree) is noted for its autumn colours, but the brilliant scarlet of *C. coggygria* makes an especially glorious sight – enhanced dramatically when reflected in water. The form *C.c.* 'Flame' is equally spectacular.

The large, ferny leaves of *Rhus typhina* (stag's horn sumach) are well known for their gorgeous shades of scarlet. *R.t.* 'Laciniata' looks even better, with its fringed leaf edges, but *R. trichocarpa* out-colours them both.

Such a wealth of autumn colour is displayed by Japanese maples that one is loath to choose. A walk through an arboretum, such as Westonbirt, where there are groves rich in reds, yellows and purples, is an unforgettable experience. Among the very best must be *Acer palmatum* 'Heptalobum Osakazuki', which comes alive with red and crimson, while *A.p.* 'Senkaki' is a reliable all-rounder, offering a delicate soft yellow colouring. The *A.p.* 'Dissectum' group contains smaller shrubs with brilliant reds and yellows.

Fothergilla major is in the front rank for autumn colour, when its mantle is a tesselation of red, orange and yellow throughout the season. Among shrubs there is none better than *Enkianthus*, especially *E. campanulatus*, which has brilliant shades of red, gold and yellow.

Among berried shrubs, *Aronia melanocarpa* (black chokeberry) has narrow leaves that turn brilliant crimson in autumn. The genus *Vaccinium* provides a wealth of autumn colour: of these, *V. arboreum* (farkleberry); *V. corymbosum* (swamp blueberry); and *V. arctostaphylos* (whortleberry) all colour well. All of them require acid soil.

There is, seemingly, no end to the list of richly-coloured trees and shrubs. Those that should certainly be included are such beauties as *Cotoneaster* 'Cornubia', *Stewartia*, *Photinia* and *Berberis*. Of the latter, the short, compact *B. thunbergii* provides especially fine colouring.

Most of the plants described may be seen at Wisley and in other great gardens and arboreta. So the wonderful hues of autumn are there for everyone to enjoy, from the first colouring of *Prunus sargentii* to the remnants of *Berberis* and yellowing willows just days before Christmas.

TREES AND SHRUBS WITH ORNAMENTAL FRUITS

An annual display of fruits or berries is the main attraction of some trees and shrubs. Pyracantha and some of the species roses are obvious examples. For others, fruiting is part of a longer display, or it may be just an irregular bonus decided by the season, the prevailing weather, or the site and soil.

A good crop of fruit is dependent on pollination by bees and other flying insects earlier in the season. It is also at the mercy of the birds, which may strip a tree in a day.

To some extent, these are matters of chance, but this does not apply to another factor that determines the set of fruits – the sex of the plants chosen. It is not always appreciated that some genera have male, female and hermaphrodite forms. Although the latter two will sometimes produce fruits on their own, results will be much better if a male is planted nearby. *Ilex* (holly) is a case in point.

By far the most spectacular and consistent fruiting is seen on plants in the family *Rosaceae*, of which the following are some examples.

Family Rosaceae The apple-blossom flowers of *Chaenomeles* (japonica) which have a delightful colour range of reds, pinks and white, later develop into quince-like fruits. Those of *C. cathayensis* can be particularly large, while those of *C. x superba* 'Crimson and Gold' are smaller but borne in great abundance.

The smaller cotoneasters seed and germinate capriciously, and the plants may be found growing in the most unexpected spots. Projecting from walls and crevices, their profusely-borne berries are alive with colour when caught by the winter sun. *Cotoneaster* 'Cornubia' is a substantial shrub which carries bunches of large and long-lasting berries. However, it is upstaged by *C. lacteus*, whose branches weep due to the volume of fruit. *C.* 'Rothschildianus' is a heavy-fruiting evergreen with a mass of yellow fruits.

The bright red fruits of *Crataegus laciniata* (ornamental thorn) contrast with the dusky silver, cut-leaf foliage before leaf-fall. *C. prunifolia* is a good all-rounder, with clusters of holly-red fruits ending the season. Another, less common, is *C. tanacetifolia* (tansy-leaved thorn) which has large yellow fruits.

Two crab apples that are smothered with yellow and red fruits, respectively, are *Malus* 'Golden Hornet' and *M.* x *robusta*.

Other equally rewarding crab apples include *M.* 'Marshal Oyama', with golf-ball-size apples that almost weigh the tree down, 'Red Jade', with cherry-like fruits, and 'Red Sentinel', with long-lasting red fruits. These are all worthy of garden space. Long acknowledged as one of the best crabs is 'John Downie', which has large, orange-red fruits.

Mespilus germanica makes a fine specimen tree, with curious fruits that remain on the tree when they have ripened. It is better known under its common name of medlar.

Although flowering cherries are not renowned for their showy fruits, one exception is *Prunus cerasifera* (myrobalan or cherry plum) which does, indeed, produce yellow and red, cherry-like plums in favourable seasons. *P. padus* (bird cherry) bears a crop of small, shiny black fruits. *P. dulcis* (common almond) carries downy green fruits.

Pyracanthas (firethorns) especially *P. coccinea*, are seen more often than not as wall plants. *P.c.* 'Lalandei' is a better form, but its superb display of red fruits is rapidly stripped by birds, leaving only the evergreen foliage. Of two fine pyracantha hedges at Wisley, one is *P. rogersiana* 'Flava', with bright yellow berries; the other is formed by a mixture of seedlings, which glow with a mass of red, yellow and orange berries.

Crataegus tanacetifolia
This bears yellow fruits in autumn.

Malus 'John Downie'
Produces oblong, orange-red fruits, excellent for crab apple jelly.

*Euonymus
europaeus*
The deep red seed
capsules split open to
reveal orange seeds.

Celastrus orbiculatus
This climber is
outstanding in
autumn, with clusters
of glistening, red and
orange fruits.

Wild pears should be mentioned, but it cannot be claimed that their fruits rival those of the crab apple. *Pyrus pashia* may do so in quantity, but the little pears are a dull russet green. The fruits of *P. ussuriensis* emit a mouth-watering aroma, especially after they have fallen.

Rose hips are among the supreme autumn fruits, both for their striking colours and for their variety. *Rosa rugosa*, and varieties, produce tomato-shaped fruits that are just as red and almost as large. Those of *R. villosa* 'Duplex' (Wolley-Dod's rose) are similar. Flagon-shaped is how the hips of *R. moyesii* are best described, while those of *R. willmottiae* are pear-shaped and orange-red.

Two climbing roses, *R. helenae* and *R. filipes* 'Kiftsgate', display a myriad of small red fruits – a legacy of summer's breath-taking display.

Of the two main species of *Sorbus*, *S. aria* is the cinderella of the family, with fruits that are not particularly outstanding. It is to *S. aucuparia* (rowan) that we usually turn for clusters of brilliantly-coloured fruits. *S. commixta* is another fine species, with large bunches of red and orange fruits. *S.* 'Joseph Rock' is an aristocrat with a double display of superb autumn tints and deep yellow, long-lasting fruits.

The large, abundantly-produced bunches of bright red fruits borne by *S. pohuashanensis* seem, at times, almost too much for the tree. The waxy, white-flushed-pink fruits of *S. vilmorinii* offer a welcome change of colour. *S.* 'Winter Cheer' is aptly named, for the fruits last right into the colder months of the year.

Other berries Aronias are among the lesser-known shrubs, but they are worth considering for their displays of black or red berries. *A. melanocarpa* 'Brilliant' has lustrous black fruits that complement its fine autumn colouring.

Aucuba and *Skimmia* may conveniently be grouped together because of their sexual characteristics related to fruiting. In both cases, some plants produce only male flowers, which will not be followed by berries, while others have female flowers.

Aucuba japonica 'Variegata' is a female plant, as are *A.j.* 'Longifolia', *A.j.* 'Salicifolia' and *A.j.* 'Sulphurea'. Two male plants are *A.j.* 'Crassifolia' and *A.j.* 'Lance Leaf'.

The same occurs with cultivars of Skimmia japonica. For satisfactory crops of red fruits, choose *S.j.* 'Foremanii', a free-fruiting female, or else *S. reevesiana*, which is an hermaphrodite.

The barberries form a particularly large group of shrubs, with a wide range of species from which to choose. A favourite is *Berberis* 'Bunch o' Grapes', aptly named for its long bunches of small but most attractive fruits. *B. dumicola* is a strong, upright evergreen with small and sparse ovoid black fruits.

Two daphnes worth noting are *D. laureola*, with bunches of small black fruits, and *D. mezereum*, which has round, scarlet fruits clasped to upright stems. The former is evergreen, the latter deciduous.

Euonymus europaeus (spindle tree) is a small tree or shrub that carries loose, cascading bunches of four-lobed red capsules. These split to reveal the seeds inside. The capsules of 'Red Cascade' are a deeper red. Other types have pink, coral or orange seed capsules.

Celastrus orbiculatus (staff vine) which belongs to the same botanical family as *Euonymus*, shows its affinity by bearing orange capsules with red seeds. There are male and female plants, and a hermaphrodite form, all with a twining habit.

That splendid shrub for coastal gardens, *Hippophae rhamnoides*, has orange berries clustered around the base of its spiny stems. They persist right through the winter. The plant is perhaps better known by its common name of sea buckthorn.

If you would like to enjoy the winter magic of hollies, remember that male and female flowers are produced on separate plants. For a full display, a male should be planted close to female plants.

This applies even to reasonably self-fertile cultivars, such as *Ilex aquifolium* 'J.G. van Tol'. Within this species there are too many named cultivars to mention. Instead, a holly to single out is *Ilex* x *altaclarensis* 'Camelliifolia', which has bold, shiny berries set against attractive, almost spineless, foliage.

Because it is so familiar, we should not overlook *Sambucus nigra*, (common elder). It flowers and fruits plentifully as well as consistently. For a change, though, one might try *S.n.* 'Fructuluteo', which has yellow fruits, and also *S. racemosa* (red-berried elder).

Viburnum opulus (guelder rose) is a shrub widely grown for its translucent berries, but these show to particular advantage in the low-growing *V.o.* 'Compactum'. *V. tinus* (laurustinus) could not be more different, for it flowers and fruits simultaneously. During the winter, heads of small, pinky-white flowers mingle with sprays of shiny black berries.

Two named forms – 'Eve Price' and 'Gwenllian' – are especially striking.

Other fruits Not all fruits are classed as berries, even though the difference is sometimes marginal. *Arbutus unedo* (strawberry tree) for instance, carries round, strawberry-like fruits, which are often on the tree at the same time as the following year's white flowers.

Single wings of *Fraxinus* (ash) hang in clusters and are very prominent. The clustered wings of *Carpinus betulus*, (hornbeam) look very much like a loose-growing hop. *Catalpa bignonioides* (Indian bean tree) has seed pods, resembling beans, that last all through the winter. Most striking of all the pod-bearing species, however, is *Cercis siliquastrum* (Judas tree) which, in a good year, is festooned with innumerable dusky-brown pods that last well into spring.

The blue berries of the shrub *Clerodendrum trichotomum* var. *fargesii* open from red calyces. *Leycesteria formosa*, a compact

Arbutus unedo
The edible orange-red, strawberry-like fruits are often retained until the next autumn crop of white flowers.

shrub with drooping branches, has dark brown berries.

Colutea arborescens, a deciduous shrub, and *Koelreuteria paniculata*, a small deciduous tree, both have similar bladder-type fruits, though not on young specimens of *Koelreuteria*.

The blue fruits of *Decaisnea fargesii*, which needs protection, might be described as a cross between a bean and a sausage. *Gaultheria procumbens* is a low-growing shrub with bright red berries. It makes a useful plant for ground cover.

Gleditsia triacanthos (honey locust) is a medium-size tree that bears twisted, dark brown seedpods right through the winter. Two other pod-bearers are *Laburnum* and *Robinia pseudoacacia* (false acacia/black locust), the fruits in both cases being of a rusty colour and split open to reveal the seeds.

Pernettya mucronata, a dense evergreen shrub, carries clusters of white to purple globular fruits right through the winter. For good berrying, set several plants close together.

Finally, the so-called snowberries have a quite distinctive texture. One of them, *Symphoricarpos orbiculatus*, has round, purple fruits clustered along the stems. *S.* x *doorenbosii* 'Mother of Pearl' is a heavy cropper, with fruits of a colour that evoke its name. *S.* x *d.* 'White Hedge' has small white berries.

Gleditsia triacanthos
The long and twisted, glossy brown seed pods stay on the bare branches through winter.

Acer grosseri hersii
This tree has richly white-marbled bark, and crimson-red autumn colours.

Betula papyrifera
The glistening white bark peels off in large flakes.

Winter is the time when eye-catching bark comes into its own. Often, it is the colour that demands attention; or it may be some aspect of the markings or texture that draws the eye during those long, leafless months. Whatever the particular appeal, these are certainly qualities to consider when choosing trees and shrubs, for the effect is much longer-lasting than that of a brief flush of flowers.

It should be noted, however, that in some instances the best colour is seen only on mature specimens, and that judicious pruning can enhance it.

Unfortunately, the full effect may be marred by a heavy growth of moss and lichen. On a small scale, scrubbing may be the answer to this problem. Spraying with a tar-oil winter wash is another possible solution, provided the position is such that other plants will not be harmed. Be sure to follow the instructions on the container.

TREES

The birch is justly prized for its delicate outline, but there are some species with bark that is no less striking. *Betula x koehnei* vies closely with *B. jacquemontii* for whiteness of trunk and stem, though the latter must surely be the more dazzling, even at an early stage in its growth.

These are not the only species of *Betula* with attractive white bark. Some are more readily obtainable than others, while not all become really striking until they reach full maturity.

B. papyrifera (paper birch or canoe birch) has paper-thin layers that lift off very easily. *B. costata* tends towards a creamy-white, while *B. utilis*, although often described as dark brown or copper-coloured, does in some cases show lighter shades. *B. albo-sinensis* and *B. a-s.* var. *septentrionalis*, *B. lenta* (with aromatic bark) and *B. lutea* all display shades of gold, orange and brown. The bark of the last-named peels attractively.

In contrast to these, *B. nigra* (river birch) has a shaggy coat which is quite arresting, especially in a multi-stemmed specimen.

Among the maples, there is a distinctive range of snake barks, which display a characteristic white striation, or marbled effect. Of these, the most popular are *Acer capillipes*, *A. davidii*, *A. grosseri*, *A. grosseri* var. *hersii* and *A. pensylvanicum*. Even young trees show these markings, so they can be selected at the nursery to suit personal preference. For a specimen tree in a lawn it would be hard to beat *Acer griseum* (paperbark maple).

There are two flowering cherries with bark worthy of note. *Prunus maackii* (Manchurian cherry) flakes and is a shiny golden-brown. Similar, and probably more common, is *P. serrula*, with new bark that is a deeper red-brown, and polished.

Eucalyptus excel in their bark effects, but there are only a few that are sufficiently hardy to be grown in the British Isles – and then only in favoured localities. *E. dalrympleana* forms a large tree, with a patchwork of creams, greys and browns on the trunk. Periodically, the bark detaches itself and slips to the ground like a cast-off skirt.

E. niphophila (snow gum) is much smaller, but the trunk markings are no less spectacular. Brown is predominant in the bark of *E. gunnii*, one of the hardier species, but it is no less attractive for that.

Eucalyptus lend themselves to 'stooling' (cutting back annually), creating a multi-stemmed tree. This gives the double advantage of keeping the tree within bounds and displaying a greater surface of bark.

Two stewartias – *S. koreana* and *S. pseudocamellia* – have remarkable flaking bark. Its shades of dark brown form a random pattern with the lighter shades of brown beneath.

The shrubby *Parrotia persica* and *Cornus kousa* both have scabby bark – more attractive than it may sound – but this is often discoloured by moss and lichen. Much the same effect, but on a greater scale, is seen on *Platanus x hispanica* (London plane).

Arbutus unedo and *A. x andrachnoides* have bold, twisting trunks of mahogany-red, with stripping flakes. The older the tree, the better the effect.

The young twigs of some trees show to advantage in winter, especially when seen against a clear blue sky. Those of large willows excel in this respect.

Among maples, *Acer cappadocicum* 'Rubrum' and *A. palmatum* 'Senkaki' have young shoots that are red – the former blood-red and the latter coral-red. The young growths of *A. pensylvanicum* 'Erythrocladum' are shrimp-pink, with lighter striations.

Alnus incana 'Aurea' has young shoots that are yellow, while those of *Populus alba* (white poplar) and *P. canescens* (grey poplar) are silvery white.

The texture of bark is a subject in itself. Familiar examples are the deeply-fissured bark of oak trees and the older willows, together with the spiralling fissures of the sweet chestnut. The twisted and furrowed brown and grey bark of *Robinia pseudoacacia* is particularly fascinating, as is the corrugated bark of *Corylus colurna* (Turkish hazel).

Although conifers are of interest in all seasons, some show up particularly well in winter, when low sunlight can penetrate their canopy and highlight the warm reds of their trunks. Of particular note are *Sequoiadendron giganteum*, *Pinus sylvestris* and *P. radiata*. Whether a plantation or a single specimen, *Picea abies* looks superb when picked out by the sun in this way.

Finally, the growth of some trees and shrubs is twisted, giving an intriguing outline or form. Two examples are *Corylus avellana* 'Contorta' (corkscrew hazel) and *Robinia pseudoacacia* 'Tortuosa', both having curiously twisted stems and branches.

SHRUBS

Some of the dogwoods – notably *Cornus alba* and *C.a.* 'Westonbirt' – have brilliant red stems in winter. Both species appreciate the moist soil at the margin of pools and streams. For the best results, cut the stems to near ground level each spring, and apply a fertilizer and mulch to encourage fresh growth for the coming season.

Certain forms of willow should be treated in much the same way, except that the 'stooling' (cutting down) and feeding is done every other year. The varieties in question are *Salix alba* 'Chermesina' (scarlet willow) and *S.a.* 'Vitellina' (golden willow), the common names aptly describing the stem colouring.

Needing similar treatment, but less well known, are *S. daphnoides* (violet willow) and *S. irrorata*, both with purple stems which become covered with a white bloom as they age. They associate well with the other willow varieties, providing a pleasing contrast.

Perovskia atriplicifolia (Afghan sage) is a small shrub of architectural elegance. Throughout the winter it bears a myriad of blue-grey shoots which, like the willows and dogwoods, need cutting down in the spring.

A mass of white-stemmed blackberries can be an arresting sight, an effect achieved by *Rubus biflorus*, *R. cockburnianus* and *R. thibetanus*. As with cultivated blackberries, the old stems should be cut out to allow new growths to mature for the next season's display. This should be accompanied by feeding.

Neillia longiracemosa is a less well-known but graceful shrub, attaining a height of about 1.8 m (6 ft) and with russet-coloured young shoots. Each year, to encourage fresh growth, cut out a few stems from the base of the plant in spring.

Prickles are seldom of visual merit, but there is an exception. *Rosa sericea* f. *pteracantha*, syn. *Rosa* omeiensis, is a strong-growing rose with long, arching stems. Its young shoots and thorns are deep red, and this effect lasts to some extent during the winter. The thorns positively glow when seen against a low sun.

Perovskia atriplicifolia
This shrub produces young, blue-grey stems.

Cornus alba
The creamy-white flower clusters are less conspicuous than the bare, bright red winter stems.

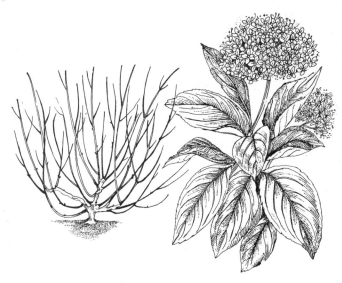

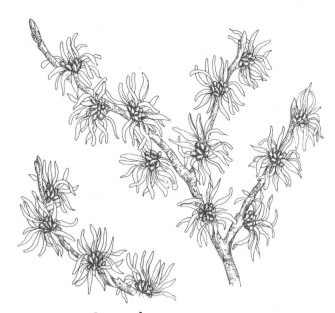

Hamamelis mollis
Rich yellow, strongly sweet-scented flowers smother the bare branches in winter.

There is no need for any garden to be devoid of interest during the winter. There are many fine trees and shrubs that flower between November and March, and these are a particularly welcome sight if they can be seen from indoors.

Unfortunately, the flowers may be damaged by cold, especially if freezing temperatures are accompanied by a strong wind. The lower the temperature and the longer the cold spell lasts, the more the flowers will suffer.

Obviously, shelter from the worst of the wind will help considerably. Damage will also be minimized if winter-flowering species are planted where the early morning sun cannot shine on them for, to camellias and rhododendrons in particular, it is rapid thawing that does the damage. A slow day-temperature rise will make all the difference.

Again, plants that carry a good many flowers over an extended period are preferable to those that bear fewer, perhaps larger, blooms. For example, *Lonicera* x *purpusii* carries many creamy-white, scented flowers throughout the winter, and those in tight bud are unharmed. In contrast, camellias have fewer flowers and these may all be open – and therefore vulnerable – at the same time.

Winter-flowering plants must continue to set their seeds even under the most unpromising conditions. Hazels are among those that bear catkins, which allow the wind to perform the task of transferring pollen. Other plants produce flowers with a very strong scent so as to attract the few insects that are still about.

One practical point to note is that any pruning of winter-flowering species should be carried out as soon as possible after flowering to allow for regrowth of shoots that will carry next year's display.

Deciding what to grow Perhaps the most frequently seen winter-flowering shrub is *Viburnum tinus*, which has been grown since the 16th century. There are several cultivars, including 'Eve Price', which has carmen buds opening to pink flowers, and 'French White', which is stronger-growing but perhaps a little more tender. *V. tinus* and its cultivars are evergreen, with dark green leathery leaves, although there is also a variegated form.

Viburnum farreri, syn. *V. fragrans*, is sweetly scented, starting to flower in early winter and continuing, between frosts, until after Christmas. Another worth considering is *V.* x *burkwoodii*, which carries on flowering where *V. farreri* leaves off. It, too, is sweetly scented.

No winter garden would be complete without a *Hamamelis* (witch hazel). The earliest to flower is *H. virginiana*, but this is less worthy of space than *H. mollis*, which is next to flower and is strongly scented. Two good forms of the latter are 'Coombe Wood', which has larger flowers, and 'Pallida', which is a lighter yellow and slightly later.

Hamamelis x *intermedia*, a cross between *H. japonica* and *H. mollis*, has given rise to many cultivars, of which 'Jelena' is one of the best. The flowers are coppery-red to orange in colour, and the shrub also provides a good show of autumn colour. *Hamamelis japonica* gives rise to perhaps the latest-flowering form, which is called 'Zuccariniana' and has pale sulphur-yellow flowers.

Hamamelis are particularly worthwhile plants, for most give a good show of flowers each year yet do not require much attention. The spider-like flowers are resistant to frost, and although, individually, not very striking, they show up well on the bare branches.

There are several daphnes worth planting. One is *D. mezereum*, which is a small, deciduous shrub that bears deep purple flowers followed by red berries. There is also a white form with translucent amber berries; the only drawback of both plants is that they are relatively short-lived.

Daphne odora is a slightly less hardy shrub, though evergreen. The sweetly-scented flowers are carried in terminal clusters, and the same is true of *D. odora* 'Aureomarginata', which has yellow leaf margins. Another evergreen, *D. pontica*, has green flowers, which appear towards the end of March.

There is a wide choice of *Prunus* species, but one outstanding plant is *Prunus subhirtella* 'Autumnalis', which flowers on and off throughout the winter. It makes a small tree, eventually, with numerous small flowers along its bare branches.

Also well worth growing are the Japanese apricots, which have typical Japanese names. One is *Prunus mume* 'Benichidori', which in late March bears double, rich pink, fragrant flowers. *P. m.* 'Omoi-no-mama' flowers at the same time, but has white flowers with occasional pink petals.

Although rhododendrons are dealt with elsewhere, there are a few worth mentioning here. In January, *R. mucronulatum* gives its all. Being deciduous, its rose-purple flowers are seen to full advantage.

For a March display there are many hybrids from which to choose: *R.* 'Bric-a-Brac' is an evergreen with white flowers that have brown stamens, the latter providing a striking contrast to the white; *R.* 'Seta' and *R.* 'Tessa Roza' do not grow to much more than 90 cm (3 ft) high and both have shell-pink flowers.

R. Nobleanum is one of the earliest to flower – before Christmas in a favourable season. It is much larger than the others and needs to be sited well back in a border.

Mahonias deserve space because, being evergreen, the leaves provide a background for other plants as well as for their own yellow flowers. *M. japonica* has yellow, fragrant, lily-of-the-valley-like flowers in terminal spikes. The leaves will colour up as well in a sunny site.

M. lomariifolia is another worthwhile species. It, too, is fragrant although slightly less hardy. Perhaps the most widely-grown of all, *M.* x 'Charity' carries long racemes of scented, deep yellow flowers and has dark green toothed leaflets. Any mahonia that outgrows its site can be cut back hard, for it will break again with new growth.

Camellias can be a good choice if the soil is acid. It is important to choose a position shaded from morning sunshine. *C. sasanqua* is perhaps the earliest to flower, starting even before the winter but continuing for a long time. The most reliable is a scented cultivar named 'Narumi-gata'.

Camellia x *williamsii* has given rise to many worthwhile cultivars. Two that should be mentioned are 'J.C. Williams', which is phlox-pink with yellow stamens, and 'Francis Hanger', a single white. One last camellia to note is 'Cornish Snow', which bears many small white flowers along its branches.

Of the other genera that flower during the winter, *Lonicera* x *purpusii* carries its flowers all along bare branches for several months. *Chimonanthus praecox* (winter sweet) has sweetly-scented flowers which are yellow and bell-shaped. *Salix daphnoides* has a white bloom on its bare stems, and silvery catkins in March.

Salix daphnoides
In early spring, the young violet stems are studded with silvery male catkins.

Camellia x *williamsii*
Named cultivars begin their glorious display of white or pink blooms in late winter.

Ribes sanguineum
Flowering currants, including *Ribes sanguineum*, do well on even heavy soils.

Clay soils are notoriously difficult for the gardener, but once improved by careful cultivation and liberal dressings of organic matter there are few plants that will not thrive. What was heavy, cold and wet becomes a very fertile growing medium.

Although clay may sometimes appear to be coarse and lumpy, the opposite is true. It is made up of very fine particles that stick together in an almost impenetrable mass. Water fills the tiny spaces between the particles, saturating the ground, in contrast to the free-draining qualities of a sandy soil made up of much coarser particles.

Evaporation from this wet mass has a cooling effect – just as one's own body cools after a swim – so coldness as well as wetness is a characteristic of clay, with an extreme reluctance to warm up in spring. Attention to drainage may be the first need, but improvements to the soil structure then follow a well-established pattern. It should be clearly understood that clay may be either acid or alkaline, depending on the locality of the garden.

Meanwhile, anyone who acquires poor clay will wish to press on with planting trees and shrubs, which are relatively slow to mature, rather than first spending years improving the soil. Fortunately, there is a good selection of species that will tolerate cold, wet conditions, provided the soil is not continuously waterlogged.

Trees All the following genera will cope quite well with cold, wet conditions *Acer* (maple); *Aesculus* (horse chestnut); *Alnus* (alder); *Betula* (birch); *Carpinus* (hornbeam); *Crataegus* (ornamental thorn); *Fraxinus* (ash); *Ilex* (holly); *Laburnum*; *Malus* (crab apple); *Populus* (poplar); *Prunus* (flowering cherry); *Quercus* (oak); *Salix* (willow); *Sorbus* (whitebeam), rowan and mountain ash; *Tilia* (lime).

Some of these are suitable only for large gardens, but many are compact enough to have a place in smaller gardens.

Alders, in particular, are closely associated with cold, moist soils, but some will not thrive in alkaline soil. Among those more tolerant to lime, making them good all-rounders, are *Alnus cordata*, *A. glutinosa* and *A. viridis*. *A. glutinosa* 'Imperialis' is a particularly attractive cut-leaf form of the common alder.

Where space permits clumps of *Betula pendula* (common silver birch) provide a striking effect. *B.p.* 'Dalecarlica' (Swedish birch) is a particularly graceful beauty, having a pendulous habit more pronounced than the type.

Poplars are fast-growing, suckering trees suitable for clay soils. *Populus* x *candicans* 'Aurora' is a medium-sized tree with attractively variegated leaves. Because variegation diminishes as the tree matures, hard pruning is needed to encourage the young growths that will maintain this decorative feature.

If you have space for an oak, our two native trees, *Quercus petraea* and *Q. robur*, will both grow in clay, but the former is to be preferred for soils that remain more or less permanently moist. An even better choice is *Q. nigra* (water oak), which is relatively small but needs a lime-free soil. However, it may not be so easy to obtain as the other two.

Shrubs With their roots closer to the surface than those of trees, shrubs are likely to benefit somewhat sooner from improvements made to the condition of the soil. Mulching is valuable, for it will help to reduce the degree of shrinking and cracking as the soil dries out.

Suitable shrubs may be divided roughly into two – those (Group A) suitable for growing in unimproved clay and others (Group B) that may be chosen when conditions improve or if given a good start in individual planting holes liberally supplied with compost.

Group A First-stage shrubs include *Aucuba*; *Berberis* (barberry); *Diervilla*; *Forsythia*; *Kerria*; *Philadelphus* (mock orange); *Pyracantha*; *Ribes* (flowering currant); *Spiraea*; *Symphoricarpos*; *Viburnum*.

Some individual species are described elsewhere, and the following are especially worth considering in the present context.

Of the several named forms of *Aucuba japonica*, a shrub often planted in difficult situations, *A.j.* 'Nana Rotundifolia', is a small female version that berries freely.

The various species of *Berberis*, both

evergreen and deciduous, will do well provided the soil is not waterlogged. A particular favourite is *B. darwinii*, an evergreen that displays masses of deep orange-yellow flowers in April and May.

Colutea arborescens (bladder senna) derives its common name from its inflated seedpods. Though rather large, growing to 4 m (13 ft), it may be pruned hard in late winter. Alternatively, if you are able to buy *C.a.* 'Bullata', this will prove denser and will grow more slowly.

There is more choice in forsythias than many realize. 'Beatrix Farrand', 'Karl Sax' and 'Lynwood' have canary-yellow flowers, those of the first-named measuring up to 2.5 cm (1 in) across. 'Arnold Dwarf' has a fairly compact habit, with a height and spread of about 90 cm × 1.8 m (3 ft × 6 ft). However, the rather sparse flowers are not particularly striking and the plant is sometimes used as ground cover.

Ribes sanguineum, a widely grown flowering currant, has several named clones. Two of the most popular are 'King Edward VII', with deep crimson flowers, and 'Pulborough Scarlet', again with deep red flowers. Also worth considering are 'Album', with white flowers, 'Flore Pleno', with double rosy-red flowers, and the lovely 'Brocklebankii', with pink flowers and golden-yellow leaves.

Depending on the variety grown, viburnums offer winter flowers, autumn colour and ornamental fruits. To allow full enjoyment of the flowers, remember to plant the shrubs where they are visible from the house.

Viburnum x *bodnantense* and *V.* x *b.* 'Dawn' flower between late autumn and late winter, the white blooms being delightfully scented. During April and May, the scent of *V. carlesii* is reminiscent of *Daphne*. Two particularly striking forms of *V. plicatum* are 'Lanarth' and 'Mariesii', their widely spreading branches, giving a layered effect, displaying heads of white flowers in early summer.

Group B Three shrubs that will grow in clay soils made really free-draining are camellias, magnolias and rhododendrons.

Of the camellias, *C. japonica* and *C.* x *williamsii* have produced numerous named cultivars. The simplest way to choose is to compare young, containerized plants while they are in flower.

Magnolia x *soulangiana* also flowers while the plant is still young and it is one of the best of its genus for growing on a clay soil. There are named forms, of which 'Lennei', with late spring flowers that are rosy-purple outside and whitish inside, is a good choice. A sport of this, 'Rustica Rubra', is rich rosy-red. *M. stellata* is a good choice for small gardens.

Magnolia* x *soulangiana Flowering while still young, it tolerates clay soil unless this is shallow.

JANUARY

Protection from birds Flowering cherries are among the trees most prone to damage from birds. As evidence, the remains of bud scales may be seen where they have been dropped under the tree or bush. In serious cases this may reduce or prevent flowering during the coming year. Sprays and bird scarers may help to reduce damage, but nets draped over the branches provide the only sure protection.

Newly-planted trees Check that recently-planted trees have not been loosened by high winds or by the soil thawing after a period of frost. If they have, tread the soil firm again as soon as it is dry enough. Check, too, that ties are secure without being over-tight.

Winter wash This month, before buds begin to swell, is the safest time to apply a winter wash in order to kill insect pests and their overwintering eggs. It will also rid the bark of moss and lichen – which is particularly worthwhile in the case of trees grown for their ornamental bark. Do not apply a winter wash during frosty or windy weather.

However, the spray will also burn any nearby grass and evergreens unless these are thoroughly covered with newspapers. If the tree is in a mixed planting, it may not be worth the risk. Grass will recover in time, but moss and weeds will appear first.

Planting With the prospect of frozen, waterlogged or snow-covered soil, any tree-planting not completed by early winter is better left until the second half of February or early March. The heavier the soil, the more worthwhile it is to wait.

Choosing trees for shape Now that the silhouettes of trees are

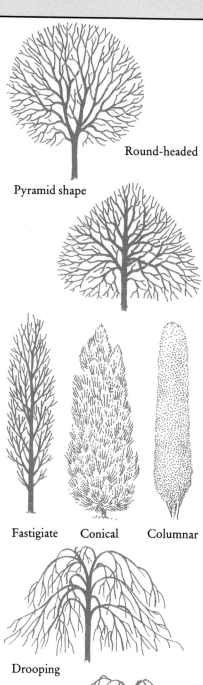

Round-headed

Pyramid shape

Fastigiate   Conical   Columnar

Drooping

Weeping

plainly visible, this is a good time to consider your choice if you are planning to plant one or more in your garden. Winter appearance is certainly a point to bear in mind, along with height, spread and rate of growth.

Some trees, such as weeping types, reveal their habit from an early stage. Others do so only as they age, but a clue may often be found in their names. 'Fastigiata' for instance, denotes an upright, narrow habit; 'Globosa' means round; 'Pyramidalis', pyramid-shaped; 'Tristis' and 'Pendula', weeping; 'Tortuosa', twisted.

However, some trees do not conform strictly to their supposed habit. For instance, a weeping laburnum is fairly constrained, retaining a mophead habit, while a weeping elm or beech is more spreading and may take over all but a really substantial garden.

It is worth noting that the height of a weeping tree can be regulated by removing the leader, and so preventing vertical growth, or by continually training upwards a strong shoot in order to gain extra height.

Another point to note is that certain varieties or cultivars are grafted on to a different rootstock, and in this case care must be taken to prevent growth from the stock from taking over. This sometimes happens with a weeping variety, the habit reverting to an upright growth. The solution is to cut out to the point of origin at the base any shoots showing signs of such reversion.

FEBRUARY

Pruning Tree surgery, especially formative pruning, should be completed by the end of this month. After this, swelling buds may be damaged by falling branches. An exception to this rule is that flowering cherries and other *Prunus* species are better left until early summer to help prevent infection by silver leaf disease. Dead, diseased, damaged or dying wood should be removed as soon as it is discovered, regardless of the time of year.

Most newly-planted trees need some formative pruning. Except in the case of multi-stemmed or weeping trees, the purpose is to ensure that the central leading shoot is kept straight and deprived of competition from secondary leaders.

To encourage straight growth it may be necessary to tie the leading shoot to a cane. If it is seriously distorted, cut it back and train in a new leader. At the same time, cut back secondary leaders in order to reduce competition.

Some ornamental apples and pears prove exceptionally vigorous, in which case the long, central shoots of each stem – those with lots of growth buds – need to be reduced by a third during the tree's earlier years. Failure to do this may result in an excessively large framework of branches. Conversely, removing the central stem will result in an open crown.

Sometimes, a tree bought as a standard will have growths emerging from the trunk or its base. Use your thumb to 'rub off' trunk growths while they are still small enough to allow this. Growths at the base of a tree can be more serious, as they may originate from the stock if it was grafted. Whether or not this is the case, remove them as soon as possible.

Major tree surgery may need the help of an expert, since it requires knowledge and experience. Chain saws, in particular, must be used with great care, and the risk of injury increases when the user is working up a tree.

Large branches should be removed in stages, mainly to prevent tearing when the final cut, nearest the trunk, is made. This last length is removed by first under-cutting it for a short distance, then cutting from the top, easing the weight with your free hand as you do so.

Planting Provided that soil conditions are suitable – neither frozen nor sticky – bare-rooted, balled and container-grown trees may be planted during the second half of the month.

MARCH

Buying trees for planting The nearer the end of the month, the greater urgency there is to complete the planting of bare-rooted trees. Make sure, however, that the ground is moist enough, if necessary watering after planting. Balled trees can be delayed for a few weeks longer (see April for details), especially if they are hessian-wrapped. Container-grown trees may be planted all the year round, subject to weather and soil conditions.

Types of trees Bare-rooted trees are those dug from open ground at the nursery during the dormant season. Although not in active growth, their roots must be protected from frost, drying winds and the sun. With this in mind, they are 'heeled in' at the nursery or their roots covered with a suitable material. Until safely planted, they must be given the same care by the purchaser – including during the journey home on a car roof-rack.

Balled trees have their roots encased in a ball of soil, the latter generally wrapped in a material such as hessian. This method is used fairly widely for both trees and shrubs with fibrous root systems, but because of the combined weight of tree and soil, professional transportation is recommended.

Container-grown trees may not always be exactly what they seem. Bare-rooted trees that remain unsold may either be replanted in nursery rows or, after drastic root pruning, placed in large pots. Until their roots grow sufficiently to fill and consolidate the soil in the containers – and this may take a full growing season – they should be called 'containerized'.

Planting a containerized specimen may result in the soil falling away from the fine hair roots. If this is done once the tree has started into growth, one is, in effect, planting a bare-rooted tree out of season.

Should this happen, the setback can be reduced by prompt planting followed by generous watering. Spraying with water will help, too, if done morning and evening and when the sun is obscured. There are proprietary sprays to reduce transpiration and therefore consequent wilting.

When buying at a nursery or garden centre you will find that container-grown trees look and feel more solid in their pots than those that are merely encased in containers.

Purchased trees
Trees sold during the dormant season are either bare-rooted (below left) or with the soil ball wrapped in hessian (centre). Container-grown plants (right) may be bought in any season.

APRIL

Planting It is now too late to plant or move bare-rooted trees. Container-grown trees may be planted at any time (see June), subject to suitable weather and soil conditions, and balled trees may be planted until about the middle of the month.

Planting balled trees The less a balled tree is moved about the better, for this may disturb the root ball. If the ball is wrapped in hessian, retain the protective covering for as long as possible. Be sure that the width and depth of the planting hole is adequate for the roots before lowering the tree into it. Place the tree so that its shape will show to best advantage from the point where it will most often be seen.

Remove the covering from the root ball by first easing the stem and ball over to one side, drawing the wrapping from beneath, then rolling it carefully the other way to complete the process. Now replace the soil, taking care that it is in all-round contact with the ball and that there are no air pockets. Water thoroughly if the ball was at all dry before planting.

Supporting a balled tree A vertical stake might damage the roots, so some other means of support is needed. This can be a single stake driven in at an angle, well clear of the roots; three or four angled stakes driven in to form a wigwam (suitable for large trees); or two vertical stakes driven in on opposite sides of the soil ball, with a batten or strap secured between them and attached to the stem.

Frost and magnolias Frost damage to *Magnolia* blooms in April is commonplace, and there is little to be done about it once the tree is planted. However, choosing a sheltered spot, especially one in woodland, will go a long way towards avoiding this trouble. In open gardens, it is advisable to avoid east-facing sites where morning sun after night frost often results in damage to buds and blooms.

Stooling for extra large leaves An unusual effect can be achieved by stooling (also known as coppicing) certain kinds of trees – that is, cutting them back almost to the ground. As a result, latent buds near the base of the tree send up fresh shoots, and these carry extra large leaves. Much the same happens in the wild on even mature oaks and horse chestnuts when the bulk of the tree has been damaged.

Trees responding particularly well to this treatment include *Ailanthus altissima, Aralia elata, Catalpa bignonioides, Fraxinus excelsior, Paulownia tomentosa, Rhus typhina* and *Robinia pseudoacacia* 'Frisia'.

In some cases, enormous leaves develop on trees restricted to just a few shoots. Eucalyptus trees respond well, resulting in fresh juvenile foliage and a bushy habit. In all cases, the energetic growth that results needs encouraging with feeding and watering.

MAY

Weed control Keep the soil around young trees weed-free, as weeds rob the trees of moisture and nourishment. Annual weeds are best kept down with a contact weedkiller. Choose a translocated type for perennial weeds.

Watering A dry spell this month may check young trees just when they need to be making growth. Give a thorough watering before the soil has dried out, applying sufficient to get right down to the roots. Merely wetting the surface will do more harm than good.

Mulching A 15 cm (6 in) layer of well-rotted manure or spent mushroom compost spread over the surface will help to conserve moisture and suppress weeds. Remove any perennial weeds first and spread the mulch when the soil is damp from rain or watering. Black plastic has the same effect but is rather unsightly.

Feeding A feed will be beneficial during this month of active growth, especially to young trees. Although specialized fertilizers are obtainable, a dressing of Growmore at about 65 g per sq m

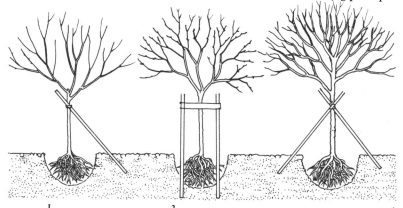

Supporting a newly planted tree
Secure the stem of a balled tree to one angled stake (1) or, for a large tree, to two stakes set as opposite sides (2). Alternatively, use upright stakes and tie the stem to a batten fastened between them (3).

(2 oz per sq yd) will suffice. Rake this into the surface and water thoroughly.

Removing stem growths If small growths appear on the trunks or base of newly-planted trees, rub these off with your thumb.

Pests Watch carefully for pests, especially for a build-up of aphids on the genus *Euonymus*. Spray as advised in *Plant and Soil Pests*.

JUNE

Check ties With young trees growing actively at this season, it is essential to examine ties regularly in case they become too tight. Some proprietary ties allow for a certain amount of expansion, but both these and twine may bite into the cambium layer unless slackened periodically.

Planting container-grown trees Trees grown in plastic containers, unlike those that are merely containerized, may be planted right through the growing season. Take care not to damage the foliage.

Moisture is the key point. Having taken out and prepared the planting hole (see November), fill it once or twice with water, allowing this to completely drain away before planting.

Plant the tree during dull weather, if possible, or else during the evening or early morning. The essential thing is to prevent the fine root hairs from being burnt, as they might be in direct sunlight. To ensure that the root ball is well soaked, stand the container in a tub of water for a short time before planting.

Often, when the plastic is cut away, it will be found that the plant is pot-bound – that is, some of the roots will have wound themselves round the inner face of the container. If this is so, tease out one or two of the longer roots away from the soil ball so that they can be laid out in the soil used to fill the space around it.

Naturally, this needs doing with care. However, if the roots of a pot-bound plant are left untouched they may continue to remain constricted, a fault that very often results in subsequent poor growth.

Stake and tie as for bare-rooted trees (see November), taking care to see that the stake does not penetrate the root ball and cause damage. During warm, dry weather, spray the leaves of any recently-planted trees with water during the evenings to help them become established.

JULY

Advice given for June also applies this month.

AUGUST

Advice given for June also applies this month.

SEPTEMBER

Feeding and watering On some trees, the following year's buds are starting to form, so they must not be allowed to suffer during a late-summer drought. This applies principally, of course, to fairly small, young trees, and these will also benefit from a high-potash feed applied before watering. If you use straight sulphate of potash, apply it at about 30 g per sq m (1 oz per sq yd). This treatment will help the wood to ripen fully and, a little later, will bring out the full autumn colours of the leaves.

OCTOBER

Preparing for planting Should you be planning a mixed planting of trees and shrubs, individually prepared planting holes will be unnecessary if the whole area is double-dug this month, with a liberal application of well-rotted manure or compost. Trees may then be planted without having to re-work the lower spit.

Root pruning Late October or November is the time for this operation, which has the object of inducing poor or non-flowering trees to bloom. Although not infallible, it sometimes works.

A trench is dug around the tree, and any thick, thongy roots are severed as they are revealed, effectively reducing the root area. Afterwards, the soil is returned to the trench and firmed into place.

Make the diameter of the trench proportionate to the size of the tree, as a rule working just within its canopy of branches. The circle around young or slender trees should not be less than 1.2 m (4 ft) in diameter. In all cases, the trench should be sufficiently deep to expose downward-growing roots.

For the tree, this can be a fairly drastic operation. To reduce the shock to large trees, spread it over two years, completing half a circle at a time. Do not allow the remaining root system to dry out during the following season, bearing in mind that the tree has, in effect, been root-balled. For the same reason, ensure that it has adequate support.

Moving a tree The process just described would also prepare a tree for removal to another site, subject to one's ability to shift the root ball. The trouble might well be justified in the case of a prized specimen.

Looking a year ahead, root-pruning a small tree – with subsequent back-filling and supporting – will result in a mass of fibrous roots developing. This would make eventual transplanting easier, especially as the root ball would be reduced in size.

NOVEMBER

Buying trees This month and next, before the soil becomes too wet and while it retains some of its summer warmth, is the ideal period for planting bare-rooted trees. (See March.)

When buying, look for a good, fibrous root system, well spread and with the stronger roots neatly cut. The roots should look plump and healthy. The bark of the trunk, too, should look plump and be free from splitting, disease or other damage.

A good main stem is straight and free from obvious kinks. The tree's head should be well balanced – that is, not growing to one side. Any grafts should look secure and healthy.

Tree forms A tree of suitable age for planting may have been trained as a bush, a half-standard or a standard, depending on the length of stem between the ground and the first branches. There are also multi-stemmed trees where, by design or accident, several main stems arise at ground level, each forming a definite leader.

Sometimes, very young trees (maidens) can be obtained or perhaps raised from seed, these having as yet no side branches and looking more like sticks emerging from the ground. From such material an enthusiast can train a tree to his or her own liking.

Planting Planting holes will have to be prepared for individual specimen trees. If these show signs of collecting and retaining water from the surrounding soil, drainage of the site must be improved before anything is planted.

Holes may be round or square, but should be large enough to lay the roots out comfortably. One measuring 0.3 m sq (4 ft sq) would not be over-generous.

In a lawn or paddock, first remove the turf and place it on one side. Good turf may be relaid; poorer turf should be dug in to the planting hole later. Dig out the topsoil and place it to one side. If the hole is insufficiently deep and will not allow the tree to be planted to its original depth, remove some subsoil and barrow it away. Take care, however, not to mix this with the topsoil.

Now dig over the subsoil, working in plenty of well-rotted manure or compost. Unless ericaceous or other lime-hating plants are to be grown, add a few handfuls of bone-meal. Firm the dug soil lightly, testing for depth by holding the tree against a piece of wood straddling the hole. The soil mark on the stem should be just below the batten.

Drive in the supporting stake or stakes before planting, remembering that a single stake should be placed on the same side as the prevailing wind, preventing the tree from damage by being blown against it. Tie the tree to it temporarily while filling the hole.

Add some peat or well-rotted compost to the topsoil when replacing it, lightly shaking the tree up and down to settle the mixture between the roots. Firm the soil at intervals. To aid watering, finish with the soil just below the level of the surrounding ground.

Adjust the height of the stake, if necessary; attach the tree-ties and also a label. If rabbits are a problem, protect the trunk with small-mesh wire netting or a proprietary tree guard.

Root pruning and moving trees These tasks, described in October, may still be undertaken during November.

DECEMBER

Advice given for November also applies this month.

Check tree-ties If this was not done at intervals during the season (see June), examine ties now in case serious damage is done.

Planting a bare-rooted tree
Position the stake before planting, setting it on the windward side. Fasten with a tie.

Specimen trees with colourful, decorative foliage are ideal for the small garden. The many attractive forms of Japanese maple (*acer*), which reach a height of about 20 ft (6.1 m), are most suitable.

Slow-growing, spreading plants that need a minimum of maintenance, such as ivy (*hedera*), make ideal ground cover in large beds, particularly in shady patches under trees or shrubs.

The huge variety of heathers available – a multitude of sizes and colours, with a range of habits and flowering times – often surprises those who have not grown them.

Foliage shrubs provide year-round colour and interest, and are useful in garden planning, as here, as a screen to provide privacy or conceal unattractive garden features such as a compost heap.

A well-chosen hedge enhances a garden in a number of ways. It can afford privacy, protection from wind, hide an unsightly view, reduce traffic noise, and provide a contrasting backdrop for flowering plants.

Even a low hedge, offering none of these advantages, will define the edge of a property in a pleasing but inconspicuous way. When planting a boundary hedge, however, make sure that it will be entirely on your side of the property line, even when mature. Your neighbours have the right to cut off any growth that encroaches on their property.

With such a wide choice of potential hedging plants, selection is worth some thought. For a start, you must take account of the type of soil and also the position – whether it is dry or wet, sunny or shady. Next, how tall a hedge do you require and how quickly do you wish it to grow? Is the hedge to provide protection from the wind or is its purpose mainly ornamental?

Closely-clipped hedges look well in formal surroundings and may be the best choice between front garden and pavement. There are many species, however, that thrive on lighter trimming, which allows them to display flowers and berries that might otherwise be lost. Evergreen hedges retain their colour and screening qualities throughout the winter, conifers, in particular, making a dense, if rather gloomy, barrier. Among deciduous hedges, beech and hornbeam hold on to their tinted autumn foliage throughout the colder months.

A hedge's effect on other plants should be considered, too. Depending on its position, a tall, dense hedge may cut out light and reduce air circulation. All but very small hedges take moisture and nourishment from quite a large area of soil, often starving plants in an adjacent border.

Finally, remember that a number of conifers form excellent hedges, some making very rapid growth and acting as effective windbreaks.

Planting Shrubs and conifers used for hedges and screens are sold in a number of different forms. This has a direct bearing on when they should be planted.

Deciduous plants are often supplied 'bare-rooted', that is, lifted directly from a nursery bed and without any protective soil around their roots. These are available during the autumn and winter and may be planted at any time from the second half of October until the end of March, provided the soil is neither sticky nor frozen.

Bare-rooted evergreens may be planted until about the end of November, subject to suitable weather and soil conditions, but

Formal hedges
If chosen with care, hedges can be incorporated happily into any size or shape of garden, where they will provide both vertical and horizontal interest.

Dense clipped hedge of *Prunus laurocerasus*

Tall barrier hedge of *Taxus baccata*

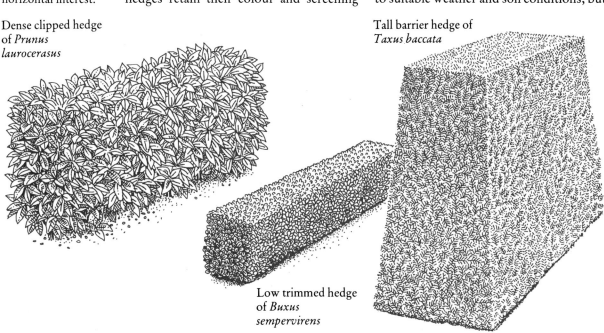

Low trimmed hedge of *Buxus sempervirens*

after this it is better to wait until the following April or May. Mid-winter planting often results in losses.

The same applies to conifers and evergreens supplied with their roots and a surrounding ball of soil wrapped in hessian. The purpose is to reduce dehydration between lifting and planting, and every effort should be made to retain the soil-ball intact when planting.

Container-grown plants, whether deciduous or evergreen, may be planted at any time of year when soil and weather conditions allow. They are usually supplied in black polythene pots, and should not be confused with plants that have simply been placed in a bag or pot after being lifted.

Trimming and pruning Pruning and shaping of hedges varies with the type of shrub, and details are given in the descriptive list, but here are some general points.

If the height of the hedge is to be restricted, remove the leading shoot a little before it reaches the height required. As an example, for a hedge that is to be 1.8 m (6 ft) high, the leader should be removed at about 1.7 m (5½ ft).

Trim the sides as required, always shaping them so that the base is a little wider than the top, which helps to prevent damage from snow. To help deciduous hedges thicken-up at the base, remove the leader at an early stage and shorten side growth.

Secateurs, which allow more precise cutting, are the most suitable tool for pruning conifers and for all informal hedges. Hand shears are quicker for yew, privet and honeysuckle, but a mechanical trimmer may be used instead, if you wish, for most formal hedges.

Hedging plants

Berberis darwinii. This beautiful, early-flowering barberry makes a dense, evergreen hedge. It has deep yellow flowers in spring and grows up to 1.5 m (5 ft) high. Though it may be cut with shears, secateurs help to maintain a more informal appearance. Cut back after flowering, removing one third of the flowered wood. It is fairly fast-growing. Plant 60 cm (2 ft) apart in an open site. It will grow in most soils.

B. thunbergii 'Atropurpurea'. This deciduous cultivar makes a superb hedge if trimmed with care. Its reddish-purple young shoots and foliage deepen as autumn approaches; it bears yellow flowers and red berries, and it makes an effective barrier up to 1.5 m (5 ft) high. It is best kept as an informal hedge, pruning with secateurs in late summer when necessary. Fairly fast-growing. Plant 60 cm (2 ft) apart in an open site. It will grow in most soils.

Buxus sempervirens (common box). A rigid evergreen that makes a dense hedge up to whatever height is needed. If cut with shears in July, a single annual trim is generally adequate. Rather slow-growing. Plant 45 cm (1½ ft) apart.

B.s. 'Suffruticosa' (edging box) is a dwarf form used mainly as an edging to paths and beds, especially in formal settings. Plant 30 cm (1 ft) apart. It will grow in any position except dense shade, and tolerates most soils.

Carpinus betulus (hornbeam). Although deciduous, the growth is dense enough to create an effective barrier throughout the year. The hedge will easily reach a height of 2.4 m (8 ft). Plant in a single row 45 cm (1½ ft) apart, or, if a really dense hedge is required, plant alternately in a double row, with 30 cm (1 ft) between the rows. Cut with shears twice a year for the first few years to thicken the hedge. In subsequent years a single trimming in late July should be sufficient.

Buxus sempervirens

If the hedge becomes too wide, cut it hard back with secateurs while dormant, first on one side and then, the following year, on the other. Speed of growth is up to 60 cm (2 ft) a year once the plants are established. Does best on an open site with good air circulation. Prefers a light, acid soil.

Cornus mas (cornelian cherry). If grown singly, it forms a large, deciduous shrub, but planted 60 cm (2 ft) apart it will also make a dense and compact hedge up to 2.1 m (7 ft) high. In late winter – February as a rule – its bare branches are covered with tiny, yellowish flowers. Later in the year, bright red edible fruits appear; in the autumn the foliage turns a reddish-purple.

Trim the hedge in the spring after flowering, using secateurs, to encourage the maximum number of flowers. Growth is 45–60 cm (1½–2 ft) a year and the plants should be set 45–60 cm (1½–2 ft) apart. It will grow in partial shade or an open position and in any well-prepared soil.

Corokia x *virgata.* A medium-sized evergreen shrub, of erect habit, that makes an attractive hedge, either formal or informal. It may not be entirely hardy in the coldest areas. The foliage is deep green above and almost white beneath. Small, yellowish flowers appear in June, followed by bright orange fruits in the autumn.

During July or August, cut formal hedges with shears, informal ones with secateurs. Speed of growth is about 45 cm (1½ ft) a year. Plant 38 cm (15 in) apart.

Hedging plants (cont.)

Cotoneaster franchetii. Although not widely grown as a hedge, it looks most effective and grows to a height of 1.8–2.7 m (6–9 ft). This is a semi-evergreen shrub, many of the leaves turning orange and scarlet in the autumn. Small, pinkish flowers are borne in clusters during June, followed by orange-scarlet fruits throughout the autumn and winter. It thrives in most positions and soils, including areas in moderate shade, but is susceptible to fireblight.

Trimming is best carried out with secateurs, as needed, in June after flowering, cutting back to expose berries to light. Speed of growth is up to 60 cm (2 ft) annually. Plant 45 cm (1½ ft) apart.

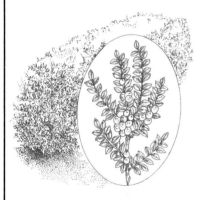

Cotoneaster franchetti

Crataegus monogyna (common hawthorn). A hardy and adaptable deciduous tree, tolerating industrial pollution and also withstanding high winds near the coast. When established it will survive extremes of dryness and moisture. As a hedge, it will eventually grow up to 2.4 m (8 ft) high.

White flowers appear in May and June, with red fruits following later. Prune with shears in July when the fruits have set, taking care not to remove the berries. Speed of growth is rather slow. Plant 50–60 cm (20–24 in) apart. It does best in an open, sunny spot. Provided the soil is well prepared, it tolerates alkaline and acid conditions. Susceptible to fireblight.

Elaeagnus x *ebbingei.* A fairly fast-growing evergreen shrub. Its large leaves are dark green but have silvery undersides, giving a most spectacular effect when moved by the wind. The whitish flowers, which appear during the autumn, are inconspicuous, but they draw attention by their gardenia-like perfume.

This is a wind-resistant shrub, which may be grown either as a hedge or as a shelter belt even in seaside areas. It will reach a height of about 3 m (10 ft). Trimming is best carried out with secateurs during the summer if grown as a hedge, but little trimming is needed for a windbreak. Speed of growth is up to 75 cm (2½ ft) annually. Place hedging plants 60 cm (2 ft) apart, those for a windbreak 90 cm–1.2 m (3–4 ft). Water young plants frequently during dry weather.

Escallonia. These lovely shrubs make excellent, dense hedges, being especially suitable for seaside gardens in the south and west. Two of the best cultivars for hedging (both evergreens) are 'C. F. Ball' and 'Langleyensis'. The former, which bears red flowers throughout the summer, can grow up to 2.4 m (8 ft) high. 'Langleyensis' has pink flowers in June and July and grows to about the same height. Both are best restricted to about 1.5 m (5 ft).

An informal growth habit is best, otherwise many of the flowers will be lost. Prune lightly after flowering. Growth of these shrubs is about 45 cm (1½ ft) a year, and they should be planted about 60 cm (2 ft) apart. They will grow in any well-drained soil and in an open position.

Fagus sylvatica 'Riversii' (purple beech). Although a number of variants are suitable for hedging, *F.s.* 'Riversii' is recommended for its deep purple foliage and spectacular autumn tints. It will form a dense, deciduous hedge that can grow up to 2.4 m (8 ft) high, and will thrive on a

Elaeagnus x *ebbingei*

chalk soil. Trim once or twice a year – in late June and, if necessary, in late August – with shears or a mechanical trimmer. Growth is steady rather than rapid, and the planting distance is 45 cm (1½ ft). Plant in any well-drained soil, in an open position.

Genista hispanica (Spanish gorse). A good choice for a sunny position, such as a dry bank. It forms a dense, deciduous barrier up to about 60 cm (2 ft) high. A mass of yellow flowers are borne during May and June. This plant grows slowly, and little pruning or trimming is needed for the first two or three years. After this, retain the shape by removing over-long growths with secateurs. The planting distance is 45 cm (1½ ft).

Escallonia 'C. F. Ball'

Hibiscus syriacus. This could be the answer if you are looking for something rather unusual. It forms an informal, deciduous hedge, with beautiful blue flowers appearing in late autumn. The growth is upright, reaching about 1.8 m (6 ft). Little or no pruning is needed. Established plants grow only 8–10 cm (3–4 in) a year. Plant 75 cm (2½ ft) apart. Although quite hardy, this hibiscus flowers more freely in the south of England than it does further north. There are a number of named forms of *Hibiscus syriacus* with variously coloured flowers.

Ilex aquifolium (common holly). Possibly the most durable of all hedging plants, the several varieties of holly will grow almost anywhere. A dense hedge, of any desired height, can be formed by sensible pruning, a single trimming with shears in July being sufficient in most years. Holly grows about 8–10 cm (3–4 in) a year when established. Plant bushes about 60 cm (2 ft) apart.

Hedging plants (cont.)

Ligustrum vulgare (common privet). Still widely planted because of its rapid growth, the variegated forms are more attractive than the familiar plain green. The shrub is deciduous or semi-evergreen and grows up to 4.5 m (15 ft) high if untrimmed. Otherwise it can be pruned to a height of 90 cm–1.8 m (3–6 ft).

A particularly attractive variegated privet is *L. lucidum* 'Excelsum Superbum', with creamy-white and deep yellow leaves. This species is evergreen.

Clip privet hedges with shears at least twice a year during the summer. Growth is rapid so place plants 60 cm (2 ft) apart.

Lonicera nitida

Lonicera nitida. With its dense habit, the shrub forms a thick evergreen hedge that will reach a height of 1.2–1.8 m (4–6 ft). The stems, which are not particularly rigid, may spread under snow, so it is a good idea to knock in a few short stakes, about 3.6 m (12 ft) apart, and run two strands of wire through the middle of the plants. They will soon be hidden by the dense growth. This hedge benefits from close clipping three times between late June and early autumn, but unfortunately it flowers very little in the British Isles. *L. nitida* 'Baggesen's Gold', a cultivar with golden foliage, makes a most attractive hedge. Speed of growth is rapid, but less so for *L.n.* 'Baggesen's Gold'. Plant 45 cm (1½ ft) apart.

Osmanthus delavayi. With its dark green leaves and, during April, white, fragrant flowers, this evergreen shrub forms an excellent low hedge, growing to about 1.2–1.5 m (4–5 ft). Its rather slow habit of growth makes it a good choice for an informal barrier. Prune with secateurs after flowering – late April or May – usually just to remove any long growths. It grows about 45 cm (1½ ft) a year. The planting distance is 60 cm (2 ft).

Photinia x *fraseri* 'Red Robin'. Although slightly vulnerable to extreme cold in exposed areas, this makes a most striking evergreen hedge and reaches a height of about 1.8 m (6 ft). The leaves are bright red at first, turning dark green. This colour sequence is repeated each time the hedge is trimmed – with either shears or secateurs – during June and late August. It grows about 60 cm (2 ft) a year. The young plants should be placed 60 cm (2 ft) apart. Grows in most soils and needs an open, sunny position for the foliage to show to best advantage.

Pittosporum tenuifolium. Although making a sound hedge, formal or informal, the hardiness of this evergreen shrub is suspect in cold areas. It grows to about 2.1 m (7 ft) high. The wavy-edged foliage is extensively used by florists; the flowers, which are small, brownish-purple and scented, appear in spring. Trim with shears for a formal hedge, with secateurs for an informal shape – in both cases during July. It grows 45 cm (1½ ft) or more annually. Plant 60 cm (2 ft) apart, preferably in spring.

Prunus cerasifera (cherry plum). Forming an excellent wind break, this shrub is easily maintained and forms a thick barrier up to 3 m (10 ft) high. An added bonus, following the white blossom in spring, are the palatable fruits that form in late summer. Trim during July with shears or a mechanical trimmer. Speed of growth is 45–60 cm (1½–2 ft) annually; the planting distance 90 cm (3 ft).

Prunus laurocerasus (cherry laurel or common laurel). A vigorous, wide-spreading evergreen, reaching 6 m (20 ft) in height. It has dark green, leathery leaves, and showy racemes of white flowers during April. These are followed by red, cherry-like fruits which eventually turn black. It makes an effective informal hedge, growing in shade and even tolerating the drip from overhanging trees. It will grow in most soils, except possibly very shallow, chalky types. There are numerous named forms with different habits and leaves.

Trim with secateurs during July. Growth is quite rapid at first, slowing down as the plants mature. For a dense hedge about 2.1 m (7 ft) high, plant 90 cm–1.2 m (3–4 ft) apart. For a taller, informal barrier, allow 1.5 m (5 ft) between plants.

Pyracantha rogersiana (firethorn). Related to the *Cotoneaster*, this evergreen shrub is easily distinguished by its thorny branches and serrated leaves. It will tolerate cold winds, shade and atmospheric pollution, and will grow in all types of fertile soil, forming a dense hedge up to 2.1–2.4 m (7–8 ft) high. Unfortunately, it is susceptible to fireblight.

Hawthorn-like flowers appear in early summer, while during late autumn there is a fine display of brilliant reddish-orange berries. If pruned with secateurs directly after flowering, removing only the parts of branches that have not flowered, the berries will be exposed to the weather and take on a deeper colour. Growth is 30–45 cm (1–1½ ft) a year. Plant 60 cm (2 ft) apart.

Rhododendron ponticum. Suitable for a shelter belt or hedge, this evergreen is one of the few plants that will thrive under beech trees. It grows up to 6 m (20 ft) high, but a hedge can be restricted to about 2.4 m (8 ft). During May and June there is a spectacular display of mauve and blue flowers. Trimming is best done with secateurs in late June, after flowering and before the seeds form, thus avoiding the removal of flower buds. Growth is about 30–45 cm (1–1½ ft) annually once the plant is established. The planting distance required to form a hedge is 1.2 m (4 ft). It requires lime-free soil and does best in light shade.

Rosa (rose). A few varieties lend themselves to creating informal deciduous hedges, among them 'Queen Elizabeth' (pink, flowering throughout the summer), 'Eyepaint' (a single rose, flowering all summer, with red petals that have white centre markings, and with large trusses of flowers on very stiff stems). If pruned in early March, they form attractive barriers, which can be up to about 1.5 m (5 ft) high

Prunus cerasifera

and provide a good display of hips in late autumn or early winter.

There are, too, the Penzance briars – 'Lord Penzance' and 'Lady Penzance' – both summer-flowering hedges with perfumed leaves. The flowers of the former are buff-coloured, with a pink flush; those of 'Lady Penzance' are copper-tinted with yellow centres. Both bear hips in autumn and early winter.

Pruning consists of removing dead growth whenever it is seen, cutting out old wood as necessary and making full use of young growth to thicken the hedge, tying this in when necessary. Watch for aphids, spraying as needed.

It will take about three years to form a reasonably dense hedge. Plant about 1.5 m (5 ft) apart, choosing a moderately sunny position in any average soil.

Spiraea thunbergii

Spiraea thunbergii. A medium-size, deciduous shrub with a twiggy habit. It will form quite a dense hedge in two or three years, reaching a height of 1.2 m (4 ft). White flowers are borne in clusters along the branches during March and April. Prune back as soon as flowering is completed. If a formal hedge is required, further trimming can be done during the summer, but most of the following year's flowers will be lost by cutting in this way. Plant 60 cm (2 ft) apart.

Weigela florida 'Foliis Purpureis'. This rather unusual, compact, deciduous shrub grows up to 1.8 m (6 ft) high. The young shoots are maroon-coloured, the foliage brownish – at first with prominent pale green veins. The flowers, borne in profusion during May and early June, are pink. Prune immediately after flowering, removing some of the older flowered stems completely. Growth is about 60 cm (2 ft) a year. Plant 45–60 cm (1½–2 ft) apart.

Conifers for hedging

Chamaecyparis lawsoniana 'Allumii'. This conifer, which has attractive grey foliage, will form a very dense hedge up to 1.5 m (5 ft) thick, and as tall as you wish. It is best cut with secateurs, because if trimmed with hand shears or a mechanical trimmer, the foliage will almost certainly turn brown at the edges. Do this during July or August. Growth is rapid. Plant 60 cm (2 ft) apart, if possible choosing plants that are about 90 cm (3 ft) tall. Any well-drained soil will do, and the hedge will grow in the open or in light shade. Support is needed for the first two years, especially in an exposed position, and frequent watering may be needed until the hedge is well established.

Cryptomeria japonica 'Elegans'. A beautiful conifer, with soft, feathery foliage that is retained throughout its life. During the winter this takes on an attractive bronze hue. Although rather slow-growing, its dense habit makes for a fine hedge up to any desired height. Any pruning should be done with secateurs in July or August. Plant 60 cm (2 ft) apart.

Cupressus macrocarpa 'Goldcrest'. A fast-growing tree that will form a good hedge in the course of two or three years, attaining a height of 1.8 m (6 ft) in that time. Two other varieties, with golden foliage are *C. m.* 'Gold Cone' and *C. m.* 'Donard Gold'.

The plants will need support for two or three years, especially in an exposed position. Trim with secateurs. On no account use hand shears or a mechanical trimmer, because *C. macrocarpa* will not tolerate being cut into a formal hedge. Plant 60 cm (2 ft) apart.

Podocarpus andinus (plum-fruited yew). A medium-sized tree or large shrub, evergreen, with leaves similar to those of the yew. They are bright green above, but twist to reveal a glaucous underside. The fruits, when they appear, are like small damsons. It grows slowly but will eventually form a hedge up to 2.1 m (7 ft) high. Trim in July with shears or a mechanical trimmer. Plant 53 cm (21 in) apart in any well-drained soil, including chalk.

Taxus baccata (common yew). Although the green varieties are most often chosen, the golden types ('Aurea', 'Elegantissima') make good hedges. Yew is the most tolerant of plants, growing in any type of soil, and in sunshine or shade. It forms a dense hedge, from 90 cm–3 m (3–10 ft) high, which should be clipped with hand shears in late spring. Plant 53 cm (21 in) apart. Although rather expensive to buy, a well-cared-for hedge will last indefinitely.

Thuja plicata (western red cedar). The shining green leaves are slightly grey on the underside, making an eye-catching hedge or screen that withstands clipping very well and will grow from 1.8 m (6 ft) to any height required. Trimming is best started early, preferably during the second growing season, to encourage dense growth. August is the best month, enabling any new growth to ripen before really cold weather arrives. Do not be too severe with the shears, leaving an inch or so of new growth at each cut.

The speed of growth is quite slow, at 20–30 cm (8–12 in) annually. Plant 60 cm (2 ft) apart in any well-drained soil and in a sunny but fairly sheltered position.

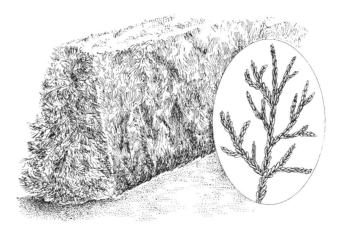

Cupressus macrocarpa

JANUARY

Established hedges Rake out fallen leaves and other debris from beneath hedges. This will expose over-wintering grubs for birds to deal with.

Remove snow from conifers and evergreens, (see December).

Cutting back Certain hedges – especially yew and privet – can be improved by cutting them back severely if they have become overgrown or developed thin patches. Provided the weather is mild, cut to within 15 cm (6 in) of the main stem. If pruning a hornbeam for the same purpose, cut back right to the main stem, or tufts of shoots will result. Prune one side one year, the other side the following year. Whatever the type of hedge, apply a general fertilizer in spring.

Pruning hedges
Overgrown hedges may be pruned hard in winter, during frost-free weather. Cut crowded shoots close to the main stem.

Roots, too, may be cut back if they are encroaching on a border. Do this with a spade, about 45 cm (1½ ft) from the centre of the hedge, thrusting the blade in vertically to its full depth along the length of the hedge. This will sever existing roots, but this will have to be repeated in subsequent years.

FEBRUARY

New hedges Plant bare-rooted, deciduous hedging plants this month in ground prepared last autumn, provided the soil is not sticky and the weather too cold. (See September and October.)

If the soil is reasonably dry, firm each plant in place with your foot. If it is on the wet side, firm it sufficiently to hold the plant secure but wait until conditions improve before completing the job.

Plant container-grown plants, subject to suitable soil and weather conditions.

If time presses, preventing you from finishing hedge planting, at least try to get flowering species, such as *Prunus cerasifera*, planted this month.

On free-draining soils, recently planted hedges may need watering during a dry period. Check whether hard frosts or high winds have loosened plants, treading them in firmly again if necessary.

Established hedges Cutting back of overgrown hedges should be completed this month.

Complete the clearance of hedge bottoms, removing weeds, fallen leaves and other debris before the beginning of another season's growth.

MARCH

New hedges Complete the planting of bare-rooted deciduous hedges by the end of this month. (See October.) Plant container-grown hedges. (See April.)

Keep an eye on newly-planted deciduous hedges, watering them if necessary. It is important not to let them dry out for the first two or three years.

If you plan to plant an evergreen hedge during April, prepare the site now. (See September and October.)

Established hedges This is the month to prune rose hedges – the first half of March in southern counties but a little later in the north. Remove any dead or weak wood and shorten remaining growths by about a third. Afterwards, spray with a fungicide as a precaution against mildew and blackspot.

Hedges that lack vigour can be stimulated with a mulch of well-rotted manure, 8 cm (3 in) deep.

APRIL

New hedges Plant evergreen and coniferous hedges and screens this month, whether the plants are bare-rooted, balled or container-grown. If the ground was not prepared last month, do this as soon as possible, following methods outlined in September and October.

In all likelihood the plants will be container-grown and it is as well to soak them thoroughly before planting. To do this, plunge each into a bucket of water and leave them until the air bubbles cease. Tease the roots out from any plants that are pot-bound.

Spray all newly-planted or pruned evergreen and coniferous hedges with water during dry weather, particularly when there are drying easterly winds.

Mulch newly-planted hedges with compost, leaving the ground bare for 15 cm (6 in) around the stems. Keep weeds under control.

Established hedges Cut back laurel hedges (*Prunus laurocerasus*) that have become overgrown. They regenerate remarkably well if pruned severely at this time.

Prune overgrown hedges of *Taxus baccata* (yew), *Ilex* (holly), and *Buxus sempervirens* (box) as soon as new buds show signs of opening. It is safe to cut back quite severely into older wood.

Prune *Spiraea thunbergii* when flowering has finished. For an informal hedge of this and other spring-flowering species, remove as much wood as possible to encourage strong new growth for carrying next year's flowers. This will allow the new wood to ripen well before the winter. Late in the month, reduce any over-long growths of *Osmanthus delavayi*.

MAY

New hedges You should complete the planting of balled evergreen and coniferous hedges this month. As a precaution against the soil drying out, fill in around the roots with a mixture of equal parts peat and soil. Unless the planting area is moist, soak it thoroughly the day before planting and again when planting is completed. If the weather remains dry, spray the hedge with water each evening.

On an exposed site, help a newly-planted hedge to become established by erecting a temporary windbreak on the windward side. Chestnut palings help to break the force of the wind, as does plastic windbreak material, sold in rolls, developed for this purpose. The object is to check and filter the wind rather than to create a solid barrier, which would result in harmful turbulence.

Established hedges When coniferous hedges have reached the height required, cut back the leaders (main stems) some 15–23 cm (6–9 in) below this level. Secondary growth developing above the cut will conceal the ugly stump.

This applies only to formal hedges, of course. Maintain informal screens by regular pruning of any protruding branches.

Hedges to prune this month, after flowering, include *Cornus mas* (cornelian cherry) and *Osmanthus delavayi*.

Moving an evergreen hedge With care, a misplaced evergreen hedge can be moved early in the month. Among others, this applies to box, laurel and yew. However, if the hedge is more than twelve years old it is advisable to prepare the plants a year in advance, using a sharp spade to cut the roots back to the proposed dimensions of the soil balls.

Having prepared the new planting position, take out a trench at each side of the hedge, just clear of the branches and about 38–45 cm (15–18 in) deep. Undercut the roots with a sharp spade and lift the hedge in short sections. It is essential that the roots remain encased with soil, so slip sacking or strong polythene underneath before attempting the move.

As you re-plant each section, pack around it a mixture of equal parts soil and peat. Water liberally afterwards. It is essential that the soil should not dry out while the hedge is re-establishing itself. During dry weather, an evening spray with water is helpful.

JUNE

New hedges Container-grown hedges may be planted, provided they are kept well watered during dry weather. (See May.)
Established hedges Hedges to trim or prune this month include *Berberis darwinii*; *Cotoneaster franchetii*; *Fagus* (beech); *Ligustrum* (privet); *Lonicera nitida* (late in month); *Photinia* x *fraseri*; *Pyracantha rogersiana* (firethorn); *Rhododendron ponticum* (late in month); *Weigela florida*; *Taxus baccata* (yew).

It is necessary to trim privet and *Lonicera* two or three times during their first year. This encourages young growth, which in turn thickens the hedge.

Prune informal flowering hedges immediately after flowering, as advised in April. Remember that any shrub flowering before the end of June does so on growth produced the previous year – hence the need now for prompt pruning.

When trimming a formal hedge, either keep the sides parallel or else taper them slightly towards the top. On no account allow the top to become wider than the base. This will make the hedge top heavy and it will open up.

When trimming a formal hedge with hand shears, keep the joint well oiled and have the blades sharpened regularly, before they become blunt. Stand with one shoulder against the clipped area – not face on to the hedge – so that you can see along the length to be cut. This will help you to avoid the bumps and hollows that can so easily spoil the result.
Weed control Hand weeding provides an effective and safe means of keeping a hedge free from weeds. With care, certain weed-killers may be used around hedging plants and other shrubs.

JULY

New hedges Container-grown hedges may be planted, provided

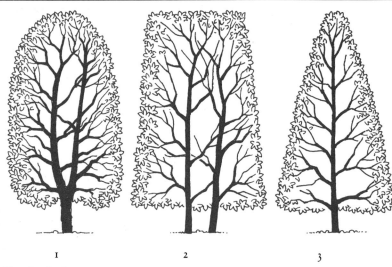

Shaping hedges
Hedges need shaping annually. Avoid a square shape which is liable to wind and snow damage; trim to a rounded form (1), a down-sloping wedge shape (2) or a conical outline (3).

they are kept well watered during dry weather. (See May.)

Trim newly-planted hedges, as necessary, to encourage them to thicken up.

Established hedges Hedges to trim or prune this month include *Buxus sempervirens* (box); *Carpinus betulus* (hornbeam); *Chamaecyparis lawsoniana*; *Corokia virgata*; *Cryptomeria japonica*; *Elaeagnus* x *ebbingei*; *Genista hispanica* (Spanish gorse); *Ilex aquifolium* (common holly); *Pittosporum tenuifolium*; *Prunus cerasifera* (cherry plum); *Prunus laurocerasus* (common laurel).

Some slow-growing hedges – notably hornbeam, box and holly – will not become unduly untidy if trimmed only once a year towards the end of this month. However, fast-growing hedges will need a further trim as soon as untidy growths start to protrude.

When trimming laurel and *Elaeagnus*, use secateurs to cut back any straggly shoots fairly hard. Clipping with shears results in cut leaves, which will turn brown and look unsightly.

Care of conifers During hot weather, spray newly-planted conifer hedges with water at regular intervals, occasionally adding a foliar feed to encourage continuing growth.

AUGUST

New hedges Container-grown plants may be purchased and planted throughout the summer. (See April and May.) However, if you propose buying bare-rooted plants between November and March – generally cheaper and in greater variety than container-grown stock – now is the time to consider choosing and ordering the plants.

It is as well to order three or four plants more than you are likely to need. There is always a chance of a few losses, and the sooner these are replaced the better. If you have to buy replacement plants, they will seldom be the same size as the rest of the hedge, whereas your spare plants will be comparable.

Spray newly-planted evergreens with water, preferably during the evening, and continue this treatment throughout the month if the weather is dry.

Established hedges Continue to keep hedge bottoms free from weeds by hand weeding or with weedkiller.

Hedges to trim or prune this month include *Berberis thunbergii*; *Chamaecyparis lawsoniana*; *Corokia virgata*; *Crataegus monogyna* (common hawthorn); *Cryptomeria japonica*; *Fagus* (beech) – late in month; *Escallonia*; *Ligustrum* (privet); *Lonicera nitida*; *Photinia* x *fraseri* – late in month; *Thuja plicata* (western red cedar).

SEPTEMBER

New hedges Container-grown plants may be purchased and planted this month (see April), but the time has also come to prepare for planting balled and bare-rooted plants during the autumn.

Having marked the line of the hedge, skim off any weeds from bare ground. If the land is grassed, either use the turves for patching a lawn or else stack them on one side for mixing in near the bottom of the planting trench.

Now dig out a trench at least 60 cm (2 ft) wide and 45 cm (1½ ft) deep, keeping the topsoil separate from the lighter-coloured subsoil. Dig the bottom of the trench, then place a 15–20 cm (6–8 in) layer of well-rotted cow manure, garden compost or other organic material. If you have turves to dispose of, place these upside down on top of the manure. Replace the soil, subsoil first.

While replacing the soil, it is a

good idea to break the sides of the trench with a fork, especially if the area is poorly drained. Failure to do this may result in the trench becoming a sump for saturated soil around it. The replaced soil will finish up some 15 cm (6 in) higher than the adjacent ground. Leave it like this, without firming it, to allow for settling.

Established hedges A healthy hedge – deciduous or evergreen – that is growing in the wrong place can be moved from the middle of the month onwards. (See May.) This will give a little time for new roots to form before the winter.

Quick-growing hedges, such as *Lonicera*, may be given a final trim before winter if they are looking untidy. *Berberis thunbergii*, grown as an informal hedge, may be pruned now to keep it tidy.

Taking cuttings For an inexpensive hedge, or an extension of an existing one, take hardwood cuttings 15–25 cm (6–10 in) long of *Ligustrum vulgare*. Insert in a sand-peat mixture, with the protection of a cold frame, planting out the rooted cuttings in a nursery bed next spring.

OCTOBER

New hedges Final preparations for planting must now be made to sites dug last month. The soil should have settled and may be quite firm. First, remove any weeds. Next, apply a balanced fertilizer, such as Growmore, at 130 g (4 oz) for each metre or yard run and mix this into the top 10 cm (4 in) of soil.

Orders placed in good time with a nurseryman should arrive from about the middle of the month. Plant evergreens without delay, but deciduous plants may be heeled-in temporarily if you are

not quite ready or the weather is unsuitable. To do this, open bare-rooted bundles and place them close together in a trench, roots covered, or else in a frost-free shed with sacking over them. Either way, they must not be allowed to dry out.

Shorten any tap roots or broken roots with secateurs before planting, making a clean cut. Set the plants so that the soil marks on their stems are just below ground level. Provided the soil is not wet, tread the plants in firmly; otherwise, firm just sufficiently to hold them upright and complete the job when the soil has dried.

Planting distances are given in the descriptions of hedging plants. However, if you wish the hedge to be particularly dense during its early stages, place the plants alter-

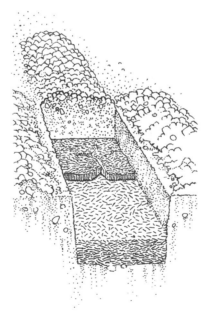

Hedge-planting preparations
Prepare the ground for a new hedge in early autumn. Double-dig a deep trench and cover the base with a layer of rotted farmyard manure, topped with any available grass turves.

nately in a double row, with 45 cm (1½ ft) between plants.

On a normal garden site, plants 60–90 cm (2–3 ft) high should not need supporting. In an exposed position, however, secure each plant to a cane to reduce the chance of wind rock. This is especially important for conifers and evergreens which offer more wind resistance.

Spread a mulch over the ground to help keep the soil frost-free.

NOVEMBER

New hedges Plant deciduous hedges, provided the soil is workable and reasonably dry. The chief danger is waterlogged soil, which may cause the roots to rot.

Do not be tempted to plant evergreen or coniferous hedges once the weather turns cold, except in the warmest, most sheltered parts of the country. Although damage may not be evident until spring, plants are liable to lose moisture more rapidly than they can regain it if they are subjected to a low temperature soon after planting. The next safe month for planting, unless they are in containers, is April.

DECEMBER

New hedges Continue to plant deciduous hedges when the weather and soil are suitable. Afterwards, mulch with organic material to help keep the soil frost-free.

Established hedges Remove snow from coniferous or evergreen hedges if it is weighing down the branches. Take great care when doing this as the branches become brittle and are easily broken in cold weather.

HEATHERS

The natural, uncomplicated beauty of the evergreen heathers makes them an asset in any garden. They create a minimum of work but they share one common dislike – lime. Even so, some do have a degree of tolerance. *Calluna vulgaris* is one that will not tolerate any lime at all, whereas *Erica herbacea* (syn. *carnea*) and *E. vagans* are not quite so fussy.

To some extent this does limit the number of gardens where heathers will thrive. They would certainly not be the first choice on chalk. On neutral or slightly alkaline soils, however, much can be achieved by adding peat, leaf-mould or leafy compost. In this way it is quite possible to create an area where heathers will grow even if the rest of the garden is not really suitable for them.

Site If one considers the places where heathers grow in the wild, it is clear that they are extremely hardy. Dartmoor, the Brecon Beacons and the Scottish Glens are not places for tender species. What these and similar locations offer is abundant light, together with a protective covering of snow during much of the winter.

It follows that heathers in the garden need an open position, away from trees. Not only do these reduce the light and cause heavy drips, their falling leaves in autumn spread a soggy blanket over the foliage. Flowering may be much reduced by overhanging trees.

Soil preparation and planting Dig the bed during September, leaving it loose and open afterwards. October and the first half of November are the best times for planting bare-rooted plants, and if this proves impossible the job is better left until March or April of the following year. Pot-grown plants may be planted at any time of the year when soil and weather conditions allow.

Pruning Trim summer-flowering heathers in March, removing only the old, flowered spikes. Trim winter-flowering heathers in April. Never cut back into old wood because, at best, you will get limited breaks. At worst, the plants may die.

Problems Given suitable growing conditions, heathers are fairly trouble-free plants, susceptible to hardly any pests and few diseases. However, two diseases that may occur are Phytophthora and honey fungus.

Phytophthora, caused by a soil-borne fungus that also attacks many other plants, first shows as some flagging or withering of young growth during the summer. On young plants, leaves on dead shoots will turn brown. Parts of older plants may continue to grow on for a while even though the remainder appears quite dead.

Heathers, especially callunas, are sometimes attacked by honey fungus, a disease that destroys many other shrubs and trees. If plants die for no apparent reason, look for the typical fungal threads in the soil.

A heather garden
This has year-round appeal, the dainty bells persisting for many weeks and the evergreen foliage associating happily with slow-growing conifers.

HEATHERS

Heather species

The sheer variety of heathers – their size, habit, colours and flowering times – often comes as a surprise to those who have not grown them before. There are relatively few species but a host of varieties.

Following are some of the more widely-grown species:

Calluna vulgaris (ling). The varieties vary in height from a ground-hugging habit to as much as 90 cm (3 ft). Flowers vary between purple and pink. The flowering period is from July until early autumn.

Daboecia cantabrica

Calluna vulgaris

Daboecia cantabrica (Connemara heath). Height is about 60 cm (2 ft). Leaves are dark green, often greyish on the underside. The flowers are mostly purple, pinkish and white, carried at the ends of the stems. The flowering period is late spring until early autumn.

Erica arborea (tree heather). The tallest of the heathers, occasionally reaching 6 m (20 ft). The flowers are greyish-white, sometimes with a pinkish tint, and produced between February and April. It tolerates some alkalinity.

Erica australis (Spanish heath). Grows to 1.2 m (4 ft). The reddish flowers, which are fragrant, are produced abundantly from May until late summer.

Erica x herbacea

Erica herbacea (syn. *carnea*). Height is 30 cm (1 ft). Some tolerance of lime. It has a spreading habit, a wide range of colours, and flowers between October and April.

Erica cinerea (bell heath). Height 25 cm (10 in). Being surface-rooting, this species needs an annual mulch or top-dressing of peat or leaf-mould. The flowers are mostly shades of purple and are carried from June until September.

Erica cinerea

Erica lusitanica (Portuguese heath). Height is 2.1–2.4 m (7–8 ft). It has feathery foliage and the pink flower buds open to white between March and May. It is best planted in groups of about five.

Erica vagans (Cornish heath). Grows to about 60 cm (2 ft). The bell-shaped flowers, predominantly pink, are borne from July to November.

Selected varieties

The heights (H) and spreads (S) are those likely to be attained after about five years, although local conditions will cause variations.

Varieties of *Calluna vulgaris*

'Alba Elata'
H 25 cm (10 in)
S 35 cm (14 in)
Medium green foliage. Single white flowers, from August.

'Alba Plena'
H 20 cm (8 in)
S 30 cm (12 in)
Medium green foliage. Double white flowers, from August.

'August Beauty'
H 25 cm (10 in)
S 30 cm (12 in)
Mature foliage is dark green. Single white flowers, from mid-July.

'County Wicklow'
H 20 cm (8 in)
S 30 cm (12 in)
Medium green foliage. Long spikes of double rose-pink flowers, from July.

'Elsie Purnell'
H 50 cm (20 in)
S 50 cm (20 in)
Grey-green foliage. Double rose-pink flowers on long spikes, from August.

'Fred J. Chapple'
H 25 cm (10 in)
S 30 cm (1 ft)
Spring foliage is dark green, with shades of gold, pink and red. Lilac-mauve flowers, from August.

'Joy Vanstone'
H 45 cm (18 in)
S 65 cm (26 in)
Pale green foliage. Single, reddish flowers, from mid-August.

'Mair's Variety'
H 58 cm (23 in)
S 75 cm (30 in)
Medium green foliage. Single white flowers, from late July.

'Mullion'
H 15 cm (6 in)
S 25 cm (10 in)
Mid-green foliage. Rose-purple flowers from August. Somewhat prostrate.

'Peter Sparkes'
H 40 cm (16 in)
S 45 cm (18 in)
Grey-green foliage. Deep pink flower spikes, from August to October.

'Radnor'
H 25 cm (10 in)
S 40 cm (16 in)
Dark green foliage. Short dense spikes of silvery-lilac flowers, from July.

'Rosalind'
H 25 cm (10 in)
S 38 cm (15 in)
Pale green foliage, golden in winter. Mauve-pink flowers, from August.

'Tib'
H 25 cm (10 in)
S 30 cm (12 in)
Dark green foliage. Cyclamen-coloured double flowers, from mid-July.

Callunas with striking foliage include:

'Beoley Gold'
H 40 cm (16 in)
S 45 cm (18 in)
Golden-yellow foliage. Pure white flowers, from late July.

'Blazeaway'
H 35 cm (14 in)
S 40 cm (16 in)
Yellow foliage, orange and red tints in winter. Pale mauve flowers, from mid-August.

'Gold Haze'
H 40 cm (16 in)
S 45 cm (18 in)
Yellow-gold foliage. Long sprays of double white flowers, from mid-August.

Selected varieties (cont.)

Varieties of *Calluna vulgaris* (with striking foliage)

'Golden Carpet'
H 15 cm (6 in)
S 40 cm (16 in)
Yellow and orange foliage. Purple flowers, from early August. Prostrate.

'Hirsuta Typica'
H 35 cm (14 in)
S 45 cm (18 in)
Grey foliage. Pale lilac flowers from mid-July. Slow to get established and flowers rather sparse.

'John F. Letts'
H 15 cm (6 in)
S 38 cm (15 in)
Yellow-gold foliage, with tints intensified by cold. Pale lavender flowers, from early August.

'Ruth Sparkes'
H 23 cm (9 in)
S 38 cm (15 in)
Golden-yellow foliage. Long sprays of double white flowers, from early August.

'Sir John Charrington'
H 30 cm (12 in)
S 45 cm (18 in)
Yellow and orange foliage. Maroon-purple flowers, from July.

'Spitfire'
H 30 cm (12 in)
S 45 cm (18 in)
Pale yellow foliage, turning red-gold. Pink flowers, from mid-August.

'Wickwar Flame'
H 35 cm (14 in)
S 45 cm (18 in)
Gold-orange foliage, deepening in winter. Rose flowers, from mid-July.

Varieties of *Daboecia*

'Bicolor'
H 45 cm (18 in)
S 50 cm (20 in)
Dark green foliage. White flowers with pale purple stripes, April to August.

'Praegerae'
H 45 cm (18 in)
S 50 cm (20 in)
Foliage is dark green above, silvery beneath. Deep pink flowers, from May. Less hardy than some others.

'Snowdrift'
H 30 cm (12 in)
S 50 cm (20 in)
Bright green foliage. White flowers, from May.

Varieties of *Erica Herbacea*, the winter-flowering group

'Alan Coates'
H 15 cm (6 in)
S 30 cm (12 in)
Mid-green foliage. Rose-purple flowers, from February.

'Ann Sparkes'
H 15 cm (6 in)
S 30 cm (12 in)
Young foliage is yellow, deepening to gold. Purple flowers, from January.

'C. J. Backhouse'
H 15–22 cm (6–9 in)
S 38–45 cm (15–18 in)
Pale pink flowers. Late flowering.

'December Red'
H 15 cm (6 in)
S 45 cm (18 in)
Deep green foliage. Rose-red flowers, from late November.

'Eileen Porter'
H 20 cm (8 in)
S 25 cm (10 in)
Deep green foliage. Carmine flowers for long period in winter. Compact.

'Heathwood'
H 22 cm (9 in)
S 38–50 cm (15–20 in)
Deep pink flowers.

'King George'
H 15–22 cm (6–9 in)
S 38–45 cm (15–18 in)

Compact, with dark green foliage. Rich pink flowers.

'Loughrigg'
H 10 cm (4 in)
S 30 cm (12 in)
Blue-green foliage. Rose-purple flowers, from early February.

'Mrs Sam Doncaster'
H 15 cm (6 in)
S 38–45 cm (15–18 in)
Greyish-green foliage of a loose habit. Rosy purple flowers.

'Myretoun Ruby'
H 20 cm (8 in)
S 30 cm (12 in)
Dark green foliage. Red-brown flower buds open to deep pink flowers, later bright red, from February.

'Pink Spangles'
H 15 cm (6 in)
S 50 cm (20 in)
Bright green foliage. Deep pink flowers, from November.

'Pirbright Rose'
H 20 cm (8 in)
S 38–50 cm (15–20 in)
Glaucous-tinged red foliage. Red-purple flowers.

'Prince of Wales'
H 15 cm (6 in)
S 25 cm (10 in)
Pale green foliage, sometimes red-tipped. Pink flowers, from February. Rather slow-growing.

'Ruby Glow'
H 25 cm (10 in)
S 50 cm (20 in)
Dark green foliage. Ruby-red flowers, from January.

'Thomas Kingscote'
H 18 cm (7 in)
S 27 cm (11 in)
Pale green foliage. Pink flowers, from January. Slow-growing.

Varieties of *E. Herbacea* with striking foliage include:

'Aurea'
H 18 cm (7 in)
S 45 cm (18 in)
Lime-green foliage turns gold in winter. Deep pink flowers, from February

'Foxhollow'
H 18 cm (7 in)
S 45 cm (18 in)
Young foliage is lime-green, maturing to yellow in winter. Red tints in cold weather. Flowers white, shading to pink, from February.

'Lesley Sparkes'
H 18 cm (7 in)
S 23 cm (9 in)
Pale yellow foliage with salmon tips. Deep pink flowers, from February.

'Sunshine Rambler'
H 20 cm (8 in)
S 38 cm (15 in)
Golden-yellow foliage. Pink flowers, from February. Spreads rather quickly.

Varieties of *Erica cinerea*

'C. D. Eason'
H 32 cm (13 in)
S 45 cm (18 in)
Dark green foliage. Abundant deep pink flowers, from June.

'C. G. Best'
H 30 cm (12 in)
S 30 cm
Salmon pink flowers on long strong stems.

'Cevennes'
H 25 cm (10 in)
S 30 cm (12 in)
Light green foliage. Lavender-rose flowers, from late June.

'Colligan Bridge'
H 35 cm (14 in)
S 45 cm (18 in)
Dark green, glossy foliage. Red-purple flowers, from June. Rather vigorous.

'Duncan Fraser'
H 30 cm (12 in)
S 30 cm (12 in)
A robust habit. White flowers tinged with soft pink.

'Glasnevin Red'
H 35 cm (14 in)

S 45 cm (18 in)
Dark green foliage. Striking ruby-red flowers, from June.

'G. Osmond'
H 30 cm (12 in)
S 30 cm (12 in)
Very pale mauve flowers.

'Pallida'
H 38 cm (15 in)
S 43 cm (17 in)
Medium green foliage. Pale lilac flowers, from June.

'Pink Foam'
H 30 cm (12 in)
S 45 cm (18 in)
Dark green foliage. Near-white flowers tinged mauve-pink, from mid-June.

'Velvet Night'
H 25 cm (10 in)
S 30 cm (12 in)
Dark green foliage. Dark maroon to purple flowers, from June.

Varieties of *Erica vagans*

'Fiddlestone'
H 45 cm (18 in)
S 45 cm (18 in)
Good grower and flowers well. Pink-cerise flowers.

'Lyonesse'
H 40 cm (16 in)
S 48 cm (19 in)
Pale green foliage. White flowers with gold anthers, from mid-July.

'Mrs. D. F. Maxwell'
H 27 cm (11 in)
S 45 cm (18 in)
Dull, dark green foliage. Cerise flowers with brown stamens, from July.

'St Keverne'
H 25 cm (10 in)
S 45 cm (18 in)
Dark green foliage. Rose-pink flowers, tinged white, from mid-July.

'Valerie Proudley'
H 15 cm (6 in)
S 25 cm (10 in)
Yellowish foliage. White flowers, from July.

JANUARY

Preventing snow damage Heavy snow can cause considerable damage to the taller heathers. Remove it carefully before it has a chance to build up, bearing in mind that the wood is brittle.

FEBRUARY

Increasing by Dropping If you have a favourite variety that has become misshapen and straggly, dig it up and replant it in a hole broad and deep enough to take the whole plant, with only the tips of the stems showing. Place the heather in the hole and gradually fill in around it with a mixture of equal parts peat and gritty sand, at the same time arranging the stems of the plant around the edge of the hole.

The heather should now be left for about a year to enable new roots to form. After this time, carefully lift the plant, cut away the old roots and plant the rooted cuttings in position.

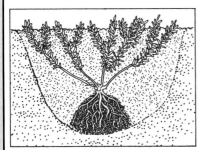

Propagating straggly heathers
Straggly heathers can be induced to form new plants by dropping them deeply, the tips just above ground.

MARCH

Trimming After their first year, heathers need trimming annually for the sake of health and tidiness. The exact timing depends on the type of heather – early March for summer-flowering kinds; late March or early April for winter-flowering; April for tree heathers.
Summer-flowering heathers Use sharp shears to remove the flowered growths. Cut no lower than the base of the flowering spike.
Winter-flowering heathers Trim lightly immediately after flowering has finished. With both types, take care not to cut back into old wood.
Move plants outdoors About late March, if the weather is suitable, move last year's rooted cuttings outdoors from the frame. Place them on a layer of sand or ashes in a light, open position, leaving space between the pots for the plants to develop. They will be ready for planting out in October.
Layering If you did not take cuttings in July or August, heathers can be propagated now by layering, following a rather different procedure from that suggested last month for misshapen plants. It will be up to a year before they can be transplanted.

Clean up the area around the plant, then scoop out a shallow layer of soil and spread equal parts of peat and gritty sand in its place. Peg the branches down on to this mixture, using a piece of bent wire, a hair grip or a flat stone, and cover with more of the mixture. Leave just the tips visible. It is unnecessary to slit the stems.

Always choose young, vigorous shoots rather than old, woody growth. Several layers can be placed from a single plant without spoiling its appearance. Normally, the rooted layers will be large enough, when severed, to plant out in their permanent positions.
Planting If planting was not completed last autumn it can be done during the last week or two of this month or during early April. (See October.) If the prepared site has become compacted during the winter, fork it over lightly to a depth of 8–10 cm (3–4 in). Spread a 5 cm (2 in) layer of leaf-mould or leafy compost.

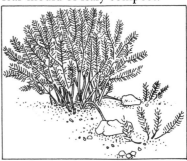

Layering heathers
Layer heathers in spring, pegging young shoots down for a year.

APRIL

Trimming Trim winter-flowering types this month if it was not done in March.
Tree heathers These need very little attention, but if they do become untidy and outgrow their position, cut them down to within 15 cm (6 in) of the ground. This job is best left until after the middle of the month, when the worst of the frosts will be over.
Weeding and feeding Remove all weeds from around the plants,

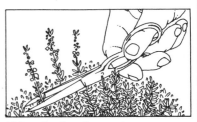

Trimming heathers
Trim faded flower sprigs, taking care not to cut into old wood.

preferably by hand-weeding. Firm any plants that have been loosened by frost. If the surface is compacted, loosen it gently with a fork. Apply a dressing of general fertilizer – 50 g per sq m (1½ oz per sq yd).

Planting Heathers may be planted up to about the middle of the month. (See October.)

MAY

Watering From now on, if the weather turns hot and dry, water the plants from time to time. If you live in a hard-water area it would be better to collect rainwater for the purpose. The lime in hard tap water may eventually cause yellowing of the foliage, or chlorosis.

Mulching Peat or leaf-mould are the best materials for mulching. Alternatively, use shredded bark. Make sure that the soil is weed-free and damp before you apply the mulch, which should be spread about 5 cm (2 in) thick.

It is important to make sure that shredded bark is fully weathered before spreading it. If in any doubt, leave it for at least six weeks to mature.

JUNE

Summer care Water the plants as necessary – both established heathers and pot-grown cuttings – and keep the area around plants weed-free. If necessary, renew or top-up the mulch applied earlier.

JULY

Propagation by cuttings A cold frame is the best place for rooting heather cuttings, but a deep box covered with a sheet of glass will do. The cuttings can either be rooted in pots of a suitable cuttings compost or else in a layer of 1 part sand and 1 part peat, 10–13 cm (4–5 in) deep, placed on the floor of the frame or box.

Because direct sunlight makes it more difficult to strike cuttings successfully, the frame or box should be sited against a north wall and the glass covered with paper or hessian on sunny days. If you use a box, turn the glass each day, taking care that the condensed water does not drip on to the cuttings.

Check that the sand used for propagating heathers does not contain lime – if necessary using a soil test kit. If you use pots, the 9 cm (3½ in) size will do nicely. When filling the pots with rooting mixture, leave sufficient room for watering. Spread a thin layer of sand over the surface before inserting the cuttings. The dibber will take some down into each hole. It acts as a mulch and holds moisture, and so keeps the compost cool.

Taking the cuttings Choose young, healthy, half-ripened shoots. There should be plenty from about the middle of July until the second half of August.

Using a sharp knife, cut the stems cleanly to give cuttings about 5 cm (2 in) long. Remove the leaves from the lower half of each cutting, then dip the ends first in water and then in hormone rooting powder. Shake off any surplus powder before inserting between six and nine round the edge of a 9 cm (3½ in) pot.

Water the pots well and place them in the frame or box. Keep

TAKING HEATHER CUTTINGS

1 In midsummer, take semi-ripe cuttings from non-flowering shoots.

2 Trim the cuttings to about 5 cm (2 in) and strip off the lower leaves.

3 Dip the cuttings in rooting powder and insert several to a pot.

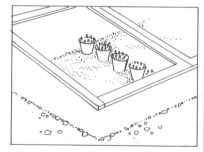

4 Place the pots in a shaded cold frame; pot singly in autumn.

this closed, to maintain a humid atmosphere, until you see signs of growth. From then on, gradually give more air, eventually removing the cover completely. Never allow the cuttings to dry out.

Drying heathers for the winter Heather makes a dainty addition to flowers dried for winter use. It keeps its colour well, although it is somewhat brittle.

Pick flowering spikes when the blooms are two thirds open. Spray each spike with hair lacquer, to prevent them from disintegrating. Take a large, firm potato, cut the heather stems on the slant to make a sharp point, then push the stems into the potato.

When sufficient have been inserted (they should not touch each other), place the potato in a dark, airy place where the temperature is not too high. The heathers will be perfectly dry within two months, retaining their beautiful soft colours.

Remove the dried flower spikes from the potato and either spray again with hair lacquer or use a purpose-made dried-flower fixative, sold in aerosol cans.

If you do not wish to use the dried heather straight away, store it in a cardboard box lined with tissue paper, placing this where it will be dry and cool. Do not store

in plastic bags or containers.

Heather can be preserved in this way at any time of the year. The winter-flowering varieties give excellent results, too, but if you wish to dry large spikes of heather, it is advisable first to pierce the skin of the potato with a skewer and soak it overnight in a pint of water to which has been added a teaspoonful of liquid Savlon. This ensures that there is sufficient moisture in the potato and that it does not start to smell unpleasant.

AUGUST

Taking cuttings Cuttings may be taken until about the middle of the month. (See July.)

SEPTEMBER

Soil preparation Now is the time to get the bed ready if you plan to plant heathers during the autumn. Dig the area over, one spit deep, adding peat, leaf-mould or a leafy compost but avoiding manure. Most heathers need an acid soil and they also react badly to one that is too rich.

Remove all perennial weeds. If left, it will be almost impossible to disentangle them from the roots of the heather plants.

Design This is also a good time to work out a plan for a new heather garden. In addition to deciding which plants to grow, you may consider varying the contours by forming ridges of soil or by including pieces of rock. Slow-growing conifers, carefully placed, will have the same effect; as will shrubs and small trees such as *Cytisus* x *praecox*, *Pernettya mucronata* or *Vaccinium vitis-idaea*. Some of the best dwarf conifers for this are *Thuja orienta-*

lis 'Aurea Nana', *Chamaecyparis obtusa* 'Nana Gracilis', *Chamaecyparis lawsoniana* 'Pygmaea Argentea' and *Thujopsis dolabrata* 'Nana'.

As to the heathers themselves, choose them with a view to getting a good continuity of colour. Remember, too, that heathers vary a good deal in height and spread – a factor to bear in mind when placing them. Another point to consider is the effectiveness of planting them in groups of five or so, which gives a much more striking result than dotting the plants about individually.

Potting cuttings Pot rooted cuttings singly into 8 cm (3 in) pots, using a mixture of 7 parts lime-free soil, 3 parts medium-grade moss peat and 2 parts sharp sand.

Water the potted cuttings well and place them in the frame, keeping this covered for a week or two until the plants show signs of growth. Increase the ventilation gradually once they are growing freely, giving a free flow of air across the cuttings whenever conditions allow.

Do not allow the pots to become frosted or saturated during the early stages. If necessary, replace the frame light, but keep it propped up with a block of wood to admit as much air as possible.

OCTOBER

Planting The ideal time for planting is from about the middle of the month until the middle of November. It is important to choose a time when conditions are right – neither frosty, too wet nor too dry. If it proves impossible to complete the task by mid-November, late March or early April will provide another opportunity.

When planting out pot-grown

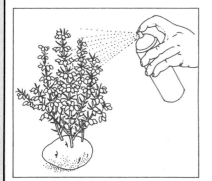

Drying heather
Dry heather sprigs, sprayed with fixative, in a dark place for 2 months.

plants, take care to tease out the roots if they are at all pot-bound. If the pots are dry, soak them in a bucket of water until the air bubbles stop rising.

If the roots have grown out through the bottom of a pot, it is better to sacrifice the pot rather than break them off. If the pot is plastic, use an old knife to cut downwards from the rim. If clay, give it a sharp tap to break it. If polythene, simply tear it.

Place a layer of leaf-mould or leafy compost all over the bed, then work this in around the roots as you plant the heathers. Make the holes with a trowel, then firm in the plants with your fingers.

Work backwards towards the path as you plant, tidying as you go and levelling the soil to remove foot-marks. This will complete the job in one operation.

Planting depth Set the soil-ball of pot-grown plants slightly below the surface. Young heathers lifted from a nursery bed in your own garden, or bought bare-rooted, should be planted in the same way. Lift them carefully, shake off some of the surplus soil and plant directly.

When laying them in position ready for planting, do not put out too many at one time. Never allow the roots to dry out, and if any delay occurs cover them with sacking. Plants from a nursery bed generally grow away more rapidly than those from containers.

Planting distance This varies with the vigour of the variety, but for most it averages 30–38 cm (12–15 in). For taller, more vigorous species, such as *Erica australis* and *E. arborea*, allow 1.2 m (4 ft).

Rabbits In country areas, winter and early spring are the worst times for rabbit damage to heathers. They are especially troublesome with young plants, which they scratch out of the ground, exposing the roots. They also nibble at the top growth.

Proprietary chemical deterrents may be used, but they are rather unpleasant in garden surroundings. Wire netting, 90 cm (3 ft) high and with the bottom 15 cm (6 in) turned outwards and buried just below the ground, is the most effective answer.

Mound layering Remove the box from plants layered last December and cut off the old plant at ground level. Separate the young rooted layers and plant them in a nursery bed to grow on for a further period before transferring them to their permanent positions.

NOVEMBER

Planting Complete planting by the middle of the month. (See October.)

DECEMBER

Removing leaves Remove fallen leaves at regular intervals; never allow them to lie on plants for any length of time. This is because a covering of wet leaves may result in rotting.

Winter care of cuttings Although most heathers are quite hardy, it is wise to protect them against the most severe weather – both wet and cold. Replace the frame covering as necessary, propping it open slightly to allow some circulation of air.

Be sure not to over-water at this time of year. If in doubt, leave the plants alone.

Mound layering This is another method of increasing heathers. You will first need to nail together four pieces of wood to form a frame, the size of which should be

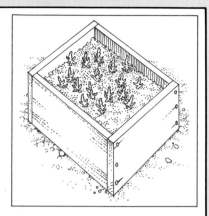

Mound-layer heathers in winter.

slightly larger than the plant selected and deep enough to accommodate it with only the tips of the branches showing.

Place this frame over the plant, then fill the box with a mixture of peat and gritty sand, in equal parts. As you fill the box, gently lift and shake the stems to ensure that the compost is spread evenly through and around the plant.

Firm the compost as you fill the box. When you have finished, only the tips of the plant should be visible. Water the compost, and subsequently keep it moist, to encourage roots to develop along the buried stems. When this type of layering is started in December, the layers should be ready for severing the following autumn.

Sever rooted layers next autumn.

Although so often grouped together, bulbs and corms are each quite distinct from the botanical viewpoint. A bulb, which is a form of underground bud, is made up of overlapping scales. In these, food is stored over the winter to nourish the following year's leaves and flowers, as yet an embryo in the centre of the bulb.

In contrast, a corm is a swollen stem. A new corm develops above the old one in readiness for the following season – as on a gladiolus, for example.

Tubers are swollen roots or stems in which food is stored and from which shoots develop. Potatoes, dahlias and some begonias grow from tubers.

Pests and diseases Although bulbs and corms are reasonably trouble-free, there are certain problems that may crop up from time to time.

Small bulbs may have their foliage eaten by slugs and snails. The key to control lies in action against these pests before the damage becomes severe.

Daffodils, snowdrops and scillas are all vulnerable to attack by the narcissus fly, which often gains entry to the bulbs through the holes left by dying foliage. The easiest way to prevent this is by raking over the surface after removing the dead leaves.

When lifting bulbs for re-planting, discard any that have holes in them; also any soft bulbs, as these will be diseased. Burn them rather than putting them on the compost heap.

Narcissus leaf scorch causes the tips of leaves to turn brown early in the season. To control it, cut off and burn the affected leaves, and spray the foliage with mancozeb.

Crocuses suffer from two separate problems, both of which can be devastating. First, there are mice, which often arrive soon after planting to feast on the corms. Traps provide the best means of control, but be careful to cover them with a box or wire netting so that birds are not trapped by mistake.

Ironically, the second problem is created by the birds themselves, which often tear the blooms to pieces. Wire netting or criss-crossed black cotton seem to be the only way to prevent this.

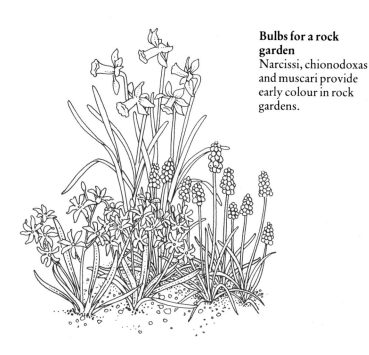

Bulbs for a rock garden
Narcissi, chionodoxas and muscari provide early colour in rock gardens.

Tulip fire (*Botrytis tulipae*) can be a problem in wet, cold weather, the plants becoming stunted and the foliage dying prematurely. Remove and burn this when the first symptoms are seen. When the plants are 5 cm (2 in) high, spray them with mancozeb and repeat at seven to ten day intervals until the flowers start to appear.

BULBS AND CORMS TO GROW OUTDOORS

Allium These are ornamental onions suitable for rock gardens, herbaceous borders and for naturalizing. They will grow in most garden soils and should be planted during October or November in a sunny position. The size of the bulbs varies considerably, the smaller ones needing to be covered with 5–8 cm (2–3 in) of soil and the larger ones with 8–10 cm (3–4 in). All are best grown in small clumps of five or six bulbs.

Height varies from as little as 15 cm (6 in) up to 1.2 m (4 ft), and flowering times are from May to August. They can be used as cut flowers, and they are also valuable for dried flower arrangements.

A. giganteum. With a height of up to 1.2 m (4 ft) this is possibly the largest flowering of all the species, having purple heads that

Allium giganteum
Easy to grow, this plant readily produces large, deep purple flowers.

are sometimes as much as 15 cm (6 in) in diameter when fully open. The flowers are long-lasting.

A. neapolitanum. The flowers are white and scented, the plant growing to a height of only 25–30 cm (10–12 in). It is suitable for rock gardens or for naturalizing.

A. moly (golden garlic). This has yellow flowers in June and reaches a height of 23–30 cm (9–12 in). Choose the planting site with care, as it spreads rapidly.

Anemone *Anemone coronaria* is often seen in florists' shops in the spring, the blooms being single or semi-double and in various shades of red, white or blue. The corms are comparatively cheap to buy and are usually replaced annually. They will grow in most garden soils and should be planted 5 cm (2 in) deep and about 10 cm (4 in) apart – during September or October for spring-flowering, and in February for summer-flowering. Soaking in water for 48 hours helps to stimulate growth.

The most widely-grown strains are De Caen and St. Brigid, but a more recent introduction, St. Piran, has shown a marked improvement, with a good range of colours on very strong stems. The flowers are excellent for cutting.

A. blanda, when grown in sun or partial shade, planted about 5–8 cm (2–3 in) deep and left undisturbed, will give a good display each spring. 'Atrocoerulea' produces abundant deep blue flowers in March. 'White Splendour' and 'White Beauty' both have large white flowers.

Colchicum The flowers of most species and hybrids are borne during the autumn, but the leaves appear during the spring and early summer. There are a number of kinds, the main ones being *C. autumnale*, *C. byzantinum* and *C. speciosum* – all flowering in September and October.

Plant the bulbs during August about 15–23 cm (6–9 in) apart, covering them with 5–8 cm (2–3 in) of soil and leaving them undisturbed for as long as possible. When dividing and replanting, do this as soon as the foliage has died down. They will not succeed if planted in heavy shade.

C. byzantinum is very free-flowering. *C. speciosum* 'Album' has large, white, goblet-shaped flowers. It may be difficult to obtain but is well worth looking for.

'Water Lily' is a distinct cultivar, having large double lilac flowers which, when fully open, resemble water lilies.

Crocus It is important to plant crocuses where they will be in full sun during the flowering period, for they will not open properly or look their best in even partial shade. Crocuses look splendid in the rock garden and when naturalized, but, as with all bulbs grown in grass, mowing should be left until the foliage has died down. When planting, cover the corms with 5–8 cm (2–3 in) of soil.

Plant the winter-flowering types during July and August, the spring-flowering sorts between August and October. Re-plant only when their performance deteriorates.

Many early-flowering crocuses bloom in February and are derived from *C. chrysanthus* and *C. biflorus*. *C. tomasinianus* and its colour variants also flower in February. They are mostly self-coloured and are followed by the larger-flowering hybrid types about March.

C. chrysanthus 'Blue Bird'. This is blue and white outside, cream inside.

C. c. 'Goldilocks' has deep yellow petals which are bronze at the base.

C. tomasinianus 'Taplow Ruby'. The reddish-purple flowers are a strong, most attractive colour.

Of the larger-flowered sorts, 'Flower Record' is a good violet-blue and free-flowering. 'Pickwick' is definitely one of the best striped varieties, being pale lilac with deeper coloured stripes and a bright orange stigma.

Crocus

Cyclamen Hardy *Cyclamen* need well-drained soil, with plenty of humus, and partial shade. Ideal situations are shady parts of the rock garden, at the foot of trees

Cyclamen coum

or under a north-facing wall. Autumn types produce flowers before the foliage, between September and November, while spring-flowering *Cyclamen* bloom in February and March. Before planting, plump the corms up in moist peat for a few days.

Take care not to plant them too deep. About 2.5 cm (1 in) is enough, except for *C. hederifolium*, which may be planted 5 cm (2 in) deep. Plant autumn-blooming types in August, spring-flowering types during August and September.

C. coum is the easiest and most popular of the late-winter and spring-flowering species. The flowers are generally smaller than those of autumn-flowering types, colours varying from white to pink but mostly with a dark blotch at the base.

C. neapolitanum, still listed under this name in most catalogues, is now correctly called *C. hederifolium*. It is very hardy, producing rose-pink flowers with a red blotch at the base during September and October, before the leaves appear. The latter are ivy-shaped, with variable marbling, and make attractive ground cover from October until April.

Daffodils If you wish to brighten your spring days with these beautiful flowers, a start must be made six months or more in advance. September is the ideal time to plant the bulbs, whether you intend to grow them in beds or borders or to naturalize them in grass.

Well before planting in bare soil, dig in a good dressing of well-rotted farmyard manure or compost, burying this 20–23 cm (8–9 in) deep. Leave the soil to settle before planting, hoeing it occasionally. When planting, using a trowel, make sure that the holes are deep enough for the bulbs to be covered with 10–15 cm (4–6 in) of soil. Odd bulbs dotted about all over the place

do not make an effective garden picture, so plant in bold clumps, leaving about 15 cm (6 in) between bulbs.

Think carefully before planting bulbs in grass for naturalizing, as they and the grass look untidy after flowering. The foliage should not be removed for at least six weeks after the last flowers have died – longer if possible. If cut earlier, the bulbs gradually become weaker, flowering is less prolific and eventually the bulbs die.

Should you decide to grow bulbs in this way, aim for an informal effect. The most effective method is to let them drop gently out of a bag and roll around, planting where they come to rest, in an informal arrangement.

If you are planting in an area of established grass, it will not be possible to prepare the soil. Also, the planting method will be a little different, a trowel being awkward to use in grass. For small bulbs, a spade can be inserted and eased each way to make a V-shaped slit. Fill the bottom with a John Innes compost, push the bulbs into this, then press the slit together with your foot. Alternatively, use a bulb planter, taking out a core of soil. Plant the bulb, then tread the core back into position. This is the most effective method as the base of the bulb is in good contact with the soil.

Dead-heading is important, because it is after flowering that bulbs build up their energy and buds are initiated for the following season. After flowering, also apply a general fertilizer such as Growmore at 100 g per sq m (3 oz per sq yd).

Bulbs grown in beds and borders will most likely require lifting and replanting after about four years, in order to prevent overcrowding.

Traditionally, one expects daffodils to be yellow, but nowadays they are available in many variations of yellow, white, orange and pink, with both early and late-flowering cultivars to extend the season. There are also many different types, with blooms of different sizes, single and double flowers, and either single or multiple flowers on each stem. The following are but a few of numerous interesting species and cultivars: *N. bulbocodium* (hoop petticoat daffodil). Height 15 cm (6 in). Golden-yellow flow-

Daffodils
These flowers are the true harbinger of spring.

Fritillaria imperialis
The common name of Crown imperial derives from the flower cluster at the top of a tall stem.

Snowdrops
Galanthus, or snowdrops, flower from late winter on, with single or double blooms.

ers, with distinctive rush-like foliage. Suitable for the rock garden or for naturalizing and does best in a damp situation.

N. cyclamineus. The cyclamen-flowered daffodil is so named because of its reflexing perianth. Height 15 cm (6 in). An early, golden-yellow daffodil suitable for the rock garden or for naturalizing.

N. 'April Tears'. Height 20 cm (8 in). Delicate yellow flowers, three or four per stem, which are scented.

N. 'Geranium'. A multi-flowered cultivar, 38 cm (15 in) high, which is pure white with a bright orange cup. It has from four to six flowers per stem and is strongly scented.

N. 'Ice Follies'. Height 45 cm (1½ ft). A good white cultivar, with a flat, saucer-shaped cup. Very free-flowering.

N. 'Passionale'. Height 45 cm (1½ ft). The blooms have a white perianth, with a frilled pink cup.

N. 'Peeping Tom' and *N.* 'February Gold'. These are both early-flowering and long-lasting. About 30 cm (1 ft) high, they naturalize well. 'Rijnvelds Early Sensation' is a cultivar which, although its flowers are not particularly outstanding, has the valuable quality of starting to bloom outdoors during January.

N. 'Tete-a-Tete'. Similar to *N. cyclamineus* in form, but slightly taller and with two or more flowers to a stem. For growing in rock gardens, beds or borders.

N. 'White Lion'. Height 45 cm (1½ ft). Large double flowers, with a mixture of white and yellow petals.

Fritillaria (fritillary) The crown imperial, *F. imperialis*, grows to a height of about 90 cm (3 ft) and bears clusters of yellow, orange-red flowers at the top of the stem. Choose a lightly shaded position and be prepared for the plants to take some time to become well established.

F. imperialis 'Maxima Lutea' is a deep lemon yellow. *F. i.* 'Maxima Rubra' is the strongest of the red shades.

F. meleagris (snake's head fritillary) grows to a height of only about 23–30 cm (9–12 in), and is suitable for a shady corner of the rock garden. It does best in sandy loam and should be left undisturbed. Plant in October, 10 cm (4 in) deep and about 15 cm (6 in) apart. The nodding, bell-shaped flowers are borne on slender stems. They are reddish-purple, chequered white. *F.m. alba* is a strong-growing white form.

Fritillarias belong to the lily family and a careful watch should be kept for the lily beetle. This can very quickly cause devastation, particularly among *F. meleagris*.

Good preparation is essential, with the soil dug two spits deep and with plenty of manure mixed into the lower spit. Plant the bulbs in October, 15 cm (6 in) deep and about 20 to 23 cm (8–9 in) apart.

Galanthus Better known as snowdrops, the bulbs can be bought from bulb nurserymen and planted in September, setting them 5–8 cm (2–3 in) deep in heavy soils and an inch or two deeper in light soils. They can be used for naturalizing in lawns, or grown in clumps in the herbaceous border or rock garden. They will increase annually and are best left undisturbed until they show signs of deterioration. However, growth is somewhat erratic and the bulbs may also take some time to settle down to a good flowering pattern.

By far the best method is to purchase them, or obtain the bulbs from friends, while the leaves are still green, or while they are still in flower during early spring. Division and planting at this time of year gives the most satisfactory results.

Most varieties are 15–23 cm (6–9 in) high. Flowering is between January and March.

Choose from the following varieties:

G. 'Atkinsii' increases rapidly and flowers in January.

G. nivalis. This is the common snowdrop, of which there are many variants, including double forms.

G. plicatus does best in woodland conditions where it will produce possibly the largest flowers of any variety.

G. 'Straffan' flowers later, in March.

Gladioli Although these plants seem to have lost some of their former popularity, they are good gap fillers for the herbaceous border and they also make excellent cut blooms. The flowering time is fairly reliable should you wish to grow for a special occasion, such as a wedding or an anniversary, the early varieties flowering approximately ninety days after planting, with up to 120 days for the very late types.

Planting can start from the end of March, depending on the state of the soil. For a succession of blooms, either use early, mid-season and late types, as listed in catalogues, or plant some early-flowering cultivars each week for five or six weeks.

The ground must be well prepared beforehand, with plenty of farmyard manure or compost added, and it must be well-drained. Gladioli need plenty of water, but avoid waterlogged soil.

When planting, the final preparation will vary according to the type of soil. On light soil, planting can be a little deeper, making holes about 15 cm (6 in) deep and with a good handful of moist peat placed in the bottom of each hole. Press the corm into the peat and cover with soil. This extra depth of planting will also help to support the flower spikes and encourage the formation of new corms.

In heavy soil, 10 cm (4 in) holes are deep enough. Place a good handful of sharp sand in the bottom, pressing the corm into this and covering with soil. In both cases, when planting is completed sprinkle John Innes base fertilizer over the surface at 100 g per sq m (3 oz per sq yd) and rake this in.

It is an advantage to stake most varieties, preferably with individual canes, as they become top-heavy as the flowering spike develops. Avoid pushing these in too close to the stems, otherwise the corms may be damaged. After flowering, give the plants foliar feeds until the leaves begin to turn yellow. This will nourish the new corms. Lift during October, before the soil becomes too wet.

There are various methods of drying the corms, including the common one of tying them in bundles of about a dozen and hanging them up to dry. However, at this rather damp time of year there is a real risk of botrytis setting in, with consequent damage to the corms.

A better practice is to trim off the upper half of the foliage, then to stand the corms in trays. This allows a better circulation of air. As soon as the foliage has dried, cut it back to within 2.5 cm (1 in) of the neck of the corm. Burn the dried leaves.

It is essential to dry the corms as quickly as possible. During the next three weeks, store them at a temperature of about 18°C (65°F), or as near to this as possible, in a well-ventilated place. When dry, remove the old corm from the base, together with the roots, and store the new corm at a temperature of 10°C (50°F). Net bags are ideal for storage but open trays are also satisfactory.

While lifting and drying you will have seen the many small cormlets that surround the base of the adult corm. These can be dried, too, and planted in rows during April to increase in size. Lifted and replanted annually, they will reach flowering size after about three years.

Gladioli are available in many colours, including shades of green. The latter are a great attraction to flower arrangers. Size varies considerably, from the smaller butterfly types to the large, exhibition blooms.

Here are a few popular varieties:

'Deciso'. A large-flowered salmon-pink, with well-spaced blooms.

'Green Woodpecker'. A butterfly type, with yellowish-green flowers that have a crimson base. It is a good garden plant and very appealing to flower arrangers.

'Peter Pears'. Good spikes of apricot-orange. Fairly early-flowering.

'Sancerre'. A pure white, with the florets closely spaced on the spikes.

'Toulouse Lautrec'. Orange, with a yellow throat. The flowers are well-spaced.

Hyacinths Although not widely grown nowadays, hyacinths are becoming a little more popular as bedding plants. They make an impressive display, with a fine scent, quite early in the season – a considerable advantage, for it allows more time for the preparation of summer bedding.

Hyacinths do best in well-prepared soil that has been enriched with manure or compost. Being early-flowering, usually during April, they need a sunny position. Plant the bulbs in October, covering them with about 8 cm (3 in) of soil.

Hyacinths are often grown with ground cover plants, such as *Bellis* or *Arabis*, these being planted first and spaces left every 30 cm (1 ft) for the bulbs. If you are planting the bulbs on their own, set them about 23 cm (9 in) apart. The flowering

Gladiolus
Butterfly type

spikes are best supported to prevent damage by wind and rain and special stakes can be bought for the purpose.

Either leave the bulbs in the soil to ripen or else lift them carefully after flowering and put them in a spare plot to dry off. Either way, they should all be lifted and dried each year. Unfortunately, hyacinths gradually deteriorate over a two or three year period, so it is as well to replace about a third of your stock each year.

Popular varieties include:

'City of Haarlem'. A late-flowering cultivar, the large blooms being primrose-yellow.

'Delft Blue'. A porcelain-blue centre, with pale mauve outside. Early-flowering.

'Lady Derby'. Shell-pink flowers on strong stems.

'L'Innocence'. Pure white and very sturdy.

'Madam Du Barry'. Crimson and scented blooms.

'Myosotis'. This has a pale blue silver centre. Very fragrant.

Iris The large-flowered bulb irises are divided into Dutch, Spanish and English types, all requiring a light, warm soil and growing to a height of 45–60 cm (1½–2 ft). Plant about 8 cm (3 in) deep and 10–15 cm (4–6 in) apart during October. Leave the bulbs undisturbed until the plants show signs of deterioration, then replant them as soon as the foliage dies down.

The predominant colours are blue, mauve, white and yellow, with varying blotches. Dutch irises flower in May and early June, with blooms up to 13 cm (5 in) across. Spanish irises, flowering a week or two later, are a little smaller. English irises, larger than either, flower at the same time as Spanish types. They include no yellow cultivars.

Of the Dutch types, 'Wedgwood' is a very popular, early variety, having light blue flowers with a pale yellow blotch. 'White Perfection' has large, pure white flowers.

In Spanish irises, 'King of the Blues' is scented, the deep blue flowers having a yellow blotch on the falls. 'Prince Harry' is bronze-coloured, with a yellow blotch on the falls.

'King of the Blues' is also a distinct cultivar of the English iris, having flecked, dark blue flowers.

Iris reticulata is a valuable dwarf species, excellent for the rock garden, which flowers in January and February. Like all irises, it needs well-drained soil, so heavy types must be improved by adding sharp sand. Plant 8 cm (3 in) deep and 8–10 cm (3–4 in) apart in early autumn. A sunny position is best. Several excellent hybrids have been raised from this species.

I. r. 'Clairette' is light blue, but with dark blue falls that are marked with white. The falls of 'Wentworth' are purple-blue with a yellow blotch, and the flowers are scented.

I. danfordiae, which belongs to the same botanical group as *I. reticulata*, has distinctively-shaped and scented bright yellow flowers, which are greenish at the base. However, there is an unfortunate tendency for the bulbs to split, in which case they will not flower.

Lilies There is great variety in lilies, in their height and form as well as in their needs. If you have never grown them before, two easy ones to start with are *Lilium regale*, growing 1.5–1.8 m (5–6 ft) high, with fragrant white blooms in July, and *L.* 'Enchantment', a hybrid plant only half this size, with speckled, orange-red flowers in June.

These and many other lilies benefit from being planted in light shade, but they will grow in full sun. Most need soil that is neutral or slightly acid, but *L. regale* thrives even in chalky soil. As soil needs vary with the species, check with the supplier when buying.

Depending on the species, lilies flower between May and October. If set among rhododendrons or other early-flowering shrubs they will extend the season of colour in that part of the garden.

The bulbs may be planted in spring or autumn (preferably the latter), first digging plenty of leaf-mould or well-rotted manure into the soil. Choose bulbs that have not been allowed to dry out. If you are unable to plant them immediately, pack them temporarily in trays or polythene bags containing moist peat.

Planting depth depends on the size of the bulb and the manner in which roots are

Iris reticulata
Ideal for the rock garden, this bears blue-purple flowers in late winter.

Lilium regale
One of the easier lilies to grow.

formed. Some produce roots from beneath the bulb only, others from the base of the stem as well. *L. regale* and *L.* 'Enchantment' are stem-rooters, needing to be covered with 15–18 cm (6–7 in) of soil. For species that do not form stem roots a covering of 10–13 cm (4–5 in) or less is sufficient.

To assist drainage, place sharp sand around the bulbs when planting. The soil must never become waterlogged, though it should retain moisture. After flowering, and as the stems turn yellow, cut the plants down gradually, but leave about 30 cm (1 ft) throughout the winter, for removal in the spring. If cut off earlier, water may enter the bulb and cause decay.

Apply a mulch of leaf-mould or rotted manure in May, helping to keep the roots cool and moist. Leave the bulbs undisturbed until vigour starts to decline, then lift and replant in fresh soil.

Lilies can be propagated from seed, though it will take from one to six years for them to flower. Other methods of propagation are by bulbils, scales and division.

Two other lilies that are easy to grow:
L. candidum (madonna lily). Height about 1.2 m (4 ft). White trumpet flowers in July.
L. lancifolium (syn. *L. tigrinum*) (tiger lily). Height 90 cm–1.2 m (3–4 ft). Orange flowers, heavily spotted in August. Very vigorous.

Muscari Grape hyacinths, as *Muscari* are often called, are at their best during March and April. They bear clusters of mainly blue flowers, about 23 cm (9 in) tall, and will thrive in most well-cultivated soils. In common with most bulbs they do not thrive in waterlogged soil, so a heavy clay must be improved with sharp sand.

As grape hyacinths produce masses of foliage in the autumn, which can become rather untidy, they are well suited to naturalizing or for growing as ground cover among shrubs. Plant them early, as they start into growth sooner than most spring bulbs. August or early September are the best times, otherwise few flowers will be produced during the first year.

Cover the bulbs with about 5 cm (2 in) of soil, spacing them about 8 cm (3 in) apart. They can then be left for many years, until

Muscari botryoides and *M. armeniacum*

flowering is reduced by overcrowding.

Three of the best varieties are:
'Blue Spike'. Height 15 cm (6 in). A large form of *M. armeniacum*, with double flowers that are scented.
M. botryoides 'Album'. Often known as pearls of Spain. Height 15 cm (6 in). Fragrant white flowers.
M. tubergenianum. Height 15 cm (6 in). A most distinctive species, the top of the flower spike being light blue and the bottom dark blue. (Therefore known as 'Oxford and Cambridge').

Scilla The cultivation of *Scilla* is much as for *Muscari*. Early planting is essential to ensure the first spring's display, but you may still plant in October if you are willing to sacrifice those first-year flowers.

They do not make such prolific growth as grape hyacinths and can therefore be used for edging borders. Plant the smaller sorts 8–10 cm (3–4 in) deep.

Two good species are:
S. sibirica. Height 10 cm (4 in). Compact, violet-blue flowers. 'Spring Beauty', with a height of 15 cm (6 in), has larger flowers which also last longer.
S. mischtschenkoana, syn. *S. tubergeniana*. Height 15 cm (6 in). It flowers well but its special value is the early, pale blue colour it provides during February and March.

Tulips It is usual, but by no means essential, to treat tulips as biennials, and any site that has been well prepared for a previous crop should need only the addition of a general fertilizer, such as Growmore. Late October or November is quite soon enough to plant. Earlier planting may mean earlier emergence in spring, and possible frost damage.

Lilium candidum
This takes time to become established, then flowers magnificently.

Lilium tigrinum splendens
Free-flowering and easy, it does best in acid soil.

After flowering, tulips may be lifted and heeled in – that is, placed in a shallow trench with their lower halves covered – until the foliage has died down, but it is better to leave them undisturbed if possible. If you do heel them in, to make space for other plants, lift them again once the foliage is dead and store ready for re-planting. Mice may damage stored bulbs, so hang them in net bags if you think there is a risk.

If you are not in a hurry to remove the bulbs from their flowering positions, they may be left undisturbed for a number of years. If this is your plan, cover them with 15–18 cm (6–7 in) of soil, instead of the normal 8–10 cm (3–4 in). If you do leave the bulbs to die down naturally where they have flowered, and all the dead heads are not removed directly after flowering, the seed pods that form can be dried and used in floral arrangements.

As with narcissi, there is a wide range of colours, heights and flowering times, from March until May. There may be single or multiple flowers on each stem and some have variegated foliage.

April-flowering tulips (earlies) have a dwarf habit, growing 30 cm (1 ft) high; they are best bedded out on their own, 10 cm (4 in) apart. May-flowering types are generally taller and are often grown in association with other plants, such as myosotis or wallflowers, and in this case spacing needs to be a little more generous. Be sure to plant the biennials first, setting the bulbs in the spaces afterwards. Popular May-flowering tulips include:

'Beauty of Apeldoorn'. Yellow and orange, on strong stems.

'Greenland'. Green and pink, a good garden flower and very desirable for the flower arranger.

'Mrs. John T. Scheepers'. An excellent yellow tulip that lasts well.

'Palestrina'. A fine salmon-pink, Cottage tulip, excellent for bedding.

'Queen of Bartigons'. A beautiful salmon-pink, with strong stems and long-lasting blooms.

'Red Riding Hood'. A dwarf cultivar with scarlet flowers. It has the added attraction of foliage variegated with purple-brown.

Tulipa Darwin Hybrid

GROWING BULBS INDOORS

Bulbs occupy a distinctive niche in the plant world. They are, in fact, modified leaf buds, each consisting of a short stem enclosed by thick, fleshy leaves. Food stored in the latter is used to trigger renewed growth after a period of dormancy. When this occurs, the lower end of the stem develops roots, while a shoot grows from the top.

As far as bulbs grown indoors are concerned, it is convenient to divide them into two sections:

Group 1. Bulbs that are bought each year and that are supplied especially for forcing. After their display they are either discarded or planted outside.

Group 2. More tender bulbs that are kept indefinitely and brought into flower indoors every year. These demand a little more attention and knowledge if they are to do well.

FORCING INDOOR BULBS

When growing bulbs indoors – narcissi, hyacinths and tulips for example – it is much better to buy bulbs specially prepared for this than to bring bulbs in from the garden or try to flower those saved from the previous year.

When producing bulbs for the house, large bowls without drainage holes are the usual choice. Ordinary pots are just as good for the bulbs, but they will need saucers beneath and do not look so attractive. Try to choose bowls in scale with the eventual size of the plants.

It is not necessary to use bulb fibre. A good, balanced potting compost, such as John Innes No. 2, is better for the bulbs as it contains nutrients that will help to nourish the bulb for flowering the following year. Usually, bulb fibre consists simply of peat, with a little oyster shell for drainage and some charcoal to keep it sweet.

However, fibre does have the advantage of being light, clean and easy to handle. It is very satisfactory unless you have high hopes for the bulbs' performance in the garden the following year.

When potting bulbs, place a little compost or well moistened fibre in the bottom of the bowl and arrange the bulbs on top. Position them quite close together, so that they are almost touching. Fill in around the bulbs with compost or fibre, pressing it in gently. Their noses should just show above the compost.

Narcissus These bulbs, which are excellent for forcing, may be divided into large-flowered and small-flowered. Large-flowered daffodils which do well indoors include 'Spellbinder', 'Home Fires' and 'Red Devon'. However, the smaller-flowered narcissi are more commonly grown indoors. These are mostly forms of *Narcissus tazetta*, including 'Cheer-fulness', 'Geranium', 'Paper White' and 'Soleil d'Or'. Most are beautifully scented.

When planting narcissi in a deep bowl it is possible to set the bulbs in a double layer, giving twice the number of flowers. Stagger the layers so there is a clear pathway for the shoots of the lower bulbs to develop.

Either pebbles or Hydroleca (expanded clay particles) may be used instead of compost or fibre for planting narcissi. The bulbs are potted in the same way, but using the pebbles or granules instead of compost. The only disadvantage is that it is difficult to see when the bulbs need watering, as the surface of the pebbles always looks dry. However, planting in a glass bowl provides a simple solution.

The water should reach only to a point just below the bases of the bulbs, encouraging the roots to work their way down into the water. A consistently higher level of water will cause the bulbs to rot.

Hyacinths Their beautiful scent and pretty colours ensure a place for these bulbs in many homes. There are varieties in shades of pink, blue, white, cream, yellow and even orange.

Several hyacinths may be placed in a fairly shallow bowl, as for narcissi, but it is not advisable to double-plant. It is also a good idea to plant hyacinth bulbs singly in 9 cm (3½ in) pots, using potting compost and with the nose of the bulb well above the soil. When these individual bulbs have been forced into flower, various pots can be selected and grouped together into bowls to suit their size and stage of development.

Often the growth of hyacinth bulbs in a bowl is uneven, and individual planting is one way of getting round the problem. Use either peat or bulb fibre around the pots to fill up the gaps.

When planting bowls of hyacinths, avoid mixing different varieties together. This is because they are likely to grow at different rates and to flower sporadically.

Special hyacinth glasses are available, providing another means of growing a bulb in water. The hyacinth bulb is placed on top of the glass above a constriction in the neck, with the water just below its base. Roots will soon develop and grow down into the water.

Jam jars of the right size may also be used, though they look less attractive.

Tulips Many different cultivars are available, both single and double, which are suitable for early flowering indoors. Five or six bulbs in a bowl give a good display, Cottage and Darwin tulips being especially recommended.

Forcing the bulbs Pot bulbs during the autumn, from September onwards. After the containers have been well soaked, place them in a cool, dark place until the bulbs' roots are well developed and they have just begun to shoot. Outdoors is ideal, with the containers wrapped in black polythene or covered by 13 cm (5 in) of peat or ashes. Leave them for about eight weeks.

During this time, inspect the bowls occasionally to ensure that the compost remains moist and also, towards the end of the eight weeks, to check on the progress of the developing shoots. These should be allowed to make about 2.5 cm (1 in) of growth before the bowls are moved either indoors or to a greenhouse. Less forward bulbs can remain in the ashes or peat and brought in later to provide a succession.

Of course, it may not be possible to put the bulbs outside. In this case a cool, dark cupboard is the best place. If the coolest spot happens also to be light, place a black plastic bag over the containers.

Darkness encourages good root growth, which is essential before the shoots are allowed to develop, while coolness delays shoot development until the roots are adequately formed.

Indoor hyacinths
Hyacinths for indoor forcing can be grown in special glasses topped up with water.

Eucharis grandiflora
This resembles a
white-flowered
daffodil, but is heavily
scented.

Haemanthus
The flowers look like
paint brushes, with
prominent stamens.

When the bulbs are first brought indoors they should not be exposed to too much light until the pale yellow shoots have turned green. From then on, good light is an advantage and will ensure a sturdier plant with better flower colour. The compost should not be allowed to dry out, nor should it stay soggy.

The bulbs do not require a high temperature. About 10°C (50°F) is ideal to begin with, gradually increasing to 18°C (64°F) if possible.

Staking and tying Some support is especially desirable if the bulbs have to be in a warmer, darker position than is ideal. This is because the leaves and flower stalks will grow longer and thinner in such conditions. In large pots or bowls, place several thin stakes around the edge and tie string around them to support the plants.

It is possible to support hyacinths with wire, choosing a type that is thin but strong. Cut the wire into lengths and thread each down through the flower stem from the top to the bottom. The wire can either go down through the bulb, or off to one side and into the compost.

This is the only unobtrusive way to support the plants, and it does them no harm for the short time they are indoors.

After-care After flowering, remove the faded blooms but not the leaves or flower stalks. Move the bowls or pots to a cool, light place – about 4°C (39°F) – and keep them watered. Plant the bulbs outside in March or April.

Alternatively, leave them in their pots to die down, remove them after the leaves have yellowed, and then keep the bulbs clean, dry and cool until the autumn, when they can be planted out in the garden.

GROWING TENDER BULBS INDOORS

Unlike forced bulbs, these are not covered after planting.

John Innes potting compost No. 2, or a similar loam-based mix, is preferable to a peat-based potting compost. This is because most of these bulbs undergo a resting period, during which the compost is quite dry, before being watered to start them into growth again. It is much easier to soak a dry, loam-based compost than a dry, peat-based mix. Also, the loam mix is altogether more stable and the pot less likely to be knocked over.

As a general guide, pot large bulbs, such as *Hippeastrum*, *Hymenocallis* and *Haemanthus*, so that their tips are above the surface. Smaller bulbs, such as *Lachenalia*, are better planted with their tips about 2.5 cm (1 in) below the surface.

The origins of these tender bulbs are various, but mostly they come from either South Africa or South America. This, in turn, has a bearing on their treatment.

South African bulbs Most bulbs in this group should be potted up in late summer. Water them in well, but allow the surface of the compost to become quite dry before watering again. This applies particularly to the stage at which the bulbs are developing their roots and beginning to produce shoots. It is very easy for them to rot away if kept in saturated soil.

It is far better for these bulbs to be in a cool greenhouse, where they will receive more light than in the house. However, a light position in the house will do if necessary. Without light, the bulbs will not do well.

They require a temperature of about 7–10°C (45–50°F), but a lower temperature will be tolerated, provided it remains above freezing point. Naturally, higher temperatures will be experienced during the summer, but a centrally-heated room in autumn or winter will do them no good. The bulbs are in full growth during the winter and spring and will become long, lanky and fail to flower if the temperature is too high.

These South African bulbs may be either deciduous or evergreen. After flowering, the leaves of the deciduous species gradually turn yellow, and watering should be reduced accordingly. Eventually, stop watering altogether and dry off the bulbs in their pots.

Many bulbs may remain in the same pot year after year. A balanced liquid feed added to the water occasionally while they are in full growth will do them good. After a few years, though, it will become necessary to split the bulbs up and repot them.

South American bulbs To do well, these usually require more warmth than the South African types.

Eucharis The Amazon lily is a beautiful bulb with very fragrant flowers. It requires quite warm conditions, between 18–21°C (65–70°F) to do well. The leaves are evergreen and, barring a short period during the autumn, the plants can be watered liberally throughout the year.

Amazon lilies need a rich potting compost, John Innes No. 3 or a peat-based equivalent being ideal. Flowering is mostly in winter and spring.

E. grandiflora, the most common species, has lovely white flowers and reaches a height of 30–60 cm (1–2 ft). Because of the high temperature needed, it is more likely to be grown indoors than in a greenhouse. However, it thrives with less light than that needed by most of the bulbs described. It also needs higher humidity, and benefits from being sprayed regularly.

Eucomis Pineapple flower or king's flower are the common names of *E. punctata*. It grows about 60 cm (2 ft) tall and bears curious spikes of green-cream flowers during the summer.

Pot the bulb in March, bringing it into growth during spring and summer and then resting it during the autumn and winter. Repotting is necessary only about once every three years. Given a very sheltered border, it is possible to grow this bulb outside.

Haemanthus There are some 50 species of the beautiful blood lily, some of which are evergreen and some deciduous. Their leaves are large and can be quite thick. Single stems carry a dense umbel of star-shaped flowers.

H. albiflos is evergreen, with hairy leaves. White flowers and bracts appear in June, having the appearance of white paint brushes dipped in yellow paint. *H. coccineus*, although deciduous and bright red, has flowers with the same bristle-like appearance. It flowers in August and September, and only after the flowers have died do the leaves begin to develop. The leaves are large, hairy and prostrate.

H. katharinae and *H. multiflorus* are both deciduous, with red flowers. They are much taller than *H. albiflos* or *H. coccinea*, attaining 30 cm (1 ft) and 45 cm (1½ ft) respectively. *H. katharinae* flowers in July and *H. multiflorus* in April.

When potting the bulbs, only just cover their necks. Once potted, it is best not to disturb them again for several years, or until they become quite pot-bound. By this time the bulbs will have forced themselves above soil level.

Hippeastrum There are many different species of *Hippeastrum*, which are often incorrectly referred to as *Amaryllis*. However, the species themselves are difficult to obtain and much work has been done on producing hybrids with flowers in a variety of colours. These are the plants referred to here.

By nature, hippeastrums are evergreen, and if kept moist throughout the year they will not lose their leaves. Even so, the bulbs perform best if rested by cutting down watering almost completely for a period. Most flower in winter or spring, so this rest period should begin about September.

Keep the plants dry, in a temperature of 4–10°C (40–50°F) until about February, when the flowers start to appear. To bring plants into flower sooner, water them and move them to a warmer place from December onwards.

After flowering, and as leaf growth starts, is the time to repot the bulbs if they require it, which is every two or three years. Use John Innes potting compost No. 2. However, established bulbs may be top-dressed instead of being repotted. This is done by removing the top 5 cm (2 in) of soil and replacing it with fresh compost.

During the most active growing season, which is from early spring until September, a minimum temperature of 16°C (60°F) is ideal. Keep the plants well watered, but not saturated, and feed them every fortnight with a liquid fertilizer. This will build the bulbs up again for the following year.

Some hippeastrums flower in summer and autumn, and these need planting in early spring. Whatever their flowering time, they all benefit from a rest period of three months before watering and growth is restarted.

Hymenocallis Better suited to growing in

Hippeastrum
With its huge trumpet flowers, this is a popular indoor plant.

Lachenalia **species**
Native to South Africa, it will flower in winter given adequate heat.

Sprekelia
The Mexican
Sprekelia is
summer-flowering.

Vallota speciosa
Best grown in the
greenhouse and taken
indoors when the
scarlet-pink flower
buds show.

the greenhouse than indoors, the bulbs should be potted in an 18–20 cm (7–8 in) pot during January or February. Use John Innes potting compost No. 2, leaving the neck of the bulb above the surface.

If you want them to flower early, maintain a temperature of about 16°C (60°F), otherwise it is sufficient just to protect them from frost at 3–4°C (37–40°F).

H. amancaes is the most commonly grown species. Originating from Chile and Peru, it will reach a height of about 60 cm (2 ft). Its large flowers, in April, are an attractive creamy-white. If grown too warm, however, the leaves and flower stem become floppy and unmanageable. The bulb is deciduous and requires a resting stage between growing periods.

Lachenalia These are small bulbs. In August or September, plant them 2.5 cm (1 in) below the surface – about seven bulbs to a 13 cm (5 in) pot. After flowering, dry them off gradually, then store them dry in their pots until repotting the bulbs the following August. They do better if repotted each year.

There are several different species to grow, *L. tricolor* (syn. *L. aloides*) and *L. bulbifera* being the most commonly available. Both have erect, strap-like leaves and racemes of narrow, tubular flowers from December until February or March. *L. tricolor* has predominantly yellow-orange flowers, while those of *L. bulbifera* are mainly purple-red.

Massonia This strange but attractive little bulb usually produces only two small leaves, which develop flat and opposite. A tuft of creamy flowers appears in the centre between February and April. Massonias do not need regular repotting and they should be watered very carefully during the growing period.

Sprekelia There is only one species, *S. formosissima*, which is known as the Jacobean lily. It comes from Mexico and reaches a height of some 45 cm (1½ ft). Beautiful red flowers are produced in June. As these fade, the leaves begin to grow and this is the best time for repotting should it be required.

A good effect can be had by planting several bulbs in a large pan of John Innes potting compost No. 2, with the necks of the bulbs just above soil level. A temperature of 7–10°C (45–50°F) is sufficient.

The plant will die down and should remain dormant during the winter. Bring it gradually back into growth in the spring by careful watering.

Vallota This is the Scarborough lily. The only species, *V. speciosa* (sometimes called *V. purpurea*), grows up to 60 cm (2 ft) tall. A cluster of bright pink flowers is carried at the top of the stem between July and September. Plant the bulbs in August, with just the tips of the bulbs protruding.

Veltheimia Though larger bulbs and plants than lachenalias, veltheimias are grown in a very similar way. Plant them so that the top half of the bulb is out of the compost, repotting every two or three years. *V. capensis* grows about 30 cm (1 ft) high and has pale pink flowers. *V. viridifolia* is a little taller, with a more purple flower. Both flower in April.

Pests and diseases As with all indoor plants, inspect bulbs regularly for pests. Mealy bugs, the most troublesome, are white and waxy, living in a sticky substance that looks like cotton wool. They nestle in the crevices where the leaves emerge from the bulb, and also on the bulbs themselves.

When spraying with insecticides, make sure that the spray really penetrates the 'wool'. Minor outbreaks can be controlled by applying methylated spirit.

Other pests to watch for are root mealy bugs, controlled by applying a drench to the pot and root ball, and also aphids, white-fly and red spider mites. However, the last three are unlikely to develop into major infestations.

Bulbs have a tendency to suffer from viruses, which result in otherwise inexplicable distorted growth. These distortions often take the form of uneven dwarfing of the growths, a shrivelled appearance, and discoloured streaks (often red) in the leaves and stems.

If virus is suspected, consult an expert to verify the attack. There is no cure, so the best plan is to burn infected plants to prevent the disease from spreading to others.

JANUARY

Protection and watering Already the first flowers will be making an appearance. Remove glass from any bulbs or corms – such as *Crocus*, *Iris* or *Cyclamen* – that have been protected for the last month or so, as these will soon be in flower.

Bulbs in frames or in the alpine house need plenty of air during the day but protection from cold during the night. Water only when the temperature is above freezing. If plants take up large amounts of water and are then exposed to a hard frost, the freezing water in the cells expands and, as a result, ruptures the cells.

Even if this does not kill the plant at once, botrytis will generally follow, eventually causing death. Pot plants, which are subject to extremes of temperature, are particularly at risk. Plants growing in open ground, where the vulnerable parts are often well below the surface, are less likely to come to harm.

Marking bulb positions If you have recently taken over a new garden, note the positions of any early-flowering bulbs. Mark with sticks or twigs the limits of the areas concerned. Then, if you wish to move the bulbs later in the year, they will be easier to find.

Beginners often make the mistake of planting large areas with bulbs that look fine early in the year but they forget what the area may look like in high summer. Large areas of dying leaves are not attractive. If you have done this, or find large areas of spring bulbs in the beds of a newly-acquired garden, careful replanting in grass, under trees or in narrow borders later in the year will help to restore the balance.

FEBRUARY

Applying fertilizer Plants that were taken indoors for display but have now finished flowering should be returned to the greenhouse or frame and fed with a potash-based liquid fertilizer. Plants that are not flowering but are in active growth should be fed, too. However, do not apply liquid fertilizer during cold weather.

Feeding naturalized bulbs Give bulbs in an alpine meadow a light sprinkling of bone-meal. Do not overdo this, however, as whatever fertilizer is applied will also stimulate the grass – something of a drawback if there are a lot of coarse grasses in the turf.

Planting anemones Plant *Anemone coronaria* (De Caen, St. Brigid and St. Piran) for flowering during the summer.

MARCH

Care after flowering Remove any remaining bowls of bulbs from the house and feed them to encourage their development for next year. Never remove leaves from any bulbs or corms before they start to go yellow naturally. Photosynthesis continues after the flowers have finished, building up a supply of starch which is concentrated in the bulb. This helps the development of next year's flower buds, so it is essential that the plants are well cared for at this time.

Moving snowdrops This is the best time to move snowdrops (*Galanthus* species). They are one of the exceptions to the rule that bulbs should not be moved while growing. Although they may look rather ungainly when first moved, they will soon recover.

Planting gladioli Start to plant gladiolus corms as soon as the soil is in a suitable condition.

APRIL

Spring planting Once the risk of hard frosts is over, planting of the later, summer-flowering bulbs such as *Allium* and *Fritillaria* may begin. Plant the bulbs in a sandy mixture if the soil is at all heavy. This will help to encourage growth of the rather delicate roots. In soil that is naturally light and sandy the bulbs need to be set quite deeply – at least two to three times the height of the bulb.

Plant *Anemone coronaria* in clay pots for display in June and July. Water well and regularly since the pots may dry out quickly at this time of year.

Continue planting gladiolus corms. Cormlets lifted with the mature bulbs last autumn may be planted in a nursery bed.

MAY

Sowing seeds Seeds of early-flowering bulbs should now be ripe. If you wish to raise new plants, collect the seeds and sow them while they are fresh and remain viable.

Moving tulips If tulips are occupying space needed for summer bedding, lift the plants and heel them in on a spare piece of ground. Leave them there until the foliage is dead, then lift the bulbs and store them in bags ready for planting in October or November.

JUNE

Moving leucojums Both spring and summer snowflakes (*Leucojum* *aestivum* and *L. vernum*) are flowering now and, like snowdrops, should, if necessary, be moved just after flowering.

Lifting bulbs after flowering Wait until the foliage has turned yellow before starting to lift spring-flowering bulbs. A few, including *Muscari* and *Scilla*, may be divided and replanted at once. Others should be dried off and stored before being replanted during the autumn.

JULY

Lily pest Although the early-flowering species have finished, the larger plants associated with high summer are now in full bloom. Lilies are perhaps the most prominent, and gardeners in southern England should watch out for infestations of the rusty red-coloured lily beetle. This troublesome pest is best eradicated by hand, or by spraying with an insecticide.

Aphids spread virus diseases in lilies, so spray regularly with a systemic insecticide to prevent infection.

Lifting daffodils and hyacinths Where daffodils are grown in beds or borders, lift and divide them every four years after the foliage has died down. Dry them under cover, then store them in a cool, airy shed, first removing any that are rotten or diseased. Avoid excessive warmth, which may result in basal rot.

Lift hyacinth bulbs, then dry and store them ready for planting in October. Discard any that are three years old.

Planting crocuses This is the right month to plant winter-flowering crocuses. You should cover the corms with a 5–8 cm (2–3 in) layer of soil.

Crocuses from seed Most spring-flowering *Crocus* species will have set seed, which should now be ripe. The easily recognized, brown, papery capsules, are divided into three compartments. Collect and sow the seeds immediately, while they are still viable. If sown in pots, leave the seedlings until they become dormant, then repot the young corms. The first flowers will appear about three years after germination. Be prepared for a lot of variation in the seedlings.

Naturalized bulbs All of the spring-flowering bulbs naturalized in an alpine meadow will have finished flowering, so this is an ideal time to cut the grass. It is important that the grass is left undisturbed while bulbs are in active growth, but it should be possible to mow your meadow once or twice more before autumn crocuses and *Colchicum* come into flower. After this, the grass can be cut as often as necessary until it stops growing. The first winter-flowering bulbs will begin to appear in the second half of December.

Most spring-flowering bulbs are fully dormant by now, so this is a good time to lift and divide plants that have been growing in open ground for the last two or three years. Lifting and division is quite important for some species, since once bulbs become overcrowded they will flower less freely.

Some large bulbs may be suitable for potting, while smaller ones can be replanted in open ground. The particular value of potted bulbs is that they can easily be taken indoors when they are at their best during the winter or spring. After flowering, they can be taken outdoors again to die down naturally.

AUGUST

Autumn-flowering bulbs It is time to start thinking about buying autumn-flowering bulbs. Though not numerous, they are worth considering since the number of plants in flower at this time of year is not that great. The two most obvious candidates are *Colchicum* and *Cyclamen*. There are also many species of autumn-flowering *Crocus*, including *C. banaticus*, *C. nudiflorus* and *C. speciosus*, all flowering before the leaves appear. *C. salzmannii* produces leaves simultaneously with its pale lilac flowers.

When buying *Cyclamen* it is best to choose plants that are in leaf. Plant them as soon as possible in their permanent site, which should be well drained and in semi-shade.

Planting crocuses and muscari Plant winter-flowering crocuses if this was not done last month. Spring-flowering types may be planted between now and October. August is also the month to plant *Muscari*.

SEPTEMBER

Propagating lilies Collect any bulbils that have developed in the leaf axils of lilies. Pot them in a mixture of peat and sand and leave them in a warm place until growth appears at surface level, which will take perhaps two or three weeks.

Autumn-flowering bulbs that are naturalized in grass will benefit from a light dressing of bone meal. Apply this at about 65 g per sq m (2 oz per sq yd).

Bulbs to plant Plant daffodils, either naturalized or in beds. Spring-flowering crocuses and cyclamen may also be planted.

Plant tubers of *Anemone coronaria*, either close to the house outdoors or else in pots for bringing indoors later on.

Forcing bulbs for mid-winter The month of September is the time to pot bulbs for flowering in the house around Christmas. Among the kinds worth considering are *Lachenalia*, *Narcissus* 'Soleil d'Or' and 'Paper White', *Hyacinthus*, *Tulipa* and dwarf *Iris*. Remember to buy so-called treated bulbs for this purpose. Having planted the bulbs in fibre or light compost, cover them with black polythene and leave for eight or nine weeks at a frost-free temperature, not exceeding 4°C (40°F), and in a dark place. Label them, noting the date planted and also the date when they are to be inspected (in two months' time).

Forcing indoor bulbs
Pot bulbs in compost or fibre, the noses just showing (1); cover with black polythene (2) and leave in a cool, dark place until shoots (3) are 2.5 cm (1 in). Move into good light when shoots have greened up (4).

OCTOBER

Bulbs to plant Planting may begin of bulbs that will flower next spring and summer. Among the more unusual species, but well worth growing, are *Cardiocrinum* and *Nomocharis*. These Himalayan members of the lily family require relatively damp conditions and therefore tend to thrive in the cooler, wetter climate of the north west. Cardiocrinums are monocarpic, meaning that they flower only once – in this case after several years – and then die. However, they do produce bulblets around the parent bulb's base, and these can be removed and grown on in pots or a nursery bed before replanting in a permanent site.

Planting dwarf bulbs For a display of colour next spring, plant raised beds, narrow borders, or small troughs with dwarf bulbs such as *Crocus*, *Chionodoxa*, *Scilla*, *Narcissus* and *Tulipa*.

Forcing bulbs for indoors If you have not already done so, it is not too late to prepare bulbs for bringing into the house in winter. You can even arrange to have a sequence of plants in flower throughout the winter by preparing a bowl of bulbs at monthly intervals.

Some October plantings Plant hyacinth bulbs, covering them with 8 cm (3 in) of soil. Also plant large-flowered bulb irises. Towards the end of the month start to plant tulips.

Lifting gladioli Lift, dry and store gladiolus corms.

Creating an alpine meadow This rather grand term describes any area set aside for growing small bulbs in grass. It can be as small as a square metre or yard, but the effect will obviously be greater if a larger area can be devoted to this rather special type of garden.

This method of growing bulbs provides the conditions in which many species are found in the wild. During the winter, the turf helps to protect the dormant bulbs from frost; in summer, the grass takes up any excess moisture, helping to keep dormant, spring-flowering bulbs in a drier state.

Bulb-planting tool
Bulb planters are specially designed for naturalizing bulbs in grass.

Planting Having cut the grass, use a spade to mark out strips of turf about 30 cm (1 ft) wide, then slide the spade beneath the turf so that most of the fibrous roots are undisturbed. The turf should be 4–5 cm (1½–2 in) deep and sufficiently flexible to roll, without cracking, in pieces about 90 cm (3 ft) long. Place these to one side and prepare the soil by lightly forking it over, adding a little coarse sand or peat, if needed, to improve its texture.

Plant the bulbs about 5–8 cm (2–3 in) below the surface, not too close to one another, and in a random manner to give a natural effect. Firm the soil and replace the turf. If it now seems a little high, roll it lightly.

Alternatively, use a bulb-planting tool. For small bulbs, a slit may be formed with a spade and used potting compost placed in the base before planting and re-firming.

Cutting the grass Wait until the flowers have seeded and the foliage has died down, if necessary leaving grass patches temporarily uncut. As a rule, make the first cut around July, the last by the end of September.

NOVEMBER

Preparing for winter Remove any rotting foliage that may still be lying around some of the sun-loving bulbs. Also, prepare to cover the more tender species, such as those in raised beds or in the rock garden, with sheets of glass. This will help to prevent the bulbs, corms or tubers from rotting through winter wet.

No special equipment is needed, just pieces of glass about 30 cm (1 ft) square and four lengths of stiff wire (metal coat-hangers will do), each about 20–30 cm (8–12 in) long. Using pliers, form a U-shaped loop at one end of each wire, push the other end into the ground until about 10 cm (4 in) is left protruding, then slot the glass into place. Allow a slight slope so that rain can drain off harmlessly, away from the bulbs. Vary the size of the structure according to the number of bulbs and the situation.

There may still be seed to collect from later-flowering bulbs.

Bulbs in pots Check any pots of bulbs that were prepared in late September. Depending on the temperature and other conditions,

some should have short growths of 4–5 cm (1½–2 in) by now. If they have, remove the polythene and take the bulbs indoors to a sunny but relatively cool position so that the shoots can develop. About 10°C (50°F) is the maximum.

For an interesting effect, sprinkle the bulb fibre with lawn grass seed. Water the bulbs when necessary, and once the leaves have elongated and the flower buds are showing, remove them to a living room with a temperature of 16–19°C (60–66°F). The grass seed will have germinated, providing an attractive backcloth to the otherwise bare stems of the bulbs.

Tulip planting Tulips planted this month are less likely to suffer from the disease called tulip fire than if planted earlier in the autumn. This is the latest month for planting.

DECEMBER

Prepare for snowdrops There is little to be done for bulbs outside at this time of year. Check that areas where snowdrops are growing are well clear of debris so that you will be able to appreciate their arrival.

Potted bulbs Check the progress of bulbs in pots that have been grown for indoor display.

The following bulbs are suitable for planting in an alpine meadow:

LARGER BULBS	FLOWERING TIME	SOIL TYPE
Lilium martagon	Summer	
Leucojum aestivum	Summer	
Tulipa sprengeri	Spring	Dry, sandy
Camassia species	Summer	Damp, heavy
Fritillaria meleagris	Spring	Damp, heavy
F. pyrenaica	Summer	Damp, heavy
Allium sphaerocephalon	Summer–Autumn	Dry, sandy
Dactylorhiza fuchsii and D. elata	Spring–Summer	
Gladiolus byzantinus	Summer	

DWARF BULBS	FLOWERING TIME	SOIL TYPE
Narcissus cyclamineus, N. bulbocodium and N. pseudonarcissus	Winter–Spring	Damp, heavy
Erythronium dens-canis	Spring	
Galanthus nivalis	Winter	
Cyclamen hederifolium	Autumn	Dry, sandy
Crocus tomasinianus	Winter	
C. chrysanthus	Winter–Spring	
Muscari species	Spring	Dry, sandy
Scilla species	Spring	Dry, sandy
Chionodoxa species	Winter	
Anemone blanda	Winter–Spring	
Colchicum species	Autumn	

These colourful beds at Wisley show how attractive a massed display of plants like tulips can be. Single plantings of bulbs or corms won't create such an impressive effect.

The spectacularly abundant flower trusses and attractive foliage of rhododendrons and azaleas make them a popular choice with many gardeners on acid soils. The colour range is extensive and the flowers can be scented.

Heated conservatories encourage extra lush growth on multi-coloured pelargoniums and trailing fuchsias; hanging baskets spill over with pelargoniums and fuchsias, and tender jasmines and other climbers scramble under the roof.

A cold alpine house gives protection to those choice plants that would succumb to a wet English winter. Dwarf forms of hardy plants, such as grape hyacinths, primulas, and pulsatillas, can be brought into early bloom.

These miniatures of the plant world provide a varied and rewarding beauty out of all proportion to their size. Many are easy to grow, others the reverse, the essential points being that all need free drainage and the majority an open, sunny spot away from the drip of trees.

The majority of alpines flower during spring or early summer. If supplied in pots, as nearly all are nowadays, they may be planted at any season except winter. Keep young plants well watered during their first spring and summer, until they have developed an extensive root system.

They are not heavy feeders. An annual spring dressing of a balanced general fertilizer, such as Growmore, at 30 g per sq m (1 oz per sq yd), will keep them growing steadily. Alternatively, apply an organic fertilizer in the form of dried blood, bone or fishmeal.

The choice in alpines is truly enormous, as a visit to any specialist nursery will show. Such a visit is a great aid to selection, provided you seek guidance from a member of staff who can pick out species most suitable for your needs. The plants listed here are merely a small selection from the vast choice available.

Rock-garden plants

Acantholimon glumaceum

Acantholimon glumaceum. A dark green cushion, 15 cm (6 in) high, of spiny leaves and, in summer, short sprays of pink flowers. These remain in an attractive 'dried' state for many weeks.
Allium beesianum. A clump-forming, bulbous plant with 23 cm (9 in) stems, each carrying pendent flowers of Wedgwood blue in mid to late summer.
Anthyllis montana 'Rubra'. In summer, rich-red, clover-like flowers lie over a mat of fern-like, grey-green leaves.
Artemisia schmidtiana 'Nana'. Finely-cut leaves of glistening silver form a low hummock during the early summer. An exquisite foliage plant.
Aubrieta 'Bressingham Pink'. Trailing mats of neat rosettes, with stemless, semi-double flowers of a clear pink. These open in earliest spring.
Campanula garganica. A clump-forming species 15 cm (6 in) high, producing

Campanula garganica

radiating stems that are loaded with blue, star-shaped flowers during June and July.
Cytisus hirsutus. This mat-forming broom has large yellow flowers in May and June, each stained mahogany-red as it matures.
Diascia rigescens. Leafy stems, some 30 cm (1 ft) high, carry open flowers of a rich salmon-pink throughout the summer.
Erodium macradenum. Produces a summer-long succession of white, finely-veined flowers, each bearing a dark-purple blotch on the upper petals. Parsley-like foliage of silvery-green. Height 23 cm (9 in).

Globularia cordifolia

Helianthemum

Euphorbia capitulata. An evergreen mat, 5 cm (2 in) high, of olive-green rosettes. Small heads of bright yellow flowers appear in spring.
Globularia cordifolia. Summer-flowering, this evergreen sub-shrub has glossy, wedge-shaped leaves, and flowers resembling blue powder puffs. It is 5–8 cm (2–3 in) high.

Haberlea rhodopensis

Helianthemum 'Ben More'. A low-growing sub-shrub to 15 cm (6 in) with narrow leaves and a mass of coppery-orange flowers for several weeks during early summer.
Haberlea rhodopensis. Thick, dark green leaves slowly form a clump 8 cm (3 in) high. Lipped flowers of pale lilac appear in May. Plant in a moist, shady spot.
Phlox 'Kelly's Eye'. A trailing mat of needle-like leaves, with masses of pale-pink flowers, each having a 'blood-shot' eye, in late spring.
Primula vulgaris var. *sibthorpii*. Crinkled leaves, with 5 cm (2 in) stems carrying lilac-coloured primroses all through the winter months. Needs light shade.
Viola 'Irish Molly'. An old variety with flowers of an unusual mixture of khaki-yellow and bronze. Spasmodic flowering all summer.

Primula vulgaris

Plants for raised beds

(T) indicates a trailing habit. (S) indicates plants suitable for the side of a bed.

Asperula lilaciflora var. *caespitosa.* (T). Deep green, heath-like foliage. Pink, tubular stars, 12 mm (½ in) high, are carried throughout the summer.

Cotoneaster congestus 'Nanus'. (T). A prostrate, twiggy mat covered in tiny, dark green leaves. Ideal to provide miniature, evergreen ground-cover. Occasional white flowers.

Erinus alpinus 'Albus'. (S). This adaptable plant is quite happy in the driest crevice, where, in May, it produces pure white flowers on 8 cm (3 in) stems.

Geranium dalmaticum. (S). Given a sunny crevice, this plant rewards with shell-pink flowers in June, and leaves that are attractively coloured in autumn.

Helianthemum lunulatum. A dwarf, shrubby species, some 20 cm (8 in) high. It has grey-green, oval leaves, and masses of yellow flowers during June and July.

Lewisia 'Trevosia'. (S). It has narrow, fleshy leaves and branched stems, 15 cm (6 in) high, that carry flowers of a salmon-red colour in May.

Primula marginata. (S). Leaves covered with powder (farina), and serrated at the edges. Blue and mauve flowers in earliest spring, scented like primroses.

Primula marginata

Salix serpyllifolia. (T). This tiny-leaved willow makes a mat of tangled, trailing stems. Attractive, yellowish bark during the winter.

Saxifraga × *apiculata* 'Alba'. A vigorous hybrid, with apple-green and white flowers on 8 cm (3 in) stems during March and April.

S. callosa 'Superba'. (S). Lovely silvery leaves form close-packed rosettes. These bear arching stems clothed with pure white flowers during May.

Sedum spurium 'Variegatum'. Forms a tangled mass of ground-hugging stems, with fleshy leaves of grey-green, margined with pink. Lovely from spring to autumn.

Thymus × *citriodorus* 'E.B. Anderson'. A rounded mat of tiny, lemon-scented leaves with the occasional sprinkling of lavender-pink flowers. Attractive golden foliage during the winter.

Veronica austriaca 'Trehane'. A plant for both flowers and foliage. Low tufts of golden-yellow leaves, with bright blue flowers on 10 cm (4 in) stems during May.

Scree plants

Achillea clavenae var. *integrifolia.* A clump-forming plant with narrow, silver-grey leaves that are aromatic. White flowers on 15 cm (6 in) stems in summer.

Anacyclus depressus. Prostrate stems carry ferny leaves and, in spring, white, daisy-like flowers that are crimson beneath.

Aquilegia bertolonii. This May-flowering columbine has dark green leaves and large, rich blue flowers, which are spurred, on 8 cm (3 in) stems.

Arenaria tetraquetra var. *granatensis.* A dense cushion of grey-green, four-angled leaves and stemless white flowers. These open in May.

Campanula cochleariifolia. With running, spreading stems, this plant produces masses of bell-like flowers throughout summer and autumn. Colours range through shades of blue to white.

Dianthus 'Boydii'. Fringed pink flowers are carried on 10 cm (4 in) stems over narrow leaves. Mainly June-flowering, it blooms spasmodically in summer.

Douglasia montana. A loose, cushion-forming species, with greyish-green, pointed leaves. In April, it carries deep pink flowers that are 2.5 cm (1 in) high.

Draba aizoides. In earliest spring, golden flowers on 5 cm (2 in) stems are carried above tufted, bristly rosettes of dark green. This is a British native plant, found on Welsh cliffs.

Gentiana saxosa. A mid to late summer-flowering gem from New Zealand. White flowers, with green veining, are borne on 10 cm (4 in) stems over dark-green, glossy leaf rosettes.

Helichrysum milfordiae. This grey, woolly, rosetted South African plant, 5 cm (2 in) high, is absolutely hardy if the drainage is perfect. Pointed, crimson buds open as white everlasting flowers in June.

Linum salsoloides 'Nanum'

Saxifraga grisebachii 'Wisley'. From beautiful rosettes of intense silver, each 2.5 cm (1 in) wide, arise bracts of a red-velvet texture. Small flowers open during April.

Plants to grow in tufa

Anchusa caespitosa. A rock-growing plant that consists of strap-shaped leaves, with vivid-blue flowers, each with a white eye, in summer. Height 5–8 cm (2 in).

Androsace villosa. Small grey-green, 5 cm (2 in) high tufts form on red-stemmed stolons, each bearing round, scented white flowers during April.

Androsace villosa

Asperula suberosa. A delicate-looking carpet of white, woolly foliage, topped with pink tubular flowers, giving a 'foam' effect. The flowers appear in May. Height 5–8 cm (2–3 in).

Douglasia vitaliana var. *praetutiana.* Greyish-green rosettes, each 12 mm (½ in) across, make a compact plant. During April, it is covered with lemon-yellow, half-open flowers.

Linum salsoloides 'Nanum'. Slender stems carry needle-like leaves and, in summer, large, pearly-white flowers. The habit is semi-trailing.

Omphalodes luciliae. A beautiful plant, about 15 cm (6 in) high, with blue-grey leaves that provide a low-domed effect. Pink buds open to soft-blue flowers, mainly during the summer.

Physoplexis comosa, syn. *Phyteuma comosum.* After its winter dormancy, sharply-toothed leaves appear, soon followed by curious claw-shaped, tubular flowers, the colour of lilac. Height and spread about 5 cm (2 in).

Potentilla nitida 'Alba'. Forms a tight mat of silver-green, hairy leaves. Stems, 5 cm (2 in) high, bear white flowers with orange stamens mainly in May and June.

Raoulia lutescens. A minute carpet of grey-green leaves, well covered with tiny, stemless yellow flowers in summer.

Saxifraga 'Jenkinsae'. A 2.5 cm (1 in) hummock of grey-leaved rosettes covered, during March and April, with near-stemless, shell-pink flowers.

JANUARY

Unheated house and frames An alpine house with accompanying frames will already have some early-flowering bulbs on display, together with the clear white flowers of *Iberis semperflorens*. Dwarf conifers, which form the backbone of any display, remain in the house for most of the year, but they will have to be moved out a little later when the main flush of bulbs and high alpines will need more space.

Ventilation Whenever possible, admit plenty of air to the house and frames, closing the side and top vents only under extremes of wet or cold. Even then, damage is more likely to occur to the house than to the plants.

The same applies to the frames. Keep them open to admit plenty of air but, if it snows, leave the frame lights off so that the snow can blanket the plants, as in the wild. Replace the lights when the snow starts to melt, giving plenty of ventilation.

Heated house and frames Frames used to supply a heated house will themselves need to be heated. Provide ventilation when the temperature is above the thermostat setting, which should be 2°C (36°F). Keep frames slightly ventilated even when the heating is on, otherwise condensation may result in damping off.

A little air is an advantage even at night, unless the temperature goes below −20 °C (−3 °F). Water only when essential, keeping the staging dry to reduce condensation.

Rock gardens, screes, raised beds There is very little to do except remove leaves, blown from elsewhere, which increase the risk of botrytis. Check glass covers to ensure that they are still secure. During wet weather, check that slug pellets have not disintegrated, replacing them if necessary.

FEBRUARY

Unheated house and frames The build-up of plants coming into the house will probably necessitate moving dwarf conifers and any other background plants to frames in order to make room for the newcomers.

At every opportunity, clean up pots in the house and frames by removing weeds and dead material. Dead and dying growth must be pulled or cut off cleanly. Use a proprietary brand of fungicide powder on any major cuts to prevent further die-back, especially on high-alpines and plants with hairy foliage.

Potting seedlings Pot up singly any seedlings that appear, preferably when they are just large enough to handle. At this stage the roots suffer very little damage. Use a gritty compost. (See March.) Surface chippings can be omitted, except for high-alpines and plants with woolly foliage, which need finer chippings to suit the smaller pots.

Place or plunge the pots in a closed frame for a few days, then ventilate when the shock of being moved has worn off.

Watering and ventilation Increase watering during mild weather. Ventilate the house and frames almost all the time, except during severe weather.

Heated house and frames Ventilate as much as possible, consistent with not wasting too much heat, and water when necessary. This will be more frequent during cold weather, when heating will tend to dry out the house and frames.

Watch out for aphids, spraying them, when seen, with a systemic insecticide for preference or a contact insecticide.

Pot up seedlings and cuttings that have rooted during the winter months.

Rock gardens, screes and raised beds The post-winter clean-up can begin on a mild day. Cut back herbaceous material, but leave woody material until later in case splitting results from a return of colder weather.

Check glass covers; renew slug pellets if necessary. Remove wind-blown leaves, and weeds, too, if the weather is not too severe.

MARCH

Unheated house and frames With the alpine house now full of plants in flower and in bud, give increased amounts of water as the weather warms up and the days lengthen appreciably. Ventilation should be provided at all times, with the doors left open on mild days. Look for aphids on young shoots, and treat as suggested for heated alpine houses in February.

Potting and dividing Continue to pot up seedlings; start repotting plants that have finished flowering and that have not been repotted for two years. For the best results, it is better to repot most plants each year. Choose a pot one size larger than the previous one, removing any crocks and as much soil as possible from the rootball.

Divide those plants that can be divided and pot the pieces singly in 5–8 cm (2–3 in) pots. Always use fresh compost when potting, making a gritty mix of John Innes potting compost No. 2, with 25% extra grit and 25% extra moss peat, and leaving at least 12 mm (½ in) of the rim exposed for easier watering. Soak the plants after re-potting unless freezing weather seems imminent.

Pot up cuttings that have rooted during the winter.

Heated house and frames The heating should come on only occasionally, in order to maintain a minimum temperature of 2°C (36 °F). The more ventilation that can be given, the more sturdily the plants will grow. Continue watering as before, but giving more to match the growing strength of the sun.

Rock gardens, screes and raised beds Complete the post-winter clean-up this month. Remove any woody material, as on fuchsias, together with herbaceous material, by pulling off the foliage. Be careful not to damage the crowns when doing so, particularly those of *Pulsatilla vulgaris*, which will shortly be in flower.

Alpines planted now will start to grow away within a month, lessening the risk of dying during dry summer weather or during cold periods next winter. Plant up sink gardens.

Replace slug pellets that have disintegrated, particularly around vulnerable young plants.

Panes of protective glass may sometimes be taken off now, but much depends on the weather. If in doubt, do not move them.

APRIL

Unheated house and frames This is the busiest time of year, with so many plants in flower and the growth of others well under way. With the house and frames fully ventilated, and the days much longer, there is a chance to enjoy the wealth of colour.

Miscellaneous jobs Watering should now be in full swing.

Although alpines appreciate good drainage, they do need plenty of water during the growing season. In the wild they would be kept moist by melting snow. Other timely jobs include potting up seedlings, repotting plants that have flowered, and also repotting those that flower in mid- to late summer.

Aphids are multiplying rapidly now and control is vital. A watch needs to be kept for whitefly, too.

If you plan to grow plants from home-saved seeds, collect them as soon as they are ripe and sow immediately, using the mix recommended for potting. Sow them thinly and cover the surface with chippings.

Cuttings may be taken now of *Dionysia* species and *Androsace* species. They are the smallest of alpine cuttings, measuring only 2 mm (1/16 in) across and up to 6 mm (1/4 in) long.

Heated house and frames From now until October, give plants the same treatment as in unheated houses and frames. Provide plenty of air, even at night, unless frost threatens.

Rock gardens, screes and raised beds It is important to keep the ground clear of weeds, because they will drop their seeds from now on if they are allowed to flourish. This is where good construction pays dividends, giving easy access for hand weeding.

Planting can continue from now until mid-summer, but the sooner this is done, the better the chance of survival.

It is still advisable to check the condition of slug pellets, especially in cold gardens, although if the weather is dry they need not be replaced.

Any glass covers still over plants should be removed now, otherwise sunshine striking

through the glass may harm the plants. By now the plants should be growing and therefore able to deal with surplus moisture, unless the season is exceptionally late.

MAY

Heated and unheated houses and frames Shading should be provided this month, following one of the recommended methods.

Watering and ventilation With many of the spring-flowering bulbs dying down, their watering should be reduced and controlled. With this in mind, replace the lights over those in frames, ventilating fully. The remaining plants will need copious watering, especially on warm days, but a plunge material does reduce the amount of water loss.

Leaving the ventilators fully open day and night – and the doors, too, on mild nights and throughout the day – will keep the air circulation going, thereby reducing the risk of botrytis at a time when much water is being applied.

It is all a question of balance. Too much shading makes the plants look drawn and out of character, and makes them vulnerable to pests and diseases. Too much water without ventilation leads to botrytis. Too little water and plenty of ventilation causes plants to become stunted and to flower poorly.

Hygiene Keeping the houses and frames clean and tidy as the year proceeds will reduce pest and disease problems. Even so, keep an eye open for aphids, which will be reproducing now every ten days until September. Prompt control is therefore vital to prevent damage to plants.

Watch also for signs of poor growth and dying foliage, perhaps accompanied by excessively wet or dry compost. This can be checked by knocking the plant out of its pot and may serve as a guide to subsequent management.

Potting and propagation This is a good month for potting up seedlings and for repotting plants that have flowered or will flower in mid- to late summer. The aim should be to maintain existing growth without a check.

Continue to collect and sow seeds. Should the seeds not be wanted at the moment, exchange them for other needed seeds as soon as possible, otherwise germination may be impaired. Petiolarid primulas, for example, can be collected ripe or just before ripening, but they must be sown immediately to have any chance at all of success.

Because these and other alpines are somewhat difficult to grow, the success rate is limited, but therein lies the challenge and satisfaction of keeping plants going in successive generations.

Propagating regularly, by seeds or cuttings, will keep the growth young and vigorous instead of allowing plants to become old and woody – or dead!

It is known that some plants grow well, flower well, then die, for no apparent reason other than that they have perhaps flowered themselves to death. The more common plants do not usually present this problem, so give your time and attention to a few difficult ones. They will provide ample reward, while the easier plants continue to give a sound return for occasional but regular attention.

Rock gardens, screes and raised beds Alpines grown outdoors are now at their peak, so time and trouble spent earlier in the year is paying off. Dwarf conifers have

their new coats of green foliage to contrast with the old; dwarf shrubs are coming into full leaf, showing colour and form after months of dormancy. Early bulbs will be dying down and those flowering in early or mid-summer will be showing good growth. Herbaceous plants will be covering the ground with new growth, joining with the shrubs in shading the ground.

Do weed under these new growths, otherwise the weeds will run to seed and spread over any bare ground. Scree areas will have more stone-covered ground than the rock garden and raised beds, so weeds should be fewer.

Slugs will not normally be a problem now, but aphids certainly will. There is a good choice of suitable sprays.

Watering Newly-planted areas may need watering, but do this only when the top 2.5 cm (1 in) or so of soil is dry. It is better to encourage roots to grow downwards, where there will be plenty of moisture, rather than sideways, which will happen when water is applied too often.

Material on the surface of a scree helps to conserve moisture for the plants. Those planted in raised beds will tend to dry out faster, and as a result will need watering more often.

Sink gardens will dry out even faster, needing water much more often. The same applies to tubs and large pots, especially those that are shallow.

Seed sowing and cuttings Seed collecting and sowing can gather pace now, with more ripe seeds becoming available from spring-flowering plants. Saxifrages and other early-flowering alpines can be propagated now by cuttings taken off their new growths. (See June.)

JUNE

Heated and unheated houses and frames Seed sowing reaches a peak this month. Bulbs, now dying down, should be producing plenty of seeds, except for crocuses, which come in July. Alpines, too, are currently producing seeds, and these ought to be sown as soon as possible.

Taking cuttings Hybrid plants, which will not come true from seed, need to be propagated vegetatively. Those forming rosettes, such as saxifrages, can be reproduced by pulling or cutting off healthy rosettes, gently peeling off the lower leaves, and dibbling the short stem in horticultural sand.

The rooting of all cuttings can be speeded by dipping the cut ends into hormone rooting powder. To prevent botrytis, water the cuttings in with Cheshunt compound.

Cuttings taken in this way, and inserted in 8 cm (3 in) plastic or clay pots will be easy to handle when rooted. Cover the pots of cuttings (each pot with a different species or cultivar, and carefully labelled and dated) with one of the clear plastic propagator cups sold for the purpose.

Place the pots on the bench or in the frame, not plunged this time because each pot is in its own little 'greenhouse'. Within a few weeks the cuttings will be ready for potting.

To propagate shrubs and plants with longer growths, take cuttings with stem lengths upwards of 2.5 cm (1 in), depending on the size of growth, with the lower leaves trimmed off and inserted in horticultural sand and treated as already described. Plants that prefer shade or, in the open ground, grow in a more acid mixture, will benefit from a 50–50 sand and moss peat mixture. This particularly suits rhododendrons.

The most suitable growths from which to take cuttings are new ones which are beginning to become firm. In the case of dwarf phlox and similar plants, softer stem cuttings are in order.

Check the cuttings as often as possible – preferably every day – for signs of damping off (botrytis) and remove any that are infected. Take off the plastic cover when they have rooted.

Bulbs Most bulbs should be left dry now for about three months, though *Galanthus, Fritillaria* and *Narcissus* may be given an occasional watering.

Rock gardens, screes and raised beds As aubrietas finish flowering, use a pair of shears to trim them back. This may seem drastic, but if all the old flowering growths are removed those made subsequently will flower much better next year. Trimming will also keep the plants within bounds, instead of becoming straggly.

Weeding is now a simple task, taking only a few minutes each week instead of hours, provided earlier weed clearance was carried out thoroughly.

JULY

Heated and unheated houses and frames The number of plants in flower will have dropped off dramatically, so keep most of the plants in open frames, without covers, whenever possible. During rainy spells this will save watering, and the plants will be cooler in the open frame than in a greenhouse.

Do not leave high-alpines out in the rain, however, as they will not enjoy our summer storms.

Continue to pot up seedlings and to repot plants that have already flowered.

Take action to control aphids.

Repotting bulbs Empty each pot in turn on to a bench and pick out the bulbs individually. Repot them in fresh compost, like that used for alpines. (See March.) Use the old soil for making up beds or lightening heavy soil in the open. Use a kitchen sieve to ensure that very small bulbs do not get thrown out with the soil.

Propagation Continue to take cuttings, if possible avoiding plants that are in flower. At this time all the plants' strength will go into making flowers instead of into rooting.

Continue to collect and sow seeds and to pot-up or repot seedlings. Rooted cuttings will need potting, too.

Rock gardens, screes and raised beds Campanulas, along with a number of other alpines, will now be coming into flower, giving beautiful shades of blue and mauve, together with white. This is a reminder that, although the bulk of alpines flower in spring, they are by no means finished then. There are others to provide a succession of flowers during the summer and berries during the autumn, with autumn-flowering crocus to follow.

As the dwarf phloxes finish their magnificent display, cut them back with shears just as the aubrietas were last month. A pair of secateurs to cut back the old, flowered growths of helianthemums will serve the same purpose, keeping the plant both more compact and helping to ensure that there are many more flowers to be enjoyed next year.

During dry weather, water newly-planted areas, raised beds and sink gardens.

AUGUST

Heated and unheated houses and frames Try to complete repotting, seed-sowing and potting, and also the potting of rooted cuttings by the end of this month. Otherwise, leave them until next year. Even in a heated house or frame there is less chance of overwintering alpines successfully if they are disturbed at this time of year.

Late-germinating seedlings, which in the wild would not appear until next spring, are at particular risk. However, this must be weighed against the greater risk of storing the seeds.

Continue to watch for pests, such as aphids and whitefly.

Rock gardens, screes and raised beds Prune late-flowering helianthemums (See July.)

Continue with weeding, watering and pest control.

Next month, when the routine work of weeding, mowing and so on tends to slacken, is a good time for constructing a rock garden, raised bed or other feature where alpines may be grown. With this in mind, now is the time to order stone and other materials. Plants may be ordered, too, for setting out this autumn.

SEPTEMBER

Heated and unheated houses and frames A heated greenhouse and frames may need to be closed at night in case of frost, but unheated structures should be left with ventilation full on. Reduce watering gradually for heated and unheated houses and frames. Water only the dry plants, giving them a good soak. Do not water over high-alpines with silver or woolly foliage.

Remain alert for aphids, spraying as necessary.

Remove shading this month as the weather dictates. This can be by stages or in one go, depending on how shading was provided.

Scrub the glass and framework on a dry day when all the plants can be removed with safety. This will ensure that maximum light is admitted during the winter. Clean frame lights individually.

Although it is worth collecting seeds from late-flowering plants, these should not be sown until late December or January.

Rock gardens, screes and raised beds New constructions, such as a rock garden or scree, started this month should be completed before the days become too short or the soil too wet. Similarly, glazed sinks can now be covered with hypertufa.

Keep existing rock gardens and beds weeded. Control aphids by spraying as necessary.

OCTOBER

Unheated house and frames Continue routine watering, weeding and cleaning as necessary. By the end of the month, however, a single, light weekly watering should be sufficient.

Place slug pellets in or near all pots to control these pests. With the protection of a frame or house, they should last all winter.

Heated house and frames Although closed at night, these must be opened fully during the day when the outside temperature is higher than the thermostat setting of 2 °C (36 °F). This will prevent the plants from becoming drawn.

Rock gardens, screes and raised beds Along with the last of the weeding start to clear any leaves blown from elsewhere on to rock gardens or other alpine sites. If left, they can lead to botrytis, so make a clearance at least weekly.

Slug pellets scattered round plants will protect them from the ravages of slugs and snails, but they will need regular renewal as the rain breaks them down. Check their condition weekly.

Constructions of all sorts should be completed. Seeds collected from late-flowering and berrying plants should not be sown until late December.

Place sheets of glass over alpines that are vulnerable to winter wet. The plants most at risk are those with silver or woolly foliage, together with those from drier areas of the world. Among widely-grown kinds are *Acantholimon;* some species of *Androsace; Calandrinia; Campanula cashmeriana; C. raineri, C. sartori;* some species of *Douglasia; Crassula sarcocaulis;* some species of *Helichrysum;* some dwarf species of *Papaver; Paraquilegia; Phlox nana* hybrids; *Primula allionii; Sempervivella.*

NOVEMBER

Unheated house and frames Give just enough water, every week or so, to prevent the pots from drying out. Full ventilation is needed, except when gale-force winds may blow rain in.

Heated house and frames Keep at least one vent open a crack, even during cold weather, so that condensation does not build up to encourage botrytis. This will increase heating costs slightly, but a temperature of 2°C (36°F) is sufficient, and the plants will remain alive and healthier.

Rock gardens, screes and raised beds Remove all wind-blown leaves weekly. At the same time, check that glass covers are secure and that slug pellets have not totally disintegrated.

DECEMBER

Unheated and heated houses Ventilate houses and frames whenever possible. Water only when absolutely necessary.

If you grow cultivars of *Primula allionii,* which flower early in the year, use tweezers to remove dead and yellow leaves in preparation for blooming.

Rock gardens, screes, and raised beds Clear up fallen leaves from areas where alpines grow, and also from gutters and along the edges of paths and beds.

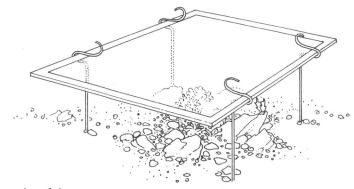

Protecting alpines
Protect silver and woolly-leaved alpines with raised sheets of glass.

Rhododendron flowers
Borne in clusters, they may be bell (1) or funnel-shaped (2), or sometimes tubular (3).

Some 600 species and thousands of cultivars make up this exceptionally large genus. It includes azaleas, which form a group of species within the overall classification.

Rhododendrons belong to the family *Ericaceae*, which indicates their need for acid soil. They are found in all parts of the world except Africa and South America, but the great majority come from Asia.

Soil Rhododendrons do not merely have a preference for acid soil; they simply will not grow when conditions are alkaline. Success is more likely if you start with soil that is naturally acid rather than try to change an alkaline soil by adding sulphur or peat. A possible exception would be if you intend to plant some of the dwarf types, where a number of plants can be grown in a comparatively small area or raised bed.

The soil should be light and open, so heavy clay needs the addition of large quantities of humus. Because the roots of rhododendrons are usually fibrous, they do not as a rule go very deep. For this reason the soil must be able to retain plenty of moisture.

When mixing in organic matter it is better to do this over the whole area rather than just in the planting pockets, or these may become sumps for water draining from the more compacted soil around. A saturated soil will kill rhododendrons.

When rhododendrons have been growing for a long time, it will be seen that their fallen leaves have gradually decomposed to form an open, light compost. This is exactly the sort of growing medium that suits them best.

Site Rhododendrons prefer partial shade to an open site, although there are some exceptions. Deciduous azaleas, for example, will tolerate a more open position. Not all gardens can provide a tree-shaded site, and, in any case, not all trees are suitable as shade trees. In addition, those such as birch have too shallow a root run, taking moisture away from the area where the rhododendron roots would be.

Again, some trees form such a dense canopy that there is insufficient light for anything much to grow. The best overhead covering is one that gives dappled shade, such as a site on the edge of woodland planting. If suitable shade is not available, the next best thing is to plant where the rhododendrons will be protected from the sun by the house or a shed during the hottest part of the day.

A further consideration is that a canopy over the plants will keep them several degrees warmer, thereby helping to avoid the worst effects of frost. This can range in severity from twisting or puckering of the leaves and death of the flower buds, to the splitting of the bark. The latter usually occurs on the main stems and often kills the whole plant.

This emphasises the importance of not planting in a frost pocket or where early morning sun can shine on plants that are still frozen. As a measure of self-protection, some rhododendrons roll their leaves around the midrib in order to protect them from desiccation when the ground is frozen or the weather frosty.

Shelter from wind is another consideration. Rather than trying to stop the wind completely, which leads to damaging turbulence, it is better to reduce its force by filtering. In other words, a hedge is better than a wall or fence, and there are also purpose-made plastic windbreaks that sift the wind rather than stop it completely.

The effect of planting in a wind tunnel, created by wind funnelled between buildings, can be disastrous. Plants may lose their leaves or be uprooted completely. Wind can also spoil the apprearance of rhododendrons by tearing their leaves, especially those of the larger-leaved species. Yet another harmful effect of wind is desiccation, due to more water being removed from the leaves than the plant is able to replace.

Soil preparation As with any permanent planting, it is essential to start with a site free from perennial weeds. This can be achieved either with the aid of chemicals or by forking them out by hand. Afterwards, when digging the soil, add as much organic material as possible. Peat and leaf-mould are excellent but not mushroom compost, which contains lime, or compost from heaps to which lime has been added. The more material added the better, as it will help give the soil a good, friable structure as well as retaining moisture during dry periods.

Planting can be carried out at any time of year, provided the ground is neither frozen nor too wet. This applies whether you buy container-grown plants or those that have been grown in open ground and then had their root-balls wrapped in hessian. Needless to say, check that the plants are specimens before you part with your money.

Planting First, check the size of the root-ball and dig a hole half as large again. Mix damp peat into the bottom of each hole – say, a couple of handfuls for a plant with a root-ball 15 cm (6 in) wide. Also mix peat into the soil taken from the hole.

Ensure that the root-ball of the plant is well and truly moist, then remove it carefully from its container. Take special care to retain the soil around a plant that has been root-balled in hessian. Check that the hole is of the right depth, so that the soil mark on the stem is level with the surrounding soil, then fill in around the root-ball with the mixed earth and peat and firm lightly.

An exception to this advice on planting depth arises with grafted plants, which may be identified by a slight swelling on the stem 5–8 cm (2–3 in) above soil level. These may be planted a little deeper, leaving a slight hollow around the stem, which, over a period, should be filled with mulch. This will eventually induce scion rooting – that is, from the stem above the point of union with the rootstock.

Water the plants in, using a can and rose, to help consolidate the soil around the roots.

After-care Ensure that the root-ball does not dry out, particularly the year after planting. It sometimes happens that the ball remains dry even though the surrounding soil is moist. This is most likely to occur with plants that are grown in a pure peat compost, which, once dry, is extremely difficult to wet again. On balance, it is better to give water when it is not needed than to miss watering when it is.

A mulch applied around the base of the

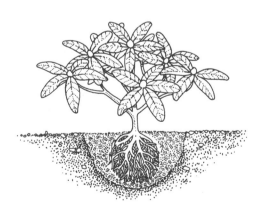
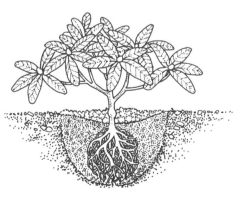

Planting rhododendrons Plant level with the previous soil mark and deep enough to accommodate the root-ball (far left). Set grafted plants deeper, with a hollow round the graft union; mulch to encourage scion rooting.

plants will help to conserve moisture, but take care not to bury their necks. The best material to use is bracken or leaf-mould, with a light and open texture.

The area mulched should be larger than the plant's own spread – preferably the whole bed. The mulch will also help to suppress weed growth.

The need for watering continues in subsequent years. As the plant grows, the leaf cover becomes more dense, tending to keep the root area dry. Probably the most effective way to water is with a slow-running, open-ended hose pipe left on for a couple of hours. In hard-water areas, and if there are only one or two plants, it is an advantage to use lime-free rainwater.

Mulching each year in the spring will help to stimulate growth. It is also good practice to give dressings of a slow-release fertilizer, once in the spring and again in July. The correct rate is about 65 g per sq m (2 oz per sq yd).

Dead-heading – that is, removing the dead blooms – is a task which, although time-consuming, pays dividends by encouraging more flowers the following year. Do it immediately the flowers have faded, so that no energy is put into seed production. It is also simpler at this time because the new growth that arises from around the old flowers may be broken off if the job is delayed. It is not so necessary to dead-head the smaller, profuse-flowering varieties after the first few years, but they certainly look better for it.

Because a number of rhododendrons are still grafted, it may be necessary to remove suckers from them. These growths arise from the rootstock and are usually fairly easy to recognize because of their different leaf shape and colour and also because of the point from which they emerge.

Remove them from as far back as possible so as to discourage the same thing occurring again. Suckering is sometimes an indication that the plant is in a poor state of health, so take steps to rectify this if necessary.

Pests and diseases There are not a great many diseases from which rhododendrons suffer, the three most important being leaf spot, bud blast and powdery mildew. As far as pests are concerned, in addition to the usual greenfly and whitefly there is a leafhopper which spreads bud blast.

Pruning There is no need to prune rhododendrons, except to remove dead wood which tends to build up within the spread of branches. Anything more, unless done very carefully, may destroy the natural shape of the plant. However, if a mature plant gets out of control and outgrows its site, it can be cut back severely, which usually results in it breaking into new growth.

Propagation The four main methods of propagation are the same for all sizes of rhododendrons.

First, species can be raised from fresh seeds sown on the surface of peat, but the difficulty is finding seed which will produce seedlings identical to the parent. If the seed is from open-pollinated plants from within a collection, there will be variations among the resultant seedlings. Another snag is that it will take from five to twenty-five years until they flower!

A second method is by taking cuttings, which will come true to the parent plant. This method is used widely, and by taking the cuttings at the correct time – from mid-July until late August – very good results can be obtained, especially from evergreen azaleas.

A third method is to graft the plants. This requires the use of a rootstock, usually *R. ponticum*, together with material from the required plant. The object is to graft the stock to the scion so that the top growth of the stock can be removed, leaving the scion to grow into a plant.

A fourth method, not much used by nurserymen, is to layer the plant. Here, a low branch is bent down into the soil and fixed there with a peg. A nick is then made in the underside of the shoot, below ground level, from which roots will emerge. After a year the layer can be cut off from the plant and left to establish for a further year. Finally, it may be lifted and planted where required.

Variety in rhododendrons Rhododendrons can be chosen to give flowers over about eight months of the year, starting in January with *R. mucronulatum* and ending

Dead-heading
Remove faded flowers by snipping them off between forefinger and thumb.

in August with *R. auriculatum*. The main flowering period is during May and June, but this varies slightly from year to year and in different parts of the country.

The colour range is very extensive, with most colours being represented in some shade or hue. Perhaps the darkest is *R.* 'Impi', which is a really dark red – almost black. The whitest is the pure white *R.* 'Bric-a-Brac'.

An added bonus to the spectacular flowers is that they are often scented. This varies from the light, delicate perfume of *R. auriculatum* to the very strong scent of *R. luteum* which, in a confined space, can be a little overpowering.

Flower size varies, too, from enormous trusses, where individual blooms of varieties such as *R. x loderi* 'King George' may be 8–10 cm (3–4 in) across, to those of *R. campylogynum* var. *myrtilloides*, which are less than 12 mm (½ in) in diameter.

The flowers are not the only attraction, for the foliage also has a lot to offer. Deciduous rhododendrons take on lovely autumn colours – especially the azaleas, whose glorious reds and yellows remain for a long time.

The foliage of some other species is particularly attractive right through the season. For example, the leaves of *R. bureavii* are dark green on top, the undersides being covered with a rusty-red down, which is also present on the young shoots. The young shoots of *R. yakushimanum* are clad with white 'wool'.

Leaf size can be another prominent feature, those of *R. sinogrande* being over 60 cm (2 ft) long. However, this species is suitable only for sheltered, moist situations in favourable parts of the country.

Another aspect to consider is size, especially where space is a limiting factor. The variation is enormous, from *R. arboreum*, which will form a tree up to 12 m (40 ft) tall to *R. radicans*, a prostrate shrub only about 10 cm (4 in) high.

Where space is not a problem, the bark of a large, mature plant itself becomes a feature as it begins to peel and flake. *R. barbatum* has a bark between red and purple; that of *R. thomsonii* is orange to cinnamon brown.

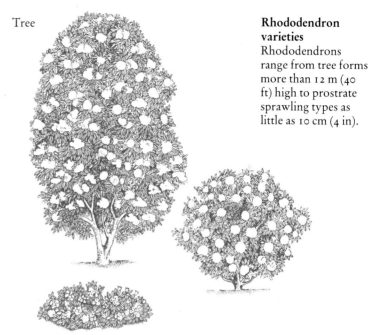

Tree

Dwarf bush

Bush

Rhododendron varieties
Rhododendrons range from tree forms more than 12 m (40 ft) high to prostrate sprawling types as little as 10 cm (4 in).

RHODODENDRONS FOR SMALL GARDENS

The smaller rhododendrons, up to 90 cm–1.2 m (3–4 ft) high, may be planted even where space is strictly limited. Whatever the size of the garden, they enable a greater range of species and hybrids to be grown in a given area. But there is also another advantage.

The smaller the area, the more practical it becomes to reduce the soil pH (make the soil more acid) if this is too high, bearing in mind that rhododendrons, like most other ericaceous plants, require a pH of 5–5.5.

The first consideration is to pick a site where water from surrounding alkaline soil will not drain into it. This is best achieved by making a raised bed, constructing the sides with stone or peat blocks. It will have to be kept well watered during dry periods, preferably with rainwater if you live in a hard-water area.

First, check the present pH with a testing kit. If it is only slightly above neutral, the addition of peat may bring it down to an acceptable level. If it is much too alkaline, the same result can be achieved, somewhat expensively, with chemicals, including sulphur.

The resistance that the soil shows to

Species and hybrids

Rhododendrons included in the following list of recommended species and hybrids are mostly medium to large size. The heights are averages for ten-year-old plants. They are evergreeen unless otherwise stated.

R. augustinii. 1.8–3 m (6–10 ft). The small leaves are dark green. The flowers, borne in trusses, are blue through pink to white, April and May.

R. fulvum. Up to 6 m (20 ft). The leaves are dark green above, and fawn-velvet below. The flowers vary from white to pink and appear in April and May.

R. glischrum. Up to 7.6 m (25 ft). The leaves are yellow to dark green above, dense, curved bristles below. The flowers are pinkish-white to plum-coloured, during April and May.

R. lutescens. Up to 3 m (10 ft). Young leaves and shoots are bright red, the older leaves bronze-coloured. The flowers, from February to April, are primrose-yellow.

R. schlippenbachii. 1.8–4.5 m (6–15 ft). The leaves are deciduous, with good autumn colouring. The saucer-shaped flowers are in shades of pink and open during April and May.

R. 'Albatross'. 1.8 m (6 ft). Scented pink to white flowers in June.

R. 'America'. 1.5 m (5 ft). Dark red flowers in May and June. A sun-tolerant plant.

R. 'Blue Peter'. 1.2–1.5 m (4–5 ft). Pale blue flowers with a dark blotch, in May.

R. 'Britannia'. 1.2 m (4 ft). A dense bush, with scarlet flowers in early June.

R. 'Crest'. 1.8 m (6 ft). Large, rich yellow flowers in May.

R. 'Lodauric Iceberg'. 1.8 m (6 ft). Scented white flowers, with a crimson blotch, in July.

R. 'Moonshine Bright'. 1.5 m (5 ft). Bright yellow flowers open in May.

R. 'Nobleanum Album'. 1.2 m (4 ft). Pure white flowers between January and March.

R. 'Pink Pearl'. 1.8 m (6 ft). Rose-pink flowers in May.

R. 'Souvenir of W. C. Slocock'. 1.2 m (4 ft). Apricot/pale yellow flowers during May.

Rhododendron 'Pink Pearl'

Rhododendron racemosum

Rhododendron yakushimanum

change will depend on how much clay and organic matter it contains. For this reason it will be easier to reduce the pH level before adding peat or any other organic material.

Altering the pH The amount of sulphur (flowers of sulphur) required to reduce the pH from 7 to 5 will depend on the soil's texture. For a sandy loam, 125 g per sq m 4 oz per sq yd) will be quite sufficient, whereas heavy loams will require double this quantity.

Aluminium or ferrous sulphate, applied at 125–250 g per sq m (4–8 oz per sq yd), will reduce the pH much more rapidly, for, unlike sulphur, these chemicals do not rely on bacterial action. (The warmer the soil is, the more rapid the action.) If you use aluminium or ferrous sulphate, it is better to apply less than the maximum dose, then to test the soil again after two or three weeks and add more if necessary. The danger otherwise is that the soil may be made unacceptably acid.

Other aspects of soil preparation and planting are the same as for larger species. One point to bear in mind, however, and especially with smaller plants, is that rhododendrons are particularly amenable to being moved. Initially, therefore, they can be planted closer than their ultimate size dictates, and then spaced out later on.

The only limiting factor is the need to lift the root-ball, but the very fibrous root system helps to hold this together, provided care is used when handling it.

Deciding which plants to grow Consider planting some of the species as well as hybrids, because they have a lot to offer. A good example is *R. yakushimanum*, which forms a compact dome about 90 cm (3 ft) high and broad. Its young growths are silvery, with dark green leaves, the undersides of which are thickly covered with brown hairs. The pink flowers are in compact trusses, and the whole plant is in many respects better than some of the hybrids which have it as a parent.

One particularly striking dwarf rhododendron is *R. glaucophyllum* var. *luteiflorum*, with leaves that are dark green above and silvery-white beneath, together with bell-shaped yellow flowers. The bark of the trunk and twigs is a rich brown and peels off in layers, leaving the unblemished bark beneath.

And then there are azaleas. These are a group of various rhododendron species, which have been put together to form a division within the larger classification. It consists of species such as *R. albrechtii*, *R. molle* and *R. luteum*, which give rise to some of the deciduous azaleas, and *R. kaempferi*, *R. malvaticum* and *R. indicum*, which are the parents of some of the evergreen azaleas. There is also a group called Azaleodendron, which are crosses between deciduous species from within the azalea sections and evergreen species from other groups.

The evergreen azaleas, which normally flower in April and May, give a really spectacular show, often with hardly a leaf showing between the flowers. For the most part they are single flowers, but some are hose-in-hose (one flower inside another), while a few are double.

Many deciduous azaleas give a splendid show of autumn leaf colour – primarily reds and golds. They are more tolerant of sun than some others, but there is a tendency for some of the colours of the flowers to become bleached. They are mostly single flowers, but there are exceptions. The range of colours is very varied, from the pastels of *R. occidentale* hybrids, including scented forms, to the bright reds and golds of the *R. mollis* hybrids.

SPECIES AND HYBRIDS FOR SMALL GARDENS

The best way to choose is by visiting specialist nurseries or by studying established collections in gardens open to the public. The following is just a small selection from the great range available:

Evergreen hybrid azaleas: 'Blue Danube', blue-purple; 'Hino Crimson', crimson-scarlet; 'Kirin', deep rose-pink, hose-in-hose; 'Orange Beauty', bright orange; 'Palestrina', white with a green eye.

Deciduous hybrid azaleas: 'Brazil', light tangerine-orange, darkening with age; 'Chocolate Ice', double, pale cream, scented, bronze foliage; 'Gibraltar', crimson-orange in bud opening to flame-orange with a yellow flash; 'Golden Oriole', deep golden-yellow, young leaves bronze; 'Persil', white with a yellow flash.

Dwarf rhododendrons for raised beds: *R. campylogynum* 'Claret', deep red; 'Curlew', yellow; *R. ferrugineum*, rose-pink; 'Intrifast', blue; 'Ptarmigan', white.

Small to medium-size rhododendrons: 'Bric-a-Brac', white; 'Diane', primrose-yellow; 'Elizabeth', bright red; *R. racemosum*, pink-white; 'Tessa', rosy-lilac. *R. yakushimanum* hybrids: 'Bambi', red opening to pink, with yellow tinge; 'Dopey', bright red; 'Grumpy', yellow tinged shell-pink; 'Hydon Ball', white, spotted light brown; 'Percy Wiseman', pink-cream fading to white.

Azaleodendrons: 'Glory of Littleworth', cream with coppery blotch; 'Govenianum', lavender-purple, scented; 'Martha Isaacson', white with pink stripe; 'Martinii', shell-pink; 'Nellie', pure white with yellow blotch, scented.

PLANTS FOR POOLS AND WATER GARDENS

Plants whose roots, and all or parts of their stems, grow under water are termed aquatic. Bog plants are those which do best with varying degrees of moisture at their roots only. There is some overlap between the two different types.

Water lilies are the principal plants in most water gardens. Apart from their beauty, they play an important part in shading the pool and so controlling the growth of algae, which turn the water green. Most need relatively deep water, and there are also some other aquatics, such as *Aponogeton distachyus*, which are also best planted in pools that are 45 cm (1½ ft) or more deep.

So-called marginal plants are those planted on shelving round the margins of a pool, for they require relatively shallow water. Alternatively, they may be set on plinths so that the containers are just covered by water.

In addition to these kinds there are oxygenating or aerating plants, which release oxygen into the water and in this way help to keep it clear. Floating plants, placed on the surface, act like water lilies in reducing the amount of light that can enter the water.

Most bog plants are herbaceous, requiring dividing and replanting every three to five years. There are also some trees, shrubs and bulbs suitable for pool-side planting.

The aquatic plants described here are particularly suitable for pools of 10 sq m (12 sq yd) or less, though they can also be grown in larger pools. The depths given are for that of the water above the container, shelves or plinths being necessary for the shallow-water (marginal) plants.

The bog plants (with the possible exception of *Gunnera manicata*) are suitable for gardens of any size and, unless otherwise stated, they need sunny situations in order to grow and flower well.

Water garden
This formal garden features the classic sunken pool planted with water lilies, flowering rushes and irises.

Marginal and deep-water aquatics

Water 5–15 cm (2–6 in) deep

Acorus gramineus 'Variegatus'. Height 20 cm (8 in). An evergreen species, with cream-variegated, iris-like leaves. This is one of very few evergreen aquatics. It rarely flowers, but the foliage is delightful. It spreads very slowly.

Iris laevigata 'Variegata'. Height 60 cm (2 ft). The foliage of this iris is white and green. It is the best variegated iris, keeping its colour all summer, unlike other water irises. Blue flowers in June. It spreads very slowly.

Iris laevigata 'Variegata'

Water 15–30 cm (6–12 in) deep

Menyanthes trifoliata (bog bean). Height 15 cm (6 in) when in flower. The three-part leaves are arranged on horizontal stems over the water. It spreads rapidly, but is easily controlled by snapping off stems after the plant has flowered in May. The fringed white flowers are pink in the bud.

Orontium aquaticum (golden club). Height 25 cm (10 in). A most striking plant, with yellow and white flowers emerging above glaucous, velvety foliage in May. Spreading very slowly, it is an excellent choice for any water garden.

Pontederia cordata (pickerel weed). Height 90 cm (3 ft). Clear blue flowers in late summer are held on short spikes above dark green, spear-shaped leaves. This plant spreads rapidly.

Water 30 cm (12 in) or more deep

Aponogeton distachyus (Cape pondweed or water hawthorn). The waxy white flowers, with black stamens, are sweetly scented. They may appear in any mild weather, summer or winter, over the oval, bronze-green leaves, which float on the surface. It spreads reasonably quickly.

Nymphaea *(water lilies)*

Water 23–60 cm (9–24 in) deep

N. 'Froebelii'. Free-flowering, with crimson blooms and neat foliage.

N. laydekeri cultivars. Shades of pink, red, red and purple, with whitish shadings.

Water 30–90 cm (1–3 ft) deep

N. 'James Brydon'. This water lily adapts to various depths of water, and even to some shade. It has large, rose-pink flowers and dark green to maroon leaves.

N. 'Marliacea Chromatella'. Large, butter-yellow flowers open later in the day than most. The green leaves are marbled with chocolate.

N. 'Masaniello'. The deep pink and cream flowers darken with age.

N. 'Rose Arey'. The flowers are small, soft and a rich pink.

N. 'William Falconer'. A popular cultivar with very dark crimson flowers.

Water 60 cm–1.2 m (2–4 ft) deep

N. 'Escarboucle'. Large, rich-red flowers. This is one of the most popular cultivars.

N. 'Sunrise'. Noted for its very large, rich yellow flowers.

Floating plants

Hydrocharis morsus-ranae (frogbit). Small, green and white flowers appear in July above the water lily-like pads. To 'plant', just place on the surface.

Aerating or oxygenating plants

Ceratophyllum demersum (hornwort). It has feathery underwater foliage, which is brittle and easily controlled.

Elodea crispa. With dark green, underwater foliage, this is a much better choice than the invasive *E. canadensis* (Canadian pond weed).

Myriophyllum aquaticum, syn. *M. proserpinacoides* (parrot feather). The light green, feathery and much-divided leaves extend above the water. Though not hardy, this plant is fast growing and excellent for reducing algae in freshly-planted ponds.

Myriophyllum aquaticum

Ceratophyllum demersum

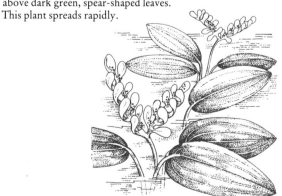

Aponogeton distachyus

Nymphaea 'Rose Arey'

Bog plants

Plants for growing in soil that remains moist all the year round, except where otherwise stated:

Astilbe simplicifolia Height (white-flowered) 15 cm (6 in); (coloured) up to 30 cm (1 ft). One hybrid form of this graceful plant has finely-cut bronze foliage and creamy-white flowers in August. Others have pink or red flowers. The plants spread slowly and prefer moist, not muddy, conditions.

Caltha palustris 'Plena'. Height 30 cm (1 ft). Double, rich-yellow flowers, in spring, are combined with a neat, compact habit. It is a much better plant than the single form and remains compact, with a slow spread.

Carex elata 'Aurea', syn. C. stricta 'Aurea', (Bowles' golden sedge). Height 90 cm (3 ft). The graceful, arching leaves have yellow variegations.

Dodecatheon species (American cowslip or shooting stars). Height 25–45 cm (10–18 in). In early summer, the red, pink, or occasionally white flowers look like shooting stars. The plants spread slowly.

Fritillaria meleagris (snake's head fritillary). Height 23–30 cm (9–12 in). Suitable for limestone soils, this bulb produces white flowers, or chequered, chocolate-coloured blooms in spring.

Hosta. Heights 30–90 cm (1–3 ft). There are many forms, with green, gold and green, or white and green foliage. In some of the larger forms it is glaucous. The flowers, which appear in summer, vary between white and mauve, and the plants spread moderately.

Leucojum aestivum 'Gravetye Giant' (snowflake). Height up to 60 cm (2 ft). The snowdrop-like flowers of this bulb, which open from April until June, have green-tipped petals. It will grow equally happily in mud or water.

Lysimachia nummularia 'Aurea' (golden creeping jenny). Height 10 cm (4 in). In July, the golden-yellow flowers are almost lost in the similar-coloured foliage. It spreads well in good soil, whether over water or ground.

Mimulus x *burnettii.* Height 10 cm (4 in). Copper-orange flowers are carried throughout the summer. It has a mat-forming habit. *M. cardinalis.* Height 60 cm (2 ft). This has an upright habit, woolly foliage and, in summer, scarlet flowers. *M. lewisii.* Height 45–60 cm (1½–2 ft). With steadily-spreading growth, the late-summer flowers are pale pink to dark red.

Polygonum affine. Height 23–30 cm (9–12 in). Though preferring muddy soil, this adaptable species may be planted in or out of water. It has ground-covering lanceolate foliage, with pink or red spiky flowers in late summer. There are several cultivars.

Primula denticulata (drumstick primula). Height 30 cm (1 ft). The mauve or white flowers appear in early spring. The plant has an upright habit and does best when grown in rich soil and divided regularly.

Saxifraga fortunei. Height 30–40 cm (12–16 in). An upright, autumn-flowering plant, with large, circular, bronze-green foliage. The dainty white flowers are pointed. A cool, shaded position is best.

Plants of medium height, too large for marginal planting:

Astilbe. There are a number of hybrids, which vary in height. A. 'Fanal', with dark crimson blooms, is 40 cm (16 in). A. *taquetii* 'Superba', which is rosy-purple, is 1.2 m (4 ft). Flowering is in mid-summer, and the soil needs to be moist rather than muddy.

Cornus alba 'Sibirica' (dogwood). Height up to 90 cm (3 ft). A shrub with bright red stems which show up in winter after leaf fall. Needs spring feeding to reach the stated height. Cut to within 8–15 cm (3–6 in) of the ground at the same time.

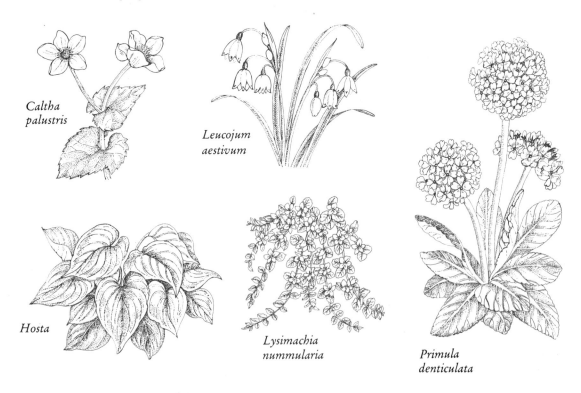

Caltha palustris

Leucojum aestivum

Hosta

Lysimachia nummularia

Primula denticulata

C. stolonifera 'Flaviramea' (dogwood). Height 90 cm (3 ft). A shrub with yellow-green stems which contrast well with those of *C. alba*. Prune stems in spring.

Iris kaempferi . Height 60 cm (2 ft). Large blue flowers, in a variety of shades, open in June. It requires moist, acid soil. The habit is upright.

I. sibirica. Height up to 75 cm (2½ ft). There are many hybrids, mostly with blue or white flowers, or combinations of the two, in June and July. The leaves are slender and the growth upright.

Lobelia cardinalis. Height 60 cm (2 ft). Mid-green leaves and bright scarlet flowers characterize this rather short-lived perennial. The flowers appear in July and August.

L. fulgens. Height up to 90 cm (3 ft). This species has shiny, purple foliage, with scarlet flowers in July and August. The habit is upright. There are a number of hybrids, some with green leaves, and flowers that range from red to purple.

Primula species. All the candelabra types are suitable for this type of planting. The two following are both 45 cm (1½ ft) high: *P. bulleyana*, orange; *P. burmanica*, reddish-purple. *P. japonica*, height 60 cm (2 ft), is carmine; *P. pulverulenta* is

similar, but has a white farina on stems and leaves. *P. sikkimensis* (Himalayan cowslip) is only 30 cm (1 ft) high and has yellow flowers. All bloom during spring or early summer, grow best in partial shade and also need rich soil.

Schizostylis coccinea. Height 60 cm (2 ft). An outstanding plant for its flowering season, which is from October onwards. It has red flowers, but cultivars are in shades of pink.

Large bog plants for ground cover:

Gunnera manicata. Height 2.7 m (9 ft). Massive leaves, excellent for ground cover and to provide a striking pool-side feature. Cut back the leaves after the first frosts and place them upside down over the crowns to provide winter protection.

Rodgersia species. Height up to 90 cm (3 ft), and with a spreading habit. The green or bronze-green foliage, somewhat like that of a horse chestnut, is their chief attraction, but there are also pinky-white flower plumes in summer.

Salix hastata 'Wehrhahnii'. Height 2.4 m (8 ft). A dwarf willow, with silver, pussy-willow catkins on dark, reddish-brown stems in April. The shape is irregular, with a tendency to spread.

Astilbe simplicifolia

Iris sibirica

Lobelia cardinalis

Rodgersia aesculifolia

JANUARY

Melting the ice If there are fish in the pool, and the surface should freeze over for a week or more, make one or two holes in the ice to allow toxic gases to escape. These are given off by rotting leaves and other plant remains, the danger being greatest in shallow pools.

It is important not to make holes by hammering the ice, as this may stun the fish. Instead, fill one or two plastic bottles with hot water and place these on the ice, first securing them with string so that they cannot sink out of sight. Refill the bottles, if necessary, until clear holes have been created. Repeat the process daily so long as the ice remains.

An alternative is to float a purpose-made heater on the surface right through the winter, switching this on during cold weather. These are sold by water-garden specialists and, with an element of about 125 watts, will maintain an ice-free patch whatever the weather. This is ideal if there is already an electric cable for supplying a pump which has been removed for the winter.

If you have left a pump in the pool, run this for a few minutes every week or two to stop it getting clogged, except when the water is frozen.

FEBRUARY

Melting the ice Advice given for January applies also to this month.

MARCH

Melting the ice In cold areas it may be necessary to continue with the procedure outlined in January.

Pumps If a pump was left in the pool during the winter, start it frequently to prevent it getting silted up.

BOG GARDENS

Pruning Cut back herbaceous growth this month, in most cases pulling or snapping off the soft or brittle stems. Failing this, use secateurs. Take care not to damage the young crowns while pruning.

Weeding Weed the bog garden while you are pruning it, treading on the wet ground as little as possible. Along with the annual weeds, remove any perennial weeds, such as bindweed, couch grass or ground elder.

Fork over the ground afterwards to improve aeration, using either a border fork or a hand fork. This is where you will be thankful for stepping stones placed in the bog garden during construction.

Dividing plants Most herbaceous bog plants will need dividing about every three to five years. When the time comes, lift the plants during March or April, together with any perennial weeds that are growing through them.

Divide the plants by placing two forks, back to back, into the crown of the plant, then lever the forks apart. Repeat this as many times as necessary to produce plants not more than about 5–8 cm (2–3 in) across, discarding the woody central crown.

At the same time, tease out and burn any perennial weeds, removing every small piece that breaks off to avoid regeneration.

Planting When the ground is clear of plants and weeds, fork in some well-rotted manure or garden compost, or, failing this, a balanced general fertilizer.

Ensure that purchased plants, or those just divided, are kept covered and not allowed to dry out. Plan their positions before planting, allowing more space between groups than between plants within a group.

WATER PLANTS

Containers Except for floating and oxygenating species, all aquatics are better planted in containers than in soil placed on the bottom of the pool. This helps to restrict their spread and makes subsequent lifting, for division or replacement, a great deal easier. The only exception is in really large pools, where containers would prove very expensive

The containers may be of any long-lasting material: plastic pots, plastic buckets and baskets, concrete tubs or clay pots. Wooden or metal containers are not recommended as they are prone to rotting or rust.

A suitable size for a container depends, of course, upon the size of the plant. Bear in mind that recommended planting depths apply to the water *above* the container, so if 30 cm (1 ft) is needed, and the pool is 60 cm (2 ft) deep, the maximum suitable depth for the container is 30 cm (1 ft). It can be as broad as you wish.

Planting water lilies
Plant in aquatic baskets and cover the planting mixture with gravel.

For maximum stability, containers for marginal plants that are to rest on shelves should be broad and shallow. This is less critical for water lilies, which will be placed on the bottom of the pool. Place water lilies with their roots in the soil, but their crowns – together with any stem – should rest on its surface.

Soil and planting A heavy loam is ideal. Lighter soil, including compost containing peat, is liable to float out of the container.

If possible, place some well-rotted cow manure at the base of the container, or, failing this, some well-rotted stable manure. Fill in the loam on top of this, putting the plant in position as the soil is added. Set the plants at their original depths, with the tops of the roots just covered.

More than one plant may be placed in each container, depending on the latter's size. After planting, place a layer of gravel over the soil to prevent disturbance by fish.

APRIL

Pumps Start and run a submersible pump frequently to prevent it from becoming clogged. If the pump has been stored for the winter, check the impeller turns freely before returning it to the pool.

Surface pumps, too, should now be re-installed, ready for summer use.

Pruning and planting Complete the removal of dead stems, leaves and weeds. Prune back the coloured stems of *Cornus* to within 8–15 cm (3–6 in) of the ground to encourage renewed growth for the following winter. Mulch the ground around them afterwards with manure or garden compost.

Continue the division and re-planting of acquatics and bog plants.

Pool cleaners This is a good month to attend to a pool that is leaking, dirty or overgrown. A warm, dry weekend should see the operation completed.

You will need a temporary container in which to place both plants and fish. Perhaps the simplest form is provided by a polythene sheet draped over a surround of blocks or bricks, up to 30 cm (1 ft) high, to form an above-ground reservoir.

Divide the plants as you remove them, placing the pieces that you wish to retain in the temporary pool. Keep some oxygenating plants, too, but only if they are of a non-invasive species. Otherwise, replace them with new, non-invasive types.

Place some closed plastic bags, partly filled with fresh water, in the temporary pool and leave them there while you clean the emptied pool. By the time you are ready to transfer the fish back again, the water in the bags will be at the same temperature as the old water.

Put the fish into the bags and place these in the fresh pool water for about three hours before releasing the occupants. In this way they will be safeguarded from sudden temperature changes.

If a leaky concrete pool was the reason for emptying, remove any sharp debris from the shell and then place a fibreglass blanket to cover the whole surface. Finally, lay a PVC or butyl liner.

MAY

Planting and weeding Container-grown bog plants may be bought and planted, but this is not a good time to re-plant existing stock as growth will be too far advanced.

Continue weeding as necessary, forking the ground afterwards.

Fish When introducing fish to a new pool, first give the plants time to become established – at least three weeks.

Golden orfe, which swim and feed close to the surface, are ideal for garden pools. Goldfish are extremely popular, too, and they breed more readily than orfe. They tend to disturb the mud, but are valuable for helping to clear duckweed.

Controlling algae New pools, and also those that have been re-filled after cleaning, must go through the 'green water' stage. Algae are the cause, a minute but prolific form of plant life that thrives in a pool where the surface is open to the sun and the water is rich in mineral salts. It will gradually disappear once the spreading leaves of water lilies and other aquatics cast shade, and when oxygenating plants in particular compete with them for the minerals.

Water lilies take time to grow, however, and a fast-growing plant that will make a great deal of difference during the first summer is *Myriophyllum aquaticum*, syn. *M. proserpinacoides* (parrot feather). It is not hardy and so will not normally survive the winter, but it will have done its job by then.

At its worst, algal growth forms a blanket on the surface – easily removed, however, by twirling a bamboo cane in it and then withdrawing it. Chemical control gives very uncertain results.

The worst mistake is to attempt to solve the problem by emptying the pool and refilling with fresh water. This will simply prolong the trouble.

JUNE

Routine jobs Weeding the bog garden and clearing blanket-weed and other algae from the pool are jobs that may need attending to throughout the summer.

Water lilies and other aquatics may be planted until mid-summer. Water lilies do best in still water, not close to a fountain or cascade, and they should be lowered to their full depth in two or three stages (placing the container on a diminishing pile of bricks) over a period of a few weeks. This reduces the shock to the plants, which may otherwise inhibit flowering during the first year.

Mature water lilies will produce a number of new leaves, the older ones dying off. Try to remove them when they become yellow, rather than leaving them to rot in the water. To avoid stepping into the pool, place a stout board across it or use a long-arm pruner.

The water level will fall, due to evaporation, during spells of warm, dry weather. Top up the pool regularly and frequently, as this is less likely to lead to a build-up of algae than if larger amounts are poured in at infrequent intervals.

A bog garden, too, will need frequent watering if it is not supplied from the pool itself.

Caring for fish Fish may become distressed, gulping air at the surface, during hot, sultry weather. To help aerate the water, either install a fountain or else trickle water on to the surface from a hose. The essential point is to create a splash, so fasten the hose to a fork handle, well above water level. Alternatively, use a spray head on the end of the hose, with the water turned full on.

JULY

The jobs listed for June still apply this month. It sometimes happens that oxygenating plants become too rampant in the warm water, but it is a simple matter to take out some of the excessive growth.

AUGUST

Continue with the summer maintenance as in June and July.

SEPTEMBER

Continue with the summer care outlined for June and July.

OCTOBER

Routine jobs Try to complete all weeding in the bog garden by the end of this month. Plants will be starting to die down – both in and out of the pool – and algae should no longer be a problem in the water. Try to remove as many dead or dying stems as possible before they can sink to the bottom.

Netting the pool Fallen leaves are a major cause of water pollution, so cover the pool with small-mesh netting if there are trees nearby. The chief danger is to fish, which may be harmed by the toxic gases given off by rotting vegetation – especially when the pool is covered by ice.

Fruit cage netting, the lighter the better, is suitable for this purpose. Secure it to pegs around the edge of the pool, removing it at least weekly to get rid of the leaves once these start to fall. If the pool is left covered with leaves, both plants and fish will suffer from the loss of light.

NOVEMBER

Routine jobs Remove the netting and leaves each week, fitting it snug to the ground again.

Protecting fish To safeguard fish during the winter it is important to maintain an ice-free patch (see December and January).

Care of pumps It is advisable, though not essential, to remove submersible pumps for the winter. After cleaning, store in a dry place. If you decide to leave the pump in the water, run it every week or two throughout the winter.

If the pump supplies a waterfall, however, do not run it during frosty weather. The risk is that ice will deflect the water away from its normal course, with a consequent loss of water.

Surface pumps, too, should be disconnected and brought indoors for the winter. Clean and dry the pump, and lubricate as advised.

DECEMBER

Routine jobs Continue running a submerged pump, if left in the pool, every week or two. Just a few minutes is sufficient.

Once all the leaves have fallen, and have been picked up from the surrounding area, the netting can be removed, dried and stored.

Preparing for ice Ice may prevent the escape of poisonous gases released by rotting vegetation (see January). These may be fatal to fish. A low-power electric heater offers the best means of maintaining an ice-free patch.

Pressure from ice may crack concrete pools, although they will not leak if fitted with a liner. To absorb the pressure, float closed plastic containers on the surface before the onset of cold weather.

The value of a greenhouse is out of proportion to the space that it occupies. Providing ideal conditions for most forms of propagation, and for raising half-hardy plants early in the season, its influence extends over the whole garden. In addition, it can be used for growing tender flowering plants that would not prosper outdoors, as well as for food crops such as tomatoes, melons, cucumbers and vines.

The controlled environment not only extends the growing season but also improves the quality of flowers and vegetables. This is due partly to their speedier growth and partly to protection from wind and heavy rain. Damage from birds and insect pests is also less of a problem or more easily controlled.

Most propagation is carried out at a comfortable working level, often in a propagator, on raised staging. Crops, such as tomatoes, are grown at ground level, either in or on the border. Many gardeners find it useful to have some of their staging hinged or removable to allow both uses.

With such a range of possibilities, it is as well to have a definite plan in mind when buying and equipping a greenhouse. Its potential is determined by whether or not it will be heated, and to what temperature.

This division into 'cold', 'cool' and 'warm' greenhouses forms the basis of the following calendars. It will serve as a reminder for beginners, but it is a good idea to make personal notes from year to year to cover particular interests and conditions.

Greenhouse fittings
A well-equipped greenhouse is fitted with staging, plant containers with bottom irrigation, and with vents and blinds.

Month by month guide for a cold (unheated) greenhouse:

JANUARY

Sow radishes and carrots in the greenhouse border, first working in some peat and a light dressing of Growmore fertilizer. Alternatively, use growing bags. The best method is to scatter (broadcast) the seeds thinly, then thin seedlings as necessary. 'French Breakfast' and 'Saxa' are suitable varieties of radish; 'Rondo' and 'Early French Frame' are good carrots for early sowing.

Spring onions, such as 'White Lisbon', may be sown in the same way at the end of the month. Maincrop onions, for growing on outdoors, should be sown in a pot or seed tray, if possible with a little warmth to aid germination, and then pricked off individually into small pots. Plant out in March.

January is a good time to plant peaches. Ensure free drainage by placing a layer of broken pots or rubble some 45 cm (1½ ft) down.

Bring in spring-flowering bulbs that were placed in an outdoor plunge bed last year in the late summer or autumn.

FEBRUARY

Sow lettuces for planting outdoors in March, Sutton's 'Fortune' being an outstanding Butterhead variety for the purpose. Sow the seeds in a pot or seedbox, pricking them out individually when the seedlings are large enough to handle.

Sow early-maturing peas, such as 'Feltham First', for planting outdoors in March or for growing on in the greenhouse. Seeds may be sown individually in 5 cm (2 in) pots to minimize root disturbance when planted out. Alternatively, lay a sheet of polythene over a seed tray and fold it into a series of corrugations, about 5 cm (2 in) wide, as you fill it with seed compost. The seeds will then germinate and grow in strips of compost, which can be slipped into a drill of the same size at planting time.

'The Sutton' is a good dwarf broad bean to sow now and grow to maturity in pots under glass. Pot on progressively, finishing in 25–30 cm (10–12 in) pots.

MARCH

Sow peas, broad beans, leeks and quick-maturing cabbages for transplanting outdoors when they are large enough. One of the best cabbages for this purpose is 'Hispi', a compact, hybrid variety with a pointed head.

If you still have bulbs in the plunge bed, these should now be brought in to provide a succession of colour.

Vines will soon be starting into growth, so make sure that pruning (see November) is completed before this happens.

Pot up corms of *Gladiolus primulinus* cultivars. A 15 cm (6 in) pot will do for a start, but pot on later into 19 cm (7½ in) and 23 cm (9 in) containers.

APRIL

Prepare the greenhouse border for tomatoes, digging in a good dressing of well-rotted manure or compost and raking a dressing of Growmore or John Innes base fertilizer into the surface. Plant the tomatoes at the end of the month, setting them 45–60 cm (1½–2 ft) apart, and erecting supports.

Sow the hardier bedding plants, such as *Alyssum*, *Phlox drummondii* and French marigolds. Sown about the middle of the month, they need no additional warmth. Less hardy sorts, such as petunias, may be sown now and the covered container should be placed on a window sill indoors.

With the sun now gaining power, ample ventilation is necessary during clear weather. Give plants plenty of water, and damp down the greenhouse surfaces freely during warm weather. Watch for early signs of attacks by aphids and whitefly, taking action without delay.

Keep vines sprayed with clear water to encourage them to break into growth.

MAY

French or African marigolds may still be sown for summer bedding. Nicotianas, petunias and other favourites raised on a window sill indoors should now be pricked out into boxes and moved to the greenhouse.

Well-grown bedding plants should be hardened-off gradually, but be ready to protect them from frost if necessary.

Make a sowing of schizanthus to provide pot plants for flowering in mid to late summer. Prick the seedlings out into a box, and subsequently into 9 cm (3½ in), then 13 or 15 cm (5 or 6 in) pots.

Tomatoes need regular watering, together with feeding once the first truss has set. If you would like to grow something a little different, try planting the dwarf tomato 'Minibel' in a hanging basket. Its mature height is only about 30 cm (1 ft).

Aubergines and sweet peppers, which will have to be purchased unless raised earlier in a heated propagator, may now be planted. Set aubergines about 60 cm (2 ft) apart, peppers a little closer at 45 cm (1½ ft). Plant cucumbers and melons, each 60 cm (2 ft) apart, at the end of the month, supporting them by tying to wires that are fastened 15 cm (6 in) apart to the glazing bars.

Tie new vine growths to wires and pinch out their tips two leaves beyond a bunch. Flowerless shoots may be left to extend to nine leaves.

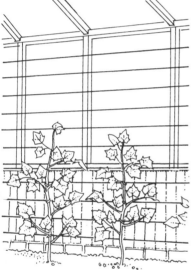

Growing cucumbers in the greenhouse
Train greenhouse cucumbers to wires fastened to the glazing bars.

JUNE

Keep cucumbers, melons and tomatoes trained or tied in, as appropriate. For these and other plants, some shading will now have to be applied to the glass if this was not done earlier.

Early peas and beans grown in pots in the greenhouse will now be ready for harvesting.

Softwood cuttings of many house plants can now be rooted.

To prevent dehydration while roots are forming, enclose each pot in a polythene bag, first inserting short, angled sticks to hold the plastic away from the foliage.

Reduce the number of grape bunches carried by individual rods. Thin the bunches themselves to allow more space and air for the remaining berries. Feed vines with a high-potash fertilizer.

A final sowing of schizanthus and nemesias will provide plants for potting next month.

Give ample ventilation and damp down frequently if the weather is hot and dry. Spray tomato plants with water at mid-day to aid setting of the fruit.

JULY

Harvest tomatoes and cucumbers regularly to aid development of further fruits. Pinch out the tips of tomato plants when there are five or six trusses of fruit on the stems. Cucumbers can be allowed to reach about 2.4 m (8 ft), or as near this as space allows.

Spray vines every fortnight as a precaution against powdery mildew.

AUGUST

The end of the month is a good time to sow some hardy annuals for spring-flowering under glass. A few popular examples are *Calendula officinalis*, *Centaurea cyanus* and *Limnanthes douglasii*.

This is also the time to consult bulb-growers' catalogues and to order bulbs for growing in pots in the greenhouse. If you buy prepared bulbs intended for forcing, pot them as soon as they are obtained and plunge them outdoors under sand or peat.

SEPTEMBER

Grapes will ripen this month, so protect the fruits from wasp and bird damage. Use fine netting or, on a small scale, muslin bags.

For top-quality sweet peas next year, sow the seeds now and transfer the seedlings to 9 cm (3½ in) pots. Overwinter the plants in the greenhouse or in a cold frame, for planting out in spring.

Continue to ventilate the greenhouse freely during the warm weather, but gradually reduce the amount of shading.

Keep a close eye on annuals sown for growing in pots, watering them carefully and potting the plants on when they show signs of outgrowing their containers.

OCTOBER

A number of herbaceous perennials, including *Aquilegia*, *Astilbe* and *Dicentra*, may now be potted in 15–23 cm (6–9 in) pots and kept in the greenhouse during the winter. Next year, they will flower well ahead of plants left outdoors.

Lift stools of early-flowering chrysanthemums and place them in boxes for the production of cuttings next spring. Just nestle them into peat or old compost, keeping this slightly moist and providing a little extra protection in the form of sacking or newspaper during severe weather.

This is the time to remove all shading from glass.

Harvest green tomatoes and store them in a cool, dark place so that they ripen gradually.

If you have a vine, give full ventilation as an aid to ripening wood that has developed during the current year.

Sow lettuces, such as 'Kloek' and 'Kwiek', for cutting in the spring. Sow and prick them out in the usual way, then plant them out in the greenhouse border.

Sow sweet peas for over-wintering in a cold frame.

NOVEMBER

Bring in pot-grown herbs now to provide a winter supply.

Have additional protection ready, such as sacking or news-papers, for slightly tender plants.

Prune vines as soon as their last leaves have fallen, shortening the current year's growth to one or two buds.

DECEMBER

Clean the framework and glass thoroughly, using household bleach as a disinfectant if it is possible to remove all plants. Also, to prevent a carry-over of diseases or pests, remove the debris of summer crops, old plant ties and the like.

Prune grape vines.

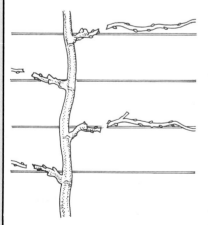

Pruning grape vines
After leaf-fall, cut vine laterals made during the current year back to 1–2 buds from the main rods.

Month by month guide for a cool (minimum 4°C/40°F) greenhouse:

JANUARY

Bring in bulbs from the outdoor plunge bed to encourage early flowering.

Keep a careful watch on over-wintering plants, such as ciner-arias and primulas, watering them as early in the day as possible to allow excess moisture to drain away before nightfall.

Check that the heating system is working well. Service it if neces-sary. Ensure, too, that any insula-tion remains intact.

FEBRUARY

Sow peas, broad beans, lettuces and summer cabbages for planting outdoors in March.

Start dahlias and early-flower-ing chrysanthemums into growth to produce cuttings. Nestle the tubers and stools into peat and keep them moist, at a temperature of 13–18°C (55–64°F).

Bring in strawberries potted last August or September and since kept in a cold frame. They should fruit in May, a month before the outdoor crop.

The first sowings of annuals for growing on in pots – schizanthus and nemesias, for instance – may be sown this month. As long as a minimum temperature of 4°C (40°F) is maintained, no extra heat is needed.

Ferns may now be divided and placed in pots.

Be sure to provide sufficient ventilation on sunny days, even at this early season.

At the end of the month, make a sowing of tomatoes in a warm propagating frame.

MARCH

Most summer bedding plants may now be sown, ready for hardening off in late April and early May and for planting out towards the end of May.

Freesias sown now, and even-tually grown in 15 cm (6 in) or 23 cm (9 in) pots, will flower in six months' time. A sowing of F_1 hybrid cyclamen, such as 'Firmament', will produce flowering plants by Christmas.

Tomatoes should be planted now, spacing them 45–60 cm (1½–2 ft) apart. Provide them with adequate supports.

Pot on or top-dress permanent plants in containers. Some, includ-ing cinerarias and calceolarias, may need shading quite early in the month but others will manage without shade for a while. Obviously, the time to apply shade depends on the weather as well as on the types of plants grown, stressing the advantage of adjustable blinds over materials applied to the glass.

Take cuttings of dahlias and chrysanthemums as soon as they are ready.

Remove dead flowers and de-caying foliage from pot plants.

APRIL

Complete the pricking out of seedlings as soon as possible. As bedding plants become well-established, move the boxes to a cold frame so that the plants have plenty of time to harden off before being planted outside.

Start to feed tomatoes as soon as the first truss of fruit has set. During warm, sunny weather, spray the plants with clear water at mid-day to encourage good pollination. Remove side-shoots regularly; give plenty of water and ventilation as the weather grows warmer.

Early in the month sow cucumbers for planting out in May. For the easiest cultivation, choose those with female flowers only.

MAY

Harden off all bedding plants, remaining ready to take precautions against late frosts.

Plant cucumbers about 60 cm (2 ft) apart as soon as the roots start to develop round the edge of the pot. They grow rapidly, so tie them in regularly and remove tendrils as they appear.

Continue to pot on all plants being grown for flowering in the greenhouse. Damp down regularly and give ample ventilation to prevent rapid temperature rises. Keep a close watch for signs of pests or diseases, taking any necessary action without delay.

Towards the end of the month, stand pot-grown chrysanthemums outdoors in their summer quarter. This should be in a sunny, open position, with the plants' supporting canes tied to horizontal wires to prevent them being blown over.

JUNE

In an average season the heating may now be turned off, but be prepared to turn it on again if the weather becomes dull and chilly.

Feed plants regularly. With growth now at its strongest, twice-daily watering may be needed during hot weather.

Towards the end of the month sow cinerarias, calceolarias and primulas for flowering in pots

next spring. By the middle of the month, make a final sowing of annuals for growing in pots.

Encourage cucumbers to keep producing by cutting the fruits as soon as they are ready.

Move pots containing azaleas, *Cytisus* x *spachianus* and cyclamen outdoors. Keep the first two growing with the aid of liquid feed, but leave cyclamen dry so that they have a complete rest.

JULY

Transfer to a shaded frame pot plants being grown for spring flowering.

It is a help to flowering plants if dead flowers and decaying foliage are removed. Turn the plants regularly to prevent one-sided growth – especially important in a lean-to greenhouse.

Remove a few of the lower leaves from tomatoes to allow a better air circulation. Stop the plants by pinching out their growing points when seven or eight trusses have formed.

Sow calceolarias, cinerarias and greenhouse primulas for flowering next spring.

Take cuttings of fuchsias and zonal pelargoniums. They root readily at this time and should be well established in small pots by autumn for over-wintering in a frost-free greenhouse.

AUGUST

Fuchsia cuttings and those of zonal pelargoniums may still be rooted this month for over-wintering as small plants.

Pot individually any plants for spring-flowering – such as cinerarias, calceolarias – that were sown last month.

Re-pot bulbs of lachenalias and veltheimias. Freesia corms planted now in large pots will start to flower in March.

At the end of the month, many half-hardy annuals may be sown to provide specimen plants in the spring. Examples are *Mimulus moschatus*, *Salpiglossis* and *Schizanthus*. Move them to the cold frame soon after they have been pricked out.

Prepared hyacinth and narcissus bulbs should be potted as soon as purchased and plunged outdoors under sand or peat.

Pot strawberries in 15 cm (6 in) pots for growing on under glass during the winter and for cropping next May.

SEPTEMBER

Re-paint and repair wooden structures. Check that heating equipment is in good working order for use towards the end of the month. Clean the inside of the house.

As temperatures fall, water the plants less and remove some or all of the shading.

Bring chrysanthemums indoors, together with any other plants that were placed outside for the summer. However, vines grown in pots in the greenhouse should be stood outdoors after they have fruited.

Bedding varieties of fuchsia should be lifted now from beds or borders, brought into the greenhouse and potted. Plant them outdoors again next spring, in late May or early June, when the danger of frost has passed.

Sow half-hardy perennials for overwintering as small plants in pots. They will give a bright display next spring.

Strawberries may still be potted for an early crop next spring.

OCTOBER

Bring in calceolarias, cinerarias and primulas from the cold frame where they have been throughout the summer. Provided matting or similar protection can be placed over the frame on cold nights, autumn-sown annuals need not be brought in until November.

Sow winter lettuces, such as 'Kloek' and 'Kwiek', for cutting in early spring. They will be a little ahead of those grown in a cold greenhouse.

NOVEMBER

Be sparing with water, applying it early in the day when needed, especially to plants in flower. Ventilate freely when necessary, but not during foggy weather.

Bring in crowns of chicory or seakale for forcing, placing them in pots or boxes of peat or old compost under the staging and keeping them as dark as possible.

Pot-on spring-flowering plants, brought into the greenhouse last month, as they outgrow their present containers.

Bring in some of the bulbs plunged during August. The sheltered conditions of the greenhouse will promote early flowering.

DECEMBER

Give plants extra protection with sacking or newspaper if severe frost threatens. Keep watering to an absolute minimum.

Check propagating equipment. Give pots, boxes and other containers a thorough cleaning.

As chrysanthemums finish flowering, cut back the main stems to about 23 cm (9 in).

Month by month guide for a warm (minimum 13°C/55°F) greenhouse:

JANUARY

Sow begonias and geraniums, either to provide bedding plants for outdoors or for growing on in pots for an indoor display. Sow sweet peas for planting out in early May.

Bring in rhubarb crowns for forcing, if possible exposing the lifted roots to frost for a few days before taking them into the greenhouse. Place the crowns in boxes, with peat, straw or old compost around them, and keep them dark with a covering of sacking. The space beneath the greenhouse staging is ideal. Water sufficiently to keep the compost and the crowns fairly moist.

Re-pot palms and ferns, or else top-dress them by replacing the upper 5 cm (2 in) of compost with fresh material.

Bring in the bulbs from the outdoor plunge bed for flowering indoors.

FEBRUARY

Sow antirrhinums and lobelias for summer bedding outdoors.

Bring in more bulbs from the outdoor plunge bed. Also take in hydrangeas in pots from the cold frame.

With *Zantedeschia aethiopica* (arum or calla lilies) now well on the move, water and feed the plants regularly.

At the end of the month, sow gloxinias and streptocarpus for flowering under glass or indoors during the summer. And this month sow zonal pelargoniums for flowering either under glass or outdoors.

Sow tomatoes for planting in the greenhouse next month. Among the best varieties for this purpose are 'Alicante' and 'Harbinger'.

MARCH

Damp down paths, walls and staging, and spray foliage plants with water, as the temperature rises.

Start achimenes, begonias and gloxinias into growth, nestling them into compost or peat and watering lightly.

Plants to sow now for outdoor bedding include ageratums, gazanias and salvias.

Plant out tomatoes in the greenhouse border, spacing them about 45–60 cm (1½–2 ft) apart and setting supports in place.

Take cuttings of fuchsias and zonal pelargoniums for a summer display. Pot on coleus raised from cuttings struck last September, using 13 cm (5 in) pots. Pinch out the terminal growing points.

APRIL

Pot begonias and gloxinias into 13 cm (5 in) pots once the root systems are well-developed. Also pot regal pelargoniums – again into 13 cm (5 in) pots – taking particular care over their watering during the early stages.

Sow celosias for providing a greenhouse display, pricking them off into small pots while the seedlings are still quite small.

Apply shading to the greenhouse, especially when foliage plants are being grown.

Pot-on coleus into their final pots. Having pinched out the terminal growing point, do the same to the lateral growths which will then develop. The object is to produce a bushy plant with abundant foliage.

Sow melons for growing in the greenhouse. Popular cultivars include 'Hero of Lockinge' and 'Emerald Gem'.

MAY

Reduce heating as appropriate, depending on the weather.

Remove the sideshoots from tomatoes. Tie their stems to supporting canes or twist the strings round them gradually.

Continue with the propagation of greenhouse plants, in particular foliage plants and climbers.

Pot on celosias, sown last month, before the root system becomes pot-bound.

Plant melons sown last month, setting them 60 cm (2 ft) apart.

Spray regularly against insect pests, taking particular care not to let whitefly become established.

JUNE

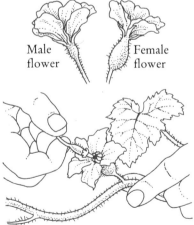

Male flower   Female flower

Strip petals from male flowers to expose the pollen-bearing anthers

Pollinating melons
Pollinate melons by hand, transferring pollen from male to female flowers.

Although the heating may as a rule be turned off, be ready to start it again, particularly at night, if the weather turns dull and cold.

Increase the amount of shading as necessary. Continue regular watering and feeding.

Move regal pelargoniums to a cold frame.

Pollinate melons by removing a male flower, stripping off its petals and pressing it against the centres of female flowers.

This is a good time to propagate many sorts of succulents from cuttings.

JULY

Although the tempo of growth will now have levelled off, continue to give plants plenty of water and to spray foliage plants with clear water during sunny weather – especially the undersides of the leaves.

Watch for any build-up of pests or diseases, taking immediate action if necessary.

AUGUST

Remove the growing tips of tomatoes at eight or nine trusses.

Pot up prepared bulbs as soon as obtained, as explained under Cool Greenhouse.

SEPTEMBER

Start to give the plants less water, but still damp down and spray regularly.

Take cuttings of named coleus for over-wintering in small pots; also propagate zonal pelargoniums for over-wintering.

This month is the ideal time to sow cyclamen seeds.

Begonia semperflorens, lifted now with a good root system from the summer bedding, can be placed in pots for display in the greenhouse.

OCTOBER

Reduce the amount of watering, and consequent humidity, but continue to ventilate the greenhouse on bright, warm days. Remove all shading and clean the glass thoroughly.

Check the heating system and fit insulation to reduce heat loss.

NOVEMBER

The brittle stems of winter-flowering begonias must be secured to canes. Now is the time to make the final ties.

When the bracts of poinsettias start to show colour, take great care to avoid under-watering or over-watering. The weight of the pot and the condition of the upper layer of compost are the best guides.

Once bulbs for forcing have made good root systems, bring them into the warmth to promote early flowering.

Although some ventilation is needed at most times, it should be very little.

DECEMBER

Double-check the heating system and insulation before the onset of the coldest weather.

Bring in seakale and chicory for forcing. (See November, Cool Greenhouse.)

Keep water away from the centre of flowering cyclamen. When removing dead flowers, take the whole stem away.

Home-grown vegetables
It is worth making space in your garden for a vegetable plot as the quality of the fresh produce it will yield can't be matched by the greengrocer.

Most gardeners have few options for choosing a site for growing vegetables. If the plot is small and rectangular, the crops are likely to be relegated to the further end, leaving the area nearest the house for flowers and, perhaps, a lawn. Even so, it is as well always to keep the ideal situation in mind, especially if the garden is large enough to permit some degree of choice.

The best results will be obtained in an open, but not exposed, position free from shade cast by buildings or trees. If possible, the rows of vegetables should run north to south to make maximum use of sunlight. This applies particularly to tall-growing crops, such as runner beans, so they do not cast continuous shade on nearby crops.

The cropping plan shows the layout of a plot to provide vegetables over as long a period as possible. In addition to the vegetables listed, such crops as radish, spinach, lettuce and spring onions may be grown on any part of the plot that is temporarily vacant – in spring, for instance, on parts of the brassica bed where broccoli and winter cabbages will not be planted until the summer. This is known as catch-cropping.

There are also such rather individual crops as tomatoes, parsley and marrows, which can be planted in spare areas after the previous crops have been harvested.

The purpose of dividing a plot into three sections is to avoid growing vegetables in any one group on the same bed within a three-year period. This rotation of crops, as it is called, helps to prevent a build-up of pests and diseases and makes it easier to feed the crops in the most beneficial way.

In the first year, Plot B should be heavily manured. Crops such as peas, beans, onion, leeks and celery need the richest soil. The residue from this manuring will continue to benefit crops in the other two groups during the next two years.

Plot A, again in the first year, carries the green crops that will be ready from late summer until the following spring. Apply fertilizer and lime to this section, first making a soil test. If you are in doubt about how much lime is needed.

Plot C completes the rotation with a range of root crops – carrots, parsnips, beetroot, for instance, and also potatoes. Apply only fertilizer to this plot. Fresh manure may cause the roots of carrots and parsnips to fork, making them of much less value in the kitchen.

During the following two years, each group of vegetables is grown on a different site, as shown. The feeding programme goes with them – that is, the pea and bean group is always given a dressing of manure, and so on.

Of course, it is not always possible to stick rigidly to such a plan, if only because the needs and the balance of the crops may vary from season to season. However, following the general principles of rotation will help to ensure that maximum use is made of the land.

Within each vegetable plot, the crops can be grown in rows with space allowed for walking between them, or they can be grown on the 'bed system'. With the former – the traditional method – plants are sometimes damaged by the gardener's feet. Also, particularly on heavy land, the soil tends to become compressed and its structure may be harmed.

With the bed system there is no need for space between the rows. The vegetables are planted closer together, the space between rows being the same as between plants in the row. Every 1.2 m (4 ft) or so a narrow path is left and from here the gardener can tend the plants. Working from either side, he or she never has to reach further than 60 cm (2 ft). It is more difficult to use a long-handled hoe, but a short-handled onion hoe, or hand-weeding, provide effective alternatives.

CROPPING PLAN			
Plot	*1st Year*	*2nd Year*	*3rd Year*
A	Cabbages Cauliflowers Sprouts Broccoli Kale Turnips	Carrots Beet Parsnips Potatoes	Peas Beans: broad, runner, French Onions Leeks Celery
B	Peas Beans: broad, runner, French Onions Leeks Celery	Cabbages Cauliflowers Sprouts Broccoli Kale Turnips	Carrots Beet Parsnips Potatoes
C	Carrots Beet Parsnips Potatoes	Peas Beans: broad, runner, French Onions Leeks Celery	Cabbages Cauliflowers Sprouts Broccoli Kale Turnips

Crop rotation

In a three-year crop rotation plan, a plot is divided into 3 sections, one of which is deeply dug and manured annually, another treated with lime and fertilizer, and a third with fertilizer only. In the first year, fertilizer and lime are applied to plot A (brassicas), manure to plot B (legumes) and fertilizer to plot C (root crops). In the second year and third year, crops and feeding programmes move to different plots so that legumes always occupy the recently manured plot and are themselves always followed by brassica crops.

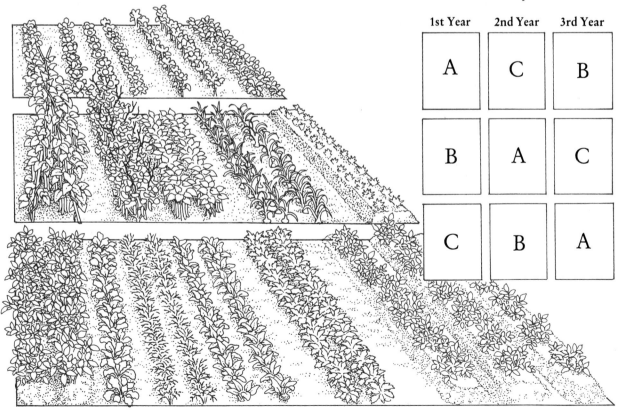

1st Year	2nd Year	3rd Year
A	C	B
B	A	C
C	B	A

QUICK-REFERENCE SOWING TABLE			
Vegetable	Time to sow	Space between plants	Space between rows
Beans, broad	November March–April	23 cm (9 in)	60 cm (2 ft)
Beans, French	May–July	15 cm (6 in)	60 cm (2 ft)
Beans, runner	May–June	60 cm (2 ft) sq. wigwam	
Beet	March–July	5–8 cm (2–3 in)	30 cm (1 ft)
Broccoli	April–May	60 cm (2 ft)	60 cm (2 ft)
Brussels sprouts	March–April	75 cm (2½ ft)	75 cm (2½ ft)
Cabbages: spring-sown autumn-sown Savoy	March–May Early Aug. April–May	45 cm (1½ ft) 45 cm (1½ ft) 60 cm (2 ft)	45 cm (1½ ft) 45 cm (1½ t) 60 cm (2 ft)
Carrots	March–July	8 cm (3 in)	30 cm (1 ft)
Cauliflowers	March–May	60 cm (2 ft)	60 cm (2 ft)
Celery (self-blanching)	March	23 cm (9 in)	23 cm (9 in)
Cucumbers (outdoor)	April (indoors)	90 cm (3 ft)	90 cm (3 ft)
Kale	April–May	60 cm (2 ft)	60 cm (2 ft)
Leeks	March	15 cm (6 in)	30 cm (1 ft)
Lettuces	March–July	23 cm (9 in)	30 cm (1 ft)
Marrows	June	90 cm (3 ft)	90 cm (3 ft)
Onions	March–Aug.	15 cm (6 in)	30 cm (1 ft)
Parsnips	Feb.–March	15 cm (6 in)	40 cm (16 in)
Peas	March–July	5 cm (2 in)	According to height
Radishes	March–Aug.	2.5 cm (1 in)	23 cm (9 in)
Spinach	March–Sept.	15 cm (6 in)	30 cm (1 ft)
Swedes	June	30 cm (1 ft)	38 cm (15 in)
Turnips	March–Sept.	15 cm (6 in)	30 cm (1 ft)

LESS-COMMON VEGETABLES

In addition to the everyday vegetables listed in the sowing table, and described in detail in the calendar on page 241–7 there are many less-common sorts that were virtually unknown here until a short time ago. Many of them are just as easy to grow as more familiar kinds, yet they provide a welcome change of flavours and textures.

The same is true of some other sorts of vegetables, such as salsify and seakale, which have been around for many years but which, for some reason, are not currently in vogue. Do consider them, along with the newcomers, when compiling your annual seed list for the vegetable garden.

Asparagus pea This vegetable is grown for its winged pods, which are at their best when about 4 cm (1½ in) long. Left longer than this, they become tough. Frequent picking is needed to prolong cropping. The plants grow to about 38 cm (15 in) high and have pretty, reddish-brown flowers.

Sow the seeds outdoors in early May, setting them about 10 cm (4 in) apart and allowing 45 cm (1½ ft) between rows. Support with twiggy sticks.

Cook the pods whole in boiling water until just tender, which takes only a few minutes.

Aubergines Also called eggplants, aubergines were little known in this country a few years ago but are now becoming more popular. Like tomatoes, they are best grown in a greenhouse, but are also worth trying in a sunny, sheltered spot outdoors.

The fruits are very tasty when stuffed or shallow-fried; two cultivars producing good-sized fruits are 'Moneymaker' and 'Slice Rite'.

To raise your own plants, sow at a temperature of about 21°C (70°F) between the end of February and early April. Prick out into individual pots when the seedlings are large enough to handle. Plant out in mid-May in a greenhouse or cold frame, or in early June outdoors. Harvest during August or September when the fruits are 10–13 cm (4–5 in) long and before they become soft.

Capsicum Variously known as the sweet pepper or the green pepper, this tender plant is becoming more popular in Britain. Depending on the cultivar, the mature fruits may be either red or yellow, and long, broad or bell-shaped. Peppers need plenty of light and warmth, and only in the milder parts of the country can they be grown unprotected. Results are more consistent when they are grown in frames or under cloches.

Fertile, moisture-retentive soil is needed, and among the most successful cultivars are 'Bell Boy', 'Merit' and 'Prolific'. Sow the seeds early in April, in gentle heat – minimum 10°C (50°F). Prick out individually into pots when the plants have three leaves, then plant out under cloches, or into a frame or greenhouse, in early May when the first flowers are showing.

Daily spraying with water helps the fruits to set.

Chinese cabbage This vegetable has found its way into greengrocers' shops and supermarkets during the last few years. A member of the cabbage family, it looks like a cross between a cabbage and a cos lettuce. The crisp, pale-coloured hearts are delicious when chopped and eaten raw, but they may also be boiled or steamed like ordinary cabbage.

Sow in drills 38 cm (15 in) apart, about the third week in July. When the seedlings are large enough to handle, thin to 30 cm (1 ft) apart. Do not transplant like ordinary cabbage. Chinese cabbages grow rapidly and are ready to eat in eight or ten weeks.

'China King', 'Nagaoka', 'Sampan' and 'Tip Top' are reliable cultivars.

Asparagus pea

Green pepper

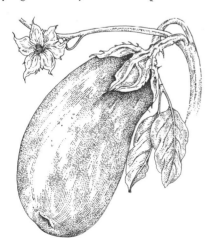

Aubergine

Chinese leaves

Florence fennel

Globe artichoke

Mange tout pea

Florence fennel or sweet fennel Grown for the swollen base of its stem, this plant does best in light, well-drained soil that has had plenty of well-rotted organic matter worked into it before sowing. It should not be confused with the perennial herb called fennel, each being a distinct species. Good cultivars include 'Perfection', 'Sweet Florence' and 'Zefa Fino'.

Sow the seeds outdoors in June or July – not earlier, as the plants may otherwise run to seed. Sow in drills 50 cm (20 in) apart, thinning the seedlings to 30 cm (1 ft). Earth the plants up when the stems begin to swell. September and October are the harvesting months.

Use the aniseed-flavoured stems raw, sliced finely in salads, or else braised as a separate vegetable. Use the leaves, fresh or dried, for seasoning.

Globe artichokes Unusually, it is the large, edible flower heads of this most striking plant that are savoured by gourmets. After being soaked in salt water for two hours, rinsed and then boiled until tender, the leaf scales are removed one by one with the fingers and dipped in melted butter or a vinaigrette dressing. The fleshy base is stripped off between the teeth.

Seed-raised artichokes are very variable. A more reliable way to acquire these perennial plants is to take offsets (rooted suckers) in March or April from plants with heads of proven quality. Alternatively, they can be bought from garden centres and nurseries.

To take offsets, slice off strong outer shoots from the main plants, setting these out 90 cm (3 ft) apart. The ground should be in full sun and enriched with compost or well-rotted manure.

Remove all but about five or six buds from each plant. Harvest the flower heads when they are well developed but before the scales open and start to lose their fresh green colour. This will be in mid-summer for mature plants; a little later for those recently propagated. Reliable cultivars are 'Large Round French Green', 'Purple Roscoff' and 'Vert de Laon'.

Golden beetroot Grown just like any other beetroot, this kind has roots with a most attractive golden-yellow colour, which is retained during cooking. It is particularly eye-catching when used in a salad. The leaves can be used in the same way as spinach, although the texture is smoother. The only listed cultivar is 'Burpee's Golden'.

Sow in succession from early April onwards, allowing 30 cm (1 ft) between rows and thinning to 13 cm (5 in).

Gourd 'Sweet Dumpling' This is an interesting plant in every way. 'Sweet Dumpling' produces small gourds, about the size of cricket balls, which have the appearance of being cut from green-veined marble. Left unopened, they make attractive decorations.

Their greatest appeal, however, is their delicious flavour when cooked, particularly when stuffed with meat and baked.

Raise plants by sowing the seeds under glass in late April, then planting outdoors at the end of May, allowing 90 cm (3 ft) between plants. Alternatively, sow the seeds *in situ* in mid-May, placing them in groups of three at 90 cm (3 ft) spacings and later thinning to the strongest seedling in each group.

Hamburg parsley The roots taste like parsnip, but with a hint of celery – nutty and sweet. The leaves may be used instead of true parsley. As the plant is hardy, the roots may be left in the soil until needed.

Sow the seeds in shallow drills, 45 cm (1½ ft) apart, between March and May. Thin to 15 cm (6 in) when the seedlings are large enough to handle.

Mangetout Also called sugar peas or snow peas, the pods and peas may be cooked and eaten either together or separately, although the pods must be allowed to swell to make shelling worthwhile. They are at their best when the pods are young and supple and the peas barely developed. The best forms are 'Sugarbon', a dwarf form of 'Sugar Snap', 'Sugar Rae' and 'Agio', all about 60 cm (2 ft) tall.

Sow the seeds from March to early June in drills that are 15 cm (6 in) wide, placing three rows in each drill and with 60 cm (2 ft) between drills. Use netting or black cotton to protect the seeds and seedlings from birds. Support the plants with sticks or netting when they develop tendrils.

A well-planned vegetable garden has orderly rows of plants and is sited in an open, but not exposed, position free from shade cast by buildings or trees.

A climbing rose, clematis and honeysuckle provide sweet-scented and colourful ornament for this old stone wall.
Train climbers and prune at the appropriate season where necessary.

The boggy ground round a garden pool is the perfect habitat for marsh marigolds and reed meadow grass, *Glyceria maxima*, whose long slender leaves are striped creamy-white and green in 'Variegata'.

An old-fashioned herb garden paints a picture of bygone times: on warm summer days, the scents of rosemary and golden balm (foreground) mingle with those of mint, contained in a tiled bed in the centre, and blue-flowered catmint.

Pick the pods as soon as they are large enough encourage further production.

New Zealand spinach The advantage of this half-hardy spinach over the ordinary kind is that it rarely runs to seed, even on poor, dry soils. It needs plenty of room, having a rather sprawling habit.

The seeds have a hard coat, so it is best to soak them in water overnight before sowing. Do this in mid-May if sowing outdoors, allowing 90 cm (3 ft) between rows and up to 60 cm (2 ft) between plants.

For an earlier crop, sow in a greenhouse during early April, prick out individually into pots and, after hardening off, plant out in late May.

Pick only the tips of the shoots, cooking these with a minimum of water, like ordinary spinach.

Salsify Also called the vegetable oyster, as a tribute to its flavour, this easily-raised winter vegetable is grown for its roots. Sow in April or May in drills 38 cm (15 in) apart, thinning to 23 cm (9 in) spacings. Do not let the soil become too dry, otherwise the plants may run to seed.

Lift as required from October onwards, first scalding the roots, then scraping them and leaving them to stand for half an hour in water to which a few drops of lemon juice have been added. After this the roots may be boiled and served with a white sauce or else fried and served with a little more lemon juice.

If a few roots remain in the ground after the winter, their mauve flowerbuds and flowering shoots may be eaten.

Scorzonera Guests will be intrigued if you serve this seldom-seen vegetable at a dinner party. It is a perennial, grown for its black-skinned roots, and these may be left in the ground for a second year if they are too thin after their first growing season. The yellow flowers are edible, too. There are only one or two cultivars, with 'Large Black' probably the most reliable.

Cultivation is the same as for salsify.

Seakale Widely grown in Victorian times, seakale is rather fussy about soil conditions. The requirements are a fertile, sandy soil containing both humus and lime. Harvesting is in April, when the blanched shoots are eaten.

Although it is possible to raise the plants from seeds, this is a slow and rather uncertain process. It is better to acquire crowns, planting these 45 cm (1½ ft) apart in each direction in March, after rubbing off all but one of the buds.

The top of the crown should be 5 cm (2 in) beneath the surface. 'Lily White' is the most popular cultivar.

Water generously during dry weather, feed occasionally with a general fertilizer and remove all flower stems as they appear. In the autumn, remove all yellowing foliage and fork over the soil lightly. In November, cover the plants with seakale pots or large buckets to exclude all light. Cut the blanched shoots during the following April when they are 15–23 cm (6–9 in) high. Cook and serve like asparagus.

After harvesting, leave the plants uncovered, apply fertilizer, and mulch with manure or good compost. Spent mushroom compost is ideal. Allow the plants to grow naturally until the autumn before covering again.

Vegetable spaghetti Looking like a pale yellow marrow, and just as easy to grow, this is a fascinating and worthwhile vegetable. After being boiled for about twenty minutes, and then cut in half, one has a plateful of 'spaghetti' which, like pasta, may be served with meat, tomato sauce, or just butter and seasoning.

Cultivation is the same as for gourds.

New Zealand spinach

Salsify

Seakale beet

'Nothing but leaves and seeds' is the disparaging comment sometimes made about the aromatic herbs. It is, indeed, easy to overlook their virtues when dazzled by the brilliant colours and perfect blooms of many of the flowering plants.

Yet herbs have a beauty of their own, a quieter, more subtle appeal that extends over many months of the year. And where would cooks and some doctors be without supplies of these 'leaves and seeds'?

In former times every garden, great or small, had its herb bed, and herbs were grown extensively by the religious communities and monasteries. In formal gardens where flowers were grown in small beds, or parterres, lavender, thyme, mint and marjoram were used for edging.

Their purpose was fourfold. Medicinal herbs were held to cure numerous ailments; pot herbs, with flavouring qualities, were grown for the kitchen; strewing herbs were sweet-smelling kinds used for spreading on floors to conceal unpleasant smells and to kill insects; yet others were used in the dyeing of wools and textiles.

Growing herbs Most herbs are easy to grow, particularly as they will thrive in practically any type of soil, with the possible exception of extremely heavy clay. Garden compost is the best organic material to add at digging time, either to improve the structure of heavy soil or to add moisture-holding humus to light soil. Herbs are not heavy feeders, and a light dressing of general fertilizer in spring will take care of their needs.

For the most part, herbs need a sunny position, although a few, including comfrey and parsley, appreciate some shade. If possible, grow your herbs near the house so that they are handy for picking. Some of the smaller kinds make good plants for a kitchen window-box.

Grow annual types, some hardy and some half-hardy, exactly as you would flowering annuals. Propagate woody

Popular herbs
Thyme (1), sage (2) and rosemary (3) are valued as much for decorative properties as for their aromatic and culinary merits.

1

2

3

types, such as sage and thyme, by taking cuttings of young shoots during August or September. Others, including mint and bergamot, can be increased by root division while they are dormant.

Drying herbs Many herbs can be kept for winter use after they have been dried. To do this successfully you should pick only perfect leaves, just before the plants come into flower. At this stage they will have the highest content of volatile oils. If possible, gather the leaves after the dew has evaporated but before the sun shines on them. Handle the leaves carefully, as they do not dry well when bruised.

Fairly rapid drying will help to retain the leaves' natural colour. An airing cupboard is a convenient place. Alternatively, place them in an oven, with the door slightly ajar, and at the lowest possible setting. Lay the herbs on muslin-covered racks, and turn them from time to time.

Herbs may also be dried in a microwave oven. Place them between sheets of kitchen paper, then put the oven on for three minutes at its lowest setting. Open the oven every half minute to turn the herbs over. Afterwards, leave them in the switched-off oven for fifteen minutes.

Instead of artificial drying, you can cut the herbs by the stems, and hang them, upside down, in small, loose bunches in a warm place, out of direct sunlight. Drying will not be quite so rapid, but not too much of the flavour or aroma should be lost.

Yet another method for storing herbs is by freezing. After collecting the leaves, place them in containers with a little water to make 'herb ice cubes'. These can be dropped into casseroles or soups as needed.

Whatever the method of drying, take care not to leave the herbs too long. If you do, they will turn brown and be of little use. Store the dried herbs in opaque containers, as they will deteriorate if they are exposed to light.

A selection of herbs

Anise (*Pimpinella anisum*). Half-hardy annual. Sow in mid-April, preferably in light, fairly rich soil. The fresh leaves give an unusual flavour to fresh fruit salads, soups and stews. Seeds are usually ready for gathering in August. After drying, use them for sprinkling on cakes and pancakes, or to flavour young carrots.

Basil (*Ocimum basilicum*). Best treated as a half-hardy annual. Sow under glass in late March, harden off and plant out when the risk of frost has gone. The slight clove-like flavour is a useful addition to tomato and sausage dishes.

For use during the winter, collect healthy leaves, wash and dry them, then pack loosely in a large jar. When within an inch of the top, pour olive oil into the jar to just cover the leaves. This will provide fresh basil all through the winter.

Bay (*Laurus nobilis*). This shrub is not altogether hardy, so plant it in a tub or large pot so that it can be moved to a protected spot during severe weather.

During the Middle Ages it was used as a strewing herb, because of its fine aroma. Many old potpourri recipes mention it, too. Nowadays, bay is used for flavouring fish and game dishes, and also for milk puddings. It is a constituent of a classic *bouquet-garni*.

Borage (*Borago officinalis*). Hardy annual. Sow the seeds in April in fairly poor soil. The leaves have a salty, cucumber-like flavour. A spray of them cooked with beans, peas or cauliflower gives an interesting taste. Use the young, fresh shoots and flowers in cold drinks for a most refreshing flavour. Borage will often seed itself.

Chervil (*Anthriscus cerefolium*). Hardy annual. Sow the seeds in succession from February to September, thinning to approximately 15 cm (6 in) apart. Remove flowering stems to encourage leaf production, which you will be able to use until the frosts.

Chervil has a slight anise flavour; it is an ingredient in the traditional *fines herbes* mixture. It also brings out the flavour of other herbs when mixed with them. It does best in a shady spot.

Chives (*Allium schoenoprasum*). A perennial which should be divided every third year. Plant 30 cm (1 ft) apart. The leaves are usually ready for use from early spring. When fresh, they have a mild onion smell and flavour. Use in egg, cheese and salad dishes.

Comfrey (*Symphytum officinale*). A herbaceous perennial that may be grown from seeds or root division. It does best in a damp, shady situation. Comfrey is reputed to have great healing properties – in particular, to check bleeding and to reduce swellings.

The leaves have a slightly bitter taste. They can be eaten like spinach, while the stalks taste good if blanched and eaten like asparagus.

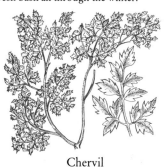
Chervil

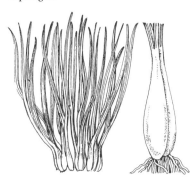
Chives

A selection of herbs (cont.)

Coriander (*Coriandrum sativum*). Hardy annual. The seeds may be sown at intervals throughout the summer, with the seedlings thinned to 30 cm (1 ft) apart. Choose a sunny position. This could well have been one of the first herbs used in cooking; more than 5000 years ago the Chinese ate the boiled roots and used the seeds for flavouring. They are still used in these ways today. Also known as Chinese parsley, the fresh leaves are a common flavouring in Eastern cooking.

The seeds are unpleasant when fresh but quite delicious when dry. Use them for flavouring meats, cheeses, soups and biscuits.

Coriander

Dill (*Peucedanum graveolens*). Hardy annual. Sow the seeds in April. Full sun is ideal but not essential. The seeds and leaves are the parts used, the seeds in pickles and sauces, the leaves in salads, with fish, with cooked green vegetables and sprinkled (finely chopped) on new potatoes.

Good King Henry (*Chenopodium bonus-henricus*). Perennial. The plants do best in a light soil, propagation being by seed or root division. This very ancient plant was once used as a nourishing vegetable, in much the same way as spinach is today. The leaves have a soft texture and, as they boil down when cooked, a large quantity is required. Add butter and lemon juice before serving. The young shoots and flower stems may be used in the same way as asparagus.

It is better to leave the plants untouched for the first year. The following season the leaves may be gathered as required, taking care not to strip the plants at any one time.

Mint There are at least 40 different types of perennial mints, but those most widely used are spearmint (*Mentha spicata*); peppermint (*Mentha x piperita*); applemint (*Mentha rotundifolia*). Because of their vigour, it is advisable to restrict the roots by planting in a bottomless box or bucket or, of course, in any ornamental container.

The different species should not be planted together as cross-flavouring may occur. Many years ago, mint was used as a strewing and medicinal herb, and there is evidence that it was used as a tooth cleaner during the sixth century.

Nasturtium (*Tropaeolum minus* or *T. majus*). Hardy annuals. Sow the seeds in April, remembering that nasturtiums prefer a sunny spot. The leaves of both species, which have a slightly peppery taste, may be used in salads. The seeds may be used as a substitute for capers if picked while young.

Parsley (*Petroselinum crispum*). A hardy biennial, but best treated as annual. Grow in a damp, shady position if possible. Use the leaves either fresh or frozen. Most of the flavour is in the stalk, so always leave a small amount with the leaves.

Rosemary (*Rosmarinus officinalis*). This is a small shrub that can be propagated by semi-hard cuttings in August. The leaves, which look like oval pine needles, are very aromatic and the flavour is strong; they are much used as a flavouring in meat and fish dishes.

At one time it was thought that rosemary strengthened the memory and it is still known as the herb of remembrance. Rosemary tea is reputed to be good for head colds. Some people also consider it a 'body reviver', simply holding a spray of the plant under the hot tap while filling their bath.

Sweet Cicely (*Myrrhis odorata*). A perennial plant about 90 cm (3 ft) high. Propagation is by the jet black seeds, which usually sow themselves very freely. Although a very dainty plant, with fern-like leaves, it has a large tap root. This may be used as a vegetable, sliced and boiled, when it develops a slight anise flavour.

As its name implies, it is a sweetening herb. If cooked with tart fruit, such as rhubarb, there is no need to use sugar – a very useful tip for slimmers and diabetics.

Sage (*Salvia officinalis*). A small shrub, with slightly hairy, grey-green leaves, and pale mauve flowers. It tends to become woody and untidy after about four years. Propagate new ones by cuttings in early summer. Alternatively, you may well get the branches to root by pegging them down on to a mound made up of mixed soil and sand.

Sage is said to be a powerful healing herb. For a sore thoat, place six leaves in a cup, half fill with boiling water and leave to cool. Remove the leaves, gargle and then swallow the liquid. Repeat four times a day. Sage is used both fresh and dried in stuffings, casseroles and cheese dishes.

Summer savory (*Satureja hortensis*). This hardy annual, which does best in a sunny position, has groups of narrow, fairly thick leaves. It is useful in all bean dishes, for it brings out their flavour without leaving any taste of its own. Sow the seeds in April.

Winter savory (*S. montana*). A perennial, has a peppery taste and is very good with pork dishes.

Tansy (*Tanacetum vulgare*). A perennial. Propagation is by root division during the winter. During mediaeval times, tansy was used as a strewing herb, and at one time it was also added to cakes and puddings. It is a decorative plant, with fern-like, bitter-tasting leaves and yellow, button-shaped flowers.

Tansy

Thyme (*Thymus vulgaris*). A shrubby perennial. There are several species of thyme, this being the most common of the culinary types. It does best in a hot, sunny spot. Propagation is by cuttings during August or September.

Thyme was one of the herbs used in olden days in tussie mussies – little posies carried to ward off infection. Nowadays it is used in a variety of savoury dishes and is one of the basic herbs in *bouquet garni*.

JANUARY

Ordering and planning The only pressing task this month is to study the seed catalogues and place orders for the coming season, not forgetting potatoes.

Draw up a plan of where crops are to be sown so that fertilizer can be applied where needed.

Sowings under glass A number of vegetables – carrots, radishes and spring onions – may be sown in the greenhouse this month.

FEBRUARY

Digging and sowing Dig and manure light land, unless it is too wet or frozen. Start preparing seedbeds in readiness for early sowing and planting. If frames or cloches are available, sow broad beans, Brussels sprouts, cabbages, radishes, peas, spinach and turnips. (See March.)

Potatoes Place seed potatoes in shallow trays, rose end upwards – that is, the end with a cluster of 'eyes', or embryo shoots. Give them as much light as possible, and keep them frost-free, as this will encourage short, strong shoots.

Parsnips Parsnips may be sown this month but are better left until March.

Sowings under glass A number of vegetables may be sown in cold and cool greenhouses this month.

Herbs Make the first sowing of chervil in the position where the plants are to grow. Thin to 30 cm (1 ft) apart.

MARCH

Asparagus To raise you own asparagus plants, sow the seeds now in drills about 5 cm (2 in) deep. If you are sowing several rows, space them 30 cm (1 ft) apart. Fertile soil is essential for this crop. Good cultivars include 'Connover's Colossal', 'Limbras', 'Lucullus' and 'Regal Pedigree'.

March or April are also the best months for planting asparagus crowns, choosing deeply-dug, well-manured soil. Plant in trenches 30 cm (1 ft) wide and 15 cm (6 in) deep, with the crowns spaced 45 cm (1½ ft) apart. Keep them well watered until they are really established.

One-year old plants are better than those that are two or three years old. The shoots or spears, can be cut in the third year after planting, just as for two- or three-year-old crowns planted at the same time, but yields will be higher because the plants will have become established more rapidly.

Do not cut shoots or spears from a new plantation during the two years following planting. In the third year, cut for six weeks from the time when the first

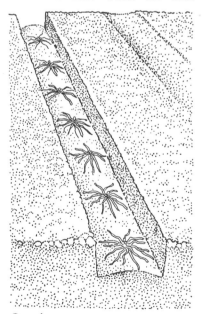

Growing asparagus
Plant one-year old asparagus crowns 45 cm (1½ ft) apart in deep trenches.

shoots appear. In the fourth and following years, cut for a period of eight weeks.

Cut when the shoots are 13–15 cm (5–6 in) high. At each cut it is essential to cut all grades of shoots, including any that are thin or crooked. This will encourage dormant buds to produce shoots. Do not cut green foliage (known as 'fern' or 'bower') for decorative purposes.

Beetroot Beetroot, or beet, can be sown near the middle of the month in drills about 2.5 cm (1 in) deep. Take care to choose suitable cultivars for this early sowing. 'Avon Early' and 'Boltardy' are particularly good, as most other cultivars will bolt (throw up a flower-spike) if sown too early.

Beet need an open site, free from shade. Soil manured the previous year suits them better than freshly-manured ground.

Other cultivars, such as 'Crimson Globe' and 'Little Ball', can follow the early sowing at intervals of three weeks throughout the summer, ensuring a continuous supply of young, succulent roots. If sown thinly there should be no need to thin the seedlings.

Carrots Sow early cultivars of carrots this month. For early roots, draw a shallow drill, 2.5 cm (1 in) deep, choosing an open site and soil that has been manured the previous year. Be patient, as carrots are slow to germinate, taking three to four weeks at this time of year.

'Amsterdam Forcing' and 'Nantes' are well-tried cultivars for this early sowing. They will provide those nice, finger-shaped carrots that look so tempting in the supermarket packs. As with beetroot, thinning is unnecessary if they are sown thinly.

Lettuces Make small sowings of lettuces in the open. For preference, choose one of the Butter-head types, round, smooth-leaved lettuces that offer a wide choice of cultivars. Sow them in shallow drills, 2 cm (¾ in) deep, with 30 cm (1 ft) between the rows.

Ten weeks from sowing is the earliest one can produce lettuces from an outdoor sowing. It is good practice to sow little and often for continuous supplies.

Reliable cultivars for sowing now include 'Fortune' and 'Unrivalled'. When the seedlings are large enough to handle, thin them to 23 cm (9 in), transplanting some of the thinnings for successional harvesting.

Broad beans It is now safe to sow broad beans in well-manured, fertile soil. For best results, sow in double drills, 23 cm (9 in) apart and 5 cm (2 in) deep, with the beans placed alternately and 23 cm (9 in) apart. This minimizes the need for staking.

Excellent long-pod cultivars are 'Hylon', 'Imperial Longpod' and 'Relon'. If space is limited, the dwarf-growing cultivar 'The Sutton' is a good choice.

During a dry spell, water once the beans start to flower, continuing throughout the pod-forming period. When at least four trusses of flowers have set, pinch out the tips of the plants as this helps the pods to form and also discourages blackfly.

Pick the pods regularly for continuous cropping. Broad beans are often the first fresh vegetables of the season.

Seedbed sowings The end of this month is a good time to start a seedbed for brassicas and leeks. Wait until the wind and sun dry the soil, enabling you to create a fine tilth. Sow the seeds in shallow drills.

Brussels sprouts (Early): 'Peer Gynt', 'Top Score'. **(Mid-season):**

MAKING SEED DRILLS

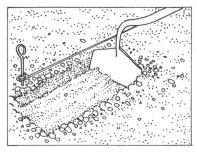

1 Make shallow seed drills with the draw hoe.

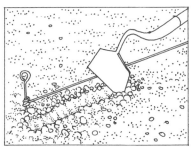

2 Use the corner of the hoe blade to take out deeper seed drills.

'Perfect Line', 'Welland'. **(Late):** 'Citadel', 'Sigmund'.

Red cabbage: 'Langedijk Red', 'Ruby Ball'.

Storable cabbage: 'Hidena', 'Minicole', 'Winter White'.

Summer cabbage: 'Derby Day', 'Quickstep', 'Stonehead'.

Calabrese: 'Corvet', 'Green Comet', 'Green Duke'.

Summer cauliflower: 'Dominant', 'Snowball', 'Snow Crown'.

Leeks: 'Blue Solaise', 'Winter Crop'.

Parsnips Parsnips sown now will germinate much quicker than those sown a month earlier, as often advised. They may have slightly smaller roots but they will be less prone to canker.

Cultivars that have some resistance to canker are 'Avon Resister' and 'White Gem'. Other worthwhile sorts are 'Cobham Marrow', 'Hollow Crown', 'Lisbonais' and 'Tender and True'.

Heavy rain will sometimes expose the shoulders of the roots. If this occurs, cover them with soil from between the rows, mounding it up slightly with a draw hoe. This will minimize the incidence of canker, which can render the crop unusable.

Peas Garden peas do best in deeply-dug, well-drained soil, with plenty of organic matter worked into the top. They do not grow well when the soil is compacted or waterlogged. Peas have root nodules containing nitrogen-fixing bacteria, so they can make some of the nitrogen they need. As garden soils usually have plenty of phosphate and potash left over from previous crops, additional fertilizer may be unnecessary, unless the ground is very poor.

Peas grow well in spring and during cool, moist summers. They can even stand slight frosts.

'Round' or 'wrinkled' are terms frequently used to describe peas – self-explanatory names when you see the different sorts. Round peas, which are the hardiest, are used for the earliest pickings, sometimes being sown in the autumn. They are not as sweet as wrinkled peas, which are more widely grown.

Although wrinkled peas are slightly less reliable for early sowings, they have a much better flavour than round-seeded peas. The cultivars are divided into early and maincrop types.

Round-seeded, hardy cultivars include 'Douce Provence', 'Feltham First' and 'Meteor', all about 60 cm (2 ft) high or less.

Early wrinkled-seeded peas, all growing to about 60 cm (2 ft) are 'Early Onward', 'Hurst Beagle' and 'Kelvedon Wonder'. For the maincrop, 'Hurst Greenshaft', 'Jof', 'Onward' and 'Sweetness' will give continuity of supply.

Celery Self-blanching celery sown this month should be ready for planting out in early June. Sow the seeds thinly in a pot and place them in full light in a warm spot in a greenhouse. Prick the seedlings out when they are large enough to handle and keep them moist at all times.

Recommended cultivars are 'Avonpearl', 'Golden Self-Blanching' and 'Lathom Self-Blanching', the latter having good resistance against running to seed.

Radishes Although one of the easiest crops to grow, radishes can cause problems if they are sown too thickly, too deeply or kept short of water. Any of these conditions will cause plants to produce excessive top growth and small roots.

Sow the seeds in a broad drill, 15 cm (6 in) wide and try to space them 12–20 mm (½–¾ in) apart. Radishes may be sown in the open from March until August.

Some recommended cultivars are 'Cherry Belle', 'French Breakfast', 'Saxa' and 'Sparkler'. Harvest the roots while they are quite young, as they become tough and woody if left too long.

Early potatoes It is worth taking a chance and planting a few early potatoes, as very few vegetables can rival them for flavour when they are freshly-dug. Set the tubers 30 cm (1 ft) apart in a drill 15 cm (6 in) deep. If you are growing more than one row, allow about 60 cm (2 ft) between them.

For the earliest crops, 'Dunluce', 'Foremost' and 'Maris Bard' are suitable cultivars.

When the plants are breaking through the soil, keep a watchful eye on the weather. If frost threatens, draw a little soil over the plants or cover them with some light material, such as plastic or newspapers.

Water is best applied at flowering time. The tubers will then be about the size of marbles and it is at this stage that they most need water for maximum cropping.

Spinach Spinach grows best in the cool conditions of spring and autumn, and in very fertile soil. It will tolerate light shade but must always be kept moist. If allowed to dry out, the plants will go to seed prematurely.

Recommended cultivars are 'Bloomsdale', 'Long Standing' and 'Sigmaleaf'.

Sow in drills 2 cm (¾ in) deep and 30 cm (1 ft) apart. The crop should be ready to harvest ten to twelve weeks after sowing. With summer spinach, individual leaves can be picked or else the whole plant can be cut about 2.5 cm (1 in) above ground level, leaving it to re-sprout.

Turnips This vegetable belongs to the cabbage family and in a rotation of crops should be on the same plot as other brassicas. It is grown chiefly for its roots, but the tops, which make excellent spring greens, may also be used.

Turnips do best in cool, moist conditions and they will tolerate light shade. They do well on land that has been manured for a previous crop but, failing this, give a top-dressing of a general fertilizer ten days before sowing. If grown well, turnips will be ready to harvest about ten or twelve weeks after sowing.

Make the drills 2.5 cm (1 in) deep, spacing the rows 30 cm (1 ft) apart. Sow thinly, thinning the seedlings as soon as they are large enough to handle. Turnips grow rapidly so prompt thinning is essential, leaving them 15 cm (6 in) apart in the row.

Turnips grown for their tops are sown in August or early September. They are best broadcast in a small batch as this will give them a certain amount of protection through the winter. They will make rapid growth in spring and will be ready to harvest when fresh greens are scarce.

Cultivars suitable for spring sowings are 'Purple Milan', 'Snow Ball', 'Tokio Cross' and 'White'. Hardy cultivars for root crops are 'Golden Ball', 'Green Top Stone' and 'Manchester Market'.

Sowings under glass Several vegetables may be sown under glass this month.

Herbs Sow basil under glass near the end of the month. A minimum temperature of 13°C (55°F) is needed. Prick out into a tray. After hardening off, plant out 30 cm (1 ft) apart when the risk of frost is over.

Sow parsley seeds, in drills or broadcast, where the plants are to grow. Subsequently, thin the seedlings to 25 cm (10 in) spacings.

Set out purchased plants of sage.

APRIL

Further sowings Continue with successional sowings of beetroot, radishes, spinach, carrots, maincrop peas and broad beans. There is still time to sow parsnips if this was not done last month.

Lettuces This is an ideal month to sow lettuces of the curly, crisp type, often referred to as Iceberg. These stand the dry, hot conditions often met with in June and July and rarely run to seed. Recommended cultivars are 'Great Lakes', 'Marmer' and 'Windermere'.

Onions Early in the month is the time to plant onion sets – immature onion bulbs about 12 mm (½ in) in diameter. If planted too early they are more likely to produce a seedhead than a bulb.

Proven cultivars are 'All-Rounder', 'Giant Fen Globe' and 'Sturon'.

Plant the sets in a drill 2.5 cm (1 in) deep, with the sets 15 cm (6 in) apart and the rows spaced 30 cm (1 ft) apart. Cover them completely. This deters the birds, particularly blackbirds, for if the tips are left showing they will pull them out and toss them on one side in their search for food.

Salad onions sown now in shallow drills, 15 cm (6 in) wide, will germinate quickly, and be ready for the salad bowl in the warm days to come.

Seakale beet Seakale beet, also known as silver beet and Swiss chard, provides a welcome change from the ordinary run of vegetables. When ready to harvest, the leaves are stripped from the stalks and cooked in the same way as spinach. The stalks or midribs can be cooked separately, as for seakale.

Sow the seeds in drills 2.5 cm (1 in) deep, with the rows 45 cm (1½ ft) apart. Sown now or in May, the crop will be ready in late summer or early winter. A further sowing can be made in July, which will give lower yields but will last throughout the winter until the following summer. With all sowings, thin the seedlings to stand 30 cm (1 ft) apart.

Of the few cultivars, 'Fordhook' crops well and is also very hardy.

Winter brassicas The end of April is about the right time to sow a seedbed of winter brassicas for planting out later in the spring.

Savoy cabbages: 'Aquarius', 'Ice Queen', 'Winter King', 'Wivoy'.

Kale: 'Dwarf Green Curled', 'Frosty', 'Tall Green Scotch Curled'.

Winter cauliflowers: 'May Queen', 'Saint George', 'Saint Keverne'.

Purple sprouting broccoli: Early and Late.

White sprouting broccoli: Early and Late.

Melons and cucumbers Melon seeds can be sown now, ready for planting, in June, when temperatures generally will be above 13°C (55°F) even at night. The best for frame or cloche culture are the small kind, called Cantaloupes, most of which have pink or orange flesh.

The easiest to grow, and probably the best cultivars, are 'Early Sweet', 'Ogen' and 'Sweetheart'.

Sow each seed 12 mm (½ in) deep in an 8 cm (3 in) pot, using a moist, peat-based compost, and cover each pot with cling-film to retain moisture. Place in the airing cupboard, where the temperature is usually over 21°C (70°F).

The seeds will germinate in three to five days, so it is important to check the pots frequently. At the first sign of growth, take them into the light and remove the cling-film, placing them on a sunny window-sill until June. By then, the plants should have at least four true leaves and will be ready to plant out in their fruiting quarters.

Raise ridge cucumbers in the same way as melons, and plant them out in late May or early June. Reliable cultivars are 'Amslic' and 'Burpee Tasty Green'.

Tomatoes To raise plants for growing outdoors, sow the seeds in the middle of the month, using 8 cm (3 in) pots or shallow trays. Sow the seeds thinly, pricking them out singly into 8 cm (3 in) pots containing John Innes potting compost No. 2.

Well-tried cultivars, suitable for growing under glass or outdoors, are 'Alicante', 'Ronaclave' and 'Sweet 100'. Reliable bush cultivars developed specifically for

outdoor culture are 'Pixie', 'Red Alert' and 'Sleaford Abundance'.

Broccoli Tender, fresh young broccoli gathered from the garden is a delicious vegetable. Closely related to the cauliflower, it was introduced into Britain from Italy. The best Italian broccoli is the green, sprouting kind called calabrese, which comes from Calabria in the sunny south. There are some excellent cultivars from which to choose.

The modern hybrids produce bumper crops on dwarf plants, which are generally ready to harvest in August or September. Any surplus can be frozen ready for later use.

Choose one or more from the special dwarf hybrids 'Corvet', 'Green Comet', 'Green Duke' and 'Mercedes'. Each produces a central green head, like a cauliflower, with numerous side-shoots or spears. 'Green Comet' alone produces a single head weighing up to 1.5 kg (3 lb), which can easily be broken into spears.

Sow the seeds in shallow drills in April or May. When the seedlings are about 10 cm (4 in) high, transplant them to their final positions in the garden. Calabrese does best in a sunny spot in rich soil with plenty of organic matter worked into it, plus a dressing of general fertilizer at the rate of 150 g (5 oz) per sq m (sq yd), well hoed into the top 10 cm (4 in).

Space the plants 45 cm (1½ ft) apart each way, planting them firmly. Cut the central head before any signs of yellow flowers appear, and the side-shoots when they are about 10 cm (4 in) long.

Herbs Sow anise outdoors, thinning to 23 cm (9 in). Other outdoor sowings include good king henry, thinning to 30 cm (1 ft); coriander, thinning to 30 cm (1 ft);

dill, thinning to 23 cm (9 in); summer savory, thinning to 23 cm (9 in); basil, thinning to 30 cm (1 ft). Also sow nasturtiums, placing two seeds at 30 cm (1 ft) intervals and removing one seedling if both germinate.

Plant mint and comfrey.

MAY

French beans These delicious beans are tender, half-hardy annuals and require an open but sheltered position as they are vulnerable to wind damage. They need soil that has been deeply dug and, although they do not require such generous feeding as runner beans, they do best on ground that has been dressed with farmyard manure or compost during the autumn or winter.

Most failures with French beans occur from sowing too early, in cold soil. The seeds will not germinate satisfactorily if the soil temperature is below 10°C (50°F), which often means about early May in the southern part of the country. Sow the seeds about the second week of the month.

Runner beans The middle to the end of the month is a good time to sow runner beans, the wigwam method of staking being preferable to the continuous row method of planting.

Each wigwam consists of four 2.4 m (8 ft) canes spaced 60 cm (2 ft) apart and tied together at the top. Two beans are sown in a short drill 5 cm (2 in) deep on the inside of each cane, and no thinning is necessary.

With this type of staking, bees have easier access to the flowers and pollination is more certain. You can expect to harvest from 4–5 kg (9–11 lb) of beans from each wigwam.

If birds cause a problem by pecking the flowers from red-flowered cultivars, try sowing one of the excellent white-flowered runner beans. Birds seem to find these less attractive. Some good white-flowered cultivars are 'Emergo', 'Desiree' and also 'Mergoles'. Recommended red-flowered cultivars are 'Achievement', 'Enorma', 'Prize Winner' and 'Red Knight'.

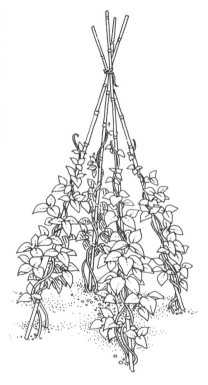

Supporting runner beans
Where space is limited, grow runner beans against a wigwam of 4–6 tall bamboo canes tied together at the top. Sow 2 seeds inside each cane.

Sweetcorn Sow sweetcorn outdoors towards the end of the month, setting two or three seeds at each station and thinning to the strongest plant as soon as they are large enough to handle.

The female flowers, or 'silks' as they are called, have to be pollinated in order to produce a well-filled cob. As successful pollination depends on the wind, sow in a block of not less than twelve stations, spacing these 38 cm (15 in) each way and sowing the seeds about 5 cm (2 in) deep.

For successional sowing, 'Earliking', 'Kelvedon Sweetheart' and 'Sundance' are reliable cultivars. For early and mid-season crops, choose 'Kelvedon Glory', 'Northern Belle' or 'Seneca Beauty'; for late crops, 'Jubilee' and 'October Gold' are good choices.

When the plants are about 30 cm (1 ft) high, draw soil around the stems – 15 cm (6 in) is ideal – as this encourages the plants to form 'buttress' roots and so prevent them from rocking in the wind. Water freely when the plants are in flower and while the cobs are forming. It is a sign that the cobs are ripening when the 'silks' turn brown.

Herbs Make a further sowing of chervil. (See February.)

JUNE

Salads Keep up successional sowings of all salad crops.

Marrows and courgettes Early this month is a good time to sow marrows. Sow three seeds at each station, spacing these 90 cm (3 ft) apart each way, and placing the seeds 5 cm (2 in) deep. Thin to the strongest plant if more than one germinates. Transplanted thinnings will not develop into plants sufficiently large to produce fruits.

Marrows are at their best when 30 cm (1 ft) long. If courgettes (which are simply immature marrows) are preferred, cut them when 10–15 cm (4–6 in) long. Plenty of water is needed for this crop, especially while the plants are fruiting.

Whether one requires marrows or courgettes, by far the best cultivars to sow are the bush types of the F₁ hybrids, such as 'Diamond', 'Zebra Cross', 'Zucchini', and the very attractive 'Gold Rush', with its banana-like fruits. Try the latter raw, thinly sliced, in place of cucumber, as it adds colour and variety to the salad bowl.

Swedes Sow swede seeds about the middle of the month in shallow drills 38 cm (15 in) apart, thinning the plants to 30 cm (1 ft) apart in the rows. Two reliable cultivars are 'Acme' and 'Marian'.

Growth will be checked if the soil is allowed to dry out, so watering will be needed during dry spells. About 9 litres per sq m (2 gal per sq yd) will increase the size and improve the quality of the roots.

One useful tip when growing swedes is to buy seed a year in advance of sowing it. Fresh young seed tends to make a lot of top growth at the expense of the roots, but the reverse is true if one-year-old seed is used.

Melons Set out the plants in cloches or frames, each on a slight mound so that water drains away freely from the stems. This helps to avoid most of the stem rots that may affect melons if water lays around the base of the stems for too long.

When planting, dig out a hole about 30 cm (1 ft) square and the depth of a spade blade, filling this with well-rotted manure or garden compost. On top of this place the soil that was removed, thus forming a mound.

When the plants have established themselves, pinch out the growing point at two true leaves – that is, excluding the seed leaves.

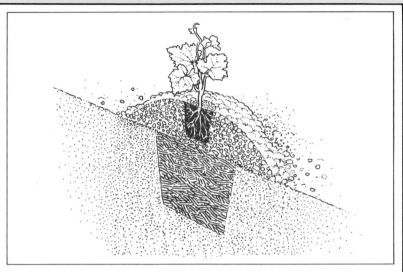

Low-growing vegetables
Melons, marrows and cucumbers grow well on mounds of soil where water can run off freely.

From these, two shoots will grow, which must be stopped at seven leaves. Sub-laterals will grow out of the leaf axils and these, in turn, must be stopped at five leaves. From these will come the fruiting laterals.

When both male and female flowers are present, open up the cloche or frames to let bees and other pollinating insects in. They will do the pollinating much better than attempts by hand.

At this stage keep the plants dry by withholding water for a while. When the fruits are set and about the size of a walnut, stop the shoots two leaves beyond the fruit and restrict the fruits to four per plant.

Tomatoes Plant outdoor tomatoes in rows spaced 90 cm (3 ft) apart, with 45 cm (1½ ft) between the plants. Put stakes in position before planting, otherwise the roots may be damaged. Water freely during dry weather.

Pinch out the side-shoots of indeterminate cultivars (those that should be stopped and have side-shoots removed) and cut off the

growing point one leaf beyond the last truss when four trusses of flowers have formed. If green tomatoes are wanted for chutney, stop at five flower trusses.

Bush tomatoes stop themselves, and all that is needed is a straw mulch when fruits are forming to keep them clean.

Brassicas Winter brassicas sown in April should be ready to plant out towards the end of this month. Plant the cabbages 45 cm (1½ ft) apart each way; the kale, winter cauliflower and sprouting broccoli 60 cm (2 ft) apart each way.

Herbs Make another sowing of coriander. (See April.) Take softwood cuttings of sage.

JULY

Harvesting This is the month when the gardener reaps his or her reward for all the effort put into the vegetable garden. Gather all crops as soon as they are ready, particularly pod crops, as this helps continued cropping and maximum yields.

Later sowings July is the latest month to sow beetroot, carrots, lettuce, turnips, spinach and sea-kale beet for harvesting this season.

Herbs Sow parsley seeds for a winter crop. Thin to 25 cm (10 in).

AUGUST

Spring cabbages If sown during the first week of this month, cabbages will be ready for planting out about mid-September. This gives the plants a chance to become established before winter. Sow in drills 2.5 cm (1 in) deep. Winter-hardy cultivars are 'Durham Early', 'Offenham', 'Pixie' and 'Spring Bounty'.

Earthing-up Draw a little soil up to the stems of winter greens, particularly the tall-growing kales and sprouting broccoli, as this helps to prevent them rocking during winter gales.

Turnips Sow turnips to harvest as spring greens. (See March.)

Harvesting Continue to gather all crops as they mature.

Herbs Gather seeds of anise. Harvest some basil leaves before the flowers open, and again before the first frosts. Take semi-ripe cuttings of rosemary and thyme.

SEPTEMBER

Sowings and plantings Spinach sown now will overwinter as seedlings and the crop will be ready about April when greens are scarce.

Turnips grown for spring greens may be sown early in the month. (See March.)

Plant spring cabbages, with 45 cm (1½ ft) spacings between rows and the plants set 23 cm (9 in) apart. Alternate plants can be cut as greens in the spring, leaving the rest 45 cm (1½ ft) apart to mature into cabbages.

Harvesting Harvest onions as soon as the tops die down.

Pull up tomato plants, with any green fruits still attached, and put them in a frost-proof place to finish ripening. Alternatively, pick the green fruits, wrap them in paper and leave them in a dark place to ripen.

Herbs Make a final sowing of chervil. (See February.) Take cuttings of thyme if this was not done in August. Sow chives where they are to grow.

OCTOBER

Harvesting Lift potatoes for storing; also beet and carrots sown before July.

Tie onions in ropes as soon as the bulbs are thoroughly ripened and hang them in a dry, well-ventilated place.

Miscellaneous jobs Remove all spent crops as soon as possible, especially the stumps of green crops.

Cut down asparagus ferns as soon as they turn yellow and before the berries fall. Burn the tops as they are unsuitable for composting.

Begin digging and manuring, applying lime where necessary.

Herbs Plant mint and comfrey. Protect July-sown parsley with a cloche to ensure a winter supply.

NOVEMBER

Broad beans Broad beans can be sown in the open, the most suitable cultivar for this autumn sowing being 'Aquadulce'.

Vegetables in store Check stored vegetables frequently and remove any showing signs of rotting.

Rhubarb Plant out rhubarb, allowing 90 cm (3 ft) in each direction. Sets with a single bud are best. Dig a hole 30 cm (1 ft) square and a spade's depth, place a good spadeful of well-rotted manure on the bottom and plant the rhubarb set so that the bud is about level with the soil surface. Two readily-available cultivars are 'Hawke's Champagne' and 'Timperley Early'.

Herbs Divide roots of tansy.

DECEMBER

Lifting and digging Lift and store swedes and late-sown carrots. Continue to remove spent crops. Dig vacant ground, applying manure or lime according to need. Try to complete the digging of heavy ground before it gets too wet.

Herbs When hard weather threatens, move pots or tubs containing bay under frost-proof cover.

Productive plot
Fences, about 1.8 m
(6 ft) high, make ideal
supports for fan-
trained peaches (H),
while wire
boundaries can be
used for cordon
apples (B) and garden
peas (I). As a feature,
train loganberry (A)
as an attractive arch.
In the central bed of
your plot, rows of
raspberries (C and
D), gooseberries (E),
red currants (F) and
black currants (G)
can be cultivated in an
area measuring about
6 m (20 ft) × 3.5 m
(12 ft). Leave space
between the rows for
growth and easy
cultivation.

There are few more satisfying
experiences for the gardener than
picking fruits that have been
allowed to ripen to the peak of
perfection from trees that have been carefully chosen and tended. Added bonuses
are the beauty of their spring blossom and
the bright colours of the fruits at harvest
time. On each of these counts, and also for
economic reasons, there is a case for
growing fruit of one or more kinds in
practically every garden, large or small.

CLIMATIC CONSIDERATIONS
Except for the harsher coastal regions and
upland areas, fruits of some kind can be
grown in most parts of Britain.

The cool, temperate fruits, such as
apples, pears, plums, cherries, hazel nuts,
and the soft fruits, will grow and crop
reasonably well almost anywhere. Fruits
such as figs, apricots, peaches and nectarines, which need a warm, temperate climate, grow best (though not exclusively) in
the southern half of Britain. A warm wall is
necessary, especially in the north, though
in particularly favoured areas they can be
grown in the open.

Nevertheless, these are general com-
ments and there are no absolutely rigid
lines of demarcation. Warm microclimates
can occur anywhere in the British Isles –
such as areas favourably influenced by the
warm Gulf Stream, and sunny, sheltered
slopes facing south. There are also artificial
microclimates, such as those found in
walled gardens and where a well-sited
windbreak keeps out strong, cold winds.
Altitude The higher the altitude, the more
limited the range of fruits that can be
grown. This is because the climate will be
cooler and the growing season shorter.
High altitude is associated with strong,
cold winds and high humidity caused by
low clouds and mists. Nevertheless, most
soft fruits grow and crop satisfactorily in
cool conditions provided these are not
extreme and the garden is sheltered. In
general, the best dessert fruits are grown in
the southern half of Britain at altitudes of
less than 120 m (400 ft) but there are, of
course, many successful fruit gardens
further north and at higher altitudes.

The temperate tree fruits are quite
amenable to cool conditions provided the
right cultivars are chosen. These are shown

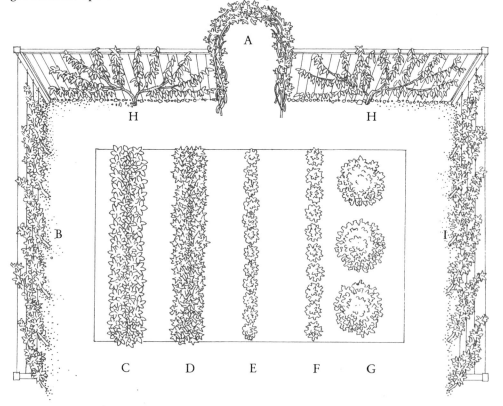

as being hardy in the descriptive lists under the relevant fruit heading.

Rainfall Low rainfall is not likely to be a problem, because usually it can be supplemented by irrigation. However, the wet conditions that go with high rainfall – that is 1 m (40 in) or more per annum – present special problems. Diseases such as scab on apples and pears, leaf spot on currants, the rotting of stone fruits and grey mould on all soft fruits are more prevalent. Fortunately, efficient fungicides are now available, giving reasonable control provided the gardener is prepared to spray at the appropriate times.

For gardeners who are reluctant to use chemicals, there are cultivars which are more tolerant of wet conditions. In particular, culinary fruits, where appearance is not so important, can be grown.

Soil The ideal, for most fruits, is a deep, slightly acid, well-drained medium loam, not less than 45 cm (1½ ft) deep and in some cases deeper. These requirements are by no means critical, however, as most fruits tolerate a wide range of soils provided there is reasonable depth and adequate drainage.

The larger the fruit tree, the deeper the soil needs to be. As a general guide, sweet cherries require fertile, well-drained soils 75 cm (2½ ft) or more deep, other tree fruits 60 cm (2 ft), bush and cane fruits 45 cm (1½ ft) and strawberries 30 cm (1 ft).

Shallow soils over a chalk base will give rise to problems such as lime-induced chlorosis and extreme dryness in times of drought. The alkalinity can be reduced by acidifying agents, such as peat, and moisture retention can be improved by adding bulky organic materials.

Good drainage is essential as waterlogging will kill the roots, leading to dieback of the above-ground parts or the possible loss of the whole plant. Apples are more liable to develop canker on badly-drained land. A few fruits, such as currants, gooseberries, blackberries, plums, damsons and culinary apples, will tolerate slightly impeded drainage below a depth of 45 cm (1½ ft), but for other fruits, especially dessert apples, raspberries and peaches, good drainage is essential.

Frost Severe frosts at blossom time can damage, reduce or completely destroy the potential crop for that year. Typical examples of damage are the 'running off' of black currants, when the flowers and fruitlets drop off; black eye in strawberries; severe circular russeting and cracking around the eye or the stalk of an apple or pear; and also malformed fruits of many kinds.

The short answer is to avoid, if at all possible, growing fruit in a frost pocket, though very few areas of Britain escape spring frosts every year. A frost pocket is a place where cold air collects. It may be a natural depression in the ground – for example, at the bottom of a valley – or it may be created artificially, often by a wall or a hedge that prevents the escape of cold air to lower ground.

Such barriers should be examined to see if they can be modified in some way to allow cold air to disperse. For example, a gap could be made in a hedge or the lower foliage removed.

Where nothing can be done about the frost itself, there are ways and means of protecting crops against it. Protection is certainly practicable on small fruits and is feasible, too, on top fruits grown on dwarfing rootstocks.

For example, protecting the blossom of black currants over the danger period will mean the difference between a heavy crop and no fruit at all.

Where sloping ground or a hollow is involved, the effect of frost can be minimized by positioning the smallest plants on the higher ground and the tallest ones lower down. Also, fruits which flower late can be planted. Raspberries, for example, and related *Rubus* species flower later than most other soft fruits. The apples 'Court Pendu Plat', 'Crawley Beauty', 'Edward VII' and 'Suntan' blossom much later than other cultivars.

The flowers of some cultivars are said to be partially frost-resistant. These include:
Dessert apples 'Beauty of Bath', 'Ellison's Orange', 'Greensleeves', 'James Grieve', 'Laxton's Fortune', 'Laxton's Superb', 'Spartan', 'Sunset', 'Worcester Pearmain'.

Frost damage Fruit trees are particularly vulnerable to frost when in blossom. To ensure good, consistent cropping, avoid planting in a frost pocket.

Cooking apples 'Emneth Early', 'Lane's Prince Albert', 'Newton Wonder', 'Wellington' ('Dumelow's Seedling').

Pears 'Conference', 'Fertility', 'Williams' Bon Chrétien'.

Plums 'Czar', 'Early Rivers', 'Laxton's Cropper', 'Marjorie's Seedling', 'Purple Pershore', 'Yellow Pershore'.

Damsons 'Crittenden', 'Prune' ('Shropshire').

Black currants (late-flowering) 'Amos Black', 'Ben Lomond', 'Ben More', 'Ben Sarek'.

Red currants 'Rondom'.

Raspberries 'Leo' (late-flowering), 'Autumn Bliss' (autumn-fruiting).

Strawberries Any perpetual cultivars, as these flower in flushes throughout the summer.

Strong winds Shelter is essential for successful fruit-growing. Strong winds can inhibit the movement of pollinating insects, damage and distort growth, flowers and fruit, and remove heat from the plants and the soil. An exposed garden needs one or more windbreaks to give protection from the prevailing and coldest winds. Take care, though, that these do not create a frost pocket.

An artificial windbreak can be permanent, such as one provided by a fence or wall surrounding the garden, or else a temporary structure formed from netting or purpose-made plastic material and placed around the fruit plot until the natural windbreak or the fruits themselves are established.

There is a wide choice in natural windbreaks. Whatever the trees chosen they should be fast-growing and, if deciduous, come into leaf early in the spring.

Where there is a choice, the windbreak should not be completely solid as this will cause buffeting. Remember, too, that natural windbreaks compete for light, nutrients and water so the fruit plants should be at least 1.8 m (6 ft) away. As a rule, the higher the windbreak the further away the plants should be.

PLANNING THE FRUIT GARDEN

Plan the plot and order trees and bushes early to make sure of getting the cultivars that you want. Likewise, buy any necessary materials and fertilizers in good time.

To avoid mistakes, it helps to draw a scale plan on graph paper. Once planted, the fruit may be in the ground for a long time – trees perhaps for a lifetime.

Walls and fences Make full use of walls and fences, especially in cooler areas, as the extra warmth and shelter they give will improve fruit quality and extend the range of fruits that can be grown.

The aspect decides the kind of fruit that can be grown. The height of the fence determines the form that can be used.

South aspect This provides the most warmth and for the longest period each day. All fruits can be grown here, though it is best reserved for the warm, temperate fruits, such as figs, apricots, peaches and nectarines, grown as fans. It is also ideal for the best dessert varieties of pears and gages.

West aspect This also is a warm aspect because it receives the afternoon sun. All fruits can be grown here, including the warm, temperate kinds, except that, in the cooler parts of the country, figs and apricots are better omitted.

East aspect This is a cool situation, receiving the morning sun and being open to easterly winds. It is often dry. Such an aspect is suitable for early and mid-season pears, apples, plums, sweet and sour cherries, gooseberries, red and white currant cordons, blackberries, raspberries and hybrid berries.

North aspect This is the coldest situation. It is suitable for gooseberries, red and white currant cordons, sour cherries, cooking apples, raspberries (not autumn-fruiting) and blackberries.

Height of wall or fence Low fences, up to 1.5 m (5 ft), are suitable for cordon gooseberries, red and white currants, and single and two-tier espaliers – both apples and pears.

Fences 1.8 m (6 ft) high and over are suitable for oblique cordons, multi-tiered espaliers and fans. Sweet cherry fans require at least 2.4 m (8 ft).

Planting in the open Bearing in mind the need to net against birds, possibly in the winter and certainly in the summer, it is best to have the plot square or rectangular.

Keep the soft fruits separate from the tree fruits, as most soft fruits ripen earlier and have different spray requirements. Plant in full sun, if possible, so that the wood is well ripened. Well-ripened wood is fruitful and winter-hardy; also, fruits in full sun have a better colour and flavour than those that are shaded.

Most fruits require sun for at least half the day but some will tolerate more shade than others. Examples of fruits that will grow in partial shade, as long as the soil is not dry and there are no overhanging trees, are raspberries, blackberries, red currants, gooseberries, the 'Morello' cherry and culinary cultivars of many tree fruits. Even so, the more sun all fruits receive the better quality they will have.

Plant the smallest kinds on the south side of the plot and the tallest on the north so that they all receive their fair share of sun. In practical terms this means planting gooseberry and red currant bushes on the south side, black currants and raspberries in the middle and tree fruits on the north.

Where space is limited, as in many modern gardens, consider planting gooseberries, and red and white currants, as cordons. These fruits must be on dwarfing or semi-dwarfing rootstocks. Closely-shaped oblique cordons are ideal for small gardens because a relatively large number can be planted, extending the season for both pollination and fruiting.

The espalier, too, is a useful form for planting along the boundary or as a screen between one part of the garden and another. Both cordons and espaliers need some form of support – for example, a post and wire fence, a wooden fence or a wall. Comparative yields are not as large as from trees grown in the open.

Where space is not so limited and a high yield is important, it is better to plant in open ground and to use one of the forms suitable for this purpose, such as the dwarf bush, bush, dwarf pyramid or spindlebush.

Standards and half-standards are unsuitable because they are grafted on to vigorous stocks and will become large trees. There is a place for them, however, as specimen or shade trees – in a lawn, for example.

Yield The number of fruits to plant, and the cultivars to choose, depend upon the family's needs and preferences relative to the amount of land available. It is not possible to give exact yields as there are so many variables involved, including soil, locality and cultivars. The chart overleaf gives average yields (in pounds) from well-grown established fruit plants.

Apples and pears No other tree fruits can offer such a wide choice of varieties, flavours and seasons of use – particularly apples, both dessert and culinary. It is not surprising that apples are our most popular tree fruits.

Plant apples and pears in full sun, if possible, or in a position which receives at least half the day's sun. Pears need more warmth than apples.

Both will tolerate a wide range of soils provided this is at least 45 cm (1½ ft) deep and is well drained. Avoid shallow soil over chalk, where the trees are likely to suffer from chlorosis and drought. Add lime to very acid soils to give a pH of between 6.5 and 6.7. If the soil is light, mix in bulky organic material to improve its texture and moisture retention.

Before buying the trees there are some important decisions to be made. These include the tree form to be used; the rootstock upon which the tree is grafted; the cultivars to plant; the pollination needs of these cultivars.

Apples
Before choosing an apple tree for the garden, consider the space you have available. Then decide on the form, rootstock and its pollination needs.

Pears
As with apples, pear trees are available in many different forms, sizes, varieties and cultivars to suit most sunny locations.

Fruit tree and bush yields (in lbs)

	Dwarf bush	Bush	Dwarf pyramid	Two-tier espalier	Single cordon	Fan
Apple	30–50	60–120	10–15	20–25	5–8	12–30
Pear	20–40	40–100	8–12	15–20	4–6	12–30
Plum	30	60	30–50			
Sweet cherry		30–100				12–50
Morello cherry		30–40	30–40			12–30
Peach/nectarine		30–60				12–30
Apricot						12–40
Fig						12–30
Black currant		10–13				
Red currant		6–12			1–3	
Gooseberry		8–10			1–2	

Fruit plant yields (in lbs)
Raspberry:
2 lb per 30 cm (1 ft) run of row.

Blackberry & hybrids:
10–15 lb per plant.

Strawberry:
½–1 lb per plant.

Tree forms There are two types: (a) restricted, and (b) non-restricted.

(a) Restricted types are the cordon, espalier, fan and dwarf pyramid, all of which are summer-pruned.

Cordon This is one of the most popular forms for small gardens because it takes up little space. It is a single-stemmed tree clothed in short fruiting spurs and is usually planted obliquely. More rarely, there are double and triple cordons. The cordon needs some kind of fence to support it. It is grafted on to a dwarfing or semi-dwarfing rootstock.

Espalier This consists of a central stem upon which are carried horizontal arms more or less opposite each other. The arms (tiers) are spaced between 30 cm (1 ft) and 45 cm (1½ ft) apart. Usually the tree is sold as a two or three-tiered espalier.

An espalier makes an attractive boundary marker and can be used to clothe low or high walls, depending upon the number of tiers. It is grafted on to a semi-dwarfing or moderately vigorous rootstock.

Fan The branch framework radiates outwards from a short central stem. It is excellent for walls 2.1 m (7 ft) or more high.

Dwarf pyramid This is a centre-leader tree for open ground, grown to a height of 1.8–2.1 m (6–7 ft). The lower branches are longer than those above, forming a pyramid shape. The tree's composition is similar to that of an upright cordon, with fruiting spurs replaced by short branches.

Pyramids are a good form for small gardens but, as the branches are closely spaced, summer pruning is crucial to prevent them from becoming overcrowded.

(b) The non-restricted types are the dwarf bush, bush and spindlebush. These are winter-pruned.

Dwarf bush and bush These traditional tree forms are the ones most widely grown. Basically, they are open-centred, goblet-shaped trees on a short trunk ranging in height from 45–75 cm (1½–2½ ft). The dwarf bush is grafted on to a dwarfing rootstock and so has less height and spread. Both are useful as orchard trees.

Spindlebush This is a relatively modern form of tree which crops well but requires a good deal of pruning skill to maintain its shape and cropping ability. It is a cone-shaped tree supported by a strong stake set about 1.8–2.1 m (6–7 ft) out of the ground.

Branches need to be at a wide angle to the main stem, so tying down of young laterals is an essential part of early training.

Rootstocks for apples The rootstock upon which a tree is grafted influences its eventual size and the time that it takes to bear. Those grafted on to dwarfing rootstocks make small trees which generally bear fruit within three or four years; those grafted on to vigorous stocks make large trees which can be slow to start cropping.

The rootstocks widely used today are as follows. The tree sizes given are no more than estimates for they will vary according to conditions.

'M.27' Extremely dwarfing. This makes a tree with a height and spread of about 1.8 m (6 ft). It is best grown as a centre leader tree (that is, as a dwarf pyramid or spindlebush) because a dwarf bush tends to collapse under the weight of fruit. 'M.27' requires a fertile soil, feeding and irrigation. The tree needs to be staked throughout its life. It is also suitable for cordons.

'M.9' Very dwarfing. This widely-used rootstock makes a dwarf bush, with a height and spread of 1.8–3 m (6–10 ft), which will start to crop within three years. 'M.9' needs a fertile soil, feeding and irrigation and the tree has to be staked throughout its life. It is used for dwarf bush, spindlebush, dwarf pyramids and cordons.

'M.26' Dwarfing. Making a bush with a height and spread of 2.4–3.6 m (8–12 ft), it is suitable for average soil conditions. A bush requires staking for the first four or five years. This rootstock is suitable for bush, dwarf pyramid, spindlebush and cordon trees and it could also be used for small espaliers and fans.

'MM.106' Semi-dwarfing. Bush trees on this rootstock will have a height and spread of 3.6–5.5 m (12–18 ft). It is suitable for most soils, except those that are poor and shallow. 'MM.106' is the most widely used apple rootstock. Bush trees need staking for the first four or five years. It is suitable for bush, spindlebush, cordon, espalier and fan trees.

'MM.111' and 'M.2' Vigorous. Both stocks make trees with a height and spread of 5.5–7.6 m (18–25 ft), depending on soil and variety. On average to good soils they make fairly large trees, but only medium-sized trees on the poorer, sandy or shallow soils. They are used by nurseries for bush, half-standards, standards, espaliers and sometimes for cordons and fans. They are too vigorous for most gardens, except where the soil is poor.

Rootstocks for pears Pears are usually grafted on to quince rootstocks, either 'Quince C' or 'Quince A'. These stocks make moderately dwarfing to moderately vigorous trees. 'C' tends to be slightly less vigorous than 'A'.

As with apples, it is possible to give only an estimate of the eventual size of the tree. Pear cultivars also differ greatly in growth, some being rather dwarf, some spreading, and others having a pronounced vigorous, upright habit. As a guide, mature bush trees on 'Quince C' have a height and spread ranging from 2.1–5.5 m (7–18 ft) and those on 'Quince A' from 2.4–6 m (8–20 ft).

A few cultivars of pear which are incompatible with quince have to be 'double worked' by the nurseryman. This means that an intermediate stock of pear, which is compatible with both, is grafted between the quince rootstock and the pear variety. The classic example of incompatibility is the pear 'William's Bon Chrétien', though there is now a compatible selection of it.

Pear rootstocks are extremely vigorous and are used only when large standard trees are wanted.

Varieties to plant The number of apple and pear cultivars is legion. There are, for example, over 2,000 different apple varieties in the National Fruit Trials at Faversham, Kent, and over 700 apple and 100 pear cultivars at Wisley. Many are old and a few are modern. Most date back to the Victorian era but some are hundreds of years old. They are, in effect, a genetic bank and a living monument to our plant breeders, past and present.

Those listed here have been noted over the years as being good garden cultivars, fairly reliable and of reasonable to good quality. Those that will give an acceptable crop in the cooler parts of the country are noted as being hardy.

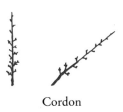

Cordon

Espalier

Fan

Pyramid

Bush

Spindlebush

Tree forms
Above, is the range of common fruit tree forms.

Good garden cultivars
In the following lists, cultivars with an especially good flavour are marked with an asterisk*. Those with a tendency towards biennial bearing are marked (B). Triploids are marked (T).

Pollination needs No apple or pear is completely self-fertile. Even those that have a reputation for setting a crop with their own pollen do better with cross pollination.

This means that at least two different cultivars, but of the same kind of fruits, should be planted and, of course, they must flower at the same time. With this in mind the pollination group of each cultivar is shown. Ideally, select cultivars within the same group, though as there is some overlap in flowering, groups immediately adjacent to each other can also be chosen.

Points to note Triploids (T), which have three sets of chromosomes, produce very little viable pollen and where these are chosen it is necessary to have two pollinators to pollinate the triploid and each other. They are extremely vigorous and are unsuitable for small gardens unless on 'M.27'.

'Family' trees have more than one cultivar grafted upon them and the cultivars chosen by the nurseryman are selected to pollinate each other. A 'family' tree, therefore, can be planted singly.

Apples – dessert Variety	Season of eating	Pollin- ation group	Comments
'Vista Bella' (B)	Late Jul.–early Aug.	2	Perfumed. Soon goes soft.
'Discovery'	Mid Aug.–mid Sept.	3	Crisp, juicy and sweet. The best early.
'James Grieve'	Sept.–Oct.	3	Crops well but canker prone. Hardy.
'Worcester Pearmain'	Sept.–Oct.	3	Sweet and chewy. Hardy and reliable. A partial tip-bearer.
'Ellison's Orange' (B)	Sept.–Oct.	4	Soft. Aniseed flavour. Hardy.
'Greensleeves'	Late Sept.–mid Nov.	3	Crisp at first. Crops heavily. Dwarfish. Hardy.
'Lord Lambourne'	Late Sept.–mid Nov.	2	Sweet. Crops well. Fairly hardy. Dwarfish.
'Egremont Russet'*	Oct.–Dec.	2	Crisp and nutty. Prone to bitter pit.
'Sunset'*	Oct.–Dec.	3	Cox-like flavour. Dwarfish. An excellent garden variety.
'Spartan'*	Oct.–Feb.	3	Crisp, vinous flavour. Canker prone. Hardy.
'Cox's Orange Pippin'*	Late Oct.–Jan.	3	First-class. Not suitable for cold situations.
'Gala'	Nov.–Jan.	4	Crisp and juicy but flavour fades. Scab prone. Hardy.
'Jupiter' (T)	Nov.–Jan.	3	Cox-like. Crops heavily. Very vigorous.
'Ashmead's Kernel'*	Dec.–Feb.	4	First-class flavour. Crops lightly.
'Fiesta'*	Jan.–Mar.	3	A promising new variety. Cox-like.
'Idared'	Nov.–Apr.	2	Flavour fair. Keeps well. Fairly hardy.
'Pixie'*	Dec.–Mar.	4	Small fruits. Crops well.

Variety	Season of eating	Pollination group	Comments
Apples – culinary 'Emneth Early' (B)	Mid Jul.–Aug.	3	Fruits small unless thinned. Hardy. Cooks frothily.
'Grenadier'	Aug.–Oct.	3	Crops well. Dwarfish. Hardy.
'Rev. W. Wilks' (B)*	Sept.–Oct.	2	Excellent cooker. Dwarfish. Compact.
'Peasgood Nonsuch'	Sept.–Nov.	3	Large, handsome fruits. Baker.
'Golden Noble'*	Oct.–Dec.	4	First-class, medium fruits. Moderate cropper.
'Bountiful'*	Sept.–Jan.	3	Crops heavily. A promising new variety.
'Blenheim Orange' (T)*	Nov.–Jan.	3	Rich, nutty, dual purpose. Extremely vigorous.
'Lane's Prince Albert'	Dec.–Mar.	3	Good cropper. Compact, hardy and reliable.
'Bramley's Seedling' (T)*	Nov.–Mar.	3	A first-class cooker. Sometimes biennial. Extremely vigorous. Fairly hardy.
'Annie Elizabeth'	Dec.–Jun.	4	Uncertain cropper. Keeps well. Hardy.
Pears – dessert 'William's Bon Chrétien'*	Early–mid Sept.	3	Excellent musky flavour. Scab prone. Fairly hardy. Will pollinate 'Doyenne du Comice' and vice versa.
'Beth'	Early–late Sept.	3	Sweet. Small fruits. Crops well.
'Onward'*	Late Sept.–early Oct.	4	First-class flavour. Unsuitable as a pollinator for 'Doyenne du Comice' and vice versa.
'Merton Pride' (T)*	Mid–late Sept.	3	Large fruits. First-class flavour.
'Beurre Hardy'*	Oct.	3	Slow to bear. Vigorous. Hardy.
'Beurre Superfin'*	Oct.	3	Moderate vigour. Good flavour.
'Conference'	Oct.–Nov.	3	Regular and reliable. Fairly hardy.
'Doyenne du Comice'*	Late Oct.–end Nov.	4	First-class pear. Requires a warm situation.
'Glou Morceau'	Dec.–Jan.	4	Requires warmth. Pollinates 'Doyenne du Comice'.
'Josephine de Malines'*	Dec.–Jan.	3	Excellent flavour. Requires a sunny position.
Pears – culinary 'Pitmaston Duchess' (T)	Oct.–Nov.	4	Very large fruits. Dual purpose. Vigorous. Unsuitable for small gardens.
'Catillac' (T)	Feb.–Apr.	4	Large fruits. A stewing pear only. Hardy.

PLUMS, GAGES AND DAMSONS

Plums, gages and damsons thrive on a high-nitrogen diet, with plenty of moisture during the summer. They need a deep, moisture-retentive soil which is slightly acid to neutral – that is, a pH range of 6.5 to 7.2. If the soil is light, irrigate during periods of drought though take care near harvest time not to give so much water that the fruits split.

Given the right conditions, all these fruits can crop regularly and well, sometimes heavily. The biggest problem arises during cold weather in the spring because these trees flower early. They may also suffer badly from bullfinches, aphids and silver leaf disease. These problems are not insurmountable, however. Certainly the trees are worth protecting against frost at blossom time, which is easiest when they are grown as fans or dwarf pyramids. Avoid a frost pocket if at all possible.

Many of the plums, and certainly the damsons, will do quite well in the cooler parts of the United Kingdom but the gages must have warmth and sun to develop their true flavour. In the north, gages are best planted against a wall and grown as fans. In the south, grow them as fans or in the open.

Most, but not all, of the plums and damsons – also some of the gages – are self-fertile and they can be planted singly. Some, particularly the gages, are self-incompatible, or partly so, and require cross-pollination to set a full crop.

In the list of recommended cultivars, these are shown either as s.f. (self-fertile), p.s.f. (partly self-fertile) or s.i. (self-incompatible). Trees in the last two categories must be planted with another, different cultivar so that cross-pollination is provided for. The partner chosen should, for preference, be in the same pollination group or else in an adjacent group.

Plant in a sunny, sheltered position and not in a frost pocket – unless protection can be given. Culinary plums will tolerate partial shade provided that this does not derive from overhanging trees and that the soil is not dry.

Rootstocks and tree forms Suitable rootstocks for plums, gages and damsons in a garden are 'St. Julien A' and 'Pixy'. Other stocks (until new ones are bred) are too vigorous for most gardens. Out in the open plums, gages and damsons are grown as bush trees, half-standards, standards and pyramids, and on walls as fans. Because of their growth habit they do not respond to the cordon or espalier methods of training.

'St. Julien A' is a semi-vigorous stock compatible with all varieties. It is suitable for bush, half-standard, pyramid and fan trees and is the stock most widely used by nurserymen. Tree sizes vary somewhat due to soil, cultivars and climate, but a mature bush or half-standard may range from 2.4–5 m (8–16 ft) in height and spread.

The pyramid, which is an excellent form for planting in the open, can be kept compact by summer pruning and on 'St. Julien A' will be about 2.1–2.4 m (7–8 ft) high, with a spread of 2.4–3 m (8–10 ft).

'Pixy' is a dwarfing stock, and relatively new, but it should make a fairly small tree with a height and spread of about 2.4–3 m (8–10 ft). It shows promise of being a most suitable stock for pyramids.

Dessert plums 'Victoria'. Fairly good flavour. The fruits are oval, large, pale red and mottled. The flesh is greeny-yellow and juicy. Late August–early September. Very heavy cropper. Prone to silver leaf disease. S.f., Group 3. Fairly hardy.

'Kirke's'. Very good flavour. The fruits are round and deep blue, with green, firm, juicy flesh. Moderate cropper. Dwarfish and spreading. Late August–early September. S.i., Group 4.

'Coe's Golden Drop'. Very sweet. Large, oval, yellow fruits with golden flesh. Juicy. An irregular cropper, making moderate growth. Late September. S.i., Group 2.

Gages 'Oullins Golden Gage'. Sweet, with a fair flavour. Large, round, yellow fruits. The flesh is pale yellow and juicy. Vigorous growth. Slow to bear but a good cropper. Fairly hardy. Mid August. S.f., Group 4.

'Early Transparent Gage'. Good flavour. The fruits are small to medium and round, being pale yellow with crimson dots. The flesh is golden and juicy. A moderate cropper with spreading growth. Mid–late August. S.f., Group 4.

Plums
Because plums flower early, frost is always a danger at blossom time. Given the right conditions, however, plums can be a good investment for the fruit garden.

'Denniston's Superb'. Good flavour. The fruits are a medium green-yellow and the flesh green and juicy. A heavy cropper and moderately vigorous. A good garden variety. Late August. S.f., Group 2.

'Cambridge Gage'. A seedling from 'Old Green Gage', and similar to that variety.

'Old Green Gage'. Excellent flavour. The small round fruits are green with russet dots. The flesh is yellow-green, syrupy-sweet and juicy. Slow to bear but vigorous. Late August–early September. S.i., Group 5 (late-flowering).

'Jefferson'. Excellent flavour. The fruits are large, oval and green, having russet dots and a pink flush. The pale yellow flesh is juicy. A moderate cropper of compact growth. Late August – early September. S.i., Group 1.

Culinary plums 'Cherry Plum'. (Myrobalan) A fair flavour. The fruits are very small and round, coloured bright red or dark purple. There is also a yellow form. This cultivar flowers very early. Very vigorous grown on its own stock. Late July. S.f., Group 1.

'Early Laxton'. Fair flavour. Small, oval, yellow and pink fruits. The flesh is golden and juicy. It has dwarfish growth and is a heavy cropper. Hardy. Late July. P.s.f., Group 3.

'Early Rivers'. Good flavour. The fruits are small, oval and purple-blue, the flesh golden and very juicy. Growth moderate. Fairly hardy. Late July–early August. P.s.f., Group 3.

'Czar'. Fair flavour. The fruits are medium in size, oval or round and dark purple. The flesh is greenish-yellow and juicy. Moderate growth and hardy. Early August. S.f., Group 3.

'Pershore'. ('Yellow Egg') Fair flavour, the fruits being of medium size, oval and golden. Yellow flesh. There is also a purple form. A heavy cropper with moderate growth. Hardy. Mid August. S.f., Group 3.

'Marjorie's Seedling'. A dual-purpose plum with a good flavour. The fruits are large, oval and purple-blue, the flesh yellow and juicy. A very good cropper. Vigorous, upright growth. Fairly hardy. Late September – early October. S.f., Group 5.

Damsons 'Prune' ('Shropshire' or 'Westmorland'). True damson flavour. The fruits are small, oval and blue-black, the flesh green-yellow. Crops well and has dwarfish growth. Late September. S.f., Group 5.

Bullaces These are round forms of the damson. They are often found growing wild in the hedgerows, but there are good cultivated forms, which may be white, golden or black.

'Golden Bullace'. Sweet, with a fair flavour. The fruits are small, round and golden, the flesh pale yellow. Growth moderate. Hardy. October. S.f.

SWEET AND DUKE CHERRIES

Unfortunately, the vigour of these lovely fruits means that they cannot, as yet, be recommended for small gardens. So far there is no dwarfing rootstock to keep them to an acceptable size, though the fruit research stations are working on the problem. The only rootstock worth considering for gardens at present is 'Colt'. This is semi-vigorous, making a bush or standard with a height and spread of about 6–9 m (20–30 ft), depending on conditions, which means that they are suitable only for large gardens. It is possible to grow them as fans, but the wall should be at least 2.4 m (8 ft) tall and allow for a spread of 4.5 m 15 ft.

Another possible solution is to try growing the sweet cherry as a pyramid on 'Colt', keeping it to a manageable size by tying down and summer pruning. Preliminary experiments at Wisley have shown that it is possible, given sufficient space, to keep it to a height of about 2.4 m (8 ft) by tying down strong, upright growths in June and July to a horizontal or weeping position. Where space is inadequate, cut back the young laterals to five leaves during June, and again in July if necessary.

Two other problems associated with the sweet cherry are that birds will take the ripe fruits – hence the importance of keeping the tree to a manageable height where it is practicable to net it effectively – and its critical pollination needs.

The Duke cherry is a cross between the sweet and sour cherry and, as one might expect, is intermediate in character and

Cherries
Perhaps not the easiest fruit tree to grow, cherries need a lot of space and have very precise pollination needs. Birds, too, can be a menace when the fruits are ripe. Netting is almost certainly a necessity.

flavour. It requires the same cultural treatment as the sweet cherry. Most cultivars are self-fertile.

Both cherries do best in the southern half of Britain but they will grow and crop reasonably well in most parts provided the site is in full sun and sheltered. Cherries flower early, so avoid frost pockets.

Cherries require a fertile, well-drained, medium to heavy soil, 60–90 cm (2–3 ft) deep and with a pH of 6.7 to 7.5. Shallow soils are unsuitable. On light soils cherries should be given plenty of irrigation during dry periods but be careful not to cause the fruits to split at ripening time.

Pollination needs At present, the only self-fertile sweet cherry is 'Stella'. All the others are self-infertile and may be incompatible with certain other cultivars. To simplify matters, suitable pollinators are grouped together in the following list:

Group 1
'Early Rivers', 'Noir de Guben'.
Group 2
'Roundel', 'Governor Wood', 'Van'.
Group 3
'Stella' is self-fertile and can, therefore, be planted singly. It will also pollinate 'Napoleon Bigarreau' or any in Group 2.

Sweet cherries 'Early Rivers'. Mid–late June. The fruits are large and dark red, the flesh red-black. Excellent flavour. Very vigorous.

'Noir de Guben'. Late June–early July. The fruits are large and dark red-brown, the flesh dark red with a fair flavour. Vigorous.

'Roundel'. Early July. Very large, dark red fruits, with flesh that is dark red. Juicy and sweet with an excellent flavour. Vigorous.

'Governor Wood'. Early July. The fruits are medium to large and dark red with yellow flesh. Has a good flavour and crops well. Moderately vigorous, making a relatively small tree.

'Van'. Late July. The fruits are large and bright red, with dark red flesh that is firm and sweet. Very vigorous.

'Stella'. Late July. The fruits are large and a dark, shiny red. The flesh is dark red and sweet with a good flavour. Vigorous, upright and then spreading.

'Napoleon Bigarreau'. Late July. Very large fruits, yellow with red mottling. The flesh is pale yellow, juicy and has a good flavour. Moderate vigour.

Duke cherries 'May Duke'. Culinary and dessert, mid-end June. The fruits are medium or large and dark red. The flesh is red, slightly acid and sweetish. Crops heavily and is vigorous.

Acid cherries This culinary fruit is excellent for pies, jam and wine. It is too sour for most people to eat raw, though some find the flavour quite refreshing.

Acid cherries have the advantage over sweet cherries that their growth is relatively dwarf, allowing them to be planted in smaller gardens. They are also self-fertile. Other points are that these cherries tolerate a certain amount of shade and are among the few fruits that will crop reasonably well on a north wall.

Acid cherries will grow in most parts of the British Isles but, as the trees flower in early spring, they require shelter against cold winds and should not be planted in a frost pocket.

The acid cherry can be grown either as a bush, a pyramid or as a fan. It is usually grafted on to 'Colt', a semi-vigorous rootstock, and when grown as a bush makes a tree with a height and spread of 2.4–3.6 m (8–12 ft).

The soil should be at least 45 cm (1½ ft) deep, slightly acid to slightly alkaline (a pH of 6.7 to 7.2), and well-drained.

The best example of the acid cherry is the 'Morello' which gives large, juicy fruits, dark red to almost black. It crops heavily.

PEACHES AND NECTARINES

To crop well, peach trees must be grown in a warm, sunny situation. For this reason, they are best grown as a fan on a south or west-facing wall, though in the south of the British Isles they can be grown in the open as bush trees.

The nectarine is a smooth-skinned form of the peach and needs slightly more warmth. Apart from this it is grown in exactly the same way, so the advice given here for peaches applies equally to nectarines. The basic need is soil that is well-drained, fertile and moisture-retentive.

Peaches
Due to their requirements of full sun and warmth, peaches are generally grown fan trained on a south or west-facing wall. In southern parts of the country, they can be grown in bush form.

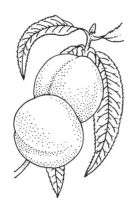

Important points to know about the peach are that it flowers very early in the spring, that it may suffer badly from peach leaf-curl disease, and that only the early and mid-season cultivars are suitable for growing outdoors, the late cultivars being unlikely to ripen.

Taking each point in turn:

Early flowering To prevent damage from spring frosts, it is essential to protect the blossom from the pink bud stage onwards until the risk is over.

As few, if any, pollinating insects are about at this time, hand pollination is needed.

Peach leaf-curl This debilitating disease attacks the leaves and, occasionally, the fruit. A bad attack will result in severe defoliation, dead wood and die-back.

The disease can be controlled by a regular spray programme or by placing a polythene lean-to over the fan to keep the framework branches dry throughout the winter and spring.

Early and mid-season cultivars Both peaches and nectarines are self-fertile, so a solitary tree can be planted if desired.

Suitable rootstocks Both peaches and nectarines may be grown on 'St. Julien A', which is semi-vigorous. An alternative is 'Mussel', which is semi-vigorous to vigorous but produces rather a lot of suckers.

Early peaches 'Duke of York'. Mid July. Excellent flavour, with tender, white flesh. The large fruits are crimson over pale yellow.

'Hale's Early'. End of July. Good flavour, pale yellow flesh. Medium yellow fruits with a red mottling and flush.

Mid-season peaches 'Peregrine'. August. A peach with an excellent flavour and green-white flesh. Large, crimson fruits. Cropping is moderate to good.

'Redhaven'. Mid August. Has a good flavour, with yellow, melting flesh that is red near the stone. The fruits are round and of medium size, being deep red over a yellow skin.

'Rochester'. August. This is the most reliable outdoor peach. A fair flavour, with yellow, juicy flesh. The medium-sized fruits are yellow with a crimson flush. It crops well and is fairly hardy.

Nectarines 'Early Rivers'. End of July. Has a rich flavour and pale yellow flesh. The large fruits are yellow with red streaks. It is best on a wall or under glass.

'Lord Napier'. Early August. Richly-flavoured fruits with white flesh. These are large, and yellow-orange with a crimson flush. It crops well but is best on a wall or under glass.

APRICOTS

This fruit is best grown against a south or west-facing fence or wall. The ideal is a warm house wall, built from brick or stone, with a substantial eave to help to ward off frost as well as to support any protective material. The apricot is a vigorous tree and needs a wall not less than 2.4 m (8 ft) high by 4.5 m (15 ft) wide. In the south of the British Isles it can be grown in the open as a bush, but because it flowers early cropping will be erratic. It is self-fertile.

The soil needs to be well-drained, moisture-retentive and slightly alkaline (a pH of 6.7 to 7.5). Light, sandy soils are not suitable unless bulky organic material is added and adequate irrigation is provided in the summer.

Rootstocks Apricots require the same stocks as plums. For a fan, the semi-vigorous 'St. Julien A' is widely used.

Recommended cultivars 'Early Moorpark'. Late July. Richly-flavoured fruits which are small to medium in size and yellow with a crimson flush. The flesh is deep orange and juicy. It crops well and is vigorous.

'Farmingdale'. Late July. Has a very good flavour. The medium-sized fruits are orange-yellow with a red flush. The flesh is orange and moderately juicy. A heavy cropper of vigorous growth. Good resistance to bacterial canker.

'Hemskerk'. Early August. A very sweet, rich flavour. Large, yellow fruits with red patches. It crops well and is moderately vigorous.

'Moorpark'. Early–mid August. The most widely-grown cultivars, with a rich, sweet flavour. The large fruits are pale yellow with a reddish-brown flush and dots. The flesh is orange, firm and juicy. Moderately vigorous.

Apricots
Apricot trees are vigorous and benefit from the warmth of a south or west-facing house wall. They are early flowering, which always brings a danger of frost damage, so a deep, sheltered eave will give additional protection.

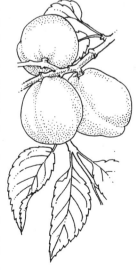

Figs
Coming as they do
from a warmer
climate, fig trees do
best against a warm
and sunny wall or
fence. They can be
successful in the
south of the country,
but are better grown
under glass in the
north.

Cobnuts
Suitable for small
gardens, cobnuts will
do well in partial
shade or full sun.
Apart from the fruits,
an added bonus is the
long yellow or claret-
red catkins borne in
late winter.

FIGS

The fig is a sun-loving fruit, from a warmer climate than that of the British Isles. Nevertheless, it can crop reasonably well here provided certain essentials are met.

It must be grown on a warm wall or fence, such as one with a south or south-westerly aspect, or in a sunny corner bounded by two walls. Although there are successful trees in the open in especially favoured sites, these are the exception rather than the rule. As might be expected, the fig is more suited to the south. Further north, it is better under glass.

Root restriction is essential, as without it the tree will tend to be vigorous, producing lanky, leafy growth and no fruits.

The embryo figs, or fruitlets, which are carried over the winter to develop and ripen the following summer, are extremely vulnerable to winter damage. Without protection they will be destroyed in a hard winter but may survive a mild one. To be certain of obtaining a crop, the branch framework which carries these young fruits must be protected against frost throughout the danger period.

Recommended cultivars 'Brown Turkey'. August–September. A reliable and widely-grown variety, with large, oval fruits. The skin is shiny brown with a blue bloom, the flesh red, rich and sweet.

'Brunswick'. Mid August. Very large fruits that are green-yellow flushed brown. The flesh is pale yellow, but red near the centre. Hardy, and a moderate cropper.

'White Marseilles'. August. Hardy and reliable and crops well. Large, pear-shaped fruits. The skin is a pale greenish-white, the flesh translucent, sweet and rich.

COBNUTS AND FILBERTS

Collectively called hazel nuts, these are ornamental trees in their own right. They produce long catkins that are yellow or claret-red, these doing much to brighten the last days of the winter, and their leaves are an attractive light green. There is also a purple-leaved form. The nuts borne in the late summer are a welcome bonus.

Botanically, cobnuts and filberts are distinct, though they are grown in exactly the same way. The difference lies in the length of the husk and the shape of the nut. In a filbert, the nut is long and the husk envelops the nut completely. The nut of the cob is a rounded oblong, while the husk is short and the nut visible. Filberts are considered to have the better flavour.

In its natural habitat the hazel nut grows in light shade provided by larger trees. The flowers, which open in February or March, are wind-pollinated, though they do not react well to strong, wet winds. They cannot withstand very hard frosts.

Though self-fertile, sometimes the catkins and female flowers do not open at the same time, or insufficient may be produced. To be sure of a full crop it is best to plant two different cultivars of either cobnuts or filberts.

Plant them in full sun or partial shade in a site sheltered from strong winds. Hazels are vigorous trees and can attain a height and spread of about 3–3.6 m (10–12 ft). However, they should be kept to a height of 1.8–2.1 m (6–7 ft) by fairly hard pruning.

Hazel nuts are lime-tolerant and will grow in almost any soil provided it is reasonably well-drained. The ideal is a medium loam over chalk, with a pH of 7.0–8.0.

Cobnuts 'Cosford'. Large, oblong nuts with a good flavour. Numerous, bright yellow catkins. A good pollinator that crops well and is vigorous.

'Nottingham Cob'. ('Pearson's Prolific') Small or medium sized nuts with a good flavour. The catkins are prolific and pale yellow. A good pollinator. Dwarfish habit and an excellent cultivar.

Filberts 'Kentish Cob'. ('Lambert's Filbert') A filbert, despite its name, and widely planted. It has a good flavour, with very long, large nuts, although it needs a pollinator. Moderately vigorous; crops well.

'Purple Filbert'. Medium sized nuts with a good flavour, in purple-red husks. Purple leaves in the spring. A highly ornamental tree, but only a moderate cropper.

'Red Filbert'. Small, long, narrow nuts with a reddish husk and an excellent flavour. The long, claret-red catkins are sparse, so a pollinator is needed. Vigorous.

'White Filbert'. Similar to 'Red Filbert', except that the husk is white.

QUINCES AND MEDLARS

Quinces Though neither is commonly grown, the quince, *Cydonia oblonga*, and the medlar, *Mespilus germanica*, are attractive trees in their own right. If there is no space for them in the orchard, they are worth planting in the ornamental part of the garden.

The quince is a relatively small, deciduous, thornless tree with a crooked, branching habit. Its flowers, borne in May, are large, solitary, pale pink or white and similar to those of the wild rose.

However, the fruits are the tree's most attractive feature. They may be apple-shaped but more often are pear-shaped. When ripe they are a beautiful golden-yellow, usually with pale grey down upon the skin. Their flavour is powerfully aromatic but sharply astringent. Though they cannot be eaten raw, they make a delightful perfumed pink jelly. Also, a slice of quince in an apple pie gives the dish an extra touch of quality.

The tree is fairly hardy but must have a sunny position for its fruits to ripen properly. In southern England it can be grown in the open, usually as a bush or standard, but further north it is better planted in a sheltered position – for example, against a warm wall or in a sunny corner. It succeeds in most soils but prefers one that is fertile and moisture-retentive. It does well when planted near water.

The quince is self-fertile and usually starts cropping when about five or six years old. If more than one is planted, space them 4.5 m (15 ft) apart.

Cultivars of quince 'Portugal' ('Lusitanica'). The pear-shaped fruits have deep yellow skins covered with grey down. Their flesh is tender, juicy and excellent for cooking and preserving. The tree is taller and more vigorous than the others but not quite so hardy. This is the best quince, but better suited to southern England.

'Vranja'. The fruit is very fragrant, of a clear, shining gold, and tender. Growth is vigorous and this is a precocious cropper. A recommended cultivar.

'Berecski'. A variety very similar to 'Vranja'.

'Champion'. Large, pear-shaped fruits with bright yellow skins. The flesh is tender when cooked, with a delicate flavour. A very productive tree that starts to bear freely when young.

'Maliformis' (apple-shaped quince). Roundish fruits, 6 cm (2½ in) in diameter and of a rich golden colour. It is very productive and will ripen in a less favourable climate than other cultivars.

Medlars The medlar, which is related to the quince, is a deciduous, long-lived tree, sometimes thorned but rarely so in the case of cultivated forms. Some have an attractive weeping habit and they are usually grown as half or full standards. When mature, trees may reach from 3.6–6 m (12–20 ft) in height, depending on the environment, rootstock and variety.

The leaves are lanceolate, dark green and downy, changing to reddish-brown in the autumn. The flowers are white or pink-tinted, very like the quince, and are borne singly in May or June at the ends of short shoots. The fruits resemble large, flattish rose hips, but they have a russety, dark brown skin.

Medlars' fruits make a superb, orange-coloured jelly, with a distinctive flavour. They can be eaten raw but are not to everyone's taste. The fruits are left until they are just beginning to decay, a process called 'bletting', when the flesh becomes brown and soft.

Medlars are hardy and can be grown in all parts of the British Isles. The site should be sunny and sheltered, however, because the leaves and flowers are easily damaged by strong winds. They tolerate a wide range of soils, provided that the drainage is good.

Cultivars of medlars 'Dutch'. The fruits are 5–6 cm (2–2½ in) in diameter, flattened, russet-brown and with a fair flavour. It makes a handsome, flat-headed and weeping tree and is the most ornamental form.

'Nottingham'. Small-fruited but with a better flavour than 'Dutch'. Each fruit has a diameter of about 4 cm (1½ in). The tree has a more upright growth habit.

'Royal'. The fruits are 4–5 cm (1½–2 in) in diameter, with a good flavour. This cultivar crops well and makes compact but fairly upright growth.

Quinces
Even if there is no room in the fruit garden, a quince would look equally at home as an ornamental tree elsewhere in the garden. It is a small tree with an attractive branching habit, and in May it bears flowers not unlike those of a wild rose.

Medlars
Cultivated forms of medlar are usually thornless and can be had in an attractive weeping form. Its flowers are similar to those of the quince, to which the medlar is related.

SOFT FRUITS

The importance of planting only healthy stock cannot be too strongly stressed. Trying to succeed with disease-ridden, unhealthy plants is hopeless.

For certain fruits there is a Ministry of Agriculture Certification Scheme. Under this arrangement, which is voluntary, nurserymen submit their plants for official inspection and, if the plants are healthy and true to name, the nurseryman receives a certificate to this effect. The plants are termed 'Certified Stock'.

Obviously, these are the kind that the gardener should obtain wherever possible, but not all soft fruits come within the scheme. At present, it covers strawberries, black currants, raspberries, certain hybrid berries and a few gooseberry cultivars. If you wish to buy other types of soft fruit, obtain them from a reputable nurseryman.

BLACK CURRANTS

This hardy, deciduous bush fruit is widely grown throughout the British Isles. The fruits make excellent pies, superb jam and fruit juice, and are rich in Vitamin C. Black currants are grown as 'stooled bushes'. This is a method in which the shoots are grown from ground level rather than from a single stem.

The chief points to note are as follows:

Certified Stock Plant only Ministry of Agriculture Certified Stock, thus ensuring that the bushes are free from big bud mite and the virus-like disease, reversion. Once planted, keep a firm control over this mite.

Site Black currants flower early, so try to avoid planting in a frost pocket. Where this is not possible, protect the bushes against frost at flowering time. Given a frost-free spring or adequate cover, a well-grown black currant bush will yield at least 4.5 kg (10 lb) of fruit.

Bushes are best planted in full sun, though they will tolerate some shade. The flowers are pollinated principally by bumble bees so it is an advantage to have a sheltered site where their movements will not be inhibited.

The soil needs to be fertile, moisture-retentive and well-drained, but the bushes will tolerate slightly impeded drainage

Black currants
This very widely grown bush fruit can be put to excellent culinary use, and it is a valuable source of Vitamin C. For best cropping, plant bushes in full sun, but they will tolerate partial shade.

below 45 cm (1½ ft). Very acid ground should be limed to bring the pH up to between 6.7 and 7.0.

Feeding and pruning Black currants bear their best fruit on wood made during the previous summer. For this reason, generous feeding and fairly hard pruning are needed so that strong young wood is produced every year.

Spacing Space the bushes 1.5–1.8 m (5–6 ft) apart, depending upon the vigour of the variety. 'Ben Sarek', which needs only 1.2 m (4 ft), is an exception.

Early black currants 'Boskoop Giant'. Large, sweet berries and a heavy cropper. It flowers early and so is prone to frost damage. It is a very vigorous bush, and is therefore unsuitable for small gardens. Space 1.8 m (6 ft) apart.

'Laxton's Giant'. This is similar to 'Boskoop Giant', the berries being very large, sweet and of good flavour. Space 1.8 m (6 ft) apart.

'Blackdown'. Has sweet berries and is a moderate cropper. The bushes are of medium size, sprawling and with lax growth. They are very resistant to mildew. Space 1.5 m (5 ft) apart.

Mid-season black currants 'Ben Lomond'. The berries are medium to large, with thick skins and a fair flavour. It crops well and has some resistance to mildew and frost. Space 1.5–1.8 m (5–6 ft) apart.

'Ben Nevis'. Crops heavily and in most respects is similar to 'Ben Lomond'.

Mid-season to late black currants 'Baldwin'. (Hilltop stock). The medium size berries have a good, acid flavour and are rich in Vitamin C. Crops well, is moderately vigorous and fairly compact. A good garden cultivar. Space 1.5 m (5 ft) apart.

'Ben More'. The large berries have an acid flavour. It forms a vigorous, upright bush, with some mildew resistance and frost hardiness. Space bushes 1.5–1.8 m (5–6 ft) apart.

'Ben Sarek'. Large berries on short sprigs, with an acid flavour. It crops heavily. This cultivar makes compact, short growth but needs support to stop it sprawling. It is suitable for small gardens and has some resistance to mildew and frost. Space 1.2 m (4 ft) apart.

Very late black currants 'Amos Black'. Medium sized to large berries, which have a fair but rather acid flavour. It forms a small bush with stiff, erect shoots and cropping tends to be light. Space 1.5 m (5 ft) apart.

RED AND WHITE CURRANTS

Though somewhat neglected in comparison with black currants, these fruits yield well and are more tolerant of cold. Red currants make excellent jelly, pies and wine and are an important ingredient of any summer pudding.

The white currant is a sport, or mutant, of the red and is grown in exactly the same way. It is slightly less vigorous, however, and the yield is not so heavy. The berries are regarded as sweeter than those of red currants.

Both are usually grown as open-centred, goblet-shaped bushes on short stems about 10–15 cm (4–6 in) high. They also make excellent cordons or, more rarely, standards and fans. There is no Certified Scheme for red and white currants, so be sure to obtain your plants from a reputable source.

Important points to note are:
Site For maximum flavour and early ripening this should be in full sun, though the bushes will tolerate partial shade. They can be grown quite successfully as cordons on a north-facing wall or fence.

These currants flower early, so avoid a frost pocket if possible, or be prepared to protect them in April and May. The site must be sheltered.
Soil These fruits tolerate a wide range of conditions but, ideally, choose a deep, moisture-retentive, light to medium loam that is slightly acid.
Feeding Red and white currants are prone to a deficiency of potassium, so this is one element that should not be omitted in the annual feeding programme. (See Calendar, February.)
Spacing Space bushes 1.5 m (5 ft) apart, with 38 cm (15 in) between cordons.
Red currants 'Jonkheer van Tets'. Very early, with a good flavour and bunches of large berries. A very heavy cropper.

'Laxton's No. 1'. An early variety, with a good flavour and medium-sized berries. Crops well and makes moderate growth.

'Red Lake'. A mid-season variety and the most widely grown, being hardy and reliable. It carries large berries and bunches and has an excellent flavour. Crops well.

'Stanza'. Mid–late season, with a good flavour and large bunches and berries. It is a heavy cropper.

'Rondom'. Late to ripen, with large berries and short sprigs. It is difficult to pick, but a heavy cropper.

'Malling Redstart'. Mid–late season. A promising new cultivar, with long sprigs on an erect and moderately heavy bush. This is a very heavy cropper.

White currants 'White Versailles'. An early white currant, with very long bunches, that makes a moderate-sized, upright bush. The berries are large, light yellow and sweet. It is widely grown and a good garden cultivar.

'White Dutch'. A mid-season cultivar with a good flavour. The bush is moderately vigorous and a little spreading. The bunches are 5–8 cm (2–3 in) long; the berries large, milky-yellow and sweet.

'White Grape'. This cultivar, which produces large clusters and large berries, is considered to be the best flavoured. The berries are a clear yellowish-white, with firm flesh, and are sweet. The bush is of medium size and spreading. It crops well.

RASPBERRIES

Few other fruits have as many attributes as the raspberry. It freezes well, is excellent as a dessert fruit and makes a lovely, perfumed jam. Raspberries give about 1 kg (2 lb) of fruit for each 30 cm (1 ft) of row, take up very little room and will grow almost anywhere in the British Isles. They are also one of our most popular fruits.
Certified Stock As raspberries are prone to all kinds of virus troubles, ensure a clean start by planting only Certified Stock.
Site A sunny but well-sheltered site is necessary. Raspberries will grow in partial shade but not under overhanging trees or in dry soil.
Soil A well-drained, moisture-retentive, fertile, slightly acid, light or medium loam is ideal. Very heavy, badly-drained soil is

White currants
Although not as widely cultivated as the black currant, white currants crop well and are more tolerant of the cold.

Raspberries
The hardy raspberry will grow just about anywhere in the country. Because of the risk of virus problems, however, buy only Certified Stock.

unsuitable because of the canes susceptibility to fungal troubles. The land should be drained before planting and, if proper drainage is not practicable, construct a soakaway of brick rubble, clinker or similar materials under the rows. In such situations it helps to plant on a slight ridge.

On alkaline soils raspberries suffer badly from lime-induced chlorosis, and in this case an acidifying agent, such as peat, should be added generously. Mulching with peat is advisable on shallow soils, too.

Training Raspberries need some kind of wire fence to support the canes.

Cultivars 'Glen Clova'. Ripens early. This is a heavy cropper, with fruits of medium size and good flavour. The canes are vigorous and abundant. It is susceptible to virus infection from 'Malling Jewel' and should not be planted with it.

'Glen Moy'. An early cultivar. The fruits are of medium size and good flavour. The canes are vigorous and stout, the fruit laterals short. It is resistant to raspberry aphids and therefore less susceptible to virus infections. Crops well.

'Delight'. Ripens early mid-season, with large, pale orange-red fruits. The canes are prolific and vigorous. It carries long fruit laterals which are susceptible to spur blight and botrytis. Resistant to some strains of raspberry aphid and crops well.

'Malling Jewel'. A mid-season cultivar, bearing good-quality, firm fruits, with compact growth but sparse cane production. For this reason, plant two canes per station, 38 cm (15 in) apart. It is tolerant of virus infection.

'Malling Admiral'. Fruits late mid-season. This is a heavy cropper, bearing good quality, medium sized berries. The canes are prolific and vigorous and the fruiting laterals long. Some resistance to spur blight, mildew and cane botrytis is shown.

'Glen Prosen'. Mid-late season. Fruits of medium size, firm and with a good flavour. They are suitable for all purposes, and there is a long picking period. The canes are moderately vigorous and resistant to aphids. Crops well.

'Leo'. A very late cultivar. The fruits are large, bright orange-red, firm, and with a good, slightly acid flavour. The canes are very vigorous but are slow to build up in number. Plant two per station. It is fairly resistant to spur blight, cane botrytis and some strains of aphid, but susceptible to cane spot. A good cropper.

AUTUMN-FRUITING RASPBERRIES

These crop at the top of the current season's canes, extending back over 30 cm (1 ft) or more. The fruits ripen from the beginning of September until they are stopped by autumn frosts.

The same conditions are needed, except that they will not tolerate shade. Choose the sunniest position available, otherwise too few fruits may ripen before the cold weather arrives.

Cultivars 'Autumn Bliss'. The fruits ripen from mid-August onwards. A promising new cultivar, with firm berries of good size and with a good flavour. The canes are short and sturdy. A heavy cropper.

'September'. Ripens from late August onwards. Flavour is good and the berries are small to medium in size. Cropping is good, the canes being very prolific but only weak to moderate in strength.

'Fallgold'. Fruits ripen from early September onwards. A yellow/orange berry with a sweet, mild flavour. The berries are small to medium, the canes vigorous and prolific.

BLACKBERRIES AND HYBRID BERRIES

Wild blackberries thrive in hedgerows throughout the British countryside. The cultivated forms have larger fruits and give a heavier yield relative to their size. Some varieties ripen much earlier, some are just as aggressively thorned while others are thornless.

Hybrid berries are of mixed *Rubus* parentage, most having the raspberry as one parent and the blackberry as the other. As might be expected, hybrid berries are intermediate in character and flavour between the two parents. Usually they are sweeter than the blackberry and ripen earlier – though not as early as the raspberry – and they are not as vigorous or as

Blackberries
Wild blackberries are a common sight in hedgerows throughout Britain. Cultivated forms, however, produce larger fruit and a heavier yield.

thorny as the blackberry. Unlike the raspberry, their canes are perennial.

Blackberries and hybrid berries are rambling, sprawling cane fruits which need some kind of support to keep the canes off the ground and the fruits clean. They are productive plants for covering walls and fences and look most attractive trained over structures such as arches and pergolas. Out in the open they are best grown on wire fences.

These fruits do best in a warm, sheltered position. This is essential for hybrid berries, but blackberries will tolerate a good deal of shade provided the soil is not dry. Both will grow in a wide range of soils provided they are reasonably deep – preferably 45 cm (1½ ft) or more. Blackberries can withstand slightly impeded soil drainage.

Source of supply Obtain the plants from a reputable source because, as with raspberries, they may otherwise be infected with virus and impossible to grow successfully. A limited Certification Scheme exists for the Tayberry. If certified it is sold as Medana Tayberry.

Choice of varieties Blackberries and hybrid berries are self-fertile and can, therefore, be planted singly. Some varieties of blackberry are very vigorous and powerfully thorned, making them quite unsuitable for small gardens. A few varieties are thornless and make fairly compact growth and these are the best ones to choose if space is limited.

Where space is limited, hybrid berries may perhaps be a better choice as most make relatively moderate growth and their taste is different. Training methods are suggested in the following list of varieties.

Blackberries 'Bedford Giant'. This is the earliest to ripen (in July), with large, shiny, blackberries of mild flavour. It crops well but the canes are extremely vigorous and thorny. It is therefore unsuitable for small gardens. Train on the rope or weaving system. Space 3.6–4.5 m (12–15 ft) apart.

'Himalaya Giant'. Early to mid-season. The large berries have a fair flavour and it crops heavily. The canes are exceedingly vigorous and thorny, so it is unsuitable for small gardens. Train on the rope or weaving system. Plant 4.5 m (15 ft) apart to allow for growth.

'Ashton Cross'. Mid-season. The medium sized berries have a true blackberry flavour. Train the vigorous, thorny, wiry canes on the rope system. Plant 3.6 m (12 ft) apart.

'Oregon Thornless'. ('Parsley' or 'Cut Leaf'). Mid-late season. A thornless form of the parsley-leaved blackberry, with a mild blackberry flavour. It has attractive leaves and, though vigorous, is easy to manage and therefore suitable for small gardens. Train on the rope system. Plant 3–4.2 m (10–14 ft) apart.

Hybrid berries 'Tayberry'. Early. The berries are medium to large, with a mild, sweet, perfumed flavour. It crops well. The prickly canes are moderately vigorous and not fully winter-hardy. Train on the rope system. Plant 2.4–3 m (8–10 ft) apart.

'Boysenberry'. Early to mid-season. The large, purplish fruits have a good acid flavour and it crops well. The canes are moderately vigorous and there are thorned and thornless forms. Train on the rope system. Plant 2.4–3 m (8–10 ft) apart.

'Tummelberry'. Early to mid-season. The fruits are large, with a sharp, acid flavour. It crops heavily. The canes are vigorous, moderately thorny and more winter-hardy than those of the 'Tayberry'. Train on the rope system. Plant 2.4–3 m (8–10 ft) apart.

'Loganberry'. Mid-season. This is the most widely grown of all the hybrid berries, the berries being medium to large and with a distinctive acid flavour. It crops well, and the canes are moderately vigorous. There are thorned (Clone LY.59) and thornless forms (L.654). Train on the rope system. Plant 2.4–3 m (8–10 ft) apart.

'Smoothstem'. Late. Large, shiny, black fruits with a sharp, acid flavour. It crops well and the canes are thornless, strong and compact. A warm, sunny position is essential, and it is unsuitable for the north. Train on the fan or rope system, planting 2.4 m (8 ft) apart.

GOOSEBERRIES

Gooseberries grow just as well in the north of the country as in the south. Indeed, they

Loganberries
A popular hybrid berry, the loganberry crops well and is moderately vigorous. Thorned and thornless forms are available.

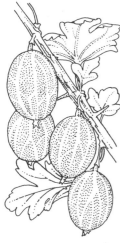

Gooseberries
An adaptable fruit, gooseberries prefer an open, sunny site, but they will tolerate moist shade if it is not too dense. Bushes are only small, so frost protection is possible.

are more popular in the northern part of Britain.

Ideally, the planting site should be in full sun, sheltered and away from overhanging trees. However, gooseberries will tolerate light shade provided the ground is not dry. They are one of the few fruits that will crop successfully against a north-facing wall or fence, though to achieve the full flavour of the dessert cultivars they are better planted in a warmer situation.

Flowering is early, so a frost pocket should be avoided if possible. Failing this, the bushes are small enough for protection to be possible. Bullfinches and sparrows can be troublesome, too, for they eat the fruit buds during the winter. Netting is the answer.

The soil needs to be well-drained and 38 cm (15 in) or more deep. Chalky soils are tolerated if sufficiently deep. Very acid soils should be limed to bring the pH up to about 6.7. If the soil is light, mix in some bulky organic material to improve moisture retention.

Grow the plant as an open-centred bush on a stem about 15 cm (6 in) long. Alternatively, it can be grown as either a single or multiple cordon, or as a fan against a wall or a fence. The cordon is an ideal form for a small garden as it allows a good selection of varieties to be grown in a relatively small area.

Thanks to the past existence of 'gooseberry clubs', in the Northern and Midland counties, there is a wide choice of cultivars – early, mid-season and late – with red, yellow, green and white fruits. Growing the largest gooseberry was the principal objective of these clubs.

Gooseberry clubs were at the peak from the start of the last century up to the first quarter of the present, and the romantic-sounding names of the cultivars they have left us are a reminder of the events taking place at the time – names such as 'Hero of the Nile', 'Roaring Lion', and 'Leveller'.

At present, the only cultivars that come within the Certified Stock Scheme are 'Invicta' and 'Jubilee'. Fortunately, though, gooseberries are not virus prone, and provided plants are obtained from a reputable source should be no problem.

Cultivars (in order of ripening)
Early (These fruits develop rapidly and can be picked green for cooking.)

'Keepsake'. Has a very good flavour, the fruits being medium to large, whitish-green and with a transparent skin. It crops well but is susceptible to mildew. Suitable for both dessert and cooking.

'May Duke'. Has a good flavour when cooked. The fruits are of medium size, oblong, and dark red when fully ripe. A good cropper, suitable for both dessert and cooking.

'Golden Drop'. Has a very good flavour. The fruits are small, round and a dull greenish-yellow. It has an upright, compact habit and is a moderate cropper. A dessert cultivar.

Mid-season 'Careless'. The virus-tested form, called 'Jubilee' or 'Jubilee Careless', should be obtained in preference. It has a good flavour, with berries that are large, oval, smooth and green milky-white. It is a reliable and good cropper. Suitable for dessert and cooking.

'Invicta'. A new cultivar, highly resistant to mildew. It has a good flavour, with large, oval berries that are greenish-white and smooth-skinned. With a vigorous, spreading habit, it crops heavily and is suitable for dessert and cooking.

'Lancashire Lad'. The flavour is fair, the fruits medium-large, dark red, oblong and hairy. It requires good soil and is a heavy cropper. A cooking variety.

'Langley Gage'. An excellent flavour; medium size, oval, smooth fruits, pale yellow in colour. A dessert cultivar that is a moderate cropper.

'Leveller'. The most widely-grown dessert gooseberry. It requires good soil but has an excellent flavour, bearing large, oval, sulphur-yellow fruits with a slightly downy skin. It is a good cropper, needing thinning if the fruits are grown for exhibition. A good choice for the latter.

'Whinham's Industry'. Widely grown and reliable, it does well on most soils. The bush is very vigorous, though prone to mildew. The fruits are large, dark red, oval and hairy, but with a sweet flavour. It crops heavily and is grown for both dessert and cooking.

'Whitesmith'. With a very good flavour, the berries are medium to large, pale green with a yellow tinge, and with a downy skin. A dessert and culinary cultivar, rigorous and with good crops.

Late 'Howards Lancer'. The well-flavoured, large berries are oval, pale greenish-white, thin-skinned and downy. This is a vigorous bush that crops well. Suitable for dessert and culinary purposes, and for exhibition.

HIGHBUSH BLUEBERRY

This deciduous North American plant belongs to the *Ericaceae* family. It is closely related to our own indigenous whinberry or bilberry but is a larger shrub that gives bigger berries and a much heavier crop. It is a delicious fruit, excellent for freezing and deservedly renowned in America for making blueberry pie. The fruits ripen from late July onwards, depending on cultivar.

Like the bilberry it is a heathland plant and must have a very acid, light to medium sandy loam. A pH of 4.0 to 5.5 is the maximum acidity. Bear in mind that the pH of acid to slightly acid soils can be brought down to the required range by using acidifying agents.

However, it is pointless to plant blueberries in neutral or alkaline soils as the plants will suffer from iron and manganese deficiencies. In such situations they can be grown in specially constructed beds filled with an acid-based compost, provided that alkaline water is prevented from permeating into the area. Alternatively, blueberries can be grown in containers, a diameter of 45 cm (1½ ft) being the minimum.

The blueberry is grown as a stooled bush. It is an ornamental plant with pretty, urn-shaped, creamy-white flowers – sometimes pink-tinted.

Blueberries will fit in quite well with rhododendrons and other calcifuge plants. The berries are extemely attractive to birds, however, and where it is grown primarily for its fruit it is better planted separately so that the plants can be netted properly.

Being winter-hardy, blueberries can be grown almost anywhere in the British Isles if given the right soil conditions. As it flowers early, a frost pocket must be avoided. The site should be sunny and sheltered, though the plants will tolerate light shade. Plenty of summer moisture is essential but it is advisable to use soft water for irrigation.

Blueberries are only partly self-fertile and for a full crop more than one cultivar should be planted.

Cultivars 'Earliblue'. Early to ripen, with large berries of good quality. Strong, upright growth and attractive autumn colouring. Cropping is moderate.

'Bluecrop'. Early to ripen. The berries are large and with a good flavour. It crops well and has vigorous, upright growth. A good garden variety.

'Ivanhoe'. Mid-season. The berries are of medium size, dark blue, sweet, and with a good flavour. It crops well and has attractive autumn colouring.

'Elizabeth'. Late. The berries are large and dark blue, with a moderate flavour. Crops heavily and is vigorous and upright. Bright autumn colouring.

'Coville'. Very late. The berries are large, light blue and with a good flavour. Makes a vigorous, spreading bush.

WORCESTERBERRIES

Though at one time this soft fruit was thought to be a hybrid between the gooseberry and the black currant, it is now considered a true species – *Ribes divaricatum*, from North America.

The bush is extremely vigorous, very thorny and hardy, and has a good degree of resistance to mildew. The berries are borne singly in a similar way to those of the gooseberry. They are slightly larger than a big black currant, a dull brownish-black and rather acid. They make excellent jam.

Worcesterberries do not crop as heavily as gooseberries, relative to their size. They are grown in exactly the same way as gooseberries.

JOSTABERRIES

The Jostaberry is a genuine hybrid between the black currant and the gooseberry. It is an extremely vigorous plant, resembling the black currant in habit but with gooseberry-like leaves. It is thornless and resistant to mildew. The berries are slightly

Blueberries
A native American plant, the blueberry will do well only in a very acid, light to medium sandy loam. Blueberries can be grown as ornamental bushes, but where the fruit is paramount, netting against birds is necessary.

larger than those of the Worcesterberry and make excellent jam. It crops well, though not as heavily as the black currant, relative to its size.

The Jostaberry bears its fruit on the old wood and also on young shoots. It is best grown as a stooled bush and treated in a similar way to the black currant. It needs plenty of room, so space the bushes 1.8 m (6 ft) apart.

STRAWBERRIES

Given a soil depth of not less than 30 cm (1 ft), together with good drainage, strawberries will grow in a fairly wide range of conditions. Drainage must be attended to if there are signs of waterlogging. On clay soils, where drainage is slow, results can be improved by planting the runners along the tops of ridges, some 5 cm (2 in) high, so that the water runs away from the plants.

Strawberries
These plants do best in a free-draining soil. To protect the fruits from soil splash and rotting, especially in clay soils, place straw over the soil and under the ripening fruits. Netting against bird attack will almost certainly be necessary.

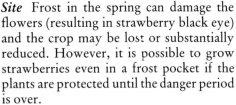

Site Frost in the spring can damage the flowers (resulting in strawberry black eye) and the crop may be lost or substantially reduced. However, it is possible to grow strawberries even in a frost pocket if the plants are protected until the danger period is over.

Overall, the important points to bear in mind are to purchase good, healthy runners, to practise soil rotation and to plant early.

Healthy runners If possible, buy Certified Stock or plants that have been propagated from Certified Stock in the very recent past. This will get you off to a good start and also enable you to propagate your own runners for the next four or five years. After this, it would be safer to buy in Certified Stock once again.

Runners from other sources may be virus-infected. If they are, the plants will never be any good, for there is nothing you can do to rid them of virus diseases.

Soil rotation All kinds of harmful organisms can multiply in the soil – especially eelworms, red core and verticillium wilt – when strawberries are grown in the same plot year after year. It makes sense, therefore, to plant runners in fresh ground as far as practicable.

This is most easily done in the vegetable plot, where soil rotation fits in well with most planting programmes. Practice a three-year rotation – that is, have one patch planted with one-year-old plants, the next with two-year-olds and the last with three-year-olds. After harvesting, dig up the three-year-old plants and plant new runners in soil that has not grown strawberries for at least three years.

Early planting This gives heavier and better-quality crops. Berries from newly-planted runners are, in any case, a little earlier and larger than those from older plants.

'Early' means July, August or September in the north of the country and not later than the middle of October in the south. However, July and August runners are expensive and more difficult to find, as they are pot-grown. Often, one has to settle for either pot-grown or open-ground runners in September or October.

Apples for storing over winter must be picked carefully from the trees as they become ready. Those at the top of orchard trees usually ripen first, followed by those at the sides.

Dark red acid Morello cherries are easier to grow than dessert varieties. They flower late and usually escape severe spring frosts; they are self-fertile and grow well on north-facing walls.

Black currants produce no berries the first summer after planting, but thereafter good crops can be expected if shoots that have fruited are cut out annually. Birds are particularly fond of the berries and should be deterred with netting.

Plums are among the earliest of tree fruits to ripen. They also flower before apples and pears, and a hard frost can ruin a year's crop. Pick the fruits as they ripen, twisting the stalks gently; damage to bark or tissues may cause fungal diseases.

Though planting is possible in November or the following spring, the plants will not be well enough established to sustain both growth and a crop during their first year and must therefore be deblossomed. Sadly, the maiden crop will be lost.

Do not plant in open ground between December and the end of March. Instead, overwinter runners in a sheltered spot – in an uncovered cold frame, for instance.

Types of strawberries There are two main types grown in Britain: the ordinary strawberry that fruits in early summer, and the perpetual kinds – or remontants, as they used to be known.

In addition, there is the alpine strawberry, a separate species closely related to our own wild strawberry. The fruits of this pretty little plant are small and dry, though their flavour is intense. It is usually grown from seed.

Ordinary cultivars New ones are introduced every year, but the following are of known performance and listed by many growers:

'Pantagruella'. Very early. Ideal for growing under polythene or glass for an even earlier crop. The flavour is good but cropping only moderate.

'Cambridge Vigour'. Second early. Fruit size deteriorates in the second and third year, so it is best grown as a maiden crop every year. The flavour is excellent and cropping good.

'Tamella'. Early in the first year, mid to late thereafter. The fruits are large and the flavour good. Cropping is very heavy.

'Royal Sovereign'. Second early. An old cultivar that has survived because of its reputation for good flavour, but it is a poor cropper. Susceptible to botrytis, mildew and virus infection.

'Red Gauntlet'. Early to mid-season. This cultivar is widely planted and reliable. If protected in the spring, or in a good summer, will give a second crop in the autumn. Flavour is poor but the variety is resistant to mildew.

'Cambridge Favourite'. Mid-season. The most widely planted and reliable variety. Flavour is fair and cropping good.

'Hapil'. Mid-season. A promising new cultivar with a reputation for giving large fruits of excellent flavour. It crops well on light soils.

'Tenira'. Mid to late. Fruit size and cropping are good in the first year but less so in the second year. It is therefore best grown for two years only. Flavour is excellent.

'Domanil'. Late. The latest of the ordinary strawberries at present. The large fruits have moderate flavour. It crops well.

Perpetual cultivars There are a few cultivars that will crop well in the summer and again in the autumn, given a warm season. These are sometimes called 'two croppers', and 'Red Gauntlet' is a typical example.

There are also the perpetual, or remontant, types, which crop in light flushes throughout the summer and autumn. They do not yield as heavily as the ordinary cultivars at any one time but it is nice to have fresh strawberries out of season. Points to bear in mind are:

1. A moisture-retentive, fertile soil and a sunny, sheltered position are essential.

2. They are not so easy to obtain as the ordinary type and are best planted not later than mid-September in the south of the country or early September in the north. Failing this, remontants should be planted in the spring.

3. To obtain a heavier late-summer crop, remove the first flowers produced during the early summer.

4. They are best grown as a maiden crop each year, as fruit size generally deteriorates badly in the second year. The cultivar 'Gento' is an exception and can be grown for two years before replanting.

5. Ample irrigation is essential during dry weather.

6. It is difficult to obtain certified stock. This is not important, provided plants are bought from a reputable source.

Some of the best cultivars include:
'Aromel'. Best grown as a maiden crop. Flavour is very good. This variety crops heavily, but only in the first year.

'Gento'. One of the few perpetuals that will give a satisfactory crop in the second year. Fruit size is good and flavour excellent. Cropping is good.

'Rapella'. A promising new cultivar.

JANUARY

Planting If there are still fruit trees, bush and cane fruits to plant, try to complete this work when soil conditions are favourable.

Liming Most fruits do best in slightly acid conditions, so do not apply lime unless the soil is very acid. If it is, add lime to bring the pH to about 6.7, using ground limestone or chalk.

Do the job in fortnightly stages, applying 130 g per sq m (4 oz per sq yd) each time. Two weeks after each application, measure the pH and apply more lime if necessary.

Pruning Try also to complete the pruning of all hardy bush, cane and tree fruits (except stone fruits). In districts where bullfinches are troublesome, leave gooseberries and red currants until March, in the meantime protecting the bushes by zig-zagging strands of black cotton from branch to branch.

Collect and burn the prunings and store the ash in a dry place. This represents a useful supply of potash for later.

Strawberries For an early crop, cover strawberry plants with cloches or polythene tunnels at any time until mid-March.

Fruit storage Inspect fruits in store frequently and remove any that are rotten. Use slightly damaged fruits immediately before they can rot.

Renovating neglected apples and pears (bush or standard) This task can be done at any time during the winter, up to the end of March. However, if there is a lot of wood to be removed, spread the operation over three winters to lessen the shock to the tree. On each occasion, work evenly over the whole head of the tree to avoid a lop-sided or imbalanced effect.

It has been found that the later a tree is pruned during the winter, the less growth-response there will be during the following summer. Therefore, a tree that is inclined to be over-vigorous is best pruned during the late winter. Conversely, a tree that lacks vigour and needs the stimulus of winter-pruning should be pruned early.

However, before starting try to find out why the tree is in poor condition. There may be other courses of action, pruning being only part of the remedy. Consider the following:

1) Damage by pests and diseases due to neglect of appropriate control or prevention.
2) Too much competition for water and nutrients from other plants, such as grass and weeds.
3) Excessive shade, due to overcrowding within the tree itself or by nearby trees or buildings.
4) Unsuitable soil conditions due to lack of depth, poor moisture retention, a hard pan beneath or poor drainage.
5) Over-pruning or lack of pruning.
6) Starvation.
7) Lack of water.
8) Damage to the framework or root system due to poor staking.
9) Damage by vermin.

There are two extremes as far as neglected trees are concerned – those that are too large and crowded and others that are weak and stunted:

Over-large and over-crowded trees First, remove dead and diseased wood. Next, prune to give adequate spacing of the main branches. As a guide, if a tree has a height and spread of 4.5 m (15 ft) or more, the main branches should be at least 60 cm (2 ft) apart when side by side at the perimeter and not less than 75 cm (2½ ft) apart when directly above each other.

This applies to large trees with many branches. Moderate the pruning proportionately for smaller trees.

Branches to remove include those that are too low, badly placed or crossing in the centre; also tall branches, including those that are vigorous and centrally placed, and consequently difficult to spray and pick.

When removing a branch, cut back to its point of origin or to a limb large enough to take up the vigour. The latter should be at least one third the diameter of the branch removed. Remove heavy limbs in stages to lessen the weight, always undercutting first and then completing the cut from above so that the falling branch does not tear the bark. Protect saw cuts with a wound paint, first paring the edges of the wound to give a smooth surface.

Such reduction in height and the cutting out of main limbs is called 'de-horning'. The aim is to achieve improved spacing of the limbs so that light and air can reach all parts of the tree. It also facilitates spraying, cultivation and picking.

Very hard winter-pruning with secateurs on a vigorous tree causes the buds to grow out as shoots instead of developing into fruit buds. If a tree has been subjected to over-pruning in the past, pruning should be relatively light. Thin out the branches, as already described, but avoid the excessive use of secateurs.

Light pruning work should be confined to dealing with laterals that cross over, to thinning out surplus leaders and to the removal of clusters of strong, unproductive laterals that are crowding other spurs. Remember, also, the technique of summer-pruning an over-vigorous tree. (See August.)
Weak and stunted trees Some-

Neglected tree before renovation
With an over-large, over-crowded tree, remove dead or diseased wood and then open out the centre.

After renovation
Once excess wood has been removed, spraying, cultivation and picking will all be easier.

times a weak tree will carry a mass of dense, complex spur systems, bearing small fruits – perhaps biennially – and making no new growth. In this case, the first task is to remove worn out and over-shading spurs and to reduce others. This will increase fruit size as well as the formation of new leaders and laterals.

Thin growth, weak fruit buds, small leaves and early leaf fall are symptomatic of starvation and, possibly, lack of water. Such trees must be fed (see February) and irrigated during dry weather.

FEBRUARY

Manuring fruit trees, bushes and canes This is the main month for feeding and mulching fruits.

The three major elements needed by fruits are nitrogen (N), phosphorous (P) and potassium (K). These must be applied in the form of fertilizers on a fairly regular basis. Occasionally, too, there is a need for some of the minor elements.

Nitrogen promotes growth and fruit size; phosphorous is required for root development; potassium for winter hardiness, fruit development and flavour.

Lime (calcium) is sometimes necessary, but this should be applied well before the other elements to avoid any risk of chemical reaction with certain types of fertilizer.

There are two main categories of fertilizers – organic and inorganic. Usually they are applied separately, but some formulations contain a mixture of the two.

Organic fertilizers In the main, this heading covers the bulky organic manures, such as farmyard manure and garden compost. There are a few non-bulky organics, such as hoof and horn, dried blood and fish meal, but for the purpose of feeding outdoor fruits only bonemeal is relevant, this being used at planting time.

The main purpose of bulky organics is not so much to supply nutrients, as to improve soil structure and moisture retention. In this respect they are invaluable.

Nevertheless, they do contain plant nutrients to a greater or lesser degree, depending upon their nature, though nothing like as much as the inorganic fertilizers when compared on a weight to weight basis.

Bulky organics are chiefly used as a mulch once the plants are in. Spent mushroom compost, being weed-free, makes an excellent mulch. However, it contains chalk and should not be used too frequently, except on very acid soils. Do not use it on raspberries.

Straw may be used as a surface mulch to conserve moisture but if mixed into the soil it should be well rotted or, alternatively, extra nitrogen must be applied.

Inorganic fertilizers Both 'straight' and 'compound' fertilizers are available. There are also 'slow release' fertilizers, both straight and compound, which release nutrients over a longer period than the ordinary ones. Straight fertilizers supply only one nutrient, although they may sometimes contain small amounts of others. Compound fertilizers contain three or more nutrients, depending on their formulation.

The straight fertilizers commonly used on fruit are:

Nitrogen: sulphate of ammonia (21% N). This has an acidifying effect, which is an advantage on soils containing an excess content of lime. On other soils, repeated heavy dressings may make the soil too acid for crops such as black currants and young apple trees. Nitro-chalk (21% N) is neutral and may be used instead.

Phosphate: superphosphate (18% P_2O_5) and triple superphosphate (47% P_2O_5). A dressing of phosphate for soils is not usually necessary more than once every three years.

Potash: sulphate of potash (48–50% K_2O). There is also muriate of potash (60% K_2O), but with this there is a risk of chloride damage to certain fruits (strawberries, raspberries, gooseberries and red currants). Its use is limited to tree fruits and black currants.

Compound fertilizers Compound or general fertilizers contain all three major elements, and sometimes some of the trace elements as well. The fertilizer may be balanced – supplying nitrogen, phosphate and potash in equal amounts – or the proportion of one nutrient may be higher in relation to the others. Usually, they are higher in either nitrogen or potash.

Growmore (7% N, 7% P, 7% K) is an easily-obtained balanced fertilizer.

Applying fertilizers and mulches
Really keen fruit-growers may prefer to use straight fertilizers, which allow greater precision regarding timing and quantities, rather than compound types. Nevertheless, a compound fertilizer may be used on a more general basis, provided that the grower adds extra nitrogen when necessary.

If Growmore is used, the recommended rate is 100–130 g per sq m (3–4 oz per sq yd), applying the higher amount on poorer soils.

In the following instances, fertilizers are applied as a top dressing – that is, on the soil surface over the rooting area, which in the case of a tree is slightly beyond the spread of the overhead branches. For smaller fruits, apply them over the whole area.

Apply mulches about 5–8 cm (2–3 in) deep over a radius of about 23–45 cm (9–18 in), depending upon the size of the plant, or as a band 30 cm (1 ft) wide along a row of closely-spaced fruits.

Taking each fruit in turn, apply fertilizer and mulches as follows:
Dessert apples Sulphate of potash at 20 g per sq m (¾ oz per sq yd) in early February. Superphosphate (every third year) at 65 g per sq m (2 oz per sq yd) in early February.

Sulphate of ammonia (Nitro-chalk if the soil is acid) at 30 g per sq m (1 oz per sq yd) in late February, but at 60 g per sq m (2 oz per sq yd) if trees are grown in grass.
Culinary apples Here, larger fruits are desired. Apply the same rates as for dessert apples, except that the amount of nitrogenous fertilizer should be doubled.
Pears These require plenty of nitrogen. Apply the fertilizers at the same rates as for culinary apples. Mulch young trees.
Peaches Apply sulphate of potash at 20 g per sq m (¾ oz per sq yd) in early February. Superphosphate is needed every third year at 60 g per sq m (2 oz per sq yd) in early February, and sulphate of ammonia or Nitro-chalk at 30 g per sq m (1 oz per sq yd) in late February. Mulch with peat, spent hops, mushroom compost or well-rotted stable manure afterwards.

Apply a high-potash liquid fertilizer every ten days from the

pink bud stage until the fruits begin to ripen.
Plums, gages and damsons All thrive on a regime of high-nitrogen feeding, with plenty of moisture during the summer. Apply at the same rates as for culinary apples, but give a little extra nitrogen by mulching with bulky organics. Mushroom compost is ideal.

Irrigate the trees in dry weather.
Cherries Give the same dressings and rates as for culinary apples.
Black currants These require heavy nitrogenous feeding with both inorganics and bulky organic fertilizers. Every year apply sulphate of potash at 15 g per sq m (½ oz per sq yd) in early February; superphosphate at 60 g per sq m (2 oz per sq yd) in early February; and sulphate of ammonia or Nitro-chalk at 60 g per sq m (2 oz per sq yd) in late February.

Mulch heavily afterwards.
Red and white currants The bushes are very susceptible to potassium deficiency. Give sulphate of potash at 30 g per sq m (1 oz per sq yd) every year in early February; super-phosphate, every third year, at 60 g per sq m (2 oz per sq yd) in early February; sulphate of ammonia or Nitro-chalk at 30 g per sq m (1 oz per sq yd) every year in late February.

Mulch young plants, and also older bushes if grown on light soil.
Gooseberries Give the same applications as for red currants. Take care when applying nitrogen, as an excess may cause soft, lush growth which is vulnerable to mildew. Mulch young plants.
Raspberries Apply the same fertilizers as for red currants, spreading two thirds of the quantities per metre or yard along a band 60 cm (2 ft) wide. Spread the rest over a wider area. Mulch lightly along each side of the row with a bulky

organic substance such as peat; avoid mushroom compost.

On very fertile soils, where cane growth is excessive, reduce the supply of nitrogen by half or eliminate it altogether. Lush growth is susceptible to spur blight.

Blackberries and hybrid berries Treat as for raspberries.

Strawberries Potash is essential for strawberries, so apply sulphate of potash at 15 g per sq m (½ oz per sq yd) in early February. No nitrogen should be necessary, assuming that the ground was manured before planting. If applied, it would induce leafy growth at the expense of fruit. Where growth has been poor, apply sulphate of ammonia at 15 g per sq m (½ oz per sq yd) in early February.

All the above recommendations are intended as a general guide. They may be modified, particularly the application of nitrogen, according to the performance of the plants.

Cobnuts and filberts (hazel nuts) The hazel nut flowers from late February into March, and sometimes as late as April. It is monoecious, meaning that it bears separate male catkins and female flowers on the same tree. Pollination is brought about by the wind.

A nut tree is grown either as an open-centred, goblet-shaped bush or as an open-centred stooled bush, with the height restricted by pruning to between 1.8 m and 2.1 m (6 ft and 7 ft).

Because the disturbance caused by pruning assists pollination, the task is left until the catkins are releasing their pollen freely and the female flowers are fully open and receptive.

Pruning Once the flowers are ready for pollination cut back strong laterals – previously brutted (broken) in August – to 5–8 cm (2–3 in). Do not prune weak laterals, as these usually carry the red female flowers.

Cut back the branch leaders to a height between 1.8–2.1 m (6–7 ft). Remove any growth crowding the centre of the tree and any suckers.

Strawberries For crops, cover the plants with a polythene tunnel or glass barn cloches if this was not done in January.

Pruning autumn-fruiting raspberries As autumn-fruiting raspberries bear their fruits at the apex of the current season's growth, they should not be allowed to crop on the two-year-old canes. This means that all canes must be cut down to ground level. New canes will grow in the spring to fruit in the autumn.

Figs: pruning fan-trained trees In late February or early March cut each alternate shoot back to one bud. This will stimulate new growth. Leave the remainder to bear fruit during the summer.

MARCH

Pruning stone fruits Now that the sap is moving upwards it is safe to proceed with the formative pruning of stone fruits, such as plums, gages, damsons, 'Morello' and sweet cherries, peaches and nectarines.

Some stone fruits – peaches, for example – produce single, double and triple buds on the one-year-old wood, these being either growth buds, flower buds or a combination of these. It is, of course, useless to prune back to a flower bud, as this will not grow. When in doubt, delay pruning until a green shoot appears, although it is quite safe to cut to a triple bud.

The formative pruning of all young stone fruits is basically the same. It is only when dealing with a cropping tree that there are some differences in pruning methods.

Always protect the cuts on a stone fruit tree with a wound paint to guard against silver leaf disease.

Bush, half-standard and full standard trees A bush should have a clean stem of about 60–90 cm (2–3 ft) beneath the head. The stem of a half-standard is 1.4 m (4½ ft) and that of a full standard 1.8 m (6 ft) or more. The pruning of the head itself is the same for all three, the only major difference being that the central stem of a standard may need to be trained up a cane or stake for a further year to achieve the necessary height. It is then headed back.

Pruning a maiden (one-year-old) Cut back the central stem to a bud or lateral at 90 cm (3 ft) for a bush, 1.4 m (4½ ft) for a half-standard and 1.8 m (6 ft) for a full standard.

If the tree has strong, well-placed laterals at the top (a feathered maiden), use these as primary branches. Select four or five and cut them back by two-thirds, pruning to an outward-facing bud. Cut back the remaining laterals flush with the main stem. Finally, cut out the central stem, pruning back to the topmost selected lateral.

If the tree is unfeathered, the top four or five buds should grow out strongly in the summer to form the first branches. Remember, in the spring, to pinch back the lower, unwanted shoots to two or three leaves. These will help to thicken the main stem but should be removed eventually.

Second year (two-year-old) If the tree was well-feathered in its first year, treat it as a three-year-old. If it was unfeathered, select four or five well-placed primary branches to make a balanced head. Cut back the leader of each selected branch by half to an outward-facing bud.

Remove the remainder flush with the main stem.

Remember, in the summer, to remove any unwanted shoots below the head.

Third year (three-year-old) and subsequently With a three-year-old tree select a further four or five branches, so that the tree has a well-balanced head of from eight to ten primary and secondary branches. Cut the leader of each by half or two-thirds to a bud facing outwards. Prune the remainder to three or four buds.

In subsequent years, little pruning is needed at this time, except that weak trees may need some formative pruning for a further one or two years. Thereafter, pruning is done in August.

Pruning to form a fan-trained tree This is often the method chosen for peaches and nectarines but it is equally suitable for other stone fruits – and even for apples and pears.

Most maiden trees of stone fruits are well-feathered. Provided that some of the growths are suitably placed, they can be used to form the primary ribs.

The number to use initially depends upon the vigour of the tree and the strength of the laterals. With a peach or nectarine only two should be used, but with a plum or cherry it is often possible to select four to form the first ribs.

A system of horizontal wires is needed for securing the ribs of the fan. The wires are spaced two brick courses apart – every 15 cm (6 in) – starting 30 cm (1 ft) from the ground. For straight growth, the primary ribs are trained along canes fixed to the wires.

Pruning a feathered maiden (one-year-old) Select two strong laterals, one to the left and one to the right, parallel with the wall. These should be about 23–30 cm (9–12 in) from the ground. Cut back the central stem to the topmost selected lateral.

If the tree is a plum or a cherry, select four shoots to form the first ribs. Cut each by two-thirds, pruning to an upward-facing bud. Tie the ribs to the canes, angled at about 25–45 degrees, so that they radiate outwards. Remove all others flush with the main stem.

In the summer, it should be possible with a two-ribbed tree to train in two more ribs on either side, so that by the autumn it consists of three on each side.

A tree which started with four ribs should have at least eight by the end of the summer.

Young shoots not wanted to form ribs are pinched back to one or two leaves in the early summer.

Pruning an unfeathered maiden (one-year-old) If the maiden tree has no laterals, cut it back to a bud on the central stem about 45 cm (1½ ft) from the ground, ensuring that there are two good buds – one to the left and one to the right – beneath it to form primary ribs.

In the summer, probably about June, when the two ribs are about 45 cm (1½ ft) long, cut out the central stem to the topmost of the two. Throughout the summer, train these ribs along canes angled about 35 degrees to the ground.

Thereafter, follow the same

Bush stone fruit

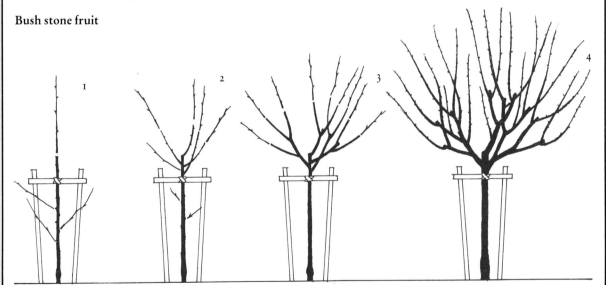

Cut back central stem of a maiden (1) to a bud or lateral at 90 cm (3 ft). In the second year (2), select four or five primaries to form the head and remove remainder flush with stem. In the third year (3), select four or five more well-placed branches for pruning. In subsequent years (4), light pruning only is needed.

pruning and tying programme as for a feathered maiden.

Formative pruning in the second and third year The aim is to fill the wall space with ribs which radiate outwards like the spokes of a wheel. As the shoots grow, train them along canes but leave the filling of the centre to the last. This is because vertical growth tends to become too dominant, at the expense of the side ribs.

Repeat the same procedure as in the first year. Prune the leaders by half to two-thirds to stimulate extension growth and new shoots to be utilized as ribs. Pinch back to one leaf any shoots that are surplus to requirements.

By the third year all wall space should have been filled in and the tree will be entering its cropping phase, though the same treatment can be repeated if necessary.

Pruning techniques applied to cropping trees differ according to type and are described under the relevant months.

Pyramid plums, gages and damsons This tree form is eminently suitable for a medium-sized garden. Bush or half-standard plum trees tend to grow too big for many gardens and they are more prone to silver leaf disease caused by branch breakages. Pyramids have a stronger branch framework, achieved by planting a well-feathered tree with naturally wide-angled side-shoots and by summer pruning. (See July.)

A self fertile variety on the dwarfing rootstock 'Pixy' is best for a small garden. Space them 1.8–2.4 m (6–8 ft) apart.

Pruning After planting, head the tree back to a bud 1.5 m (5 ft) from the ground. Prune any branches (feather shoots) to half their length, but remove those less than 38 cm (15 in) from the ground. Thereafter, prune to shape in April and again in July.

Planting This is the last month to plant bare-rooted tree, bush and cane fruits. Container-grown fruits may be planted at any time.

Alpine strawberries Sow alpine strawberry seed under glass, ready for planting out in May. Alpine strawberries make a pretty border plant, as well as yielding highly perfumed, though dry, fruits.

Perpetual and ordinary strawberries Plant out over-wintered strawberry runners now, ready for de-blossoming in May.

Gooseberries and red currants Established gooseberry and red currant bushes should now be pruned to minimize loss due to birds.

Heading back-budded rootstocks Cut back rootstocks immediately above the bud (see July). This will induce the bud to grow and form a maiden tree by the autumn. Throughout the summer, train it up a cane and remove side growth.

Hand pollination: trees on walls Hand pollination is essential for early-flowering trees as few pollinating insects are about.

Use a soft camel-hair brush, gently transferring the pollen from one flower to the next. This is best done in the middle of every day until flowering is over.

Pruning blueberries During the

Fan-training a feathered maiden tree

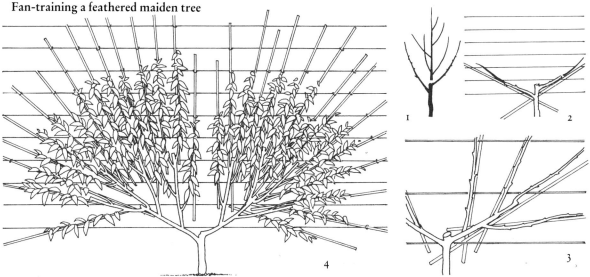

With a feathered maiden for fan-training (1), select and prune two strong laterals and cut back central stem (2). In summer (3), tie in two more ribs on either side, making six in all. Formative pruning in the second and third years (4) is designed to fill all available wall space with outwardly radiating ribs.

first four years after planting, blueberries are pruned lightly if at all – just sufficient to cut out any dead or broken wood. As with many other fruits, they crop best on the young wood and from the fourth year onwards it will be necessary to cut out some of the oldest wood to stimulate new growth, ideally from the base.

Pruning is best done this month because at this stage it can be seen which wood is carrying the most flowers. Remove the oldest, weakest and least productive growth by cutting down to the base or to a strong upright shoot. Cut out no more than one quarter of the bush.

Hybrid berries and blackberries Untie the young canes that were bundled together for winter protection (see October) and train them according to the preferred systems.

Pyramid plums: Pruning after planting Cut back the central leader to a bud at about 1.5 m (5 ft) from ground level in late March. Halve the length on the maiden tree branches cutting to a downward or outward-facing bud. Re-

move branches within 45 cm (1½ ft) of the ground.

Protection against frost Fruits grown outdoors in the United Kingdom are winter-hardy, with the possible exception of the fig. It is when the flower buds start to open in spring that they become vulnerable, and the more advanced their growth the greater the chance that they will be damaged by cold and frost. A severe frost while they are in full blossom can destroy the crop for that year.

For most fruits the danger period is from mid-April until the end of May. However, wall-trained fruits, such as apricots and peaches, as well as forced strawberries, may flower earlier. For these, protection may be necessary from March onwards.

The Meteorological Office issues warnings when frosts are anticipated, enabling preventive measures to be taken in good time. As forecasts are not infallible, cautious gardeners may prefer to protect their fruits every night until the risk is past.

The usual method of protection

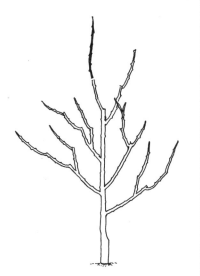

Pruning a newly-planted pyramid plum
Cut back central leader and halve length of branches. Remove those within 45 cm (1½ ft) of the ground.

is to cover the plant with a material thick enough to keep out the frost. If this is opaque it should be removed during the day to allow light and pollinating insects to reach the plant. This does not apply to clear material, such as glass, so long as provision is made for pollination.

Small plants are easier to protect than large ones, hence the advantage of growing tree fruits on dwarfing rootstocks whenever possible. Rows of cordons, espaliers, dwarf trees and both bush and cane fruits can be draped with hessian, lace curtaining or with two or three layers of bird netting – the heavier the material, the greater the protection given.

It is essential that it does not rub against the flowers. This calls for some kind of framework to hold the material just clear of the blossom. Canes held together with rubber uni-joints are ideal for this purpose. For wall-trained fruits, a

Hand pollination
Use a soft brush to transfer pollen from one flower to the next.

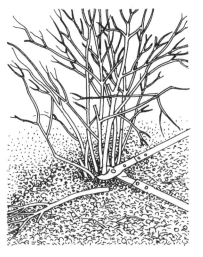

Pruning blueberries
With blueberries, just cut out dead or broken wood for first four years.

roll of hessian held at the top is best, for it can be unfurled at night and rolled up the next morning.

Strawberries in the open can be covered with something light, without the need for a framework. Straw is suitable, or two or three layers of newspaper. Glass cloches provide some protection but thin polythene gives practically none at all. When a severe frost is threatened, extra covering is advisable.

Because of the cost, artificial heat provided by oil or paraffin burners is best reserved for fruits under glass, though it might be a practicable system for wall-trained fruits that have a polythene lean-to over them.

Another means of frost protection relies upon the principle that latent heat is released when water freezes. This is a commercial practice and can be adopted in the garden provided permission is obtained, if necessary, from the local water authority.

The plants must be kept sprinkled with water, the droplets the size of raindrops, throughout the period of frost. By the morning they may be covered by quite a heavy layer of ice, so the branch framework must be strong and the weaker branches propped up. Good soil drainage is needed to avoid the risk of waterlogging.

APRIL

Routine tasks Continue frost protection and hand pollination of early-flowering fruits.

On sunny days, ventilate strawberries under cloches and polythene to prevent the temperature getting too high and to provide access for pollinating insects.

Control weeds throughout the fruit garden.

Harden off in a cold frame alpine strawberry seedlings sown in March.

Liquid feeding Start giving liquid fertilizer to plants in containers and on walls, such as peaches, nectarines, apricots and figs. The fertilizer should be rich in potassium, so a tomato type is ideal. Give each between a half and a full watering can.

Pruning pyramid plums One year after planting, shorten the central leader by two thirds, cutting to a bud. Repeat this pruning every year until the tree has reached 1.8–2.1 m (6–7 ft) if on 'Pixy' rootstock, or 2.4–2.7 m (8–9 ft) if on 'St. Julien A'. Thereafter, shorten the central leader (previous summer's growth) to 2.5 cm (1 in) or less to keep the tree to this height. Remove any vertical shoot competing with the leader.

Pruning a one-year-old pyramid plum
Shorten central leader by two thirds, cutting back to a bud.

MAY

Alpine strawberries Plant out alpine strawberry seedlings 30 cm (1 ft) apart in rows 75 cm (2½ ft) apart, or as an edging to a flower border. They will grow in full sun or in partial shade. Incorporate a little peat and some Growmore fertilizer at about 60 g per sq m (2 oz per sq yd) before planting.

Alpine strawberries are best grown for no more than two years before replanting with new seedlings, as after this they usually deteriorate with virus infection.

Perpetual and ordinary strawberries Remove the blossom from spring-planted runners to ensure that they become well established, with strong crowns, for future cropping.

It should be possible to pick the first of the protected fruits from mature plants towards the end of the month.

Thinning gooseberries Where there has been a heavy set, thin the fruits large enough for cooking and freezing. Remove every other one along the branches.

Repeat this thinning procedure whenever more fruits are needed, but leaving sufficient to ripen fully for dessert use.

Pruning restricted trees Once restricted forms have reached the desired length or height – for example, the length of espalier arms or the height of cordons and dwarf pyramids – cut back the leaders (the previous summer's growth) to 12 mm (½ in).

With oblique cordons, it is possible to grow the main stem a little longer by carefully lowering them and their canes, five degrees at a time, once a year. Finish at 35 degrees to the ground, as there is a chance they may break if trained lower than this.

Frost protection and hand pollination Continue protection techniques until the danger of frost is completely over.

Uncover frost-protected figs at the end of the month. Re-train the branches if necessary.

Continue the hand pollinating of peaches and nectarines if they are still carrying flowers.

Fruit cages Remove the netting from one side of fruit cages to provide easier access for pollinating insects.

Feeding and irrigating wall-trained trees Continue the liquid feeding of wall-trained trees. Ensure that no fruit suffers from lack of water. Remember that the soil at the base of a wall is often shielded from rain and therefore needs special attention.

Pruning established fan-trained peaches and nectarines It is important to know the cropping habit of peaches and nectarines in order to understand the pruning of fan-trained forms.

Peaches flower only on growth made during the previous summer, so the aim in pruning, as well as in feeding, is to obtain a succession of strong young shoots year by year. It is on this young growth that the fruits are carried in the second year. To achieve this, peaches are pruned on the replacement system. (See August.)

Looking at a tree in the spring, the fan can be seen to consist of the basic framework and the fruiting laterals – the previous summer's growth. These, in turn, are now carrying the flowers or fruitlets. Also, at this stage, young green shoots are starting to appear, some of which will be next year's fruiting laterals.

The task in May and June is to thin out the young shoots and to tie in those that are kept – a process called 'de-shooting'.

Start on the fruiting laterals first. Ensure that a young shoot is left at the base of each (the replacement shoot) together with one in the middle as a reserve. Pinch out all the others, back to one leaf. Stop the extension growth – the fruiting lateral itself – at six leaves. This stage may not be reached until June.

Finally, deal with any remaining young shoots. Thin them by pinching back so that they are spaced 10 cm (4 in) apart. Pinch back unwanted shoots to one leaf.

Wall-trained cherries, plums, gages and damsons Tie in the young shoots of fan-trained trees parallel to the wall where there is room. Remove altogether those growing directly towards the structure.

JUNE

Soft fruits and the fruit cage The first of the raspberries, dessert gooseberries, and both red and white currants should be ready for picking towards the end of this month. Before this happens, it is necessary to protect the crop from birds with netting. This can be of plastic, terylene or some other man-made fibre, with a 12 or 18 mm (½ or ¾ in) mesh.

A ready-made cage of tubular metal can be bought – a simple, though rather expensive solution. Alternatively, the cage can be home-made. A small cage to cover a few bushes can be constructed of stout bamboo canes held together by rubber uni-joints, but for a taller and larger cage it is better to use wooden posts to support the net.

The height is important. A cage should be high enough to allow picking in comfort and to avoid the plants growing through. A structure 1.2 m (4 ft) high will do for strawberries, but for cane and bush fruits it should be 2–2.1 m (6½–7 ft).

Drive in the posts at 1.8 m (6 ft) intervals along the centre and run horizontal wires or thick string from post to post, draping the netting over this. It will help to prevent the net snagging if a plastic plant pot is placed over the top of each post.

The sides can be of plastic or galvanized wire netting. Do not use wire netting on the top because of the risk of zinc toxicity.

Irrigation Water tree, bush and cane fruits during dry weather. Apply not less than 20 litres per sq m (4½ gal per sq yd) – the equivalent of 2.5 cm (1 in) – once every ten days until rain restores the balance. Large trees can be left for longer periods, but apply double the above quantity every three weeks. Keep the grass short and weeds under control.

Peaches Continue de-shooting wall-trained peaches and nectarines. (See May.) Tie the retained shoots to the wires.

Thin the fruits in two stages, first when they are the size of hazel nuts and finally when the size of walnuts. Thin those that are badly placed, malformed or diseased, and reduce pairs of fruits to one. Initially, space the fruits to 10 cm (4 in) apart, with a final spacing of 23 cm (9 in) for peaches and 15 cm (6 in) for nectarines.

Plums, gages and apricots Thin plums, gages and apricots in two stages, in early June and again in late June. The final spacing should be 8 cm (3 in) apart.

Fan-trained apricots, sweet cherries, plums and gages Continue removing shoots growing directly towards the wall from fan-trained sweet cherries and plums. Stop those that are projecting directly outwards at six leaves so that they form spurs. If shoots are growing parallel with the wall, tie them in if there is room, or stop them at one or two leaves.

Fan-trained and bush figs Pinch out the apical (top) bud on the young shoots to induce them to break lower down and so produce more shoots upon which the embryo figs will develop.

Raspberries Some varieties are too prolific in the production of new canes (suckers). In this event, thin them out to 5 cm (2 in) apart so as to divert energy into the remainder. Hoe out suckers growing too far away from the row to be useful.

Remove the 23 cm (9 in) stub from newly-planted raspberries as soon as sucker growth has appeared from the base.

Blackberries and hybrid berries Tie in the new canes as necessary to reduce the risk of damage by wind or cultivation.

Bush and cordon gooseberries; red and white currants At the end of the month start summer-pruning of gooseberries and currants, both red and white. Spread the operation over four weeks, aiming to complete the job by the third week of July. The purpose is to open up the plants to light and air, helping to ripen the wood and fruits. This also helps to get rid of mildew and greenfly.

Prune the young shoots (cur-rent season's growth) back to five leaves. Cut the longest laterals first, together with those crowding the centre in the case of a bush and any that are drooping towards the ground. Remove altogether basal and sucker growth on the 15 cm (6 in) leg of cordon or bush.

Do not prune the leaders of a bush unless they are affected by mildew. Cordon leaders should be summer-pruned in the same way as the laterals once they have reached the desired height, not before.

Strawberries: straw beds Before strawberries ripen it is necessary to spread straw beneath them in order to keep the fruits clean. Do not do this too early, as it increases the risk of frost damage to the flowers. Before starting, scatter slug pellets around the plants and between the rows.

The softest straw is barley, but wheat will do. Oat is not recommended as there is a risk of eelworms infecting the land. Tuck the straw under the trusses and across the row.

Alternative materials to straw are dry bracken, strawberry mats and black polythene.

Strawberry runners If you plan to grow new plants from your

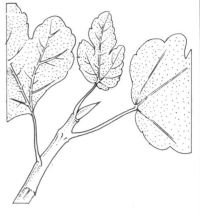

Pinching out figs
To encourage a bushy shape, pinch out the apical buds.

own runners, the earlier they are planted the better the crop the following year. To secure early runners, peg them down as soon as they are produced by a healthy mother plant. These new runners, or plantlets, start to appear about the end of June.

Pegging down, so that the plantlets make good contact with the soil, aids rapid rooting. Peg each new runner down into a 9 cm (3½ in) plastic pot filled with John Innes potting compost No. 1, or a peat-based compost, with the pot plunged level with the soil surface. Take no more than five runners from each parent plant and pinch out the stolon beyond the runner. U-shaped pegs can be made from straightened paper clips.

Pot-grown runners transplant better than open-ground runners at this time of year, when the weather is hot, because there is less root disturbance. Even so, runners pegged down into open ground usually transplant fairly well. Whichever method you choose, keep the plants well watered. After about three weeks they should have made sufficient roots to allow them to be severed from the parent plant and set out.

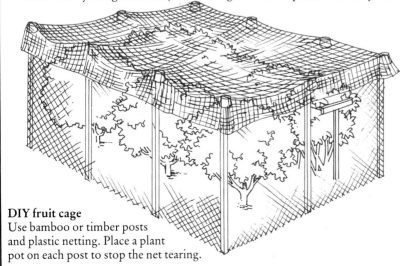

DIY fruit cage
Use bamboo or timber posts and plastic netting. Place a plant pot on each post to stop the net tearing.

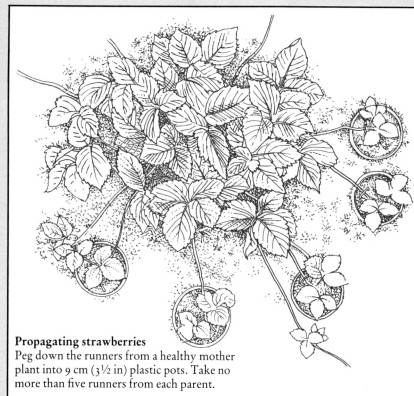

Propagating strawberries
Peg down the runners from a healthy mother plant into 9 cm (3½ in) plastic pots. Take no more than five runners from each parent.

Preparing a new strawberry bed
First, get rid of perennial weeds by forking them out or by spraying them with a weedkiller such as glyphosate.

With the weeds removed or killed, spread a 2.5–5 cm (1–2 in) layer of well-rotted manure, peat or compost and dig it in. This should be done at least three weeks before planting to give the soil time to settle.

JULY

Harvesting The soft fruit harvest is now in full swing. Although strawberries are coming to an end, gooseberries, raspberries and currants are at their best; blackberries and hybrid berries are starting to ripen. Sweet and acid cherries are also ready, while early plums, peaches, pears and apples are now developing their colours. Pick all these fruits gently so as not to bruise them.

It is difficult to judge when peaches and nectarines are fully ripe. When ready, the fruits should look bright and well-coloured, with a yellowish or pink-white background. Even so, some fruits with this appearance may still be hard. The surest way to tell is to press the shoulder of the peach gently. If it gives slightly the fruit is ready. It should also leave the spur easily.

Hard fruits picked in error will usually soften after a few days at room temperature, provided they were not excessively under-ripe when picked. Keep fruits in a cool, dark place until needed.

Pruning pyramid plums *First summer* Prune in the third week of July when the young shoots have finished growing. Shorten all the branch leaders to 20 cm (8 in), pruning to a downward or an outward-pointing bud. Cut all the young side-shoots of the current season to six leaves.

Subsequent years Shorten branch leaders to 20 cm (8 in), pruning to a downward or outward-facing bud in the axil of the leaf, and laterals to six leaves. Also cut back to six leaves any strong, young vertical shots at the top of the tree if they compete with the leader.

Supporting plums In some years the branches of plum trees are liable to break under the weight of fruit unless supported. This can lead to the killer disease silver leaf entering through the wounds.

The branch can either be propped up with a forked length of wood, like a clothes prop, or else the tree can be 'maypoled'. A stout pole is driven into the ground near the centre of the tree and thick string or rope is led from the top of the stake to each branch.

Fan-training Continue the fan-training of bushes and trees. Where there is space, tie young shoots to the wires parallel with the wall so that they radiate out-

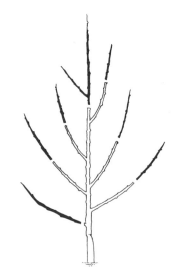

Pruning two-year-old plums
Shorten branch leaders to 20 cm (8 in) and laterals to six leaves.

wards like the ribs of a fan. Where they are crowded, thin them out by cutting the unwanted shoots back to one leaf.

Thinning apples and pears If a great many fruitlets have set, thinning is needed to avoid overtaxing the tree's strength. Failure to thin may result in undersized fruits and start the tree into biennial bearing – that is, cropping one year and resting the next.

Wait until the natural fruit drop has occurred, for very little thinning may be needed after this natural shedding of fruitlets. Although called the 'June drop', it usually happens in early July.

Pay special attention to young trees, for all their energies must be channelled into creating a strong framework of branches. Newly-planted trees should have all their fruitlets removed.

How much established trees should be thinned depends on their state of health. A vigorous tree with a good show of healthy leaves can carry more fruit than one that is weak or stunted, where

Supporting branches
In heavy cropping years, the branches of plums may need supporting. Either prop them using forked lengths of wood or use a maypole arrangement.

Effects of thinning
Thinning prevents over-taxing the tree and yields larger fruits.

the leaves are generally small, sparse or poorly coloured.

As a general guide, thin dessert apples to 10–15 cm (4–6 in) apart – about one per cluster, but occasionally two. Cookers must be thinned more severely to obtain large fruits, and a good average is 15–23 cm (6–9 in) apart.

Remove the poorest fruitlets first – those that are blemished, malformed or under-sized.

Pears must be thinned, too, using the same guidelines except that two fruitlets can be left per cluster. Do not thin until the fruitlets have turned downwards, by which time the natural drop should be over.

Planting strawberries This is the best month to plant new runners, so that the strawberries are well established by the autumn and have developed strong crowns to yield a good maiden crop next summer. The difficulty is that runners are scarce and expensive at this time, unless you have propagated your own. (See June.) All is not lost, if runners are not available.

Although July planting is best, you can still get a crop next year from runners planted by mid-October in the south and by the end of September in the north.

Complete the soil preparation if this was not done in June. Just before planting, rake Growmore fertilizer into the top 10 cm (4 in) of soil at 60 g per sq m (2 oz per sq yd). No additional feeding will be needed during the life of the strawberries, except for some sulphate of potash applied in early February. Finally, give the bed a thorough soaking.

Space the plants 30–38 cm (12–15 in) apart in the rows and leave ¾–1 m (2½–3 ft) between rows. The lesser spacing is on light, sandy soils. Use a line to ensure that the rows are straight, a piece of cane or a measuring rod as a spacer, and a trowel to take out the holes. Spread the roots out well, and firm the soil with your knuckles to ensure that it makes good contact with the roots.

Plant the runners with their crowns just level with the soil. If planted too deep, they may rot during the winter; if too shallow, the runners may dry out in hot weather. Rake the ground level, tidy up and water the plants in. Alternatively, they may be inserted through holes in black polythene.

Weed control The choice is between weeding by hand, using herbicides or planting through slits in black polythene sheeting. Weed control is essential to prevent competition for water, light and nutrients.

If you decide to use weedkillers, the first one that can be applied is propachlor, which is sprinkled over the soil surface after planting. Later, in December, simazine may be used. It is effective for a longer period.

Black polythene not only suppresses weeds but also serves as a substitute for straw, which otherwise has to be spread under the foliage to keep the ripening berries clean. Being black, it absorbs heat so the berries ripen two or three days earlier. However, the crop is over more rapidly and watering has to be watched very carefully.

Use heavy-duty polythene cut into strips 90 cm (3 ft) wide. Plain polythene will serve, and there is also a perforated type with numerous tiny slits that admit air and moisture but do not allow weed seedlings to grow through.

Lay the polythene before planting, first forming a slight ridge where each row will be and then soaking the soil thoroughly. Press the edges of the polythene about 8 cm (3 in) deep into the ground, using a spade. Leave a 15 cm (6 in) gap between sheets to allow water to permeate towards the roots. At each planting station slit the polythene with a sharp knife, making a diagonal cross, each slit about 5 cm (2 in) long. Plant through these as already described.

Propagation by budding Few tree fruits are grown on their own roots but are propagated by budding or grafting the variety (the scion) on to a different rootstock. The main purpose is to control the eventual size of the fruit tree, for it is the rootstock more than any other factor that influences the size and vigour of the plant. So, if a small tree is wanted, the scion is budded or grafted on to a dwarfing rootstock.

Budding is done in July, August or not later than the middle of September on rootstocks planted the previous winter. There are two main budding techniques – chip budding and T-cut budding, the former being the more important of the two.

Chip budding Necessary equipment and materials include a sharp budding knife; a length of polythene tape 2.5 cm (1 in) wide; a piece of clean, damp sacking; a pair of sharp secateurs to collect the budwood (scion wood); a sharpening stone, oil and rag; marker pen; pencil and labels.

Budwood The budwood, or budstick, should be a healthy shoot of the current season's growth, which must be about pencil thick, well ripened and well-budded.

Collect the budstick from the outside part of a healthy parent tree where the growth is well exposed to the sun and more likely to be ripe: nut-brown and woody over most of the shoot's length. Usually, an apple budstick is about 30 cm (1 ft) or more long and will have twelve or more buds on it.

Each bud is in the axil of a leaf. They should be well developed by July but, if not, delay budding until August.

Preparing the budstick Remove all leaves with secateurs, leaving about 6 mm (¼ in) of leaf stalk in each case. Also cut off the soft, green, immature tip of the bud-stick. To prevent the shoot from drying out, wrap it in damp sacking until ready to bud.

Rootstock Remove all side shoots on the stock up to, and slightly beyond, the height where budding will take place. The usual height is 15–30 cm (6–12 in) from the ground, preferably the latter.

Budding Straddle the rootstock and hold the head of the stock between your knees to stop it waving about. Select a smooth piece of stem at least 5 cm (2 in) long. Make the first cut at an angle of 20 degrees into the stem, and to a depth of about 3 mm (⅛ in), to form an acute lip. Make the second cut about 38 mm (1½ in) above the first – a shallow cut about 6 mm (¼ in) wide – sufficient to remove the bark and directed downwards to meet the first cut.

The chip bud is made in the same way and should, ideally, be of the same length and width so that it fits the cut on the stock exactly. Place the bud on to the cut on the stock, sliding it under the lip so that it is held firmly during tying.

Should the cut on the stock be wider than the chip bud, place the bud to one side of the stock cut. The important point is that the exposed cambium of the bud should press against the exposed cambium of the stock to ensure a successful union.

Tying Secure the bud to the stock by tying. Wrap the bud completely with polythene tape, exerting maximum pressure above and below the bud and with a slightly slacker, but still firm, pressure pass over the bud itself.

Tie release After about five or six weeks, remove the tie by carefully slicing the polythene at the back of the stock (away from the bud) so that the tape falls away easily without disturbing the bud. No

BUDDING

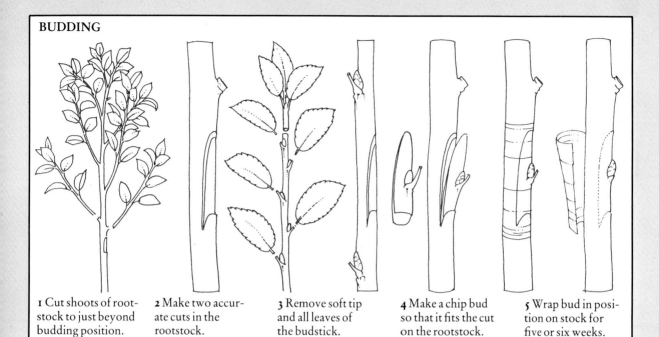

1 Cut shoots of root-stock to just beyond budding position.

2 Make two accurate cuts in the rootstock.

3 Remove soft tip and all leaves of the budstick.

4 Make a chip bud so that it fits the cut on the rootstock.

5 Wrap bud in position on stock for five or six weeks.

further attention is needed until next spring, apart from general cultivation such as watering.

T-cut budding In this technique a T cut is made on the stock, and the flaps of the rind (bark) are lifted so that the bud can be slid underneath. The essential point about the method is that the bark of the stock should lift easily. This condition is usually reached in July and T-cut budding remains possible until September.

AUGUST

Harvesting There are still some soft fruits to be gathered, including remontant strawberries, late raspberries, blackberries and hybrid berries, as well as the last of the currants and gooseberries.

Early top fruits are ripening – plums and gages, peaches, figs, early apples and pears.

To test whether an apple is ready, lift it gently in the palm of your hand. When given a slight twist it should leave the spur. Use colour as a guide, too, for not all the fruits will be ready at once.

Eat early apples within a few days of picking, because they will not keep. Gather pears while they are still firm and slightly under-ripe. They will become more mellow off the tree. Examine them frequently, however, as they soon go 'sleepy' – become mealy.

Strawberries Immediately the crop of ordinary (not remontant) strawberries is finished, cut off the old leaves about 10 cm (4 in) above the crown. Cut off all the runners, except any that are needed to fill gaps in the row. Rake off the straw, leaves and weeds, and burn the lot.

Apply Growmore fertilizer between the rows at 30 g per sq m (1 oz per sq yd). Fork up the soil, then rake it to a fine tilth so that the weed-killer simazine can be applied.

Strawberries are best dug up and burnt after their third harvest.

Summer-pruning restricted forms of apples and pears In all but wet areas, prune pears in early August and apples in mid-August. In areas of high rainfall, delay pruning until September so as to avoid too much secondary growth.

Cut to three leaves – about 8 cm (3 in) – all mature shoots of the current season's growth that are longer than 23 cm (9 in) and arise directly from the main stem. Cut to one leaf – about 2.5 cm (1 in) – shoots that grow from spurs. Leave immature shoots, and those less than 23 cm (9 in) long, until the wood is ripe and they have made more growth.

Leave the leaders of cordons and espaliers unpruned, but stop the branch leaders of dwarf pyramids at five leaves.

Propagation Continue propagating strawberries (see June) and budding fruit trees. (See July.)

Over-vigorous, unfruitful apple trees Summer-pruning checks growth, opens up the tree and induces fruitfulness. Do not prune trees that are weak.

Cut to five leaves any laterals (current season's growth) that are longer than 30 cm (1 ft). Spread this task over the whole month, starting with the longest laterals.

Plums, bush, half-standard and full standard In late August remove any broken branches and dead wood, cutting back to healthy wood. Pare wounds clean and apply a wound paint to guard against silver leaf. If the tree is crowded, remove some of the thin, twiggy growth.

Plum, gage and damson pyramids Early in the month, prune the branch leaders to 20 cm (8 in), cutting to a leaf on the underside. Reduce current laterals to six leaves. Stop the central leader at 1.8 m (6 ft) if the tree is on 'Pixy' rootstock, or 2.4 m (8 ft) if it is on 'St. Julien A'.

Cut to one leaf any vigorous, upright laterals at the top.

Fan-trained sweet cherries, plums and gages In late August cut all young laterals back to three leaves to encourage spur formation. However, leave unpruned any shoots that are needed to fill in uncovered wall space. Tie these to the wires.

Fan-trained peaches and nectarines Immediately fruiting is over, untie the old laterals that carried the fruit and cut them out by pruning back to young replacement shoots near the base. Tie in the young replacements to the wires, along with any others needed to fill in wall space.

The average spacing should be about 20 cm (8 in) along the branch framework.

Raspberries As soon as the crop is finished, the old fruiting canes should be cut down to ground level. Tie in the strongest young canes, spacing them 8–10 cm (3–4 in) apart along the wires. Lace them in place with soft string, or use twist ties.

Finally, cut out the surplus young canes, rake off debris and burn.

Plums, gages, apples and pears Remove fruits affected by brown rot and bird pecks to prevent infection spreading.

Top fruits can be protected from birds by enclosing them in old nylon tights or polythene bags, cutting holes in the bags to allow water to drain away.

Cobnuts and filberts Break (about half-way) the strong young shoots growing from the branches and leave them hanging. The purpose of this is to reduce vigour and induce the production of female flowers at their base. Remove suckers around the base.

SEPTEMBER

Harvesting Mid-season apples and pears are now ripening, and the later keeping varieties will soon be ready for picking. Now is a good time to check on your storage arrangements.

Clean storage trays and boxes and tidy up the storehouse. If necessary, obtain wooden tomato trays and apple boxes from a greengrocer. Moulded fibre or polystyrene trays are suitable, too.

Autumn raspberries are ready, and perpetual (remontant) strawberries are coming to an end. To extend the season, cover the remontant strawberries with a polythene tunnel or glass cloches.

Planting and budding Finish planting strawberries and budding fruit trees by mid-September (see July).

Pruning 'Morello' cherries The 'Morello' crops on wood made during the previous year. To prevent the tree cropping only on its outside, and to stimulate new growth, it is necessary to cut out some of the older wood.

Prune a fan-trained 'Morello' in the same way as a peach (see August). To prune a bush 'Morello', cut out about a quarter of the old wood by pruning a proportion of two-year-old and three-year-old branches back to strong, young growth. Paint the cuts with a wound healing compound.

Ordering new bushes and trees Order early while a good selection is still available.

Liming The main preparations for planting are carried out in October, but where lime is needed to raise the pH this should be applied now.

Summer-pruning restricted forms of apples and pears If you live in a high rainfall area, and therefore postponed summer-pruning last month, this can now go ahead.

OCTOBER

Harvesting The picking of late apples and pears is now in full swing. Most cultivars should be off the trees by the third week but there are a few which are left until next month – 'Sturmer Pippin', 'D'Arcy Spice', 'Wagener', 'Idared' and 'Granny Smith'.

Pick with the stalk intact and handle the fruit gently. Damaged and blemished fruits will not keep, so use them right away.

Very late apples are unripe when picked. Ripeness develops in storage according to season.

Storage The essential conditions are coolness, darkness and a little ventilation. Too much ventilation will cause shrivelling, too little will cause the flesh to break down. The ideal fruit store is a cool, dark, frost-free shed, cellar or garage.

The containers, too, must provide for air circulation. Wooden apple boxes, tomato trays, moulded fibre and polystyrene trays are all satisfactory. Although not essential, tissue or waxed paper wraps for dessert apples, and newspapers for cookers, extend the storage life.

Another good storage method is to keep the apples in clear polythene bags, each holding 2.5 kg (5 lb) of fruit. Punch holes in the bag first – two pencil holes for every ½ kg (1 lb) of apples. Do not seal, but fold the top cover.

Load the store in the evening when the fruits are cool. Open up the storeroom at night to reduce the temperature. Keep the different cultivars separate, and those ripening mid-season well away from the late ones; the gases they give off speed the ripening process.

Store pears unwrapped, ideally in single layers. Small quantities could be kept in the vegetable compartment of a refrigerator. When they are wanted for dessert, according to their season, bring them into normal living room temperature where they will soon mellow.

Examine fruits regularly to remove rotten ones and prevent the spread of spores.

Pruning blackberries and hybrid berries In late October, when the last fruits have been picked, untie and cut to ground level the old canes that have fruited. However, if young replacement canes are scarce, leave the best old canes in.

Tie the replacement canes to the wires, according to the chosen training system; in very cold districts it is better to defer training until March. In the meantime, loosely bundle the canes together for mutual protection and secure them to the lowest wires until the winter is over.

Training Although the canes of these fruits are perennial, they produce their best fruit on the young growth made during the previous summer. To ensure a succession of strong, young, pro-ductive growth they are pruned on the replacement system in a similar way to raspberries. Each year, the canes that have fruited are cut out at ground level and the best of the new young canes are tied in to replace them. These will fruit during the next summer.

This should be done in the late autumn once the harvest is over, and not later than the end of November. However, in areas where the winters are very hard and there is a risk of the young canes being killed by severe frost it is wise to defer training until March. In the meantime, the young canes should be loosely bundled together for mutual protection and secured to one of the lower wires. Cut out the old canes.

Brambles are rambling plants and it is necessary to have some kind of training system to keep them tidy, to hold the fruits clear of the ground and to make pruning easier.

The three most widely used systems are as follows:

Fan This is the quickest and simplest way and suitable for varieties that produce thick, rigid canes that do not easily bend. Suitable sorts include the blackberries 'Smoothstem' and 'Thornfree', and the hybrid berry 'King's Acre'. The canes are secured to all the wires in a fan-like pattern, with space left in the middle for the young canes which will be taken up the centre.

Rope This method is suitable for blackberries and hybrid berries of moderate growth which produce flexible canes capable of being bent over parallel with the wires. Varieties within this category are most of the hybrid berries, the Japanese wineberry and the blackberry 'Ashton Cross'.

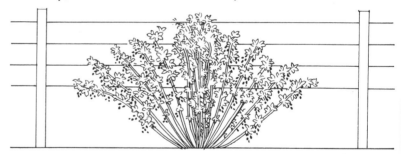

Fan-training
This method is ideal for varieties with rigid canes. Secure canes to wire in a fan shape and leave room for young canes in the centre.

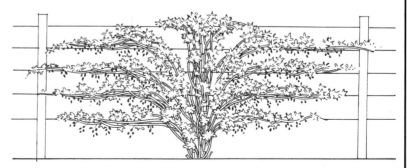

Rope training
This method suits more flexible canes; tie three or four canes to each wire, but leave the top wire free for current season's growth.

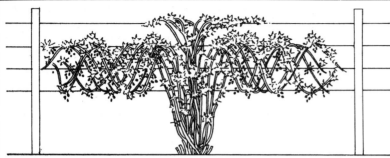

Weaving
This training method is ideal with long, strong canes. It does, however, require most handling of the canes. Again, leave the top wire free for new growth.

Three or four canes are tied to each wire, to the left and right, but leaving the top wire free for young canes during the summer.

Weaving This system requires more training than the others and is recommended only for varieties that make long, strong canes. It involves a good deal of handling the canes. Suitable varieties are 'Himalayan Giant', 'Bedford Giant' and 'Oregon Thornless'. The canes are woven over the lower wires and, as in the rope system, the top wire is left free for securing the young growth.

Ordering plants Order early so that you have a wider choice. Wherever possible buy Certified Stock. These are plants that have been certified by the Ministry of Agriculture as being healthy and true to name.

Not all fruits come within the Ministry Certification Scheme – only those that are commercially important. At the moment it applies to strawberries, raspberries, black currants, a few cultivars of hybrid berries and gooseberries and all the well-known cultivars of apples, pears, plums and cherries.

Always obtain plants from a reputable source.

Preparing for planting Mark out the land. Kill all perennial weeds using the weedkiller glyphosate early in the month. When the weeds are dead, or three weeks after spraying, dig the ground.

Raspberries need special treatment, as good ground preparation is the foundation for successful cropping for many years to come. Take out a trench along the intended row, one spade depth and three spades width. Into the bottom of the trench mix thoroughly an 8 cm (3 in) layer of well-rotted manure or garden compost. The canes are intolerant of poorly-drained land. To improve such ground, first incorporate builders' rubble or similar open material along the row below the rooting area – about 45 cm (1½ ft) down. If the ground is still suspect after such treatment, plant the canes along an 8 cm (3 in) ridge.

During the final preparations, fork in a compound fertilizer, such as Growmore, at 100 g per sq m (3 oz per sq yd).

Virgin land, such as grassland, will need double digging before planting any kind of fruit, and so will ground with a hard, impermeable layer (a 'pan') beneath. Cultivated ground should be single dug. Impoverished land will need some bulky organic material, such as manure or compost, incorporated during the digging process. Spread a 5 cm (2 in) layer of this, or about 2.5 cm (1 in) of peat, and then dig it in.

The whole plot will need preparing in this fashion before planting soft fruits or closely-spaced trees, such as cordons. For widely-spaced trees it will be sufficient to dig an area 75 cm (2½ ft) square at each site.

Place any old turf at the bottom of the planting hole, chopping it into small pieces.

Propagating gooseberries, black currants and red currants Each of these soft fruits is propagated by hardwood cuttings. The method differs with each case.

Gooseberries Select strong, straight, well-ripened, one-year-old shoots of pencil thickness taken from healthy bushes. The cuttings should be 30 cm (1 ft) long.

Cut to just above a bud at the top, with a slanting cut away from the bud. Make a straight cut just below a bud at the base. Remove any leaves, except for two or three at the top which will help in root production. Leave all the buds on, but snip off the thorns from the bottom 15 cm (6 in) to make the cuttings easier to insert. Dip the

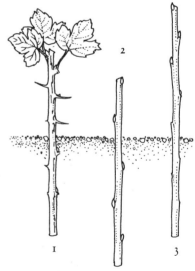

Cuttings from: gooseberry (1), black currant (2) and red currant (3).

base of each cutting in a hormone rooting powder or liquid.

Insert the cuttings 15 cm (6 in) deep, preferably in well-prepared, light, sandy soil, with some bonemeal added, and firm around them. In heavy ground take out a narrow, straight-sided trench and put in some sharp sand to help drainage. Space the cuttings 15 cm (6 in) apart in the row, with 75 cm (2½ ft) between the rows.

A year later, dig up the rooted cuttings and remove any suckers and unwanted basal shoots to create a clean stem 15 cm (6 in) long. Plant out 30 cm (1 ft) apart in nursery rows.

Black currants Select strong, straight, well-ripened, one-year-old, healthy shoots taken from Certified Stock bushes. The cuttings should be 25 cm (10 in) long, cut to just above a bud at the top and just below a bud at the base. Remove any leaves but not buds.

Black currants are adaptable and will root in most types of soil that are reasonably well-drained and weed-free. Fork in some bonemeal, at 130 g per sq m (4 oz per sq yd).

Take out a straight-sided trench 25 cm (10 in) deep. Insert the cuttings about 20 cm (8 in) deep, with no more than two buds showing above the ground. Space them 15 cm (6 in) apart in the row, with 90 cm (3 ft) between the rows. Fill in and firm the soil.

A year later, dig up the rooted cuttings and either plant them out in their permanent stations or grow them on for another year, 30 cm (1 ft) apart, in nursery rows. Prune them down to 2.5 cm (1 in) above ground level.

Red currants The propagation of red currants is similar to gooseberries except that, being a more vigorous plant, the cuttings may be up to 38 cm (15 in) long.

They root easily. Remove all the buds except the top four, together with any leaves. Insert them to about half their length, 15 cm (6 in) apart in the row and with 90 cm (3 ft) between rows. A year later they can be dug up and planted in their permanent positions.

NOVEMBER

Planting: tree fruits The usual time to plant trees – and, indeed, bushes and canes – is between November and March, while they are dormant. For preference, plant in the early winter while the soil is still warm and easy to work. Container-grown fruits may be planted at any time, weather and soil conditions permitting.

The dormant season – after leaf-fall and before bud-break – is also the right time to prune most fruits. Stone fruits such as plums are an exception, because of the greater risk of silver leaf disease entering the pruning cuts if these are made during the winter. Young stone fruits are pruned in the spring (see March). Established trees bearing crops are pruned, if necessary, immediately after the fruit is gathered.

Heeling in If conditions are too wet for planting when your fruit trees arrive, heel the plants in temporarily in a sheltered part of the garden.

To do this, take out a shallow trench to contain the roots. Place the trees in this, closely spaced, after untying them and removing any packing. If they were wrapped in straw, spread this over the soil to help prevent it from freezing.

If planting has to be delayed because the ground is frozen, place the plants in a cool but frost-free shed or garage for the time being. Unpack any wrapping

from their above-ground parts but leave the roots covered. It is important not to allow the roots to dry out or be exposed to frost.

Planting in the open First, fork fertilizer into the topsoil. For each sq metre (sq yard) apply 100 g (3 oz) of Growmore and 200 g (6 oz) of bonemeal.

Now mark out the planting positions. Following are the recommended spacings for bush apple and pear trees:

Dwarf bush apples on 'M.27' rootstock, 1.8–2.4m (6–8 ft); on 'M.9', 2.4–3 m (8–10 ft). Bush apples on 'M.26', 3–3.6 m (10–12 ft); on 'MM.106', 3.6–5.5 m (12–18 ft); on 'MM.111', 5.5–7.6 m (18–25 ft).

Bush pears on 'Quince C', 3–4.2 m (10–14 ft); on 'Quince A', 3.6–4.5 m (12–15 ft).

The lesser spacings are for light, sandy soils or weaker varieties.

The next job is to drive in a vertical stake on the windward side of each planting position. All fruit trees need staking for at least the first four years, and dwarf trees require permanent support.

Use stakes 5–6 cm (2–2½ in) in diameter that have been treated against rot. Their length depends on the type of tree. For bush and standard trees the stake must be just clear of branches on that side, to avoid rubbing. For trees with a centre leader, such as the pyramid or spindlebush, it must be 1.8–2.1 m (6–7 ft) out of the ground.

To these lengths must be added the part that will be in the ground – 45 cm (1½ ft) in heavy soil and 60 cm (2 ft) in light soil.

Dig a hole wide and deep enough to take the root system well spread out. Plant the tree – with a helper, if possible – to the same depth that it was in the nursery, ensuring that the graft union between the rootstock and

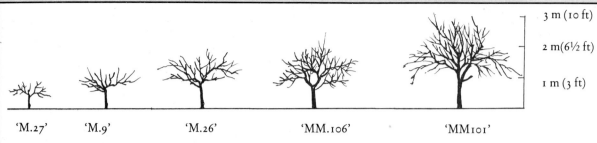

'M.27'   'M.9'   'M.26'   'MM.106'   'MM101'

Effect of rootstock on eventual size of tree (all 12-year-old stocks).

the scion (variety) is at least 10 cm (4 in) above the soil to prevent scion rooting. The stem should be 8 cm (3 in) away from the stake.

Fill in the hole, shaking the tree a little to ensure that soil falls between the roots. Firm gently while filling, finally levelling off and raking the surface.

Secure the tree to the stake with a proprietary tree tie, which provides a cushion between the tree and the stake. Standard and pyramid trees need two ties, one at the top and the other halfway down.

Finally, spread a circle of well-rotted manure, compost or peat. This should be 90 cm (3 ft) across and 5 cm (2 in) deep.

Planting against a wall or fence (espaliers, etc.)

Soil preparation The soil at the base of a wall can become very dry in the summer. At planting time, improve moisture retention by mixing in some bulky organic material, such as peat or well-rotted manure. Apply a 5–8 cm (2–3 in) layer over a 45 cm (1½ ft) radius and fork it in, along with 85 g (3 oz) of Growmore fertilizer at each of the planting sites.

Wiring the structure The trees need support, the usual method being to secure horizontal wires to the wall or fence.

Planting the tree Take out a hole deep and wide enough to contain the root system with the roots well spread out.

Plant the tree to the same depth as it was in the nursery, ensuring that the union between stock and scion is at least 10 cm (4 in) above ground level. This prevents scion rooting, which would destroy the dwarfing effect of the stock.

Set the tree 15–23 cm (6–9 in) away from the structure, to allow for expansion, with the top inclined slightly towards it and the roots radiating outwards. Cover the roots with soil and firm gently as you fill in. Finally, mulch the tree to a depth of 8 cm (3 in) over a radius of 38 cm (15 in), but keep the material just clear of the stem.

Restricted tree forms The restricted tree forms are so called because they are confined, usually by pruning, in some way or another. Cordons, for example, are restricted to a narrow band along the row. Espaliers and fans are confined to a narrow space against a wall or fence, though they are usually allowed plenty of lateral room.

Such restriction is achieved by summer-pruning. However, all tree fruits, no matter what the form, are planted in the winter (unless container-grown) and most require a certain amount of formative winter-pruning at planting time and for a few years afterwards.

Although planted while dormant, stone fruits are not pruned formatively until the spring, when the sap is rising.

Cordon apples and pears Cordons may be grown against walls or fences, or in the open. Planting is the same as for other trees, already described. Before this can be done, however, it is necessary to erect supporting wires.

On a wall or fence, use vine eyes to secure the horizontal wires 10 cm (4 in) away from the support. Three wires are needed – 60 cm (2 ft), 1.2 m (4 ft) and 1.8 m (6 ft) from the ground. Use 10 gauge galvanized wire.

In the open, posts are needed to support the wires at these same intervals. These may be of concrete, 10–13 cm (4–5 in) timber, or 4 cm × 4 cm × 6 mm (1½ in × 1½ in × ¼ in) angle iron. Set the posts at 3.6 m (12 ft) intervals, 60 cm (2 ft) deep, and strut the end posts so that they will not shift under tension. Allow 1.8 m (6 ft) between rows. Attach straining bolts at one end so that the wires can be pulled taut.

Cordons may be planted and trained either vertically or, for preference, at an angle of 45 degrees. It is better, though not essential, that the rows should run north–south, with the tops of the trees inclined towards the north if they are planted obliquely.

Rootstocks Because the cordon is a restricted form of tree it should be grafted on to a dwarfing or semi-dwarfing rootstock. For apples, the most widely-used is 'MM.106' (semi-dwarfing). 'M.26' (dwarfing) or 'M.9' (very dwarfing) are also used but both require a deep, fertile soil. 'M.27' (extremely dwarfing) is also available, making a small, compact cordon, but it requires a good deal of extra care and attention.

Pear cordons are grafted on to either 'Quince A' or 'Quince C'. The latter is slightly less vigorous, but both are acceptable.

Planting Space cordons 75 cm (2½ ft) apart in the row, with a cane secured to the wires at each planting station. For oblique cordons, secure the canes at 45 degrees. Ensure that the graft union of rootstock and scion is at least 10 cm (4 in) above the soil.

Tie the cordon to the cane, using three figure-of-eight ties. Plastic chain-lock strapping is ideal for this purpose.

If the cordon has side-shoots, shorten those over 15 cm (6 in) to three or four buds. This is all the pruning needed at planting time. Subsequently, prune in August.

Pruning established cordons August is the usual month for pruning cordons, but winter-pruning is better in areas of high rainfall, where secondary growth is more prolific following summer-pruning. Follow the method described in August.

A weak cordon that is not producing sufficient side-shoots can be induced to do so by pruning the leaders (last summer's growth) by half to two thirds during the winter.

Winter-pruning will also bring a neglected cordon back into shape. The method is to reduce over-long or complicated spur systems back to two or three fruit buds. Summer pruning can be reintroduced the following year.

Lowering cordons When cordons reach the top wire, they may be lowered to increase the length of the stems. Do this not more than five degrees at a time, and never lower than 35 degrees to the horizontal, otherwise there is a risk of breaking the stem.

Espaliers This attractive tree form for apples and pears makes an ideal divider between one part of the garden and another. It is also an excellent choice for covering walls and fences.

An espalier consists of horizontal arms or tiers. Usually the nurseryman supplies a two- or three-tier espalier, leaving it to the gardener to train in more tiers.

Choice of rootstock Apples are grown on 'MM.106' (semi-dwarfing), or on 'MM.111' (vigorous) if the soil is poor. Pears are grown on 'Quince A' or 'C'.

The usual spacing is 3.6–4.5 m (12–15 ft) apart.

Support system On a wall or fence, fix horizontal wires to correspond with the arms, which are usually about 38 cm (15 in) apart. Use 10 gauge galvanized fencing wire, and 15 cm (6 in) lead wall or vine eyes spaced every 1.5 m (5 ft) to hold the wires.

Away from a wall or fence, a post-and-wire structure, as for cordons, is needed. Space the wooden posts 3.6–4.5 m (12–15 ft) apart, and plant the espaliers between the posts.

Training and pruning Tie the tiers to the wires with figure of eight ties, three on either side of each tier.

Prune the horizontal leaders by one quarter to an upward-facing bud. This is to stimulate extension growth and side-shoots during the following summer. Existing side-shoots on the tiers and main stem (except the central one on the topmost tier if further tiers are wanted) should be cut to a bud at about 10 cm (4 in); any side-shoot on the trunk below the first tier must be removed entirely.

Pruning to create more tiers In this case the central, upright leader is not removed but is trained up a cane fixed to the wires.

Once this leader has reached the next wire, cut it to a bud just above

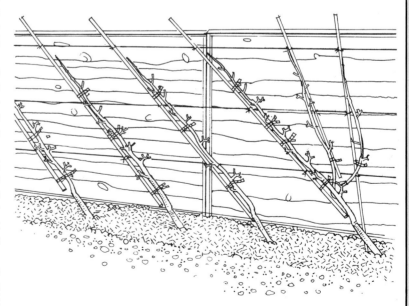

Apple and pear cordons
Tie oblique apple and pear cordons to canes secured to wires. Train the first in the row as a multiple cordon to fill the available space.

the wire, first ensuring there are two good buds, one to the left and one to the right, immediately beneath it. These two buds will grow in the spring to form the new tiers. Train the top bud vertically to the cane as it grows. Thereafter, prune the espalier during August.

Dwarf pyramid apples and pears

The dwarf pyramid is a tree with a central leader, pyramidal in shape – like a Christmas tree – as the name suggests. Being a closely-spaced, dwarf form for planting in the open, it is ideal for small gardens because it is possible to plant a number of varieties in a relatively limited area.

Choice of rootstock For apples, 'M.27' (extremely dwarfing), 'M.9' (very dwarfing) or 'M.26' (dwarfing) are suitable. For pears, select 'Quince C' (semi-dwarfing) or 'Quince A' (semi-vigorous).

Spacing Apples grown on 'M.27' need to be 1.2 m (4 ft) apart. On 'M.9' the spacing can be increased to 1.5 m (5 ft). On 'M.26', a spacing of 1.8 m (6 ft) is usual.

Pears on 'Quince C' should be planted 1.5 m (5 ft) apart; on 'Quince A', 1.8 m (6 ft).

Space the rows 2.1 m (7 ft) apart and ideally, though not essentially, align them north–south.

Support system If there are only one or two trees, stake them individually. The stakes need to be 2.3 m (7½ ft) long, with a 4 cm (1½ in) diameter and driven in 45 cm (1½ ft). For rows of trees, run two horizontal wires down each row, one at 60 cm (2 ft) and the other at 1 m (3½ ft). Secure the trees to the wires with figure of eight ties.

Pruning and training: first winter – maiden whip Cut back to a strong, healthy bud at 50 cm (20 in) from the ground, with a sloping cut away from the bud.

Pruning: first winter – feathered maiden Select three or four laterals 30–38 cm (12–15 in) from the ground and cut each to within 20 cm (8 in) of the trunk, pruning to a bud. Remove all other side-shoots flush with the trunk, and protect the cuts with a wound paint. Cut back the central stem at three buds above the topmost lateral.

Remember, during the spring and summer, to train up the central leader and tie it to the stake as and when necessary.

Pruning: second winter Prune the central leader to leave about 23 cm (9 in) of the previous summer's growth. Cut to a bud on the opposite side to the first year's pruning in order to maintain a straight trunk. Prune the side branches to downward-facing buds to leave about 20 cm (8 in) of extension growth.

Such pruning of the main side branches and the central leader should induce more extension growth and new laterals during the following summer.

From this point onwards the dwarf pyramid is pruned during the summer as well as the winter.

Pruning: third and subsequent winters Continue to prune the central leader – the previous summer's growth – to leave 23 cm (9 in) of extension growth, cutting to a bud on the opposite side to the previous year's cut, zig-zag fashion, until it has reached the desired height of between 1.8 and 2.1 m (6 and 7 ft). Thereafter, maintain it at this height by pruning in May.

Prune the leaders of the side branches to eight buds while extension growth and new laterals are needed. Once the desired width has been reached, prune these also in May. Also, remove vigorous, upright shoots at the top, and stop branch leaders from growing into neighbouring trees.

Thereafter, very little winter-pruning should be necessary, the main pruning being done during August. Maintain the pyramid

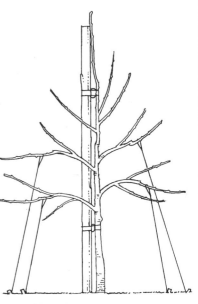

Spindlebush shape
This is achieved by tying 3–4 shoots to the horizontal.

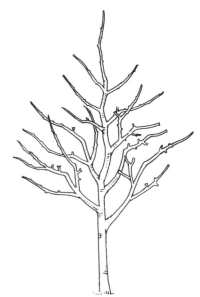

Planning a dwarf pyramid
Winter-prune central leader and main side branches on a young dwarf pyramid.

shape by selective cuts wherever necessary. Remove any secondary growth which may occur after summer-pruning.

Spindlebush apple or pear trees The spindlebush is a cone-shaped tree with a strong central stem. Along its length, starting at about 45 cm (1½ ft), are borne evenly-spaced branches and laterals. Those at the bottom are longer than those at the top. The tree is supported by a tall stake.

The success of this form depends upon the tree being well furnished with wide-angled branches and laterals. Tying down is practised to achieve near horizontal branches, which tend to be more fruitful than upright growth. For preference, start with a feathered maiden (a one-year-old tree with side-shoots) rather than a maiden whip, because the laterals on such a tree are formed naturally at the correct angle.

Rootstocks and spacing Suitable rootstocks for apples are 'M.9' (very dwarfing), 'M.26' (dwarfing) or 'MM.106' (semi-dwarfing). For pears, 'Quince C' (semi-dwarfing) or 'Quince A' (semi-vigorous) are suitable.

Apples on 'M.9' (or, in light soils, on 'M.26') need a spacing of 1.8–2.1 m (6–7 ft) × 3.6 m (12 ft). Plant those on 'M.26' and 'MM.106', on good soils, with distances of 2.3–2.6 m (7½–8½ ft) between the trees and 3.6–4.2 m (12–14 ft) between the rows.

Pears on 'Quince C' need spacing at 2.1 m × 3.6 m (7 ft × 12 ft), and on 'Quince A' at 2.4 m × 4 m (8 ft × 13 ft).

Formation pruning at planting time: maiden whip Cut back to a bud at 90 cm (3 ft).

Pruning: feathered maiden Select three or four laterals at not less than 45 cm (1½ ft) from the ground to form the first branches, then cut each by half to a downward-facing bud. Remove the remaining laterals close to the main stem. Cut back the central stem at three buds above the topmost lateral. In the summer, the topmost bud will be trained up the stake as the central leader.

Pruning: second year Cut back the central leader (the previous summer's growth) by about a third, to a bud on the opposite side to that of the previous year. Remove any upright shoots at the top that are competing with the central leader. Check the ties and remove those where the branches have set at the desired angle.

Removing secondary growth from cordon, espalier and fan-trained apples and pears Secondary growth is the regrowth that may occur in the same summer, after summer-pruning, from pruned shoots on restricted tree forms of apples and pears. Secondary growth may appear if the trees have been pruned too early or if heavy rain falls after pruning. Such growth should not be left, as it is too soft and immature to withstand winter frosts.

Remove it by pruning back to a bud on mature, nut-brown wood. This will generally be on the lower part of the secondary growth, but it may sometimes be necessary to cut back to older wood.

Cobnuts and filberts These can be grown as stooled bushes. However, the simplest form to maintain, and also the most attractive, is the open-centred, goblet-shaped tree.

The ideal is a tree with a head of six or seven main branches on a 30 cm (1 ft) clean stem. The tree is kept to a height of 1.8–2.1 m (6–7 ft) by late-winter pruning.

Generally the nurseryman supplies trees two or three years old.

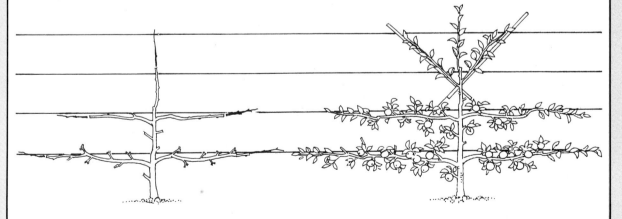

Training an espalier
At planting time, cut a two-tier espalier back by a quarter, the central stem to just above a wire. In the third summer, tie side shoots for a third tier to canes secured to the wires; train them to the horizontal in winter. Tip the other tier branches.

Space these 4.5 m (15 ft) apart.

Staking and planting As it is a small plant at the start, a stout 1.5 m (5 ft) cane or thin stake will suffice to support it. Plant to the same depth as it was in the nursery, spreading the roots outwards. Firm the soil after planting.

Pruning: first winter If the plant consists of a single stem, head it back to about 38 cm (15 in), pruning to a bud. This will stimulate the remaining buds to break in the next growing season to form the first branches.

Where the plant has a number of laterals, select five or six that are well placed to form the primary branches. Prune these by half to outward-facing buds. Cut back unwanted laterals flush with the main stem and remove any suckers from the base to leave a single trunk of about 23–38 cm (9–15 in).

Pruning: subsequent winters Carry on this formative pruning for the next three or four years, by which time a strong goblet shape should have been formed. Remember to keep the centre open and to remove any sucker growths from the base, as well as laterals on the trunk below the head.

Suckers, if they are young, can be pulled and twisted off; if old, the easiest way is to cut them with an old pair of secateurs or a spade just below soil level. It is important not to allow the tree to develop into a stooled bush.

Once it has started cropping, prune the tree when the male catkins are shedding their pollen.

Figs The fig is a sun-loving plant. When grown outside, it is best as a fan-trained tree against a south or west-facing wall. As it is also extremely vigorous, root restriction is essential to stop the tree becoming over-large and unfruitful. This is provided by planting it in some kind of container.

On a patio or in a greenhouse, a fig is an excellent subject for growing in a pot, which might be a 45 cm (18 in) plastic pot filled with John Innes potting compost No. No. 3. Against a wall, the usual way is to construct an open-based trough with a 2.5 cm (1 in) rim above the soil surface. The rim is essential for watering and it also prevents the roots escaping.

All kinds of materials can be used for its construction – for example, corrugated iron, asbestos or plastic, or it might even be a galvanized tank sunk into the ground. The ideal trough is one made of either bricks or concrete paving slabs. A border, 60–90 cm (2–3 ft) wide, bounded on one side by the wall and the other by a concrete path also provides the necessary restriction.

Construction of the trough The size of the trough governs the eventual size of the fan. If it is intended to cover a wall about 2.4 m (8 ft) tall by 4.5 m (15 ft) wide, the trough should contain about ½ cu m (13.5 cu ft) of compost and drainage materials. For a wall or wooden fence 1.8 m (6 ft) high by 3 m (10 ft) wide, a 0.054 cu m (2 cu ft) box constructed of paving slabs is sufficient.

To allow drainage, the trough must have an open base. Pack the bottom tightly, to a depth of 23 cm (9 in) with broken bricks and mortar rubble or lumpy chalk. Then fill the container with John Innes potting compost No. 3. Remember to mulch the tree with a 5 cm (2 in) layer of manure or compost, as this will help to protect the roots against winter frosts.

Pruning This is done in May or June, after the hard frosts.

Winter protection The framework branches of a young fig are very prone to frost damage, as are the fruit-carrying laterals on a mature tree. It is therefore a wise policy to protect the branches

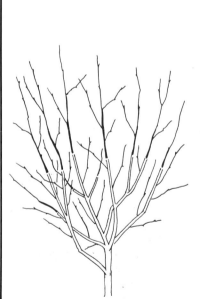

Pruning young nut trees
Prune a young nut tree to goblet shape, retaining six main branches only.

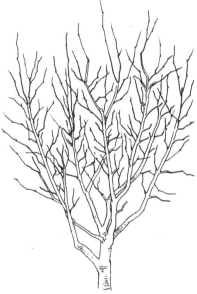

Pruning established nut trees
On established trees, remove unwanted laterals to maintain an open centre.

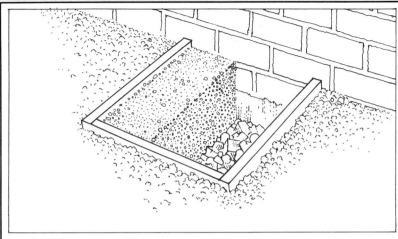

Fig-tree trough
Restrict the roots of a wall-trained fig tree be planting it in a hole lined with bricks or paving slabs and filled with rubble.

throughout the winter. Do this with a loose, open thatching of something like bracken or spruce boughs. The material should dry quickly after rain.

To protect the roots, cover the trough with a thick layer of straw.

Soft fruit

Planting and winter-pruning black currants Black currants crop best on young wood and for this reason need generous feeding and hard pruning. They flower early, so be prepared to protect bushes at that time to ensure regular cropping and heavy yields. A well-grown bush will give 4.5–7 kg (10–15 lb) of fruit.

Black currants are tolerant of a wide range of soils, but very acid land should be limed to bring the pH to between 6.7 and 7.0.

The scourge of black currants is big bud mite, so buy only certified stock and take regular control measures against this pest. They are grown as stooled bushes and are sold as two-year-old plants.

Spacing Set the plants 1.5–1.8 m (5–6 ft) apart. Use the wider spacing for the vigorous varieties, but plant the new compact variety,

'Ben Sarek', only 1.2 m (4 ft) apart.
Planting and pruning Just before planting, fork into the top 10 cm (4 in) a compound fertilizer, such as Growmore, at 130 g per sq m (4 oz per sq yd) over the whole area. Plant 2.5 cm (1 in) deeper than the bush was in the nursery.

Cut all shoots down to 2.5 cm (1 in). This is to stimulate strong new shoots from the base but it means that no fruit will be borne in the first summer. Finally, mulch each plant with well-rotted manure, compost or peat 5–8 cm (2–3 in) deep, but avoid burying the pruned stubs.

Pruning: second winter There should be between four and eight strong new shoots, which will crop in the coming summer. No pruning is necessary except to remove, between November and March, any very weak growth.

Pruning: third winter Again, very little pruning is necessary; but remove, between November and March, any low-lying branches and weak shoots.

Pruning an established bush: fourth winter onwards The black currant is now coming into full production and from this point is

treated as an established plant. Remove about a quarter to a third of the bush each winter, cutting out the oldest unproductive wood and the low-lying branches.

Make the cuts low down to stimulate strong growth from or near the base, pruning to ground level or back to a well-placed, strong, young upright shoot. Use limb-loppers or a saw for the heavy wood. Finally, take out any weak and dead growth.

Planting and winter-pruning red and white currants The red currant bears its fruit buds in clusters on the older wood and at the base of one-year shoots. It is most commonly grown as an open-centred, goblet-shaped bush on a 10–15 cm (4–6 in) clean stem but it can also be grown as a cordon in single or multiple form and, more rarely, as a standard or fan. In the first and last forms it is suitable for a wall or fence. The white currant is a sport of the red and is treated in exactly the same way.

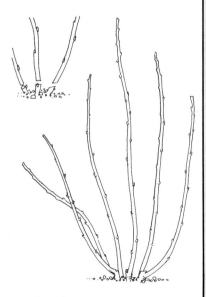

Pruning black currants
Restrict black currants to strong main stems after initial hard pruning.

Planting and pruning young bushes Red and white currants are sold by nurserymen as one- or two-year-old bushes. Choose a plant with an evenly-balanced head of three to six shoots on a clean stem 10–15 cm (4–6 in) long.

For the initial soil preparation, see October. Just before planting, fork into the top 10 cm (4 in), at 100 g per sq m (3 oz per sq yd), a compound fertilizer such as Growmore; also, at 30 g per sq m (1 oz per sq yd), a dressing of sulphate of potash. Apply both over the whole area.

Space the bushes 1.5 m (5 ft) apart if more than one is planted. Plant to the same depth as the bushes were grown in the nursery. Spread the roots out well and firm the soil gently during the filling-in process. Finally, mulch with good compost, manure or peat to a depth of about 2.5–5 cm (1–2 in) over a radius of 23 cm (9 in).

With pruning, the objective is to create an open-centred, goblet-shaped bush with eight to ten main branches growing upwards and outwards. Prune each branch leader by half, to an outward-facing bud, to encourage extension growth and the formation of new branches.

Remove any suckers or side-shoots arising from the main stem below the head. Keep the centre open, but cut back any centrally placed shoots to 2.5 cm (1 in).

Repeat this formative pruning during the next two winters, by which time the main framework should have been formed and the bush will have started to crop. Thereafter, prune it as an established bush.

Pruning established bushes Red currants are spur-pruned to induce the formation of short spur systems along the framework branches. To achieve this, the young side-shoots (the previous

summer's growth) are cut back to a bud at about 2.5 cm (1 in). The branch leaders are pruned by half, to a bud facing outwards.

Cut out old, unproductive and badly-placed branches, allowing young growth to replace them. Keep the centre open.

Planting and pruning cordons Red currant cordons are usually grown vertically and taken to a height of about 1.7 m (5½ ft), though they can be grown higher than this if desired. They are excellent for boundary walls or fences, and will crop quite well even with a north-facing aspect. In this case the fruit will ripen later.

Out in the open, cordons need a post-and-wire fence, with horizontal wires at 60 cm and 1.2 m (2 ft and 4 ft) to support the plants and to hold the canes along which they are trained.

The first task is to fix bamboo canes to the wires at each planting station. Space single cordons 38 cm (15 in) apart; doubles, 75 cm (2½ ft).

Plant the cordon and tie it to the cane with soft string. Cut the central leader by half, to a bud facing away from the cane. This is to stimulate extension growth and the production of side-shoots, which will eventually form spurs. Prune all laterals (the previous summer's growth) back to 2.5 cm (1 in) and remove any lower than 10 cm (4 in).

Repeat the pruning of the leader each November until it has reached the required height, then stop it in May. The cordon should start to crop in its second year.

Pruning established cordons These are pruned in both winter and summer.

Winter-pruning consists of pruning the side-shoots (the previous summer's growth) back to a bud at 2.5 cm (1 in). Remove any

Pruning red and white currants

At planting time, prune main shoots by half, to outward-facing buds, to encourage an open centre.

In second and third winters, reduce all main stems to half. Remove weak side shoots and any stem suckers.

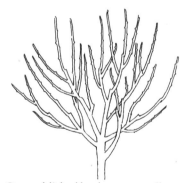

On established bushes, prune all leaders by half and cut fruiting spurs back to about 2.5 cm (1 in).

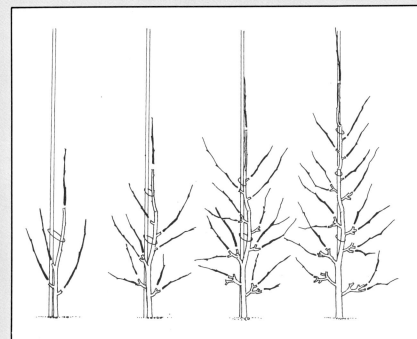

Pruning red currant cordons
On red currant cordons, trained to canes, prune the leader by half, side shoots to one bud. Repeat for three or four winters until the desired height is reached, to encourage short fruiting spurs on the laterals.

growth lower than 10 cm (4 in) and any suckers around the base.

After a number of years it will be necessary to simplify and shorten any spur systems that have become over-long and congested, by cutting into the older wood. Paint such cuts with a wound-healing compound.

Planting and pruning gooseberries
Like red currants, gooseberries bear their fruit buds on spurs on the older wood and at the base of the one-year-old laterals. For this reason, a permanent framework of branches is retained in the same way as on an apple or pear tree.

A gooseberry is usually grown as an open-centred, goblet-shaped bush on a clean stem 10–15 cm (4–6 in) high, with a head of from six to eight main branches. It may also be grown as a cordon, in single or multiple form, and in this case is ideal for wooden fences – even one facing north.

More rarely, gooseberries are grown as fans or standards.

Soil preparation was described in October, but can be carried out now if necessary. Just before planting, fork in a compound fertilizer, such as Growmore, at 100 g per sq m (3 oz per sq yd), plus sulphate of potash at 30 g per sq m (1 oz per sq yd), over the whole area.

Planting and pruning a young bush A gooseberry is sold by the nurseryman as a two- or three-year-old bush. Select a plant with a well-balanced head of about three to six primary branches on a clean stem 10–15 cm (4–6 in) long. Plant the bushes 1.2 m (4 ft) apart in the row and 1.5 m (5 ft) between rows.

Plant the bush to the same depth as it was in the nursery, ensuring that the roots are well spread out. Firm the soil as planting proceeds. Finally, mulch with a 2.5–5 cm (1–2 in) layer of peat, manure or compost over a 20 cm (8 in) radius around each plant. This will help to retain soil moisture.

As with red currants, the objective is to maintain an open-centred bush, with the leaders of the main branches growing upwards and outwards. Many gooseberry varieties have a drooping habit, so the leaders are usually pruned to buds facing inwards or upwards, or back to more upright laterals, to maintain an erect compact form.

Prune each branch leader by half, cutting to a bud or lateral, whichever is necessary. Shoots crowding and growing over the centre must be cut back to about 2.5 cm (1 in). Remove any suckers around the base and shoots growing from the main stem below the head.

Repeat this formative pruning each winter for the next two years, or longer if necessary, until a strong, well-balanced head has been formed and the bush has started to crop.

Pruning established bushes If bullfinches are troublesome and the bushes are not netted, delay pruning until the spring, when it can be seen which buds are alive.

The bush is spur-pruned, and pruned hard, if large dessert fruits are required; less so if smaller fruits are needed for cooking or freezing.

Prune the leaders by half, to a bud facing in the required growth direction. If the branch is too spreading, prune to a suitable upright lateral, which will then become the new leader. The laterals (the previous summer's growth) are cut back to two buds where large berries are wanted or to three or four buds for cooking fruits.

Cut out weak, dead and diseased wood, and any growth crowding the centre. As the bush ages it will be necessary to thin out some of the older wood which has become congested and unproduc-

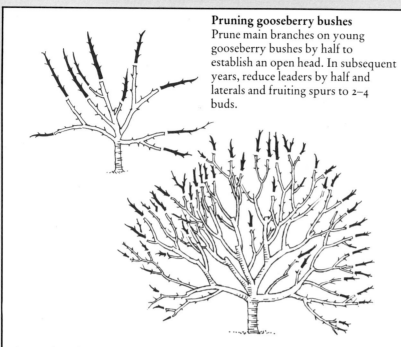

Pruning gooseberry bushes
Prune main branches on young gooseberry bushes by half to establish an open head. In subsequent years, reduce leaders by half and laterals and fruiting spurs to 2–4 buds.

tive and to leave vigorous young shoots to replace them.

Planting and pruning gooseberry cordons The wire-fence system, including cane supports, planting and pruning, is the same as for red currants, except that the less vigorous gooseberry should be planted 30 cm (1 ft) apart for a single cordon and 60 cm (2 ft) for a double cordon.

The Worcesterberry *(Ribes divaricatum)* Although a different species, with a growth habit and leaves strongly resembling the gooseberry, this soft fruit is more vigorous and very thorny. For cultural purposes, treat it in exactly the same way as the gooseberry.

Planting raspberries The initial ground preparation and trenching (see October) can be carried out at planting time if necessary. If more than one row is planted, the rows should run north to south to prevent excessive shading of one row by another.

Raspberries need support to prevent the canes bowing over and breaking off under the weight of the fruit. There are various ways to achieve this, the two most widely used being the single wire and the parallel wire fence systems. Of the two, the single wire fence is the better because it takes up less room, the canes are held secure and get plenty of light and air, and picking is easy.

Nevertheless, some growers prefer parallel wires because no individual tying of the canes is required; this system is obviously not advisable in a windy situation. It is easiest to erect the fence at planting but it can be done at any time during the first year.

Single wire fence This consists of horizontal wires stretched taut at 75 cm, 1 m and 1.7 m (2½ ft, 3½ ft and 5½ ft) from the ground and held by posts spaced 3.6–4.5 m (12–15 ft) apart. The posts are 2.3 m (7½ ft) long, driven 45 cm (1½ ft) deep and the wire should be galvanized, gauge 14.

Parallel wires system This consists of two sets of parallel wires spaced 60 cm (2 ft) apart at 90 cm (3 ft) and 1.5 m (5 ft) from the ground. Drive in 2 m (6½ ft) posts spaced 3.6–4.5 m (12–15 ft) apart, 45 cm (1½ ft) deep, and fix 5 cm sq (2 in sq), 75 cm (2½ ft) long battens to the posts as T pieces to hold the wires. Cross ties of wire are also necessary every 60 cm (2 ft) on both sets to prevent the canes falling over in the row.

Planting and spacing Space raspberry canes 38–45 cm (15–18 in) apart in the row, with the rows 1.8 m (6 ft) apart.

Plant the canes shallowly, about 8 cm (3 in) deep, and spread the roots out well. Over-deep planting will inhibit the production of new canes from the root system.

Next, cut the canes to a bud at 23–30 cm (9–12 in) from the ground. This will mean foregoing a first summer crop, but will help plants to become established and to produce strong new canes in the first and subsequent summers.

Finally, mulch with a 2.5 cm (1 in) layer of peat, or a 5 cm (2 in) layer of well-rotted manure or compost, over a continuous band 15 cm (6 in) wide along each side of the row.

Autumn-fruiting raspberries These raspberries bear their fruit at the top of the current season's canes, extending over 30–45 cm (1–1½ ft). The pruning of the established plants differs from that of ordinary raspberries in that *all* the canes are pruned down to ground level in February.

Most of the cultural treatment is the same, including soil preparation, spacing, mulching and pruning at planting time. The canes are cut down initially to 23 cm (9 in). However, as the canes are not so tall and do not grow for longer than one year, they can be allowed to grow a little closer – 5 cm (2 in). They are most easily grown between parallel wires, as described under ordinary raspberries.

Blackberries and hybrid berries
Blackberries and hybrid berries are cane fruits with a rambling habit. Like the raspberry, they need some kind of support to hold the canes clear of the ground. They are ornamental as well as utilitarian plants, suitable for growing over pergolas and archways and against walls and fences.

Out in the open, brambles (as they are collectively called) are best grown on a wire fence and a training system is used to keep the plants manageable and tidy.

Support system Various materials can be used, but a system of wooden posts and galvanized fencing-wire is probably the cheapest and simplest to erect. Use wooden posts 2.4 m (8 ft) long, with 8 cm (3 in) diameter tops (peeled, pointed and thoroughly impregnated with wood preservative) and 10 gauge galvanized wire. Space the posts 3.6 m (12 ft) apart, driving them 45 cm (1½ ft) into the ground.

For runs longer than 3.6 m (12 ft) strut the end posts for extra stability and fit straining bolts at one end to draw the wires taut. Use wire staples on the intermediate posts to hold the wires. Altogether, four wires are needed, spaced 90 cm, 1.2 m, 1.5 m and 1.8 m apart (3 ft, 4 ft, 5 ft and 6 ft).

Spacing Nurserymen usually supply one-year-old rooted tips. Vigorous varieties, such as the blackberries 'Oregon Thornless', 'Himalaya Giant' and 'Bedford Giant', need spacing 3.6 m (12 ft) apart on light to medium soil, but 4.5 m (15 ft) on very fertile soil. Hybrid berries should be spaced 3–3.6 m (10–12 ft) apart. Allow 1.8 m (6 ft) between rows.

Soil preparation, planting and initial pruning Complete the initial soil preparation, if not done in October. Just before planting, fork in a compound fertilizer, such as Growmore, at each planting site. A suitable rate is 100 g per sq m (3 oz per sq yd).

Plant not more than 8 cm (3 in) deep, so as not to inhibit the production of new canes. Spread the roots out well and firm the soil gently around them. After planting, prune the canes to 25 cm (10 in) above the ground.

Finally, mulch with a layer of peat, compost or well-rotted manure, about 2.5–5 cm (1–2 in) deep over a radius of 23 cm (9 in).

High bush blueberries This heathland plant will thrive and crop well only in very acid soil. Ideally, it should have a light, sandy soil with a pH between 4.0 and 5.5. It will not thrive in neutral or alkaline soils. Usually, two- or three-year-old plants, container-grown, are supplied by the nurseryman.

Soil preparation It is essential that the rooting medium has an acid, highly organic content. Before planting, mix into the top 23 cm (9 in) a generous quantity of peat or acid leaf-mould. If the soil is very heavy, add sharp sand to help lighten it; spread an 8 cm (3 in) layer over the area and fork it in.

Finally, rake in hoof and horn at 130 g per sq m (4 oz per sq yd) and sulphate of potash at 20 g per sq m (¾ oz per sq yd).

Spacing and planting The blueberry is grown as a stooled bush. Set the plants at 1.5 m × 1.5 m (5 ft × 5 ft) spacings.

Carefully knock each plant out of its container, without breaking the rootball, then gently free and comb outwards some of the outer roots. Spread these out in the planting hole and, while filling in, ensure that the rootball is surrounded by a roughly 50/50 mixture of peat and soil.

Finally, mulch each bush with a 5 cm (2 in) layer of peat, sawdust, pulverized bark or pine needles over a radius of 45 cm (1½ ft). You must not carry out any pruning at this stage.

TRAINING RASPBERRIES

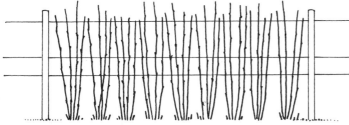

Tie raspberry canes to single wires between posts; cut out fruited canes at soil level, allowing up to 8 new canes to develop on each plant.

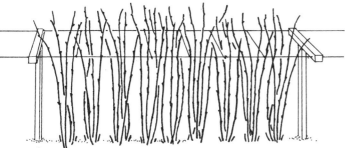

Alternatively, grow raspberries on the parallel wires system, 60 cm (2 ft) apart in the rows and secured to stout posts and cross battens.

Tree fruits: formative pruning
Young bush, standard and spindle-bush apple and pear trees are pruned in winter, both at planting time and for several winters afterwards, until a framework of branches has been built up that is sufficiently strong to bear heavy crops from then on. This formative pruning is best carried out in the early part of the winter, when the growth response to the cuts next spring and summer will be stronger.

Although stone fruits, such as cherries and plums, are planted in the winter, they are not formatively pruned until March to reduce the risk of silver leaf disease.

Bush trees

One-year-old maiden trees The objective in pruning is to create an open-centred, goblet-shaped bush tree on a clean trunk 45–60 cm (1½–2 ft) long.

There are two types of one-year-olds – those without side-shoots (whips) and those with side-shoots (feathered maidens). Of the two, the feathered maiden is the better choice because the side-shoots, if suitably placed, can be used as primary branches. This saves a year in the formative pruning.

Pruning a one-year-old without side-shoots At planting time, cut the maiden to a bud at about 60 cm (2 ft) for a dwarf bush and at about 75 cm (2½ ft) for a bush, ensuring that there are not less than three good buds beneath it. Make a sloping cut away from the bud.

This heading back will stimulate the top buds to grow in the following summer to form the primary branches. Paint the cuts with a wound paint.

Pruning a feathered maiden Cut back the main stem to a lateral at about 60 cm (2 ft) for a dwarf bush or 75 cm (2½ ft) for a bush, ensuring that there are three or four well-placed laterals just beneath the cut. Remove the remain-der flush with the main stem and prune the retained laterals by about two thirds, each to an outward-facing bud. Protect the cuts with a wound paint.

Pruning a two-year-old tree Choose three or four strong laterals at the top to form the primary branches. Select those that are well placed and form a wide angle with the main trunk, but nevertheless grow upwards and outwards.

Sometimes, the topmost shoot is too upright, because it is naturally dominant. In this case, cut it out, provided there are alternative leaders. Failing this, tie it down to an angle of 30 degrees for one growing season, by which time it should have set at the desired angle.

Remove all the unwanted laterals flush with the main trunk and protect the cuts. Prune the retained laterals (primary branches) by two thirds if they are weak, or by one half if they are strong,

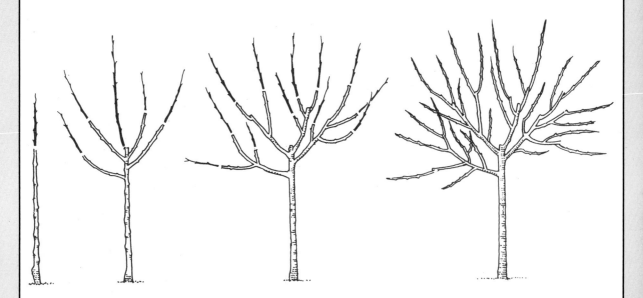

Pruning bush fruit trees
Formative pruning begins with maiden trees, headed back at planting time to strong buds. The following year, cut out the upright leader and reduce main branches by half. The next year, allow strong, well-balanced laterals to develop, pruning them by half. Thereafter, lightly tip all main branches, to encourage the formation of fruiting spurs and extension shoots.

cutting to an outward-facing bud. (If trees were feathered maidens in their first winter, treat them as three-year-olds in their second winter.)

Pruning a three-year-old bush tree Select between two and four more, widely-spaced and well-placed strong laterals to form secondary branches. The framework should now consist of about six to eight branches, forming the basic head of the tree. Cut these by about one half to two thirds, depending on their vigour, to a bud facing in the required growth direction.

Prune any remaining laterals not needed as branches, to about four buds. These will eventually form spurs. However, remove entirely any laterals crowding and crossing the centre. Remember, also, that the technique of tying down strong, upright laterals can be practised if they can usefully fill a gap in the tree's framework.

Pruning a four-year-old bush tree With the tree now beginning to bear reasonably well, the pruning should be moderate unless growth is weak and the stimulus of hard pruning is needed.

Lightly tip the leaders to encourage extension growth and the production of more side-shoots which will, if needed, eventually form spur systems or secondary branches. From now on, winter prune the tree as an established bush. (See December.)

Standard apples and pears Most are grafted on to vigorous rootstocks and are therefore unsuitable for small gardens. However, if they are planted in lawns – perhaps as shade trees – or in a large orchard, prune them in exactly the same way as a bush apple.

Other tasks Pick the last of the very late apple varieties, such as 'Sturmer Pippin', 'Granny Smith' and 'D'Arcy Spice'.

Check the fruit store and remove any rotting fruits to prevent the trouble spreading.

Inspect the fruit cage to ensure that it is proof against bullfinches, but remove the roof netting whenever heavy snowfalls are forecast.

Check tree ties and stakes. The ties should be firm but not constricting.

DECEMBER

Methods of pruning There are three basic methods of winter pruning a spur-bearing tree, all or any of which can be applied as circumstances dictate. The three methods are regulated, spur and renewal.

Regulated pruning This is the most straightforward method and the one which should generally be used. It quickly brings the tree into bearing, without a great deal of complicated pruning.

Regulated pruning consists of removing diseased, crowded and crossing branches and of removing or shortening laterals where there is insufficient space or where they are competing with the branch leaders.

The centre of the tree is kept open but not completely devoid of growth. If the tree has a drooping or spreading habit, some laterals are left at or near the centre to become replacement branches. In later years it may be necessary to cut back to these if the original branches become too low or spreading.

Branches which rub against each other or cross the centre are shortened or removed. Laterals on the outside of the tree are left unpruned, provided there is space, so that they can develop fruit buds along their full length in the following year.

In later years the size of fruit on trees so pruned may become too small, and the tree lacking in new growth and vigour. If this occurs it is necessary to prune harder by thinning out some of the fruiting laterals, shortening some of the spur systems and practising some renewal pruning.

Spur-pruning (Pruning to form spurs.) This is based on the principle that spur-bearing varieties develop fruit buds on two-year-old wood and form spur systems on the older wood.

Spur-pruning consists of cutting back the young laterals (shoots made in the previous year) to between four and ten buds. The more vigorous the tree, the longer the length of lateral left.

In the second year, the lower buds on the pruned lateral should have developed into fruit buds, while the topmost buds (usually two or three) have grown into shoots. The gardener must then decide whether to extend this 'induced spur' by spur-pruning the new shoots, as in the first year, or to stop it by cutting back to a fruit bud on the wood that is now two years old. If there is room, the spur can be extended; if not, it should be stopped.

If you are uncertain whether to 'cut short or to cut long', the effect of previous years' spur pruning should be studied. Or experiment with a variety of cuts and observe, in due course, which system has produced the most fruit buds and then adopt it in future years.

Renewal pruning (Pruning to obtain new growth.) Renewal pruning is applied when new growth is needed – for example, where the old wood has become unproductive and needs replacing. It relies on the principle that dormant basal buds within the wood can be stimulated into growth by hard pruning.

Renewal pruning is carried out on wood up to and including growth that is three years old. It is not normally practised on older wood, because of the large wounds such cuts would make.

It consists of cutting out the wood, leaving a stub 2.5 cm (1 in) long, by making a long, sloping cut on the underside. In the following summer, new growth will spring from the stub and may be used to form a new branch or spur if necessary.

Renewal pruning is regularly practised on spindlebush trees.

Applying the principles With a young tree, it will be necessary for a number of years after the initial, formative pruning to continue pruning the branch leaders. Cut by a quarter to a third, pruning to a bud facing in the required growth direction. This is usually outwards, but with a drooping branch it will be upwards. If necessary, cut back to an upright lateral, which then becomes the new leader.

The purpose of all this is to obtain strong extension growth and stout new side-branches. Cut short or remove laterals competing with the leaders. Spur-prune laterals lower down the branch. Later, as the tree becomes bigger, prune the branch leaders lightly, or not at all. Similarly, the laterals may be spur-pruned or left unpruned.

With an old tree it may be necessary to thin out fairly large limbs which are rubbing, too close or crowding the centre. (See January.) Remove the branch, either back to its point of origin or to a replacement branch.

The replacement branch must be large enough to take up the vigour; as a reliable guide it should be not less than one third the diameter of the removed limb. Do not leave a stub which leads to 'die-back'.

Remove heavy branches in stages to lessen the weight. When making the final cut, undercut first to avoid any risk of tearing the bark as the limb falls.

Saw close to, but not absolutely flush with, the main trunk. Cutting flush makes too large a wound and removes healing tissue. Pare the edges of the cut smooth with a knife, then paint with a proprietary wound paint. Apply a second coat fourteen days later.

Pruning a 'tip bearer' A tree of this type is best pruned on the regulated system, to ensure that the tree does not become overcrowded, so assisting air movement and light.

Most of the young laterals should be left unpruned, because they carry fruit buds at their tips. Nevertheless, vigorous shoots longer than 23 cm (9 in) should be pruned by half their length, cutting to a bud. While this will result in some loss of fruit buds, it will stimulate the pruned shoots to produce more tip-bearing shoots during the following summer.

Similarly, all branch leaders should be pruned. This is to obtain extension growth, more laterals and to prevent long stretches of bare wood.

In later years some fruit-bud thinning may be necessary if too many small fruits are being produced.

Pruning a spindlebush (from year three onwards) A spindlebush is pruned on the renewal system, to ensure a continual supply of good cropping wood.

Keep the branches at the top shorter than those below, so maintaining a cone shape, and keep the height of the tree at about 1.8–2.1 m (6–7 ft). Keep the side branches as near to horizontal as possible by tying them down and by selective pruning. The weight of fruit on the branches also helps to keep the branches down.

In practice, this means removing or tying down strong-growing, upright laterals at the top of the tree that are competing with the leader and spoiling the cone shape. Whenever necessary, maintain the height of 1.8–2.1 m (6–7 ft) by cutting the central leader back to a weaker side-branch or lateral lower down. Tie this 'replacement' upwards to a supporting stake.

The lowest three or four main branches are more or less permanent, but prune the growth that they carry on a renewal basis. The branches above are also replaced by renewal pruning whenever necessary – for example, if they have become too crowded, unproductive or are casting too much shade on the branches below.

Old or neglected cordons and espaliers Now is a good time to renovate neglected cordons, espaliers and other trained forms of apples and pears, bringing them back into shape by hard pruning. Simplify complicated and congested spur-systems by shortening, if necessary removing them altogether. Thereafter, restrict pruning to the summer.

Planting Continue to plant bush, cane and tree fruits, provided soil conditions are favourable. Try to complete this before the end of the year while the ground is still relatively warm.

Burning Burn all prunings and store the ash in a dry place. It provides a useful supply of potash and lime.

Figs Protect all wall-grown fig trees well before the end of the month.

Fruit store Examine the fruits in store regularly and remove all fruits showing any signs of decay.

Dwarf conifers are popular as lawn specimen trees in small gardens, in rockeries and among heather plantings. Slow-growing rather than true miniatures, they take many years to outgrow their allotted space.

House plants with attractive variegated foliage can be grouped together to good effect. This collection includes the eponymous indoor specimen – the spider plant (*chlorophytum*).

Town dwellers without a garden need not forfeit the pleasure of growing plants if they have a balcony. Pots and tubs of colourful flowering plants will hide an ugly city view.

The lawn forms the centrepiece of most gardens. A great deal of care and attention has gone into producing this particularly fine result.

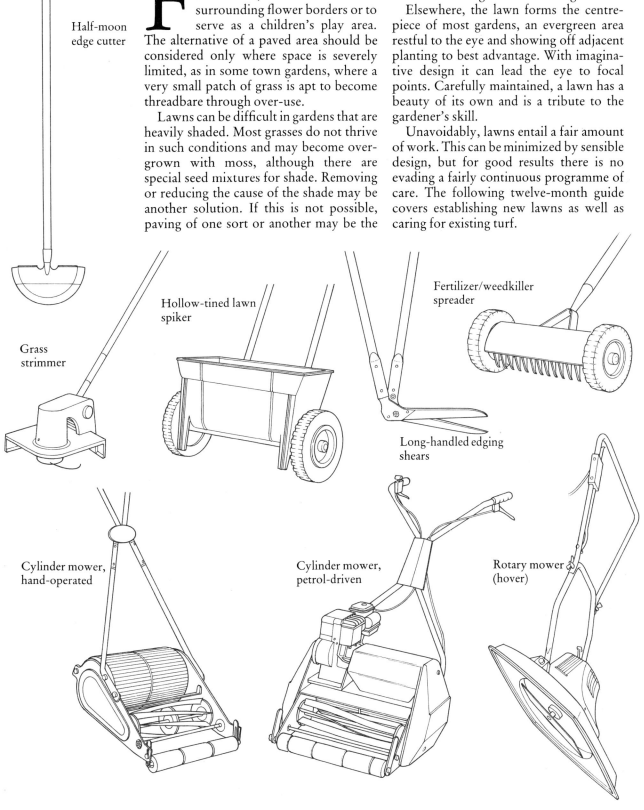

Half-moon
edge cutter

Few gardens are without a lawn of some kind, whether to set off surrounding flower borders or to serve as a children's play area. The alternative of a paved area should be considered only where space is severely limited, as in some town gardens, where a very small patch of grass is apt to become threadbare through over-use.

Lawns can be difficult in gardens that are heavily shaded. Most grasses do not thrive in such conditions and may become over-grown with moss, although there are special seed mixtures for shade. Removing or reducing the cause of the shade may be another solution. If this is not possible, paving of one sort or another may be the answer, thus providing a place for access, as well as for sitting and entertaining.

Elsewhere, the lawn forms the centre-piece of most gardens, an evergreen area restful to the eye and showing off adjacent planting to best advantage. With imagina-tive design it can lead the eye to focal points. Carefully maintained, a lawn has a beauty of its own and is a tribute to the gardener's skill.

Unavoidably, lawns entail a fair amount of work. This can be minimized by sensible design, but for good results there is no evading a fairly continuous programme of care. The following twelve-month guide covers establishing new lawns as well as caring for existing turf.

Hollow-tined lawn
spiker

Fertilizer/weedkiller
spreader

Grass
strimmer

Long-handled edging
shears

Cylinder mower,
hand-operated

Cylinder mower,
petrol-driven

Rotary mower
(hover)

JANUARY

New lawns Turves may be laid on prepared ground whenever weather conditions allow. The soil should be neither frozen nor sticky.

Routine jobs Remove any dead leaves, twigs or other debris from the lawn.

Overhaul your mower; or have the job done by a specialist. There is likely to be a delay if left until the mowing season.

If water remains on the lawn surface for some time after rain, check that the outlets of any drains are not blocked. If these are clear, it may be possible to locate the drains and check at intervals for blockages caused by roots or other debris. If there is no drainage system, make plans to put such work in hand.

FEBRUARY

New lawns Try to complete turf-laying by the end of this month. The next suitable time is October, although it is possible to lay turves during the spring and even the summer if you are prepared to irrigate during dry weather.

Towards the end of the month, soil conditions permitting, start preparing the site if you plan to sow grass seed in April or May. If the ground was dug in November or December, a pronged cultivator will break down any remaining lumps.

The decision whether to sow or turf a new lawn is not always easy. Site preparation should be carried out with the same thoroughness in each case. (See July and September.)

Successful seed-sowing has an element of chance about it, for it depends to an extent on good weather – that is, it must be neither too wet nor too dry. Birds and cats are a hazard, too.

Turf gives an 'instant' lawn, but it is more expensive. Good quality turf is often difficult to obtain, while laying it requires time, effort and considerable care.

Routine jobs Scatter worm casts periodically, using a besom or a long, thin bamboo cane. If worms are particularly troublesome, control them by watering the turf with chlordane. This chemical kills the worms beneath the surface and provides control for about a year.

Check for signs of unhealthy turf.

If the weather is mild and settled, moss-killer may be applied late in the month. Otherwise, wait until March.

Choosing a mower With grass-cutting due to start in a few weeks, now is a good time to consider buying a new mower if your present machine needs replacing.

The basic choice is between cylinder mowers and rotary mowers. The former shear the grass, scissor-fashion, between a series of curved, moving blades and a static blade positioned beneath them. Rotary mowers work with a scythe-like action, having two or more blades that depend on their high speed to slash the grass rather than shear it.

Both hover mowers and wheeled rotary grass-cutters work on exactly the same principle.

The narrow, spiral blades of a cylinder mower are arranged around a central, horizontal shaft. The fineness of cut is related to the number of blades on the cylinder and to the gear ratio. The greater the number of blades, the more cuts the mower gives per yard of travel – and so the neater the trim.

For instance, a mower with four blades gives 30–40 cuts per metre (yd) whereas twelve blades may give 140–150 cuts per metre (yd) – a finish fit for a bowling green.

The blades of a rotary mower take the form of a bar with sharpened edges, or small individual blades may be attached to a rotating disc. In both cases they move at high speed under a protective canopy.

Rotary mowers give quite a neat finish, and have the advantage that they can cut grass that is considerably overgrown. They are particularly useful where areas of rough grass require occasional mowing, and they will also maintain lawns to a reasonable standard.

However, the scissor-like action of a cylinder mower does give a superior finish and they are to be preferred for all areas of really fine ornamental turf.

Whatever the type of mower, width of cut is an important consideration. The wider the cut, the less time is needed to mow a given area. Usually a 30–35 cm (12–14 in) width of cut is satisfactory for the smaller sizes of lawn.

As a rough guide, it will take about thirty minutes to cut approximately 400 sq m (500 sq yds) with a 30 cm (1 ft) mower, 800 sq m (1000 yds) with a 40 cm (16 in) mower, or 1200 sq m (1500 sq yds) with a 60 cm (2 ft) mower.

MARCH

Mowing This month usually sees the start of the mowing season. Choose a day when the grass is dry and the weather mild.

Check first for worm casts on the surface. Large numbers of casts will blunt the mower blades and will also look unsightly after being flattened by the mower wheels or roller. Weeds may soon grow on them. If left until fairly dry and crumbly, they can be scattered with a besom or a flexible cane. Although worm activity can improve the drainage of heavy soil, a worm-killer (chlordane) may have to be applied if casts are numerous.

Roll the lawn before mowing if it has been lifted by frost. Mow with the blades set high.

Collecting the clippings It saves time not to collect the clippings, but on the whole it is much better to do so. If left, the lawn gradually deteriorates due to clogging and loss of air to the roots.

The least harm results from short mowings left during dry weather on an alkaline soil. If you decide not to collect the clippings for a while, check frequently to see whether they are building up excessively. If they are, loosen them with a wire rake and collect them. Also, keep the lawn weed-free. Short clippings of creeping weeds, such as speedwell, may be scattered widely and they will root readily in moist soil.

Feeding lawns Regular close mowing of lawns, which restricts the natural development of the grasses, has a weakening effect. Nutrients taken up from the soil by the grass are removed when the mowings are collected, and to compensate for this lawns should be fed at least once annually.

Lawns that are never fed will usually decline in health and vigour, weak turf being more susceptible to disease and also to moss and weed infestation. Undernourished lawns are less drought-resistant and more likely to be damaged by heavy use. Perhaps the only disadvantage of feeding is that it increases the rate of growth, necessitating more frequent mowing.

When to feed The best time to apply a lawn fertilizer is in early spring when the grass is beginning to grow freely. The nutrients will then be used at once. In southern Britain this is usually late March; in northern Britain, early April. However, if weather conditions are unsuitable, feeding can be delayed for two or three weeks.

A single annual dressing of a fertilizer containing nitrogen, phosphate and potash will supply the lawn's phosphate and potash needs for a season. To maintain vigour and a good colour it may be necessary to give additional nitrogen in late spring and early summer, unless the original dressing contained a slow-release type.

The simplest method is to use a proprietary lawn fertilizer formulated for spring and summer use. However, products vary considerably both in content and in cost. Some contain weed-killers; in others, the fertilizer is combined with a peat-based organic top-dressing. Both add to the cost of treating a lawn.

An analysis of about 5 to 7% nitrogen, 10 to 15% phosphate and 2 to 4% potash provides a suitable and economical balance of nutrients. Although less work is involved in applying a combined fertilizer/weedkiller, weed control may be more effective if both the grass and the weeds are growing vigorously, in response to feeding, before weedkiller is applied as a spray.

As the season progresses and the nitrogen is used up, the grass will decline in vigour and lose its spring freshness, life and colour. The extent to which this happens depends on the type of soil and the particular season. However, the turf can be revitalized by summer feeding in May

and July, provided it receives adequate rainfall or irrigation. It will then maintain its attractive appearance until the autumn, when growth slows down naturally with lower night temperatures.

Applying fertilizers If applying fertilizer by hand, mark out strips 90 cm (3 ft) wide, using canes and a garden line. Apply the product at half the recommended rate, working lengthways, then repeat the procedure working crossways. When using a fertilizer drill or distributor, the wheel-tracks serve as guide lines.

Avoid overlapping, as too-high concentrations of fertilizer can damage the turf. Where possible, spread matting or newspapers along the end of the lawn, turning on them rather than on the lawn itself.

APRIL

Mowing Increase the frequency of mowing to suit the speed at which the grass is growing. Both this and the height of cut have a major bearing on the quality of a lawn.

Turf is weakened if it is regularly mown closer than 5 mm (3⁄16 in), resulting in a build-up of moss and creeping weeds. The coarser grasses can soon become dominant as a result of irregular mowing or if the grass is not kept to 4 cm (1½ in) or below.

During the spring and summer, medium-quality lawns may be cut to a little over 12 mm (½ in), utility-type lawns to 2.5 cm (1 in) and well-nurtured, fine lawns to 5 mm (3⁄16 in). Cylinder mowers give a closer cut than do rotary or hover mowers.

During the autumn, when growth has slowed down or virtually ceased, raise the height of cut by 6 mm (¼ in). The same applies during a summer drought, when little growth will be made and slightly longer grass will help to prevent the surface from drying out. It also holds good in the unlikely event of a winter cut being needed.

Between April and August, when the grass is growing vigorously, mow frequently. Ideally, average lawns need cutting every three to five days, utility lawns every seven days and fine-quality turf every two or three days. However, few gardeners have the time for such frequent mowing. Reduce the frequency as the growth rate slows in September.

From October or early November onwards there will usually be little need for mowing – possibly an occasional light trim during a mild winter, or in the milder coastal areas.

Whenever possible, vary the pattern of mowing – alternately lengthways and crossways. This helps to reduce localized compaction caused by a fixed mowing pattern and is more effective in keeping coarser grasses and creeping weeds in check.

Feeding In the colder and more northerly parts of the country, give a spring feed during the early or middle part of the month. (See March.) This also applies elsewhere if the job was not done last month.

Weeds and coarse grasses If there are weeds in the lawn, apply a selective weedkiller as soon as the fertilizer has stimulated both the grass and the weeds into vigorous growth.

Check the lawn for coarse grasses. They must be removed by hand as there is no weedkiller sufficiently selective to kill them while leaving the finer grasses unharmed. Use a hand fork or a potato fork, depending on the size of the clumps or tufts.

After removing coarse grasses, carefully refirm the soil, adding a little where necessary to restore a level surface. If bare or thin patches are left, scatter grass seeds over them and rake lightly. Mark with canes so that the seeds are not disturbed when next you mow.

Repairing edges Where an unsupported lawn edge has crumbled, cut out a square of turf containing the damaged section and turn it through 180 degrees to give a new, firm edge. Make good the damaged patch with ordinary soil, firm it lightly and re-seed.

New lawns Check the joints and levels of recently-laid turves. Top-dress with fine soil to fill any slight hollows or to make good any open joints.

New lawns may be sown towards the end of the month, or in early May, when weather and soil conditions allow.

MAY

Routine jobs Early in the month, adjust the mower to its summer cutting height and start to mow more frequently.

Some four to six weeks after the April weedkiller treatment, give a further application to any surviving weeds. Apply moss-killer, if necessary.

Watering Strong, healthy, deep-rooted turf is resistant to drought, whereas neglected turf may soon show signs of distress. First indications are a general dullness and blueness, with the grass losing its resilience. Growth ceases and, if not watered, the leaves will soon shrivel and turn brown and the roots wither and die.

The length of time between the last appreciable rainfall and the first signs of drought depends on the time of year, the condition of the turf and the type of soil. Sandy soils dry out more rapidly than heavy soils. They generally need watering about once a week.

At the first signs of drought, irrigate to wet the soil thoroughly to a depth of at least 15 cm (6 in). Frequent light waterings are harmful. Carefully bore a test hole to see how long this takes, using this as a guide for subsequent waterings. If water soon gathers on the surface, turn the water off and allow it to soak in before continuing.

To help the grass retain its colour and keep growing strongly, apply a light dressing of a nitrogenous fertilizer towards the end of the month. Sulphate of ammonia applied at ½–1 tablespoon per sq m (sq yd) is effective.

To ensure even distribution and to guard against damage from scorch, mix the fertilizer first with sandy soil at the rate of 100–125 g per sq m (4 oz per sq yd). Apply during cool, damp weather, not while it is hot and dry.

New lawns Complete the sowing of new lawns early in the month.

JUNE

Routine jobs Mow frequently, scarifying the surface lightly before mowing if creeping weeds are troublesome.

Check regularly for signs of drought during dry periods, irrigating when necessary. Also check for compacted areas and heavy wear. Remedy by spiking deeply, followed by a light top-dressing of soil and thorough irrigation.

New lawns If you are planning to make a new lawn during the autumn, you will need to start preparing the site next month. In the meantime, it would be as well to give some thought to its position and design.

Where possible, it should be in a sunny part of the garden. Grass is difficult to establish and maintain in deep shade.

Try to keep the shape of the lawn simple, avoiding sharp angles and tight curves. These, along with small, scattered flower beds, make for difficult mowing. Separate beds also entail a good deal of tedious edge trimming.

Grass paths and narrow access points are another source of difficulty, for the surface will soon deteriorate with frequent use. If either is unavoidable, place stepping stones at strategic points.

JULY

Routine jobs Under normal conditions mow regularly – but do so less frequently, and with the blades set higher, during dry weather if you are unable to irrigate.

Feed again lightly with a nitrogenous fertilizer.

If necessary, give a third application of weedkiller.

New lawns The best season for both sowing and turfing is approaching, and towards the end of this month is the time to start preparing the site. Completing the initial work will give the soil time to settle, a considerable aid in securing and maintaining a level surface.

The first steps are to clear away rubble, kill perennial weeds and check the drainage. Then adjust the overall level, if necessary, and either dig or cultivate the soil.

Levels and soil depth A gently sloping or undulating lawn can be quite attractive, but an uneven surface is not. If significant hill-

ocks or hollows have to be corrected, first move the topsoil to one side, then level the subsoil and, finally, replace the topsoil. This can represent a great deal of work, but there is no simple alternative.

Ideally, there should be at least 23 cm (9 in) of good topsoil, but earth-moving by builders may leave a new garden either with little topsoil or with one of varying depth.

Try to achieve a uniform depth. Lacking this, the grass may grow unevenly, giving the lawn a patchy appearance. If there is less than 15 cm (6 in), add topsoil to bring it up to at least this depth.

Soil preparation Dig the soil, or turn it with a powered cultivator, at the same time working in some organic matter such as well-rotted manure, leaf-mould or peat. Heavy clay soils, chalk and the lighter, sandy soils will all benefit from a dressing of about 7 kg per sq m (14 lb per sq yd). The texture and surface drainage of clay soils will also be improved by adding sharp grit or coarse, gritty sand.

Final preparation of the soil must wait until a short time before sowing or turfing.

AUGUST

Routine jobs Keep mowing regularly, varying the blade height and the frequency of mowing to match the growth rate. If you return from holiday to find an overgrown lawn, raise the blades for the first cut and lower them gradually to their normal height over the next week or two.

A final summer feed may be given, if necessary, about mid-month. Do not apply nitrogenous summer feeds after the end of

August. Autumn applications may encourage lush growth just as the weather becomes cooler, leaving the grass more susceptible to disease should the autumn be wet.

Complete weedkilling by the end of the month. Although later treatments can be attempted, they may be less effective as growth slows in the autumn.

New lawns In colder areas, lawn seed may be sown during the second half of the month in preference to September.

SEPTEMBER

Mowing With the rate of growth slowing, towards the end of the month the blades should be raised by a little over 6 mm (¼ in) in order to leave the grass slightly longer. Disperse worm casts before mowing.

New lawns This is the ideal month to sow new lawns in the milder parts of the country. If possible, do this during cool, settled weather, for preference before the middle of the month.

Soil preparation Start the final soil preparations when the soil is fairly dry, breaking down any clods with a garden fork or the back of a garden rake.

Next, the soil will need firming, either with a roller or by treading. The latter, which is the better method for small areas, involves taking short, overlapping steps, with one's weight mainly over the heels. Follow this by raking and further treading until the surface is level and uniformly firm.

Unless the site has been manured or dressed with fertilizer quite recently, apply a balanced mixture a few days before you sow. This could consist of 1 tablespoon sulphate of ammonia, 2 tablespoons superphosphate, ½ tablespoon

SOWING A NEW LAWN

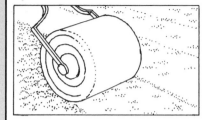

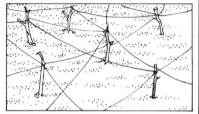

1 Firm the seed bed for a new lawn by rolling (top); rake in to produce a fine tilth.

2 Divide the plot into strips and sow seeds, half crossways, half lengthways.

3 Rake bed lightly (top) and protect against birds with criss-crossed thread.

sulphate of potash – all amounts per sq m or yd.

Seed mixtures The most satisfactory choice for fine ornamental lawns is a mixture of 80% *Festuca rubra* var. *commutata* (Chewing fescue) and 20% *Agrostis tenuis* (browntop bent). Together, these will form a fine-bladed, dense, compact turf tolerant of close mowing.

This combination forms the basis of most fine lawn mixtures, for it will grow well in a wide range of soils. *Festuca rubra* ssp. *rubra* (creeping red fescue) which tolerates both wet and dry conditions, is sometimes included.

Hard-wearing mixtures for utility lawns include dwarf, leafy strains of *Lolium perenne* (perennial rye grass) a coarser, hard-wearing grass, together with *Poa pratensis* (smooth-stalked meadow grass). Neither of these likes close mowing.

All grasses grow reasonably well in light shade. Some seedsmen supply mixtures for deeper shade, perhaps under trees, but the grasses are unlikely to survive for long if close-mown. If longer grass is unacceptable in the shaded area, plant shade-tolerant ground-cover plants instead.

Sowing Seed may be sown by hand or with a fertilizer drill designed for this dual function. For more even distribution, sow half the seed lengthways, half crossways. When hand-sowing, sow in strips a metre or a yard wide, using a line and marker canes.

After sowing, rake over the seedbed lightly so that the seeds are just below the surface. If buried deeply, the seeds may not germinate. Do not roll after raking. Irrigate gently but thoroughly if no rain falls and the surface of the seedbed begins to dry.

Birds may be troublesome, dust-bathing in the loose soil or eating the seeds. Before either happens, protect the area with brushwood or with black thread criss-crossed 8–10 cm (3–4 in) above the surface.

If the surface soil is lifted slightly by the germinating seeds, roll lightly when the grass is about 5 cm (2 in) high. Give a light first cut two or three days later with a sharp-bladed mower. If the mower has a removable front roller, take it off first. Remove only 12 mm (½ in) of grass.

Dealing with lawn problems

Moss Check early in the month for signs of moss. Although traces can be found in most established lawns, it is necessary to use a moss-killer if a considerable amount is present.

There are a number of proprietary moss-killers, including lawn sand. If the latter contains sulphate of ammonia, however, it is better avoided at this time of year, because of the stimulus it gives to leaf growth. Rake out the dead moss after a week or two.

Thatch Between the roots and the foliage of all established lawns there is a layer of fibrous organic material, some living and some dead. This consists of stems, stolons, rhizomes, decomposing mowings and other debris, an accumulation that goes under the collective name of 'thatch'. On acid soils, where bacterial activity is low, it may accumulate to form a deep, carpet-like 'pile'.

Routine raking, together with the use of a grass-box on the mower, will keep thatch in check in most cases. Indeed, in moderation it acts as a mulch, keeping the surface moist and giving a resilience to the turf. Further, it helps to protect it against wear.

However, if the thatch is thicker than about 12 mm (½ in) it may impede the penetration of moisture. As a result, prolonged rain or watering may be needed to penetrate through to the soil. Fertilizers are slower to reach the roots, and the turf may become less resistant to drought and disease.

A spring-tine rake or a long-handled scarifying tool will deal effectively with thatch. Alternatively, small electric scarifiers can be purchased or hired. Handle them with care, for if used too vigorously they can cause serious damage to the turf.

Add the rakings to the compost heap, but do this in fairly small quantities, well mixed with other materials.

Thatch is most likely to be a problem on acid soils or where drainage is poor. Here, bacterial activity is low and organic matter decays slowly.

Where thatch builds up rapidly, improve the drainage, if necessary, by laying land-drains in late October or November, when regular mowing has ended. If the soil is strongly acid (below pH 5) apply a light dressing of calcium carbonate (ground chalk or ground limestone) during the winter, at up to 60 g per sq m (2 oz per sq yd) on light, sandy soils, and up to 125 g per sq m (4 oz per sq yd) on heavy soils.

Where the soil is only moderately acid, regular light top-dressing in autumn with good quality loam may be enough to help the thatch decompose.

Compaction Many lawns suffer, to some degree, from compaction after a summer of use. This may be local – for example, where deck-chairs are placed or where the newsboy takes a short-cut across the lawn – or it may be more general, due to regular mowing with a heavy mower.

Among other effects, compaction impedes air movement through the soil, in extreme case killing the turf. Compaction can also impede moisture penetration and drainage, encouraging a build-up of moss and thatch during wet weather.

Compaction can be relieved by aeration. Spiking with a garden fork or a purpose-made tool may be carried out at any time during the spring and summer, repeating this every four or five weeks if the lawn is used a lot. Water thoroughly afterwards.

Drive the fork in for at least half its depth at regular, closely-spaced intervals. Light wheeled tools or hand tools that penetrate only 2.5–5 cm (1–2 in) can be useful for dealing with shallow compaction or surface capping, but tools that penetrate 8–15 cm (3–6 in) may be needed in cases where there is deeper compaction.

Powered aerators, including types with changeable tines and blades, are often available from hire firms.

The most difficult soil to aerate is heavy clay. For this, a hollow-tine fork or aerator is needed. Each insertion removes a plug or core of soil which is then expelled on to the surface. After brushing up the cores, top-dress with a sandy soil mixture, working it into the holes with a brush or a twiggy besom.

New roots will soon grow into the shafts of lighter-textured soil. The process can be repeated on heavier soils every third or fourth year; it has little value on light soil.

Top-dressing The main value of top-dressing, using a mixture of loam, sand and organic matter, is to achieve and maintain an even and level surface. It will eliminate minor unevenness that may come about during the year – for example, where children have played, or where the weight of a mower has magnified slight variations in the firmness of the surface.

On poorer soils, top-dressing will improve surface fertility, encouraging better rooting of desirable grasses, and so improving the density of the turf.

A good basic mixture is three parts sieved loam, six parts sand, and one part granulated peat (all parts by weight). The sand should be lime-free, if possible with a particle size of 2–5 mm (1/16–3/16 in). Sieved leaf-mould or well-decomposed garden compost may be used instead of peat, but do not use compost known to contain viable weed seeds.

On heavier soils, sand alone may be used. Peat may also be used on its own as a top-dressing, but too-frequent use of peat can build up a spongy surface, particularly on acid soils. This will dry out and become moisture-resistant during dry weather, and will hold excessive surface moisture during the winter, encouraging moss. Repeated heavy dressings of sand can create an unstable surface layer.

Mow the grass before applying a top-dressing, and do not be in a hurry to start if the grass is still growing vigorously. Wait, too, for settled, dry conditions.

Apply top-dressing materials by spreading or 'broadcasting' them with a shovel. An average dressing is about 2 kg per sq m (4 lb per sq yd), but this can be increased to 3–3.5 kg per sq m (6–7 lb per sq yd) where the ground is very irregular.

Distribute the dressing evenly, working the mixture into the turf with the back of a broad rake so that the blades of grass remain visible. Grasses which are completely covered may not survive, so do not attempt to correct major irregularities in a single season.

Once a true level has been achieved there is no need for regular top-dressing, though it can be given annually on poor soils.

Autumn feeding Under normal conditions, and where the lawn is strong and healthy, autumn feeding is not essential. However, if the turf has suffered from compaction or from summer drought – both conditions that damage the roots – it is worth applying a fertilizer dressing this month, after scarifying, aerating and spiking, but before top-dressing.

The purpose of an autumn lawn fertilizer is to encourage root growth, not leaf growth. It should therefore have only a low nitrogen content but a good level of phosphate and potash.

A suitable formula (all parts by weight) is: 25 parts superphosphate; 50 parts fine bonemeal; 15 parts sulphate of potash; 10 parts sandy soil.

Mix well, then apply at 60 g per sq m (2 oz per sq yd).

OCTOBER

Mowing With the speed of growth slowing down, set the mower to its winter height and continue mowing as necessary.

Ideally, and an hour or two before mowing, remove the early morning dew with a supple bamboo cane or switch and leave the grass to dry.

Routine jobs During fine weather, remove the dew daily, if possible, as this lessens the likelihood of disease. For the same reason, remove fallen leaves regularly.

Scarify, spike and top-dress if you were unable to do so in September, preferably early in the month.

Kill worms with chlordane if the casts become troublesome.

LAYING TURF

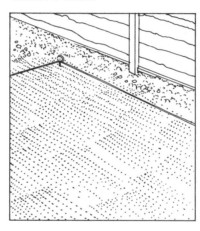

1 Rake and level plot in preparation for the turves.

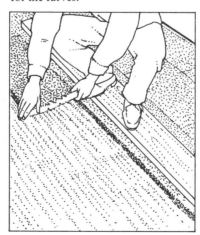

3 Work from a board across laid turves.

New lawns Although it is now past the best time for sowing a new lawn, the turf-laying season is just beginning. It continues, subject to weather and soil conditions, until about the end of February.

Buying turf Turves are a relatively expensive means of creating a lawn, so try to examine them before ordering and again when they are delivered. Sub-standard turves may be difficult to lay and may also contain both weeds and unsuitable grasses.

The most important points to look for are the quality of the

2 Lay turves from one edge of the area.

4 Firm lawn and work in top dressing.

grass, the soil and the roots. The grass should have a uniform appearance, with no broad-bladed, coarser types present. It should have been mown, for long, shaggy grass may hide defects.

The soil should be loamy, not light and sandy nor a heavy clay. A clay soil, in particular, could adversely affect the lawn later on.

The turves should have a good root system, with a reasonable level of dark, fibrous, organic matter. If there is too little organic matter, the turf may break up when handled. On the other hand, too high a level may result in poor rooting, leading to later problems.

The turves should be weed-free, or virtually so. If there are many weeds present, it indicates that the turves have been poorly managed. They will usually break apart when handled, and, once laid, weeds will be an immediate problem.

The final point to check is that the size and thickness of the turves is uniform. They may be 30 cm (1 ft) square, 45 cm × 30 cm (1½ × 1 ft) or 90 cm × 30 cm (3 ft × 1 ft). The smallest size is the simplest to lay. For preference, the turves should be 2.5–4 cm (1–1½ in) thick. Thinner turf will establish satisfactorily if of good quality, with well-developed roots, but more care is needed both when laying and while the lawn becomes established.

If the turf is thicker or irregular, it will have to be trimmed to an even and satisfactory thickness. To do this, lay each turf grass-side down in an open-ended box of appropriate depth. Then, using a long-bladed knife – preferably one with two handles – shave off the excess soil.

A fairly recent development in the production of turf is the flotation or roll-down method. The turf is raised rapidly by sowing seeds on floating beds of soil-less rooting medium. The resultant product, sold in small rolls, is quite easy to lay, but site preparation must be to a high standard.

A level, fine-particle surface is needed to ensure rapid rooting into the soil. This type of turf is more prone to drying out while becoming established, so check frequently in dry periods, watering thoroughly as necessary.

Laying turf Mark out the site in advance, using a tautly-stretched line to mark the base-line and sides. Allow an extra 2.5–5 cm (1–2 in) all round so that the established turf can eventually be given a true and accurate edge with a half-moon turf cutter or a sharp spade.

Keep some sandy loam handy for packing under any thinner turves. You will also need a rake to make minor adjustments to the level of the bed as laying proceeds, and planks on which to stand.

Check the turves when they arrive, rejecting any that are of poor quality. If the weather prevents an immediate start, the turves may be left for two or three days – rolled, folded, or stacked three or four deep – out of the sun. If there is likely to be a longer delay, lay them flat, singly, in the shade and keep them well watered.

Start laying from the most accessible side, facing the unturfed area. Do not walk on the prepared bed at any time while turfing.

Set each turf as closely as possible to its neighbour, bonding them row by row, like bricks in a wall. This will mean staggering successive rows of turves, and using half-turves to complete each alternate row.

From the second row onwards, work from planks placed on the newly-laid turf. This will spread your weight and avoid damage.

When you have finished, gently firm with a light roller or a home-made turfing board – a piece of thick board measuring about 23 × 38 cm (9 × 15 in), with a broomstick handle attached vertically. It is not advisable to firm by pounding with the back of a spade.

The final step is to apply a light overall dressing of sandy loam, working this well into any spaces between the turves with the back of a rake.

Irrigate thoroughly and regularly during any dry periods. When the grass begins to grow in spring, top it lightly at first before getting into the normal mowing routine. If possible, avoid using the lawn until early summer.

NOVEMBER

Mowing A final cut may be needed, but do not attempt this during frosty weather or when the surface is wet after rain. Brush off the dew first. (See October).

New lawns Turves may be laid whenever weather and soil conditions allow. If you plan to sow lawn seed next spring, dig the soil now and leave it in rough clods for the frost to crumble.

Routine jobs Rake up fallen leaves and stack them to form leaf-mould. Some rotary grasscutters make efficient leaf collectors.

DECEMBER

New lawns Turves may be laid whenever weather and soil conditions allow. If you plan to sow lawn seed next spring, and have not already dug the site, do this now so that it will be exposed to frost action during the winter.

Routine jobs Rake up leaves and stack to form leaf-mould.

Contrasting forms
The variety of beautiful contrasting forms and colours of dwarf conifers make them ideal specimens for a rock or scree garden, raised beds or for container growing.

The term 'dwarf conifer' can be misleading. Although it implies that the plant is small, it is often used for forms that are simply smaller than others of the same species. They may not be true dwarfs at all. So choose carefully, making sure that your selected plants will not grow above a given size in a given time.

The ones described here are suitable for rock gardens, raised beds, screes and small gardens, but they can be planted elsewhere if desired. They constitute the backbone of any alpine and small-garden planting, providing evergreen forms in different hues of green, blue-green and bronze.

Some are upright, others spreading, but most tend to be rounded or bun-shaped, with a neat habit. Try to plant them, and also dwarf shrubs, before other plants, to give form to the site.

Use the taller kinds near the base of a rock garden or scree, with the more spreading types towards the top, or else in a raised bed. The plants listed will normally grow no more than about 75 cm (2½ ft) high or wide during their first ten years, but they will continue to grow after this time and you should be prepared to take them out if they get too large.

The majority of the plants described are readily available, and specialist nurseries should be able to supply more rare forms.

Selected dwarf conifers

The sizes given in this list will be attained in about ten years under normal conditions. H refers to height, S to spread.
Abies balsamea 'Globosa'. H and S 60 cm (2 ft). A strange-looking plant, having a flattish top, yet with upright, rounded growth. The large needles are dark green, tinged with yellow.
A.b. 'Hudsonia'. H 30 cm (12 in), S 50 cm (20 in). This form has dark green, flattish, broad needles, white underneath, and a compact and rounded habit.
Abies cephalonica 'Nana'. H 40 cm (16 in), S 70 cm (28 in). The silvery undersides of the shiny, dark green needles show up well, standing upright on horizontally spreading branches.
Abies koreana 'Brevifolia'. H and S 75 cm (2½ ft). Shiny, broad, dark green leaves are arranged neatly around stiff stems, which have a spreading habit. The needles have prominent white undersides.
Abies nordmanniana 'Golden Spreader'. H 30 cm (12 in), S 50 cm (20 in). Golden, broad foliage and a stiff, bushy habit. This cultivar should be protected from intense sunlight when young.

Abies pinsapo 'Horstmann's Nana'. H 50 cm (20 in), S 70 cm (28 in). Bright, blue-green, medium-sized needles are arranged neatly on this irregularly-shaped plant. It is more heavily branched at the top than at the base.
Abies procera 'Glauca Nobel'. H 30 cm (1 ft), S 60 cm (2 ft). Small needles of an intense blue are carried on loose, spreading branches. The winter colour is excellent.
Cedrus libani 'Sargentii'. S 75 cm (2½ ft). This spreading, ground-hugging plant is ideal for growing over rocks. There is some yellowing of the ends of the blue-green needles, especially in winter.
Chamaecyparis lawsoniana 'Aurea Densa'. H 50 cm (20 in), S 30 cm (12 in). Dense, small, golden-yellow foliage covers this rounded bush, which has a pointed top. The colour is exceptional throughout the year.
C.l. 'Ellwood's Pillar'. H 75 cm (2½ ft), S 30 cm (1 ft). The growth forms a squat column, with a loosely-rounded top of feathery, darkish-green foliage. This has a touch of bronze-yellow during the winter.

C.l. 'Gimbornii'. H and S 60 cm (2 ft). The shape is rounded, and wider near the top than the base. The foliage has a blue-green tinge.
C.l. 'Gnome'. H 20 cm (8 in), S 30 cm (12 in). For a form of this species, the foliage is uncharacteristically tiny and dark green. The habit is squat, with loose top growth.
C.l. 'Green Globe'. H and S 30 cm (1 ft). The small, medium-green foliage is tinged with blue. It is carried in tight balls, with slightly spiky tips.
C.l. 'Minima Aurea'. H 60 cm (2 ft), S 50 cm (20 in). Small, bright, golden foliage is carried on a compact, rounded pyramid.
C.l. 'Minima Glauca'. H and S 60 cm (2 ft). This form makes a sea-green globe; the almost-flat sprays are compact.
C.l. 'Pygmaea Argentea'. H 30 cm (12 in), S 40 cm (16 in). The habit is squat and rounded, the foliage dark green with silvery tips.
Chamaecyparis obtusa 'Nana Aurea'. H and S 75 cm (2½ ft). This plant has a loose shape, with green or golden-green foliage carried on slightly drooping sprays.

Selected dwarf conifers (cont.)

C.o. 'Nana Lutea'. H 50 cm (20 in), S 30 cm (12 in). Golden sprays of shell-shaped foliage are carried like droplets, the plant being slightly pointed at the top.

C.o. 'Tonia'. H and S 40 cm (16 in). The shell-shaped sprays of bright green foliage are tipped with white and borne on a loosely-rounded pyramid. The white tips may not appear until the plant is mature.

Chamaecyparis pisifera 'Sungold'. H and S 60 cm (2 ft). Bright golden, feathery foliage, and a loose, weeping habit, forms a ball-shaped plant.

Chamaecyparis thyoides 'Andelyensis Nana'. H 60 cm (24 in), S 20 cm (8 in). The habit is columnar, the foliage an intense, soft bronze-blue, especially in winter.

C.t. 'Ericoides'. H 60 cm (2 ft), S 30 cm (1 ft). The bronze-green foliage is tinged with mauve in winter. The habit is conical, with soft growths.

C.t. 'Rubicon'. H 60 cm (24 in), S 20 cm (8 in). The intense bronze-green foliage becomes fully bronze in winter. Growth is upright, with soft needles.

Pinus mugo

Cryptomeria japonica 'Spiralis'. H and S 60 cm (2 ft). Twisted in spirals, the stems have bright green leaves arranged tightly round them. The plant has a slightly drooping habit, especially when older.

C.j. 'Vilmoriniana'. H and S 40 cm (16 in). With a rounded habit, the plant carries light-green foliage that turns an attractive bronze in winter.

Juniperus communis 'Compressa'. H 45 cm (1½ ft), S 15 cm (6 in). A perfectly shaped spire of blue-green needles, closely packed like a clipped hedge.

Juniperus recurva 'Densa'. H 30 cm (1 ft), S 60 cm (2 ft). Bright green the year round, the dense foliage is carried close to the stems. The habit is spreading and irregular.

Juniperus squamata 'Pygmaea'. H and S 40 cm (16 in). Blue-green, medium-sized needles are borne on ascending shoots that weep at the tips.

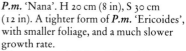

Chamaecyparis lawsoniana

Picea abies 'Clanbrassilliana'. H 20 cm (8 in), S 30 cm (12 in). A miniature, squat Christmas tree with a pyramidal habit. The medium-green needles are closely packed.

P.a. 'Gregoryana'. H and S 20 cm (8 in). A tiny spruce with a rounded habit and long, bright green needles.

P.a. 'Little Gem'. H 25 cm (10 in), S 35 cm (14 in). Tiny, medium-green needles form a compact, broad mound.

P.a. 'Nidiformis'. H 30 cm (12 in), S 50 cm (20 in). Dark-green needles cover horizontally held branches on this flat-topped, spreading plant.

Picea glauca 'Alberta Globe'. H 50 cm (20 in), S 40 cm (16 in). Medium-green needles are tightly packed over this neat, pyramidal plant, which has a pointed top.

P.g. 'Laurin'. H 25 cm (10 in), S 10 cm (4 in). A very tight, upright conifer with medium-green needles.

Picea mariana 'Ericoides'. H 40 cm (16 in), S 60 cm (24 in). The hazy, green-blue needles, large for the size of plant, are softer to the touch than other spruces. It has a squat habit, with horizontal branches.

P.m. 'Nana'. H 20 cm (8 in), S 30 cm (12 in). A tighter form of *P.m.* 'Ericoides', with smaller foliage, and a much slower growth rate.

Picea pungens 'Globosa'. H and S 50 cm (20 in). A globular, pointed-topped plant with attractive, intense blue needles of medium size.

Pinus mugo 'Humpy'. H 30 cm (12 in), S 40 cm (16 in). Small, medium-green needles on a plant that has a rounded appearance, and looks tighter with age.

P.m. 'Mops'. H 40 cm (16 in), S 60 cm (24 in). With an overall rounded, gently spreading appearance, the medium-sized matt-green needles grow on tightly-clad upright growths.

P.m. 'Ophir'. H 40 cm (16 in), S 60 cm (24 in). The medium-sized needles are green at the base but golden above on this plant of neatly rounded, spreading habit.

Pinus sylvestris 'Doone Valley'. H 40 cm (16 in), S 30 cm (12 in). Matt-blue, medium-sized needles are carried on upright growths. The habit is rounded, spreading with age, and the plant bears small cones.

P. s. 'Gold Coin'. H and S 60 cm (24 in). With pyramidal growth, this plant has a looser appearance than most dwarf conifers. It bears small cones, and large, bright and golden needles.

Taxus baccata 'Adpressa Aurea'. H 60 cm (24 in), S 50 cm (20 in). Small, dark green leaves are topped by bright, golden foliage on stiff, irregular branches that spread with age.

Thuja occidentalis 'Danica'. H 45 cm (18 in), S 60 cm (24 in). The vertical, flattened sprays of green foliage are tipped with bronze in winter, and the plant has a neat, rounded habit.

T.o. 'Recurva Nana'. H 30 cm (12 in), S 50 cm (20 in). The green foliage is carried in crimpled sprays on a flat-topped bush; the branches recurve at the tips.

Tsuga canadensis 'Jeddeloh'. H 40 cm (16 in), S 60 cm (24 in). The dark green leaves, with silvery undersides, show up well on a plant that weeps readily even when young.

Juniperus communis

Colour variations can occur in most types of garden plants, including annuals, hardy perennials, shrubs, trees and alpines, as well as in house plants. It takes the form of spotting, streaking or some other distinctive marking of the leaves or petals, often giving a most attractive effect.

It may come about in a number of ways. For instance, leaves may develop red or yellow margins, or suffer from a form of chlorosis, when certain nutrients are lacking in the soil. Such variations have little or no ornamental value, but they at least provide a useful pointer to nutrient deficiencies.

Most variations, however, are due to failure of the plant to produce sufficient chlorophyll – the green colouring matter in leaves. As a result, the plant cells do not form in the normal way, the type of variation depending on the manner in which the cells are arranged.

It may take the form of variously striped formations, leaves with varying degrees of green or yellow, or others where the two sides of a leaf have different colours. Sometimes, parts of a plant will revert to their normal green colouring, and such shoots should be removed by pruning.

Although variegated plants are not to everyone's taste, they are becoming increasingly popular, especially among flower arrangers. There is even a Variegated Plant Contact Group, set up with the aim of producing a register of all variegated forms.

Earlier reservations about such plants owed something to the belief that all forms of variegation were caused by virus diseases, and better destroyed. This has proved to be untrue, for only about three per cent of such plants show positive signs of virus disease.

One of the advantages of these plants is that they provide interest for long periods – throughout the year in the case of evergreens. With some, the intensity of the colour seems to increase during the dull, drab days of winter.

Although a few variegated plants can be raised from seed, most must be propagated vegetatively.

Following are some of the many variegated plants available. All are reasonably easy to obtain and grow.

Conservatory and house plants

Coleus blumei. A popular pot and bedding plant, with many and varied leaf colourings. Grown solely for its foliage, any flowers should be removed in order to help maintain leaf colour. Though it can be grown from seed, only cuttings will produce plants identical to the parent.

Hypoestes sanguinolenta. The dark green leaves have pink spots.

Sansevieria trifasciata 'Laurentii' (mother-in-law's tongue). The sword-shaped leaves of this plant, some 60–75 cm (2–2½ ft) long, have yellow margins.

Tradescantia albiflora 'Albovittata' (wandering jew). Easy to grow and propagate (from cuttings), this widely-grown house plant has yellow and cream striped leaves.

Zebrina pendula, syn. *Tradescantia zebrina.* The silvery-green leaves of this trailing plant have reddish-purple margins.

Aphelandra squarrosa 'Louisae'. One of many species in this genus, it is particularly striking for the intense silver stripe along and across each leaf – also for the four-sided spurs of yellow flowers.

Maranta leuconeura 'Kerchoveana'. Dark blotches on each side of the central leaf vein are a feature of this dwarf plant.

Peperomia metallica. The leaves, carried on reddish-brown stems, are dark green with a metallic lustre and have white stripes along their mid-ribs.

Pilea cadierei (aluminium plant). The leaves of this easily-grown species, which grows to only about 30 cm (1 ft), have irregular, silvery-white variations.

Zebrina pendula

Shrubs

Cornus alba 'Elegantissima' (dogwood). This deciduous species has variegated silvery foliage, with red stems in winter. Prune hard in March to promote new growth.

Elaeagnus pungens 'Maculata'. The gold-splashed leaves of this vigorous evergreen shrub will brighten any winter's day.

Fuchsia magellanica 'Gracilis Variegata'. Edged with creamy-yellow, the leaves are flushed with pink. It flowers until the frosts, and will grow from the base again even if the foliage is cut down by cold weather.

Maranta leuconeura

Shrubs (cont.)

Philadelphus coronarius 'Variegatus' (mock orange). Leaves with creamy-white variegations, somewhat irregular, are a feature of this bushy, deciduous shrub.

Pieris japonica 'Variegata'. The silver-variegated form of this evergreen shrub is comparatively slow-growing. It does best in acid soil, sheltered from the wind and full sun.

Climbers

Actinidia kolomikta. Preferring a sunny wall, this vigorous, deciduous climber, which carries white flowers in early summer, has white and pink variegation on its leaves.

Hedera canariensis 'Gloire de Marengo'. A fast-growing climber, with large leaves that have silvery-white margins. *H. colchica* 'Dentata Variegata', large leaves with light yellow edges. *H. helix* 'Goldheart', fairly small, dark green leaves with bright yellow centres. It looks brilliant on a winter's day.

Lonicera japonica 'Aureoreticulata' (Japanese honeysuckle). An evergreen climber with leaves that are netted with gold.

Hedges

Ligustrum ovalifolium 'Aureum' (golden privet). So much more attractive than the plain green type, the leaves have yellow edges.

Prunus lusitanica 'Variegata' (Portugal laurel). The silvery variegations of the leaves make this an attractive hedging plant.

Ground cover

Euonymus fortunei 'Emerald Gaiety'. A trailing, evergreen species, with silver-variegated leaves. The young foliage of *E.f.* 'Emerald 'n' Gold' is a bright gold. Both benefit from an occasional light trimming.

Lamium galeobdolon 'Variegatum' is very rampant; the evergreen silvery leaves turn bronze in the autumn. It has yellow flowers in May and June.

Pachysandra terminalis 'Variegata'. An evergreen with white-edged leaves that grows best in semi-shade.

Vinca major 'Variegata' (greater periwinkle). The leaves of this popular ground-cover plant, which thrives in dry shade, are blotched and edged with creamy-white. It has bright blue flowers in late spring. The leaves of *V. minor* 'Aureo Variegata' are yellow and green. More compact than *V. major*, with blue or white flowers.

Actinidia kolomikta

Hedera canariensis 'Gloire de Marengo'

Hosta fortunei 'Albopicta'

Phormium tenax 'Maori Chief'

Trees

Acer negundo 'Variegatum' (box elder). The leaves of this medium-sized deciduous tree, growing to about 6 m (20 ft), have white margins. Suitable for small gardens.

Ilex aquifolium 'Argenteo Marginata' (holly). Both male and female forms have silver-edged foliage; the female bears berries in abundance. Can be grown as a tree or a large bush.

Annuals

Abutilon striatum 'Thompsonii'. Although strictly a greenhouse plant, cuttings taken in August can be planted among annuals the following season. The leaves have mottled yellow variegations.

Humulus japonicus 'Variegatus'. With its green and white foliage, this quick-growing plant will soon cover a screen or fence.

Ornamental cabbage. These plants are increasingly grown in flower borders, because of their curled and fringed, creamy-white and rose-coloured leaves.

Pelargonium. The boldly-zoned foliage of many cultivars complements the beauty of the flowers. Although perennial it is used for bedding.

Herbaceous plants

Hosta fortunei 'Albopicta'. The leaves have pale green edges and bright yellow centres. Best grown in a moist, shady spot; there are many other variegated cultivars.

Phormium tenax 'Maori Chief' (New Zealand flax). This plant has sword-shaped leaves, striped pink and bronze, but there are many other cultivars with different variegations. Not hardy enough for cold areas but will survive most winters in the south and west of Britain.

Pulmonaria saccharata 'Mrs Moon' or *P.s.* 'Bowles Red'. Both have marbled white foliage and will grow in sun or shade. The pink and blue flowers come in April or May.

Alpines

Ajuga reptans 'Variegata' (bugle). It makes a carpet of light green and buff foliage, with blue flowers in late spring.

Aubrieta deltoidea 'Variegata'. The purple flowers, from April to May, stem from a carpet of green and gold leaves.

Thymus x *citriodorus* (lemon-scented thyme). There are a number of cultivars with silver-margined leaves, including 'Silver Posie' and 'Silver Queen'. Pale lilac flowers are borne during the summer.

Ideal specimen
Some plants, such as
Armeria maritima,
advertise their
preference for
location. Also known
as sea pink, this
attractive dwarf
perennial has linear,
strap-like leaves and
bears heads of pink
flowers from late
spring.

Mild coastal areas
Although the coast is
not as prone to frost
as inland areas, winter
is still a testing time
for plants. Those that
can be grown with
reasonable confidence
include *Eryngium
maritimum, Buddleia
colvillei* and *Grevillea
rosmarinifolia*.

The hostile elements of wind, salt and sand present a real challenge to coastal gardeners. The exact nature of that challenge depends on whether one has to cope with cold, blustery winds from the north; penetrating and drying east winds; persistent, rain-bearing winds from the west; or the warmer, sometimes balmy, winds of southern coasts.

Salt-laden winds from the sea are damaging enough, but those carrying whipped-up sand have an abrasive effect on stems and leaves. Some plants have become adapted to cope with such conditions, developing needle-shaped leaves or tough, leathery surfaces, while others have a protective covering of hairs.

Important though such plants are, they offer only a small selection compared to those available to the inland gardener. However, the range of suitable plants increases dramatically if the garden can be given some protection. Indeed, the low incidence of frost in gardens on southern and some western coasts allows, with suitable protection, a range of plants to be grown that are difficult, or even impossible, to cultivate in inland gardens.

Nevertheless, it must be recognized that, sooner or later, severe weather will strike even these favoured areas. When this happens, as it does at least once in most decades, one's treasured, carefully nurtured plants may be lost.

Protective screening can be formed by living materials, such as a hedge, or by a man-made structure, such as wattle fencing. On an exposed site the latter comes first, enabling a second line of defence – a living windbreak – to gain a hold.

The fact to keep in mind is that the purpose of a screen is to filter the wind rather than to attempt to stop it dead. On the leeward side of a solid wall there are eddies and damaging turbulence, whereas trellis, slatted panels or wattle hurdles achieve their object by robbing the wind of its initial force.

Plastic windbreaks, sold in rolls of varying heights and grades, are particularly effective. Supported by stout poles, they are not especially attractive but they will have served their purpose once the living screen planted in their lee has become established.

Two plants especially suitable for screening are *Cupressus macrocarpa* and x *Cupressocyparis leylandii*. Hedges that, once established, make admirable windbreaks include *Aucuba japonica; Elaeagnus* x *ebbingei; Escallonia* 'Crimson Spire'; *Griselinia littoralis* (not fully frost-hardy); *Hippophae rhamnoides* (sea buckthorn); *Lonicera ledebourii; Quercus ilex* (evergreen oak); *Ribes alpinum; Senecio rotundifolius; Ulex europaeus* (common gorse) and *U.e.* 'Flore Pleno', the double form.

Arundinaria japonica (bamboo) makes an effective filter. It is a rather untidy,

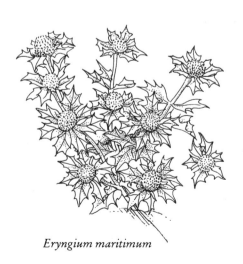

Eryngium maritimum

Buddleia colvillei

Grevillea rosmarinifolia

somewhat invasive plant, however, and a lot of work is involved if, at a later stage, you should wish to get rid of it.

Plants with specific and common names that tell of their association with the sea are *Armeria maritima* (sea pink); *Crambe maritima* (sea kale); *Eryngium maritimum* (sea holly); *Hippophae rhamnoides* (sea buckthorn) and *Limonium vulgare* (sea lavender). These, and that favourite coastal plant, *Tamarix anglica* (tamarisk) are reliable choices. So also are *Senecio cineraria*, syn. *S. maritimus* (sea ragwort) and, except in very cold areas, *S. laxifolius*.

In the warmer south, where there is less chance of frost damage, plants that can be grown with reasonable confidence include the charming *Grevillea rosmarinifolia*, the large-flowered hebes and pittosporums. For a sunny, well-sheltered spot, try the handsome *Buddleia colvillei*.

Of course, not all coastal gardens are exposed to the full force of wind, salt and sand. A little further inland, perhaps sheltered by houses or other gardens, much better conditions can prevail. Here, climbers and wall plants that are at risk on even a 'warm' wall inland may be planted with greater confidence. Among these are *Campsis radicans* (trumpet vine) and the larger-flowered *C. grandiflora*, with their deep orange-scarlet, trumpet-shaped blooms. *Passiflora caerulea* (passion flower) will stand a better chance of ripening its fruit. *Sollya heterophylla* is

worth growing for its sky-blue flowers. *Trachelospermum jasminoides* is a Chinese plant with a delightful scent. The flowers of *Clianthus puniceus* are crimson, and shaped to warrant its common names of lobster-claw or parrot's bill. *Fremontodendron californicum* has felted leaves and lovely yellow flowers.

A mild, coastal climate has a marked effect on some plants. Species normally considered herbaceous may prove to be evergreen. Half-hardy perennials may survive the winter outdoors. In the west, especially, growth and foliage benefit from the moist atmosphere and lawns grow particularly well.

Trees must be well supported and it would be wise to concentrate on the shorter kinds. Where wind remains a problem, in spite of shelter, it would be better to avoid plants with brittle stems and shoots. The taller dahlias and other large-flowered plants are particularly at risk.

Hardy perennials worth considering are *Achillea* species and hybrids, forms of *Chrysanthemum maximum*, *Iris unguicularis*, *Kniphofia* species and hybrids, *Sedum spectabile* and *Veronica spicata*.

Rock garden plants attuned to seaside conditions include *Aethionema* species and hybrids, forms of *Aubrieta deltoidea*, *Dianthus* species and hybrids, *Hypericum olympicum*, forms of *Iris pumila*, *Polygonum affine*, *Silene schafta* and *Zauschneria* species.

Stately form
A hardy perennial, whose stately form would grace any garden, is *Iris unguicularis*.

Sheltered coastal areas
Move just a little further inland and your choice of plants increases greatly. Here, *Campsis radicans*, *Fremontodendron californicum* and *Kniphofia* are among the many that can be grown.

Campsis radicans

Fremontodendron californicum

Kniphofia

As a rule, keen gardeners are very aware of the soil quality when choosing a new property. Rhododendron-lovers, for instance, will go to great lengths to ensure that the land is suitably acid. However, it is not always possible to get exactly what you want, and a limy or chalky soil need not be limiting when it comes to choosing interesting and beautiful plants.

All the plants listed here are hardy and perennial, their main need being good drainage, especially during their resting time. Colour, foliage and form have been taken into consideration with a view to providing continuing, year-round interest.

Most of the plants mentioned will be found at larger garden centres. For others, it may be necessary to track down specialist nurserymen.

Foliage plants

Astrantia 'Sunningdale Variegated'. Height 25 cm (10 in). Perennial. Divided leaves, variegated yellow and cream, which look their best in spring.
Aubrieta deltoidea 'Aureovariegata'. Height 5 cm (2 in). Evergreen. Compact gold and green rosettes, with light purple flowers in spring.
Daphne cneorum 'Variegata' (garland flower). Height 15 cm (6 in). Prostrate shrub. Evergreen leaves with yellow margins. Pink, fragrant flowers in May.
Euryops acraeus. Height 30 cm (1 ft). Evergreen shrub. Intense silvery leaves; bright yellow, daisy-like flowers in May.

Hebe ochracea 'James Stirling'. Height 45 cm (1½ ft). Shrub. The foliage has an old gold colour. Occasional white flowers.
Mertensia asiatica. Trailing. Herbaceous. Bluish-grey leaves, with drooping, tubular, blue flowers in June.
Ribes alpinum 'Aureum'. Height 38 cm (15 in). Deciduous shrub. The young leaves are a soft yellow. Attractive leaf-buds in winter.
Santolina chamaecyparissus 'Weston' (cotton lavender). Height 38 cm (15 in). Evergreen shrub. Annual pruning of this grey-leaved bushlet serves to intensify the colour.
Saxifraga moschata 'Cloth of Gold'. Height 5 cm (2 in). Evergreen perennial. Bright yellow 'mossy' rosettes, with white flowers in April or May. Grow in light shade.

Sedum 'Vera Jameson'. Height 20 cm (8 in). Herbaceous. Dusky pink flower-heads, in late summer, over fleshy, glaucous-purple leaves.
Spiraea x *bumalda* 'Goldflame'. Height 60–90 cm (2–3 ft). Deciduous shrub. The new leaves are a glowing orange-red, becoming golden later. Regular pruning produces dense growth with fine colouring.
Veronica incana. Height 23 cm (9 in). Herbaceous. A mat-forming plant with silver-grey leaves. Spikes of blue flowers during June.

Dwarf shrubs

Berberis thunbergii 'Bagatelle'. Height 38 cm (15 in). Deciduous. A real pygmy with coppery-red leaves. Annual growth is about 2.5 cm (1 in).
Hebe cupressoides 'Boughton Dome'. Height 45 cm (1½ ft). Evergreen. A conifer-like, slow-growing shrub.
Jasminum parkeri. Height 30 cm (1 ft). Evergreen. This jasmine is sprinkled with tubular yellow flowers in June, followed by black berries.
Penstemon newberyi. Height 30 cm (1 ft). Sub-shrub. Spreading stems and narrow leaves. The flowers, in June, are ruby-red and tubular.
Prunus tenella 'Firehill'. Height 90 cm (3 ft). Deciduous. A slow suckering almond, with erect, slender stems. Deep pink flowers on bare stems in April.
Salix helvetica. Height 90 cm (3 ft). Deciduous. The new leaves on this attractive bushy willow are intensely silver-grey, with a downy texture. Good catkins in March.
Syringa afghanica. Height 90 cm (3 ft). Deciduous. This dwarf lilac is grown principally for its dissected foliage. Typical lilac flowers in May.
Verbascum 'Letitia'. Height 30 cm (1 ft). Shrubby. Upright woody stems with grey-green leaves. Clear yellow mullein flowers over a long period in summer.

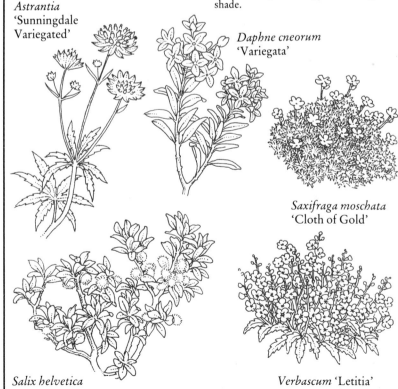

Astrantia 'Sunningdale Variegated'

Daphne cneorum 'Variegata'

Saxifraga moschata 'Cloth of Gold'

Salix helvetica

Verbascum 'Letitia'

Alpine beds

Aethionema pulchellum. Height 23 cm (9 in). Evergreen perennial. A low bush of steel-blue leaves. Rounded, sugar-pink flower-heads from May to July.

Campanula 'Elizabeth Oliver'. Height 8 cm (3 in). Herbaceous. Completely double flowers of a curious silvery-blue in July. Modest spreading habit.

Daphne retusa. Height to 60 cm (2 ft). An evergreen shrub with glossy leaves and sweetly-scented, rose-purple flowers in May.

Diascia 'Ruby Field'. Height 23 cm (9 in). Herbaceous. Produces a summer-long succession of glowing pink flowers.

Dicentra 'Stuart Boothman'. Height 23 cm (9 in). Herbaceous. A vigorous plant for sun or shade. Finely cut blue-grey leaves, and pink flowers in April.

Gentiana asclepiadea. Height 60 cm (2 ft). Herbaceous. A plant for light shade. A blue, trumpet-shaped flower emerges from each leaf axil in late summer.

Geranium farreri. Height 10 cm (4 in). Herbaceous. Crinkled leaves, followed by soft pink, black-anthered flowers throughout the summer.

Hacquetia epipactis. Height 8 cm (3 in). Herbaceous. Low tufts of trifoliate leaves and apple-green bracts, on which sit yellow flowers in February.

Leucanthemum hosmariense (syn. *Chrysanthemum hosmariense*). Height 30 cm (1 ft). Shrub. Snow-white, golden-eyed daisies are borne in March over cut, silver-green leaves. A mild winter will produce a 'bonus' crop of flowers.

Lithodora oleifolia. Height 15 cm (6 in). Sub-shrub. Silvery-green leaves; pendent blue flowers throughout summer. Increases by underground runners.

Oenothera glaber. Height 30 cm (1 ft). Herbaceous. Woody stems clothed with mahogany-coloured leaves. Clustered, rich yellow flowers in early summer.

Origanum 'Kent Beauty'. Height 15 cm (6 in). Herbaceous. Short stems carry papery, apple-green and pink bracts. Tubular pink flowers during late summer.

Penstemon heterophyllus 'Blue Spire'. Height 38 cm (15 in). Deciduous shrub. Clear blue, tubular flowers, with just a hint of pink, in June and July.

Phlox 'Daniel's Cushion'. Height 5 cm (2 in). Herbaceous. A good mat-forming plant, with enormous rose-pink flowers in May. 'Russet' has coloured foliage during the winter.

Polygonatum hookeri. Height 8 cm (3 in). Herbaceous. Masses of pointed leaves. Starry-pink flowers in May.

Polygonum tenuicaule. Height 10 cm (4 in). Herbaceous. A shade-loving plant producing dense spikes of white flowers over dark green leaves in early spring.

Pulsatilla vulgaris 'Alba Superba'. Height 23 cm (9 in). Herbaceous. Pure white, almost tubular, flowers during April and May. Fresh green leaves soon follow.

Ranunculus calandrinoides. Height 15 cm (6 in). Herbaceous. A summer dormancy precedes the long, grey-green leaves that appear in September and October. They are followed by clear pink buttercups, some 5 cm (2 in) across, throughout mild winters, and in spring.

Roscoea cautleoides 'Grandiflora'. Height 23 cm (9 in). Herbaceous. This plant does not emerge until the end of May. The orchid-like flowers, soft yellow in colour, open in June and July.

Satureja montana var. *subspicata.* Height 23 cm (9 in). Sub-shrub. This aromatic-leaved plant has lavender-coloured flowers in late summer.

Sedum kamtschaticum 'Variegatum'. Height 8 cm (3 in). Herbaceous. Gold and green leaves. Yellow flower-heads, ageing to crimson, in late summer.

Sisyrinchium bellum 'Album'. Height 10 cm (4 in). Herbaceous and clump-forming. Small iris-like leaves, and large white flowers over a long period during the summer.

Zauschneria californica 'Dublin' (Californian fuchsia). Height up to 30 cm (1 ft). Herbaceous. A bushlet with narrow, grey-green leaves. Vivid, orange-red tubular flowers as autumn approaches.

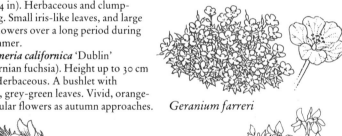

Aethionema pulchellum

Gentiana asclepiadea

Geranium farreri

Pulsatilla vulgaris 'Alba Superba'

Roscoea cautleoides 'Grandiflora'

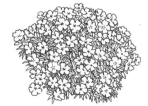

Phlox 'Daniel's Cushion'

Daphne retusa

Window dressing
A wide range of house plants can be grown if given the right conditions and, when grouped together and arranged properly, they add an elegant finishing touch to any room in the house.

Double potting
Where necessary, increase humidity by placing the plant and pot inside a larger container packed with moist sphagnum moss.

Though most house plants are not difficult to grow, they will remain healthy and attractive only if given the correct care. The way they are displayed is important, too, including their grouping, the choice of pot holders, regular cleaning, and the neat staking and tying of climbing plants.

House plants fall into two main categories. The first consists of pot plants, grown on a seasonal basis, that are either discarded after they have flowered or else moved to the garden or greenhouse. The ones for discarding include *Calceolaria*, *Celosia*, *Cineraria* and *Solanum*. Those for moving elsewhere comprise such plants as azaleas, primroses and bulbs. The second category is made up of flowering or foliage plants that provide a more or less continuous display. The aim should be to have a combination of both types.

CARING FOR HOUSE PLANTS

When choosing and positioning plants, the most important points to note are their particular needs in terms of light, temperature and humidity. Having attended to these, it is vital to water them correctly.

Positioning Photosynthesis is the process by which plants acquire the energy to grow and flower. Light is an essential factor, but this is severely reduced in most rooms. Fortunately, the light requirements of individual plants vary considerably and there are species for most places, except where there is no light at all.

Most of the pot plants in the first, seasonal category need cool, light conditions in order to flower well for a long time. In a dark corner of a hot, dry living room, the flowers will almost certainly fade and not be replaced by new ones. An azalea in this position would soon begin to drop its leaves and die.

House plants that remain indoors permanently will mostly manage with less light, many having their origins in tropical forests. Some of these plants, adapted to shade, will flower indoors in a relatively dull position. Most climbing plants, however, need some direct light in order to flower, for in their natural surroundings they would attain a position at the tops of trees where the sun would initiate the flower buds.

In addition, other house plants are derived from species that grow on open grass plains, in Mediterranean coastal areas or in deserts. Naturally, these need some direct light if their foliage is not to become pale and drawn.

Where light comes from one direction only – from a nearby window, for instance – the plant should be turned regularly so that growth does not lean to one side. Bear in mind, too, that plants with variegated or brightly-coloured leaves need an extra share of light in order to show to best advantage.

Humidity House plants from the tropics do best in warm, moist conditions, but the average living room provides a hot, dry environment. The following steps will increase humidity:

1. Syringe plants regularly, dispersing a fine, mist-like spray over the leaves.

2. Stand the pots in larger containers, with moistened pebbles under and around them, so that water can evaporate around the plants without the pots becoming unduly wet.

3. Alternatively, use a large, tall container and pack around the pot with moist sphagnum moss.

4. Group several pot plants in a container of moist peat, plunging the pots to their rims.

5. If the air is particularly dry, keep small plants in bottle gardens or terraria to provide a moist micro-environment.

6. If even these steps prove inadequate, move moisture-lovers to a steamy bathroom or kitchen.

Watering It is inadvisable to water plants only from beneath, and better to water carefully from the top, giving sufficient to soak right through the pot.

In either case, the most important thing is to make sure that plants do not stand in water for any length of time. Their roots, as well as the visible parts of the plant, need to breathe, and to make this possible the soil must dry out sufficiently between waterings for air to get into the tiny spaces around the roots. In soil that is continually waterlogged, pot plants are liable to wilt, as if they were dry, because the roots are dying and can no longer take up water.

The best rule is to wait until the top inch of soil starts to become dry and crumbly before watering the plant again, and it should then be given a good soak. Judge by touching the compost with your fingers and feeling the weight of the pot. Avoid watering little and often.

If plants become bone dry, plunge them into a deep container, submerging the pot until it is thoroughly soaked. Generally, but particularly with cuttings and seedlings, use water at room temperature.

There are some plants that dislike tapwater, especially in hard-water areas. Noted for this are ericas, azaleas and carnivorous plants. Try to save rainwater, which contains no lime, for such plants.

Holiday times give rise to the biggest watering problems, especially in the absence of helpful neighbours. If plants have to be left unattended for a week or two, move them away from windows and direct sunlight. Although contrary to normal practice, leave plenty of water in the containers, perhaps standing several plants in a bath of shallow water. Various 'automatic' watering systems involving a reservoir, tubes and capillary matting can be bought, but none is really fail-safe.

A simple method, though reliable only with plastic pots, is to fill the kitchen sink and place one end of a piece of wet capillary matting in the water, with the remainder lying on the draining board. If clay pots are used, insert short wicks of matting through the drainage holes. Place the plants on the matting, making sure that they are well watered, and draw the curtains half way across the window.

If you are likely to be away for long periods it would be wise to stick to cacti, succulents and such plants as *Sansevieria* (mother-in-law's-tongue) or *Dracaena*, which can survive for long periods without water.

The alternative would be to make use of hydroponics. The equipment can be bought as sets, the containers having a sightglass and an indicator to show when the water reservoir needs topping up. This should be required only every few weeks, and fertilizer is added to the system every six months.

Feeding Most pot plants in active growth will need feeding when their roots have filled the pots and taken up all the fertilizer in the compost. This is done by means of a liquid feed, a foliar feed, a slow-release fertilizer or a top dressing. Feeding is needed after about six weeks for soil-less composts, two or three months for John Innes composts.

When buying fertilizer you should be able to find on the label a breakdown of the ratio of N (Nitrogen) to P (Phosphorous) to K (Potassium), and a list of trace elements. This is useful, for there are times when you may wish to vary the ratios given. In summer, for instance, when much leafy growth is desirable, a feed rich in nitrogen is preferable. In contrast, the application of a fertilizer with abundant potassium (potash) will give a better flowering performance. Tomato fertilizers are suitable for this.

Liquid feed is mixed with water and applied during a routine watering, though plants that are either very dry or very wet should not be fed. In the former case, the fertilizer may be too strong for the roots; in the latter, the fertilizer will not be taken up by the saturated soil.

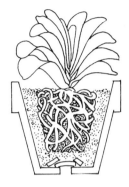

Potting on
When a house plant's compost is full of root, it is time to pot it on. This should be done when the plant is in active growth. Take care never to move a plant into a pot that is too large.

Moistened pebbles
Humidity can be increased locally by standing the plant pot on a bed of moistened pebbles or gravel.

Foliar feed is applied as a spray to the plants' leaves, which will absorb it. Some liquid feeds have foliar properties, also, and can be taken up by the plant in both ways.

Slow-release fertilizers are added to the soil as tablets or sticks which release their contents into the soil gradually as the plant requires it.

Top dressing is the addition of compost and fertilizer to the surface of a large pot. The fertilizer may be instantly available or of a slow-release type, and the method is particularly useful with large plants that are too big to be potted on further. Loosen and scrape off the surface of the old soil before adding a couple of inches of fresh compost and fertilizer.

Plants which are resting during the winter, such as cacti or *Bougainvillea*, do not require feeding. Neither will flowering specimens of such plants as *Cineraria*, because they are at the end of their lives.

COMPOST AND POTTING

Both peat-based and loam-based composts are suitable for house plants, but there are a number of points to be made about each. Most proprietary peat-based composts contain some fine sand and fertilizers as well as the peat. They are very light and fine and, although ideal for many plants – especially the more permanent kinds – they do have some disadvantages. Being light, if the plant is very tall or one-sided the pot may become unstable. Also, when dry it is often difficult to soak the compost again.

A good compost can be made by mixing the following ingredients thoroughly:

3 parts fine, moist peat.
1 part sharp sand or grit.
A well-balanced fertilizer with trace elements, preferably one with slow-release properties. (Follow the manufacturer's instructions as to quantity.)
Some ground chalk, the quantity of which will be indicated with the fertilizer instructions. Omit this for acid-loving plants.

Note that sharp sand or grit is used in this mixture instead of fine sand. It gives more stability, and assists the passage of water through the soil.

Slow-release fertilizer
At the start of the growing season, insert a stick of slow-release fertilizer well into the soil.

The most widely-available loam-based compost is John Innes, which is sold in three different grades, 1 to 3. The numbers denote different fertilizer contents, the amount rising with the number. This compost was developed at the John Innes Institute and, when made correctly with good quality ingredients, is excellent. In practice, quality does vary with the supplier. The supply of nutrients in John Innes compost lasts longer than with peat-based composts, while the compost's weight provides a more secure anchor for plants.

One of the reasons for variable quality is the loam itself. Ideally, it should be made by cutting turves and stacking them, grass side down, until well rotted. The sieved results of this provide a good, fibrous ingredient. However, most of the loam now used is really just top soil, which can vary a great deal, depending on its origins.

If a reliable source of compost is available, with the product feeling fibrous, not sticky, and smelling fresh, then use it. The best safeguard is to look on the bag for the seal of approval of the John Innes Manufacturers' Association. Otherwise, switch to a peat-based mix as these are always of dependable quality.

Potting When potting plants, there are a few basic rules to observe:

1. Never pot a plant into a pot that is too large for it. Generally, a small cutting or seedling, depending on size, should go into a 6 cm, 8 cm or 9 cm (2½ in, 3 in, or 3½ in) pot. Once that pot is full of root, then a plant in an 8 cm (3 in) pot would be potted on to an 11 cm (4½ in) pot, a 9 cm (3½ in) to a 13 cm (5 in) pot, and so on. The amount of roots and the need for repotting can be checked by inverting the plant and pot, supporting the soil ball with one hand while the pot is removed with the other.

2. It is better not to repot a plant which has been dormant, or while the temperature is low. Wait until it shows signs of active growth, with new shoots and leaves forming, before potting.

3. Either clay or plastic pots may be used. Those made of plastic are lighter and easier to handle, but being less porous there is a greater risk of over-watering. Plants in clay pots dry out faster.

4. Always use a clean pot. If old soil is clinging to the sides it will be hard to knock the plant out cleanly when the time comes to pot it on again. There is also a risk of spreading pests and diseases. If fungus diseases have been a problem, it is worth sterilizing the pots as well.

5. Never pot on a dry plant, and always water a fresh-potted house plant immediately. For this, use a can with a rose to settle the compost around the roots.

6. If the plant is very pot-bound, so that the roots are packed around the side, tease out a few roots to aid their penetration into the new compost.

7. Try to keep the plant at its original level in the new pot.

8. When potting with a peat-based mix, avoid firming the compost too thoroughly around the old root ball. It will become firm enough when watered in. However, always pot firmly when using a loam-based mix.

PRUNING

House plant growers seem loath to take up their secateurs to prune their plants. Nevertheless, correct pruning keeps plants compact and bushy and promotes greater vigour. Make pruning cuts above a node (the positions on the stem from which leaves arise) because a shoot will then develop from the bud in the axil of the leaf.

Pruning also encourages the production of strong new shoots for propagation by cuttings, especially with old, woody plants where the material for cuttings would otherwise be very hard and much slower to root. Some climbing plants in the house need regular pruning if they are to do well over a long period.

The following common house plants all benefit from pruning:

Allamanda cathartica (golden trumpet). A golden-flowered climber, this plant should be cut back by about two thirds in February and trained over a frame or trellis. Retain several long main shoots, shortening these to the top of the frame.

Younger growths arising from the main stems should be spurred back to within one or two buds. The plant will subsequently flower on growths arising from the cuts.

Aphelandra (zebra plant). Cut the plant down to within 5–8 cm (2–3 in) of the soil after the yellow flowers and bracts have faded. The shoots that result will grow and flower again, or they can be used as cuttings.

Ardisia crenata (coral berry). An upright, leathery-leaved plant which bears masses of red, long-lasting berries. After several years the plant will become very tall and, although continuing to flower and berry, will have a long woody stem.

When it becomes unattractive, cut it down to within a few inches of the soil, making the cut above a node, as usual. Fresh shoots will arise to grow and produce berries. Shoots from the top of the old plant may be used as cuttings, and seeds from old berries may be sown.

Bougainvillea. Cut hard back in February after a resting period during the colder months. During this time, keep the plants in a cool room, though with the temperature above freezing, and also very dry. Most of the leaves will drop off.

After their first year when grown from a cutting, make the cut about 2.5 cm (1 in) from the surface of the soil, leaving at least two buds on the stem. After another year's growth, during which time the buds will have produced strong shoots and flowers, cut the shoots back to within a bud of the older wood, leaving small spurs. In this way the plants can be kept small and tidy.

The flowering wood can be staked and tied easily. If desired, a few long shoots may be retained, and growths arising from them spurred back to within one or two buds to allow the plant to climb over a larger area.

Citrus. These plants may become rather unruly if not pruned every year, so shorten the shoots by about two thirds in spring. If an old plant is very untidy it is quite safe to cut it back harder into relatively old wood. Always cut above a node and water very carefully until new growth resumes.

Clerodendrum thomsoniae. A rest period is needed during the winter, when the plant must be kept cooler and drier than normal. After this period, and as it begins to produce new shoots, prune it back by half of the previous year's growth.

Pruning for flowers
With the boldly striped *Aphelandra*, cut back hard when the flowers and bracts have faded. This will encourage additional flowers.

Pruning for shape
To maintain a healthy and bushy shape, prune *Citrus* back by about two-thirds in spring.

Hanging basket
Columnea is a good specimen for a hanging basket. To prevent it from becoming woody, however, prune it back to the rim of the basket when the flowers have faded.

Columnea. Whether they are grown in pots or hanging baskets, trim these trailing plants after flowering or else they will become very old and woody. Trim the growths back to a point around the rim of the pot or basket. Keep the plants a little drier than usual until new shoots develop.

Dieffenbachia (dumb cane). After a while, these plants become very tall, with the leaves at the base turning yellow and dropping off. When they become unattractive, cut the succulent stem down to within a few inches of the soil above a node. Watered moderately, without allowing the soil to dry out completely, new shoots will grow to make a fresh plant.

Note that the sap is poisonous, causing the mouth and tongue to become swollen and painful if brought into contact with the sap.

Euphorbia pulcherrima (poinsettia). Generally known by its common name, the brightly-coloured bracts of this plant are prominent in the shops at Christmas time. It can be brought on for a further year by the following means.

After the bracts have faded, allow the compost to become almost dry. If the plant is kept in a cool place, most of the leaves will fall. In April, prune it back to within about 8 cm (3 in) of the base and water well. Place the plant in a warmer position and water it carefully until new growth begins. If you wish, some of the resulting growths may be used as cuttings.

Bear in mind that, with natural lighting, poinsettias will produce colourful bracts for Christmas. However, if they are kept in artificial light, make sure that the plants are in total, uninterrupted darkness for fourteen hours each day over an eight-week period.

Hibiscus. If not pruned regularly, these plants will grow into large, woody shrubs. In spring, cut back all the growths to within about 15 cm (6 in) of the base.

Hypoestes sanguinolenta (polka dot plant). The many shoots of this plant have spotted leaves, but after a season's growth the foliage becomes dull and tangled. Wait until new shoots appear at the base under the old leaves, then cut away all the old growth and let the new take over.

Jasminum polyanthum. When the plant becomes woody and unattractive, do not hesitate to prune all the shoots back by at least two thirds to encourage new growth. Do this after flowering, about June.

Mandevilla splendens. Flowering on the current year's growth, most of this needs to be cut away during the autumn when flowering is nearly over. Keep the plant drier and cooler during the winter, then gradually increase the watering in spring to promote the new season's shoots and flowers.

If the plant is trained as a climber, it can be left unpruned until it starts to exceed its boundaries.

Monstera deliciosa. There is a tendency for these plants to take over whole rooms, so do not hesitate to cut back very hard to within three or four nodes of the base if necessary. Shoots will either be there waiting, or will be readily produced to replace the old ones.

It does not damage the plant to trim off its aerial roots either. However, the best way to grow them is by providing a moss pole for the plant to cling to. If the moss is kept moist by syringing, the aerial roots will cling to it.

Nerium oleander. Often grown as a reminder of Mediterranean holidays, neriums will become very large if not pruned. Plenty of flowers can be produced by quite small but manageable plants.

After a plant raised from a cutting has grown and flowered, cut it hard back to within 15–30 cm (6–12 in) of the soil. New shoots will produce a much more branched plant. After every flowering season, shorten the shoots by at least half.

Pachystachys lutea. Their bright yellow bracts have helped these plants to become very popular in the home. Kept in bright, but not direct, light and in reasonable warmth, they will flower almost continuously, but eventually will become rather tall and woody.

At this point, cut them back by a good two-thirds, then give them a short rest period of cooler, drier conditions before bringing them on again. Time this renewal to coincide with spring so that they may benefit from the increased light.

Passiflora caerulea. This is the most commonly grown passion flower, but the same information applies to other species. Strong, young, established plants should be cut down to within about 15 cm (6 in) of the soil in spring, and main shoots pruned thereafter to keep them within the bounds of their trellis or frame. Prune side branches to 5–8 cm (2–3 in). Old, very tangly plants can be cut hard back quite safely to promote a complete replacement by new growth.

Philodendron. Prune as for *Monstera.*

Tradescantia. When they become straggly and unattractive, trim them right back to the top of the pot. A mass of new stems will result very quickly. This also applies to related plants, such as *Callisia* and *Zebrina.*

PROPAGATION

In the home, it is difficult but by no means impossible to provide the light, warmth and humidity necessary for most methods of propagation. The purchase of a small propagating unit, with controlled heating, will help, and will allow a larger range of plants and methods to be tried.

Hormone rooting compounds applied to cut surfaces will promote root development. Many of the powders contain a fungicide to reduce the risk of disease. Since these compounds lose their effectiveness if they are stored for too long a period, buy them in small quantities and use while fresh.

Propagation is either vegetative or by seed, the simplest form of vegetative propagation being by division.

Division This method is used to increase plants, such as *Aspidistra, Maranta* and *Spathiphyllum,* which form clumps of growths in their pots. It is usually done when the original plant has grown too large for its pot.

Knock the plant out and prise the old clump apart into several smaller ones. Frequently, this is hard to do as the old root-ball is virtually solid. In this case, take the plant outside and use two forks back to back to prise the clump apart, in much the same way as when dividing herbaceous plants. On a small scale, use handforks.

With this stage completed, pot the resulting plants in good compost and water them in. Allow the surface of the soil to become dry before watering again, for it is critical not to allow the soil to become waterlogged at this point. Wet soil discourages root development.

Offsets Frequently, plants such as *Sansevieria* and bromeliads produce offsets. To make use of them, take the original plant out of its pot, separate the offsets and sever them from the parent with a sharp knife. The offsets can then be potted up.

If they have a few roots, John Innes potting compost No. 1 may be used. However, if there are no roots it is better to use a cuttings compost. (See Shoot Cuttings.)

Root cuttings This technique also is carried out while the parent plant is out of the pot. Plants suitable for this method of propagation usually have thread-like roots, which should be detached and cut into sections measuring 1.3–2.5 cm (½–1 in). Lay these on the surface of some cuttings compost and cover with at least 13 mm (½ in) of the mixture. Water them in and keep moist.

After a few weeks, shoots will grow up from the roots. *Plumbago indica* and *Phyllanthus nivosus* can be propagated in this way.

Toes If you examine the base of the root-ball of an *Aspidistra* or *Cordyline* it is possible to find fleshy knobs instead of the normal fibrous root growth. These may be detached, about 1.3–5 cm (½–2 in) long, depending on the thickness, and potted about 2.5 cm (1 in) below the surface of a good potting compost.

Shoot cuttings These are what most people think of as 'ordinary' cuttings. Select strong, healthy shoots, and, if the plant is variegated, choose those showing good, balanced variegation.

Make a clean cut beneath a node, and trim away the bottom leaves of the cutting to make insertion into the cuttings mix easier. It is important not to make the cutting too long, an average length being 8 cm (3 in). The extra leaves on long cuttings result in excessive loss of moisture which cannot be replaced.

Stem cuttings
With plants such as *Dieffenbachia*, cut a stem with two or three nodes. Remove any leaves and lay the stem section horizontally on compost or insert it vertically to half its length.

Leaf cuttings
Plants such as *Begonia* can be propagated by leaf cuttings. Take a strong, healthy leaf from the parent plant and cut the prominent veins in several places. Lay the leaf on cuttings mix and weight it down to keep it in contact with the soil.

If the cuttings have very long leaves, trim these shorter so that the cuttings are not top-heavy and so that five or six of average size can be placed around the edge of an 8–10 cm (3–4 in) pot. Rooting is always better if the pot is full of cuttings.

Cuttings mix This should consist of 50% peat, together with 50% grit, sharp sand, Perlite or a mixture of these. The peat should be quite fine, and well-moistened before use. The drainage ingredient is a matter of personal choice and availability, but one or other of those listed is vital to ensure that water runs through the compost, as opposed to clogging it. Mix the ingredients well.

Most cuttings need more humidity than is available in a normal room. Water is continuously leaving the plant through the leaves, and there is as yet no root system to replace it fast enough. This is another reason why only sufficient leaves are left on the cutting to provide food for growth.

If you do not have a propagating case, place a polythene bag over the pot. Alternatively, a plastic top for an individual pot can be made by screwing the lid back onto an empty plastic squash bottle and cutting off the top 18 cm (7 in) or so.

Most cuttings should be kept as warm and moist as possible. However, there are a few that do not require humidity to root. Pelargoniums will rot if covered, and should be left open in good light. Cacti and succulents, too, prefer a dry environment.

It is quite possible to root a wide range of cuttings in water, *Tradescantia* and *Impatiens* being particularly well known for this. Other cuttings which seem more than happy in water have been exploited as aquarium plants and, given good lighting, they survive in aquaria for long periods. Examples include *Alternanthera*, *Fittonia*, *Pilea* and *Syngonium*.

Stem cuttings Stem sections of plants such as *Dieffenbachia* and *Dracaena*, each containing two to three nodes, will provide cuttings. No leaves are required on them. Stems are either laid on the compost horizontally or inserted upright to half their length. In each case, water them in and keep them warm and humid until roots and shoots appear.

x *Fatshedera* can be propagated by means of sections of stem containing two nodes, with cuts below the bottom one and above the top one. The top leaf is left on, the bottom one removed, and the cuttings inserted in the normal way.

Aphelandra can be propagated by making a cut above and below one node, with the leaf left on. Push this leaf-bud cutting into the cuttings mix so that the roots will grow down and the shoot will grow out from the leaf axil. If stock is scarce, slit the stem lengthways to obtain two cuttings.

Leaf cuttings With all types, choose leaves that are strong and healthy.

Saintpaulia and *Peperomia* root from the leaf stalk or petiole, so cut them from the parent plant with 2.5 cm (1 in) of stalk attached and insert them almost up to the leaf in cuttings mix.

Keep the cuttings warm and humid, waiting until small plantlets appear before disturbing them. Saintpaulias also root quite readily in water.

Begonia rex and *B. masoniana* leaves may be used entire. Cut the prominent veins in several places and place the leaf flat on the surface of a tray of cuttings mix. Hold it in place with pebbles.

Alternatively, leaves can be cut into sections the size of large postage stamps. Each should contain a main vein and be placed flat on the cuttings mix.

The place where the strongest roots occur is the area of thick veins where the leaf stalk is attached. Triangular cuttings, each containing a section of this vein, are possible. Insert upright in the compost.

With the first two methods it is essential to water the cuttings mix first. With all three methods the cuttings should be watered afterwards.

Streptocarpus leaves may be used for cuttings, too. Either cut a whole leaf into sections, each 4 cm (1½ in) long and inserted upright, or else cut the leaf lengthways down the vein. The vein is discarded, leaving two long strips of leaf. Insert each of these about 13 mm (½ in) deep, with the cut edges of the veins downwards. When the small plantlets that arise at the ends of the veins are large enough to handle, separate them and pot into small pots.

Air layering This method is used for propagating large plants with thick, woody stems that are too mature to root easily as ordinary cuttings. *Ficus bengalensis*, *F. benjamina* and *F. elastica* (rubber plant) may be propagated in this way.

Cut two rings around the stem, 13 mm (½ in) apart, and peel the bark away. Brush hormone rooting powder gently onto the cut surface.

Tie one end of a piece of sheet plastic below the cut, fill with moist sphagnum moss, packing it around the cut, then tie the other end tightly around the top above the cut to seal the area filled with moist moss. When roots become visible, cut off and pot the rooted cutting.

Plantlets Plants such as *Saxifraga stolonifera* and *Chlorophytum*, that produce plantlets, can be propagated by removing these little growths and pushing them firmly into a cuttings mix (see Shoot Cuttings), watering them and providing a warm, but not too humid environment until they have rooted and begun to grow on their own.

Alternatively, the plantlets can be rooted while still on the parent, severing the runner after roots have formed.

Some grow plantlets on their leaves or fronds, which may be similarly detached and rooted. Examples include *Tolmiea menziesii* (pick-a-back plant) *Asplenium bulbiferum* and *Bryophyllum daigremontianum* syn. *Kalanchoe daigremontiana* (Mexican hat plant).

Tubers Some plants form underground tubers, which are used for propagation. Many species in the family *Gesneriaceae*, such as *Achimenes*, *Sinningia* and *Kohleria*, have this characteristic, as do members of the ginger family, *Zingiberaceae*. The Aroids, such as large and small species and varieties of *Zantedeschia*, *Caladium* and *Alocasia*, also form tubers.

Most of these plants die down in the autumn, and remain dormant during the winter, when they should be kept almost completely dry in their pots before being lifted out in February. At this stage they are completely dormant and need replanting in fresh potting compost either about 4 cm (1½ in) deep, as in the case of *Achimenes*,

or with the top of the tuber just showing, as for the Aroids. They are then watered in thoroughly, and thereafter very carefully, until growth appears.

Propagation by seed It is possible to germinate seeds indoors, but light is the determining factor. The seedlings, once germinated, must be given as much light as possible without scorching them.

PESTS

Though pests are not usually a major problem with house plants a constant watch must be kept as it is so much easier to control them before they become established in large numbers. Watch for leaf discoloration and for sticky deposits.

Having identified the pest, if necessary with the aid of a magnifying glass, obtain the necessary pesticide to control the infestation. Do not vary the recommended dilution rate. Unless the pesticide is provided in an aerosol, a small sprayer will be needed. Take the plants outside before spraying.

The pests most liable to attack house plants include: aphids, whitefly, mealy bugs, root mealy bugs, scale insects, red spider mites, tarsonemid mites, leaf miners and vine weevils.

All except the tarsonemid mite and vine weevil are easily controlled. If either of these is diagnosed it will probably be best to get rid of the plant.

DISEASES

The most common disease affecting house plants is mildew, which often attacks members of the *Begonia* family. It is easy to control if spotted early enough and treated with the appropriate fungicide.

PLANTS FOR PARTICULAR POSITIONS

The chart (right) is a rough guide to plants suitable for a particular location. L means that the plant requires a well-lit position to do well. D denotes that the plant will tolerate a comparatively dark position. Obviously, artificial lighting will have to be provided for really dark corners, as even the toughest plant needs a certain level of light.

Warm, centrally-heated room

Aechmea L
Asparagus D
Aspidistra D
Asplenium D
Billbergia D
Clivia L
Dracaena D
Ficus D
Hibiscus L
Hippeastrum L
Hoya L
Palms D
Philodendron D
Pilea L
Sansevieria D
Streptocarpus L
Yucca D

Cold room with only occasional heat

Azalea L
Begonia L
Bulbs L
Calceolaria L
Cineraria L
Cyclamen L
x *Fatshedera* D
Fatsia D
Ferns D
Hedera D
Jasminum L
Primula L

Sunny windowsill

Beloperone
Cacti and succulents
Coleus
Cuphea
Fuchsia
Impatiens
Iresine
Pelargonium

Bathroom or steamy kitchen

Anthurium D
Bromeliads D
Fittonia L
Ferns D
Maranta D
Peperomia D
Philodendron D
Stephanotis L

Dark hallway

Aspidistra
x *Fatshedera*
Fatsia
Some ferns
Hedera
Sansevieria

All too often relegated to some dreary, dark area of the garden where 'nothing else will grow', ferns tend to be underrated in today's gardens. Yet many of them are most useful and attractive plants that will enhance any suitable site. Being rather primitive plants, with no flowers, their beauty comes entirely from the remarkable variation in the shapes and colours of their leaves (generally called fronds).

Ferns can form an attractive feature in their own right, but they also provide a beautiful foil for more flamboyant flowering plants. Although too often associated with dark, dank corners, they will grow well in most situations that are not too dry or sunny. They may be used on their own to form a fernery, but are more often planted in a mixed fern border, together with other plants in order to promote contrast and interest.

Many woodland herbaceous plants associate well with ferns. Examples are willow gentians, hostas, alchemillas, epimediums, wood anemones and periwinkles, which all blend well and introduce some variation in colour.

Some ferns are completely deciduous, but the fronds of many others remain green throughout the winter. Both sorts are of value, and many of the former colour up well during the autumn.

General cultivation In their natural habitat, most ferns are woodland plants. In the garden, too, they are best suited to positions in light shade, with a neutral or slightly acid soil that is humus-rich, moist but reasonably well-drained.

They may be planted at any time of the year, except during severe frost or drought. Early spring and late summer are particularly good times, since the soil then is warm enough to stimulate root growth and help them become established.

To prepare a site for planting, dig it over, remove any perennial weeds and mix in some well-rotted leaf-mould or coarse peat, together with a sprinkling of bone meal. After firming the area with your feet it will be ready for planting.

Tease out, just a little, the root-balls of pot-grown ferns, then firm the soil round the roots. The crowns of tufted ferns should be just above ground level; the rhizomes of creeping species should be only thinly buried.

Water newly-planted ferns freely and regularly during their first spring and summer.

Propagation Since ferns are not flowering plants, they do not produce seeds. In the wild they reproduce by spores, by the creeping rhizomes that are typical of certain species or by the production of offsets from the main rosette. These same methods may be used in the garden to increase your stock.

Dividing ferns The easiest means of increasing a stock of ferns is by division. This is done in autumn or spring, in much the same way as for herbaceous plants.

Ferns with creeping rhizomes quickly cover a substantial area, and it is a simple matter to remove a well-rooted portion of the patch. Most of the more garden-worthy ferns, however, are clump-forming, producing shuttlecock-like tufts or crowns of fronds.

With ferns of this type it is easy to see whether a clump is composed of several crowns, and therefore ready to be divided. They are best kept to a single crown to promote a good slope.

To divide such a plant, first lift the whole clump. The roots will be tightly intertwined, so insert a pair of hand-forks or border-forks back to back between the crowns to help ease them apart.

With large and old clumps, most of the blackish fibrous roots will be dead, the live roots being mostly hidden under the bases of the old leaf-stalks. It is therefore a good idea to pull off some of these lower stalk bases carefully before replanting the separated crowns in suitably prepared soil. Small offsets can be potted up for growing on for a year or so.

How to sow spores Raising ferns from spores is perhaps less easy than growing other plants from seeds, but it does provide a means of raising large numbers of plants.

Most ferns produce their spores in small heaps or lines, on the undersides of the mature fronds, during the summer. *Osmunda regalis* (royal fern) is a notable exception in that it bears its spores conspicuously on the modified ends of the fronds. When ripe, the spore heaps of most ferns are a deep brown or black, only becoming a pale rusty-brown colour when the spores have fallen.

To collect spores, remove a small piece of spore-bearing frond and place it immediately in a paper envelope. If this is left in a living room for a day or so, and then opened carefully, any spores present will have settled in the bottom of the packet as a dust-like brown powder. The spores may then be sown in pots prepared in the following way:

Fill an 8 cm (3 in) plastic pot to within 13 mm (½ in) of the top with either John Innes seed compost or John Innes No. 1 potting compost. Place a disc of newspaper on the compost and gently pour boiling water on to it from a kettle. When the water coming out from the bottom of the pot is really hot, any stray fungus or moss spores on the surface should have been killed.

Cover the pot with a piece of glass or plastic until it is cold, then remove the glass and the disc of paper and sprinkle the spores very thinly over the surface of the compost. Immediately cover the pot with a piece of clear polythene and tie it in place with string.

Write the fern's name on the pot with a permanent, waterproof marker pen, or attach a waterproof label. Leave the pot undisturbed in a lightly-shaded cold frame, a cool greenhouse or on a cool windowsill. Do not remove the top until the young sporelings are large enough to be pricked out easily.

After a period, which may be a month or as long as several months, a green film will be visible through the cover, on the soil surface. This will gradually resolve itself into distinct filmy green structures, the prothalli.

Later still, the first, tiny true fronds will appear from these and, when two or three such fronds are visible, the sporelings may be pricked out into new pots of sterilized potting compost and grown on in similar conditions.

In two or three years, with careful attention, the young ferns will be large enough to plant out in the garden.

Propagating ferns
Sowing fern spores requires patience, since it may take as long as three years before ferns are ready for planting out in the garden. You can, however, increase your stock dramatically using this technique.

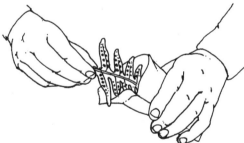

1 Remove some ripe spore-bearing frond and leave it in a dry envelope for a day, or until spores have settled to the bottom.

2 Kill fungus or moss spores with boiling water before sowing.

3 When compost is cold, sow fern spores thinly over the soil.

4 Identify the fern. Cover the pot with polythene.

5 Leave in a shaded cold frame or greenhouse.

6 Leave undisturbed until the sporelings can be pricked out.

7 Place sporlings in individual pots of compost and cover.

8 Grow on young fern plants in new pots of sterilized compost.

Fern bulbils
Some ferns produce bulbils along the midrib of the fronds. Peg the frond down, and in about one year the plants will have rooted and be ready for detaching and growing on.

Unusual ferns
Not all ferns are delicate and lacy. *Osmunda regalis* (1) is large and bold; and *Adiantum candatum* (2) has rounded leaves to its fronds. *Phylitis scolupendrium* (3) has undivided, strap-like fronds.

A few ferns, mainly cultivars of *Polystichum setiferum* (soft shield fern) develop small bulbils along the midrib of the frond. If such a frond is pegged down on to the soil, the bulbils will eventually root into it. After a year or so the young plants will be large enough to be detached and grown on.

A selection of ferns Many hardy ferns are best suited to the slightly shady, cool conditions that resemble their natural woodland habitats. Probably the most handsome are the larger clump-forming types, which produce shuttlecocks between 45 cm–1.2 m (1½–4 ft) high.

Some of these are deciduous, their foliage dying down in winter, and among these is, *Athyrium filix-femina* (lady fern), a beautiful species that has given rise to numerous cultivars. These vary in size and in the lace-like dissection of their fronds.

Osmunda regalis (royal fern) can exceed 1.8 m (6 ft) in ideal conditions and has the added virtue of fine autumn colour as the foliage dies down. This species will form magnificent clumps when planted beside water and its fronds are much bolder in form than the delicate lacy growth of the lady fern.

Dryopteris filix-mas (common male fern) can appear rather coarse, but it is suitable for a wild-garden setting and also has some pleasant cultivars.

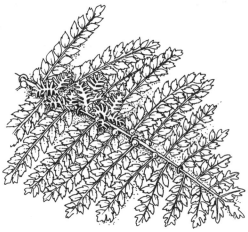

Two striking species, well worth a place in the fernery, are *Dryopteris affinis*, syn. *D. borreri* or *D. pseudomas*, (golden-scaled male fern) and *D. austriaca*, syn. *D. dilatata*, (broad buckler fern). The fronds of both, though deciduous, remain green in winter.

D. affinis derives its common name from the abundant scales on the midrib, which are most conspicuous as the fronds unfurl in the spring. A related fern from Japan is *D. erythrosora*, often notable for a pink tinge in the young foliage and for its bright red spore heaps.

D. oreopteris, syn. *Thelypteris limbosperma* (mountain fern) grows wild on wet stream banks in moorland areas and does not always persist in the garden. It is intolerant of limy soils, but has fragrant, almost lemon-scented fronds.

Matteuccia struthiopteris (shuttlecock fern) forms extensive colonies of erect tufts that die down at the first touch of frost. A great beauty for a sheltered site is *Adiantum pedatum* (maidenhair fern) which is native to Japan and western North America.

Another Japanese species that is highly desirable is *Athyrium nipponicum* 'Pictum', syn. *A. goeringianum* 'Pictum'. This cultivar is most distinct in the colouring of its fronds, which are a light greyish-green, with a paler zone either side of the dull crimson midrib.

Perhaps more attractive still are those species with fronds that remain green through the winter. *Polystichum setiferum*

1
2
3

and *P. aculeatum* (both shield ferns) are very variable in form, some of their cultivars being amongst the finest hardy species. The Plumosum and Divisilobum groups of *P. setiferum*, especially, produce the most elegant fronds which are, in some cultivars, of outstanding laciness.

In complete contrast, *Asplenium scolopendrium*, syn. *Phyllitis scolopendrium*, (hart's-tongue) has undivided, strap-like fronds. These are a familiar sight in the lanes of the West Country, where they may reach 60 cm (2 ft) in length. Like many of the British species of ferns, the hart's-tongue has produced many curious and often attractive forms that are now named as cultivars.

A smaller, evergreen species of compact growth is *Blechnum spicant* (hard fern). This demands acid or neutral conditions, in which it forms a neat rosette of dark green, pinnate leaves, with ladder-like, erect, fertile fronds.

Some ferns have a questing, branching rhizome from which the fronds arise singly, and by means of which they may colonize a considerable area. *Pteridium aquilinum* (bracken) is the best known species, but it is a rampant grower, difficult to eradicate and unsuitable for ordinary gardens. More restrained species with this type of rhizome can be useful ground-cover plants, and may be a particularly effective underplanting for taller flowering plants, such as lilies and hostas.

The evergreen *Blechnum chilense*, syn. *B. tabulare*, has dark green upright fronds which, in suitably damp conditions, can reach 90 cm (3 ft) in height. On the other hand, *Polypodium vulgare* and its varieties seldom exceed 30 cm (1 ft), slowly spreading to produce a mat of light, olive-green fronds.

Deciduous creeping species include *Onoclea sensibilis* (sensitive fern) with broad, rather pale fronds quite unlike those of other ferns. As its name suggests, the fronds are killed by the first frost.

Gymnocarpium dryopteris (oak fern) and *Phegopteris connectilis* (beech fern) are two gems for leafy, acid soils, the former having 15 cm (6 in) triangular fronds of delicate texture, on long, thin stalks. Beech

fern has pale, slightly hairy fronds of a similar size, but narrower.

Dennstaedtia punctilobula and *Hypolepis millefolia*, although quite low-growing, are capable of spreading extensively and are therefore better suited to a large, shady bed than to, say, a shaded part of the rock garden.

In their natural habitat, several ferns are confined to screes, rock crevices and walls, and these species can be a charming feature of a rock garden or peat wall, or even of a trough planted with alpines. Several evergreen spleenworts, such as *Asplenium trichomanes*, *A. adiantum-nigrum* and *A. ceterach* (rusty-back fern), will grow well in these situations.

Another attractive evergreen species is *Blechnum penna-marina*, from New Zealand. It grows slowly into a mat of fronds 8–15 cm (3–6 in) high, the young ones being tinted with bronze.

The deciduous bladder ferns (species of *Cystopteris*) are also good crevice plants, looking well with rock garden plants. *C. fragilis* and *C. dickieana* seldom exceed 15–20 cm (6–8 in), but the North American *C. bulbifera* has narrow, erect fronds 30–45 cm (1–1½ ft) high.

Small, pea-like bulbils are produced on the undersides of the fronds of this species, providing an easy means of raising new plants. Another hardy fern, the Himalayan maidenhair, *Adiantum venustum*, forms mounds of pretty foliage from its slowly-spreading rhizomes.

Although moisture-loving, most ferns require a well-drained soil; some larger species, however, thrive on the margins of ponds or streams. Apart from the royal fern, *Blechnum chilense* and *Onoclea sensibilis* make bold waterside features. *Thelypteris palustris* (marsh fern) has a thong-like rhizome from which deciduous fronds, 60 cm (2 ft) high, are produced.

Most of the ferns mentioned here are native to Europe, but many species from North America and north-east Asia are equally hardy and attractive. It is worthwhile finding sources for these rarer plants because a fern border, large or small, can form a feature of great beauty and interest and requires relatively little maintenance.

Common fern
Although rather coarse in appearance, *Dryopteris filix-mas* (common male fern) is hardy and looks excellent, for example, growing from a rock crevice in a wild garden.

Evergreen fern
The evergreen spleenwort *Asplenium adiantum-nigrum* makes a fine plant for the rock garden, peat wall or alpine trough.

Dendrobium nobile
This orchid is an ideal specimen for growing on bark in the kitchen or bathroom, where the humidity is high.

Even accomplished house plant growers may be put off orchids by their reputation for being expensive and difficult. However, the cost of a plant is being reduced by modern micro propagation techniques, while a considerable number can be kept at quite low temperatures – about 7°C (45°F) – in spite of the tropical origin of some species. Though it is a challenge to have orchids flowering well each year, they are by no means difficult and certainly merit a place among other indoor plants.

Understanding orchids Before getting closely involved, one should have a basic understanding of this intriguing family of plants. Obviously, they will be easier to grow if one knows something about the natural conditions to which they have adapted.

The first overwhelming fact is their sheer abundance and diversity, for there are thousands of known species and thousands more hybrids. Some orchids are terrestial, meaning that they grow normally in the ground; many others, however, are epiphytic, which means that they use supports, such as trees, rocks or even telegraph poles, on which to live.

This latter group usually grow in very humid conditions and have roots which either cling to the support or hang in the air. Note that they are not parasitic, for they do not take any nourishment from their support. They obtain everything they need from the moisture in the air and from any nearby decaying matter.

Many orchids have storage structures known as pseudobulbs, which are swellings at the base of the leaves. Their purpose is to store sufficient food and moisture to get the plant into growth and, often, to flower at the end of a dry period. Orchids with these structures generally require a rest period at some stage during their growing cycle, when little or no water and nourishment should be given. It is unlikely that continued growth would kill the plant, but it might prevent it from flowering.

All orchids have interesting flowers. Some are extremely beautiful; others are small and delicate, or merely curious. Their primary purpose is to assist in pollination of the plant, and some flowers actually resemble the bees or butterflies that are attracted to them.

Composts As most orchids are epiphytic, or grow in very light soils, they require an open, free-draining compost that will allow as much air to the roots as possible. Few will grow well in ordinary potting compost, whether based on loam or peat. Ready-mixed composts are available, or you can prepare your own from the following – a mixture that will suit most orchids:

Bark chippings (orchid grade)	4 parts
Charcoal	2 parts
Perlite	1 part

Orchids need repotting whenever the compost begins to break down and lose its openness, or when the plants become too large and roots escape from the pot.

Growing on supports An alternative to planting epiphytic orchids in pots is to grow them on a support, much as they would naturally. This can be either a dead tree branch, some cork bark or a piece of osmunda fibre. The method is to secure the main part of the plant with a large staple, then, using thin wire or nylon fishing line, to attach the remainder of the plant.

Watering can be a problem if orchids are grown in the home on such supports. They have to be sprayed regularly, up to twice a day, which means moving the plants each time or else growing them where moisture will not harm the furnishings – not necessarily the best place for the plants. Things are easier in a greenhouse or conservatory, however, where attractive arrangements of epiphytic orchids on trees can be made, along with other compatible plants.

Watering There is no simple guide as to how often orchids should be watered. When in active growth, the plants should not be allowed to dry out completely, but the compost should always have begun to dry before more water is added. Particularly with the epiphytic species, it is essential for the roots to have air around them and not to be waterlogged.

As the compost is so open and full of bark it is impossible to gauge its water content by examining the surface. The only sure way is to feel the weight of the pot, and to water only when it becomes very light. Use soft water, if possible.

Feeding As there is no nutrient in the recommended compost, a well-balanced liquid fertilizer must be applied weekly. This should contain trace elements, vital for plant growth though needed only in very small amounts. If the fertilizer also acts as a foliar feed, so much the better. Occasionally, especially when coming into flower, a high-potash feed should be given.

One feed in four should be omitted, and water given instead, to ensure that there is no build-up of harmful salts in the compost. When the plants are resting, give no more feeds until growth resumes.

General care As with other plants, observation is one of the keys to success with orchids. Look over all the plants regularly, checking for pests and diseases, new growths, flower buds or any sign that the plant is becoming dormant.

If a plant has gone into a decline it will probably be due to overwatering, so do not hesitate to get it out of its pot. Trim off any dead roots and pot it into some fresh compost. Very careful watering will probably then encourage new root growth and the plant should survive.

Orchids as houseplants It is possible to grow quite a wide range of orchids in the home, provided the right combination of temperature and light can be found. Following are a few easily-obtained orchids which are suitable for beginners to try:

Cymbidium. After flowering in winter, keep the plants at a temperature of 10°C (50°F) in good, but not direct, light. Shoots will form at this stage and the plants continue in active growth. In the spring, if the plant is large or the compost is becoming very broken down, repot into the recommended compost. Any old, dead pseudobulbs should be cut off, but the growing part of the plant should be backed up by two or three green pseudobulbs.

If the plant is very large, it can be split at this time and potted firmly. During the hottest months of summer, cymbidiums will benefit from being placed in the garden in a position of good, but not direct, sunlight. An open cold frame, with slats that can be drawn over during the brightest days, is ideal. This will have the effect of 'ripening' the plant, which will encourage it to flower later on. Keeping the plant slightly drier during August and September will also aid the future development of flower spikes.

Make sure that the plant is brought back inside again well before the cold weather starts. If a minimum temperature of 10°C (50°F) is maintained, flower spikes will begin to appear during the winter. When flowering starts, change the liquid feed to one with a high-potash content.

Cymbidium cuerum This winter-flowering orchid requires a temperature of at least 10°C (50°F) before flower spikes will appear. Apart from routine care, it is an easy plant for beginners to try.

Dendrobium. There are many different species of this epiphytic genus, some deciduous, some evergreen. Small ones are easily grown in pots but some of the larger ones will either become very top-heavy or will trail and pull the pot over. They are ideal orchids to grow on bark in the bathroom or kitchen, where humidity is not a problem.

Most dendrobiums require a resting period of several months, from about November, during which they need only infrequent watering. After the dormant stage they will produce new shoots, and leaves will grow and stems swell until finally a terminal leaf appears on the shoot, with no signs of any growth beyond it.

Now is the time to stop watering. Failure to impose a drought on these orchids will not kill them, but they will produce offsets instead of flowers.

Masdevallia. Mostly terrestial orchids, the flowers are curious rather than beautiful. Provided they are given reasonable light and ventilation, a minimum temperature of 10°C (50°F), and watered carefully, they should flower regularly.

Paphiopedilum. These require a minimum of 13°C (55°F) to do well, and should stay indoors all the year round in a position where the light is good but not direct. The plants do not require a resting period, but they need very careful watering as they cannot stand being waterlogged.

Phalaenopsis. Requiring a minimum of 16°C (60°F) to do well, these orchids do not undergo a dormant phase but need water and feed all the year round. They are suitable for growing in pots or on bark, though in pots the roots do have a tendency to climb over the top.

Do not cut off the flower stalk after the flower has died, for fresh buds will appear until the stalk dies naturally.

Growing under glass A landscaped epiphytic display, using trees and bark, can be most attractive, but during the summer it may be difficult to maintain a sufficiently humid atmosphere. An orchid grown on bark, with its roots in the air, may need damping down as many as four times on a really hot day.

Displays of orchids can also be grown in pots on staging. Ideally, the staging should be of slats over a gravel tray, which will keep the air round the plants humid.

Shading is most important, for orchids are very prone to scorch. Provide some light shading as soon as the sun begins to brighten in spring, and add to this as the sun's strength increases. This can be done with a proprietary shading paint, a shading material, or both. All parts of the greenhouse or conservatory should be shaded – the sides, doors and vents, as well as the roof. Remove it gradually as the light fades in autumn. Plenty of ventilation is needed in summer to prevent extremes of temperature. When choosing a house for orchid growing, make sure that there is ample ventilation space in the sides as well as at ridge level.

Exotic forms
Despite the fact that the needs of orchids tend to be a little more precise than those of other plants, the beauty of their exotic forms makes them worth persevering with.

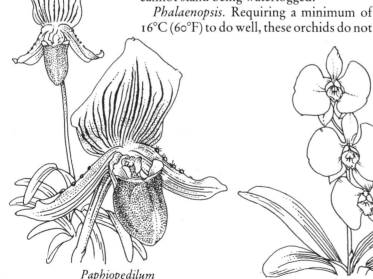

Paphiopedilum callosum

Phalaenopsis amabilis

Paphiopedilum insigne

The rock face has been used as a planting area in this sloping cliff-top coastal garden. It is essential to choose salt tolerant plants for seaside sites.

Stone sinks or troughs provide excellent miniature landscapes for growing a selection of alpines, and have the advantage of raising plants to a more comfortable working level.

A scree bed is designed to simulate the litter of stones found on a mountain side. It has the advantage of allowing rock garden plants to be grown on a gentle slope.

All sorts and sizes of pots, in plastic, clay or stone, can be used to grow plants in. And found containers like this outmoded wooden wheelbarrow make particularly attractive homes for flowering specimens.

CHAPTER FOUR

PLANT HEALTH AND WEED CONTROL

Every gardener wages an on-going battle against the often invisible enemies that distort leaves and shoots, spoil flowers and fruit, and sometimes cause the death of favourite plants. This chapter is about plant care – it shows how to recognize the tell-tale signs of specific plant pests and diseases and gives advice on controlling them and preventing further damage.

Healthy, strong-growing plants withstand pest and disease attacks far better than sickly specimens, and good cultural care can do much to minimize the need for chemical sprays. Such maintenance also includes the suppression of weeds which compete with cultivated plants for water, nutrients, air circulation and light.

Plant names and gardening parlance have their own special terminology. A short compendium lists the technical terms the gardener will most often encounter and explains the logic behind the botanical nomenclature that distinguishes one species – and one cultivar – from another.

Finally, a quick at-a-glance guide summarizes the tasks that are part of the pleasures of the gardening year.

Awide range of pests feed on cultivated plants, although not all cause sufficient damage to require control measures. In all cases, sound methods of cultivation will produce strong plants that are better able to withstand attacks. However, timely use of an insecticide may also be needed to deal with the more important sorts, such as those that reduce the yield and quality of fruits and vegetables or spoil ornamental plants.

Soil-dwelling pests

Ants Forming large underground nests in lawns and flower borders, ants are a nuisance rather than a pest. They feed mainly on other insects, and on sweet substances, such as honeydew, collected from aphids. Their nest-building activities can cause indirect damage to plants by loosening soil from the roots, and low-growing plants may suffer from partial burial by excavated soil.

Eradication of ants is rarely possible, so confine control measures to nests that are causing actual harm to plants. The nest area should be drenched or dusted with either HCH, carbaryl or pirimiphos-methyl.

Chafer grubs and leatherjackets These are mainly lawn pests, although they also eat the roots of vegetables and ornamental plants.

Leatherjackets are the more widespread and troublesome, causing yellowish-brown patches in lawns in mid-summer. They are greyish-brown, legless maggots up to 4 cm (1½ in) long.

Chafer grubs occur mainly in sandy soils and are plump white grubs, curved like a letter C, with brown heads and three pairs of legs. Chafer damage occurs in the autumn, when magpies and crows may be seen ripping up the turf in order to feed on the grubs.

HCH or carbaryl will control these pests, although they need to be used while the grubs are small if damage is to be avoided. For leatherjackets, early October is the correct time, while early June and early August are the times to treat chafers.

Cutworms and wireworms Both of these pests are found most frequently in newly-dug ground or neglected, weedy plots. After the soil has been cultivated for several years these pests will become much less abundant.

Cutworms are the soil-dwelling caterpillars of various moths and they either sever roots or gnaw away the outer tissues from the base of stems. This causes sudden wilting and death especially of lettuces, asters and other annuals.

Wireworms are thin, stiff-bodied, light brown larvae up to 2.5 cm (1 in) long which bore into potato tubers and the roots of many other plants. Where damage occurs, some reduction in these pests can be achieved by mixing diazinon, bromophos or phoxim granules into the soil.

Millipedes and woodlice Decaying plant tissues form most of the diet of these common inhabitants of the soil. They are numerous in compost heaps or where dead leaves have accumulated, and in these situations they are of some benefit in assisting the process of recycling nutrients. Their weak mouthparts cannot make much impression on established plants, but they can damage seedlings and soft shoot tips. They also enlarge damage started by slugs.

Vegetable root flies Carrot fly maggots bore into the tap roots of carrots, parsley and parsnips, causing rusty-brown tunnels beneath the skin. Young plants may be killed or stunted, and tunnelled

parts of the root develop an unpleasant taste.

Brassicas, including turnips and swedes, and onions are attacked during the summer by several generations of other species of root fly. The larvae are white, legless maggots up to 8 mm (⅓ in) long. They destroy the roots, and damage varies from a slowing of growth to wilting and dying.

With each of these pests, young plants in seed-beds and any recently transplanted are the ones most susceptible to damage. Protect during the early stages of growth by treating seed rows and the soil around transplants with diazinon, bromophos or phoxim granules. Attacks by later generations on established plants can be checked by watering with spray-strength pirimiphos-methyl.

Vine weevil The adult beetles eat irregular notches at night from the leaves of rhododendrons and other shrubs. Their larvae live in the soil, where they eat the roots and corms of many plants. They damage garden plants, including strawberries, primulas and sedums, but are most frequently found among the roots of house plants and other plants grown in pots, tubs and windowboxes.

The legless, slightly curved grubs, up to 12 mm (½ in) long, are white with light brown heads. Damage occurs mainly during the autumn and spring, and often the first indication of the grubs' presence is when a cherished plant collapses and dies. Examination of the soil may reveal a dozen or more larvae where the roots used to be.

The older larvae are tolerant of pesticides, so it is best to water susceptible plants during July and August with HCH or permethrin in order to kill the young larvae. These insecticides can also be sprayed at dusk during the summer if the adults are causing significant damage to shrubs.

Sap-feeding pests These have needle-like mouthparts that are inserted into the vascular tissues of leaves or stems. Some pests that feed on sap, especially aphids, whiteflies, scales and mealybugs, excrete a sweet, sticky liquid known as honeydew.

Ants are attracted by this honeydew, which coats the upper leaf surfaces, and allows the growth of a non-parasitic sooty mould. This unsightly fungus is difficult to remove without sponging individual leaves, so it is advisable to control the pest causing the problem.

Aphids Also known as greenfly and blackfly, aphids are among the most troublesome of the common garden pests. Over 500 species occur in Britain, so few plants escape their attentions.

Dense colonies can develop, particularly on young leaves, shoot tips and flower buds. Some species, such as the woolly aphids on apple and beech, disguise themselves by secreting fluffy white fibres from their bodies. Heavy infestations often result in curled foliage and distorted growth.

Some virus diseases of soft fruits and ornamentals are spread by the mouthparts of aphids when they transfer from diseased to healthy plants. Early treatment, before heavy infestations develop, is necessary if damage is to be avoided.

Overwintering eggs of aphids on fruit trees and bushes can be destroyed by thorough spraying with tar oil while the plants are fully dormant. Many pesticides will control aphids, but systemic compounds, such as dimethoate or heptenophos, are particularly

suitable as they penetrate into the sap. In this way they reach aphids hidden under curled leaves that contact pesticides would miss.

Pirimicarb is partly systemic and is a selective insecticide that kills aphids while leaving bees and many aphid predators unharmed.

Spray fruit trees and bushes shortly before the blossom period – except for pears and peaches, which should be sprayed shortly after petal fall. Inspect vegetables and ornamentals regularly and treat when necessary.

Capsid bugs These are pale green or brown agile insects up to 6 mm (¼ in) long that suck sap from young leaves and flower buds. They have a toxic saliva that causes some plant cells to die. When the leaves expand to their full size, the dead areas tear into many small holes, making the foliage tattered and distorted.

Flower buds of dahlias and chrysanthemums develop unevenly into flowers where not all the petals expand; those of hardy fuchsias abort. Other plants likely to show foliage damage include bush fruits, roses, hydrangeas, caryopteris and clematis.

Capsids are active from May until late summer and control is not easy, since by the time obvious symptoms develop the pest may have moved on. Sprays based on HCH, dimethoate or permethrin should be applied at the first sign of damage. Hydrangeas are scorched by most insecticides, so it is best to tolerate capsids on this plant.

Mealybugs Cacti and succulents are the main host plants, but mealybugs also infest many other indoor plants. They are soft-bodied, pinkish-grey insects up to 3 mm (⅛ in) long, but may be difficult to see as they cluster in leaf axils and other inaccessible

parts of the plant. This helps protect them from insecticides, as does their habit of secreting a fluffy white, waxy substance over themselves and their eggs.

Thorough spraying with malathion will control them, as will the old remedy of dabbing the mealybugs with methylated spirits. This latter method is best for succulents, such as species of *Crassula*, which are damaged by insecticides.

Red spider mites The fruit tree red spider mite found on apples and plums, and the glasshouse red spider mite are the most troublesome examples of this group. The latter attacks most greenhouse plants and, in hot summers, many outdoor plants as well. Both mites are only just visible to the naked eye. Despite their name, they are yellow-green, with darker markings during the summer.

Both species live underneath leaves and cause a fine, mottled discoloration of the upper surface. Heavy infestations cause leaves to turn yellow and fall off, and a fine silk webbing is spun over the plant. Hot, dry conditions encourage red spider mites to breed rapidly.

Neither pest is easy to control, but thorough spraying with malathion, pirimiphos-methyl or dimethoate before heavy infestations have developed may work. Three applications at seven-day intervals are advisable. However, strains of mite resistant to pesticides do occur.

An alternative means of controlling glasshouse red spider is to use biological control by introducing a predatory mite called *Phytoseiulus persimilis* on to the plants. Further details are available from suppliers such as Natural Pest Control, Yapton Road, Barnham, Bognor Regis, Sussex, and Bunting and Sons, The Nurseries, Great Horkesley, Colchester, Essex.

Scale insects Various species of scale insects attack both greenhouse and outdoor plants. They vary in size, shape and colour, but are all relatively immobile and covered by a scale. They sometimes resemble miniature shellfish.

The two species most commonly encountered are soft scale and brown scale. The former is a flat, oval, yellowish-brown scale up to 3 mm (⅛ in) long, which occurs on the undersides of leaves next to the larger veins. Bay, ivy, camellias, citrus, ferns and many house plants are attacked, and soiled with honeydew and sooty mould. Brown scale is a dark brown, convex scale up to 6 mm (¼ in) long, and is found on the stems of greenhouse vines and peaches, and on many outdoor shrubs.

Spraying with malathion is effective, especially if timed to coincide with the hatching of the scales' eggs. Outdoors, this will be in early or late June, depending on species. Under glass, it may be at any time of year. Infestations on deciduous trees and shrubs can be controlled by using tar oil in December.

Whiteflies The main problem is glasshouse whitefly, which attacks tomatoes, cucumbers and many indoor ornamentals. Another species, the cabbage whitefly, occurs on brassicas throughout the year.

The tiny white adult insects fly up from beneath the leaves when disturbed. Their immobile, scale-like nymphs and pupae also feed on the lower leaf surface. Honeydew is excreted, and both foliage and fruits become soiled with sooty mould.

Early treatment is necessary for good control, using permethrin, pirimiphos-methyl or pyrethrum on two or more occasions at seven-day intervals. Pesticide resistance may arise with glasshouse whitefly and, as an alternative, use biological control by the parasitic wasp *Encarsia formosa*. Suppliers are listed under Red Spider Mites.

Leaf-eating pests

Beetles Seedlings of brassicas, turnips, swedes and radishes are damaged by adult flea beetles. They scallop small holes in the leaves, and seedlings may be killed in heavy attacks, especially if growth is delayed by drought or cold weather.

Flea beetles are 2 mm (1/12 in) long and metallic-blue or black with a yellow stripe on their wing cases. They can be controlled with HCH seed dressings or by dusting the seedlings with HCH, derris or pirimiphos-methyl.

Asparagus may be defoliated between May and September by the adults and larvae of the asparagus beetle. The adults are coloured red, yellow and black and are 6 mm (¼ in) long. The larvae are greyish-black grubs, and there are two or three generations during the summer. Damaged plants become yellowish-white where the stems and leaves have been gnawed.

Closely related is the scarlet lily beetle, which is confined mainly to the Surrey, Hampshire and Berkshire areas. The bright red beetles are 9 mm (⅜ in) long, and present from late March until October. Their grubs are orange-red and covered by a slimy black excreta. Lilies and fritillaries can be severely defoliated.

Control lily and asparagus beetles by spraying with permethrin, HCH or fenitrothion.

Caterpillars (see also Sawflies) Many species can attack garden plants. Brassicas are the host plants of the large and small cabbage white butterflies and cabbage moth. Early treatment is necessary, otherwise caterpillars bore into the heart leaves, where they are beyond the reach of pesticides.

Fruit trees and many deciduous trees and shrubs are attacked during the spring by the pale green looper caterpillars of winter moths. They are the principal cause of holed leaves on such plants during the summer.

Larvae of the carnation tortrix moth feed on many house plants by binding two leaves together with silk webbing and then grazing away the inner surfaces.

Caterpillars can be controlled by spraying with permethrin, fenitrothion, pirimiphos-methyl or derris. Some reduction in winter moth attacks can be achieved by putting sticky grease bands round tree trunks in late October. This stops some of the emerging flightless females from climbing the trunk to lay eggs.

Earwigs These pests feed at night on the young leaves and flowers of clematis, dahlias, chrysanthemums and other plants. HCH, fenitrothion or permethrin sprayed at dusk on warm evenings will control them, but several applications may be required during the summer.

Leaf miners A distinctive type of damage is caused by the larvae of certain flies, moths, beetles and sawflies. They tunnel within leaves, causing white or brown lines, circles or irregular blotches as the damaged tissues dry up. Chrysanthemum leaf mining fly causes sinuous narrow mines, while a related species causes irregular blotches on holly leaves.

Celery, parsnip and lovage also have a leaf mining fly that causes large areas of the leaves to turn brown and become shrivelled. A leaf mining moth attacks lilac and privet, causing brown blotch mines and rolling of the leaf tips.

These and other leaf miners can be dealt with by spraying with HCH or pirimiphos-methyl (not on celery) or malathion.

Sawflies The larvae of sawflies closely resemble moth caterpillars, but the adults belong to the same order of insects as ants, bees and wasps. Gooseberries, currants, willows, aquilegias, geums, *Aruncus dioicus* and Solomon's seal all attract sawfly larvae that eat the leaves, often to the extent of the plants being completely defoliated.

They are relatively easy to control, provided they are spotted before the damage is too far advanced. They are killed by most contact insecticides, including derris, pyrethrum, permethrin and malathion.

The rose leaf-rolling sawfly is less easily dealt with as the larvae are hidden inside rolled leaves. The leaf curling is caused by chemicals injected into leaves by the females as they lay eggs in May or June. Light infestations can be checked by removing affected leaflets; otherwise spray forcibly with pirimiphos-methyl or fenitrothion.

Slugs and snails Most plants are at risk, but especially seedlings and soft young shoots. They can be protected with pellets or sprays based on either metaldehyde or methiocarb. The latter is the more effective under damp conditions, when slug and snail activity is greatest.

Some slugs live underground, where they tunnel into bulbs and root vegetables, especially maincrop potato tubers. Early lifting helps to limit damage.

Potato varieties vary in their susceptibility to slugs. 'Pentland Dell' and 'Pentland Ivory' are less

vulnerable, while 'Maris Piper', 'Cara' and 'Pentland Crown' may be badly damaged. Soil-dwelling slugs come on to the surface on warm days after heavy rain, and methiocarb pellets used at such times will reduce their numbers.

Galls These abnormal growths are produced by plants in response to attacks by pests or diseases. Oak trees are affected by many species of gall wasps that gall the leaves, buds, catkins and acorns. None causes serious damage, and control measures are unnecessary.

Other trees, such as *Acer* and lime, are affected by gall mites that cause red, raised structures on the leaves. These are harmless and should be tolerated. Some gall mites do, however, adversely affect their host plant.

One causes big bud of black currant, affected buds fail to open in the spring. Another galls the *Cytisus* buds, converting them into cauliflower-like structures.

Gall mites are little affected by insecticides available to the amateur, but the fungicide benomyl may check them if applied on three occasions at two-week intervals, starting in early April. Pick off and burn galled buds; replace with new plants if infestations become too bad.

Fruit and seed pests

Black currant big bud mite Big bud is caused by microscopic gall mites which feed inside the buds, causing them to become swollen and rounded. Such buds often fail to develop in spring and the mites can further reduce plant vigour by spreading reversion disease.

No insecticides available to amateurs give good control of big bud. Picking off and burning the rounded buds in winter will limit light infestations. Spraying with the fungicide benomyl when the flowers first open, with two furth-

er treatments at two-week intervals, will also help. Heavily infested plants that are cropping poorly should be scrapped.

Codling moth The larvae of this moth are the cause of maggoty apples in late summer. Thorough spraying with permethrin or fenitrothion in mid-June, and again three weeks later, will kill the recently-hatched larvae.

Pea moth This lays its eggs on peas which are in flower, so late or early sowings that flower outside the moth's flight period of late June to August escape damage.

The pest can be controlled by spraying vulnerable peas with permethrin or fenitrothion when in full flower and again ten days later.

Pear midge These tiny flies lay eggs in the flower buds. The larvae are whitish-orange maggots, up to 2 mm ($\frac{1}{12}$ in) long, which feed inside the young fruitlets. These soon turn black and drop.

In gardens where pear midge has occurred in the previous year, spray with HCH or fenitrothion at the white bud stage.

Raspberry beetle The small, brownish-white grubs of this beetle damage the stalk ends of raspberry, loganberry and blackberry fruits, causing them to dry up. Damage can be prevented by spraying thoroughly at dusk with derris, malathion or fenitrothion.

Raspberries are sprayed at first pink fruit stage and again two weeks later; loganberries at eighty per cent petal fall and two weeks later; blackberries as the first flowers open.

Wasps In some years, wasps damage many fruits of plums, apples, pears and grapes. Protect fruit by enclosing the trusses in bags made from old nylon tights or muslin.

Destroy wasp nests by putting carbaryl dust in the entrance.

Diseases of plants are caused by various types of parasitic organisms, the most important being fungi, bacteria and viruses. Their effect is to spoil the appearance of ornamental plants and to reduce both the yields and quality of fruit and vegetable crops.

Plant diseases can be classified either by the type of organism causing the trouble or by the symptoms produced, as described here. Though the active ingredients of fungicides are mentioned, rates of application are omitted as they *must* be applied according to manufacturers' instructions. Nor are any proprietary names given as they go out-of-date at regular intervals.

Downy mildews Although these fungi are not very obvious, they cause serious diseases on some types of plants. A greyish-white or purplish bloom of spores may show on the lower leaf surfaces, but the more obvious symptoms are discoloured foliage of seedling brassicas, severe distortion of wallflowers and rotting of lettuces. Affected onion leaves wither and fall over.

As downy mildews are really troublesome only where the seedlings are overcrowded and aeration is poor, they can usually be prevented by sowing thinly on a fresh site each year, in well-drained soil where the tilth is good. At the first signs of trouble, remove and burn diseased tissues and spray plants with an appropriate fungicide – either Bordeaux mixture or mancozeb.

Powdery mildews In most cases these diseases are easily recognized, for they show as a white powdery coating on the leaves, stems, flowers and fruits of many types of plants, especially apples, gooseberries, begonias, roses and also Michaelmas daisies. Rhododendron powdery mildew is an exception to this rule, however. For though it may cause severe discoloration of the plant's leaves, followed by premature leaf-fall, the fungus, which is found on the undersides of the leaves, can barely be seen with the naked eye. Inspect suspect plants carefully.

Some powdery mildews of herbaceous plants may attack a wide range of plants, including weeds, whereas others are specific to only one type of plant – begonias, for example. The fungi flourish where the atmosphere is moist, and in greenhouses can be checked by careful ventilation to reduce humidity. On trees and shrubs, pruning regularly to keep the centres open will help to improve the circulation of air, which reduces humidity.

Remove and burn diseased shoots of fruit crops as the first symptoms appear, and as most powdery mildew fungi overwinter in buds or on shoots, destroy infected shoots at the end of the season.

Plants are more susceptible to infection when they are dry at the roots, so mulching and watering, especially of plants grown on walls, should help to prevent infection.

When a powdery mildew appears, spray with benomyl, carbendazim, propiconazole, thiophanate-methyl or triforine with bupirimate. Pyrazophos may be used to treat these diseases on pot plants. And copper or sulphur sprays are the most effective treatment on herbaceous plants and on shrubby plants in hedges.

Moulds Amateurs use the terms 'mildews' and 'moulds' rather loosely, but the only true mildews that affect plants are the powdery and downy types that have been mentioned already.

However, there are many fungi which can be classified as moulds that do infect plants, the commonest being:

Grey mould (Botrytis cinerea)
This disease is most familiar on strawberries, but it can also be troublesome on greenhouse plants, particularly tomatoes, grapes, chrysanthemums and cyclamen. Lettuces are also very susceptible to grey mould infection; the affected plants will wilt at ground level.

The fungus causes tissues to rot, showing on them as a greyish-brown mould or, occasionally, as small, roundish, hard, black structures, which are its resting bodies (sclerotia).

The fungus can also cause dieback of woody shoots which have been injured, especially on roses, acers, lilacs, magnolias and ceanothus. Spores of the fungus, which are always present in the air, infect plants through wounds and damaged or dying tissues, including the stamens and petals of flowers of soft fruit crops. Infection can also occur, however, by contact between diseased and healthy tissues.

Remove and burn all diseased or dying parts, cutting back to clean, living tissues. No further treatment is required on woody plants. As the fungus is encouraged by a humid atmosphere, it is important to ventilate greenhouses well and, in addition, fumigate them with tecnazene smokes.

Benomyl, carbendazim and thiophanate-methyl can be used to control grey mould once it has appeared, but too-regular use of these fungicides, which are related, could lead to the build-up of strains of the fungus which are resistant to them. Thiram can also be used, except on fruit to be preserved.

Spray soft fruit crops before the disease is seen – that is, as first flowers open. Repeat two or three times at fortnightly intervals.

Other Botrytis species Several other *Botrytis* species can attack plants, especially bulbous crops. Most are specific to one type of host plant. For example, *Botrytis elliptica* and *B. paeoniae* cause lily disease and peony wilt, respectively. These diseases show as brown blotches on the leaves, followed by collapse of the stems. This is due to rotting of the tissues, which may become covered with a greyish-brown mould. Small, roundish, black resting bodies of the fungus may then develop.

Remove all diseased parts and dust the crowns of plants with dry Bordeaux powder. Spray the developing leaves and shoots with a copper fungicide. Benomyl, carbendazim or thiophanate-methyl may be used effectively on occasion.

Other moulds Tomato and potato blights cause a blackish blotching of leaves, shoots, fruit and tubers, which rot rapidly in wet weather. Prevent infection with a copper fungicide, mancozeb, maneb or zineb, spraying maincrop potatoes before the haulms meet in the rows, and tomatoes in July (in the west) or August (in the east). However, control may be impossible in wet seasons and, in this case, destroy all rotting parts.

Tomato leaf mould affects the foliage of tomatoes in cold, humid greenhouses. It shows as yellow blotches, with a greenish mould on the undersides of leaves. As a precaution, grow Cladosporium-resistant cultivars and ventilate freely. Spraying with one of the fungicides recommended for blight may check the disease.

Rusts Although gardeners may refer to any brown blotch as 'rust', true rust diseases are caused by fungi, which usually affect the leaves but can also attack the shoots, flowers and fruits. Yellow, orange, brown or black powdery masses of spores are produced, either scattered or in small pustules that are often arranged in concentric rings. The colour depends on the rust, the host and the season, as most rust fungi produce more than one type of spore during the year.

Weak plum trees, birches, willows and other trees may be affected by rusts in late summer, resulting in premature defoliation. However, such rusts can usually be prevented by mulching, watering and feeding the trees. Rake up and burn diseased leaves, no matter what the host.

Most rusts are difficult to control, but rose rust and, possibly, antirrhinum rust, can be partially controlled by spraying with thiram, zineb or propiconazole. These fungicides can also be used to control pelargonium and fuchsia rusts (though growth of some fuchsia cultivars may be retarded by propiconazole), provided the greenhouse is well ventilated to reduce humidity.

Raise new hollyhock plants every second year; do not grow sweet williams too soft; burn over mint beds at the end of the season, or cut off all old shoots, to reduce infection. No other control measures are satisfactory on these troublesome hosts.

Leaf spots Most types of plant can be affected by a leaf spot fungus, but, as a rule, the fungi are troublesome only on plants lacking in vigour due to incorrect planting, unsuitable soil conditions or malnutrition. This applies even to the rose black spot fungus, which causes roundish black blotches, without definite margins, and finally premature leaffall, the symptoms being worse on weak bushes. This fungus attacks only roses, and most leaf-spotting fungi are specific to certain hosts.

Some leaf spots do not have definite margins, because the fungus grows out as fine threads over the leaf surface, as in black spots. Some spots are large and spread outwards in concentric circles – hellebore leaf blotch, for example – but others are very small, as in weeping willow anthracnose. The fruiting bodies of some fungi show as pin-head sized, black structures on the leaf spots, as in chrysanthemum leaf blotch.

To control leaf spot diseases spray with benomyl, carbendazim, mancozeb or thiophanate-methyl, repeating as necessary. In severe cases spray also with a foliar feed to encourage vigour.

As most leaf-spotting fungi overwinter on fallen leaves, they should be raked up and burned. Winter treatments against black spot have not proved effective at Wisley, so start spraying roses and other plants which have suffered from leaf spot as soon as the new leaves develop in the spring.

Leaf distortion Peach leaf curl and azalea gall both cause distortion of leaves. In these diseases the leaves become very swollen and distorted, at first pinkish in colour, later covered with a white bloom of spores, then finally becoming brown. Diseased peach, nectarine and almond leaves fall prematurely.

Remove and burn diseased leaves before they turn white. After removal, spray indoor azaleas with copper or mancozeb, but spray outdoor shrubs the following spring as the new leaves appear. Spray peaches and related plants with copper in January or early February, repeating a fortnight later and just before leaf-fall. Trees grown against walls can be protected against peach leaf curl with a polythene covering, open at both ends. This allows good aeration while keeping away moisture needed by the fungal spores.

Cankers The most troublesome disease of this type is apple canker, which affects the branches. The inner tissues are exposed by deep cankers, which cause die-back if the stem is girdled. Cut out and burn all dying branches and diseased tissues and paint the wounds with a canker paint containing thiophanate-methyl.

The fungus can enter through wounds caused by other diseases and pests, so control these as well. Spray severely diseased trees with a copper fungicide just before leaf-fall, half-way through leaf-fall, and with thiophanate-methyl at bud burst.

So many small cankers are produced by willow anthracnose that it is impossible to remove cankered shoots. Some control may be achieved by spraying with a copper fungicide or thiophanate-methyl at bud burst, repeating two or three times at fortnightly intervals. Diseased leaves should be raked up and burnt, and this is the only treatment possible for large trees, apart from trying to encourage greater vigour by cultural methods.

Cane diseases All cane fruits can be affected by cane blight and, more importantly, by spur blight, but raspberries are the most susceptible to infection. Spur blight causes the death of buds or die-back of shoots, but cane blight kills complete canes, causing them to become so brittle that they snap at ground level.

Cut off diseased canes below soil level. Spray with benomyl, carbendazim, copper or thiophanate-methyl as new canes develop, repeating at fortnightly intervals until flowering ceases.

Other fruit diseases A rapid decay of top fruits on trees and in store is caused by brown rot, which shows as cushions of white fungus spores on the brown, rotting tissues. Diseased fruits dry up, and the fungus overwinters on the mummified fruits on the tree or ground and also on small shoot cankers.

Destroy all rotten or withered fruits and cut out dead shoots. No other measures are effective.

Wound parasites Many types of woody plants, including roses, rhododendrons and, very commonly, plums, are susceptible to infection by the silver leaf fungus. This causes silvering of the foliage on an infected branch, followed by progressive die-back of the tree or shrub.

Coral spot fungus is also a troublesome wound parasite, being most common on acers, elaeagnus, figs and red currants. Considerable die-back, even the complete death of plants, may occur after infection, and the fungus develops on the dead shoots as coral-red pustules of spores.

Cut out affected branches to a point at least 10 cm (4 in) below the apparently diseased tissues. In the case of silver leaf, a stain is visible in the wood. Paint wounds with a paint containing thiophanate-methyl. Destroy all woody debris on which the fungi can live as saprophytes.

Soil-borne diseases The most common and troublesome root parasite is the honey fungus, which causes the rapid death of woody plants. The fungus develops beneath the bark of the roots and the main stem of the

plant at and just above ground level. It shows there as a white growth, often fan-shaped, but it also produces brownish-black, root-like structures, known as rhizomorphs, which grow out through the soil and cause new infections. Honey-coloured toadstools may appear in autumn at the base of a dying plant.

Dig out dead and dying plants, together with as many of the roots as possible. Then treat the soil with a proprietary phenolic emulsion, or change it completely before replanting.

The two latter treatments are the only effective measures that can be taken against the root disease of woody plants caused by the fungus *Phytophthora cinnamomi*. Well-known for causing heather wilt, it has a wide host range. Diseased plants die back as a result of a rot at ground level, but no fungal growth develops.

Beans, peas, tomatoes, sweet peas, pansies, petunias, polyanthus and China asters are also susceptible to infection by soil-borne fungi which attack the roots and cause the plants to wilt. Prevent such troubles by growing bedding plants, as well as vegetables, on a rotation system. As the fungi produce resting spores which remain viable in the soil for many years, soil sterilization is the only effective control measure.

Sowing seed thinly and the use of sterile compost and clean water will prevent damping-off. This disease causes the collapse of seedlings at ground level, particularly where they are overcrowded.

Club root of brassicas and wallflowers occurs where susceptible crops are grown on the same site year after year in acid soils. Plant wilt or collapse due to swelling and distortion of the roots.

This is a difficult disease to

control, but rotation of crops, the liming of soil and the use of a benomyl or thiophanate-methyl dip will help to prevent infection of healthy plants which have been raised in sterile compost.

Bulb diseases Soil-borne diseases also affect bulbous plants of all types. Tulip fire is probably the most troublesome, as it causes rotting of leaves, shoots and flowers on which a grey mould may develop. No shoots emerge, however, if tulip and hyacinth bulbs are affected by grey bulb rot, because they rot in the soil.

Narcissus bulbs infected with basal rot may rot in the soil or in store. Storage rots of gladiolus corms are also common, and the foliage turns yellow or collapses completely when they are affected by soil-borne diseases during the growing season.

Lift unhealthy plants and examine the bulbs or corms, and also examine them regularly in store. Destroy any which are rotting or bear fungal resting bodies, the latter showing as small, hard, black structures on or between the scales. Dip bulbs and corms within 24 hours of lifting in a solution of benomyl, carbendazim or thiophanate-methyl. Dry off and store in an airy, cool but frost-free place. Replant on a fresh site the following season.

Turf diseases Several fungal diseases can cause browning or even death of turf. In general, they can be controlled by applying benomyl, carbendazim, thiophanate-methyl or a proprietary turf fungicide. However, red thread and snow mould are encouraged by completely opposite cultural conditions, so specialist advice should be sought if there is any doubt as to the exact cause of the trouble.

Bacterial diseases The most im-portant bacterial plant diseases can be divided broadly into three main groups, according to the type of tissues affected and the effects produced.

A soft rot, which is usually wet and foul-smelling, occurs when the fleshy tissues of celery, carrots, potatoes, rhizomes, bulbs, and even the crowns of plants are attacked. Such bacterial rots are usually secondary and follow injury by frost, diseases such as potato blight or by pests such as slugs. Prevent soft rot, therefore, by growing crops well, avoiding injuries by pests, diseases or mechanical damage and by the correct storage of root crops and bulbs.

There is usually no cure for soft rot, so destroy badly affected vegetables and plants. However, in the case of irises affected by rhizome rot, cut out diseased tissues and dust the cut surfaces and healthy clumps with dry Bordeaux powder. This fungicide may also save cucumbers affected by stem canker, which is similar.

A canker is the most common symptom when woody tissues are affected by bacteria. Bacterial canker of *Prunus* species, including plums and cherries, shows as flattening of the branches, which bear exudations of gum and which finally die back. Cut out all dying branches and spray with a copper fungicide in mid-August, September and October.

Fireblight looks similar to bacterial canker but is found only on pears, apples and related ornamentals such as *Crataegus*, *Cotoneaster* and *Sorbus*. As the infected shoots die back progressively, the brown and withered leaves remain.

This is a notifiable disease, and the owner of a suspect tree or shrub is obliged by law to notify the local Ministry of Agriculture office. In most cases, instructions will be given to cut out affected branches 60 cm (2 ft) below the apparently diseased tissues, disinfecting the pruning implement between each cut, and to burn the diseased wood.

Tumours or galls are formed when the outermost layers of dividing cells are infected, as they are stimulated to reproduce abnormally. Crown gall, which is not considered to be a serious disease, shows as one large gall or a chain of smaller galls on the roots of many woody plants or on the shoots of roses, cane fruits and daphnes.

Leafy gall is a much more troublesome disease as it affects herbaceous plants, such as chrysanthemums, sweet peas, pelargoniums and dahlias. It results in the production of a mass of abortive, leafy shoots at ground level. Destroy any galled plant.

Viruses and virus-like organisms These organisms affect all types of plants, but the most susceptible to infection are marrows, tomatoes, sweet peas, lilies, strawberries and raspberries. The main symptoms are stunting, distortion, mottling or striping of leaves, deformation of flowers (which may show white or dark stripes) and poor cropping.

Destroy poorly growing plants showing any of these symptoms. Control aphids, as these pests frequently transmit viruses – especially cucumber mosaic virus, which has an enormous host range. Also, destroy weeds, as many of these harbour viruses.

When planting soft fruit, use only plants which are certified to be free from virus infection. Grow them on a fresh site, but bear in mind that they, too, could become infected within a year or so.

PLANT DISORDERS

Plants are very sensitive to their environment. For a plant to reach its maximum potential, the light must be of the right intensity and duration, the temperature, atmosphere and water supply must be correct, and all food materials must be supplied throughout its life. If any of these conditions are abnormal, a physiological disorder will occur.

In general, affected plants show discoloration of foliage, lack of growth, poor cropping and even die-back. However, certain specific disorders are associated with cultural conditions that are definitely unsuitable.

Light

Thin, weak, drawn and colourless plants, which may fail to flower and which are known as etiolated, develop where the light is of low intensity. Such conditions are likely to occur among seedlings where the seed was sown too thickly; also in overcrowded greenhouses where the plants do not receive much sunlight, particularly during long, dark winters. Given more light, affected plants should recover.

Temperature

High temperatures Scorching of leaves, which shows as pale brown blotches, can be caused by hot sun striking through glass on to moist foliage. If the shoulders of tomato fruits are injured in this way, the tissues become hard and stay green, the trouble being known as greenback. Such problems can be prevented by adequate shading and ventilation of greenhouses, and in the case of tomatoes by growing resistant cultivars.

Leaf scorch can also occur on house plants growing close to glass which is faceted, as in a porch or bathroom, or where there is a flaw in the window glass. In both cases the distorted glass acts as a lens, intensifying the sun's rays.

Where this type of scorching occurs, the discoloured patches, either pale brown or, occasionally, creamy-coloured – depending on the type of plant – usually form a pattern of stripes across the injured leaves. This type of damage can be avoided by moving the plant away from the glass or by turning it around a little way each day so that the same leaf is not exposed continually to the sun.

During hot summers, scalding of fruits – particularly of gooseberries, plums and apples – can occur, causing creamy, sunken blotches on the skin. There is no method of preventing scald on outdoor fruits. However, careful ventilation should prevent it on greenhouse grapes, where scald shows as sunken, discoloured patches.

Bulbs stored or forced at too high temperatures may be completely blind the following spring or produce withered flowers.

Low temperatures Frost damage results in symptoms of various types. When young fruits, particularly apples, are injured, russeting of the skin occurs. This is visible as discoloured, roughened patches on the fruits, especially around the eyes.

Evergreen leaves become distorted and often show parallel rows of small holes on either side of the main vein. Leaves injured in the bud or when very young become more and more distorted as they grow. In the case of deciduous leaves, especially of apple, quince and chrysanthemums, those affected curl, while the lower leaf surfaces lift so that they can be peeled off easily.

Frost can also cause longitudinal splitting of the bark on stems which, in severe cases, will die back. If seen early enough it may be possible to save an affected shoot by binding it with grafting tape. This must be removed once the wound has healed.

Tender plants should not be grown in frost pockets. Small plants can be protected when frost is forecast, but half-hardy perennials need protection throughout the winter – for instance, by using a cover made by packing bracken between wire netting.

It should also be remembered that container-grown bulbs or plants can be killed in a very severe winter if the soil ball is frozen solid. During a hard spell, keep them where the temperature will not drop very far below freezing point.

When there are great extremes between day and night temperatures, the leaves may become white, as in *Ipomoea*, silvered or purple as in the case of tomatoes, or yellow as with the young, soft foliage of magnolias. The affected discoloured leaves will never turn dark green.

Cold, drying winds can cause scorching of the young leaves of beech, *Acer* species and variegated trees and shrubs.

Little can be done to prevent weather damage on outdoor plants, but where severe symptoms occur again every year it is better to move them to a less exposed position. As weak plants suffer most, encourage vigour in all types of plants by suitable cultural treatment. Injured plants will usually benefit from applications of a foliar feed.

Atmosphere

High humidity Apart from encouraging many diseases, such as grey mould and tomato leaf mould, a very humid atmosphere under glass may cause oedema or dropsy, which shows as raised, corky patches on the undersurfaces of leaves, particularly those of ivy-leaved pelargoniums, and on the shoots and fruits of vines.

Do not remove affected leaves, as this will only make matters worse. Ventilate greenhouses well and water, syringe or spray early so that plant tissues can dry off before night.

Low humidity Poor growth, bud drop and leaf browning can be caused by too dry an atmosphere in greenhouses and dwelling houses. Any plants that need humid conditions should be syringed daily in hot weather. In centrally-heated houses, stand pot plants in larger containers which can be packed with moist peat or moss, or stand them on pebbles in water.

Water supply

Growing plants need a continuous supply of water, but the amounts required for different stages of growth may vary. Troubles arise when the water supply is deficient, irregular or in excess of the plants' requirements.

Water deficient – sudden drought A sudden and acute deficiency of water, likely to occur on a hot day, results in wilting. An affected plant usually recovers its turgidity by morning and no further trouble should occur if the plant is watered. However, if the leaves of a large-leaved tree, such as *Catalpa* or *Aesculus*, wilt it indicates that many of the roots have been injured and that recovery will be slow. The tree may not be restored to its former vigour until the following season.

Water deficient – long drought A chronic lack of water results in the stunting of plants, and the leaves may show 'autumn' tints of yellow, red or brown. Such leaves fall prematurely and crop yields are greatly reduced.

Lack of water at critical times Drought when flower buds are beginning to develop can result in bud drop at flowering time. Thus, camellias affected by a lack of water in August or September may lose all their flower buds the following spring. Flower drop of tomatoes, withering of cucumber fruits and split stone of peaches may also be due to drought conditions and the sudden drying out of the soil.

When bulbous plants are affected by drought in early spring, they may suffer from blindness, with the flower buds withering without opening. This trouble occurs most frequently in double narcissi.

Sporadic water supply If the soil is watered sporadically, but is allowed to dry out in between, fruits and root crops may split and the latter, particularly potatoes, may have hollow centres or develop strange shapes. Tomatoes affected in this way develop blossom end rot, which shows as a brownish sunken blemish at the blossom end of the fruits.

Plants in growing bags are particularly susceptible to this trouble, as on very hot days it may be necessary to water as often as five times in order to keep the compost moist. There should be no need for the fruit on later trusses to be affected once watering is attended to, providing the plants have well-developed root systems.

Prevent all the above troubles by mulching plants well with peat, leaf-mould or other organic materials to conserve moisture. Water in dry periods before the soil dries out completely – even in cold weather if there are drying winds. This is particularly important for plants growing against walls, as the soil in such situations can remain dry even in periods of

heavy rain if the prevailing wind is not in the right direction.

Water in excess Waterlogging of soil kills the roots, due to lack of oxygen. They show a bluish-black discoloration, sometimes accompanied by peeling of the outer tissues, leaving just the central cores. Affected plants may show a variety of symptoms, such as oedema (see High Humidity) or yellowing between the veins on yew and pot plant foliage.

Shoots of waterlogged plants occasionally show corky patches due to bursting of the lenticels (breathing pores), or knobbly, gall-like structures due to the development of clusters of incipient roots. Peeling of the bark, which becomes papery, may also occur. In severe cases a general discoloration of foliage and die-back of shoots, or even complete death, may occur.

It is not always possible to prevent waterlogging during prolonged or heavy rain, even on light soils. Where waterlogging occurs regularly, however, incorporate some system of drainage if possible. Alternatively, grow plants on beds raised to a height of about 15 cm (6 in).

Improve the texture of heavy soils over a wide area and not just in planting holes, otherwise these will act as sumps into which water from the surrounding, heavier soil will flow. Dig out planting holes with a fork, not a spade or trowel, to prevent compaction of the sides, through which the roots may not be able to penetrate.

Plants affected by waterlogging may possibly be saved by spraying with a foliar feed throughout the growing season. Remove all dead and dying shoots.

Nutrition

Most plants require feeding at some stage of their growth, but perennial plants, including trees, ornamental shrubs and fruit crops, should be fed at least once a year, according to their requirements. Though many food materials are required, few are likely to become deficient, except when plants grown in soil-less composts are not fed correctly. In gardens, specific deficiencies of the major nutrients – nitrogen, potassium and phosphorus – are less likely to occur than is general malnutrition caused by neglect.

Plants which have been neglected show discoloured foliage, premature leaf-fall, die-back and poor cropping. When specific nutrients are deficient, however, certain symptoms are produced, though they are not necessarily as clear-cut as described here. Except where specific treatment is recommended, the following deficiencies can be corrected by applying appropriate fertilizers, the rate of application depending on the type of plant affected.

Nitrogen deficiency This trouble occurs mainly on plants growing in light soils lacking organic matter, and it may also show on pot-bound plants. Affected plants are spindly and upright, with short and thin shoots. The leaves are at first small and pale yellow but later become highly-coloured, with tints of yellow, orange, red or purple. Fruits are also small and highly-coloured, and there is a great reduction in the yields of fruits and vegetables.

Phosphorus deficiency The symptoms are somewhat similar to those caused by nitrogen deficiency and are therefore not easily distinguished. However, the leaf colour is dull bluish-green, with purpling rather than yellowing or reddening. In black currants it shows as a dull bronzing, with purple or brown spots. In pota-

toes, the leaf margins are scorched.

Affected trees produce fruits with soft flesh, acid in flavour and of poor keeping quality; the skin is green but may be highly flushed. These symptoms occur most frequently in high-rainfall districts of the west and north, and on clay soils.

Potassium deficiency Some crops require a lot of potassium, especially tomatoes, chrysanthemums, potatoes, beans and fruit crops. On these, deficiency symptoms may occur on plants growing in clay soils but more frequently the trouble arises on light, sandy, peat or chalk soils.

Affected plants are stunted and bear dull, bluish-green leaves which may show browning as small spots around the margins or at the tips. The leaves may also curl down towards the undersurface. Poor flowering and/or poor berrying of ornamental plants is often due to a deficiency of potassium.

Magnesium deficiency This is probably the most common deficiency, occurring on all types of plants, as magnesium is easily leached from the soil during periods of heavy rain. Plants such as tomatoes and chrysanthemums that are grown in soil containing a lot of bonfire ash or are fed with high-potash fertilizers frequently show the symptoms, as excess potassium in the soil makes magnesium unavailable.

Chlorosis (yellowing) between the veins is the commonest symptom, but brilliant orange, red, purple or brown tints may also develop. The symptoms appear first on the older leaves and spread upwards progressively, the discoloured leaves falling prematurely. Affected apple, black currant and gooseberry fruits are small, immature and woody.

The quickest method of overcoming this trouble is to spray with a solution of magnesium sulphate at the rate of 250 gr in 11 litres of water (½ lb in 2½ gal), to which is added a wetter and spreader, such as soft soap or a few drops of a mild liquid detergent. Spray tomatoes at the first signs of trouble and repeat this at ten to fourteen-day intervals.

Even with this treatment some discoloration may persist on tomatoes which are fed correctly, but they will produce good crops of high-quality fruits. Other types of plants should also be sprayed as the first symptoms appear, repeating two or three times at fortnightly intervals. Petal fall is the time to spray top fruits.

Manganese deficiency Soils which are generally deficient in manganese are sands, fen peats or alluvial silts and clays, when these have a pH of over 6.5 and are high in organic matter. Manganese may, indeed, be present but be made unavailable to plants in soils having a very high pH (over 7.5), so that the trouble is frequently linked with a deficiency of iron.

It can also be made unavailable if the soil is very wet, so deficiency symptoms may appear after a spell of heavy rain.

In general, the symptoms are similar to those caused by magnesium deficiency – that is, interveinal chlorosis, but without the additional tints. The terminal leaves on a shoot are less chlorotic or remain green.

Among fruit crops, cherries, apples and raspberries are affected most frequently. In peas, the most common symptom is seen only if the seeds are split open, when they show a dark, rusty-red spot or cavity in the centre, the trouble being known as marsh spot.

Beetroot and related crops are

also affected by a specific disorder known as speckled yellows, in which the leaves become triangular in outline. They show yellow blotches between the veins and have a tendency to roll inwards at their edges. In severe cases, whole leaves become pale yellow.

When the trouble is diagnosed, spray with 60 g of manganese sulphate in 11 litres of water (2 oz in 2½ gal), plus a spreader, such as soft soap, or a few drops of a mild liquid detergent. Repeat once or twice at fortnightly intervals, as necessary, to restore the green colour to the foliage. A chelated compound or fritted trace elements could be used as an alternative method of treatment.

Iron deficiency This trouble, which shows on the leaves as yellowing between the veins, is almost always induced by very alkaline conditions, in which the pH is 7.5 or over. The condition is often known as lime-induced chlorosis. The youngest leaves are always the most severely affected. Scorching of the leaf margins and tips occurs in extreme cases, on leaves which may be almost white.

Plants which frequently show severe symptoms, where the pH is about 7.5, are peaches, raspberries, hydrangeas, *Ceanothus* and *Chaenomeles*, but almost any type of plant may be affected if the pH is 8.0, especially if it is lacking in vigour due to some other adverse factor. Acid-loving plants, such as rhododendrons, camellias and most heathers, will show lime-induced chlorosis when growing in soil having a pH above 7.0; between 5.5 and 7.0 they will probably merely look poorly.

As it can be difficult to distinguish between iron, manganese and magnesium deficiencies, it is essential, if a plant shows chlorotic foliage, to determine the pH of the soil so that the correct treatment can be given. If the pH is found to be too high, try to reduce it by digging in pulverized bark, peat or crushed bracken.

Around growing plants, flowers of sulphur can be used on sandy loams at 130 g per sq m (4 oz per sq yd) and twice this rate on heavy loams. However, it is better to apply just a small quantity at first, test for pH after a few months and repeat the application as necessary until the pH of the surrounding soil is reduced to the required level.

On vacant ground, aluminium sulphate or ferrous sulphate can be applied at 130 g to 250 g per sq m (4–8 oz per sq yd). Rake the chemical in well and water in dry weather. Test for pH after two or three weeks and, if it has not fallen by the desired amount, repeat the process until the right pH is obtained. Note that phosphate may be made unavailable to plants through the use of either of these two chemicals.

Even with these treatments it is unlikely that it will be possible to reduce a pH of over 7.5 to as low as 5.5, as required by acid-loving plants, so an annual application of a proprietary product containing chelated compounds or fritted trace elements will be required. It is also unlikely that regular use of these latter materials alone, without some soil treatment, will restore the green colour to the foliage of chlorotic plants.

Calcium deficiency Calcium is unlikely to be deficient in gardens, even in areas that have acid soils. It may be short, however, in very acid, peat-based composts of the type used in growing bags, and blossom end rot of tomatoes may then occur. Even then, it can be overcome by avoiding sporadic watering.

A localised deficiency of calcium within the fruits of apples, but not in the soil, and induced by a shortage of water at a critical time when there are wide fluctuations in rainfall and temperature, results in the disorder known as bitter pit. Slightly sunken pits develop on the surface of the skin of the fruit, with small brown areas of tissue immediately beneath them and scattered throughout the flesh.

Some fruits may be affected while still on the tree, but most symptoms develop in storage. Brown patches near the skin can be removed by peeling, but in severely affected apples the flesh has a bitter taste, making them inedible.

Bitter pit can be prevented to a certain extent by mulching well to conserve moisture (though the use of straw will aggravate the trouble), and by watering during dry periods. Its incidence can be reduced considerably by applying sprays of hydrated calcium nitrate, used at the rate of 30 g in 9 litres of water (1 oz in 2 gal) in mid-June. Repeat this ten days later. After a further ten days treat with a double strength solution (60 g in 9 litres, or 2 oz in 2 gal) of hydrated calcium nitrate, repeating the treatment at least three times at ten-day intervals.

Alternatively, give a first spray of 125 g in 18 litres (4 oz in 5 gal) in mid-June. Spray again three weeks later at 250 g in 18 litres (8 oz in 5 gal), and repeat twice at this rate at three-weekly intervals.

Boron deficiency Boron may be leached out of sandy or chalk soils in heavy rain or can be made unavailable by over-liming normally acid soils. Boron deficiency affects pear trees, causing the bark to have a roughened and pimpled appearance and leading to the die-back of some shoots, while on others the leaves are small and mis-shapen. The fruits on most branches are distorted and have brown spots in the flesh.

Where this is a recurrent problem, spray at petal-fall with 70 g borax (sodium tetraborate) in 18 litres of water (2½ oz in 5 gal), adding a spreader such as soft soap or a few drops of a mild liquid detergent.

Vegetables may also suffer from a deficiency of boron. In celery, for instance, brown horizontal cracks develop across the stalks, leading to poor growth, with yellowing and death of the leaves.

Swedes and turnips are affected by a disorder known as brown heart. This shows only when affected roots are cut across, the flesh in the lower part of the root showing clearly-defined greyish or brownish discoloured areas, often in concentric rings. Affected plants show no other symptoms, and the roots do not rot but become hard, stringy and tasteless in cooking.

Heart rot of beet, also due to boron deficiency, shows as browning of the inner tissues of the root, which sometimes turns black, and also at the crown, where the tissues may become sunken. Most of the leaves die and only small deformed leaves remain. In severe cases, rotting of the outer tissues of the root may occur, causing cankers.

Where boron deficiency symptoms occur in vegetables every year, rake borax (sodium tetraborate) into the soil before sowing, applying it at the rate of 30 g to about 17 sq m (1 oz for every 20 sq yds). The borax should be well mixed with a large quantity of light sand before it is spread over the soil, to ensure that the chemical is evenly distributed.

Molybdenum deficiency This deficiency, which occurs only occasionally in acid soils, affects only brassicas, causing the disorder known as whiptail. The leaves of broccoli and cauliflowers become ruffled, thin and strap-like, while the curds of affected plants are poor or fail to develop.

Where this trouble is known to occur, apply a solution of sodium molybdate to the soil, using 30 g in 9 litres of water per 8 sq m (1 oz in 2 gal per 10 sq yds).

Combination of adverse factors
As already indicated, many troubles produce similar symptoms, and it is sometimes difficult to determine the exact cause of a disorder that is affecting a plant. Furthermore, one unsuitable cultural condition can result in other troubles, so that plants may suffer from a combination of adverse factors.

Thus, faulty root action may be due to injury to the roots caused by too wet or too dry soil conditions but, because the injured roots are unable to take in food materials, the damaged plant will also be affected by malnutrition.

Poor planting – that is, failure to spread the roots out well in all directions, or too-deep planting – will also result in an inefficient root system. As a consequence, the plant will be unable to take in sufficient water and nourishment.

Bitter pit of apples and blossom end rot of tomatoes, both already described, are really due to a combination of adverse factors. Similarly, shanking of grapes is due to overcropping of a vine, the root system of which is functioning inadequately. The stalk of the berry shrivels gradually until it is completely girdled. As the grapes ripen, odd berries or groups of berries fail to colour normally, those on white cultivars remaining translucent while those on black varieties turn red. The grapes do not swell and are watery and sour.

When shanking occurs early in the season, cut out the withered bunches, spray with a foliar feed and improve cultural conditions as necessary. Reduce the crop for a year or two until the vine has regained its vigour.

Peach split stone can also be due to one or more adverse factors. Affected fruits have a deeper suture than normal and are cracked at the stalk end, the hole sometimes being big enough to allow the entry of earwigs. The stone of such a fruit is split in two and the kernel, if formed, rots.

Peaches with this disorder fail to ripen normally, and rot as a result of infection by the brown rot fungus or other secondary organisms. Split stone can be caused by lack of water at a critical stage of growth, but it can also be due to poor pollination, so pollinate the flowers by hand when possible.

A lack of lime may also cause the stone to split. Therefore, lime acid soils in autumn to raise the pH to 6.7–7.0. General malnutrition or excess feeding after stoning may also result in peach split stone disorder.

Chemical injury Some fungicides that can be used with safety on most types of plants may nevertheless cause damage on sensitive plants. Thus, sulphur sprays can cause russeting of the fruit on some apples, defoliation of some gooseberry cultivars and brown blotches on black currant leaves. The leaves of weak rose bushes and of rhododendrons may be scorched by copper sprays.

Chemicals which cause such injuries to sensitive plants are said to be phytotoxic. Several insecticides of this type can also cause discoloured foliage or leaf-fall. Sensitive plants are usually listed on proprietary packs of chemicals, so always read the label before using an insecticide or fungicide to make quite sure that it can be used with safety on a particular plant.

Most chemical injury to plants occurs as a result of the mis-use of weedkillers. Damage can be caused by the drifting of a herbicide used on a windy day, but plants can also be injured as a result of using a badly-rinsed watering can or sprayer which is contaminated with a weedkiller. Keep special apparatus for applying herbicides and do not wash it out in a water butt or tank used for irrigation.

Hormone weedkillers, such as 2,4–D and mecoprop, cause most damage to plants, especially to roses, vines and tomatoes. The symptoms caused by this type of herbicide are twisting and distortion of the shoots, and leaves which may become very narrow and cup-shaped. In severe cases, small nodules may appear on the shoots of shrubs and herbaceous plants, such as chrysanthemums, and also on tomatoes. This is due to the development of incipient roots.

These symptoms occur most frequently as a result of drifting, or the storage of herbicides in a greenhouse. They can arise, however, on a plant that has been mulched with compost containing cuttings from a lawn treated with a hormone weedkiller, so do not put the first mowings after treatment on to a compost heap nor use them as a mulch.

Fortunately, plants affected by the hormone weedkillers available to amateur gardeners usually grow out of the symptoms in due course, and the crops will be edible, though in the case of tomatoes they may prove to be hollow and plum-shaped.

However, brassicas affected by a hormone weedkiller do not recover, and they should be destroyed. They do not show the typical distortion of the leaves, but large, gall-like outgrowths develop on the stems. Although these may occur near ground level, they should not be confused with the distortion caused by club root, which affects only the roots.

Other weedkillers can also damage plants. Aminotriazole and simazine can cause yellow blotches or chlorosis between the veins, especially on the leaves of certain trees and shrubs.

A mixture of paraquat and diquat can cause complete yellowing of the leaves of bulbous plants during the season following treatment. This occurs if weedkiller is applied around the plants before the foliage has died down completely and the necks of the bulbs are still open. In order to prevent this trouble the bulbs should be covered with soil before treating the area with weedkiller.

Glyphosate can seriously injure roses, raspberries and other woody plants if taken in by suckers. The affected plants do not produce normal leaves, but at each node a small cluster of abortive shoots, like a small witches' broom, will develop, and these will soon die.

Use all weedkillers with care and follow the makers' instructions at all times, particularly with regard to the types of plants which may be injured by chemicals. If in doubt, seek professional advice before use.

Mechanical injury Heavy snow can break branches, so remove deposits of snow from evergreens as frequently as possible. Little can be done to prevent wind damage, however, which can also break branches and tatter large leaves, such as those of the horse chestnut. And weather damage from hail, which can cause small pits in fruit or holes in leaves, cannot be prevented.

Most man-made injuries are obvious, as when plants are damaged by hoeing or trees are accidentally hit by lawn mowers. Clean up any large wound on a woody plant so that no ragged tissues are left, and take care not to leave snags when pruning.

Wounds which are easily overlooked, however, are those made by tight ties, which can result in die-back of woody shoots. Keep a careful watch on any ties and labels as the plants grow, because you may need to loosen them so that they do not become embedded in the tissues, thus strangling the shoots.

If the growing point of a plant is injured early, whether by frost, hoeing, slugs or an early insect attack, the resulting growth, whether a shoot or flower stalk, may be flattened. This condition, known as fasciation, is seen most frequently on forsythia, *Prunus subhirtella* 'Autumnalis' and some herbaceous plants.

Once flattening occurs, the affected part will continue to grow in a flattened manner. Though a shoot may branch, it will still produce leaves and flowers on the fasciated area.

With forsythia and *Prunus*, the only treatment necessary for this condition is to cut off the affected shoot a short distance below the point at which the fasciation starts. No treatment is necessary for fasciated herbaceous plants as these will probably grow normally the following year unless the garden is in a frost pocket.

The seeds of many wild plants – weeds, to the gardener – are carried by the wind into gardens or deposited there by birds. Many are brought to the surface, ready to germinate, during digging operations. Small but viable sections of such plants may be imported in loads of manure or topsoil, or among the roots of plants acquired from friends. For all these reasons, weed control is a never-ending problem.

There are two basic ways of dealing with weeds – cultural and chemical. In a small garden devoted largely to flower borders and a lawn, there may be little need for weedkillers other than on the lawn and for localised spot treatments. Hoeing and hand-weeding, especially in conjunction with mulching, will keep things under control. In larger gardens, however, sensible use of weedkillers on paths, in the fruit garden and in other troublesome areas can reduce substantially the time spent on maintenance.

CULTURAL CONTROL

A well-fed and regularly-mown lawn is more resistant to weeds than one that is neglected, and the same principle applies to planted areas of the garden.

Always remove perennial weeds before planting or sowing. Buy only healthy, well-rooted plants as these are better able to compete with weeds. Plant or sow at suitable spacings so that there are no wide gaps between plants. Maintain healthy growth by regular feeding, mulching and pruning, and by spraying to control pests and diseases.

Organic mulches are effective in promoting weed control, as well as helping to conserve moisture. They provide a cooler root run for plants and may also supply nutrients and trace elements as the materials decompose.

Deep mulches of well-rotted farm manure, leaf-mould or moist peat will bury small weed seeds to a depth at which they will not germinate. Wind-borne or bird-carried seeds germinating in the loose material can easily be dislodged with a hoe.

Processed tree bark is another suitable material. It is stable, long-lasting and attractive to look at.

Black polythene laid around newly-planted ornamental and fruiting trees and shrubs is very effective in controlling weeds. Sheets 90 cm (3 ft) wide are suitable for row crops; 90 cm (3 ft) squares may be placed around individual trees or bushes, digging in the edges so as to anchor them in the soil. This method also makes for rapid root establishment and vigorous growth.

Hoeing or weedkillers? Hoeing and hand-weeding are perfectly valid methods of weed control, but both have their drawbacks.

When hand-weeding around young plants there is a danger of disturbing their roots. Also, weed seeds may be brought near the surface, where they can germinate.

Hoeing relies upon fine, dry weather to kill the weeds. Many may become re-established if the use of the hoe is followed by wet weather. Also, hoeing is only partly effective against perennial weeds, as their roots will generate fresh growth. There is, too, a risk that the sharp blade may damage the roots of plants. For all these reasons, hand-weeding has the advantage. The roots of perennial weeds are removed completely, with minimal damage to plants.

When weedkillers are used, the soil is not disturbed at all. As a result, plants generally grow better than after either hoeing or hand-weeding.

Stale seedbed method Weeds can be particularly troublesome in beds or vegetable plots that have been neglected for a time, during which weeds have been allowed to grow and seed freely. There will be numerous weed seeds in the soil, some of which will be brought close to the surface and will germinate each time the soil is disturbed. Within a few days of sowing or planting flowers or vegetables, the earth may be a green carpet of weeds, smothering the crop seedlings.

Where this seems likely, try the stale seedbed method. Given suitable soil and weather conditions, prepare the seedbed (or planting bed) ten to fourteen days before the planned sowing or planting date, raking it to a fine tilth.

The weed seedlings that will appear after a few days can be killed by spraying with a weedkiller that contains paraquat as its active ingredient, or else by hoeing very lightly with a well-sharpened hoe. Paraquat leaves no residue harmful to seeds sown subsequently. Sowing or planting may go ahead when the weeds are dead.

To avoid bringing more weed seeds close to the surface, disturb the seedbed as little as possible when spraying and sowing. If possible, work from a board so as to avoid walking on the seedbed.

WEEDKILLERS

Weedkillers may enter weeds (or garden plants) through their roots, stems or leaves. Although they kill in different ways they do not all have the same effect. Some destroy all plant growth, above and below ground, others, such as some leaf-acting weedkillers, kill green plant matter but are neutralized on contact with the soil. Leaf-acting weedkillers can be further divided into contact-acting and translocated types.

A few are more complex, killing through the soil and also to a lesser extent through the leaves, or vice-versa. Some are selective, killing some plants by disrupting vital processes – daisies in a lawn, without damaging the turf, for instance – while other plants remain unaffected. Others are selective because, at low dosage rates, they penetrate the soil for only an inch or two, killing germinating weed seeds and shallow-rooting weeds, but not coming into contact with most of the root systems of deeper-rooting plants.

Following are some examples from each category, the kinds mentioned being readily available to amateur gardeners:

Soil-acting weedkillers These weedkillers are absorbed by the roots and transmitted to the above-ground parts of plants. Apply them in the early stages of growth or during the growing season, not while the weeds are dormant.

Soil-acting, non-selective weedkillers Ammonium sulphamate is applied as a spray and is effective against woody weeds and many herbaceous perennials. It remains active for up to twelve weeks. It corrodes metal, so use plastic sprayers or cans. Do not use on cultivated land.

Sodium chlorate, too, is applied as a spray, and is active for up to twelve months or more. It is corrosive to metal. This chemical is moderately soluble, and, like ammonium sulphamate, should not be used in areas where there are underlying tree and shrub roots. Both chemicals are useful for unplanted areas and waste ground.

Dichlobenil and simazine are both non-selective when used at full strength and they persist for several months. Dichlobenil, a granular formulation, is particularly useful for spot treatment, such as weeds in crevices or in crazy paving.

Soil-acting, selective weedkillers Propachlor is a low-strength weedkiller and stays active for a few weeks only. It is useful for controlling annual weeds at seed-germination stage among bulbs, certain vegetable crops and after planting out bedding plants like wallflowers.

Simazine is non-selective at full strength, but at low dosage rates can be used amongst various plants, including asparagus, to kill almost all weed seeds as they germinate. It is supplied as a soluble powder and persists for several months.

Dichlobenil is non-selective at full strength, but at low dosage rates can be used amongst some woody plants to kill weed seeds as they germinate, to control established annual and shallow-rooted perennial weeds, and also to check deeper-rooting perennials. It persists for several months and is applied as granules. Dichlobenil should not be used around tolerant woody plants until these have been established for two years.

With both dichlobenil and simazine there is more risk of damage on light, sandy and silty soils and where the organic content is low.

Contact weedkillers Weedkillers in this category destroy only the green parts – foliage and stems – with which they come into contact. Annual weeds are killed if the spray coverage is thorough. The foliage of perennial weeds is also destroyed but, as there is little or no effect on their roots, re-growth soon occurs.

An example of this type of weedkiller is paraquat with diquat, available to gardeners as soluble granules in measured dose sachets.

Paraquat with diquat is non-selective, and quickly kills green plant tissue it comes into contact with. It rapidly becomes inactive on contact with the soil and therefore does not harm the roots of plants. Application can be made at any time of year.

It can be used to kill annual weeds which appear in the time between site preparation and planting. Seeds may be sown immediately after treatment, but planting should not be carried out until twenty-four hours have elapsed.

Translocated, foliage-applied weedkillers Weedkillers of this type are absorbed through leaves and green stems, then transferred to underground roots and rhizomes. Weeds are usually killed in two or three weeks after treatment, most products causing the weeds to become contorted before they die.

Some, such as 2,4–D, mecoprop and dichlorprop, are selective, killing broadleaved lawn weeds without harming grasses – although grasses may occasionally be scorched.

They are most effectively used during the spring and summer, when lawn weeds are in strong, vigorous growth. Do not spray in hot or windy conditions as spray drift or vapour may harm nearby garden plants.

Other types are non-selective. One of them, glyphosate, is effective against many perennial plants and has the added advantage of being inactivated on contact with the soil. Glyphosate is most effective from the onset of flowering, when food reserves in the roots are low, and in late summer when weeds are rebuilding food reserves in their roots.

Safety precautions Many different weedkillers are used in agriculture and commercial horticulture. Only a few of these eventually reach the amateur market, having been cleared for safe use in the garden under the Pesticides Safety Precautions Scheme after considerable commercial experience and thorough assessment of safety and environmental factors. The agreed precautions take into account the safety of the person applying the weedkiller, and of domestic animals, pets and wild life. Also the safety of consumers is considered where use of the weedkiller is approved on food crops.

Safety is, to a large extent, based on common sense, but in addition to following the precautions printed on the product label one should remember to keep all weedkillers away from children, preferably in a locked cabinet. Do not mix indoors, and do not leave part-used containers or bottles within reach of children while spraying. Never transfer one chemical to another container, or obtain small quantities of commercial, and possibly dangerous, formulations from farmers.

Do not spray in windy weather or when weeds in flower are being visited by bees. Wear rubber gloves when mixing and applying weedkillers. Thoroughly wash out all equipment after use.

Applying weedkillers Most weedkillers available to gardeners are in the form of a liquid, a soluble powder or granules. Liquids and powders are applied either with a pressure sprayer or with a suitably adapted watering can. A wheeled distributor is best for applying granules to a large area. For small areas, make holes in the lid of a screw-top jar, fill with sufficient weedkiller for 1–2 sq m (or yds), then shake evenly over the carefully measured area.

Other means of applying weedkiller include aerosols and wax solids, both useful for the spot treatment of isolated lawn-weeds. When applying weedkillers close to garden plants, either cover individual plants or else use a portable screen, such as a piece of hardboard attached to a broom handle.

APPLICATION OF WEEDKILLERS

New lawns Do not use selective lawn weedkillers, such as 2,4–D or mecoprop, during the first six months after germination of a seeded lawn. Similarly, do not use them on newly-turfed lawns sooner than six months after laying, by which time the turf should be well established.

If broad-leaved weed seedlings appear in a newly-seeded lawn they can be kept in check by regular mowing until it is safe to begin using weedkillers. If coarse-grass weeds appear, then hand-weed.

Established lawns There are two basic groups of broad-leaved lawn weeds: those with a rosette-forming habit, such as plantain, and those with a creeping habit. There are also grassy-leaved weeds, such as annual meadow grass; coarse-leaved grasses, such as Yorkshire fog and field woodrush; and mosses.

Apply lawn weedkillers during good growing weather and when rain is not anticipated for several hours. The best time is when both grass and weeds are responding to a spring-applied lawn fertilizer. As the weeds die, the grasses will recolonize the weedy areas, though re-seeding may be needed if there are large bare patches.

Lawn weedkillers are usually selective in action, killing broad-leaved weeds without harming the grasses. However, in lawn sands ferrous sulphate is contact in action, and can be used to check the growth of persistent weeds as well as moss.

Most lawn weedkillers contain two, sometimes three, active ingredients, providing control of a wider range of weeds than would be possible with a single ingredient. Daisies, dandelions and plantains are most effectively controlled by products containing 2,4–D, but clovers, yarrow and pearlwort are better treated with products containing mecoprop, dicamba or dichlorprop.

If a lawn has various kinds of weeds, use mixtures which combine 2,4–D with either mecoprop, dicamba, dichlorprop or fenoprop.

If some weeds are not killed by a single application, repeat after a month or six weeks. If some survive even a second application, try to identify them. It may then be found that they are more susceptible to a particular weedkiller mixture, or that some cultural measure will help to weaken the weed. Occasionally, weed is resistant to lawn weedkillers and must be removed by hand.

Speedwells are resistant to lawn weedkillers. However, repeated use of lawn sands can gradually reduce severity of infestation. Tar oil (phenols) applied in late winter to individual patches will often kill or severely check infestations, though grasses may be temporarily scorched. Use 142 ml. (5 fl. oz.) in 9 litres (2 gallons) water, applied to 6 sq. m. (20 sq. yds.).

Soleirolia soleirolii (Helxine, or Mind-your-own-business) is similarly resistant. Lawn sands or tar oil can be used. Small areas are best returved.

Field woodrush usually occurs in very acid soil, often where there is a build-up of thatch. Scarifying to remove the thatch is the first step, followed by a winter dressing of ground chalk or limestone if the soil is acid. Repeated spraying with mecoprop may check the weed, but is unlikely to give control unless cultural steps are also carried out.

Moss in lawns A number of different mosses may occur in lawns – cushion-forming, soft trailing types, and others that are short, bristly and matted. Large amounts of moss suggest that the grass itself is in poor condition.

Moss can be given a temporary check by applying moss-killers or lawn sands based on chelated iron or ferrous sulphate. There are also lawn moss killers combined with fertilizer (which should not be used during the autumn) or dichlorophen. With the exception mentioned, apply during fine weather at any time of the year, though preferably in autumn or early spring.

For complete, long-term control, encourage healthy, vigorous turf by attending, as necessary, to drainage, aeration, liming (if very acid), or a reduction in shade. Also, feed and irrigate the turf throughout the active growing season, and do not mow too closely.

Ornamental trees and shrubs Simazine applied at a low dosage rate to clean, moist soil in late winter will control almost all germinating weeds for several months.

With some widely-grown trees and shrubs, however, such as *Choisya*, *Forsythia* and *Kolkwitzia*, there is a significant risk of damage. To a lesser extent this may also occur with others, such as *Cotoneaster*, *Diervilla*, *Prunus*, *Spiraea* and *Viburnum*. It is therefore essential to check manufacturers' recommendations very carefully before use. If any susceptible plants are killed, replace with simazine-tolerant species or revert to hand-weeding.

Dichlobenil may safely be used, at low dosage rates, around many trees and shrubs to control weeds at the seed germination stage; also to kill established annual weeds and to kill or check many perennial types. However, as with simazine, some trees and shrubs are susceptible, though not the same ones. *Forsythia* and *Spiraea*, for example, are tolerant of dichlobenil.

Apply the granules in late autumn or in winter, before growth buds show signs of life and also while plants are dry, so that granules do not lodge against buds or in leaf axils. Trees and shrubs should have been established for at least two years before using dichlobenil.

Propachlor may be applied in early spring to control some annual weeds as they germinate. The effect is short-term, but the treatment can be repeated.

Alloxydim-sodium, applied as an overall spray, will give selective control of couch grass and other perennial grasses that appear among growing shrubby plants, such as heathers.

Paraquat with diquat will kill annual weeds at any time of the year, but the spray must be directed with care.

Glyphosate is suitable for very careful spot treatment of a range of perennial weeds, including couch grass.

Established roses Roses that are kept well mulched should remain fairly free from weeds. Even so, occasional hand-weeding or disturbance of the mulch with a hoe may be needed to remove developing weed seedlings, usually before renewing the mulch in spring. Never hoe or fork deeply, for suckers may develop at the point where the rose roots are damaged.

If mulching is not part of your routine, remove over-wintering annual weeds in late winter, either by hand-weeding or by applying paraquat/diquat carefully with a dribble-bar. Follow either treatment with an overall, low-dosage spray of simazine. Repeat this procedure annually.

If perennial weeds become established, apply dichlobenil at a low dosage rate in late winter. Repeat annually until the weeds are controlled, then resume treatment with simazine. If there are only couch or other perennial grasses, and no other perennial weeds, apply simazine in late winter, then alloxydim-sodium when the grasses are growing strongly. Note that alloxydim-sodium will not control annual meadow grass.

Fruit

Apples and pears As a basic annual programme, apply simazine to clean, moist soil in February or March. This will control nearly all weeds at the germinating stage, though any over-wintering annuals should first be killed with paraquat/diquat. Although paraquat will not penetrate mature bark, it is important to avoid spray contact with stems that are less than three years old.

Alternatively, if perennial weeds become established, apply dichlobenil in March, distributing the granules evenly over the soil surface. Do not apply under trees within two years of planting.

If couch grass or other perennial grasses become troublesome, spot-treat in autumn or early spring with alloxydim-sodium or apply dalapon as a directed spray. Do not use dalapon among trees established for less than four years, and avoid excessive run-off into the soil. If broad-leaved weeds, such as docks or bindweed, become troublesome, it is best to spot-treat very carefully with glyphosate.

Plums and cherries Both of these fruits are intolerant of simazine and dichlobenil, but propachlor will give short-term control of germinating annual weeds. Paraquat or alloxydim-sodium may be used, as for apples and pears.

Bush fruits Use simazine, as for apples and pears; also paraquat/diquat. Dichlobenil may be used, too, but not within two years of planting or within one year of being cut down. Dalapon may be used to control grass weeds, including the perennial couch grass, between leaf-fall and the end of December.

Cane fruits Annually, apply simazine to clean, moist soil in February or March to kill germinating weeds. Any over-wintering annual weeds should be killed first with paraquat/diquat. Dichlobenil is suitable, too, but not within two years of planting. Apply it before the buds begin to show signs of life and before the emergence of suckers.

Strawberries Simazine may be applied in December to clean, moist, firm soil as an overall spray on plants that have been established for at least four months. Do not use on sandy soils. Repeat the treatment after the harvest, in July or August, following defoliation and a general clean-up of weeds and runners.

Apply paraquat/diquat, to kill annual weeds and unwanted runners, by careful application with a dribble-bar between the rows. Do this between the end of picking and the start of flowering times.

With this crop, in particular, it is important to follow precisely the manufacturers' recommendations regarding application rates and timing.

Vegetables Regular cultivations, as when preparing for planting or when lifting root crops, will usually clear perennial weeds from a new vegetable plot reasonably quickly, and thereafter keep it free from such weeds.

Annual weeds can be very troublesome, however. Some, such as shepherd's purse, mature rapidly and produce large numbers of seeds, which may remain viable in the soil for years. Each time the soil is cultivated, fresh seeds are brought close to the surface, where they may germinate.

Where a site is known to be heavily infested with annual weeds, try the stale seedbed method of weed control. Prepare the sowing or planting bed carefully, but some ten or fourteen days before the planned sowing dates. This allows time for weed seeds to germinate, and the seedlings can then be killed by light hoeing or by spraying with paraquat/diquat.

When sowing or planting the plot, work from a board, if possible, to avoid disturbing the soil and so bringing more weed seeds to the surface.

Paraquat/diquat, which acts by contact, may also be used following the sowing of slow-germinating vegetable seeds, such as carrot and parsley, where a lot of weed seedlings appear shortly after sowing. This method must be used with great care, however. If the weedkiller is applied just before the appearance of the vegetable crop, the seedlings, too, may be damaged, particularly if they are sown in light soil.

Propachlor, which is soil-acting and persists for only a few weeks, may be used following the sowing or planting of a number of crops, including shallots, onions and brassicas.

Paths Apply simazine to weed-free gravel paths, in late winter. If over-wintering annuals and perennial weeds are present, use a proprietary path-weedkiller containing simazine and aminotriazole. Spot-treat perennials, where necessary, with dichlobenil granules or glyphosate. Where there are path-side hedges, check their tolerance to simazine and dichlobenil.

Problem weeds There are a number of weeds that may prove very difficult to eradicate, owing to their deep roots or their easily-fragmented rootstocks. Such problem plants include bracken, creeping thistle, field bindweed and large bindweed (bellbind), horsetail and Japanese knotweed, as well as the bulbil-forming oxalis.

Where it can be used with safety, dichlobenil may check such weeds to a useful degree. Additionally, apply glyphosate as localised or spot treatments when weeds are growing strongly, repeating the treatment if re-growth occurs. If necessary, continue these treatments in subsequent seasons.

Plants are generally referred to in this book by their scientific, or botanical, names. Common names in general use in Britain are given also, although, they apply to only a limited number of plants. It is also true that so-called common names have many disadvantages, in spite of the supposed difficulty of using Latin names.

Common names Because they do not conform to any agreed rules, common names are frequently ambiguous, and their use is often local. For instance, some plants have one name in England and quite a different one in Scotland, and there are many examples of even more local usage.

A further drawback to common names is that they are often misleading. For example, it may come as a surprise to learn that the so-called evening primrose is in no way related to the ordinary primrose that we all know and love so well.

Scientific plant names In contrast to common names, botanical names are relatively stable, are internationally understood without any ambiguity, and they also give a clear and pecise indication of the relationships between plants. Instead of being fored arbitrarily, they have clear and precise meanings which are often helpful in describing some notable plant feature or association.

Many plant names, for example, describe the flower colour, habit of growth or origin of the plant, while others may bear the name of the plant's discoverer or some other notable person.

The giant water lily, *Victoria amazonica*, was named in honour of Queen Victoria, while its name also indicates that it was originally found growing wild in the Amazon region.

The common snowdrop is called *Galanthus nivalis*. *Galanthus* means 'milk flower', in reference to the milky-white flowers, while the word *nivalis* means snowy, presumably alluding to its winter-flowering habit.

Classification of plants The term 'plant' covers primitive horsetails and ferns no less than the relatively more advanced flowering types. Over the two centuries since the Swedish botanist, Linnaues, began the scientific study of plants and their classification, botanists have come to perceive certain similarities and relationships between different species, and this has enabled them to work out a scheme of classification to encompass all plants.

This scheme attempts to reflect the natural relationships between different species, so that plants considered to have evolved from a common ancestor are placed together in groups. Three of these groups – species, genus and family – are of direct significance to gardeners.

When we talk of a particular plant in precise terms – for example, a cowslip or a primrose – we are usually referring to a species (a word that can be either plural or singular). Some groups of species, while clearly distinguishable as distinct entities, have certain characters in common. These are therefore placed together in the same genus (the plural is 'genera'). Cowslips, oxlips, primroses and drumstick primulas are classified together in the genus *Primula*.

Likewise, similarities in flower structure, fruits or other characters allow related genera to be placed together within a larger group, the family. This hierarchy of divisions within the plant kingdom has several other, broader categories, but these three –

family, genus and species – are the ones that are of most importance to gardeners.

Cultivars The foregoing are all botanical categories, dealing primarily with wild plants. But a further category, most important in the horticultural world, is the cultivar. This term is used for plants that differ from the typical (wild) form in some way that is horticulturally different, and sometimes desirable. Cultivars may arise by chance, in the wild or in gardens, or they may be the result of deliberate breeding or selection. A cultivar may be a single clone (that is, a number of identical, vegetatively reproduced individuals), or a group of clones of similar appearance. The main characteristic of cultivars, regardless of their origin, is that they persist, and are propagated, only by the intervention of man.

Calluna vulgaris, the common heather or ling, has produced many seedling variants and 'sports' of garden value, showing variations in flower colour, or shape, or foliage colour. Many of these have been introduced into cultivation and given cultivar names. For example, *Calluna vulgaris* 'Robert Chapman' is distinct in its reddish foliage; 'County Wicklow' in its compactness and double pink flowers; and 'Silver Queen' in its greyish, hairy foliage.

The formation of plant names Linnaeus developed a 'binomial' (two-named) system for naming plants – the basis of that in use today – in which each plant is known by a two-word name. The first word is the name of the genus (the generic name) and is normally a noun. The second, which is usually an adjective describing some attribute of the plant, indicates the species and is known as the specific epithet.

As an example, the botanical name for the primrose is *Primula vulgaris* – *Primula* being the genus and *vulgaris* the specific epithet. Clearly, although a quite distinct plant, the cowslip is closely allied to the primrose, and it is therefore regarded as a separate species of *Primula* – *P. veris*. Primulas, cyclamen and loosestrifes share certain similarities of structure, and for this reason they are placed together in the same family, *Primulaceae*.

Some species are rather variable, either in the wild state or in cultivation, and it is then necessary to subdivide the species. Although, in Britain, wild primroses are invariably yellow, a pink form occurs regularly in parts of the Balkan area and Turkey. This is distinguished as *Primula vulgaris* subsp. *sibthorpii* – a wild variant.

Such variations within a species may be considered to be of greater or lesser significance, and the category used for them – 'ssp.' (subspecies), 'var.' (*varietas* or variety), or 'f.' (*forma* or form) – reflects this. In general, a minor difference, often in a single character such as an albino variant, will be treated as a forma. In contrast, both ssp. and var. are usually distinguished by a combination of several characters.

Species normally remain quite distinct in the wild state. Occasionally, however, natural hybrids occur and these sometimes receive species-like names, but distinguished by a multiplication sign. Thus, the natural hybrid between *Geum urbanum* (wood avens) and *C. rivale* (water avens) is called *Geum* x *intermedium*.

Rules of plant naming The names of species, varieties and cultivars are not given in an un-controlled way, but are governed by internationally accepted rules – the International Code of Botanical Nomenclature and the International Code of Nomenclature for Cultivated Plants.

The first of these sets of rules applies to the names of wild plants. It details the method for publishing valid new botanical names and the correct style of usage. These are almost invariably in Latin form, as in the examples given above, and they follow the rules of Latin grammar in that the endings of the generic and specific names must agree in gender.

Similarly, the Cultivated Code provides a clear set of rules for the formation and use of cultivar names. One of the most important of these states that new cultivar names must not be in Latin form, but must be in a modern language.

While the names of species are generally printed in italics, cultivar names are always printed in Roman type, with a capital initial letter, and they are enclosed within single quotation marks – for instance, *Calluna vulgaris* 'Robert Chapman'.

Why plant names change One aspect of scientific plant names that many people find quite infuriating is the occasional instance of a well-known name being replaced of an unfamiliar one. There are many examples of this, but such changes are seldom made without good reason.

Plant names are usually changed either for taxonomic reasons (those concerned with reassessments of the relationships between plants) or for nomenclatural reasons (those necessitated by the application of the rules of nomenclature).

A rule common to both Codes, for example, is that (in most cases) the correct name for a plant is the earliest one published for it. It sometimes occurs that in the course of researching a group of plants, a student will find a correctly published name for a particular species that predates the more well-known name. Generally, the familiar name will be ousted in favour of the earlier one.

GARDENING AND PLANT TERMS EXPLAINED

Acid Soils with a pH below 7 are classed as acid.

Adventitious buds Growth buds which arise on the stem, not in the leaf axils, usually in response to a wound.

Adventitious roots Roots that develop from stems above ground level.

Aeration Used to describe the piercing of lawns with a garden fork or a purpose-made tool, allowing air to enter the soil and relieve compaction.

Alkaline Soils with a pH 7 or above are classed as alkaline.

Annual A plant that completes its life-cycle within twelve months from germination.

Anther The pollen-bearing parts of the stamen that constitute the male reproductive organ of a flower.

Anti-desiccant Chemical that is sprayed on to plants to reduce water loss when transplanting. Often used with evergreens, especially conifers.

Axil The upper angle between a leaf or branch and the stem.

Axillary Produced in the axil – e.g. an axillary bud.

Balled Plant lifted from the open ground with soil around its roots, the root-ball then being wrapped, usually in hessian.

Bare-root plant Nursery plant lifted from the open ground, usually with little or no soil around the roots.

Base dressing Fertilizer applied immediately before sowing or planting and mixed into the soil.

Bedding plant One used for a temporary display. Examples include wallflowers planted in autumn for flowering the following spring, and half-hardy annuals planted in spring for flowering during the summer.

Biennial A plant that completes its life-cycle within two years, flowering during the second growing season.

Biennial bearing The habit among fruit trees of bearing a good crop of fruit one year but almost nothing the next.

Blanching The exclusion of light from a plant to whiten the stems or leaves – e.g. celery, leek.

Blindness A condition in which a shoot or bud, usually a flower bud, fails to develop properly and aborts.

Bole The trunk of a tree.

Bolting Premature flowering, especially in vegetables.

Bottom heat Artificial warmth provided at the base of plants growing in compost. It is most often used to encourage the rooting of cuttings. The heat source may be either beneath the compost or, as with electric cables, embedded in it.

Bract A modified, usually reduced, leaf which grows just beneath the flower head – e.g. *Cornus*, poinsettia.

Brassica The genus grown widely as vegetables that includes cabbages, cauliflowers, Brussels sprouts and turnips.

Break The development of a lateral shoot as a result of pruning a shoot to an axillary bud.

Broadcast A method of sowing seeds thinly and evenly over the soil.

Bud An embryo shoot or flower which, with a suitable stimulus, will develop.

Bud burst The period when buds begin to swell and produce leaves or flowers.

Budding A method of uniting two different plants by inserting a single growth bud from one into a stem of the other.

Bulb An underground storage organ consisting of a short stem bearing a number of swollen, fleshy leaves or leaf bases, the whole enclosing the following year's flower bud(s). *Narcissus* is an example.

Bushel An Imperial measure of volume equal to 1.28 cu ft – for example, the amount of compost required to fill a box measuring 22 in × 10 in × 10 in.

Callus Tissue growth induced in response to wounding.

Calyx The outer series of flower parts, formed of individual sepals.

Catch crop A fast-maturing crop grown between harvesting one vegetable and sowing or planting the next in the same piece of ground.

Central leader The central, upright and dominant stem of a tree.

Chitting The germination or sprouting of seeds prior to sowing. Also, the sprouting of seed potatoes.

Chlorosis Leaf-yellowing due to failure of the chlorophyll-making process. The commonest cause of this disorder is a mineral deficiency, often aggravated by alkaline soil conditions.

Cloche A low, transparent structure, made from glass or polythene. Used to protect plants from bad weather and so assist growth.

Clone All of the identical plants propagated vegetatively (e.g. by cuttings) from the same parent.

Compost (garden) Rotted organic matter.

Compost (potting or seed) Rooting medium of organic or inorganic materials used for growing plants in containers. The materials that make up the compost may include loam, peat and sand.

Compound fertilizer One that contains more than one nutrient, usually the three major elements required for healthy growth – nitrogen, phosphorus, potassium.

Conifer A plant that bears its seeds in cones.

Contact insecticide One that kills pests by direct contact.

Container-grown A plant that has been grown in a pot or container in the nursery, for subsequent sale.

Containerized A plant that has been grown in the open ground for most of its life and has only recently been planted in a container prior to sale.

Cordon A tree or shrub usually restricted to a single main stem and spur-pruned.

Corm A solid, swollen stem-base that acts as a storage organ. Crocus and cyclamen are examples.

Corolla The inner whorl of flower parts (petals), usually of a different colour to the calyx.

Cotyledon A seed leaf – the first to appear after germination has taken place.

Crocking Placing small pieces of broken clay pots over the drainage hole in a clay pot to prevent the soil becoming too wet.

Crown The base of a herbaceous perennial from which roots and shoots grow. Also, the main branch system of a tree.

Cultivar Plant selected from the wild form for its desirable characters and so retained and propagated by man. For example, *Hedera helix* 'Buttercup' is a golden-leaved cultivar of *Hedera helix* (ivy).

Cutting A piece of stem, leaf or root taken for the purpose of propagating a new plant.

Damping down Wetting the floor and walls of a greenhouse in summer in order to reduce the temperature and increase humidity.

Dead-head To remove spent flowers or unripe seed capsules from a plant. The main purpose is to prolong the flowering period.

Deciduous A plant that loses all its leaves at the end of each growing season.

Dibber A tool in the form of a round-ended stick of varying size that is pushed into the soil or compost to make a hole for the purpose of planting or pricking-out young plants.

Dicotyledon A plant that produces two seed leaves (cotyledons) at germination.

Die-back The death of branches or shoots, beginning at the tips and spreading back towards the trunk or stem.

Disbudding The removal of surplus buds or shoots as they begin to grow. The purpose is to obtain larger flowers or to train fruit trees.

Dioecious Plants that have male and female flowers on separate plants.

Drill A straight furrow in the soil in which seeds are sown. It may be as shallow as 2 cm (¾ in) for small seeds, such as lettuces, or 5 cm (2 in) deep for large ones, such as broad beans.

Earth up To mound soil around the base and stems of plants. This may help to support them, ensure that their roots are adequately covered or induce blanching – e.g. potatoes, celery.

Epiphyte A plant that grows on another, but obtains only support, not nourishment from it. Many orchids are epiphytic.

Espalier Tree, usually fruit, trained on wire supports with tiers of parallel, horizontal branches.

Evergreen A plant that retains its leaves throughout the year.

Eye A growth bud on vines and roses.

Fallowing Allowing land to remain uncropped for a period.

Fan Trees and shrubs with main branches trained like a fan against a wall or a fence.

Fastigiate A tree form, with branches erect and close together.

Fertilizer A material that provides plant nutrients. It may be organic, deriving from decayed plants or animal matter, or inorganic, based on chemicals.

Flushes Irregular, successive crops of flowers or fruits.

Foliar feed A liquid fertilizer sprayed on to, and partially absorbed through, the leaves.

Fungicide A chemical used to control diseases caused by fungi and some bacteria.

Gall An abnormal growth of plant tissue caused by the feeding of certain insects or other pests.

Germination The development of the embryo within a seed into a seedling.

Grafting Uniting a shoot (or bud) of one plant with another.

Growth bud One that gives rise to a shoot.

Half-hardy A plant that is unable to survive the winter without protection.

Half-standard A tree with 90 cm–1.2 m (3–4 ft) of clear stem.

Harden off To acclimatize gradually plants raised in warm conditions to outdoor conditions.

Hardy A plant that will survive the winter unprotected.

Heeling-in A temporary measure for storing woody, bare-rooted plants; also certain bulbs after flowering. The roots are covered with soil until they can be planted.

Herbaceous perennial See **Perennial**

Herbicide Synonym for weedkiller.

Humus Organic matter in an advanced state of decay.

Hybrid A plant derived from a cross between (usually) two species. However, a bigeneric hybrid results from a cross between two genera. F_1 hybrids of flowers and vegetables, noted for their vigour and uniformity, result from controlled pollination between selected parent lines.

John Innes composts Standard mixtures for raising young plants, to a formula developed at the John Innes Horticultural Institute in 1939. They are all loam-based composts.

Joint see **Node**

Lateral A side-growth that develops at an angle from the main stem of a tree.

Layering Propagation by inducing shoots to form roots while they are still attached to the parent plant.

Leaching The removal of soluble minerals from the soil by water draining through it.

Leader shoot The main shoot which extends the growth of a branch.

Leaf-fall The period when deciduous plants shed their leaves.

Leaf-mould Well-rotted leaves. The material may be used as a mulch or added to the soil to improve its texture.

Light The glass or polythene covering of a cold frame.

Lime A compound that contains calcium and/or magnesium. It is added to the soil in order to reduce acidity.

Line out To plant out young plants or cuttings in a temporary garden site.

Long Tom A pot about half as deep again as a standard pot.

Maiden A one-year-old tree or shrub.

Manure Bulky material of plant or animal origin added to the soil to improve its structure.

Monocarpic Usually applied to plants that die naturally after their first flowering and fruiting.

Monocotyledon A flowering plant that produces only a single seed leaf.

Monoecious Male or female flowers that are separate but carried on the same plant.

Mulch A top dressing of organic or inorganic matter applied to the surface of the soil.

Naturalized Plants, particularly bulbs, established in what look like their natural surroundings – often grass. Here, they increase of their own accord and need little maintenance.

Node The position where a leaf is attached to a stem. Also known as a joint.

Nut A non-splitting, one-seeded, hard fruit.

Organic matter Any material consisting of, or derived from, living organisms. Examples include farmyard manure and leaf-mould.

Ornamental A plant grown in the garden primarily for its decorative qualities.

Pan A hard layer of subsoil which obstructs drainage and root penetration. Or, a shallow container for seed-sowing.

Pelleted seeds Small seeds coated with pesticide or other inert material to make them easier to handle for space sowing.

Perennial A plant that lives for more than three seasons. The term is used mainly for herbaceous plants, which die down each autumn and make fresh growth the following spring.

Perianth The outer parts of the flower (calyx and corolla) which enclose the reproductive parts.

pH A measure of the degree of acidity or alkalinity in the soil. Below 7 on the pH scale is acid, above is alkaline.

Pinching The removal of the growing tip of a plant's shoot in order to encourage branching lower down or assist the development of flower buds. Also known as 'stopping'.

Plunge To bury container-grown plants up to their pot rims in ash, peat or sand. This helps to conserve moisture and to maintain a more even temperature around the plants' roots.

Pollination The transference of pollen from the male to the female parts of a flower.

Pot-bound The condition reached by a pot plant when its roots have filled the pot and exhausted the available nutrients.

Potting on Transferring a plant into the next larger size of pot – e.g. from an 11 cm (4½ in) pot into a 15 cm (6 in) pot.

Pricking out The transplanting and spacing out of seedlings to allow for growth.

Propagation The production of a new plant from an existing one. Achieved either sexually (by seeds) or asexually – for example, by cuttings.

Ramblers Roses that produce long, flexible basal canes and are usually trained against walls, fences or screens.

Recurrent flowering The production of several crops of flowers in succession during one season. (See also *Flushes*.)

Repotting Replacing with fresh material some of the compost around the roots of a pot-grown plant. It does not involve moving to a larger pot, as in potting on.

Resistant Describes a plant that is able to overcome completely or partially the effect of a parasitic organism or disorder, or that is able to withstand frost, wind, salt, etc. It also describes a pest or disease that can no longer be controlled by a particular pesticide or fungicide.

Rhizome A perennial, horizontal, underground stem that acts as a storage organ.

Rhizomorph A root-like mass of fungal threads by means of which certain fungi spread their growth through the soil.

Rod The main, woody stem of a vine.

Root ball The soil or compost ball formed among and around the roots of a plant.

Rootstock A plant on to which another (the scion) is grafted; it provides the root system.

Runner A rooting stem that grows along the surface of the soil. Strawberries are an example of this type of rooting system.

Run-off When spraying, the point at which a plant becomes saturated and excess liquid runs off.

Scarifying The process of raking a lawn vigorously in order to remove old dead-grass and other compacted matter.

Seedcoat The tough, protective layer around an embryo.

Seed dressing An insecticide or fungicide applied as a fine powder to seeds before sowing to protect them from pests or diseases.

Seed leaf The first leaf or leaves produced by a germinating seed. Also known as cotyledon.

Self-sterile Describes a plant with pollen that cannot fertilize its own female parts.

Sepal Part of the leaf-like outer covering of a flower.

Sets Whole or part bulbs or tubers used for propagating – e.g. onions.

Scion A shoot grafted on to the rootstock of another plant.

Shrub A perennial plant with persistent woody stems, branching from the base.

Snag A short stump of a branch left after incorrect pruning.

Space sowing Sowing seeds individually at predetermined spacing in the site where they are to grow to maturity.

Spit When digging, the depth of a spade – about 25 cm (10 in).

Spot-treat To treat a small, defined area or a particular plant, usually with weedkiller, a fungicide or a pesticide.

Spreader A substance, such as detergent, added to a spray to assist its even distribution over the target area.

Spur A short branch system that carries clusters of flower buds. The fern is applied particularly to fruit trees.

Stamen The male reproductive organ of a flower, comprising a stalk with anther.

Standard A tree grown with 1.5–2.1 m (5–7 ft) of clear stem.

Stolon A prostrate stem that roots at its tip to form a further plant. Blackberries increase this way.

Stool The base of a plant, such as a raspberry or chrysanthemum, that produces new shoots.

Stopping See **Pinching**

Sucker A shoot growing from a root below ground level.

Systemic An insecticide, fungicide or weedkiller absorbed into the plant's sap stream and carried throughout the plant.

Thatch A layer of dead or living organic matter found covering the soil between the roots and foliage of lawn grasses. It tends to stifle new growth of grass, and so needs to be removed regularly.

Thin To reduce the number of seedlings, buds, flowers, fruitlets or branches.

Tilth A fine, crumbly layer of surface soil produced by weathering and thorough cultivation.

Topsoil The upper layer of dark, fertile soil in which plants grow. Below this lies lighter-coloured subsoil, which lacks organic matter and is often low in nutrients.

Trace elements Nutrients required by plants in only very small amounts.

Transpiration The continual loss of water vapour from the leaves of plants and trees.

Transplanting The transference of young plants to another site.

True leaves Leaves typical of the mature plant, in contrast to the simpler seed leaves.

Truss A cluster of flowers or fruits.

Tuber A swollen underground stem or root that acts as a storage organ and from which new plants or tubers may develop. The potato is an example.

Turgid Plant material that contains its full complement of water and is therefore not under stress.

Union The join between rootstock and scion, or between two scions grafted together.

Variegated Describes leaves with coloured markings, due to an absence of chlorophyll.

Vegetative growth Leaf and stem growth, as opposed to that of flowers and fruit.

Water shoot A vigorous, sappy shoot which grows from an adventitious bud.

Weedkiller, contact action A weedkiller that kills only the green parts of plants.

Weedkiller, hormone A weedkiller that affects growth, often causing the stem to extend rapidly before the plant collapses and dies.

Weedkiller, residual A weedkiller that remains as a layer in or on the soil for weeks or months, killing emerging weed seedlings or the shoots of perennial weeds.

Weedkiller, selective A chemical that kills only certain types of plants, leaving others unharmed.

Weedkiller, translocated (systemic) A weedkiller that is absorbed through the leaves and stems and is carried through the sap-stream to kill the whole plant.

Wetting agent A chemical added to a spray liquid to improve the spray's adherence to a plant.

White bud stage Just before the flower buds actually open.

Wilting Occurs when plants are short of water and under stress.

Wind-rock The loosening of a plant's root system (usually of a tree) by strong winds.

GENERAL INDEX

INDEX OF PLANTS

INDEX OF PLANTS

Picture credits
Barnaby's Picture Library: 270, 272.
Pat Brindley: 126, 306.
Linda Burgess: 236, 269.
John Glover: 20, 54, 55, 91, 308, 344.
Tania Midgley: 18, 199.
Photos Horticultural: 17, 53, 90, 127, 162, 164,
200, 305, 341, 343.
R.H.S. Wisley: 128, 163, 197, 198, 233, 271.
Harry Smith Horticultural Photographic
Collection: 19, 56, 89, 92, 125, 234, 235, 307,
342.
Zefa: 161.

Illustrations by: Peter Bull, David Cook, Vana
Haggerty